Computers AND STUFF Made Easy

Never again ask:
IS THIS THING ON?

Computers AND STUFF Made Easy

Stay Connected to Family and Friends with Hundreds of Tips and Tricks for Your Computers, Tablets, and Cell Phones

ABBY STOKES
20+ Year Teacher of Computer Skills to Students of All Levels

RODALE

This book was previously published as *Is This Thing On?* by Workman in 2008, 2011, and 2015. Published by arrangement with Workman Publishing Company. Rodale exclusive edition published in January 2017.

Printed in the United States of America

Rodale Inc. makes every effort to use acid-free ∞, recycled paper ♻.

Book design by Janet Vicario

Library of Congress Cataloging-in-Publication Data is on file with the publisher.

ISBN 978–1–62336–931–6 direct mail hardcover

2 4 6 8 10 9 7 5 3 1

RODALE.

We inspire health, healing, happiness, and love in the world.
Starting with you.

To my mother . . .
who tried and succeeded
and will always be my inspiration.

Thank You, Thank You, Thank You

I thank my lucky stars every day for the incredible group of family and friends that I am privileged to call my loved ones. My lucky stars also have me dividing my time between the most exciting city in the world and a little piece of heaven on the water. Above and beyond my lucky stars I thank the following people: Mom, Eve, and Sherri, whose unwavering support is always felt and appreciated; Dan Tucker, whose sage advice guided me through every aspect of the book; Suzie Bolotin, Margot Herrera, Michael Rockliff, and Janet Vicario, along with their colleagues Orlando Adiao, Danny Cooper, Heather Schwedel, Joan Giurdanella, Beth Levy, Emily Krasner, Jenny Mandel, Deborah McGovern, Selina Meere, and Patrick Scafidi; illustrators Michael Sloan and Susan Hunt Yule; the amazing digital team of Andrea Fleck-Nesbit, Kate Travers, Molly Kay Upton, Anthony Foti, and the folks at Being Wicked for all of their help designing *AskAbbyStokes.com;* and the entire Workman family for over a decade and a half of support and enthusiasm. I'd also like to thank the team at Rodale, specifically Anne Egan, Shea Zukowski, and Kristina Gonzalez. And to all of my students, who make going to work a pleasure, and above all, you, the reader, for having enough faith in this book to open your wallet or being smart enough to know someone who would buy it for you, thank you!

Contents

Appendices

Here's What You Can Expect . . .

This exclusive Rodale edition is a "total tech" guide,, whether you're using a computer, tablet, smartphone, or ALL THREE. As in my previous *Is This Thing On?* books, I'll hold your hand, help you decide which tech device would benefit you most, and stay by your side while you make your purchase and bring the new addition to your family home or workplace.

We'll set it up together and get familiar with how everything works. This book is intended to demystify technology, not explain the gory inner workings of it. Every day, we use contraptions such as a car, telephone, and TV, but have no idea how they really work. Technology is no different. You don't need to know how it works in order to operate it.

Be forewarned that once you arrive at Chapter 10, it is all hands-on instruction and might be overwhelming if you try to visualize what is being discussed without having the actual technology in front of you. Go ahead, though, and scan each chapter to pick up some basic and helpful information, but be sure to return to the chapters when you have your technology in hand. Later in the book, we'll delve into digital photos, social networking, file management, and streaming movies and TV shows, along with wearable technologies and voice recognition.

If, when you look at your tech toy, you find that what's described in the book differs a bit from what you see, don't panic. Websites and technology change. I'm going to regularly encourage you to visit my website, *AskAbbyStokes.com*, for the most current, step-by-step video tutorials specifically tailored to your device and the task at hand. It's the next best thing to me being in the room beside you.

Take a deep breath and let's begin our journey. You're going to be pleasantly surprised by how soon you will skillfully "surf the net," email your friends, take photos to share online, and conquer your fear of technology!

Abby

THERE IS
NOTHING TO FEAR
BUT FEAR ITSELF

CHAPTER 1

BRING THE WORLD TO YOUR FINGERTIPS

Research, find, and buy anything you can imagine, and communicate with loved ones, without leaving home—what technology and the Internet offer

My mother still can't reset her clock radio after daylight saving time. She just adds or subtracts an hour until I come home for a visit. And the first week after she buys a new car, she only drives it in the Stop & Shop parking lot. Once she feels comfortable enough to take it on the road, it's still a few months before the windshield wipers stop being activated whenever she means to signal a right turn. Considering her lack of technical savvy and anxiety about new devices, I am incredibly proud of her for joining the community of computer users. Mom had never shown any interest in technology, but like so many seniors, she knew she was missing out on something when she began to notice that every article she read ended with "For more information, go to *www.[insert almost anything here].com.*"

"I had no idea what the Internet could do for me, but I knew that if I didn't try it soon, I never would. Now I use it for everything. . . . I write the newsletter and maintain the mailing list for my church. I love finding out all kinds of information online and I'm a big fan of email."
—Marsha

"Peach, what is a website?" she asked me.

"Think of a computer or tablet as a combination television set and typewriter. Then think of the Internet as a library. You can find information on absolutely anything you can dream up on the Internet by accessing different websites—as you would books in a library. Just type in what you want to learn about, and it will appear in front of you in the form of pictures, text, and sound" was my answer.

A website is like a book. Instead of going to the library and looking up a title in the card catalog (which is now on a computer), you go to the Internet and type in a website address.

Because there can be more than one website for a given subject, you'll have many choices available to you. Each website is designed individually, just as books are written individually by different authors.

Anyone can have a website—even you. All that is needed is the desire to convey information and the willingness to pay a small annual fee to a company to register the name of your website. If you don't mind piggybacking on another website or having advertisements on your site, you may be able to have a website at no cost.

A few months later, Mom visited me in New York and wanted to see a Broadway musical. This was the perfect opportunity to show her what the Internet has to offer and how I make my living. (I teach computer skills to digital immigrants—those not born with a keyboard or a mouse in their hand.) I turned on my computer, connected to the Internet, and then typed in *playbill.com* (the website address of a company that sells theater tickets), and like magic, their website appeared on my screen. I picked the show we wanted to see and the date that was best for us. Next, the seating chart appeared on the screen and we chose our seats. Then I ordered the tickets and typed in my email address, where I would receive the e-tickets (electronic tickets), and printed them on my printer at home.

Mom was impressed. I've been teaching people how to maneuver around the Internet for more than two decades now, and it continues to amaze me with the infinite ways that it can benefit those who use it. The Internet allows you to track investments, research family genealogy, contact buddies, purchase a new car, auction a coin collection, search for the best deal on airline tickets, and so much more.

"The Internet allows us to get up-to-date stock quotes, access detailed information on a company of interest, and directly buy and sell stocks any time we want. We even access the *Wall Street Journal* online. All this has increased our enjoyment and the value of our investments. Who can argue with that?"
—Cy and Ruth

Convincing Mom Continues . . .

The ease with which we were able to purchase the theater tickets on the computer had my mother intrigued.

"What else can the Internet do?"

"I can't tell you everything it can do, Mom, because it's constantly evolving. I don't think anyone really knows its full capabilities. But I'll give you some examples of what I think is fun and practical about it."

Mom had lost track of a dear friend of hers several years before and, after much effort, sadly gave up on finding her. I signed on to the Internet and typed in *whitepages.com* (a website where you can search for people and businesses, much in the way you would with a phone book). Within a few seconds, there were seven listings of people with the same name as Mom's long-lost friend, one of whom was unmistakably her. The listings that appeared included telephone numbers and street addresses. The happy ending is that Mom found her friend. From that moment on, she was sold on the Internet.

Shirley, one of my mother's friends, suffers from a very rare cancer. Once she learned how to get online, she found detailed information about her specific form of cancer and alternative treatment ideas, but she also found a group of people with the same condition. She now communicates with some of them daily. All of this is done through the Internet, which enables her to be involved in the world around her even when she is housebound.

TABLET VS. LAPTOP OR DESKTOP COMPUTER

All of these devices will connect to the Internet, check email, and offer photo sharing. Tablets are small, lightweight, and easy to carry with you. Computers have more processing power than tablets. There isn't necessarily a "winner," only a more preferable choice for your specific needs.

To say that the Internet can give you information on just about anything you can dream up may sound like a huge overstatement, but it's true.

A Taste of What Some People Do with the Internet

One of my students, Graciela, always has an interesting list of things she wants to find out about on the Internet. During one lesson, we visited websites with information about renting a house on Martha's Vineyard, tracked down an artist whose work she wanted to buy, and found a doormat with Jack Russell terriers emblazoned on it.

By typing "Martha's Vineyard rentals" into a search engine (which I'll explain to you later), we came upon more than a dozen websites, many of them with photos of the interiors and exteriors of the houses available. While looking at a photo of one of the rentals, we noticed the words "how to get here" on the screen. We clicked on the words and a different website appeared that offered us driving directions and a map that showed the best route. Graciela printed the directions and set them aside to put in her car's glove compartment.

Then came the mission of tracking down the artist whose work she liked. First, we typed in the artist's name, but because Graciela couldn't remember the exact spelling, that didn't work. But she did remember what gallery showed his work and typed that in. Not only did it give us contact information, but the website featured one of his paintings, as well.

On to the doormat. That took a little ingenuity. We searched for "doormats" and "doormats with dogs." We found tons of doormats and a surprising number of doormats with dogs, but not the right kind of dog. Then we searched for "Jack Russell terrier doormat." We found a great-looking mat and bought it over the Internet with her credit card. It was delivered the next week. We both had ear-to-ear grins of satisfaction.

What More Does the Internet Offer?

Another really great feature of the information superhighway is that you can communicate inexpensively with other people all over the world. I remember when we would call my grandparents and have just enough time to say, "Hello. How are things?" before my grandfather would say, "OK. Enough, ladies. This is long distance. Say good-bye now." I don't mean to make light of the cost of a telephone call or how hard my grandfather worked for his money, but wasn't that why they invented long distance, so we could talk to one another? Well, thank heaven for digital technology. I have students who communicate with friends and family across the globe every day. If it wasn't for the Internet, this would be financially impossible for most of us.

"I'm sure when my son gave me my tablet he thought I might never use it. I guess I wasn't sure either. But I've always been a tinkerer, and the tablet became a new challenge. Last month, I gave my son advice about websites to check out for buying a new car. That felt good."
—*Peter*

Email = ?

Email, or electronic mail, is the same idea as sending a letter (now lovingly referred to as snail mail), but rather than waiting for it to go from a mailbox to your local post office to get sorted, sent to another post office, and then delivered to the recipient, you send your message through the computer by way of your phone line or a high-speed connection to the Internet. This all happens in a matter of seconds rather than days.

Still confused? Well, email confused me, too, until I could actually see how it all worked. So if things in this book get a bit murky, have faith that when you get in front of a computer and see what I'm talking about, it will all make sense.

What Else Can a Computer or Tablet Do for Me?

It's hard to deny that along with all the other things you can accomplish on a computer or tablet, it is the Internet, with its access to the information superhighway, that has made digital technology a must-have over the years.

"Technology is such a part of my grandchildren's lives—I wanted to know what it was about. Once I got online, they started to send me weekly emails. We used to see one another only at holidays and talk only on birthdays. It's the last thing I expected, but it has brought us closer together."
—*Lev*

However, having a computer or tablet offers you much more than the Internet. You will have the ability to organize your address book, create a family newsletter, and, if you want to, simulate flying a plane or master chess. Some of my students track their frequent-flyer miles, inventory their collectibles, and design their own stationery. The computer can consolidate your paperwork, create order in your world, and track your finances.

There is no end to how technology can organize, simplify, and enhance your life. But first you need to learn a bit more about computers and tablets, decide what you want to buy, and get it up and running. The whole undertaking of buying these devices can seem overwhelming, but don't get discouraged. This book will guide you through the entire process. You'll be pleasantly surprised by how easy it will be to make an educated purchase and how quickly you will learn to use and love your buy.

In Conclusion

Mom now emails me every day. She sends and receives attachments (which I'll describe to you later) from the various committees she volunteers on. She has also become our family's online detective. When my brother, Jeff, was looking into summer camp for his four kids, Mom did all of the research for him online. She investigated the location of each camp and learned what they offered. Once my brother chose one, she gave him printouts from the local chamber of commerce and tourism websites with hotel and restaurant recommendations, highlighting the best places to buy a lobster roll! She printed driving directions and an area map. She found all this while surfing the Web.

This world that you keep hearing about is not passing you by—it's just waiting for you to come along. What technology can offer you is amazing and boundless, but you're not alone if it seems elusive and intimidating. Most of my students are over fifty and new to all this tech stuff, and I can't explain to you how exciting it is for them (and me) when they start to zoom around the Internet and begin to enjoy what the digital realm has to offer.

Before you know it, the world will be your oyster. Trust me, if my mother can do it, you can, too! (I'm only teasing you, Mom.)

Q: I've just bought a computer for my parents. The last thing I want to do is scare them when they're already so tentative. What things should I avoid discussing so I don't confuse or intimidate them?

A: There are no topics to avoid discussing with your parents. But what you *do* want to avoid is using computer jargon. You'll know when you've done it because their eyes will start to glaze over. The other crucial thing is to take your time. You may be in a rush, but they are not. Rushing people who are fearful or overwhelmed only makes them retreat.

For more tips on how to teach your parents, read **"10 Tips for Teaching Computers to Future Silver Surfers"** on my website, ***AskAbbyStokes.com/blog*** (you can find the article in the "First Steps" section). Good luck!

Q: What's the difference between the World Wide Web and the Internet, if there is one?

A: Commonly, we think of the World Wide Web (also known as the Web) and the Internet as being synonymous, but technically they are not. The term Internet was originally coined in the 1970s and refers to a massive network of networks globally connecting millions of computers, as well as devices like tablets and smartphones. The Web is one of the networks within the Internet. There are other networks on the Internet that convey information between computers for different governments and businesses. Most of us don't visit the other networks on the Internet and that's why we think of the Internet and the Web as being one. Think of the Internet as an umbrella. The Web is under that umbrella as are all other networks that convey information from computing device to computing device.

Q: Where can I test a computer or tablet before deciding to buy one?

A: Your local library should offer free access to computers and many have tablets or e-readers for you to try. If the computers at the library are very busy, there may be a sign-in sheet where you can reserve a time slot. Ask the librarian if they offer any technology classes. If they don't, contact your nearest community center about classes. A lot of adult education programs offer technology classes as well. All of these are good options if you're looking for a chance to play around on a computer or tablet and see if you might want to venture further.

CHAPTER 2

HARDWARE: THE THIGH BONE'S CONNECTED TO THE . . .

A simple introduction to the parts of a computer and how they relate to one another

You probably aren't concerned with how the engine of your car works or what the parts are called. What's important is that it gets you where you want to go. The focus for technology should be the same—not on how it works, but on how to work it. Computers and tablets are very much like cars—they come in different sizes, styles, and colors, but they all have the same basic components and do the same thing. By performing the tasks you command, computer technology gets you from one piece of information to another. In the same way that you decide where to go for a Sunday drive, you decide where to go on the computer or tablet and, before long, you'll enjoy yourself along the way. But first let's get familiar with the machine.

"I have an enormous family, and come Christmas my computer is my personal assistant. It keeps a list of who I sent cards to and who I get them from. It also keeps track of what gifts I gave to my 13 (!) grandchildren and, of course, who has been naughty and who has been nice."
—Joan

In this chapter, we'll first look at the parts of a computer. Even if you have your heart set on a tablet (an all-in-one handheld device with no parts to connect), consider reading this chapter to understand the essence of computer technology. We'll talk a bit about tablets on page 20, and we'll compare them to computers on page 35.

The Hardware of the Computer

Hardware is the machinery of the computer. Whatever kind of computer you get, the basic parts of the machine and what they do will be the same. You do not need to understand how the parts of a computer work to use one, but it can be helpful to know what they are called. Just read through the following information and know that it is here for reference if you need it later on.

DESKTOP

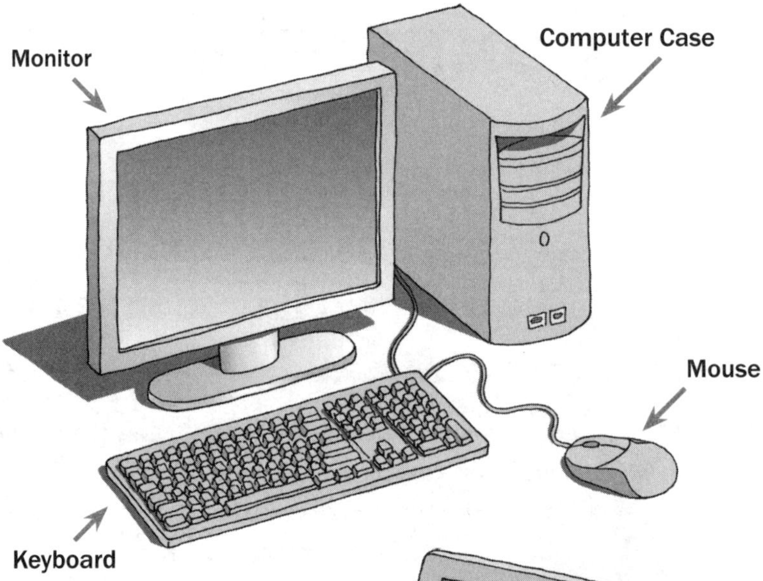

LAPTOP

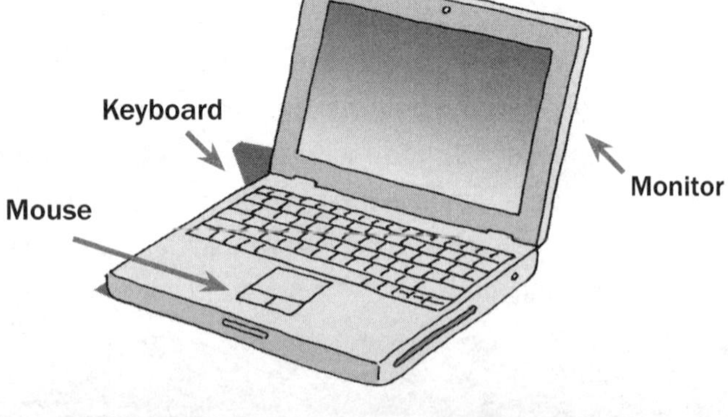

The Monitor

The monitor houses the screen of the computer. It is where any information in your computer is viewed. For example, as you type a letter using the keyboard of your computer, the words will appear on the screen of your monitor.

You can get monitors in as many different sizes as you can buy television sets, but you probably don't want a monitor that's too large. For most tasks, a monitor somewhere between 14 and 27 inches is sufficient. The monitor size is measured diagonally from a top corner to the opposite bottom corner of the screen itself. When we narrow down what is the best computer for you, we'll talk more about screen options.

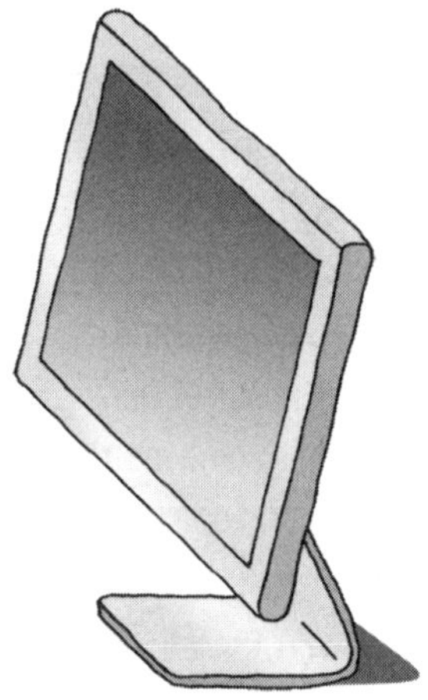

Monitors come in a variety of styles and sizes, including this flat-screen model.

The Mouse

A mouse is basically a hand-operated device that controls the movement of a pointer that appears on your monitor's screen. This pointer can appear in different shapes depending on what its function is at a given time. It can also be referred to as the arrow, mouse arrow, or cursor.

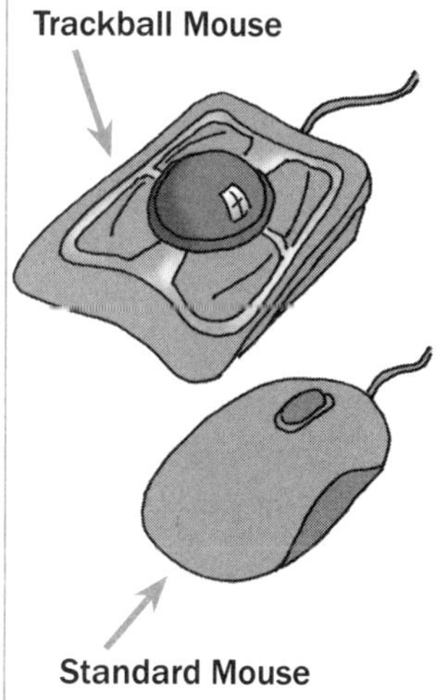

The mouse controls the pointer that appears on the computer screen. You can choose from among several mouse styles.

"The hardest part for me was learning to use the mouse. I never thought I would figure it out. But I kept practicing and making mistakes and practicing some more. It isn't second nature yet, but I'm getting there."
—*Martin*

Mice come in a variety of shapes and sizes, but all perform in the same way. You rest your hand or finger on the mouse, and when you move your hand, a ball or light sensor on the bottom of the mouse detects your movements. When you move the mouse, it sends a message either through a cable or wirelessly to the brain of the computer, and the pointer or arrow on your screen moves accordingly. You press and release a button (or buttons) on the top of the mouse to perform an action. A slight click might be heard when you do this, so people often refer to the motion as "clicking the mouse." Not all mice make a clicking sound.

The original name for the mouse was "X-Y position indicator for a display system." What a mouthful! It didn't take long for the little gray device with the long tail (the cord connected to the computer) to be renamed a mouse. Eureka!

IT'S ALL IN THE TOUCH
A touch screen allows you to simply tap on the screen to take an action rather than clicking the mouse. I'll help you decide later on whether a touch screen might be right for you.

The Keyboard

The keyboard on a computer is very similar to the keyboard on a typewriter. The alphabet and number keys are set up in exactly the same pattern as on your old Smith Corona and function in the same way. Whatever you type on the keyboard will appear on your monitor's screen.

However, the computer keyboard is not used just for typing. There are several other keys beyond the numbers and the letters, such as arrow keys that allow you to move around the screen, much as you do with the mouse. There is either an **Enter** key, on a PC, or a **Return** key, on a Mac, as well as some additional keys that are called function keys.

The **Enter** and **Return** keys are significant because you can use them to instruct the computer to carry out a task. Hitting them is like giving the computer the green light to take an action. If you depress a specific key, you can tell the computer to move a paragraph, delete

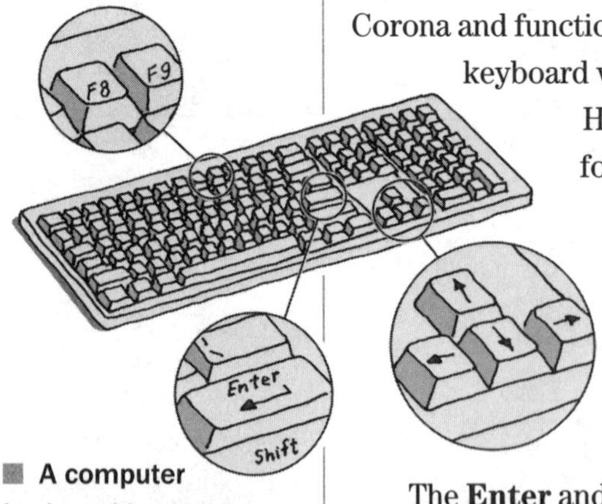

■ **A computer keyboard is set up much like a standard typewriter, with additional keys that perform specific tasks.**

a sentence, or access a piece of information. *A word of caution:* You don't want to use the **Enter** or **Return** keys without knowing what the result will be. It is hard to visualize this without having a computer in front of you, so enough said on that for now. You'll see what I mean when you start working with an actual keyboard.

Even though the mouse and keyboard are physically very different, many functions can be carried out by using either of them. For example, if you want to move from the top to the bottom of a page, you can use either the keyboard or the mouse to get the job done. When you are on the Internet, most of your activity will be controlled by the mouse, but the keyboard will remain essential for typing information.

The monitor, keyboard, and mouse are the most straightforward parts of a computer. Each of them plays a major role in allowing you to view, access, and manipulate information.

One other thing worth mentioning: I don't know how to type. I use the "Columbus Method"—find the key and land on it. I am sharing this with you in case you think that you can't use a computer if you don't know how to type. Poppycock. It's how I make my living.

NO CABLES, NO PROBLEM

Nowadays you can buy a mouse, keyboard, and even a printer that will work wirelessly (no unsightly cables to get tangled) with your computer.

The Brain of the Computer

Several components make up the brain of the computer. All of the components discussed here work together to gather, identify, move, and store information.

The Computer Case

A computer case is nothing more than a plastic box, but it houses the most important and most expensive part of your computer—the central processing unit (CPU), the hard drive (C:), and the random access memory (RAM). (In a laptop, these components are inside the laptop itself.)

Sounds complicated already, doesn't it? Fear not. This combination of CPU, hard drive, and RAM is simply the brain of

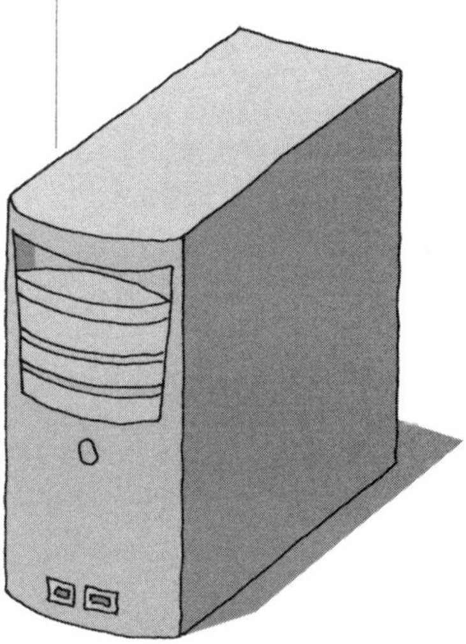

The computer case houses the brain of the computer. Cases come in various shapes and sizes. This vertical box is called a tower case.

HOW DOES IT MEASURE UP?

HERTZ

Hertz is a measurement of speed. (Think Hertz car rental = speed.) The CPU (central processing unit) has a speed measured in hertz—the more (i.e., faster), the better.

BYTES

A byte is a measurement of space. (Think bites of a sandwich filling the space in your stomach.) The hard drive and the RAM (random access memory) are storage spaces measured in bytes—the more, the better.

Don't get bogged down if you don't quite grasp the concept of bytes or hertz. It's not necessary to understand either to use a computer.

your machine. Some users refer to the computer case as a BUB (big ugly box)!

The Central Processing Unit (CPU) is the pathway for all of the information in your computer. The CPU is to information on the computer what the post office is to a letter. The information has to go through the CPU to get to its proper place. When you hear references to megahertz or gigahertz, people are talking about the speed of the CPU, or how quickly it moves information through your computer. The more megahertz, the faster the computer will operate. It's not unlike your car—the more horsepower it has, the faster it goes from 0 to 60.

The Hard Drive (C: Drive) is the permanent memory of your computer. The information that you type into the computer lives on the hard drive, as does the software that has been installed. (I'll explain software in the next chapter.) Even when your computer is turned off, the information remains stored on the hard drive.

A peek inside a standard computer case . . . eek!

Random Access Memory (RAM) is the memory used to open up programs or images only while the computer is on. The amount of RAM is important when we get on the Internet. Websites are made up of pictures, and to help those pictures appear on the screen, your computer uses the power of the RAM.

In summary, the CPU is the organizer and messenger of all information in the computer. The hard drive and RAM both store information. The hard drive is your permanent memory, and RAM is the temporary memory used only when the computer is on.

The Brain's Memory

Information stored in a computer—both on the hard drive and in its RAM—takes up space. This space is measured in bytes.

- A megabyte can store about as much text as *Moby-Dick*.
- A gigabyte is capable of storing about 1,000 copies of *Moby-Dick*.

So if you're planning to write a fat book about a whale and follow up with 999 sequels, you'll want a computer with a hard drive of at least a gigabyte! I'll explain how many bytes you'll really need for your hard drive and RAM when we're closer to shopping for your machine.

On older models, the A: drive is where a floppy disk was inserted. Newer computers don't have this drive. The D: drive is for a CD or DVD. Most, but not all, computers have this drive.

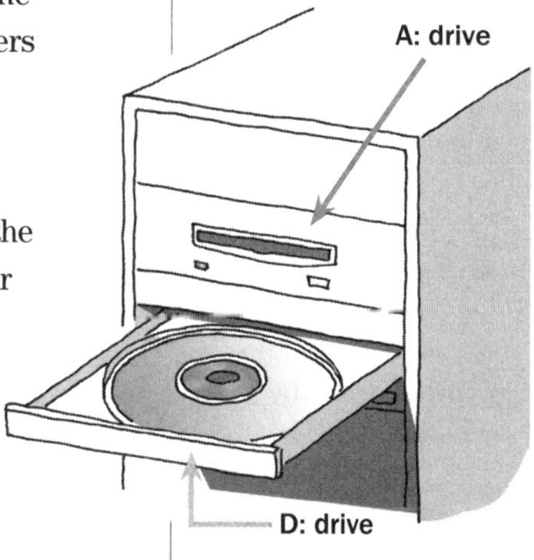

Other Parts of the Computer

In this section, we'll review some other essential parts of the computer. Each of the components described here transfers information onto the brain of the computer.

Additional Drives

As I said before, the hard drive, also sometimes referred to as the C: drive, is where all information is permanently stored on your computer. Many computers also have a D: drive (on some computers it's referred to as the E: drive) where information can be fed or "installed" into the computer. A CD or DVD is inserted into the D: or E: drive (which may also be called the media drive) in the same way you put a CD into a compact

A NOTE WHEN YOU'RE SHOPPING

Some desktop and laptop computers come with a CD/DVD (media) drive. These drives enable you to install software that comes on CDs, listen to music on a CD, or watch a movie on a DVD. I recommend you get a computer with a CD/DVD drive. Some laptop computers don't have a media drive, to minimize their weight. In that case, if you wanted to watch movies on a DVD or listen to music on a CD, you would need to buy an external drive to plug into the laptop.

disc player. This is all theoretical at the moment, but when you get near a computer—whether it's in a store, at a friend's, or at your local library—take a look at these drives. You'll see that they're really quite simple.

Modem

A modem is a device that connects your computer to the Internet, which in turn connects your computer to the outside world. This allows you to access websites and send email. You cannot access the Internet or send email without a modem. New computers come with a modem inside the computer case, along with the CPU, hard drive, and RAM.

Most people use DSL (digital subscriber line) or cable connections to access the Internet because they are fast and don't tie up the phone line. Your local telephone company probably offers DSL. Your cable TV provider almost certainly offers a cable connection to the Internet. DSL and cable connections are referred to as high-speed or broadband connections. Ask family and friends who are already surfing the net which Internet service they recommend.

Without adding to your possible confusion, you should also know that you can connect to the Internet wirelessly. Almost all new laptops offer this feature. Wi-fi (wireless fidelity) is discussed in greater detail in Chapter 13. Hang tight and it will all make sense to you as you keep reading.

How Does It All Get Connected?

Let's review the hardware that makes up a desktop computer before we get into how it is connected. There is a monitor, mouse, and keyboard. There is also the computer case, which houses the brain of the computer, the modem, and the disk drives. The pieces of hardware must be connected to have information conveyed from one part to another.

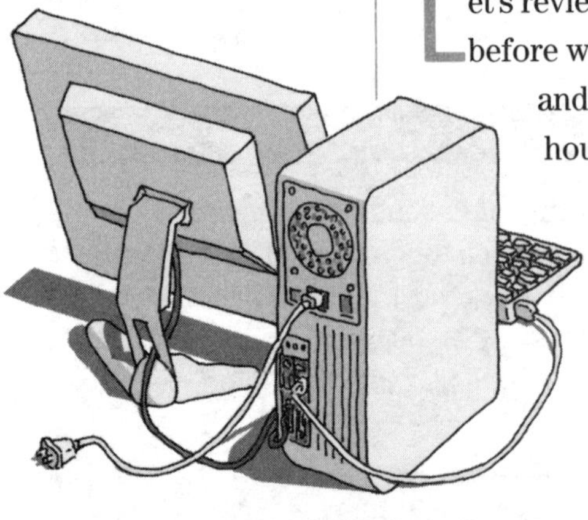

The monitor, like the keyboard and mouse, is connected to the computer case by a cable.

Ports

Desktop computers have a bunch of ports at the back of the case where the cords that connect each piece of hardware are plugged in. For example, the monitor must be connected to the case before you can view the information that your computer has stored. The connection between the monitor and the computer case is made by way of a port. A cable coming from the back of the monitor is plugged into a port on the computer case. The same is true for the keyboard, mouse, and any additional equipment you may choose to have, such as a printer. On the computer case there is also a place to plug in an electrical cord to bring electricity to the computer.

Each piece of hardware has a different-shaped plug to match a specific port. This makes it difficult to plug things in incorrectly, which makes connecting the parts of a computer easier than you would expect. Laptops have fewer ports because most pieces are already connected inside the computer, but the ports they do have are on the sides or back.

Having said all that, there are also all-in-one desktop computers, as shown below, where the computer brain is built into the hardware of the monitor. All-in-ones are lean and space-saving, but a bit more expensive.

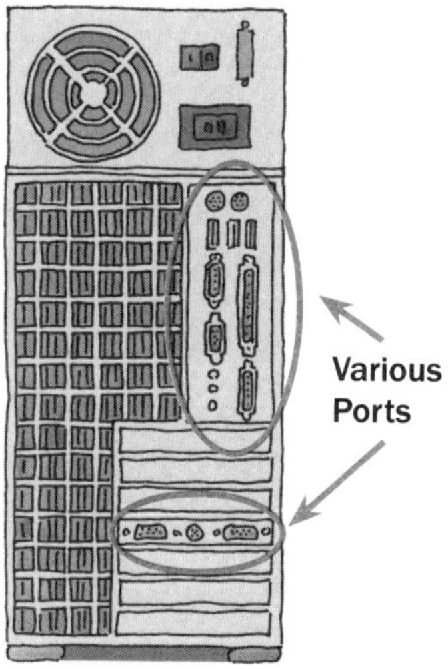

The cables that connect the various parts of the computer are plugged into ports in the back of the computer case. Thank heaven, the ports have different shapes. It makes plugging in cables a whole lot easier.

All-in-one desktop

"With every email from my kids that I print out for my mother, she gets closer and closer to wanting a computer of her own."
—***Evelyn***

Tablets

OK, time to talk tablets. A tablet computer, or simply a tablet, is a computer contained in a single panel capable of doing almost anything a desktop or laptop computer can do. Tablets are operated by fingers or a stylus, with a touch screen replacing the need for an external mouse and keyboard. You can type on a tablet by tapping on its on-screen keyboard. Most tablets are equipped with a built-in camera, microphone, and speakers. They are smaller and weigh less than a laptop so are particularly good for carrying around. We'll discuss the pros and cons of tablets in Chapter 4.

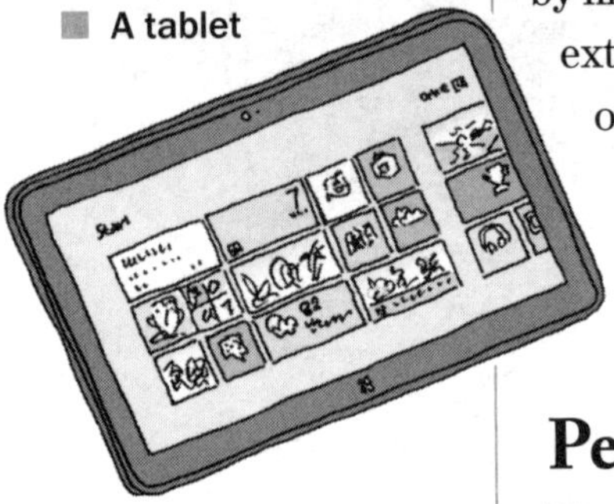

A tablet

Peripherals

Peripherals are pieces of hardware that you can use with your computer above and beyond the basic pieces we've already discussed. (For example, you might add a scanner or webcam.) These can be added at any time, so there is no urgency to buy them when you make your computer purchase. But a printer is pretty essential and I think you'd regret not having one from the get-go.

Printer

The printer will print whatever you ask it to print from the computer. For example, you can print the letters or recipes you've written or an email you've received. You can also print the information from the websites that you've pulled up on the Internet or a photo you've taken digitally or received in an email. Perhaps you have accessed a website that sells antique weather vanes. Before you make your purchase, you might print out several that appeal to you so your spouse can have a say in the decision.

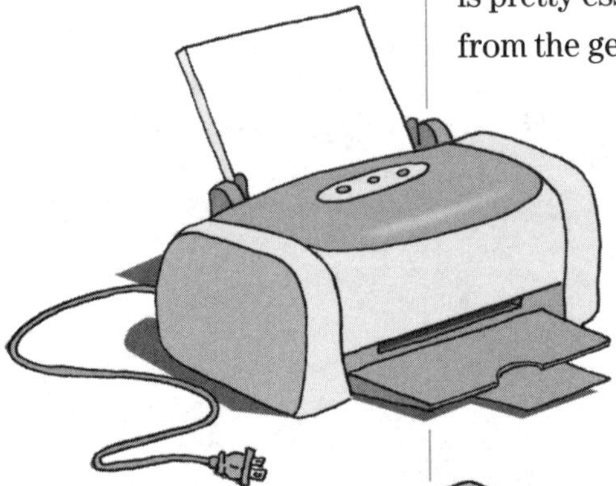

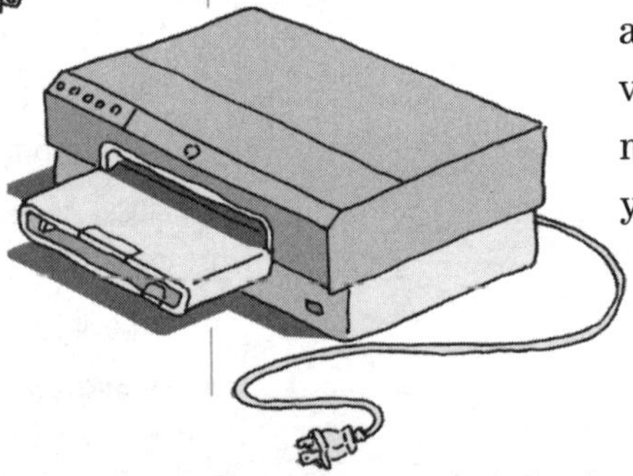

Printers, like the two here, are designed in a variety of styles and sizes.

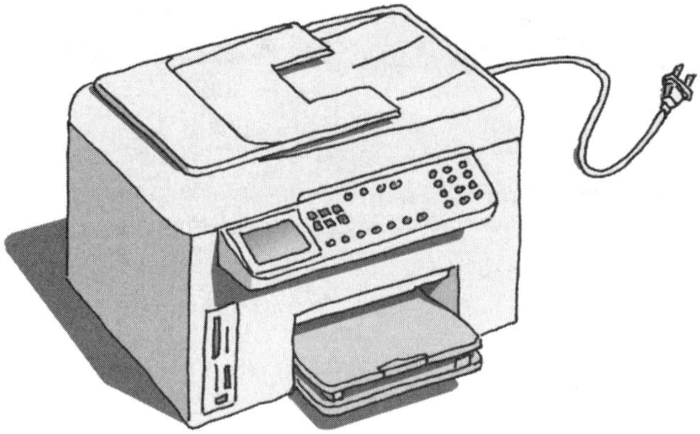

A combination printer, scanner, copier, and fax

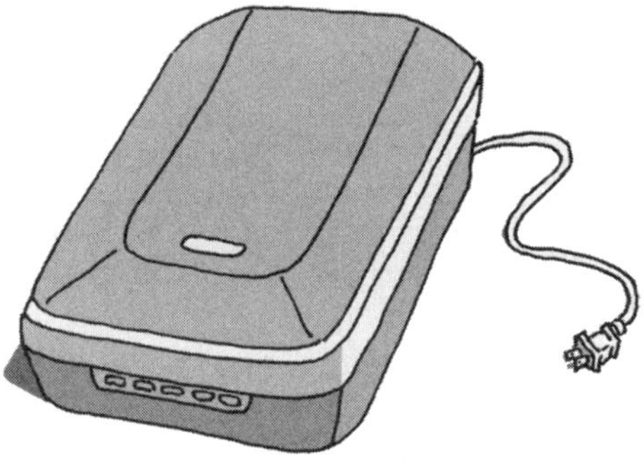

A flatbed scanner

Scanner

A scanner is a bit like a photocopier. It scans an image and sends a copy of that image to your computer. Once the image is in your computer, you can make changes to it, print it, or even send it as an email attachment. I have a student who had a basement full of boxes and boxes of family photos that no one ever looked at. She selected the best pictures, scanned them, and created a photo album that anyone in the family could access online and enjoy.

A scanner can also scan documents. This same student scanned all of the letters her husband had sent her when he was stationed in Europe during World War II. The letters were beginning to fall apart, and she didn't want to risk losing them forever.

Webcam

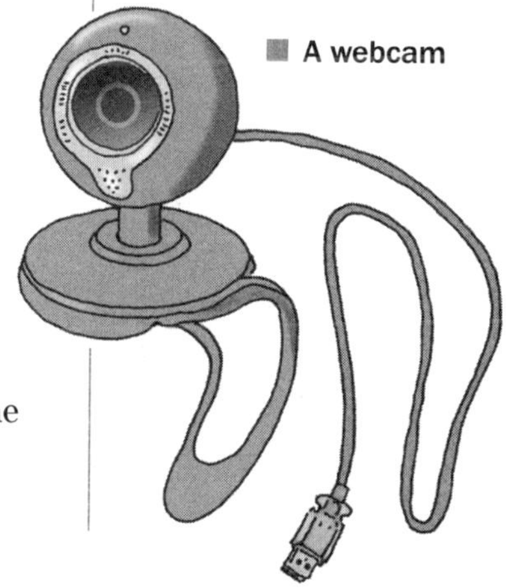

A webcam

A webcam records sounds and moving images just like a video camera does, but it can send the video over the Internet in what is referred to as "real time." Some computers have a webcam built in. It enables you to see and hear a person who also has a webcam and for them to see you in the moment that it is really happening. If you have relatives or friends who live far away and you rarely get to see one another, a webcam can bring everyone into the same room at the same time. See page 359 for more about communicating using a webcam.

LET'S REVIEW

arrow keys
features of the keyboard; allow movement around the screen

bytes
measurement of space

CD
contains software to be installed, documents, images, or music to listen to on the computer

click
depressing the mouse button to take an action

computer case
contains the CPU, hard drive, RAM, modem, and disk drives

CPU (central processing unit)
the processing part of the computer

D: drive (or E: or media drive)
the place to insert CDs or DVDs

DVD
contains software to be installed, documents, images, music to listen to, or a movie to watch on the computer

Enter or Return and function keys
features of the keyboard; hitting them allows you to perform desired actions

hard drive (or C: drive)
where information is permanently stored

hertz
measurement of speed

keyboard
used to type information into the computer

modem
communicates through a phone line or TV cable to connect to the Internet

monitor
houses the screen where information is viewed

mouse
device to move the pointer on the screen

peripherals
additional pieces of hardware, such as a printer or scanner, attached to the computer

pointer (or cursor)
appears on the screen and moves according to the manipulation of the mouse

port
where cords that connect the different computer parts are plugged in

printer
prints information from the computer

RAM (random access memory)
temporary memory used when the computer is on

scanner
copies images and text into the computer

touch screen
responds to the touch of a finger or stylus (so you don't have to type all your commands)

webcam
sends and receives video in real time through the Internet

wi-fi (wireless fidelity)
allows access to the Internet without wires or cables

Don't fret if you feel overwhelmed by the technical aspect of this information. How many of us can actually describe how our telephone works? Do you have any problem using a telephone? I don't think so!

Q: Can I use my TV set instead of buying a monitor?

A: Some new TVs allow you to use them as a computer monitor, and some computer monitors allow you to watch TV on them. But keep in mind: Where is the TV in relationship to where you'd like to use it as a computer? Can you really read an email comfortably from your sofa?

Q: Is there a keyboard designed for the visually impaired?

A: Yes, there are keyboards designed to make viewing and use easier for the visually impaired. Contact the American Foundation for the Blind (1-800-232-5463) or the American Council of the Blind (1-800-424-8666) for advice about where to order or buy exactly what you require.

Q: I'm not sure I can use a mouse because of my Parkinson's. Are there any other options?

A: Yes, you do have options. Computers didn't always use a mouse to navigate. Before the mouse came along, the keyboard was used for all tasks on the computer. There are keyboard shortcuts that allow you to use a mouse-free computer. At the back of the book is a list of shortcuts. If the touch screen of a tablet is too difficult to navigate, consider purchasing a stylus, which allows greater control. You hold it like a pencil and tap the screen with the rubber tip.

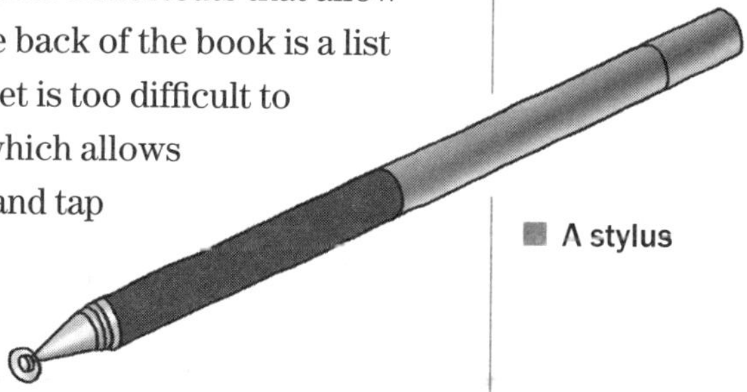

A stylus

CHAPTER 3

SOFTWARE: FEEDING THE COMPUTER'S OR TABLET'S BRAIN

An explanation of software and how it is used

For a computer or tablet to function, it must have software added to its brain. Think of it this way: Hardware is the machinery and brain of the computer. The machinery and brain are useless unless intelligence or information is added to it. Software is the information or intelligence of the brain. Without software, a computer or tablet is nothing more than a chunk of plastic. It's like the telephone: The phone is the hardware; our voices are the software.

You do not need to completely understand software to be able to use technology. My guess is that, unless you are a brain surgeon, you've been using your brain all this time without really understanding how it works in any detail. Again, the goal is to be able to use the computer, not dismantle and reassemble it!

Operating Software vs. Application Software

There are two types of software: operating software and application software. Your computer or tablet will come with operating software already stored on the hard drive. (Remember, the hard drive is the permanent memory of the device.) Operating software organizes and manages your computer. Think of it as the computer's filing system and library.

In Chapter 2, we became familiar with the central processing unit (CPU)—the hardware that organizes the flow of information. Well, the operating software works hand in hand with the CPU. A computer or tablet would not be able to function without operating software. It would be like having the lumber (hardware) to make a house, but no foundation and no blueprints (operating software).

Application software, with the help of the operating software, enables you to perform certain tasks. For example, word-processing application software allows you to use the computer as a typewriter with advanced editing tools. Other application software allows you to practice your Spanish, set up your taxes, or play chess. There are hundreds of thousands of different application software programs on the market that let you type a letter, store photos, design a website, or even chart your family genealogy.

APP = APPLICATION

The term *application software* is often shortened to *software* when referring to programs added to a computer. The nickname *app* (short for *application*) is most commonly used when referring to software added to a tablet.

DIFFERENT KINDS OF APPLICATION SOFTWARE

Communication
enables you to send email, explore the Internet

Educational
offers you typing instruction, language lessons, reference materials, and much more

Entertainment
lets you play games, music, movies, videos

Financial Management
helps you track accounts, print checks, pay bills, figure out taxes

Graphics
lets you create pictures and design cards and invitations

Organizational
helps you maintain a calendar, address book, home inventory

Word Processing
lets you type and edit letters, recipes, a novel—anything you write

WHY CAN'T I STICK WITH MY OLD UNDERWOOD?

If you make a mistake on a typewriter, you have to remove the error with correction tape or Wite-Out, or, even worse, type it all again. With a computer you can make tons of changes to a document and view it in its entirety on the screen to make sure it's just the way you want it before you print it out. The computer will even check the spelling and grammar for you.

How Does the Software Get into the Computer?

Software needs to be transferred to the brain of the computer. This is done by way of a CD or DVD or by transferring (aka downloading) the software from a website onto your computer. The computer reads the information off these disks or downloads and stores it in the brain.

A CD or DVD is inserted into the D: drive (aka the media drive). Once the disk is inserted, the computer can read its contents.

CDs and DVDs

A CD or DVD with software on it looks just like a compact disc for a stereo or a DVD with a film on it. Like a movie DVD, software discs are capable of holding sound, text, and images (even moving images), which you can access through your computer's monitor and speakers. A CD can store the equivalent of an entire set of encyclopedias, and a DVD can store up to 26 times that much information.

Installing Software from a CD or DVD

Before you can use application software, it needs to be added to the brain of the computer. To add software to your computer, your computer transfers the information stored on a CD or DVD or downloaded from the Internet onto the hard drive. This process of transferring the software to the hard drive is referred to as "installing" software. Once the software has been installed, it is stored permanently on the hard drive.

To install software from a CD or DVD, you first insert either disk into its proper drive (see the illustration to the left). The drive for the CD or DVD works in one of two ways: There may be a button you push to open the drive. What looks like a shallow version of the cup holder in your car will slide out. You will place the CD or DVD on this tray, label side up, and push the button again to close the tray. This particular piece of the computer can be quite fragile. *You never want to force the CD or DVD tray to close. Always use the open and close button.* Alternatively, your computer may not have a button to open the drive but instead a slot where you insert the CD or DVD (label side up). After part of the disk is inserted, the computer will grab the CD or DVD. You don't need to use any force.

Once the disk is inserted, you will either follow the instructions that will automatically appear on the screen of your computer or the written instructions included with the software. Through this process the hard drive will transfer and store the information from the CD or DVD into the brain of the computer. You may also hear people refer to this transferring of data as "reading" the software onto the computer.

Downloading Software

Another common option for installing software is to transfer it from the Internet or "download it." There are some computers (the MacBook Air, netbook computers, and tablets, for instance) that don't

WHERE TO GET SOFTWARE

Online

- Can often sample the software on your computer.
- Can be purchased and transferred from the Internet onto your hard drive.

In Stores

- Often have competitive prices.
- Good ones have informed salespeople.
- Offer face-to-face contact.
- Generally have a fair return policy, but do check before buying, especially opened/unopened package.

Mail-Order Catalogs

- Often have competitive prices.
- Generally have well-informed salespeople you can talk to on the phone.
- Be sure to ask if they have a money-back guarantee!

Pirating

- Unlawful to accepting unauthorized copies of software.
- No technical support from the manufacturer.

have a CD or DVD (media) drive. With these devices, your only option for installing a program is to access a website that offers the software program you seek and follow the instructions for downloading or copying the software from the site onto your computer.

How Else Can a CD or DVD Be Used?

CDs and DVDs all store information. A DVD stores 26 times as much as a CD.

We've discussed putting information into the computer, but what if you want to take information out of the computer? A CD or DVD can work in two ways. Information can be transferred from the CD or DVD onto the computer, and the reverse is also true: You can take information from the computer and store it on a CD or DVD.

Let's say that you want to give your publisher a copy of the autobiography you've typed on the computer. You could print out the whole book and lug it to the publisher's office. Or you could copy it (aka burn it) onto a blank CD, called a CD-R (for recordable), slip the disk into your pocket, and stroll over to deliver it. At that point, your publisher would copy the information from the CD onto the hard drive of his or her computer.

What's a Flash Drive?

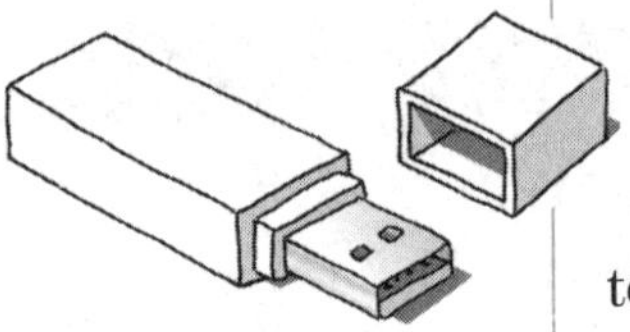

A USB flash drive

A flash drive (also called a thumb drive or a memory stick) is another method for moving information onto or off of a computer. The flash drive is plugged into a port on the computer to add or remove information. I'll describe how to do this on page 358.

Upgrading Software

Even as you install your new software, a group of diligent computer researchers (aka computer geeks) may be fast at work improving that software. So within a relatively short period of time, there might be a new and improved version of what you have purchased. This is true for application and operating software. Both are constantly being improved and changed to better meet your needs.

It may be that the upgrade (another term used for an upgrade is update) is just cosmetic or that the company corrected glitches people complained about. Rather than buying a whole new version of the software, you can get an upgrade from the manufacturer. Most manufacturers offer their upgrades for free; others may offer them at a reduced price.

Most upgrades can be installed directly from a website. Once you install the upgrade, it will automatically make changes to the existing software on your hard drive to reflect the improvements.

You do not need to upgrade your software unless you need to or want to. When the time comes, you will know whether you are interested in the improvements that are being touted. If there is any uncertainty, ask a friend with more computer experience for his or her advice or experience with upgrading.

REGISTER YOUR GOODS

It is a good idea to fill out and send in the product registration information that comes with your software. That way, the manufacturer can reach you to notify you of an upgrade for their product.

LET'S REVIEW

application software (aka app)
lets you perform specialized tasks, such as word processing

CD
contains software to be installed, documents, images, or music to listen to on the computer

CD-R (recordable)
a blank CD you can use to copy information from your computer

CD-RW (rewritable)
a blank CD you can use over and over again to copy information from your computer

DVD
contains software to be installed, documents, images, music to listen to, or a movie to watch

DVD-R (recordable)
a blank DVD you can use to copy information from your computer

DVD-RW (rewritable)
a blank DVD you can use over and over again to copy information from your computer

flash drive (aka thumb drive or memory stick)
used to copy information from or to a computer

installation process
where software is read and stored on the hard drive

operating software
the system that organizes and manages your computer

upgrade
new and improved generation of an existing software program

Q: How expensive is most software?

A: That's kind of like asking "how expensive is a car?" The price varies depending on what you're buying. Some software is actually free. I would say the cheapest personal software to purchase is around $19.99, and the costliest I've run across is close to $400. Apps—software for a tablet—can be free or purchased for as little as 99 cents or as much as $999.

Q: Will the store where I buy my computer or software install it on my computer?

A: The store where you buy your computer may be willing to install the software you purchase from them at the time of purchase. Because you're making a fairly large purchase, they should do it for free. It is certainly worth asking.

Q: My son bought Microsoft Office for his computer. Can I borrow it and install it on mine?

A: Using software that you have not paid for is called "pirating software" and is against the law. Many software manufacturers protect their product so it can be installed only once and then never again. Some programs allow for several installations. If the latter is the case with your son's software, then you can legally install it on your computer without a problem (providing your computer is compatible with that software—ask your son to check).

Q: Is it always safe to upgrade or update software?

A: You are so wise to be cautious. Instead of clicking on the notice that says your software needs to be updated, it is safer to visit the product's website and download the most recent version directly from the site.

WHERE WILL IT SLEEP AND HOW OFTEN DO I NEED TO WATER IT?

CHAPTER 4

THERE'S NO PLACE LIKE HOME VS. TAKING YOUR SHOW ON THE ROAD

Desktop vs. laptop vs. tablet

Can you picture yourself sitting in your backyard watching the roses bloom while "surfing the net"? Or perhaps you're traveling on a plane with your tablet tucked into your carry-on luggage. Maybe you're even snuggled up all comfy in your bed answering emails. On the other hand, you might be sure you'll use the computer only in the warmth of your den and have no intention of moving it. This chapter will help you decide whether a desktop, laptop, or tablet best suits your needs, based on how you think you might want to use it. If at the end of this chapter you're still on the fence, don't lose hope; we'll be test-driving your options in Chapter 7. I'm confident that when it's time to acquire your device you'll have all the information necessary to make the perfect purchase.

■ Desktop and laptop computers do the same things. The main difference is size and portability.

How Are Desktops and Laptops Alike?

First, let's talk about the two types of computers, starting with their similarities. A desktop and a laptop function in exactly the same way, using the same software and allowing you to access the Internet. They both have the same basic hardware (monitor, keyboard, and mouse) and they think alike—using the CPU (central processing unit), hard drive, and RAM (random access memory). Many have a drive to read CDs and DVDs. Software is installed on both types of computers in the same manner. They also have the capability of being linked to a printer or other peripherals using ports. (To brush up on these parts of the computer, look over the "Let's Review" sections at the ends of Chapters 2 and 3.)

KEEPING THE BATTERY CHARGED

A laptop computer's battery recharges when you plug the machine into an electrical outlet, just like your Dustbuster does. The computer doesn't need to be turned on to recharge (but your surge protector does). For maximum battery life, let the battery fully run down every month.

■ The average laptop is about the same size as a small stack of magazines and weighs between 4 and 7 pounds. Some swankier designs are even lighter.

How Is a Laptop Different from a Desktop?

Laptops and desktops differ primarily in portability. A desktop is created to stay in one place. Laptops were given their name because they are small enough and light enough to carry with you and to sit comfortably on your lap when you use them. (That said, actually having your laptop on your lap for an extended period of time isn't a great idea. A laptop can get hot when there isn't enough circulation around the computer. It's always best to have the computer on a tabletop.) A laptop can also be referred to as a "notebook" because theoretically it's about the same size as a notebook. To be realistic, many laptop computers are a little too big and heavy to slip under your arm as you would a real notebook, but they continue to get smaller and lighter every year. There are no cables connecting the monitor, keyboard, and mouse on a laptop because these parts are all contained within the machine.

How Does a Tablet Compare to a Computer?

A tablet *is* a computer. The distinction is that a tablet is fully contained in a single panel and it utilizes touch screen technology. So instead of using a mouse to navigate, you simply tap the screen to take an action. The keyboard is even integrated into the touch screen. A tablet can do pretty much anything a desktop or laptop computer can do, but it generally doesn't have as much processing power. In addition, the only way to add software (referred to as apps) to a tablet is to download it from the Internet (there is no CD or DVD drive). The other significant difference is portability. As small and light as a laptop may be, a tablet can be slipped into a handbag or even a large pocket.

The sacrifice that you make for having something portable like a laptop or tablet is that everything is smaller. On a laptop, both the monitor and keyboard are usually smaller than on a desktop—in fact, you may find some laptop screens difficult to view. If a laptop screen feels too small for you, a tablet screen might seem impossible. And if your hands are large, you may feel cramped using the keyboard or mouse on a laptop or the touch screen on a tablet. But for some people, it is infinitely more important that they can take the computer with them, even if it is a little less comfortable to use. Read on—there are some other things to consider.

"I didn't think of myself as a gadget person but I've fallen in love with my iPad. It's gorgeous and so easy to use."
—***Carolyn***

A tablet can be as small as 7.5 inches by a bit more than 5 inches and weigh slightly more than a half pound or as large as 13 inches by just under 9 inches and weigh nearly 2 pounds.

Freedom of Movement

Laptops and tablets can be plugged into a wall outlet or they can run off a battery. On average, laptops run for a few hours on a fully charged battery. Some newer models boast more than 10 hours of battery life. The battery life of a tablet can range from 5 to 13 hours. This is wonderful for people who want to use a computer while en route and who don't have access to a wall outlet. Another battery bonus: If you are plugged into a wall outlet and you lose electricity, the machine won't shut down (potentially losing the document you are working on). Instead, the battery will kick in automatically and the computer will keep going.

Unlike a desktop computer, a laptop doesn't come with an external mouse. A laptop mouse is usually either a touch pad or touch point.

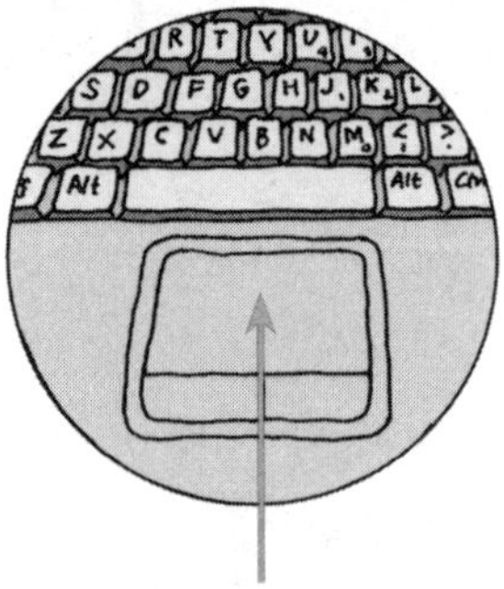

Touch Pad

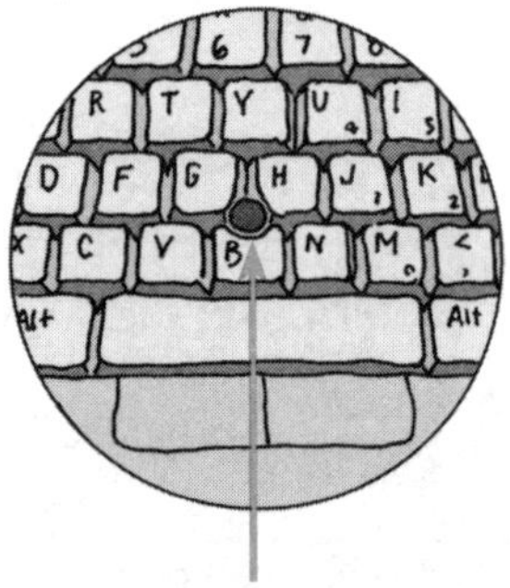

Touch Point

The Cost of Freedom

The weight of laptop computers varies. The lightest one out now is about 2 pounds, but most average about 6 pounds and may be too heavy to carry around for very long. The perk of a tablet is that the average weight is 1 pound. Remember, when you transport your compact computer, you will also have to take along the electrical cord and a case to carry it all.

There are possible disadvantages to taking your technology with you. You risk dropping it, losing it, or having it stolen. To be on the safe side, my laptop is covered under my renter's policy in case it disappears while I'm on the road.

Space Saving/Visual Appeal

A laptop may appeal to you even if you're not thinking of traveling with it. It will take up less space in your home than a desktop computer. There is a big difference between the look of a monitor, keyboard, and bulky computer case with all their messy cable attachments and that of a box the size of a small stack of magazines. Many tablet users also enjoy the ease of using their tablet to watch a movie anywhere in their home.

Let's Talk Touch Screen

Tablets utilize touch screen technology, which allows the user to tap or drag a finger or fingers on the screen to take an action—even typing. The touch screen also negates the need for a mouse. There are some desktops and laptops available with the touch screen design innovation. Using the touch screen can be difficult if you have an unsteady hand or very dry fingertips. If that's the case, you can use a stylus. For most people, it just takes a little practice on the touch screen to get the hang of it.

Stylus

Mouse Types for a Laptop

A desktop comes with a standard external mouse. This is not true of a laptop. Laptops usually come with either a touch pad or a touch point. Some manufacturers have just one type of mouse, and others offer a choice. If you're interested in purchasing a laptop, it is vital that you try out each type of mouse to see how it feels. By no means should you expect to find it easy to manipulate either of these mouse options without practice, but you may favor one over the other by its feel. Be assured that over time you will be able to use whichever mouse you choose with great dexterity.

Expense

At the moment, laptops are more expensive than desktops. Smaller parts = more technology = more $$$. Over time, this may level off. Some people play a waiting game with computers, asking themselves, "If I wait long enough, will it get cheaper?" The answer is probably yes, but as long as you shop wisely, it is very possible to buy something now and still feel like you got a good value for years to come.

QUESTIONS TO ASK YOURSELF

1. Do you want to be able to use your computer anywhere?

2. Do you want a large screen?

3. Do you need a standard-size keyboard?

4. Do you have a very limited amount of space at home?

5. Do you want to spend as little as possible for as much speed and power as you can get?

6. Do you have a bad back and shouldn't carry anything heavy?

7. Do you want portability with a built-in keyboard?

8. Do you want a computer you can slip in your pocket?

Answers if "yes": 1. Laptop or Tablet; 2. Desktop; 3. Desktop; 4. Laptop or Tablet; 5. Desktop; 6. Desktop or Tablet; 7. Laptop; 8. Tablet.

Having Said All This . . .

I didn't mean to hold out on you, but I wanted you to really weigh your basic options before I tell you how you can have it both ways. If you want to buy a laptop because it's portable, but you're concerned about the comfort of working on a laptop while at home, you could plug a larger monitor and a standard keyboard into your laptop

It is possible to attach an external mouse, keyboard, and/or monitor to a laptop so you can enjoy the larger features of a desktop.

through ports in the machine. And if you don't like the mouse on your laptop, you can even attach an external mouse.

You may now know which type of computer (laptop, desktop, or tablet) is best for you. But if you don't, have no fear. Once you've seen and touched a variety of devices, you will instinctively feel what is right for you. Just keep reading and we'll get there together. For those of you who already know what kind you want to buy, stick with us—there's still more to consider.

Q: What is the difference between a notebook and a laptop?

A: I once posed a similar question to a farmer when visiting the Berkshires. "What's the difference between a pig and a hog?" I asked. "Way you spell it," he answered. That is the same answer for the difference between a notebook and a laptop computer. Two names for the same thing.

Q: Is a netbook different from a laptop?

A: A netbook (don't mistake it for a notebook) is a small, lightweight, and inexpensive laptop. Netbooks average 2 to 3 pounds and the screens are quite small—they measure between 5 and 10 inches. Their keyboards are also small and they do not have the ability to read CDs or DVDs. Netbooks are less expensive than laptops and can be purchased for as little as $200.

Q: Is there a better time of year to buy a computer?

A: Good question. My experience is that after Christmas, computer salespeople are often willing to negotiate prices.

Q: Is it wrong to buy a laptop if I'm never going to move it from my desk?

A: No, not at all. A laptop takes up less space than a desktop. If space is at a premium, buy whatever fits into your home and lifestyle.

Q: Why wouldn't I buy a tablet if I wanted something portable?

A: If you're working with complex spreadsheets, heavily designed documents, or lots of typing, the smaller format of a tablet can make the task more difficult to manage than it would on a laptop. Also, if you need to use a particular software program, be sure there is a tablet version available online.

"Within a few months, we both loved the computer so much that we decided to buy a laptop so we could take it with us when we travel, and so when we're home we don't fight over whose turn it is to use the desktop computer!"

—Marie and Larry

CHAPTER 5

CREATING A COMPUTER COMFORT ZONE

Tips on finding a comfortable and safe work area

Some people don't need to designate a space in their home for a computer. With a tablet or laptop, they can hop from the sofa to their deck to the bed and stay connected. With a desktop, they need to think through where their computer will live in their home. One of my students converted a closet into a small home office; she opens the closet door and pulls up a chair to work on the computer. Another student utilizes an old armoire in a similar way. When she's done working, she just closes the doors and her "little secret" is hidden in the living room. Setting up shop inside an extra closet may work for one person but may not be very pleasant for another.

Assuming you can use the dining room table and move all your things in time for dinner isn't realistic. Using that spare storage room may seem like a great idea, but if you leave all those musty boxes in there with you, you're probably not going to want to spend much time in there, either. Take a few minutes to stroll around your home. Scan the space for possible work areas. Ideally, where you put your desktop will be a space where you like to be.

What You Need to Check Out

You'll want to choose a spot near an electrical outlet. If your setup is not near an electrical outlet, you will end up with extension cords for the computer, as well as whatever peripherals you may buy, snaking all over the floor.

The Wi-Fi Question

Wi-fi allows communication to happen between your computer or tablet and the Internet without the computer having to be plugged into a modem for the signal. I'll go into more detail about wi-fi in Chapter 13. If you don't use wi-fi technology, the location of your computer will be dependent on where the modem is located in your home.

The Computer Desk

Even though a laptop is smaller than a desktop, it, too, needs a happy and safe home. One of my students confessed that she sits on the sofa with her computer on her lap while watching television. (It *is* called a laptop, isn't it?) This is fine every once in a while, but even a laptop

THE THREE LITTLE BEARS TEST
Set a chair where you think you might like to put your computer workstation. Sit in the chair for a bit—read a chapter of this book, check out the sports section, or browse a magazine. Does the space feel right to you? Is it too noisy? Is it too drafty? Or is it just right?

All-in-one desktop computers are designed to take up less space.

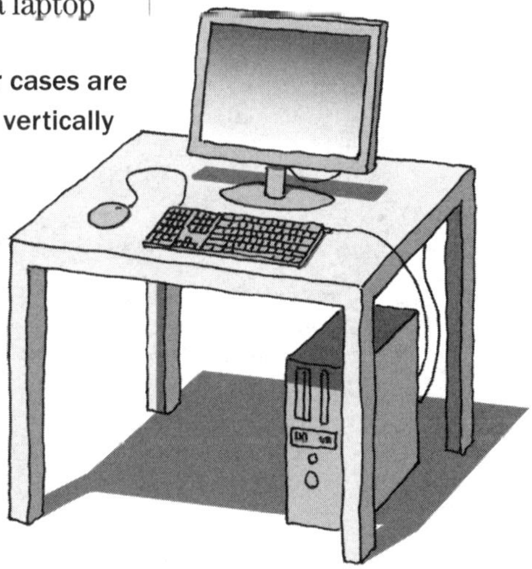

Tower computer cases are designed to stand vertically under a desk.

should have a designated work area. It will make your time at the computer more efficient and enjoyable.

If your computer is a desktop, you'll need a table or desk large enough to hold the monitor, keyboard, and, depending on the model, the computer case.

Tower computer cases stand vertically and can fit under a desk, thereby saving a great deal of desktop space. No matter where your case is, be sure it is positioned within reach (not a big stretch) from where you will sit so you can easily turn it on and insert a CD or DVD.

All-in-one computers are designed to house all components within the body of the monitor or on the base that holds the monitor. Whether you choose a laptop or a desktop, you'll also need to have enough empty space on your desk to hold a book or any papers you might refer to while you're at the computer.

A standard old-fashioned desk is usually too high for proper computer posture. Ideally, your thighs should be at about a 90-degree angle to your calves and, with your hands resting on the keyboard, your elbows should be at a 90-degree angle as well. This can be achieved in three different ways.

Watch your posture and your distance from the screen. Your elbows, knees, and hips should be at 90-degree angles.

1. If possible, adjust the height of your chair to put your body higher than you would normally sit at the desk. Unfortunately, this may cramp your leg space.

2. Invest in a computer desk or workstation. Not only is it designed to accommodate peripherals (such as your printer), thereby giving you a single unit where all the parts of your computer can be together, but your keyboard will also be at the proper height in a holder attached below the desktop. The position of the keyboard is significant because

you prevent wrist injury when you maintain a straight line from elbow to fingertips.

3. If you don't want to invest in a special computer desk, you can buy a keyboard holder that can be installed under your current desk. This will put the keyboard at a healthier height and free up more desk space.

A retractable keyboard shelf fits under a desk or computer table.

You don't have to have your computer space set up perfectly in the beginning. I'm just letting you know that the more you use the computer, the more you'll have to be careful not to strain yourself in any way. If all you have at the moment is a card table in the corner of your living room, start there. My computer is set up on an antique tea cart in my dining room with the printer on the shelf below. I use a dining room chair with two pillows on it. Because this is not the best arrangement for my back, I make sure to get up and walk around every half hour or so.

Some Other Things You Need to Consider

Certain health issues should not be ignored when choosing where you set up your computer. "Ergonomically correct" is a phrase becoming almost as popular as "politically correct." It refers to creating a healthy work environment and positioning your body properly to accomplish the task at hand without injury.

Monitor: Your monitor should be at a 15-degree angle below your sight line. Flat-panel monitors often have an adjustable neck to allow you to find the perfect height. If you set the monitor on the computer case, that may or may not bring it to the correct height. If it doesn't, try setting the monitor on a large phone book or a dictionary, instead. Be sure the monitor is stable.

Chair: The chair you sit on is extremely important. Make sure you have proper back support. If you want to make the investment, an adjustable office chair is the best choice. Used office furniture can often be found through your local classified section or online if you have a friend or family member to help you shop on the Internet.

Footrest: You also want to make sure you don't cut off circulation to the backs of your legs. If you need to raise your feet, an open file drawer, a wastebasket, or a couple of books make a great inexpensive footrest.

To avoid eyestrain, it is essential to position the monitor properly.

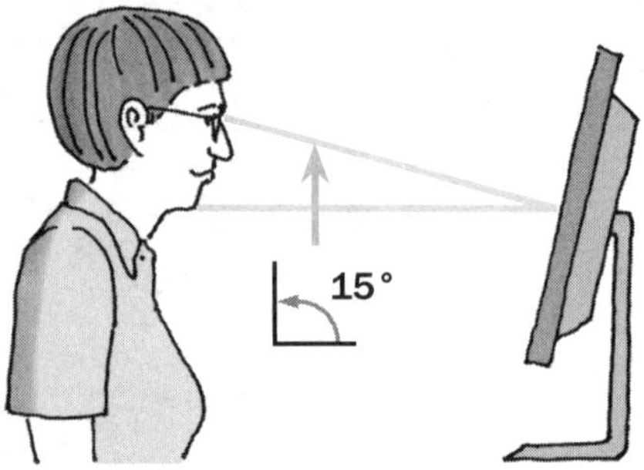

Glasses: If you wear glasses (especially bifocals or progressives), you may want to visit your eye doctor to be sure your prescription will be accurate for the computer. I have several students who have a separate pair of glasses that they use exclusively for the computer.

Keyboard: Your keyboard should be at a height where your elbows are at a 90-degree angle and there is an unbroken line from your wrists to your fingertips. Try adding a cushion to your chair, if you need to sit higher.

To avoid wrist strain, keep a straight line from your elbow to your fingertips.

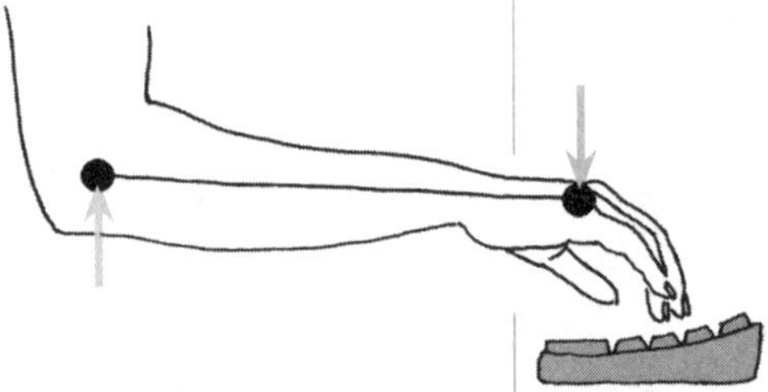

Injuring yourself while sitting at a computer may seem a bit odd to you, but it's not uncommon. Bad posture, repetitive motion, and eyestrain can take a real toll. Many people lose track of time when they're in front of a computer. Before they know it, they've been staring at the screen for two solid hours without ever moving their body from its slightly slumped position.

We'll review safety issues again when you are actually using the computer.

BUILD IN BREAKS

The National Institute of Occupational Safety and Health recommends that you take at least one 15-minute break for every hour that you are at the computer. You need to relax your eyes and move your body a bit. Something as simple as going to the kitchen to get a drink of water is enough to ease strain.

A Few Don'ts

Besides making sure you're physically comfortable at the computer, there are a few potential problems to watch out for when setting things up.

Don't place the computer in too tight a space. A computer generates a fair amount of heat, and you want to make sure that air can circulate around it.

Don't place the computer by an open window. The glare from the sun may make it difficult to view the screen. Also, constant direct sunlight on the computer can make the computer too warm when in use. And all of the microscopic things that blow in the window (whether it is grit in New York City or pollen in Nebraska) can eventually damage the inner workings of the computer.

Don't let your animals get too friendly with your computer. Cats in particular are attracted to the heat emitted by the computer case and monitor. Unfortunately, animal fur can really muck up your system.

Don't put your computer equipment in a room with thick carpeting. Very thick carpeting can conduct excessive static electricity, which can be harmful to the computer. If you choose to get a tower computer case, do not set it directly on carpeting. There are trays you can buy to hold it, or simply set it on a wooden board.

Don't place any magnets near the computer or the software. Magnets have been known to damage monitors. Crazy, but true.

Don't place any kind of liquid near the computer. Spilling fluids on the keyboard can cause serious and expensive damage. This includes cereal and milk. I had to have my computer repaired after breakfast didn't make it from the bowl to my mouth. If my computer hadn't still been under warranty, I'd have been crying over spilt milk.

What Else?

You've chosen your work area and decided the best way to arrange everything once you make your purchase. Be sure to measure your workspace before you go computer shopping. Bring the measurements with you and refer to them to ensure a perfect fit. One last thing: You will need a small amount of easy-access storage space near your work area. A shelf in a bookcase or a file box will do. You'll want a place to store assembly instructions, instruction manuals (although most of these materials are available online), installation CDs and DVDs, as well as other office supplies, such as paper and replacement ink cartridges for your printer.

Addressing the issues of your workspace before you go into a store ensures that your computer will have a good home. Now we can get to the business of deciding what kind of computer is right for you.

Q: What are some tips for preventing back pain and other discomfort when using a computer?

A: The best thing you can do is take a 15-minute break every hour. Walk around and stretch before you sit down again. Be very aware of your posture, as well.

Q: My cat loves to sleep on top of the CPU. Is that bad?

A: Yes, that's bad! It isn't good for your computer *and* I doubt it is healthy for your cat. Set a large bowl on top of the CPU to dissuade the cat from curling up there. Just don't put anything liquid into the bowl. That would be dangerous near the equipment.

Q: Can I put my computer in front of my air conditioner?

A: The real enemy of a computer is heat, not cold. Nonetheless, my concern is the air blowing onto the computer. I'd imagine unwanted particles would be more apt to get into your computer in that location. Try to find a spot that's not directly in front of your AC.

Q: How do I avoid bad posture with a tablet?

A: Rather than buying a computer desk, you can buy an easel-like reading table. These are usually adjustable so you can have it at the perfect height and angle for you. When you are away from home, try to get in the habit of holding the tablet at eye level. It's good exercise for your arms and it imposes regular breaks because your arms will get tired.

Watch your posture when using a tablet.

GO FOR A TEST-DRIVE

CHAPTER 6

APPLES AND ORANGES

Mac vs. PC

Perhaps you've decided that a desktop or a laptop computer best meets your needs, and you're not considering a tablet right now. And you've scoped out your home for the perfect place to set up shop. The next big question is—should you buy a Mac or a PC computer?

Personal computers made by Apple are referred to as Macs (as in Macintosh, the first personal computer the company brought out) and, as you have probably seen, their logo is an apple.

Macs were the first computers designed for personal use that used visuals (or icons) as a way to get from one piece of information on the computer to another. They also introduced the mouse and menus (lists of options). These innovations were intended to make the Mac easy, fun to use, and less confusing.

In the 1980s, IBM came out with a model called the IBM PC (IBM Personal Computer). For a while people referred to other non-Mac brands as IBM compatible, but that didn't make for catchy advertising, so the partial name PC (personal computer) stuck.

"I had no idea that my daughter used a different type of computer than I did. I thought they all worked the same. When I called her in a panic and she couldn't help me, I felt lost. Luckily, my neighbor also has a PC, and he came to my rescue."
—*Dan*

Technically, a Mac is also a personal computer (PC), but it has the prestige of carrying its own brand name. For our purposes an Apple computer is a Mac, and everything else is a PC.

Many companies followed in the footsteps of the original IBM PC and actually surpassed IBM in sales. Some of the manufacturers' names might be familiar to you: Hewlett-Packard (HP), Dell, and Toshiba, among others.

What Makes a PC and a Mac So Different?

When Apple introduced the first Macintosh in 1984, the differences between its system and that of the PC were enormous. Mac had an incredibly easy operating system (remember, the operating system is what manages the information you have in your machine) and became known as the company that made computers user-friendly. That translates to being easy to use, less intimidating, and more fun. They accomplished this through creative graphic design and the use of visual cues to access information on the computer.

Apple made the decision not to share its operating system with any other manufacturers. Think of it this way: Macs speak a special language all their own. The pickle is that Macs and PCs have different operating systems. When software is designed, it needs to be designed in one version for Macs to understand and in another version for all other PCs to understand. When Apple decided *not* to

THE PROS AND CONS OF MACS AND PCS

Pros

Macs
- still considered more user-friendly
- great service record
- used by most graphic designers

PCs
- less expensive
- software may hit the market first
- more brands available

Cons

Macs
- more expensive, but prices are dropping
- not always compatible with non-Mac software
- software can take longer to come to market

PCs
- design is still catching up to the Mac
- operating system is more of a target for viruses

share its operating system, this left the door open for someone else to enter the market to create another "user-friendly" operating system. That is exactly what Microsoft did when it came out with Windows 95 (an ancestor of Windows XP, Vista, Windows 7, and the great-great-great-great-grandfather of Windows 8). Microsoft designed a PC operating system based on a lot of the Mac's original ideas. The creation of Windows 95 gave PCs an operating system as straightforward and user-friendly as the Mac's.

Up until recently, there were close to eight PC computer owners for every Mac owner. Tablets have changed that ratio, with Apple dominating the tablet market. This is significant because if most people are buying software for a PC, naturally the priority for manufacturers is to create software for the majority. Now, however, most software is designed for both Macs and PCs more or less simultaneously. That said, if you have specific software that you know you'll be using, be sure it is compatible with whichever brand of computer you choose to purchase.

From a teaching and learning point of view, having only one operating system for all computers would make our technological lives so much easier. That way, we could all speak the same language. You'll see what I mean later when I describe how to use a computer if you have a PC, then how to use it if you have a Mac.

The basic pieces of hardware are the same on both systems. However, the ports where you plug in the monitor and other peripherals may be different. That means that you can't always plug a Mac peripheral into a PC and vice versa without some kind of adapter, unless the peripheral plugs into a USB port. This is another reason why the division between

USB cable

USB = UNIVERSAL SERIAL BUS
Universal is the key word. A USB cable will plug into both a Mac and a PC.

PC

Some of the ports at the back of a PC.

the two is hard to bridge. It is more seamless if you commit to one or the other—they don't always mix well.

The dispute between Mac users and PC users is legendary. If you haven't experienced it, just ask Mac users if they would change to a PC, and they will more than likely square their shoulders and give you a powerful "never." A PC user might even offer you a knuckle sandwich. I know it sounds ridiculous, but it's true.

Enough Already. Which Should I Buy?

One big consideration is what your friends and family have—not because you can't march to a different drummer, but because if you find yourself calling someone at 3:00 p.m. on a Sunday with a computer problem, that person's ability to advise you will be limited if he or she has a different operating system than you. What if your daughter wanted to give you her old monitor or share some software, but she has a Mac and you have a PC? You'd be out of luck. That said: Don't make a mountain out of a molehill. You will learn to use and love whatever computer you decide to buy. This is a win-win situation. There are more happy PC users in the world than blades of grass in your backyard, and the same is true for Mac users.

LET'S REVIEW

Apple
brand of personal computer with a unique operating system

Mac
nickname for Apple personal computers

PC
personal computer; used as a name for any computer other than a Mac

Windows
the operating system currently used on PCs

Q: If I learn on a Mac, will I be able to use a PC at some point?

A: Sure. You can learn anything. There are some differences in how things look on the screen and how to organize documents, but I have total faith that you can make the transition. And once you're on the Internet there are very few differences between the two.

Q: How can I tell an Apple computer from a Mac computer?

A: You can't tell one from the other because they are one and the same. Apple and Mac are two names for the same brand of computer.

Q: I have an iPhone and am ready for a computer. Should I buy an Apple or a PC?

A: You'll be able to learn to use either a PC or a Mac, but since you are already in the Apple "family" with your iPhone, purchasing an Apple computer would prevent any compatibility issues.

Q: Do I need to buy an Apple computer from an Apple store?

A: Apple computers can be purchased from non-Apple computer stores. However, if you do so, make sure the store allows you to also buy AppleCare, which provides you with Apple's tech support services (which are very good) and makes you eligible to take Apple's in-store classes (which are also very good).

POPULARITY CONTEST

If all your friends have Macs, get a Mac. If they all have PCs, get a PC, but don't limit yourself to purchasing the same brand as all your friends. All PCs work the same way, no matter who manufactures them.

CHAPTER 7

WOULD YOU BUY A CAR WITHOUT TEST-DRIVING IT?

What to look for when you get behind a keyboard

On more than one occasion I have received calls from students who want me to "choose whatever technology you think is best for me." For the same reasons that it is unwise to buy a car without a test-drive, it is unwise to buy a computer or tablet without taking a few different models for a spin. As with a car, you're looking for comfort, ease, speed, and quality at the best price possible. How can you know about comfort and ease until you actually touch the machine? Speed and quality, however, can be determined through research, which includes talking with computer-using friends and family.

What makes one person buy a Cadillac and another a VW bug? I can tell you what kind of computer I like, but my hands may be smaller, my eyesight worse, and my needs entirely different from yours. No matter how tempting it is or how much easier it seems, *don't have someone else make your technology-buying decisions for you.* An experienced computer user can give you great advice, but you have to get your hands on the machine before you make the final decision. Your adviser is not the one who is going to sit in front of the device and use it. You are. Would you buy a pair of shoes without trying them on?

"I think I was more scared buying my first computer than when I went in for surgery. So, I brought a friend for support. In the end, it wasn't that bad."
—*Eliza*

Preparation for Your Test-Drive

Here is a little homework that you need to do before you step into a store to test-drive computers.

Try out the technology of your friends and family. Keep in mind that people are usually very loyal to the tech gadget they use and think it is the *only* choice. For your research assignment, the more variety, the better. If no one you know has a computer, go to your local library, community center, or even high school. I guarantee you'll find someone around who is proud of his or her computer skills and eager to show off their tech toys.

Do research. An eager salesperson can send you reeling with too much information, so it's best to go into the store with a few computer brands in mind. The salesperson might very well show you a gem that you didn't know about, but you're always better off having done some research on your own.

Look through computer magazines to get an idea of what computers you're interested in seeing. Call the magazine publisher and see which issue has the most recent list of the top-ten computers or tablets to buy. Get a copy of that issue and narrow your choice to three or four of their top recommendations. Mark the articles so that you remember which computers you want to see. Don't try to read the entire magazine unless you're very interested. It can be confusing (and boring) and may put you off buying a new device.

You might want to call several computer mail-order stores listed in the back of this book. Feel free to ask whatever questions you have. The telephone salespeople are usually very helpful and informative. Give them a call, but do not make a purchase yet. It is still important that you go into a store and test-drive different

"I can't remember what book I read last week. Without my notes, I would never have been able to make the right computer choice."
—*Claire*

machines—although you may ultimately decide to buy your computer through the mail.

Take notes in advance. It's so easy to become confused or forget details. Write down the size of your available workspace, the components you know you're interested in, what information you would like explained, and the brands you want to test-drive. It is a great way to keep organized, and it may make a salesperson stand a little bit more at attention.

In addition to the marked articles, you'll want to take a note like the one below with you.

WHAT I WANT MY COMPUTER TO HAVE

Must-Haves

- *No less than 4 GB of RAM, more than 8 GB unnecessary*
- *Scanner (may be included with printer)*
- *Bare-bones word-processing software*

Questions

- *Is there an extended warranty policy?*
- *Can someone come to my house and set it up? How much will that cost?*

Workspace

- *Old teacher's desk with space underneath: 24 inches high by 30 inches wide*

Be prepared to take notes while you're shopping. There is nothing worse than spending a whole afternoon shopping for a new device, checking out a half-dozen possibilities, and then returning home and not being able to remember one from the other. You definitely don't want to have that happen. There's a form beginning on page 60 that you can use to take down the information you gathered on your expedition. Later you will be able to review your notes and discuss your choices with others without mixing up the details.

The task at hand is to find out what feels and looks right to you. You are on an information-gathering mission.

> "Laptop. Desktop. Tablet. I had no idea what I wanted. The moment I saw them all in the store, I knew a laptop was for me."
> —*Mario*

If You Haven't Decided Between a Desktop or a Laptop or a Tablet . . .

If you still haven't decided which is best for you, make a trip to the computer store solely to help you determine which device you should buy. Try a couple of models of each. While you're at it, think about your workspace and how you're planning to use the machine. Keep in mind that all the basic hardware components are the same on a laptop or a desktop and between tablets. What you're considering is whether the size of each type of device suits your needs and whether you want something portable. Once you think you've made a choice, or if you're feeling overwhelmed, leave the store. Either go have lunch and return in the afternoon or come back another day to continue your field trip. If you feel you've absorbed all you can, take a break. This is an important decision, and you want to make a thoughtful choice. If you're still confused after your trip, take another look at the questions in Chapter 4 to help you make your decision.

It's Only a Test-Drive

Before we prepare for your excursion, I want to make sure you're clear about the purpose of this adventure. Test-driving is not the same as buying. No matter how tempting, *do not buy* your device the same day that you test-drive it. You still have more to learn. At the end of Chapter 8, you can put this book down and go shopping.

That said, my mother has friends who have gone through a whole course of computer lessons at her senior center and still haven't bought a computer because they're intimidated by the computer store. The sad thing is that without a device to practice on, they have forgotten all they had learned. Promise yourself that you will go to the store before finishing the entire book. This way you will make the trip, realize it isn't such a big deal, and then continue learning more about the available technologies before you make your investment.

It's empowering to know that this is nothing more than a research expedition. No obligation, no financial outlay, no decision making. If you don't want to go back, there is always the option of mail order or purchasing from the store by phone so you never have to reenter the place. And remember, if the salesperson you are dealing with really doesn't appeal to you, give him the brush off, let him get out of sight, smile sweetly at another salesperson, and watch her come running.

Initially, the computer store can sometimes add to any confusion you might have, especially after you get home and try to remember all you saw. The Test-Drive Form that follows will give you a written record to reference at your own pace in your own home. Copy these pages to bring with you to the store. If it's easier, rip the pages out to make the copies. (Yup, you have my permission.)

TEST-DRIVE FORM

1. **Store:**____________________

   Salesperson: ____________________

   Note the address and phone number of the store and the name of the salesperson you spoke with.

2. **Brand & Model of Computer or Tablet:** ____________

   Include any numbers that follow the brand name—this will indicate the model. For example: Dell Inspiron 15 3000.

3. **Cost:** ____________________

   Note the basic cost and any additional costs. For example: $499 plus $50 for RAM upgrade = $549.

SYSTEM INFORMATION

4. **Computer Case:** ☐ All-in-One ☐ Tower

   If you're buying a desktop, is the computer case an all-in-one or a tower model that will go on the floor?

5. CPU Speed: ________________ Upgradable ☐ Yes ☐ No

Remember, the central processing unit (CPU) speed is measured in gigahertz (GHz). You will need a CPU with at least 1.7 GHz, but if you want to splurge, you could go as high as 3 GHz, or even higher. Tablets don't allow for as much customization as computers do. Comparing CPU speed is only for computer buyers.

6. RAM: ____________________ Upgradable ☐ Yes ☐ No

The random access memory (RAM) size is measured in bytes—specifically gigabytes (GB) for RAM. You will want a RAM size of at least 4 GB—but 8 GB or higher is more fun because you can have more programs open at the same time.

7. Hard Drive: ________________ Upgradable ☐ Yes ☐ No

The hard drive size is also measured in bytes—these days usually in gigabytes (GB), but it can go as high as a terabyte (TB = 1,000 GB). With a computer, I recommend that you start with at least 250 GB. I doubt you'll require as much as a terabyte, but it all depends on how many photos and videos or how much music you store on your computer. With a tablet, the low end for the hard drive is 16 GB, but you can go as high as 512 GB. Again, your decision is based on how much you want to store on the device.

8. Monitor Size: ____

Monitor size is measured in diagonal inches from a top corner to the opposite bottom corner of the screen itself. For most, a bigger computer screen is better, but compact and portable may be what you want. You can judge what suits you best by checking out several different sizes.

9. Touch Screen: ☐ Yes ☐ No

Touch screen technology is not limited to tablets. Many new laptop and desktop computers offer touch screens as well. Touch for yourself and see if you have a preference.

"Even with all the choices in the store, there were only a couple of computers that appealed to me. My son helped me decide which of these few was the best."

—*Bert*

"I'm glad I didn't have someone else buy my tablet for me. I learned so much when I visited the computer store."
—*Kreeson*

10. Media (CD/DVD) or Optical Drive: ☐ Yes ☐ No

Media or Optical Drives allow your computer to read CDs or DVDs. It's a two-way operation. You can copy information from the CD or DVD onto the computer or copy information from the computer onto a CD or DVD. Tablets and netbooks do not have built-in media drives. Fewer laptop and desktop computers have a media drive now as most people download movies or programs directly from the Internet. If you want to watch your DVD collection on your computer, be sure that it has media/optical drive (also called a DVD drive).

---

11. Number of USB Ports: ______________________

USB stands for "Universal Serial Bus." It is today's most commonly used type of computer port to plug in a mouse, keyboard, printer, or scanner. It's also where you insert a flash drive (see page 53). If you're buying a computer, you want to be sure your computer has at least two USB ports. If it has only one USB port, you can purchase a USB hub, which offers additional USB ports off the hub, but a computer with additional USB ports is preferable. Tablets vary. Some do and some don't have ports, and that might make your decision right there.

---

12. Ethernet: ☐ Yes ☐ No

This port is used to connect your computer to an external DSL or cable modem for a high-speed Internet connection. An ethernet port looks like a phone jack, but it is slightly wider. Even if you aren't interested in a high-speed Internet connection at the moment, you'll want your computer to have the capacity for it down the road. Tablets don't use an ethernet port.

---

13. Wireless: ☐ Wireless ☐ Cellular Data

A tablet uses wireless technology to connect to the Internet. Some tablets offer wi-fi only, and some also offer cellular connection. With the latter, you will have the choice of using its wi-fi capability (which limits you to connecting only when wi-fi is available) or paying a monthly fee for cellular data, which gives you a connection 24/7. Be sure to ask if the tablet is limited to wi-fi or offers both.

14. **Speakers Included:** ☐ Yes ☐ No

15. **Webcam Built-In:** ☐ Yes ☐ No

16. **Type of Mouse:** ____________ **Notes on Feel:** ____________

If you are buying a desktop, it will come with a standard mouse. If you are buying a laptop, note which kind of mouse it comes with (touch pad or touch point). Jot down some notes on the feel of each. Remember, you can't be expected to master the mouse at this point, but you will have an impression of how it feels. Is the mouse positioned in a place that seems easy to access or is your hand cramped while using it? Your mouse will be your constant companion when you're on the computer, so it must be comfortable to access and control. But generally speaking, control will come with practice.

17. **Notes on Keyboard:** ____________________________

Note the feel of the keyboard. Do the keys feel mushy? Are they too resistant? Or are they just right?

18. **How Will It Fit in Your Workspace?** ____________________

Take notes on how you picture your computer system in your home.

SUPPORT

19. **Warranty:** ____________________________________

The length of the warranty will be in months. What parts fall under the warranty? Ask if the screen is covered. It is the most fragile part of the device.

"I was apprehensive about our class field trip to a nearby computer store. It seemed much more than I could handle. But once I tried a couple of different computers, I knew that it was the right thing to do. I still wouldn't stroll into a computer store for fun, but it helped me make a more informed decision."
—*Vance*

20. Extended Warranty: ____________________

Cost: ____________________

It's more than likely that the computer store where you make your purchase will offer you an extended warranty. This is an agreement with the store or mail-order company, not the manufacturer. The agreement is valid only if the store is open and in business for as long as the extended warranty—a good reason to make sure you are shopping at a reputable store. Because a single repair on a computer can run into the hundreds of dollars, consider a warranty.

---

21. Money-Back Guarantee: ☐ Yes ☐ No

This may be an agreement with the manufacturer that you have a certain number of days to return the machine—kind of like the lemon law. Beware: Some manufacturers will not exchange a computer even if it is defective. They may offer only to repair the machine. In that case, you may want to engage your credit card company as an advocate for you. Or, before contacting the manufacturer, call the store you purchased it from and ask if it is willing to exchange the defective computer.

---

22. Technical Support: ☐ Yes ☐ No

This is crucial. You want to make sure that the store or mail-order company you purchase from has technical support. The last thing you want to have to do is pack up your computer and mail it to the manufacturer. It is irritating enough to have to bring it to the store for repairs. Ask specifically about telephone technical support. A lot of questions or problems can be answered by a telephone call to a technician.

You should be getting free support for the length of your warranty, whether you have a problem with your computer or you have a question about how to use the machine.

If the manufacturer, not the store, provides the technical support, ask your salesperson for the technical repair numbers of the manufacturers you are considering. When you are home, call the numbers and see how long it takes for you to speak to a technician.

I've been on hold with some for over 20 minutes. This could be a deciding factor in determining which computer you purchase.

23. **On-Site Repair:** ☐ Yes ☐ No **Cost:** ________

Can someone come to your home to repair your computer? How much will it cost if it is still under warranty? What if the warranty has expired?

24. **On-Site Installation:** ☐ Yes ☐ No **Cost:** ________

Can someone come to your house to install your system? (This is more relevant for desktops than for laptops or tablets.)

SOFTWARE

Note: Software questions are only for computers, not tablets.

25. **Operating System:** ____________________

Preinstalled Software: ____________________

Note the operating system in the computer (Windows 8.1 or 10, Mac Mavericks, Yosemite, other) and any preinstalled application software. For example, many computers come with a basic word-processing program, such as WordPad or NotePad, already installed.

26. **Additional Software:** ____________ **Cost:** ________

Additional Software: ____________ **Cost:** ________

You may want to buy word-processing software or some other software, based on your interests. We'll talk about this choice in Chapter 8.

PRINTER

27. **Brand Name & Model:** ____________________

Include any numbers that follow the brand name—they will indicate the model.

28. **Cost:** ____________________

"I almost skipped computer class the day of the field trip to the store. It made me think of going to the dentist. But it wasn't that bad at all. I've already gone back twice on my own to ask more questions."

—*Nicole*

29. Type of Printer: ☐ Ink-jet ☐ Laser-jet

An ink-jet printer is less expensive at purchase time, but a laser printer proves cheaper over the long term because it uses toner cartridges, which last much longer than ink cartridges purchased for the ink-jet. However, that only proves true if you're doing a large volume of printing. Most individuals opt for an ink-jet printer, and most businesses purchase a laser-jet.

---

30. Features: ☐ Color ☐ Black & White Only
☐ Fax/Copy ☐ Scanner

You will choose features based on your specific needs. Some printers send faxes and/or make copies. A color printer and scanner might be helpful if you decide to create something like a family newsletter or your own greeting cards. Color is definitely fun if you're printing from a website or want to print pictures. With a color printer, you have to purchase both a black ink cartridge and a color ink cartridge. Be prepared; cartridges can be pricey.

---

31. Paper Loading: ☐ Top ☐ Front

It is important to note whether the printer is front or top loading so you can arrange your workspace accordingly.

---

32. Wireless: ☐ Yes ☐ No

Some newer printers don't require a cable between computer and printer. It is possible to print from a tablet, if you purchase a wireless printer.

---

33. Number of Pages Printed per Minute: ____________________

If you are anticipating a lot of printing, how quickly the printer works may be quite important to you.

---

34. Number of Pages Printed per Ink Cartridge: _______________

This is an important issue. I have a student who was interested in having a small portable printer. She was unpleasantly surprised when her ink cartridge ran out after fewer than 50 pages were printed and a replacement cartridge cost over $20.

35. Cost of Ink Cartridge Replacements: ____________

36. Length of Warranty: ____________

37. Extended Warranty: ____________ **Cost:** ________

To repeat point 20, it's more than likely that the computer store where you make your purchase will offer you an extended warranty. This is an agreement with the store, not the manufacturer. The agreement is valid only if the store is in business for the duration of the extended warranty—a good reason to make sure you're shopping at a reputable store.

38. Money-Back Guarantee: ☐ Full refund ☐ Store credit

Again, this is an agreement with the manufacturer that you have a certain number of days to return the machine. Ask the store if you get a full refund or just store credit.

39. Toll-Free Support: ☐ Yes ☐ No

Remember, this is crucial. You want to make sure that the store or manufacturer you purchase from has technical support. You should be getting free support for the length of your warranty.

40. On-Site Repair: ☐ Yes ☐ No **Cost:** ________

Ask if someone can come to your home to repair the printer if you have trouble with it.

41. Did You Ask if All of the Peripherals Are Compatible?

Make sure that the printer you are buying is compatible with your computer. Have your salesperson confirm this and note his or her name in case the person is wrong.

Filling out this form may seem like a lot of work—perhaps more work than you've done buying anything else. This isn't just a way to have you make an educated purchase; it is also a way for you to learn about the machine you will be using. By the time you go through this process and get the device home, you'll be much more knowledgeable than the average consumer. Your friends and family will be calling *you* for guidance!

Think of your first trip to the computer store as a dress rehearsal. What a relief to go in knowing that you don't have to make any big decisions or spend any money. You're just sightseeing. Bask in all the attention from the salesperson and get as much information as you can, but feel no purchase pressure. Remember: This is only a test-drive.

On Your Mark, Get Set, Go!

OK. Let's make sure you have everything you need for your test-drive.

- You have a copy of the Test-Drive Form, whether it's a photocopy or the pages in this book.
- You have a sense of where you want to set up your computer and a note with any necessary measurements.
- You have thought about whether you want a desktop, laptop, or tablet and whether it will be a Mac or a PC.
- You are equipped with recommendations from friends and/or magazine articles in which you have flagged the computers and software that interest you.
- You have brought something to write with.
- You have adopted the right attitude. Remember, you're in control. You may not completely understand what you're looking at, but that's fine. Make your salesperson prove his or her worth by helping you understand.

- You have chosen a nice place to have lunch. You deserve a lovely treat after all your hard work!

It's helpful to keep in mind that the performance pressure is on the salespeople, not you. When you get inside the store, the responsibility is on them to make you feel at home and to help you decide which computer best meets your needs. All you have to do is listen, take notes, and ask questions (if you have any). Certainly it isn't necessary, but it wouldn't be a bad idea to bring along a computer-literate friend or family member who can act as a translator if the high-tech jargon gets too thick. And one last thing: *Enjoy yourself!* Remember, you don't have to make any decisions. Just look, listen, and learn.

DON'T BUY BEFORE YOU'RE READY

Carol, one of my students, bought her computer but didn't want to get started for a couple of months. This meant that she ran the risk of not being able to use the free assistance the manufacturer offered at the time of purchase.

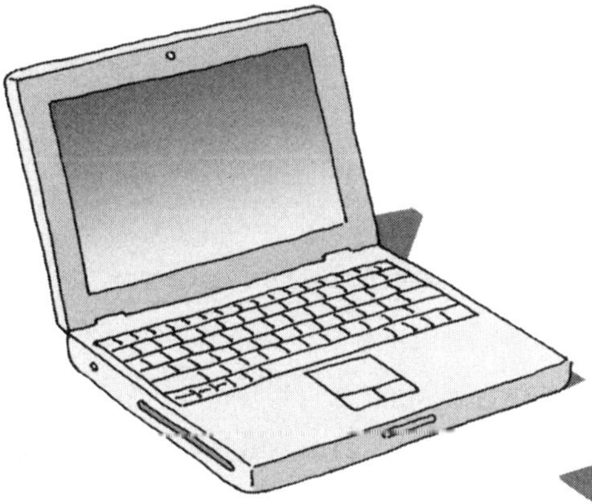

Laptops are portable and don't take up much space, but all the components are smaller.

Desktops can be more comfortable to use, but they take up quite a bit of space.

Tablets can be small enough to fit in a large pocket, but they aren't as versatile as a computer.

Q: How long will I keep my computer?

A: That is a hard question to answer. I had my first computer for nearly ten years and my second for seven. However, the average length of ownership is eighteen months! I think that number is so low because executives trade in their computers when technology makes a new leap. I have never really cared about the latest and greatest. I just want a computer that accomplishes the tasks I require. Figure you'll be able to keep your computer for at least three years, maybe even five to seven years.

Q: What do you consider the best three laptop companies to do business with?

A: Personally, I'm very fond of Sony, Apple, and Dell. But my preferences are not scientific. Keep your eyes open for computer magazines that have cover stories on the top-ten best computers, and so on. They will have tested all the laptops to make their conclusions.

Q: I really dread going into a computer store. Do you have any suggestions to make it easier?

A: Release yourself from any buying pressure. It is just an outing, nothing more. Bring a friend or family member with you for comfort and support. And plan something fun for after your visit.

Q: What is an SSD and is it better than a hard drive?

A: Solid State Drives (SSDs) have become much more common in recent years. As a result, SSD computers can be smaller, thinner, and lighter and last much longer on a single battery charge. All of that makes a computer with an SSD more expensive. You can weigh the perks against your wallet.

CHAPTER 8

CHOOSING THE BEST ROUTE

What software and Internet connections fit you best

With the test-drive behind you, we can now discuss your software and Internet connection options. However, before we talk further about software, you might want to review Chapter 3, which gives an explanation of software and how it is used.

What Software Will Come with Your Computer or Tablet?

Regardless of whether you buy a desktop or a laptop, or a PC, Mac, or tablet, your device will already have the operating software stored in its brain. Even though the operating software on a PC is different from on a Mac, both offer some features that let you get started right away. However, these are bare-bones features. You will probably want to investigate adding some application software to your computer or tablet at the time of purchase or

SOFTWARE INCLUDED
All computers and tablets come with preinstalled operating software. The operating software functions as the road map and filing system of your computer. A device *must* have operating software to function. Most computers also come with some application software included as well.

shortly thereafter. (Remember: Different types of application software enable you to type a letter, design a website, chart your family genealogy, and much more.)

Often, the manufacturer of your computer will have already added some application software to your device. Just to toss some jargon your way, a salesperson might say, "It already has software *loaded* on it." That means some application software has already been installed on your computer or tablet. There will likely be some sort of word-processing program. Sometimes financial management software (such as Quicken) and often some fun stuff (simulated golf, solitaire, etc.) will also be preinstalled on a new computer. Preinstalled application software is also referred to as "bundled software."

As I mentioned in Chapter 3, a software program added to a tablet is referred to as an app. There are apps for almost anything you can imagine, with more than 1 million available to date. Some tablet apps mirror software installed on a laptop or desktop computer. I'll be more specific about how to install apps in Chapter 12.

Buyer Beware

When a store offers to sell you a computer "bundled" with software, it may sound convenient, but it does have a downside. When you do not buy the software outright—by that I mean you actually own the installation disk or have downloaded it from the Internet to your computer—you may have trouble getting technical assistance if you need it. Each purchase has a serial or registration number. With this number, the manufacturer confirms that you qualify for technical assistance. This is how manufacturers protect themselves against people who have "pirated" software (not bought, but "borrowed" and installed).

It is tempting to say yes when someone offers to bundle software with your computer purchase. However, I strongly advise that you consider making the extra investment of buying the software so you have the security of technical assistance, in case you need it.

"My son bought me software so that I could create a family tree and track our genealogy. It is marvelous. Once I'm done I'll be able to give copies to all the kids."
—***Martina***

Some software manufacturers also offer a "trial version" of their software that is preinstalled on the computer at the time of purchase. At the end of the trial period, you sign up and pay for the software online and it is yours to keep on the computer. The downside to this is that when you replace your computer you will have to purchase the software all over again because you don't actually own the installation disks to install it on the new computer.

"My reason for wanting a computer was email—I had no idea there were so many other things I could do with it."
—*Sonny*

What If You Want to Buy Additional Software?

Whatever application software you may be interested in, here are some things you should check out before you make a purchase.

Compatibility: You *must* make sure that the software is compatible with your computer. On the outside of the software box, or on the website where you're purchasing and downloading the software, it will indicate which operating system it is friendly with (Mac or Windows). Make sure your operating system is listed. The manufacturer may also post how much space, speed, or RAM it needs to operate properly. (When you buy your computer you'll record the size of your hard drive and the speed of your CPU. Always have this information handy when you go shopping for software.)

There are no compatibility issues with a tablet because apps are downloaded directly from the "store" on the device.

Popularity: It's valuable to find out what the top-selling software is. It still may not be the right choice for you, but there is a reason why it is so popular. Ask your salesperson why a particular software dominates the market.

Friends and family: Again, if your friends or family have computers, ask which software they're using and why. Have they been happy with it? Can they do a little show-and-tell for you? Keep in mind that people are very loyal to their choice of software. This sense of loyalty should not convince you; the performance of the software should.

Subscriptions: Rather than paying to own the software, more and more manufacturers offer an annual subscription.

Salespeople: Ask them about software products and have them give you a demonstration. They really do have your best interests in mind. Also ask if they can install it for you and what that will cost. Installing software isn't difficult to do on your own, but if you buy it at the same time you buy your computer, the store may install it for you as a courtesy.

Help: Find out if the software manufacturer offers technical support. Is it free? For how long is it free? Some software manufacturers offer free support for the first 90 days after purchase. If that is the case, it's a good idea to play with the software right away to work out any bugs and take advantage of the free help.

Cost: Some software is surprisingly expensive. If it seems out of your price range, ask your salesperson if he or she can recommend something similar without all the bells and whistles. The same manufacturer that designed the expensive software may offer a pared-down version for substantially less.

A REMINDER ABOUT SOME DIFFERENT KINDS OF APPLICATION SOFTWARE

App Compatibility
You may need to update your tablet's operating system (ios/os) to be compatible with a new app.

Educational
offers you typing instruction, language lessons, reference materials, and much more

Entertainment
offers games, music, or movies

Financial Management
helps you track accounts, print checks, pay bills, or figure out taxes

Graphics
lets you create pictures, design cards, or make invitations

Organizational
helps you maintain a calendar, address book, or home inventory

Word Processing
lets you type letters, recipes, a novel—anything you write

Software or Apps for Your Tablet

All of the above considerations apply when adding software programs or apps to your tablet, with the exception of compatibility. You won't be purchasing an app on your tablet from an outside store. The manufacturer of your device offers a preinstalled "store" on your device. For example, if you own an iPad, which is Apple's tablet, you visit the App Store to purchase an app. If you have a Surface, Microsoft's tablet, you'll visit the Microsoft Store to purchase an app. If you have an Android (that is any non-Apple or Microsoft tablet), you will visit the Play Store which is owned by Google. (*Sheesh* . . . that can all seem confusing, but when you have the tablet in your hand, it will all make sense.)

Connecting Your Home to the Internet

To be able to connect to the Internet in your home, you'll pay a monthly fee to either your telephone or cable TV service provider. If you don't know which provider to choose from, call both and see what kind of pricing they offer. You might get a better deal if you bundle all your services—TV, Internet, and telephone. Ask your neighbors which company they use to connect to the Internet and if they're happy with the service.

A few suggestions when you call to place your order: Tell the sales representative that you're in the market to get a high-speed or DSL connection—not dial-up. Dial-up is much slower and is no longer competitively priced. (Most Internet service providers won't even offer you a dial-up connection, but be specific just in case.) Even if you don't think you'll need a wireless connection (wi-fi) to the Internet, ask that the modem they send you, or install, be wi-fi capable. It won't cost you any more money and it means if someone visits with their computer or tablet, they can connect to the Internet while in your home. In Chapter 13, we'll go over the specifics of how to set up the Internet connection in your home.

Connecting to the Internet When You're Not at Home

As I mentioned on the Test-Drive Form, some types of tablets may connect to the Internet only if there's a wi-fi signal. Alternatively, you can opt to purchase a tablet with access to the Internet both through wi-fi and a cellular data plan. The latter means that you will pay a service carrier (AT&T, Sprint, Verizon, or T-Mobile, to mention a few) to provide you with a signal so you can access the Internet from anywhere their signal reaches, 24 hours a day and 7 days a week. You will pay a monthly fee for this service.

If you want to connect to the Internet using your laptop when you're away from home, you have a couple of choices. You could pick up a wi-fi signal, if one is available. Most libraries offer free wi-fi, as do many coffee shops nowadays. Or, you can carry an Internet signal with you by purchasing a mi-fi card (mi-fi, not wi-fi.) or a wi-fi/remote hotspot. There's a monthly charge for the service (again with AT&T, Sprint, Verizon, T-Mobile, etc.). Your smartphone may also be activated as a hotspot, but be sure that you don't exceed your data plan or your monthly bill can be higher than expected. All of the above provide a signal to the Internet—usually for up to five devices within its range. (Not to worry—no strangers will be able to piggyback on your signal—there will be a password to gain access.) It's as though you are carrying the Internet in your pocket.

Again, it's all theory for now. It'll make sense when you have your tech toy in your hand and you're setting everything up to connect to the Internet.

Q: What if I buy my computer and it doesn't have operating software on it?

A: Well, if it didn't have operating software on it, it wouldn't turn on. Or, if it turned on, you wouldn't be able to operate the computer.

At that point, you would return the computer for a replacement. Fortunately, it is extremely unlikely that this would ever happen.

Q: What are the pros and cons of downloading software rather than owning the CD?

A: Downloading or transferring software from a website onto your computer may be necessary if your computer doesn't have a CD or DVD drive. Those of us with a CD or DVD drive usually have the choice of buying the actual software, so we own the physical CD or DVD, or we can choose to download the software from the Internet. The upside of downloading software is that it is instantaneous—you can start using it right away. The downside is that if your computer glitches and loses everything, you don't have a CD to reinstall from. You'll also have to use your credit card online, which is an issue for some people.

Q: What does DSL stand for?

A: Digital subscriber line. DSL offers a high-speed connection to the Internet.

Q: Do I need to sign a contract with these Internet providers?

A: That is such a wise question. Always ask when you initialize your account. Most providers do not require a contract and they usually allow you to change your plan in any given month (for instance if you are traveling internationally or expect to be using the device more away from home).

LET THE SHOPPING BEGIN

CHAPTER 9

MAKE YOUR PURCHASE

Old vs. new, extended warranties, store vs. mail order, and what questions to ask

Now that you're armed with the experience of your test-drive and have thought through your application software choices, let's address a few more options before you make your big purchase. Some decisions involve a little gambling, but with careful thought and consideration, you'll never have to say, "I can't believe I took such a chance." We'll go over all the bets, sure and otherwise, and I'll tell you what the odds favor. I promise, if you do your homework, you'll love your technology choice.

Hand-Me-Downs

There are always people looking to sell their used computers or tablets to finance the purchase of the newest device on the market. Because technology evolves so quickly, a computer or tablet can begin to look like a dinosaur in just a couple of years. However, that's really an issue only for

MISSING PARTS

When you buy used equipment, be very sure that all the parts end up in your hands. Cables may run from one piece of equipment to another, so make a deal with the seller to set up the device for you, turn it on, and connect it to the Internet. This way you can make sure everything you need is there and that it all works. Do your best to also get any manuals that came with the equipment and any installation disks for the software.

people who use all the features on their device to the fullest. For most of us, that's not the case.

People sell perfectly good used technology not because anything is wrong with it but because they want the latest and greatest. Perhaps they want more speed, more hard drive space, or some new feature their old machine doesn't have. Their old machine may be just right for you. That said, be cautious about whom you purchase used equipment from. You don't want to buy someone else's headache. Never buy a used device without knowing its history.

It is probably safest to buy only from a friend or family member. If one of your kids wants to buy a new computer and sell the old one, forge ahead! If your local high school is looking to replace its computers, you might get a great deal and personal technical support. Ask if one of the students can set it up for you and give you a demonstration. But if you're answering an ad in the newspaper, think twice. What is your recourse if it breaks down? Probably none. The odds are not in your favor if you buy your device from a total stranger.

Guidelines to Buying Used Equipment

Before you opt to buy a used computer, consider the following:

1. *Is the CPU at least 2.2 GHz?* **Translation:** The CPU, as we have discussed, is what guides everything on your computer. The speed of it should be no less than 2.2 GHz (gigahertz). Anything slower will hinder your use of the Internet, and you might have problems adding software in the future.

2. *Does it have at least 2 GB of RAM?* **Translation:** The RAM is the memory used when the computer is on. To open websites on the Internet and send email, you will need at least 2 GB of RAM.

3. *If it is a PC, does it have Windows 7?* **Translation:** Windows 7 is an operating system to help organize your files

and documents. You need to have at least Windows 8 or 8.1 to buy any software. If it is a Mac, does it have at least Yosemite or El Capitan?

4. *Is the hard drive at least 128 GB?* **Translation:** The hard drive is where everything on your computer is stored. 128 GB = 128 gigabytes. That is the minimum space you should have. Any less space than that and you'll have problems adding software.

5. If you are looking at used printers, have the seller print a page from the printer for you. Do you like the quality of the print? How long did it take to print a page? If it's a black-and-white printer, was your heart set on getting one that can print in color? If you decide to go ahead, make sure the seller includes all the cables and software for the printer (ideally the manual, too). There should be a cord that goes from the printer to the computer and one that goes from the printer to the electrical outlet. Remember your workspace: Does the printer fit where you want to put it?

6. *How much does it cost?* As a general rule of thumb, any used PC that costs $200 or more is likely too much. You can buy a new PC desktop that fits the criteria just described for around $400. (You won't find a new Apple desktop for less than $1,000, so you may be willing to pay a higher price for a used Mac.) And a new computer will come with some type of warranty and technical support. A used computer bought for the same price without that support would be a foolish purchase. Any used printer for $30 or more is too much. You can buy a new color ink-jet printer starting at around $60.

7. *Can it be upgraded?* Ask about the maximum CPU, hard drive, and RAM capacities. If the previous owner has upgraded the computer to its highest capacity—brought the CPU, hard drive, and RAM to the maximum—you might outgrow the machine, and you won't have the option to beef it up.

"I figured I had nothing to lose if I bought a cheap used computer. I wasn't even sure I was going to like it. I did the math and decided it was worth it, even if I replaced it a year later with something better."
—*Harvey*

A USB cable can connect your printer to your computer.

"The thought of buying a used computer and having something go wrong with it made me too nervous. I chose to buy a new computer instead."
—Charlotte

8. Trust your instincts. If something smells fishy with the used machine, say, "Thanks, but no thanks," and walk away. No obligation. If it smells sweet, buy it and enjoy.

Upgrading . . . Infuriating

It all sounds fine and dandy that an older computer can be upgraded, but it isn't that simple. Once someone opens up the machine to make an adjustment, you run the risk of something being damaged. The inside of a computer is very fragile, and the components there have a relationship to one another that should be left alone if at all possible. On more than one occasion, I've had students whose upgrades turned into low-grade headaches. Tread carefully if someone says that the machine just needs an upgrade to meet your specifications. Upgrading the computer will also entail your taking the machine to a store for the work to be done.

Something else to keep in mind: When you upgrade a laptop, it can cost more than upgrading a desktop computer. Some manufacturers don't design their laptops to be compatible with other manufacturers' hardware. For example, if you want to increase the RAM in your laptop, you might only be able to buy your laptop manufacturer's upgrade—at their price. It's the old monopoly game. This policy is less common with desktop models.

If New Is the Only Thing for You

I just gave you the minimums that you should accept for a used computer. If you're buying a new computer, use the following criteria as your minimums, but feel free to surpass them. (Once your computer purchase is made, you won't have to think about all this technical mumbo jumbo.)

- **Hard Drive**—500 GB to 1 TB
- **RAM**—4 GB to 18 GB
- **PC Operating System**—Windows 10

- **Mac Operating System**—OS Sierra
- **Webcam**

One of the great advantages when you buy a new computer is the warranty and technical service offered. Most new machines have a limited warranty of 30, 60, or 90 days offered by the manufacturer.

Are Extended Warranties Warranted?

An extended warranty will probably be from the store where you made your purchase, not the manufacturer. Double-check with your salesperson whether a warranty is from the store or from the manufacturer. Regardless of who offers the warranty, make sure you understand the terms. There is no advantage to the warranty being from one or the other. You just want to be sure that whoever offers the warranty is going to stay in business for the time that you have the computer.

Ask questions: How long has the store been in existence? Is it part of a chain? What is their reputation? When I bought my television, I purchased an extended warranty. In less than six months, the store I bought it from went out of business. At that point, the manufacturer had the option of honoring my warranty. They chose not to. Surprise, surprise. Lucky for me, I've never had any problems with the set.

Once you've determined that the store is reputable, be sure to ask your salesperson what the extended warranty covers and what it costs. If it sounds good, I advise you to buy it. When things go wrong with a computer, it can be mighty expensive to repair. The episode I mentioned in Chapter 5, where I spilled milk on my laptop, could have set me back several hundred dollars, but thankfully, I was still under warranty. (By the way, you don't always need to let the technical support person know you were foolish enough to eat or drink by your computer. Your confession may affect whether your warranty is honored. In describing how the injury to your computer or tablet occurred, less is more.)

IF YOU NEED A TECHNICIAN

Ask friends and family if they know of a computer whiz who makes house calls. My mother was given a great recommendation through the computer class at her local senior center. The person she hired came to her house, and my mother paid a lot less than she would have at a technical service department.

THE REBATE DEBATE
Know thyself . . . A rebate is only a savings if you're really going to follow up and submit the necessary paperwork. If you know that you'll never get around to mailing the rebate in, do not take the rebate into cost consideration. If you are going to send in the rebate, don't throw away any of the computer or printer boxes, because usually the bar code printed directly on the box is necessary. Also, make copies of everything you send in to follow up in case you don't hear back.

Some extended warranties are based on the price of your total purchase. Others are based on the prices of individual items. For example, one store may offer an extended warranty of a certain price for purchases, say, from $1,500 to $2,000 (combining the costs of your computer and printer). Another store may require that you purchase separate warranties for each item. You will save money by purchasing a single extended warranty based on the total cost of your purchase if the store allows that. Some salespeople may not tell you this is their store policy and will instead offer you two separate warranties. Be sure to investigate.

Also ask if the preinstalled application software (probably something like NotePad and Quicken) is covered under the extended warranty. Remember when I warned you about bundled software on page 72 in Chapter 8? Some stores offer to give you support for the bundled software under their warranty. If this is the case, you can ignore the warnings I gave earlier.

WHAT ARE FRIENDS FOR?
Shopping, of course! You may not be shopping on the Internet *yet*, but I bet you know someone who is. Invite yourself over for a computer-shopping "excursion." Don't forget your credit card so you can pay for your purchases, and it might be nice to bring flowers for your host. (See Chapter 23 for more information about making online purchases.)

The last thing you need to check out is where any repair work will be done. Can they come to your house? What is the charge for an on-site visit? An on-site visit is obviously the most convenient choice, but it's likely also the most expensive. If it's too expensive, do you have to bring the machine to the location where you bought it? Does it need to be mailed somewhere else to be repaired? Mail-in repair may not suit you. It probably means that you need to keep the original boxes for packing so you can schlep it from your house to the post office—and you'll be without the machine longer because of mailing time.

Mail Order

Now that you've gone for a test-drive and have a feel for several different computers or tablets, you can think about the pros and cons of buying your machine by mail order. As with purchasing a device in a store, buying mail order without test-driving is definitely not recommended.

Mail order is not limited to finding what you need in a catalog, picking up a phone, and placing your order. If someone you know is already on the Internet, have him or her help you visit the manufacturer's website so you can view the technology, configure your ideal device, and order it on the spot. Delivery usually takes a week to 10 days.

Mail order can be a very convenient way to shop, but there is a downside. Most of the mail-order tech manufacturers do not offer on-site repair unless you buy one of their more expensive machines or pay extra for the service. If you don't want to make that kind of investment, your options are to hire someone to come to your home or to try to correct the problem yourself over the phone with a support technician. If you can't fix it with one of those options, you'll have to send the machine to the manufacturer . . . and you know what that entails. For me, that's a real turnoff.

Buyer's Remorse

Hold off on registering your device until you're sure it's working properly. Once a computer or tablet is registered, the manufacturer may not be willing to replace it, but instead will offer to repair it if there is a problem. Contact the store you bought it from. The store should be willing to make an exchange, if you haven't registered with the manufacturer yet. Ask your salesperson about the store's return policy before you seal the deal. If the computer or tablet has any bugs, you will discover them immediately. That's why it is so important to use the machine right away.

Additional Accessories

There are a few small items that you should purchase when you buy a used or new computer or tablet. All are relatively inexpensive, and it will be easier to get them at the same time that you make your "big" purchase.

■ If you are using a laptop or tablet and it is plugged into a surge protector, the surge protector needs to remain on for the battery to be able to charge.

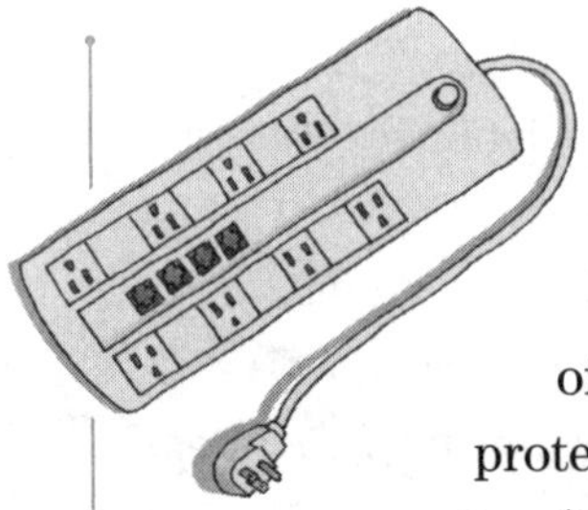

Surge Protector

The electrical cords for your computer or tablet and any peripherals should be plugged into a surge protector. It maintains a constant flow of power to whatever is plugged into it, thereby protecting your equipment from irregular power surges. A change in the flow of electrical power can cause damage to your computer.

Wrist Rest

A wrist rest allows you to maintain an unbroken line from elbows to fingertips when working on the keyboard. This keeps you from straining your wrists and helps prevent discomfort and, more specifically, carpal tunnel syndrome, a wrist injury that results from inflammation of the tendons. Carpal tunnel syndrome is common among tennis players, pianists, and computer users.

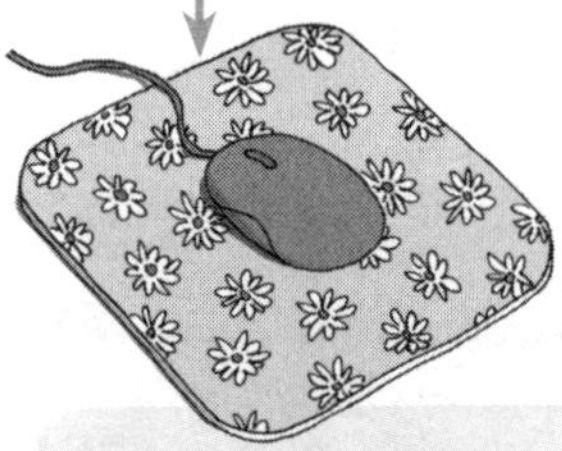

Mouse Pad

A mouse pad helps you have better control of the mouse. It's a smooth pad similar in dimension to a facecloth and about ¼ inch thick. You manipulate the mouse by sliding it on top of the pad. It can be difficult to control a mouse without one.

RUBBER NO MORE
Used to be that mouse pads were about as fun as a flat tire and didn't look much better. Now you can get them printed with your favorite photo or made of paper that you can actually write on.

Stylus

A stylus can prove more steady and accurate than the touch of your finger(s). Consider a stylus if you purchase a tablet or your new computer has a touch screen.

Now What?

Well, it's finally time to go back to the store for your purchase, get on the phone, or have someone access a website where you can buy a computer or tablet. For this shopping trip, you need many of the same things that you used for the test-drive.

- A blank piece of paper and something to write with.

- The measurements of your workspace.
- A list of what your device must have to suit your needs.
- Your filled-in Test-Drive Form and your marked magazine articles. (If you have already decided on the computer you want to buy, you may not need to bring these with you.)
- A blank Test-Drive Form. Have your salesperson fill this in with the details of your new computer. If you are ordering over the phone, you can still go over the form with your salesperson. If you are ordering over the Internet, the website should provide you with all the necessary information to fill out the form.
- Means to pay for your purchase, such as a credit card and proper photo identification.
- If you are buying at a store, bring a friend, if for no better reason than to help you carry things to the car.
- Butterflies in your stomach. It's only natural when you're about to embark on a new adventure.

"I went back to the computer store with more questions and a friend. We gave the salesman a run for his money. . . . I don't think he expected us to know as much as we did. It all ended happily—I went home with a computer and my friend a tablet. So he made two big sales."
—***Phyllis***

Get the Most Out of Your Salesperson

Never let a salesperson smooth-talk you into something you feel is excessive or that you're not comfortable with. You always have the prerogative to go home and think it over or to say no on the spot. There is no need to be impulsive. Take all the time you need to make your decision, and ask all the questions you need answered to be well informed. The person selling to you needs you more than you need him or her.

Here are some suggestions on how to take control of your shopping experience and have the salesperson do the best for you.

Set the scene. Give salespeople as much information as you can. If they start to lead you around the store before you've explained exactly what you want, halt the process. Just stop in your tracks

TAKE YOUR TIME
These suggestions for getting the most out of your salesperson hold true if you're purchasing by telephone as well. Let the salesperson know you have all the time in the world to make the right decision.

and say, "First let's talk about what I know I want and some questions I have." In the middle of a crazy day, people can run on automatic—bring them back to a human level. I've seen salespeople relax when given a chance to deviate from their "routine speech." Look them in the eye, and let them see you as an individual who needs their expert guidance.

Be honest. Let them know that you've done research. You can even show them your notes. If you're uneasy with something, tell them. Perhaps you're concerned about how to connect the cords to the ports at the back of the computer when you get home. Upon hearing this, your sympathetic salesperson might offer to send someone over to help you. Or instead, the salesperson may give you an in-store demonstration. Feel free to ask for such a demonstration. A refusal would be the worst that can happen, and it may be an indication you should take your business elsewhere.

Slow the process down. Salespeople often miss the mark because they assume we're all comfortable with technology and understand the jargon that goes along with it. I've been working with computers for 20 years and still find myself asking salespeople to slow down and explain themselves in plain English.

If, as you tell your salesperson what you need, he or she looks ready to start a 10-yard dash, state that you're not in any rush. "If you can't give me the time I need, I'd be happy to speak with someone else." I know it sounds a bit harsh, but the salesperson is probably used to people who want to come in, make their purchase, and get out. Asking the salesperson to slow down will come as a surprise, but it may be a welcome one—it gives him or her a chance to relax and not "work" so hard.

If You Still Aren't Sure

If after all your research you still haven't decided which computer you want, ask the salesperson to show you the top two computers that interest you. Then ask to see the models just higher and lower in price to get a better feel for what's right for you. Don't deviate from your budget, but do make sure you're buying a computer that meets all your needs.

REVIEW WHAT YOU'RE INTERESTED IN BUYING

Before you set foot into your local computer store to buy a machine, decide on the following:

- Laptop vs. desktop vs. tablet (Review Chapter 4)
- Mac vs. PC (Review Chapter 6)

Here are a few other things that you should have done by now:

- Checked out the tech gadgets of friends and family
- Researched technology magazines for their recommendations
- Gone for a test-drive
- Reviewed your filled-in Test-Drive Form

Return Policy

What is the store's return policy? There may be a certain number of days during which you can return your computer for no better reason than you've changed your mind or you don't like the color. However, if you want to take advantage of this, you'd better get the new machine up and running in that amount of time. No procrastinating on this or you will be in the soup! Be delicate with the packaging. Some stores won't accept returns if the package is damaged.

Keeping Track of Things

Be sure to ask your salesperson for a couple of business cards. If you have any questions down the road, his or her telephone number will be at your fingertips. Also ask the salesperson to fill in the blank Test-Drive Form. This will prove a helpful record of the computer and peripherals you have bought.

At this point, the success of your shopping trip is not based on luck. You have all the information that you need to make a wise computer purchase. I wasn't as well informed when I bought my first computer, and it served me well for seven years. Go to your computer store confident that you know more about computers than the average customer. When you get home with your new machine and you want to set it up, I will be waiting for you in Chapter 10.

Q: How long should I wait to buy a new computer when I hear something new is coming out?

A: It is hard to know. I don't like to jump on the new technology right after it's been released. I want someone else to figure out the flaws and have the manufacturer update it accordingly, and then I start shopping around.

Q: I've been offered a used computer. Should I buy it?

A: Someone with more computer experience than you should definitely test-drive the machine for you first. A used computer can prove a very nice start-up machine for someone, but you may outgrow it sooner than you think. There is a reason it's being sold, and it may be that the computer is slow. Is it worth the hassles of uncertainty when you can buy a new PC for close to $400?

Q: What criteria do you use to choose a salesperson?

A: I want a salesperson who can explain things clearly and who I get an instinctively good feeling about. If there isn't anyone around who fits that description, it may not be the store where I want to shop.

BABY'S FIRST DAY HOME

CHAPTER 10

COUNTING FINGERS AND TOES

Taking your new technology out of the box and connecting all the parts

You are now in all likelihood the proud owner of a computer or tablet. Congratulations on the new addition to your home! Give yourself a pat on the back (or a pink cigar) from me. Just as you would with the arrival of a newborn child, you might be feeling a little nervous about whether you'll have what it takes to be a good technology parent. Don't give it another thought. You're a natural . . . you just don't know it yet.

From this point forward, we'll be doing hands-on work with your device. Don't worry, I know you'll do great. You can read through the chapter if you want, but then come back to the beginning and follow the instructions step by step. Illustrated setup instructions may also be included with your new arrival. (Be forewarned—these may be harder to follow than your tax return.) The instructions here will help simplify the process. Read them along with the instructions that came in the box.

"Some people may feel comfortable setting up their own computer, but I would rather spend the money to have someone come and do it for me."
—*Kathy*

Set the Scene

There are three things that you must do before you even open your computer or tablet boxes.

1. Find a large (at least 8-inch by 12-inch) mailing envelope or a 1-gallon self-sealing plastic bag that can be closed securely. Label it "Computer (or Tablet) Information." Put all your sales receipts and any other paperwork from the computer store into the envelope or bag. If your salesperson filled out the Test-Drive Form when you made your purchase, you can skip the next steps. If you don't have a filled-out Test-Drive Form, take a clean piece of paper and write down the following information on it:

   - The date of purchase. (If you do have a Test-Drive Form, write the date of purchase at the top.)
   - The store where you made your purchase, as well as the phone number and name of your salesperson (or staple the salesperson's card to the piece of paper).
   - The length of the warranty and extended warranty, if you purchased one.
   - The brand name of your computer or tablet and any numbers or letters that follow—this indicates the model. (Look on the outside of your computer or tablet's packing box. It will probably have a description of your device.) The speed of your CPU, size of your hard drive, and speed of your RAM may also appear on the outside of the box. Note these as well. Last but not least, write down any peripherals you bought—printer, scanner, etc. (include brand and model). If this information isn't on the packing boxes, you can get the details when you set up the computer or tablet.

   Put this documentation inside your envelope or bag.

2. The next thing you have to do is make space, especially if you are now the proud owner of a desktop. Don't try to set up the desktop computer in an area where there's a lot of clutter.

A clean, open workspace not only makes for a pleasant work environment, but it also lets the computer get proper ventilation. Look at the workspace that you want to use for the desktop computer, and move everything that's in your way to the other end of the room. You can move things back eventually, but it's much easier to keep track of what you're doing (and much less frustrating) if you have plenty of space to work in. If you are unsure of your workspace, go back to Chapter 5 for a quick review of some factors to consider in choosing one.

3. Finally, have a pair of scissors, box of rubber bands, wastebasket, roll of masking tape, Sharpie, and small box or an available section of a bookshelf at the ready.

"I wanted to put it together myself. I figured it was the best way to get to know the machine. I did it very slowly." —*Ralph*

Before you connect all the parts, feel free to ask a computer- or tablet-owning friend or family member to help you. This is not a test of your ability to last four days in the forest alone. If someone in the know is willing to set up your new stuff, it's perfectly fine to let them do it. Maybe you've even convinced someone from the store—or a high school student—to help. Just be sure that you pay attention to what's done. Take notes or pictures if you want to. There may come a time when you'll move the desktop computer, and it will be helpful to understand how it's all connected.

The Moment We've Been Waiting For

If you've bought a laptop computer or tablet, the unpacking stage is quite simple. There will only be your device, an electrical cord, and a few incidental items to unpack. However, if you've bought a desktop, there will be several large items—a monitor, the computer case, the keyboard, and several cords to connect everything.

1. Use scissors to cut open the box. *Be gentle.* Not only is your investment inside, but if you do have buyer's remorse, you'll have to return the computer in its original packaging. Try not to destroy the box or the big pieces of packing materials. My sister saves all her equipment boxes. She has moved several

Labeling the cords that connect the parts of the computer proves helpful if you ever have to move the computer.

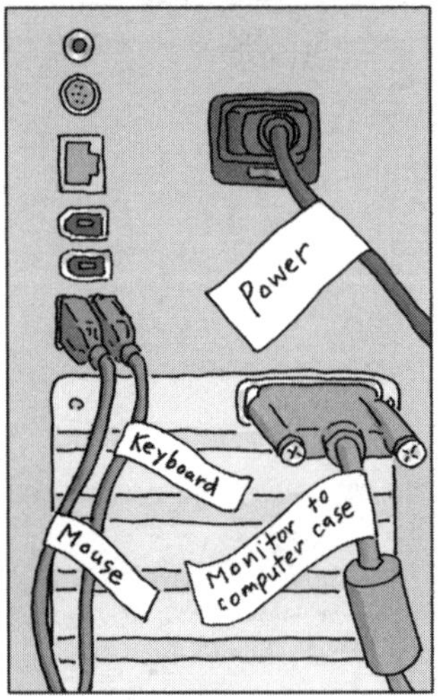

times, and it gives her great comfort to have her computer happily secured in its original boxes— safe from the dangers of careless movers.

2. If you've bought a desktop, be aware that the computer case and the monitor can be quite heavy and unwieldy. It is a good idea to set the box gently on its side and drag the piece of equipment out of the box along the floor. If you think it's too heavy for you, do *not* try to take it out of the box yourself. You don't want to hurt yourself or damage the computer. If it all seems manageable, gently remove the computer parts from their boxes and set them carefully on the floor.

3. Each packing box will also contain the proper cords. As an extra precaution, you can stop now and label each cord with masking tape. For example, mark "Monitor to outlet" on the cord that plugs into the wall and "Monitor to computer case" on the other cord. "Keyboard to computer case" and so on. That way, if you move the computer, there'll be no confusion about which cord goes to which part.

The main components of your desktop computer are the computer case, monitor, keyboard, and mouse.

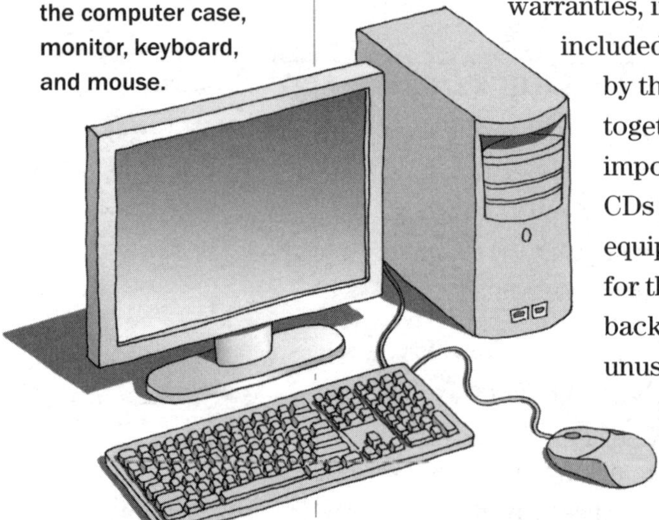

4. Until all the parts are situated, it's safest to have them where they can't be knocked over. The instructional books, warranties, installation disks, and small parts included with your computer should be placed by the parts they came with and kept together with a rubber band. It's very important that you don't misplace any of the CDs or DVDs that may have come with your equipment. These are the installation disks for the operating software and are used as backup if your computer breaks down. It is unusual, but there is always the chance that your computer might have a major failure and lose everything stored in its memory. If for some reason the

software (either operating or application) is affected, you can use these disks to reinstall. Eventually, all these things will be stored in the box that you set aside or on the available space on your bookshelf. If there is anything really tiny that might get lost, put it in your "Computer Information" envelope.

5. On each piece of equipment, there is a serial number (usually on the back or bottom). Take the piece of paper with all your computer information on it and jot down these serial numbers. Be clear about which serial number goes with which item. It's much easier to record these numbers now than after everything has been set up. This is also the time to record the brand and model if it wasn't on the box.

Once all the parts of your purchase are out of the box, sit down. Take a few minutes and just look at everything. Admire your new companion. Soon you'll be playing with and enjoying it.

Also set aside any registration cards that came with your equipment. They should be filled out and sent in after you're sure everything is in working order. The piece of paper where you recorded all the serial numbers will be your resource to complete the registration cards.

Take time to look over the written material that came with your device, including the illustrated brochure on how to set everything up. No matter how tempting it is to forge ahead and hook everything up, don't. It is very important that you follow the instructions that the manufacturer has given, along with the steps here. Once a mistake has been made and something is hooked up improperly, it is a bear to backtrack and make a correction.

COMPATIBILITY
It is very important that whatever extras you buy for your computer or tablet are compatible with your system. If you get home and discover the salesclerk was wrong, and the parts are not compatible, take them back to the store!

Examine the Ports

Before you plug anything in, get acquainted with the ports at the back or side of your device. Notice that the cords and ports are designed as pairs; the number of holes in one port corresponds to the number of prongs on one of the cords. If, when you begin plugging

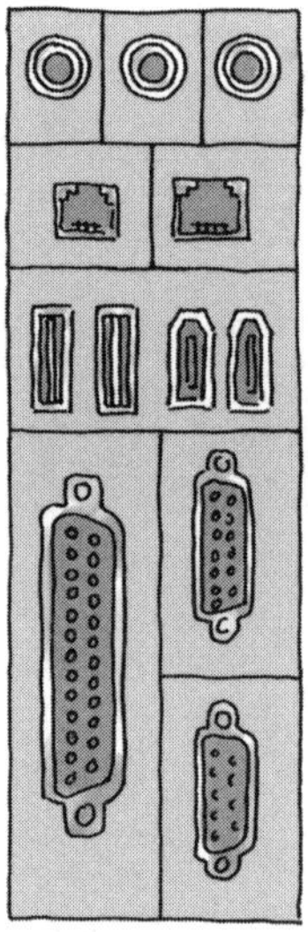

The ports at the back of the computer case are where the cords plug in.

things in, you feel any resistance, remove the cord and confirm that it matches the port. Be aware that the prongs on the cords are very delicate. If you bend one of the prongs, gently, very gently, urge it back to its original position.

Putting It All Together

If you have chosen a laptop computer, setup is very simple: Set the device on your desk and plug the electrical cord into it. *Do not* plug it into the wall yet.

Most tablets are pre-charged out of the box. That also allows you to set it up while you're still in the store. Why not ask your salesclerk to help since you've got his or her attention and the store has your money?

If you have a desktop, the procedure for attaching all the parts of the computer is the same, whether you have purchased a Mac or a PC. Before you follow these directions, read the manufacturer's instructions.

HANDLE YOUR LAPTOP OR TABLET WITH CARE!
The screen of a laptop or tablet is very fragile, and some of them are not covered under the warranty. If by chance you damage the screen, the fun may be over. Repairing a screen can cost almost as much as it would to replace the entire device. Be careful!

1. Gently and carefully pick up the **computer case** and place it where you want it. (Remember: Don't place the computer case directly on carpeting because it may generate static electricity that can harm the unit.) Don't forget you're going to want the computer case where you can easily reach it. Position it so that the ports at the back are still within reach. You will swing it into its final position once everything is plugged in. Attach the electrical cord to the back of the computer case, but *do not* plug it into the wall outlet yet.

2. The **monitor** should be placed either on top of your desk or on top of the computer case on your desk. The monitor is very fragile. If you can't manage it, leave it where it is and ask someone to help you. Attach the cord that connects the monitor to the computer case. Then take the electrical cord for the monitor and plug it into the back of the monitor. *Do not* plug it into the outlet yet.

3. The **keyboard** should be placed on your desk or pull-out shelf and plugged into the appropriate port on the computer case.

4. Set the **mouse** to the right of the keyboard and plug it in. Usually the mouse plugs into the computer case. If it doesn't, it will plug into the keyboard or sometimes even the monitor. Refer to the setup page in the instruction book that came with your computer to be sure. If you have a mouse pad, place it under the mouse.

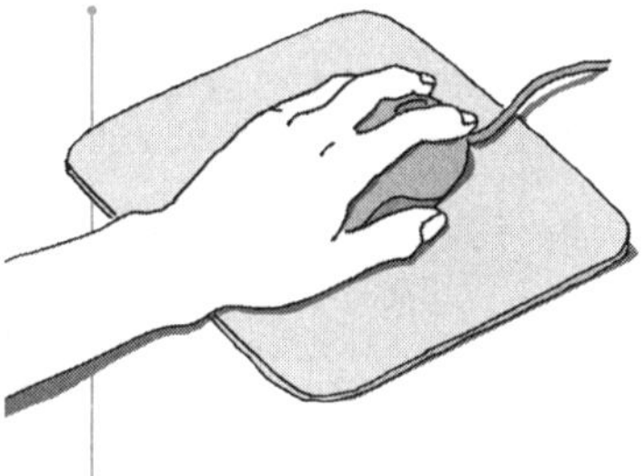

The mouse is positioned with the "tail" pointing away from you.

ATTENTION, SOUTHPAWS

The mouse can also be positioned to the left of your keyboard. However, if you bought a PC, the function of the mouse buttons will be reversed. We're going to rectify that in Chapter 12. You might want to leave the mouse on the right side of the computer until then. If you bought a Mac, you can set the mouse on either side of the keyboard. I have several students who write with their left hand but manipulate the mouse with their right. Try it both ways to see which you prefer.

5. If you have bought a **printer**, a **scanner**, or any other peripheral, place it where you want it to be. Follow the manufacturer's instructions for proper installation. It is important that you plug the cords in to the computer only when instructed.

Before you plug anything into the electrical outlet, let's review what we have done so far.

- The monitor and keyboard are plugged into the back of your computer case.
- The mouse is plugged into either the computer case, monitor, or keyboard.
- The monitor and computer case also have cords that will eventually plug into an electrical source.

WIRELESS KEYBOARD OR MOUSE

There will be no cables to plug in with a wireless keyboard or mouse, but you may need to insert batteries and turn it on.

Sit back and view your creation. Take a break now and do something else, or if you're up to it, you can take the next big step of plugging it in, as described below.

Plug It In, Plug It In

OK, are you ready to take the final steps before turning the computer on? Here goes.

- Take the surge protector and position it near all the power cords. Do not plug it into the wall yet.
- Plug the monitor, computer case, printer, and any other peripherals into the surge protector.
- Finally: Plug the surge protector into the wall outlet! There may be an indicator light on the surge protector to let you know that it is connected. If that light is not lit, there should be an on/off switch on the surge protector; flip the switch and the light should go on.

At this point, all the parts of the computer are attached and they are plugged into a power source. In the next chapter, you will turn the computer on and begin to learn what an incredible resource it really is. Congratulations!

OOPS—SOMETHING'S MISSING

Are you missing a cord? Before you call the store, make sure that you've looked in all your boxes and on the floor where you unpacked everything. It is unusual for a cord not to be packed with the equipment, but it isn't impossible. Once you're sure the cord isn't hiding somewhere, inform your salesperson that you are missing a cord. It's a drag, but you will probably have to go back to the store to pick it up.

Sit Safely

Before we begin working on the computer, it's a good idea to know how to sit safely. For your well-being and good health, keep the following ergonomic guidelines in mind:

1. Your knees, hips, and elbows should be at 90-degree angles.

2. There should be an unbroken line from your elbows to your fingertips—no breaking at the wrists.

3. Your hands should be relaxed when using the keyboard and the mouse—no claws or strain.

4. Be very aware of your posture—it is easy to "sink into" the machine over time.

5. The monitor should be an arm's length away. To see the screen properly, you may need to wear prescription glasses or to adjust your existing progressives.

6. *Take a break!* Do not sit at the computer for more than 45 minutes without taking a break to stretch and rest your eyes.

Q: I didn't save the original boxes, and unfortunately I want to return the computer. What can I do?

A: Each store has a different policy, but if you are within the window of time for returning a purchase, the boxes (or lack thereof) shouldn't be a deal breaker.

Q: Help! I can't find the cable to connect the printer to the computer.

A: That's because neither the printer nor the computer comes with that cable. You need to buy it separately. Return to the store where you bought the printer, with receipt in hand, to be sure they sell you the correct cable. Make a point, before going to the store, of measuring how long the cable needs to be.

STEER CLEAR OF . . .

For your computer's health and well-being, keep it away from:

1. Extreme heat or cold
2. Liquids of any kind
3. Dirt, dust, and animal hair
4. Magnets
5. High-pile carpeting

CHAPTER 11

SHAKING HANDS

Meet your device

The time has come to turn on your new arrival. It may seem unnecessary to have part of a chapter devoted to turning on your device, but it is a bit involved and can be a little confusing. You're about to embark on a wonderful new adventure, and I will be by your side through the whole process. However, feel free to have a friend or family member also join you during any part of this journey.

The Ground Rules

My experience with students is that most people ask too much of themselves during the learning process. If I'm teaching you how to use a computer or tablet, here are my rules for you to follow.

- Do *not* try to memorize what we do. Eventually, it will become second nature. Just follow the instructions—time and repetition will take care of the rest.

- Do *not* get hung up on understanding everything. I don't understand exactly how the computer works, but I know how to make it work.

- Trying can be trying. If you've hit your saturation point or you're frustrated, simply stop. Put down the book. Leave the new arrival as it is and go do something else. If you don't return to the computer or tablet for an hour or a few days, it doesn't matter. The device isn't going anywhere on its own. Eventually, your tech toy is where you'll go for fun, but at the beginning it can seem more like work.

"For three months I was afraid to turn my tablet on. I would see the unopened box and feel increasingly defeated. How times have changed—I just set up a friend's tablet without a glitch!"
—*Mark*

Turning It On

If you've bought a tablet or laptop, there will be an "on" button that turns on the device. Run your finger along the edges of your tablet to find it. You may have to hold down the button for a count of five for the screen to illuminate. If you can't find the button, refer to the instruction information that came with your machine.

There is no hard-and-fast rule about which parts of a desktop computer should be turned on in what order, but I always turn on the monitor, then any peripherals, and finally the computer case. Refer to the instructions included with your computer to confirm the precise procedure for your machine.

Instructional manuals may have been provided to you by the computer manufacturer and enclosed with your new purchase, but more likely you'll have nothing more than a diagram of how to connect the parts. Feel free to sit back and read whatever was

CLICK AND GO

1. Turn on monitor.
2. Turn on printer.
3. Turn on computer.

"I knew I had time for the computer, but I was terrified of the technology. Sometimes I still have trouble with my answering machine. But now, I've been scanning family photos to design a website. My grandchildren love it when I email them pictures of when their dad was their age . . . and so skinny!"
—*Margaret*

provided to you at this time. Don't be surprised if you find the information confusing—most people do. You might want to read what you've been given in tandem with my instructions that follow.

1. If the monitor is not on, turn it on. A monitor's "on" switch is often, but not always, located in its lower front right corner. A light should indicate it's on, but nothing will show on the monitor until the brain of the computer in the computer case is up and running. So sit tight and eventually something will appear.

2. If you bought yourself a printer, turn it on. The "on" switch can be located at the front, back, top, or side. Again, refer to the machine's literature if necessary.

3. Find the "on" button for your computer case. The "on" switch can usually be found on the front of the computer case near the CD-ROM (D:) drive. This switch will activate the operating system, keyboard, and mouse. Press it, slide it, toggle it—whatever is the proper way to activate the switch. An indicator light, usually located on the front of the computer case, will light up when the unit is on. (The keyboard may also have an indicator light, but the mouse may not.) Give each computer component time to warm up—they don't always come to life immediately. Repeatedly pressing the "on" switch will only cause you to lose track of whether it's supposed to be on or off.

IF IT ISN'T WORKING . . .

One of the most common problems with computers and tablets is also the easiest to fix . . . believe it or not. If the screen is blank or the mouse or keyboard isn't working on a desktop, check to make sure they are properly plugged into the computer case and wall outlet. Sounds too easy, but it works nine times out of ten.

If that doesn't do the trick, or if it's a laptop or tablet, hold down the "on" switch and start counting to 30. By the time you get to 10, the device should turn off. Give it a full minute before trying to turn it back on.

Be sure to read Chapter 25 for troubleshooting tips. Remember, if you've purchased a new machine, you're entitled to call for technical service under the warranty.

You may hear a sort of whirring or soft grinding sound as the hard drive in the computer case warms up. This can also be true throughout the time that you use the computer—the hard drive will periodically make a noise as it works. It's less disconcerting than it sounds and indicates that the computer is hard at work, which is a good thing.

Staying Turned On

If at any time you need to step away from your device to answer the phone or run an errand, you can leave everything on without harming the machine. Some people never turn their technology off. Computers do, however, generate a certain amount of heat, and leaving them on unnecessarily is a waste of energy and battery life. If you plan to leave your machine on most of the time, make sure the area around the equipment has good ventilation.

With a laptop or tablet, make sure there is circulation under the machine. If there are retractable legs on the bottom of the computer, use them to raise the computer. If not, use a small paperback or something similar under the back of the laptop to allow air circulation. This also angles the keyboard in a way that may be slightly more comfortable for you. Try it and see. However, I don't suggest leaving a laptop or tablet turned on indefinitely, as you might a desktop. Neither gets the same circulation as a desktop.

Note: The screen may appear different after you let it sit for a while. It may even seem that the device has shut off. Most screens go into a standby or "sleep" mode, or a screen saver may appear. (We'll talk more about screen savers in Chapter 12.) Simply move the mouse, hit any keyboard key, or tap a touch screen to bring the screen back to life.

As I explained in Chapter 6, Macs and PCs have different operating systems (the mastermind that organizes everything in your computer), but all computers can do essentially the same things—create documents, connect to the Internet, send email, and so on. However, there are different computer instructions for PCs and Macs as there are for different manufacturers of tablets. If you've bought a PC, turn to page 120, and I'll join you there. If you purchased a Mac computer, turn to page 138. All computer and tablet users will meet up again on page 157. If you've bought a tablet, stay right where you are and keep reading.

THE COMPUTER WILL NOT EXPLODE

With earlier computers, there was a lot of talk about them crashing and dying, which simply meant the computer shut off for no apparent reason and, in the worst-case scenario, couldn't be turned on again.

Those earlier machines were much less stable than the ones today. It just isn't that easy to hurt your computer. If you treat it gently and be sure to read what's on the screen before you take an action, you'll do no damage.

"Crashing" and "dying" are unfortunate descriptives because they cause unnecessary anxiety. Chalk it up to dramatic excess and don't lose sleep over it.

Welcome, Tablet Users

As your tablet starts up, the background of your screen may remain dark as a series of start-up messages appears. They might appear and disappear so quickly that you can't read what they say. That's OK. If by chance you can read what they say, they won't make any sense anyway. This is a process the device goes through to make sure everything is in working order.

The First Step

If you're turning on a new tablet for the very first time, there are some one-time-only setup procedures that you must go through. Go nice and slow and read everything on the screen. There's no need to rush. The appearance of a progressive circle , a spinning circle , or a line of dots tells you that the tablet is working on something and it is best not to use the touch screen until the symbol goes away.

GET THEE TO A TABLET

If you haven't yet purchased a tablet but want to continue reading—*beware*. Much of the book from this point forward is based on information that will appear on the screen. You will become *very* confused if you do not have a device as a point of reference. Get yourself to someone's tablet so you can follow along.

Identify Yourself

The next few things to appear on your screen may ask you to accept the license terms, choose a time zone, confirm the date and time, and even choose a language. Your tablet may ask you to choose a user or computer name. The device will lead you through the process—follow the instructions step-by-step. Once you've completed a step, you move on to the next by tapping on either an arrow, the word **Next**, or the word **Continue** in the bottom right-hand corner of the screen. If any of this becomes too much for you, call a friend to walk you through the steps or have the store where you purchased the tablet help with signing on the first time. (But I suspect you'll do just fine on your own.)

For example:

Type whatever name you want to give the tablet. If you want to have the first letters of the name capitalized, you need to use the cap (or shift) key , as you would on a typewriter. (There are two cap keys —one near the bottom left of your touchscreen, next to the **Z** key, and one on the right, next to the ?/ key. It doesn't matter which one you use.) Depress and release the cap key before you type the letter that you want capitalized. If you make a mistake, use the backspace key. Remember to use the space bar to add spaces between words.

If you are asked to enter a password, you don't have to. The password feature is especially helpful with a mobile device, however, since a tablet may be used outside of your home and has a much higher risk of theft or loss. I provide more information in the section that follows, but if you choose to skip setting up a password now, you can visit my website and watch a video tutorial later.

Wait patiently while this setup process takes place. There may be times when the computer takes several minutes to do its work. You may be asked to register your computer or to set up your Internet connection; skip both of these steps for now.

As your computer starts up, you may hear a sort of *ping*. That's the computer's way of saying "hello." Several different screens may appear briefly before the computer comes to a rest at the Start screen.

To learn how to **Protect Your Mobile Device with a Passcode,** visit ***AskAbbyStokes.com***. Click on Video Tutorials at the top, then click on Video #1.

OOPS—I MADE A MISTAKE

If you make a mistake, you can erase your typing (from right to left) by using the backspace key. (It can usually be found on the upper right section of your keyboard near the **P** key.) Depress it once for each letter that you want to erase. You'll see that it moves from right to left, deleting whatever precedes it on the screen. If you hold your finger down on the key, it will continue to move and delete to the left until you lift your finger. You definitely have more control when you depress and release the key with each character rather than when you hold the key down.

Protect Your Mobile Device with a Passcode

A passcode offers you a way to protect the information you store on your tablet or smartphone. In case your device is lost or stolen, nobody will be able to open it without knowing the code you have created. If you choose to have a passcode, please be sure to write it down and include it in the packet where you plan to store all your tablet information. No one will be able to help you recover your passcode if you forget it.

There are two sets of step-by-step instructions below. The first set is for the iPhone or iPad. The second set of instructions is for an Android device using Google's operating system.

iPhone and iPad Instructions

Before you begin, think about a four-character passcode. Please do not use your birth date or any other public information. Write down your passcode (aka PIN) before you type it in.

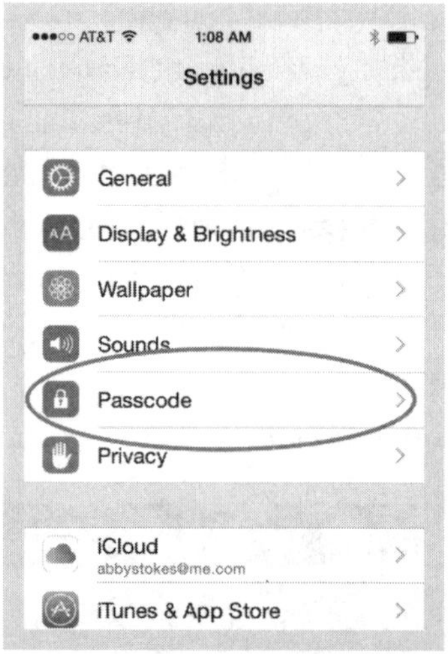

1. Tap **Settings**. 
2. Tap **Passcode** or **Touch & Passcode**.
3. Tap **Turn on Passcode**.
4. Tap your four-character PIN.
5. Re-tap your four-character PIN (to double-check that you tapped what you intended).

That's it. A+! So, from now on you'll need to enter your PIN in order to access your iPhone or iPad.

Android Smartphone and Tablet Instructions

You're going to have a choice of which method to use to protect your smartphone or tablet. You could use your face (Face Unlock) to identify you. Surprisingly, Face Unlock is not the most secure choice as there are people who share your facial characteristics. You could choose Pattern, where you drag your finger across the screen in a particular pattern, or you could type in a PIN (usually numeric) or a password (usually a combination of letters, numbers, and even symbols). Both the PIN and password must be at least 4 characters long, but no longer than 17 characters.

1. Tap **Settings Cog**. 

2. Tap **Security**.

3. Tap **Screen Lock**.

4. Choose between **Face Unlock**, **Pattern**, **PIN**, or **Password**. Tap on your choice. Type or swipe your code.

5. Tap **Continue**.

6. Re-tap your code (to double-check that you tapped what you intended).

7. Tap **OK**.

Well done! So, from now on you'll need to tap your pattern, PIN, or password to access your device.

Mastering the Touch Screen

Getting the feel for how to use a touch screen is not unlike learning how to drive a standard-shift automobile. Do you remember how awkward it was trying to figure out when the clutch was in the right position to give the car gas or hit the brake? And do you remember how many times the car stalled before you got the clutch timing right? Well, welcome to a touch screen. As you eventually conquered the clutch, you will eventually conquer the touch screen. I promise.

As I said, you press and release the pad of your finger (not your fingernail) on a touch screen with a gentle but firm touch. It'll take a little practice, but soon you'll be tapping away with abandon. There are several other gestures used with a tablet. Below is a sampling of the most common gestures.

■ Press and release

Tap and drag. Slide your finger along the screen. Most tablets utilize this move to unlock the screen. It can also be used to move an object.

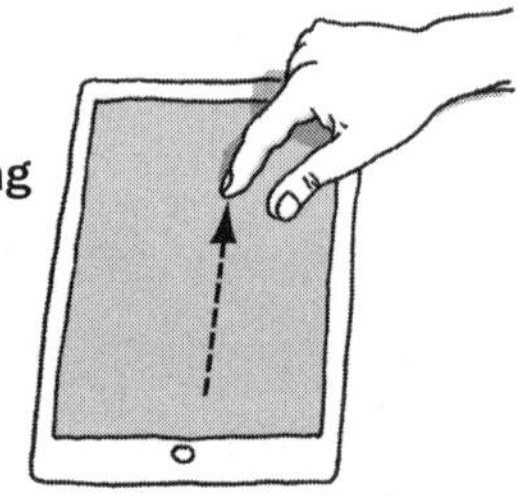

■ Tap and drag

Tap and hold. Press and hold your finger down to enable editing tools like moving where you want to type, or to copy and paste (which we will discuss in detail in Chapter 15 on page 250).

■ Tap and hold

Spread. Place two fingers beside each other and pull them away from each other while maintaining continuous contact with the screen. This allows you to enlarge whatever is on the screen.

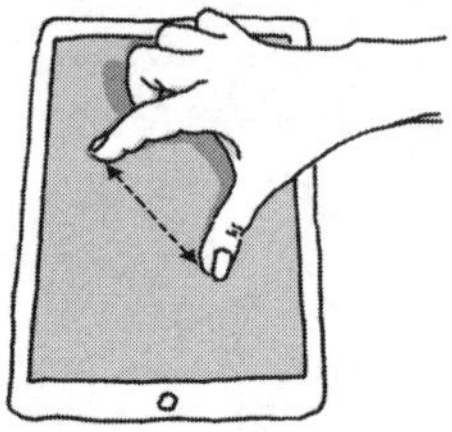

■ Spread

Pinch. Place two fingers at a distance from each other and draw them together while your fingers remain in contact with the screen. This pulls you farther away from whatever is on the screen. An example of this would be when you want to see a larger area of a map rather than zooming in on a smaller area.

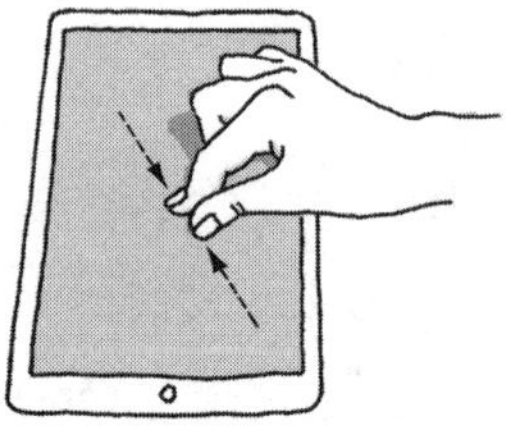

■ Pinch

We'll get to practice more mouse skills in the next chapter, but for now let's try to get a little practice under our belts.

If you're the proud owner of an Android, meet me on page 115. If you purchased a Microsoft Surface, meet me on page 116. We'll start right here for those who have an Apple iPad. All tablet users will reunite on page 117.

Welcome to the Apple iPad

On an iPad, the **Home** button is the second-most important navigation tool besides your fingers. The Home button is located at the bottom center of your iPad. It is an actual button that requires firmer pressure than when you tap the touch screen. Again, a little practice will make perfect. If you lose your way with the iPad, depress and release the Home button to return to a familiar place.

The Home button brings you to the **home page** screen, which allows you access to all of the programs or apps that live on your tablet. If you're familiar with a computer, the home page screen is similar to the Desktop screen on a computer. The small pictures, or icons, on your home page are referred to as apps. These apps offer access to different programs and settings on your tablet. You will get to know each of these icons and their capabilities in due time.

TENSION IS YOUR ENEMY

There's no reason for you to feel any tension or strain in your hand. Using a touch screen is a task that requires accuracy, not strength. If you feel strain, your hand is not relaxed, and it should be. You're probably concentrating too hard, or your hand is in an awkward position. Periodically stop what you're doing and focus on your hand. If you feel any strain, relax your hand and try a slightly different position.

Your home page screen may appear slightly different from this one, but it will offer the same basic features.

We're going to play with the brightness of your screen to find a level that works best for you.

1. Depress and release the **Home** button.
2. Find the **Settings** icon and tap on it to open the Settings window.
3. Look down the sidebar on the left and tap on **Display & Brightness.**

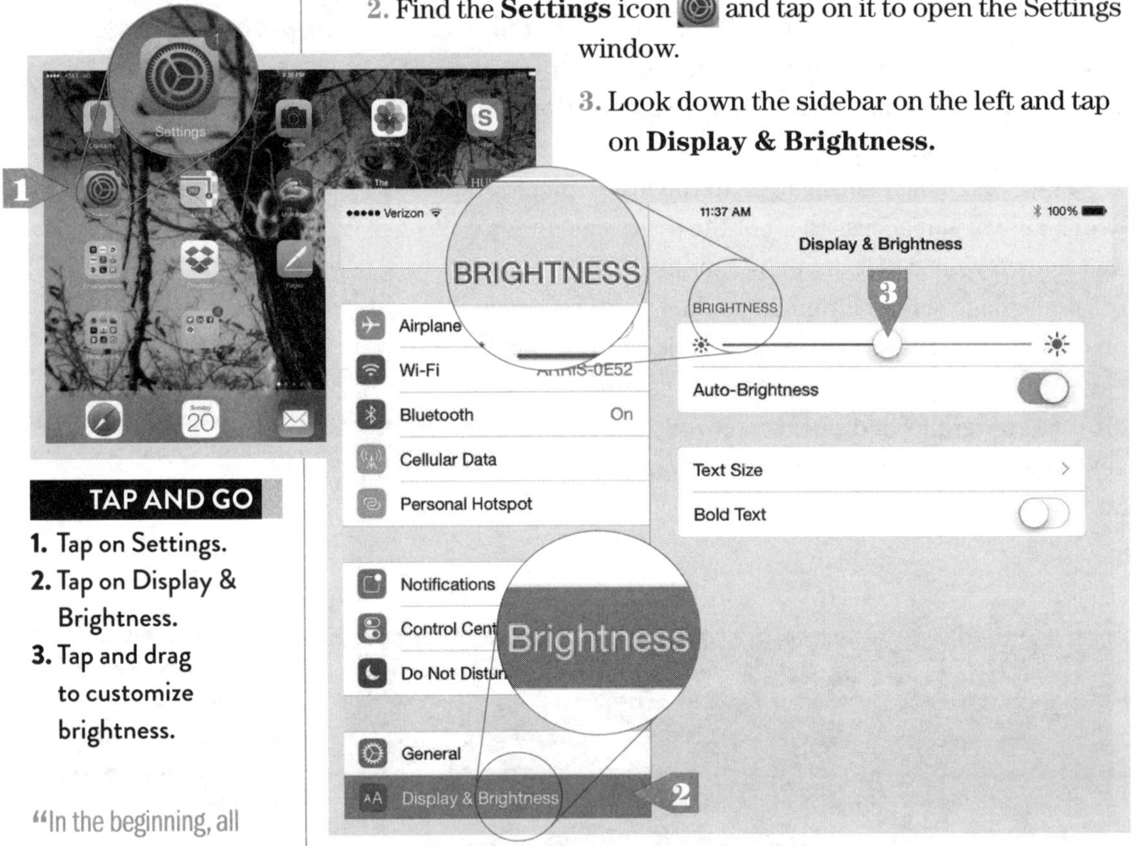

TAP AND GO

1. Tap on Settings.
2. Tap on Display & Brightness.
3. Tap and drag to customize brightness.

"In the beginning, all sorts of things would appear on the screen and I couldn't figure out how they got there. As I calmed down and got more proficient, I realized I had been clicking on things without knowing it."

—*Fred*

4. Tap and drag the circle on the Brightness bar to increase or decrease the brightness.
5. Depress and release the Home button to return to the home page.

Where in the World Are You?

Now we're going to open a Maps program, which is included on every tablet.

To access Maps on an iPad:

- Tap on the Maps icon.

Now that you have Maps on your screen, meet me on page 117 at "Tablet Travelers, Unite!"

Welcome to the Android

Google designed the Android operating system, which runs on most tablets other than the Apple iPad (which you just met) and the Microsoft Surface (which you'll see next). The Android **Home** button is the second-most-important navigation tool besides your fingers. The Home button is located at the bottom center of your device. The trick is that the button isn't visible until you touch the screen.

It may not seem like a button, as it is flush with the surface of the device. Again, a little practice will make perfect. If you lose your way on an Android, tap the Home button to return to a familiar place.

The Home button brings you to the **home page**, which allows you access to all of the programs or apps that live on your tablet. If you're familiar with a computer, the home page is similar to the desktop on a computer. The small pictures, or icons, on your home page are referred to as apps. These apps offer access to different programs and settings on your tablet. You will get to know each of these icons and their capabilities in due time.

We're going to play with the brightness of your screen to find a level that works best for you.

- Tap anywhere on the screen.
- Tap and release the Home button.
- Find the **Brightness** icon and tap on it to change the brightness.
- Tap and release the Home button to return to the home page.

Your home page screen may appear slightly different from this one, but it will offer the same basic features.

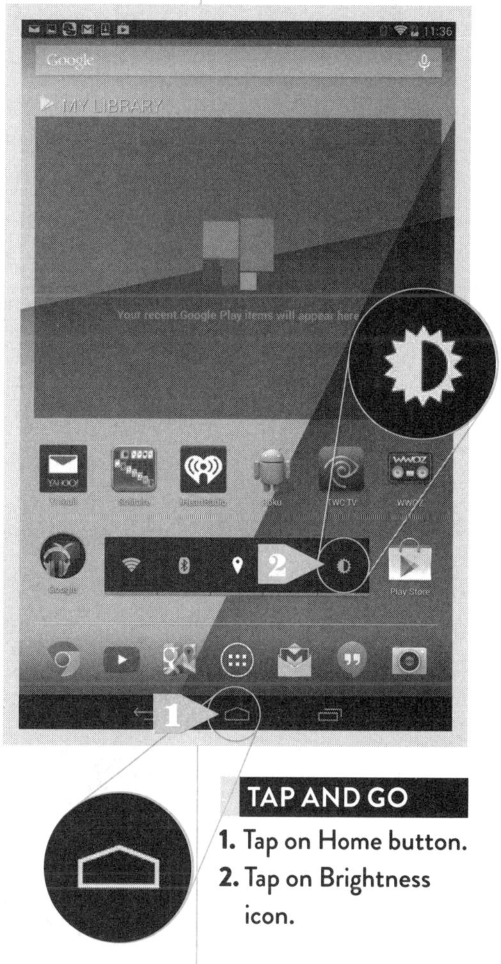

TAP AND GO

1. Tap on Home button.
2. Tap on Brightness icon.

Where in the World Are You?

Now we're going to open a Maps program, which is included on every tablet.

To access Google Maps on the Android:

- Tap on the Maps icon.

Now that you have Maps on your screen, meet me at the bottom of the opposite page at "Tablet Travelers, Unite!"

Welcome to the Microsoft Surface

On the Surface, the **Home** button is the second-most-important navigation tool besides your fingers. The Home button is located at the bottom center of your Surface. It may not seem like a button, as it is flush with the surface of the device.

Tap on the Home button to visit the **home page**, which allows you access to all of the programs or apps that live on your tablet. If you're familiar with a computer, the home page is similar to the Desktop screen on a computer. The small pictures, or icons, on your home page are referred to as apps. These apps offer access to different programs and settings on your tablet. You will get to know each of these icons and their capabilities in due time. If you lose your way

Your home page screen may appear slightly different from this one, but it will offer the same basic features.

with the Surface, depress and release the Home button to return to a familiar place.

We're going to play with the brightness of your screen to find a level that works best for you.

- Depress and release the Home button.
- Tap and drag the right side of the tablet.
- The Charm Bar will appear.
- Tap on Settings.
- Tap on Screen in the menu.
- Tap and drag the bar to customize brightness.
- Depress and release the Home button to return to the home page.

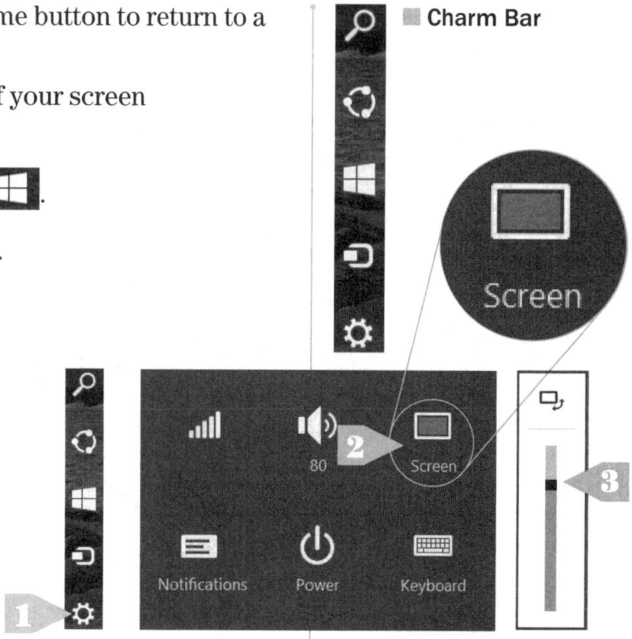

TAP AND GO

Tap and drag the right side of tablet.

1. Tap on Settings.
2. Tap on Screen.
3. Tap and drag bar to customize brightness.

Where in the World Are You?

Now we're going to open a Maps program, which is included on every tablet.

To access Maps on the Surface:

- Tap on the Maps icon.

Now that you have Maps on your screen, let's join forces with those other tablets.

Tablet Travelers, Unite!

So here we are with the **Maps** window opened. Let's review the touch screen gestures and then we can play around.

- You may be asked if you want to turn on Location Services or Share Your Location. By approving this you will allow the Maps app to utilize the GPS (global positioning system) aspect and actually find where you are on the map.

■ **Practice your tablet gestures with the Maps app.**

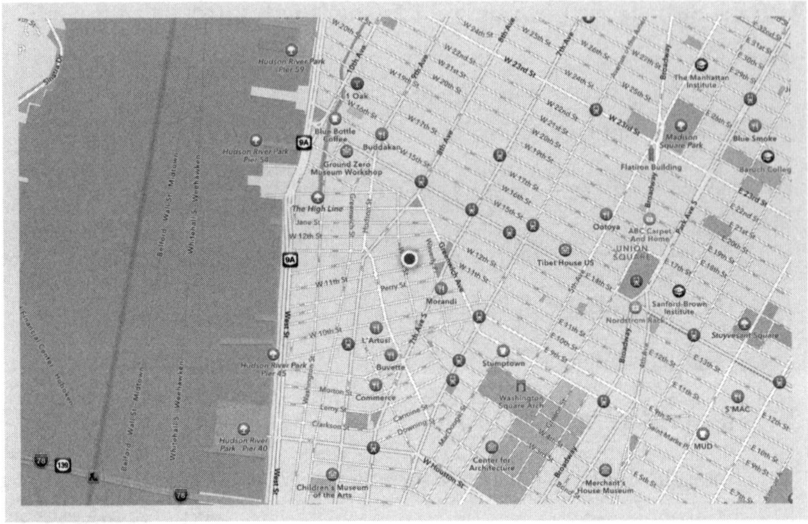

- Tap and drag to move the map around—up and down and side to side.
- Practice the pinch maneuver to view a larger area on the map.
- Now try spreading your fingers to zoom in on the map.

Remember the Goal

Play with Maps for at least 15 minutes every day for a week. If you choose to spend more time, make sure you take five-minute breaks every half hour or so. What you are really doing is mastering the touch screen. Once you feel like a pro, go on to the next chapter. Remember, it is practice and only practice that will allow you to conquer the touch screen or any other aspect of the tablet.

Exit Maps

To exit maps, press and release the Home button.

- Reminder, if you have an iPad, it looks like this: .
- If you have an Android, such as Google Nexus, it looks like this: .
- If you have a Surface, it looks like this: .

MAP YOUR JOURNEY
Your navigation journey doesn't end here. We'll look at finding your way around with a map app in Chapter 18. Stay tuned.

Ready to Call It a Day?

Get into the habit of shutting down your tablet every so often. It's good for the tablet to restart from fresh, and it saves your battery.

Putting the Tablet to Bed

The process of shutting down a tablet begins by holding down the Power button. From there, each tablet has a different method for powering off.

On the Apple iPad, you tap and drag **Slide to Power Off** from left to right.

With the Android, tap on **Power Off**, then **OK**.

The Surface shuts down after you tap and drag your finger from the far right of the tablet onto the screen area to reveal the **Charm Bar**. Tap on **Settings**, then **Power**, and finally **Shut Down**.

Bravo!

You're almost done. Meet up on page 157 at the "All Together Now!" section.

TAP AND DRAG . . . IS IT A DRAG?

Are you having some trouble with the finger gestures on the tablet? Let's review.

Tap and drag. Press down and slide your finger along the screen. Most tablets utilize this gesture to unlock the screen. It can also be used to move an object.

Tap and hold. Press and hold your finger down to enable editing tools like moving to where you want to type, or to copy and paste (which we will discuss in detail on page 250).

Spread. Place two fingers beside each other and pull them away from each other while maintaining continuous contact with the screen. This allows you to enlarge whatever is on the screen.

Pinch. Place two fingers at a distance from each other and draw them together while your fingers remain in contact with the screen. This pulls you farther away from whatever is on the screen. An example of this would be when you want to see a larger area of a map rather than zooming in on a smaller area.

My advice is keep playing with Maps! It may seem silly (or drive you nuts), but it is the best way to master the touch screen.

Welcome, PC Users

As your computer starts up, the background of your screen may remain dark as a series of start-up messages appears. They might appear and disappear so quickly that you can't read what they say. That's OK. If by chance you can read what they say, they won't make any sense anyway. This is a process the computer goes through to make sure everything is in working order.

The First Step

If you're turning on a new PC for the very first time, there are some one-time-only setup procedures that you must go through.

Go nice and slow and read everything on the screen. There's no need to rush. You may be instructed to type in the "Product ID" or "Product Key" number located on your Microsoft "Certificate of Authenticity" on the cover of the Microsoft book packaged with your computer. Don't confuse the "Product ID" with the "Product Key." These are two different numbers. This information has to be *exactly* correct, so take your time as you type it in.

The appearance of an hourglass  or a spinning circle  in place of or along with the mouse's indicator arrow tells you that the computer is working on something and it is best not to use the keyboard or mouse until the hourglass goes away. For example, if you have just typed in your Product ID or Product Key number, the computer may take a moment to process that information—hence the hourglass or circle, indicating that time is needed.

GET THEE TO A COMPUTER

If you haven't purchased a computer yet but want to continue reading—*beware*. Much of the book from this point forward is based on information that will appear on a computer screen. You will become *very* confused if you do not have a computer as a point of reference. Get yourself to someone's computer so you can follow along.

Identify Yourself

The next few things to appear on your screen may ask you to accept the license terms, choose a time zone, confirm the date and time, and even choose a language. The computer may ask you to choose a user or computer name. The machine will lead you through the process—follow the instructions step-by-step. Once you've completed a step, you move on to the next, clicking on either an arrow, the word **Next**, or the word **Continue** in the bottom right-hand corner of the screen. If any of this becomes too much for you, call a friend to walk you through the steps, but I suspect you'll do just fine.

For example: Type whatever name you want to give the computer. If you want to capitalize the first letter of the name, use the **Shift** key, as you would on a typewriter. (There are two **Shift** keys—one near the bottom left of your keyboard, next to the **Z** key, and one on the right, next to the ? / key. It doesn't matter which one you use.) Hold **Shift** down as you type the letter that you want capitalized. If you make a mistake, use **BkSp** or the **Backspace** key. Remember to use the space bar to add a space between words.

If you are asked to enter a password, you don't have to. The password feature is helpful if you're going to have confidential information on your computer that you don't want anyone else to access or if you travel a lot and there's risk of loss or theft. For the average at-home user, using a password means having to remember

A GENTLE TOUCH

If you hold down a key on the keyboard, it will keep tttttttttyping. Use a quick depress and release to hit the key you want without having it rrrrrrepeat.

WHICH WINDOWS ARE YOU LOOKING AT?

The Windows operating system shown in this book is Windows 8.1.

For those of you transitioning to Microsoft Windows 8.1 from Windows 7, click on the Desktop app (usually in the bottom left of all the boxes on the Start screen) to navigate to what looks more familiar to you.

You'll find information on page 126 to help get you started if you are using Windows 10, the newest version.

it and type it in every time you turn on the computer, which is unnecessary. So instead of typing anything in the box, click on **Skip**. This will instruct the computer to accept that there is not a password. If you choose to have a password, be sure to write it down and put it in the packet where you plan to store all your computer information. No one will be able to help you recover your password if you forget it.

Wait patiently while this setup process takes place. There may be times that several minutes will go by while the computer is working. You may be asked to register your computer or to set up your Internet connection; skip both of these steps for now.

Welcome to Windows

As your computer starts up you may hear a sort of *ping*. That's the computer's way of saying "hello." Several different screens may appear briefly before the computer comes to a rest at the Start screen.

Microsoft Windows 8.1 Start screen

Desktop

Manipulating the Mouse

Learning how to use the mouse is not unlike learning how to drive a standard-shift automobile. Do you remember how awkward it was trying to figure out when the clutch was in the right position to give the car gas or hit the brake? And do you remember how many times the car stalled before you got the clutch timing right? Well, welcome to the mouse. As you eventually conquered the clutch, you will eventually conquer the mouse. I promise.

Here we go:

- If you bought a desktop computer, gently rest your hand on the mouse with your index finger positioned over the button on the upper left side of the mouse. If you bought a laptop with a touch pad, trackball, or touch point, place your index or middle finger on the pad, ball, or point.
- *Slowly* move the mouse around on the mouse pad or your finger on the laptop mouse, and you'll notice that the arrow on the screen moves according to your manipulation of the mouse. If you have a desktop computer, lift the mouse off the desk or mouse pad and move it around. You'll notice that when the ball or light on the bottom of the mouse doesn't have contact with a surface, there's no movement of the arrow on the screen. Place the mouse back on the desk or mouse pad. If you find yourself without enough surface space on the mouse pad, simply lift the mouse off the pad (your arrow will stay in place on the screen) and reposition it in the center of the pad.
- Do *not* press any of the buttons on the mouse yet, and be careful not to accidentally put pressure on the mouse buttons while you move it around or you may click on and activate something unintentionally. If the mouse seems out of control, use very small hand or finger movements to make it move *much* slower. Over time you can go faster, but for now we are striving for optimum control of movement.
- *Slowly* move the mouse arrow to the upper left corner of your screen. Now move it to the upper right, lower left, and lower right corners. Did the arrow ever disappear off the edge of the screen? Did something pop up on the screen? Sometimes that

AN INDICATOR ARROW BY ANY OTHER NAME . . .

There are many names for what appears on your screen and moves according to how you manipulate the mouse. I tend to call it the mouse arrow, the arrow, or the mouse (e.g., move the mouse arrow to the happy face). You may find it called the pointer, indicator, or cursor elsewhere. Whatever it's called, it gets the job done.

Whatever type of mouse you use, try to keep your hand relaxed and tension-free. It takes very little physical effort to move the mouse.

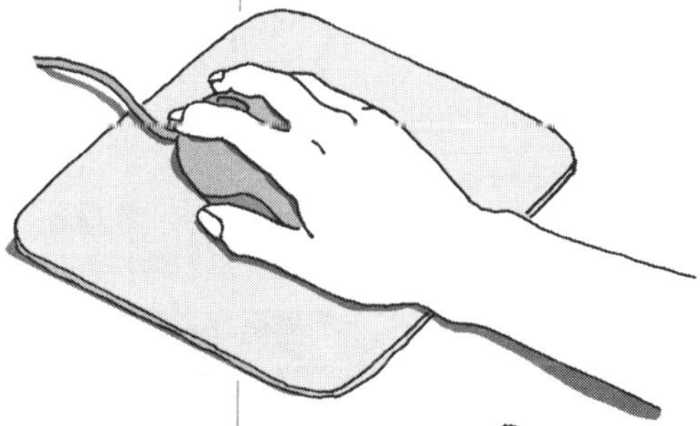

happens when you get close to the edge of the screen. No harm done—gently move the mouse around a bit and the arrow will reappear on the screen. Don't ask me where it goes when this happens—it is the computer's version of hide-and-seek. Notice what pops up on the screen and when. It gets less surprising and off-putting each time, doesn't it?

- Most of our practicing will happen on the Desktop screen. If you have Windows 8.1, you're seeing the Start screen as shown previously. Look at the bottom left corner. There is a box or an app named **Desktop**. Move your mouse onto the Desktop image and click. *Poof!* You're now at the Desktop screen. To return to the Start screen, move your mouse to the bottom left corner and click on the **Start** symbol ⊞. Try it all again by clicking on **Desktop**. Another way to get to the Start screen, at any time, is to depress and release the keyboard key marked with the same **Start** symbol on the bottom left of your keyboard. Try that. From the Start screen there's a way to return to whatever the last window was you were looking at (in this case, the Desktop). Simply depress and release the **Esc** (escape) key at the top left of your keyboard. Go back and forth between the Start and Desktop screens until it feels familiar. You'll be moving from Start to Desktop virtually every time you play with your computer, so you may as well get comfortable with the action as soon as possible.

TENSION IS YOUR ENEMY

There's no reason for you to feel any tension or strain in your hand. Manipulating the mouse is a task that requires accuracy, not strength. If you feel strain, your hand is not relaxed, and it should be. You're probably concentrating too hard or your hand is in an awkward position. Periodically stop what you're doing and focus on your hand. If you feel any strain, relax your hand and try a slightly different position.

OOPS—I MADE A MISTAKE

If you make a mistake, you can erase your typing (from right to left) by using the **BkSp** or **Backspace** key. (It can usually be found on the upper right section of your keyboard next to the ± key.) Depress it once for each letter that you want to erase. You'll see that it moves from right to left, deleting whatever precedes it on the screen. If you hold your finger down on the key, it will continue to move and delete to the left until you lift your finger. You definitely have more control when you depress and release the key with each character than when you hold the key down. If you want to delete from left to right, use the **Delete** or **Del** key on the keyboard.

- Now *slowly* move the mouse arrow onto the little picture  (which is called an icon) above the words **Recycle Bin**. The tip of the mouse arrow needs to be right on the icon, not on the edge of the icon or the words below. If you're using a desktop or an external mouse, push on the button under your index finger and release. This is clicking the mouse. There may also be a button on the upper middle and right. I want you to depress only the button on the upper left. If you're using a touch pad or trackball mouse, use your thumb to depress the button to the left of the pad or ball (above or below it) and release. If you're using a touch point, use your thumb to depress the left of the two buttons at the base of your computer. There is no need for the mouse to move when you depress the button. Keep your eye on the screen and your hand steady so the arrow won't move from its position. If you're having trouble hitting your mark, take your hand off the mouse. Give your hand a rest; maybe shake it a bit. For some people, manipulating the mouse is easy, and for others it takes a few tries. When you're ready, try again.

- Keep your eye on the mouse arrow on the screen and do not move the arrow when you depress the left button of the mouse. It's very common to move the mouse as you depress the button. That will unfortunately make the mouse click off-target. Keep trying—you'll get it eventually. Remember, it is like driving a car: Keep your eye on the road (the screen), not the steering wheel (the mouse).

CLICK AND GO

1. Move mouse to upper right corner.
2. Move mouse to lower left corner.
3. Move mouse to lower right corner.
4. Click on Recycle Bin icon.

"In the beginning, all sorts of things would appear on the screen, and I couldn't figure out how they got there. As I calmed down and got more proficient with the mouse I realized I had been clicking on things without knowing it."
—Fred

What About the Other Buttons on the Mouse?

For now, I want you to depress only the upper left button of the mouse. The other buttons perform advanced actions that we aren't ready for. Be very careful not to let your fingers depress the buttons in the center or right by accident. Nothing bad will happen, but unfamiliar things will appear on your screen.

If something appears on your screen that you didn't intend to have there, either click on the **Close Box** ☒ or, if there is no Close Box, move the mouse to a blank space on the screen and click once with the left mouse button. That should get rid of whatever happened when you hit the wrong button.

Windows 10

Windows 10 is the latest operating system (revisit page 25 if you just asked "What is the operating system?") from Microsoft. Windows 10 is now the brains behind any new PC computer. For those of you with an older computer, you are probably familiar with Windows 7 or 8.1, or even XP, as the operating system, and you'll find that most of the directions throughout this book correspond to these versions. However, you may have upgraded to Windows 10 during their free upgrade period. If you didn't upgrade and you want to, it will now cost $119. But fear not, if your computer is running fine and meeting your needs, you don't have to upgrade if you don't want to.

Part of the motivation for Microsoft to create Windows 10 was that so many people really hated Windows 8.1. Many of the design features in 10 revert back to what people liked in version 7. Honestly, for most of us—who cares? As long as I understand how to accomplish what I want to do on the computer and the thing works, I don't really care what operating system it is—I'm not a computer geek who is invested in what's inside the brain of the device. Most reviews of Windows 10 are very favorable, and there are some treats that you might enjoy. Anything new takes a little getting used to, and you'll probably fumble around this new operating system the same way I did, but it will eventually become second nature.

Let's Start with Start

One of the huge complaints about Windows 8.1 was that the **Start Menu**—what you get when you click on the Microsoft logo in the bottom left corner—disappeared. The Start Menu was what so many of us used as a tool to get to everything else on the computer, and "poof!" it was no more with Windows 8.1. Thankfully, the Start Menu is back in Windows 10 by popular demand.

The most immediate function, when you click on the Microsoft logo, is that it toggles between the desktop view and a screen with an assortment of boxes (also referred to as tiles), which are direct links to programs, photos, websites, and more. I prefer to work with the desktop view, but to each his or her own.

Personally, I don't like how the tile page was originally set up. So I made a tweak and you might want to do so as well. Here are the steps to personalizing Start.

1. Click on the **Start** button in the lower left corner.
2. Click on the 3 lines in the top left corner.
3. Click on **Settings**. Settings
4. Click on **Personalization**.
5. In the left-hand sidebar of the Personalization window that opened, click on **Start**.
6. Turn off **Show More Tiles** by clicking on the little circle to the left of **On.** The word **On** is replaced with **Off**.

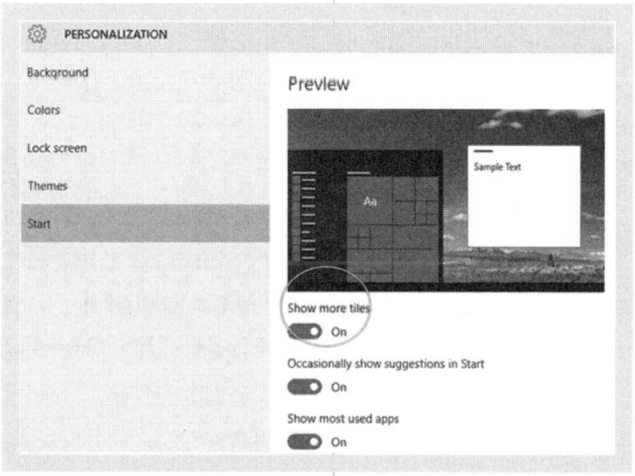

You can customize how your Start screen appears.

Now that's a simple change. As you can see, when you visited the Personalization page, there's a lot of customization you can do. There's really no better way to get to know your computer and feel more comfortable with it than by fiddling around with it. Keep in mind, however, that it's a good idea to write down what the original settings are before you change them, in case you want to change things back and your memory is like mine.

Let's meet one of the most innovative features of Windows 10.

Meet Cortana, Your Personal Assistant

Cortana is Microsoft's Personal Assistant. "She" (yes, I'm giving her a gender) competes with **Siri** (Apple's assistant) and **Google Now** (Android/Google's assistant). Cortana's text box appears at the bottom left of your screen beside the Start Menu button.

■ You can type your communication with Cortana in the box of the Task Bar. You can either type what you seek in the text box or you can activate Cortana so that the two of you can speak to each other. Cortana is pretty mind-boggling. Not only can you instruct her to email the spreadsheet you were working on "yesterday afternoon" and she'll know which one it is, but she'll also alert you that an appointment you're making conflicts with an event already in your calendar. And that's just the start.

Cortana can be synced with your Android or Microsoft smartphone or tablet so that not only is information cross-pollinated between the two devices, but you can also control the handheld devices by way of Cortana. Here's what I mean: You're sitting at the computer and Cortana is on. Your Android or Microsoft smartphone is in the other room. The battery is getting low on your phone. Who knew? Cortana, that's who! Cortana detects the low battery and warns you. Don't worry. You don't have to stop what you're doing and go into the other room. You can simply tell Cortana to shut down the phone and she will. WHAT?!?! Yup.

Customize Cortana

To get familiar with what Cortana can do for you, click on the circle in the left of the text box at the bottom of your screen. A sidebar now opens that offers you a guided tour of what Cortana can do for you. Click **Next** to see more or **Not Interested** if you're, well . . . not interested.

Click on the **Settings** cog to customize Cortana. Here's an example of a change that I made.

At the very top of the Settings it offers: **Cortana can give you suggestions, ideas, reminders, alerts, and more.** I opted to turn this off. I'd rather go to Cortana than have her constantly coming to me with her ideas. (This decision could reflect how we each deal with our live personal relationships. Please don't judge me!) Skim down this sidebar to see what you might want to change.

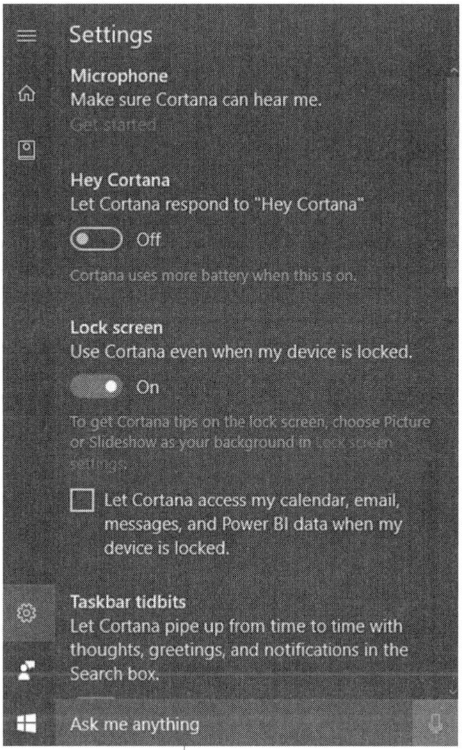

Play nice with Cortana, but do play with her so that you can get familiar with what she has to offer. Again, it's a good idea to write down what the original settings are before you make any changes.

Windows 10 has so many features, but take it in small bites so that you don't get overwhelmed. This is a leaping-off place for you to dig deeper and see what else Windows 10 can do for you in time. Have fun!

The Windows Desktop

A non-laptop computer is called a "desktop" computer. The screen display of your computer (whether it is on a desktop or laptop) is also called the "Desktop." Isn't the English language a beautiful thing?

Your screen is now displaying the Desktop. Think of it as the top of your desk in a virtual office. From this screen, you can access everything that your computer has to offer, just as you can access what you need on your office desk. You'll decide which you'll consider home base—the Start screen or the Desktop screen. As long as you can get from one to the other, you're all set.

We're going to play with the brightness of your screen. It could be that there is a dial or button somewhere on the bottom or side edge of the monitor. Fiddle with the control until the brightness of the screen is right for you. There may not be a brightness control on the monitor itself—instead it may be indicated on the keys of your keyboard. Look for a small image on a key that resembles a sun. If the key with the sun has an **F** on it that means you have to hold down the **Fn** key (bottom left) of your keyboard in order to access the brightness function.

There is one way anyone with Windows 8.1 can adjust their screen brightness.

- Move the mouse to the bottom right corner—all the way into the corner—and five images should pop up in a sidebar on the right side of the screen: **Search**, **Share**, **Start**, **Devices**, and **Settings**. These symbols all live in what Microsoft dubbed the **Charm Bar**. Initially, I called it "those weird things that pop up on the right." They're not so weird now that I understand what they do. Click on the Settings icon. Oops! Did the Charm Bar disappear? It does that after about five seconds or when you move the mouse out of the far bottom right corner. Move your mouse back in the corner and click on the Settings icon. You can also access the Charm Bar by holding down the Start key (bottom left on your keyboard) and keeping it depressed while you depress and release the C key. Once the Charm Bar appears, release the Start key, too.
- Take a second to read everything that is available in Settings. Now click on the Brightness icon. You can click in the vertical bar to brighten or darken your screen. Once you have it set where you like it, move your mouse out onto the Desktop and click once. The sidebar will disappear.

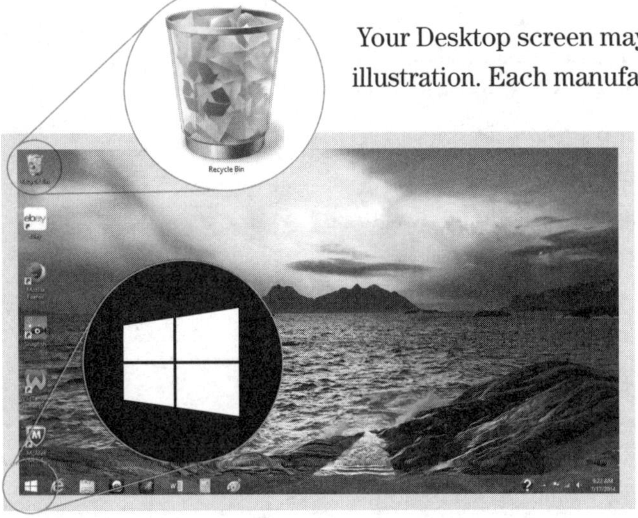

■ Your Desktop screen may appear slightly different from this one, but it will offer the same basic features, including a Recycle Bin and Start icon.

Your Desktop screen may not exactly match the screen in the illustration. Each manufacturer configures how the Desktop looks, so yours may have some of the same components, but they may appear slightly different.

The small pictures on your Desktop are referred to as icons. These icons offer access to different programs and parts of your computer. They are like doors, but instead of knock-knocking to open the doors, you click-click, or "double-click" on them. You will get to know each of these icons and their capabilities in due time. But for now let's learn more about how to move about the computer.

Eek! It's a Mouse!

The mouse has a variety of functions. All of the tasks that the mouse performs are accomplished by moving the mouse to the designated area and depressing and releasing the button on the mouse.

In some ways, it is more chameleon than mouse. You won't see its many mutations until later, but in the box on page 132 are the different faces and what they mean.

To Click or to Double-Click, That Is the Question

As I've said, to click the mouse means to depress and release one of its buttons. Clicking the mouse instructs the computer to perform a task (such as to open a document). You can click either the left button or the right button on the mouse, but you will never click them simultaneously. For now, however, unless I instruct you otherwise, you will use only the left button.

With the left button, you can either single-click or double-click. A single-click is accomplished by depressing and quickly releasing the button. To double-click, you depress, release, depress, release in quick succession. (The right button will require only a single-click.)

There's no clear way to explain when to single- or double-click. Generally, you double-click on an icon to open it, allowing you to access an application software program. Remember, think of it as a knock-knock to allow entry to the program. Usually, when you're in a program (typing a letter or playing a game), you single-click on something to perform a task. You'll get the feel for what's best to do when. If you single-click when a double-click is necessary, you'll know because you won't accomplish your desired task. If you double-click when a single-click is called for, nine times out of ten nothing is affected. On occasion, the double-click opens another window

I THINK I CAN, I THINK I CAN, BUT MAYBE I CAN'T DOUBLE-CLICK

It may be that double-clicking is giving you some trouble. You have a second option. When you're required to double-click to open an icon, you can single-click (to highlight the icon) and then depress and release the Enter key on your keyboard.

WHAT IT MEANS	
	This is the most common look for the mouse arrow. In this form, it tells the computer where to take an action. When you move the mouse arrow, you need to be sure that the point of the arrow is on whatever you want to click on.
	When you move the mouse arrow into a text area, it changes into an I-beam. This shape can be positioned easily between letters or numbers to mark where you want to make editing changes. This shape can be referred to as the cursor.
	The hourglass or circle indicates that the computer is busy performing a task. You shouldn't use the keyboard or the mouse until the hourglass or circle changes back to an arrow.
	The combination of an hourglass and an arrow indicates that the computer is "multitasking," but you can still use the mouse. However, whatever you do may happen more slowly than usual.
	An up-and-down arrow appears when the mouse is at the top or bottom edge of a window. This will allow you to click and drag to increase or decrease the height of the window (for more on this, see page 170).
	An arrow going right and left appears when the mouse is at the left or right edge of a window. This will allow you to click and drag to increase or decrease the width of the window.
	A two-ended arrow at an angle appears when the mouse is at the corner of a window. This will allow you to click and drag so you can change the window's height and width.
	A hand with the index finger pointing indicates that if you press the mouse button, more information will become available. It is the *finger* of the hand that must be on the item desired—just as it is the point of the arrow.
	A "don't" icon indicates that you're not allowed to take any action at this time. You're either in an area where you're prohibited from taking an action, or the computer is busy and will let you know when you can resume.

unexpectedly, but you can press **Esc** (the Escape key—upper left on the keyboard) to correct things or click on the **Close Box** or a blank area on the screen to get rid of the unwanted window.

Let's Experiment

It's time to experiment with the mouse arrow on your Desktop screen and become familiar with its movement. If you've taken a break and returned, follow the instructions from earlier in the chapter to get from the Start screen to the Desktop.

1. Place your hand on the mouse (with the tail or cord of the mouse pointing away from you), and move the mouse arrow to a blank space on the Desktop screen. (Don't click on an icon yet.)

2. Click the left mouse button by depressing and releasing it with your finger.

3. Now depress and release the left button two times. Do it again as fast as you can. Continue double-clicking until you're comfortable with the action. For some people, double-clicking can be tricky.

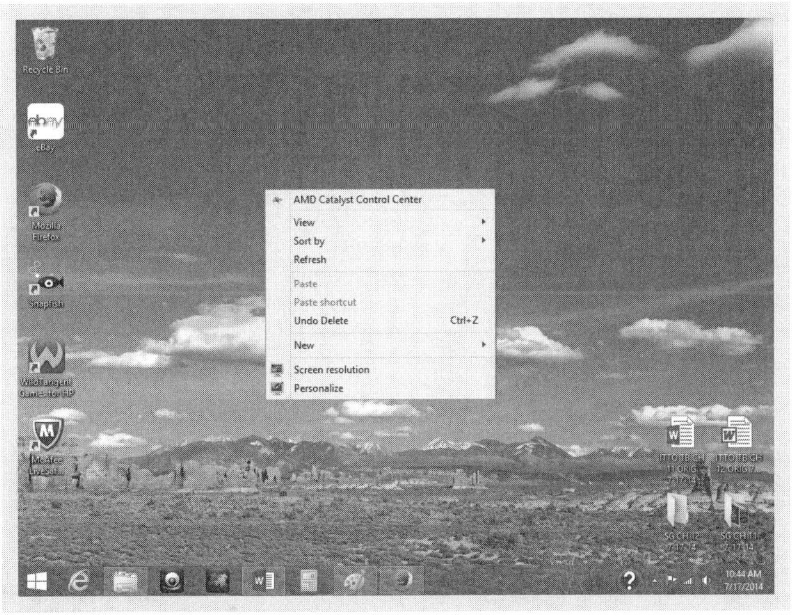

4. Once you've had enough of that, click once on the *right* mouse button just for fun. The little gray box that appeared on the screen has advanced options that we don't want to get into yet. To get rid of the box, move the mouse arrow

■ If you right-click by accident, a box will open. To get rid of the box, move the mouse arrow anywhere on a blank area of your Desktop screen and click once with the left button.

For the downloadable guide **Microsoft's Apps in Windows 8,** visit ***AskAbbyStokes.com*.** Click on Resources at the top, then click on Helpful Guides, and lastly click on Guide #1.

anywhere on a blank area of your Desktop screen and click once with the *left* button.

If at any point you goof up and your mouse careens around the screen, don't worry. Just relax and try again. Move the mouse arrow to a blank spot on your Desktop and click the left button once. If you opened another program by accident, move the mouse arrow to the **Close Box** and click once to get rid of it.

Learning the Parts of a Window

Let's test the waters a bit more with the mouse and discover what a window is and how it works. On the Desktop, find the Recycle Bin again. Move your mouse onto the image and double-click. Don't lose hope if your double-clicking is spotty. You'll improve with time.

Look at the Recycle Bin window. The top blue bar, or the **Title Bar**, contains the name of the program you are now in. In this case, it indicates that we are in the Recycle Bin window. The words in gray below the Title Bar are contained in the **Menu Bar.**

Most PC windows have a Title Bar, Menu Bar, Minimize Box, Maximize Box, and Close Box.

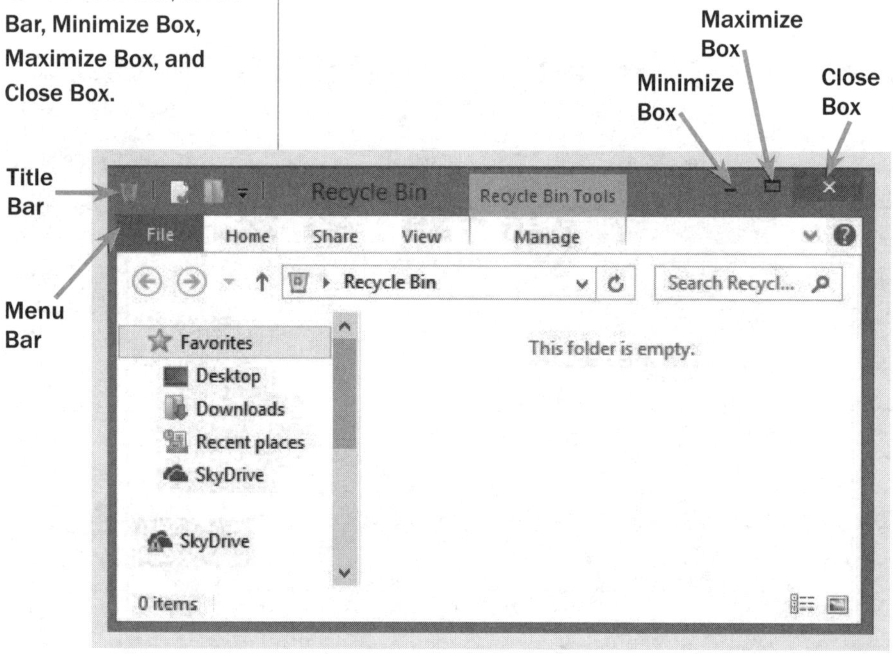

At the far right corner of the Title Bar are three small boxes. You remember that the **Close Box** is to the far right. The **Maximize Box** is in the middle. And the **Minimize Box** is the box to the left.

These same features will appear on nearly every window that you open from the Desktop on your computer. (When you open up an app on the Start screen, it will not have the same design and functionality.)

The Title Bar at the top tells you which window you are viewing. There will be a Menu Bar, and a Close, a Maximize, and a Minimize Box. Once you learn how to use these features within the Recycle Bin window, you will be able to use them on any window you open.

The Maximize Box

To maximize a window is to make the size of the window as large as possible. The advantage of this is that you will see more of what is contained in that window.

Move the mouse arrow into the Maximize Box and click once. It's a little tricky to position the arrow exactly inside the box. If the Recycle Bin window disappears, you probably clicked the **Close Box** by accident. No harm done. Just find the Recycle Bin icon on the Desktop and double-click to open it. That's what we were going to do soon anyway—you just get a little extra practice.

If you have clicked successfully on the Maximize Box, the window will now take up the whole screen. It is maximized! Now look at the Maximize Box. It has changed to look like this: . It has now become the **Restore Box**.

The Restore Box

To restore a window is to bring it back to its original size, which is smaller than when it is maximized. This allows you to view other items on the screen at the same time that you view part of what is contained in the restored window.

Move the mouse arrow onto the **Restore Box**, and click once to restore the Recycle Bin window to the size it was before you maximized it. Did the window return to the size it was when you started? If the window disappeared, you might have clicked on one of the other boxes on the Title Bar instead. Not to worry. Go back and open the Recycle Bin. If it didn't disappear, you did it right.

The Minimize Box

To minimize a window is to shrink the window to its smallest form and store it in the **Task Bar** at the bottom of your screen. The advantage of this is that you can access the window quickly, but it isn't taking up space on your screen.

Let's see the Minimize Box in action. Move the mouse arrow onto the **Minimize Box** and click once. If you click on the correct button, the Recycle Bin window seems to disappear, but it doesn't really. You'll see what looks like a folder in the Task Bar at the bottom of your screen. This is the Systems Folder. Move your mouse over the folder. You don't need to click. By simply moving your mouse over the folder you'll see the Recycle Bin window. Now move your mouse onto the window and click. Voilà! The Recycle Bin window is back.

The advantage of minimizing a window is that you can, in one click, get the window off the screen so you can view other items, then just go to the Systems folder to open it again.

Now we're going to use the Close Box. Move the mouse arrow to the **Close Box** and click once. Good-bye, Recycle Bin window. If that was rough going, don't despair. This is your first time playing with the mouse and accessing a window. It's all about practice, practice, practice. With that in mind, go back to the start of this section and repeat everything until you feel more comfortable with the mouse and your computer.

Place Your Bets

We're now going to open your Solitaire program, which is included in most Microsoft operating systems. The **Start** button (at the bottom left of your screen) offers you access to everything on your computer, including any of your applications software programs, or apps, preinstalled on your computer.

Follow these steps to access Solitaire.

- Move the mouse arrow to the Start button , located at the bottom left corner of your screen, and click once. *Remember, unless I instruct you otherwise, always click with the left button on your mouse.* What has now appeared on the screen is called the Start screen. The Start screen lists what is available on the computer.

- Look for the **Microsoft Solitaire Collection** app. It looks like this: . Once you find it, click on the app. If you accidentally click on the wrong app, not to worry. Depress and release the **Start** button , or move your mouse to the bottom left corner and click on the Start symbol.

If any requests pop up on the screen to access your contacts or register in any way, click on **No**. You can't blame Microsoft for trying to have you share information with them, but you have no obligation. If it gets too confusing, simply click on Start and try again from scratch.

There will be several Solitaire options. We are going to play Klondike solitaire, which is very basic. Click on Klondike. On my computer it appears on the left. You may have to wait a minute before either your Solitaire choices or Klondike opens up on the screen. It's the first time and the program needs to wake up, so don't start clicking and clicking—that only confuses the computer. A good rule of thumb is to wait a solid 10 seconds after you click the mouse before you decide to click again. Patience always pays off with technology.

Now that you have Solitaire on your screen, meet me on page 151.

Welcome, Mac Users

As your computer starts up, you will hear a *ding*, or perhaps more of a *bing*—you get the idea. That's the Mac's way of saying "hello." The first thing to appear on your screen will probably be the Mac logo with a spinning circle below it.

GET THEE TO A COMPUTER

If you haven't purchased a computer yet but want to continue reading—*beware*. Much of the book from this point forward is based on information that will appear on a computer screen. You will become very confused if you do not have a computer as a point of reference. Get yourself to someone's computer so you can follow along.

The First Step

As the Mac starts up, the screen looks something like this.

If you're turning on a new Mac for the very first time, there are some one-time-only setup procedures that you must go through.

If an Everything Mac guide came with your Mac, consult it. Read it along with these simplified instructions. The appearance of a round spinning ball in place of the mouse's indicator arrow tells you that the computer is working on something and it is best not to use the keyboard or mouse until the spinning ball goes away.

Identify Yourself

The next thing to appear on your screen may ask you to accept the license terms, then choose the location of the computer (i.e., United States). The computer may ask you to choose an Apple ID. Follow the instructions step-by-step. Once you've completed a step, move to the next by clicking on an arrow, the word **Next**, or the word **Continue** found on the bottom right of the screen. If any of this becomes too much for you, call a friend over to walk you through the steps, but I suspect you'll do just fine.

For example: Type whatever ID you want to have on the computer. (You can name it after yourself or your cat—anything you want.) If you want to have the first letter of the name capitalized, you need to use the **Shift** key, as you would on a typewriter. (There are two **Shift** keys—one near the bottom left of your keyboard, next to the **Z** key, and one on the right, next to the ?/ key. It doesn't matter which one you use.) Depress **Shift** and hold it down as you type the letter that you want capitalized. If you make a mistake, use the **Delete** key.

If you are asked to enter a password, you don't have to. The password feature is helpful if you're going to have confidential information on your computer that you don't want anyone else to access or if you travel a lot and there's risk of loss or theft.

For the average at-home user, having a password means having to remember it and type it in every time you turn on the computer, which is unnecessary. You can instruct the computer to accept that there is not a password. If you choose to have a password, please be sure to write it down and include it in the packet where you will be storing all your computer information. No one will be able to help you rediscover your password if you forget it.

Wait patiently while this setup process takes place. There may be times that several minutes will go by while the computer is working. You may be asked to register your computer or to set up your Internet connection. Skip both of those steps for now.

Macbook laptop

iMac Desktop

The Mac Desktop

A non-laptop computer is called a "desktop" computer. The screen display of your computer (whether it is on a desktop or laptop) is also called the "Desktop." Isn't the English language a beautiful thing?

Your screen is now displaying the Desktop. Think of it as the top of your desk in a virtual office. From this screen, you can access everything that your computer has to offer, just as you can access what you need on your office desk. The Desktop is your home base.

While you are here, find the brightness control on your monitor. On an Apple computer, the brightness control is also usually located on one of the keys of your keyboard. Look at the top row of keys, above the number keys. To the far left there are two keys that resemble a sun—one smaller than the other. Fiddle around with the controls until the brightness of the screen is right for you. There is no standard

A GENTLE TOUCH

If you hold down a key on the keyboard, it will keep tttttttttyping. Use a quick depress and release to hit the key you want without having it rrrrrepeat.

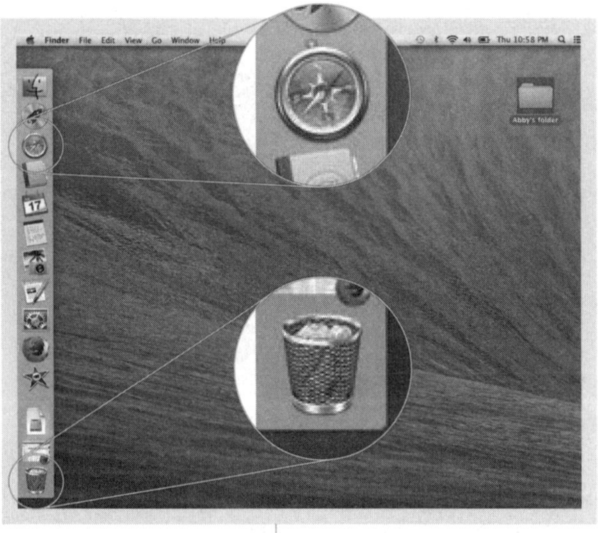

■ **Your Desktop may appear slightly different from this one, but it will offer the same basic features, including an icon for the browser Safari and one for Trash.**

for the appropriate level of brightness—it's what you find comfortable and what doesn't strain your eyes.

What you see in this illustration may not exactly match your screen. The small icons offer access to different programs and parts of your computer. They are like doors, but instead of knocking to open the doors, you click-click, or "double-click" on them. You will get to know each of these icons and their capabilities in due time. But for now, let's learn more about how to move around the computer.

OOPS—I MADE A MISTAKE

If you make a mistake, you can erase your typing (from right to left) by using the **Delete** key. (It can usually be found on the upper right section of your keyboard, next to the ± key.) Depress it once for each letter that you want to erase. You'll see that it moves from right to left, deleting whatever precedes it on the screen. If you hold your finger down on the key, it will continue to move and delete to the left until you lift your finger. You definitely have more control when you depress and release the key with each character than when you hold the key down.

Manipulating the Mouse

Learning how to use the mouse is not unlike learning how to drive a standard-shift automobile. Do you remember how awkward it was trying to figure out when the clutch was in the right position to give the car gas or hit the brake? And do you remember how many times the car stalled before you got the clutch timing right? Well, welcome to the mouse. As you eventually conquered the clutch, you will eventually conquer the mouse. I promise. Let's try.

Do yourself a favor—lower the bar for how user-friendly the mouse is . . . or isn't. It used to be that the mouse had three simple actions—single-click, double-click, and click-and-drag. Apple decided to beef up the capabilities of the mouse for both their desktops (dubbed "Magic Mouse") and the trackpads on their laptops. It matters now if two fingers tap on the mouse as opposed to only one. If you swoop two fingers left and right, that will perform a very different task than if you pull your finger down on the mouse. All of that is well and good unless you don't know how sensitive the mouse is, and that's when frustration sets in. Right now we're going to concentrate on the basics. In the next chapter, I'll lead you to where you can customize your mouse functions to meet your needs.

For now the best rule of thumb is to hover your hand over the mouse, but avoid touching the mouse until you are ready to take an action.

TENSION IS YOUR ENEMY

There's no reason for you to feel any tension or strain in your hand. Manipulating the mouse is a task that requires accuracy, not strength. If you feel strain, your hand is not relaxed, and it should be. You're probably concentrating too hard or your hand is in an awkward position. Periodically stop what you're doing and focus on your hand. If you feel any strain, relax your hand and try a slightly different position.

- If you bought a desktop computer, gently rest your hand on the mouse with your index finger positioned on the upper portion of the mouse. If you bought a laptop with a touch pad, place your index or middle finger on the pad.
- *Slowly* move the mouse or your finger around, and you'll notice that the arrow on the screen moves according to your manipulation of the mouse. If you have a desktop computer, lift the mouse off the desk or mouse pad and move it around. You'll notice that when the bottom of the mouse doesn't have contact with a surface, there's no movement of the arrow on the screen. Place the mouse back on the desk or mouse pad. If you find you don't have

AN INDICATOR ARROW BY ANY OTHER NAME . . .

There are many names for what appears on your screen and moves according to how you manipulate the mouse. I tend to call it the mouse arrow, the arrow, or the mouse (e.g., move the mouse arrow to the happy face). You may find it called the pointer, indicator, or cursor elsewhere. Whatever it's called, it gets the job done.

enough surface space on the mouse pad, simply lift the mouse off the pad (your arrow will stay in place on the screen), and reposition the mouse on the center of the pad.

- Do *not* press down on the mouse yet, and be careful not to accidentally put pressure on the mouse while you move it around. If the mouse seems out of control, use very small hand or finger movements to make it move *much* slower. Over time, you can go faster, but for now we are striving for optimum control of movement.
- Slowly move the mouse arrow to the upper left corner of your screen. Now move it to the upper right, lower left, and lower right corners. Did the arrow ever disappear off the edge of the screen? This can happen if you get close to the edge of the screen. No harm done. Gently move the mouse around a bit and the arrow will reappear on the screen. Don't ask me where it goes—it's the computer's version of hide-and-seek.

CLICK AND GO

1. Move mouse to upper right corner.
2. Move mouse to lower left corner.
3. Move mouse to lower right corner.
4. Move to top left and click on File.
5. Click on New Folder.
6. Click on Untitled Folder.
7. Click on File.
8. Click on Open.
9. Click on Close.

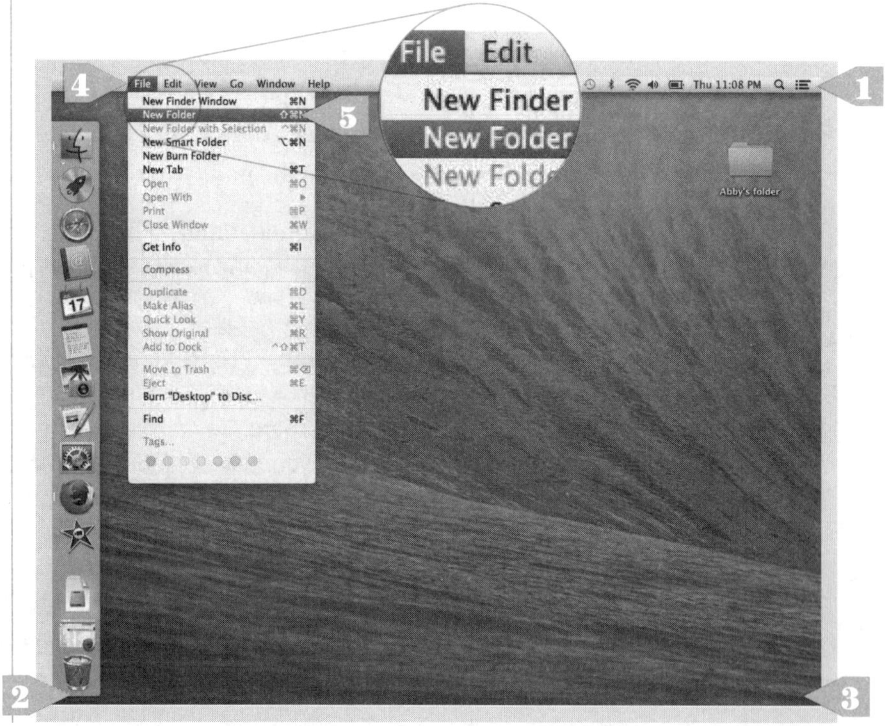

- Now slowly move the mouse arrow to the word **File** at the top left of your screen. *If you're using a desktop computer or an external mouse*, depress and release the button under your index finger. *If you're using a touch pad*, use your thumb to depress the button below the pad and release. There is no need for the mouse to move when you depress the button. Keep your eye on the screen and your hand steady.
- Now move the mouse arrow onto the words **New Folder**, and then release the button. Keep your hand very steady so the arrow won't move from its position. If you're having trouble hitting your mark, take your hand off the mouse. Give your hand a rest; maybe shake it a bit. For some people this is easy, and for others it takes a few tries. When you're ready, try again.
- When you release the mouse button, a new icon that looks like a file folder with the words **Untitled Folder** enclosed in

a box below it should appear on the screen. We need to open this folder to produce a window. Move the mouse arrow onto the folder itself (not the words below) and depress the mouse button and release. The folder should now be highlighted.

- Move the mouse arrow back up to the word **File** (at the top left of the screen). Depress and release the mouse button. Now move the mouse arrow down to the word **Open** and depress and release the mouse button. You have just opened a window on your computer screen!
- Now we're going to close the window. Find the red circle box in the upper left corner of the window. This is the **Close Box**. Move the mouse arrow *inside* the Close Box. An X appears in the circle. It is important that the tip of the arrow is inside the Close Box, not on the edge of the box. Keep your hand steady so the mouse won't move from its position. Depress and release your mouse button. The **Untitled Folder** window has now disappeared. Well done.

If the box hasn't disappeared, there is nothing wrong with you or the computer; you simply didn't click the mouse correctly inside the Close Box. Keep your eye on the mouse arrow on the screen, and do not move the arrow when you depress the left button of the mouse. It's very common to move the mouse as you depress the button. That will unfortunately make the mouse click off-target. Keep trying—you'll get it eventually. Remember: It is like driving a car—keep your eye on the road (the screen), not the steering wheel (the mouse).

"I thought I would never be able to control the mouse. It took me a long time to feel comfortable with the clicking and the movement. I made a lot of mistakes along the way, but eventually it got easier. Sometimes I don't even think about it now—I just do it."
—Eileen

Eek! It's a Mouse!

The mouse has a variety of functions. All of the tasks that the mouse performs are accomplished by moving the mouse to the designated area and depressing the button.

In some ways, it is more chameleon than mouse. You won't see its many mutations until later, but the chart below shows the different faces and what they mean.

To Click or to Double-Click, That Is the Question

As I've said before, to click the mouse means to depress and release the button. Clicking the mouse instructs the computer to perform a task (such as open a document). This can take a single- or a double-click. A single-click is accomplished by depressing and then quickly releasing the button. To double-click, you depress, release, depress, release in quick succession.

There is no clear way to explain when to single- or double-click. Generally, you double-click on an icon to open it, allowing you to access an application software program. Remember, you can think of it as a knock-knock to allow entry to the program. Usually when you're in a program (typing a letter or playing a game), you single-click on something to perform a task. You'll get the feel for what's best to do when. If you single-click when a double-click is

WHAT IT MEANS

This is the most common look for the mouse arrow. In this form, it tells the computer where to take an action. When you move the mouse arrow, you need to be sure that the point of the arrow is on whatever you want to click on.

When you move the mouse arrow into a text area, it changes into an I-beam. This shape can be positioned easily between letters or numbers to mark where you want to make editing changes. This shape can be referred to as the cursor.

This round spinning ball indicates that the computer is busy performing a task. You shouldn't use the keyboard or the mouse until the ball changes back to an arrow.

A hand with the index finger pointing indicates that if you press the mouse button, more information will become available. This configuration is seen often when you're on the Internet. It is the finger of the hand that must be on the item desired—just as it is with the point of the arrow.

necessary, you'll know because you won't accomplish your desired task.

If you double-click when a single-click is called for, nine times out of ten nothing is affected. On occasion, the double-click opens another window unexpectedly, but you can press **Esc** (the Escape key—upper left on the keyboard) to correct things or click on the **Close Box** ⊗ or a blank area on the screen to get rid of the unwanted window.

Let's Experiment

It's time to experiment with the mouse arrow on your Desktop screen to become familiar with its movement.

1. Place your hand on the mouse (with the tail or cord of the mouse pointing away from you or the Apple symbol at the bottom of the mouse nearest you), and move the mouse arrow to a blank space on the Desktop screen. (Don't click on an icon yet.)

2. Click the mouse button by depressing and releasing it with your finger.

3. Now depress and release the mouse button two times. Try it again and do it as fast as you can. Continue double-clicking until you're comfortable with the action. For some people, double-clicking can be kind of tricky.

Learning the Parts of a Window

Reopen the **Untitled Folder** that you created on page 143 by moving the mouse onto the folder (not the words below) and double-clicking. If you are having trouble with the double-click, you can single-click on the folder to highlight it, then click on the word **File** at the top left and single-click on the word **Open**. Your Untitled Folder window should now be open.

Look at the window. The words at the top of the screen are contained in the **Title Bar**. In the far left corner of the Title Bar is the

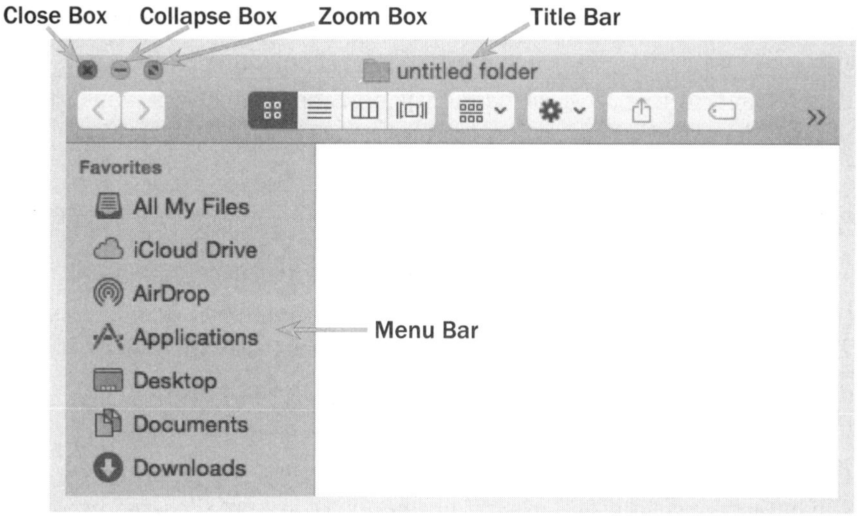

Close Box. In the left corner of the Title Bar are two more circles. The green circle on the right is the **Zoom Box**, and the yellow circle in the middle is the **Collapse Box**.

These same features will appear on most windows that you open on your computer. There will always be a Title Bar at the top that tells you which window you are viewing. There will always be a Menu Bar, a Close Box, a Zoom Box, and a Collapse Box. Once you learn to use these features in this window, you will be able to use them on any window.

The Zoom Box

When you use the Zoom Box, it makes the size of the window as large as possible. The advantage of this is that you will see more of what is contained in that window. Move the mouse arrow to the **Zoom Box** and click once. It's a little tricky to position the arrow exactly inside the box. If you've clicked successfully on the Zoom Box, you'll see that the **Untitled Folder** window now takes up more of the screen. Note: Sometimes the window thinks it's maximized, but it isn't taking up the entire screen. In that case, the window can be maximized by clicking and dragging the window's edges. We'll play with that later. To restore the **Untitled Folder** window to the size it was when you started, move the arrow back onto the **Zoom Box** and click once. If the window is now the original size, you did it right.

The Collapse Box

When you use the Collapse Box, it shrinks the window to its smallest form on the Dock at the bottom or left of your screen next to the Trash. The advantage of this is that you can access the window quickly but it isn't taking up space on your screen. Let's see the Collapse Box in action. Move the mouse arrow onto the **Collapse Box** and click once. If it seems as though the box has disappeared, you have successfully collapsed the window. To restore the window to its original size, move the mouse arrow onto the Dock and click on the **Untitled Folder** once. The **Untitled Folder** window is back on your screen.

The Close Box

To close the window completely, move the mouse arrow into the **Close Box** and click once. Good-bye, **Untitled Folder** window. If that was rough going, don't worry. This is your first time playing with the mouse. It's all about practice, practice, practice.

Mouse Play

Playing solitaire is a great way to practice your mouse skills. But unlike a PC with a Microsoft operating system, a Mac doesn't come with Solitaire preinstalled on the hard drive. If you purchased Solitaire software when you bought your computer, you can skip this section and go directly to "Place Your Bets" (page 150) to play Solitaire.

If you don't have Solitaire, hone you mouse skills by following the steps here as often as you can. Once you've mastered the mouse, go on to the next chapter. Remember, it is practice and only practice that will allow you to conquer the mouse or any other aspect of the computer. So, let's try it again.

To access a new folder:

- Move the mouse arrow up to the top of the screen.
- Click on the word **File** at the top of the screen.
- A menu will have opened. Move the mouse down into the menu, and click on the words **New Folder**.
- Take a look at the desktop, and you will notice that there is now a folder there with the name **Untitled Folder**.

CLICK AND GO

1. Click File.
2. Click New Folder.

My goal here is to have you learn to click and drag the mouse. It is a mouse skill that you will use later when you are on the Internet.

Here's what I would like you to do:

- Double-click (as you did on page 146) on the **Untitled Folder**.
- The folder has now opened to a window. Move your mouse onto the title bar where it says **Untitled Folder**.
- Depress the mouse button and keep it depressed while you move the **Untitled Folder** to the left, then to the right.

TRIVIA

There are many versions of Solitaire and many names for each game. The familiar version is often called Klondike. It most likely dates back to the Klondike gold rush in the late 19th century.

CLICK AND GO

1. Double-click on Untitled Folder.
2. Move mouse onto Title Bar.
3. Click and drag Untitled Folder window.

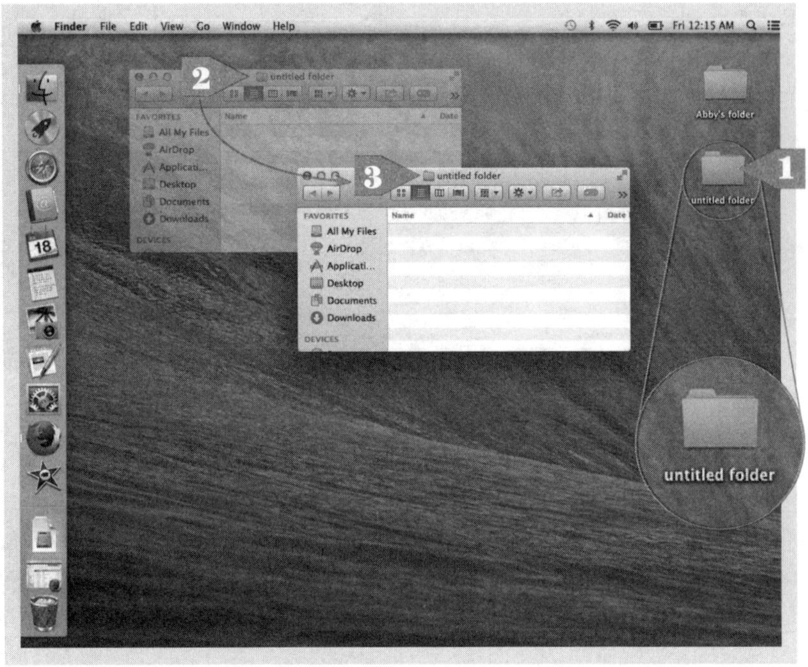

- Release the mouse. You'll notice the folder remains where you moved it.

Good! Before you know it you will have mastered the mouse. Remember, it is practice that allows you to conquer the mouse or any other aspect of the computer. Repeat this exercise every time you visit your computer.

Place Your Bets

As I mentioned, Mac computers don't come with Solitaire preinstalled. If you want to practice using the mouse by playing Solitaire, now is a good time to ask a friend to help you download the game. But if getting Solitaire isn't an option for you, fear not. You'll get plenty of practice with the mouse as we move forward. If you do get Solitaire installed, open the program using the following steps:

1. If there is a **Solitaire** icon on your Desktop screen, move the mouse arrow onto the icon and double-click. It is important that the arrow be on the icon and not on the words below.

2. If there isn't an icon, move the mouse arrow to the **Finder** icon and click.

3. Find the **Application** folder. Move the mouse arrow onto that folder and click.

4. Now find the **Solitaire** folder. Move the mouse arrow onto that folder and double-click. The Solitaire window is now opened.

MAC USERS: AVERSION TO DIFFERENT VERSIONS
Your version of Solitaire may differ slightly from what we describe here. This is true of any software package. Follow my instructions as best you can, but when in doubt, refer to your software manual.

PC and Mac Card Sharks, Unite!

So here we are with the **Solitaire** window opened. Let's review the rules of Solitaire, and then we can play a hand. If you already know how to play Solitaire, skip this section and we'll catch up with you at "How Do the Cards Get Moved?" (page 153).

- The ultimate goal of Solitaire is to have all the cards in four piles in the empty spots of the Solitaire window. Each stack must be of a single suit and in ascending order, with the ace on the bottom and the king on top (ace, 2, 3 . . . jack, queen, king).

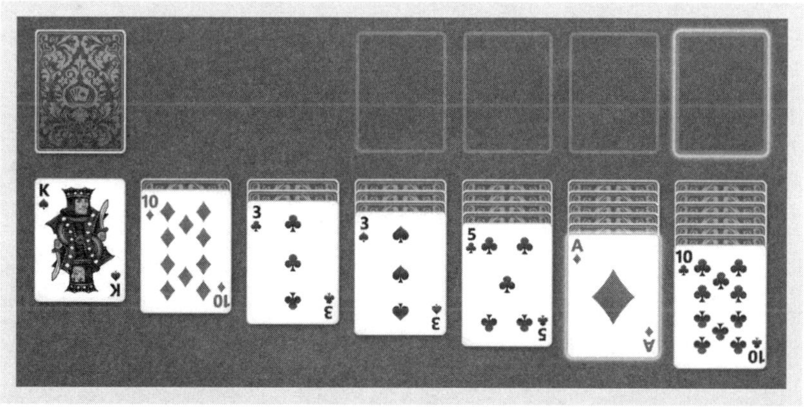

A PC Solitaire window

- Along the way, your challenge is to build on the cards that are faceup in the seven piles. You add cards to these piles moving down in value (10, 9, 8 . . .), but you must alternate in color (black, red, black, red).
- You can play the top card in any of the seven piles or play the card that is faceup in the draw pile. When you take a card from the draw pile, the card below will be revealed and may then be played.
- As you use a card from the seven piles, the card below it can be played. If an empty space is created, only a king can be moved to that spot; then you can start building on the king in the same

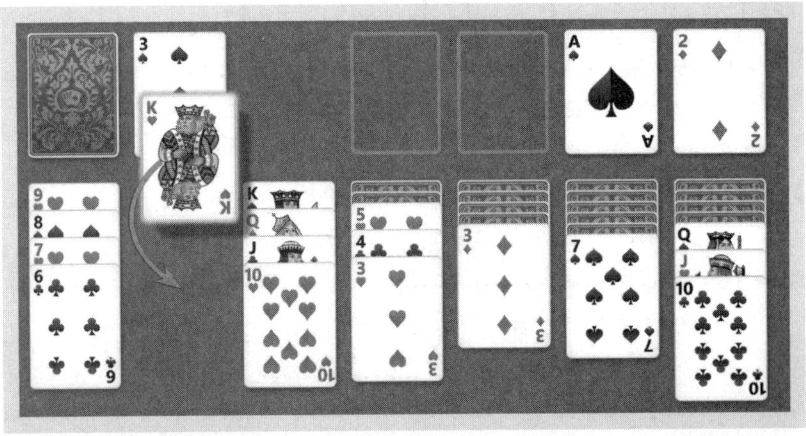

A king is the only card that can be moved to an empty space.

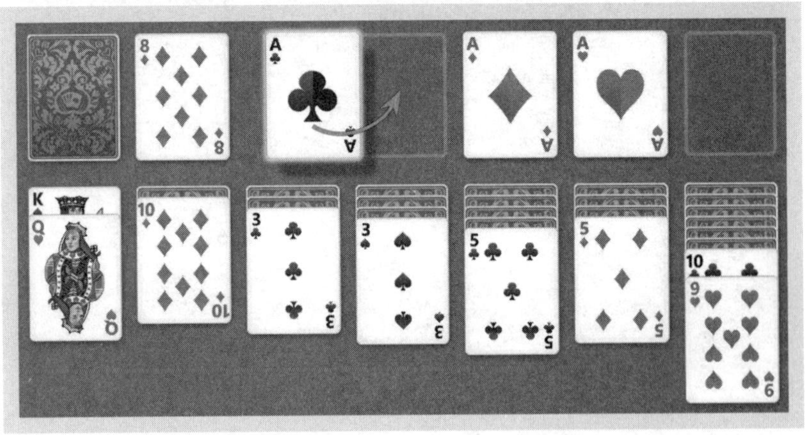

Aces are moved to the spaces at the top right of the window.

way the other piles are built (king, queen, jack . . . alternating red and black).

- If you come upon an ace, move it to one of the open four spots at the top right and build up your stacks by suit (ace, 2, 3 . . .).
- A series of cards can be moved together. For example, if you have a black queen revealed in one pile and in another stack you have built a series with a red jack, black 10, and red 9, you can move the series, starting with the red jack, onto the black queen.
- Keep in mind, the strategy in Solitaire is to try to expose as many facedown cards as possible.

Don't get frustrated if you don't often win. If you win one out of five games, you're doing quite well. Remember: It isn't whether you win or lose, it's how you control the mouse.

How Do the Cards Get Moved?

To move a card, you must click and drag it. Place the mouse arrow on the card that you want to move. Press the mouse button, and, without lifting your finger, drag the card to where you want it to be. Then let go of the button on the mouse.

HUH? WHAT HAPPENED?
You'll discover that the computer will not allow you to make a mistake or cheat! If you choose a card and try to play it on another card incorrectly, the computer will send your choice flying back to its original spot as soon as you release the mouse button.

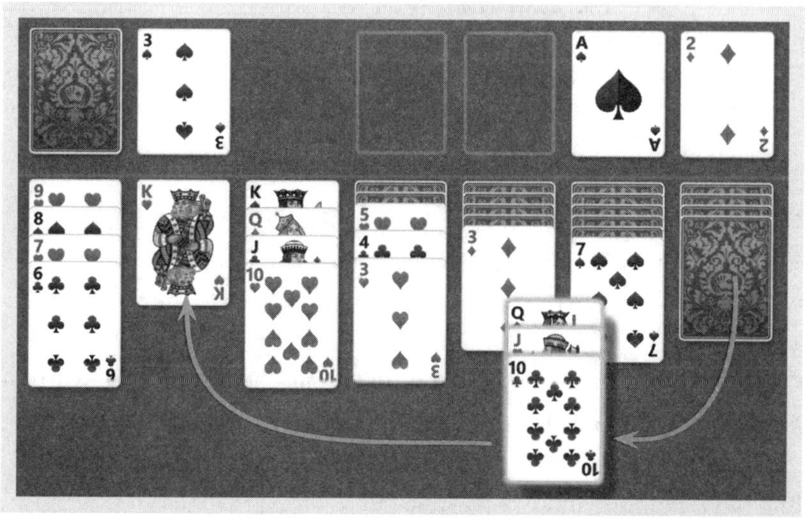

A series of cards can be moved together by clicking on the highest card of the series and dragging it to the appropriate spot. All the cards in the series will move together.

CLICK AND DRAG . . . IS IT A DRAG?

Are you having some trouble with the click-and-drag maneuver? Let's review:

- Place the mouse arrow on the object you want to move and depress the mouse button.
- Keep the mouse button depressed while you drag the object by moving the mouse to where you desire.
- Take your finger off the mouse and the object will remain where it has been moved.

My advice is, keep playing Solitaire! It may seem silly (or drive you nuts), but it is the best way to master the mouse.

To flip over a card from the draw pile, move the mouse arrow onto the card and click once. If you double-click here, you will turn over two cards, so be careful.

Let the Games Begin

Look at the cards that are faceup in your seven piles. If there is an ace, move the mouse arrow onto the ace. Press down the mouse button. With the mouse button held down, move the card onto one of the four designated blank spots. Take your finger off the mouse button. If this didn't work, give it another try.

Look for a card one less in number than any of the cards faceup in the seven piles. Is the color different? (The cards must alternate black and red.)

- If you have a card to move, move the mouse arrow to that card and click and drag the card to its new position.
- If you don't have a card to move, can you play the faceup card in the draw pile?
- If you can't play that card, click once on the facedown pile. Can you use that card? Keep flipping cards until there's a card to play. If the draw pile is depleted, click once on the empty area so you can go through the pile again.

The game continues like this until you can't play any of the cards available to you. Unfortunately, that means you've lost. But if you manage to complete the four piles by suit from ace to king, that means you've won.

If you want to play again, move the mouse arrow onto the word **Game** (in Apple) or **Menu** (in the bottom left on Windows 8.1) and click. Then move to **Deal** in the Menu Bar (in Apple) or **New Deal** and plus sign (in Windows 8.1) and click.

Remember the Goal

Play Solitaire for at least half an hour every day for a week. If you choose to play more, make sure you take five-minute breaks every half hour or so. What you are really doing is mastering the mouse. Once you've mastered the mouse, go on to the next chapter. Remember, it is practice and only practice that will allow you to conquer the mouse or any other aspect of the computer.

Exit Solitaire

If you have a PC with Windows 8.1, move your mouse arrow to the Close Box of the Solitaire window and click once.
If you have a Mac, move your mouse arrow to the Close Box of the Solitaire window and click once.

Ready to Call It a Day?

Get into the habit of shutting down your computer properly. You must try to avoid simply turning the power off instead of going through the shut-down process. If you do not go through the proper shut-down procedures, you can damage the computer. It is best to close all the windows that are open and quit any programs that you are in. If you forget to do this, the computer will remind you.

CLICK AND GO

1. Click .
2. Click Power.
3. Click Shut Down.

Putting the Computer to Bed

If you have a PC:

1. Move your mouse to the bottom left corner of your screen and click on the **Start** button .

2. Move your mouse onto **Power** and click once.

3. Click on **Shut down.**

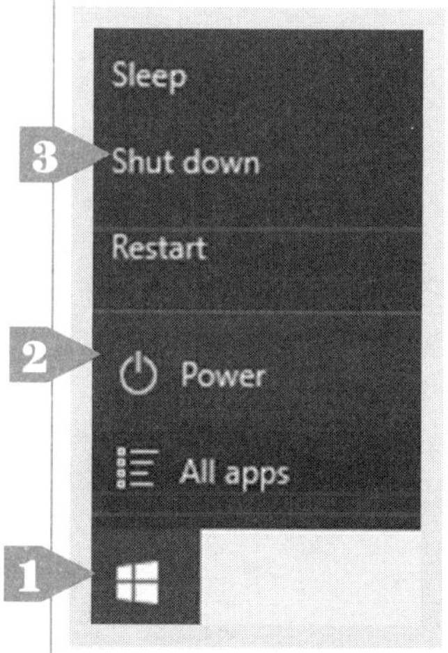

If you have a Mac:

1. Move your mouse arrow to the in the top left corner and click once, then to the words **Shut Down** and click once.

2. Click on **Shut Down** in the little window that has opened. This will instruct the computer to shut down.

3. Turn off any peripherals that may still be on—your monitor, the printer, and so on.

CLICK AND GO

1. Click on Apple logo.
2. Click Shut Down.
3. Click Shut Down.

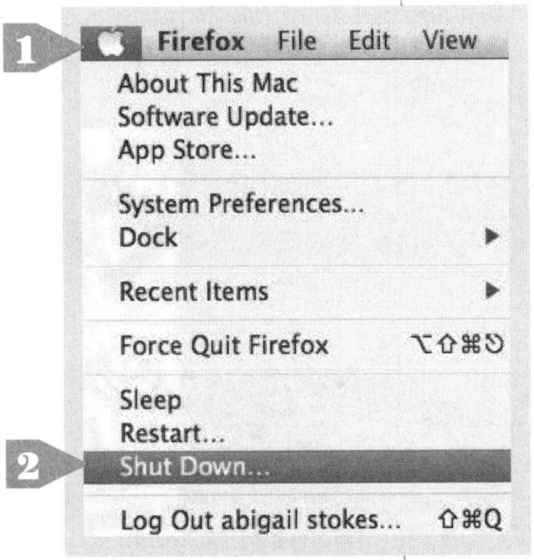

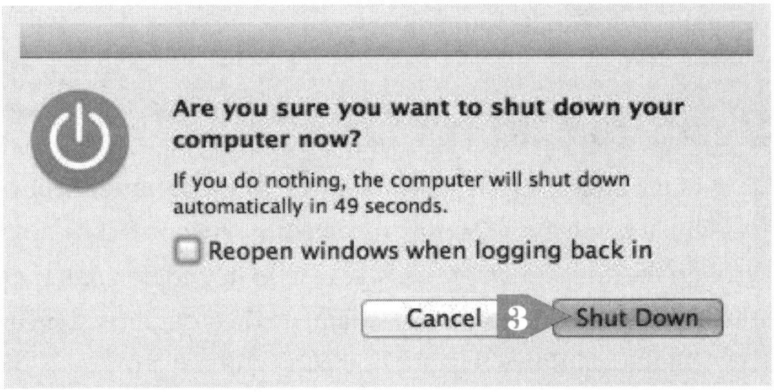

If You Have a Laptop:

Be sure to close the cover after completing the preceding steps.

LET'S REVIEW FOR COMPUTERS

Here is a quick guide to get you up and running with Solitaire (or opening a new folder for Mac users).

If you are using a PC

To Access Solitaire:

- Turn on the computer and wait for it to warm up.
- Depress and release the **Start** key on the keyboard.
- Move the mouse onto **Microsoft Solitaire Collection** and click.
- Click on **Klondike**. Have fun!

To Shut Down:

- Move your mouse to the bottom left corner of your screen and click on the Start button.
- Move the mouse arrow to **Power** and click.
- Move the mouse to **Shut Down** and click once.

If you are using a Mac

To Open a Folder:

- Turn on the computer and wait for it to warm up.
- Click on **File** in the Menu Bar.
- Click on **New Folder**.
- Double-click on the new **Untitled Folder**.

To Click and Drag:

- Move the mouse onto the words **Untitled Folder**.
- Depress the mouse and keep it depressed as you move (or drag) the window around the screen.

To Shut Down:

- Close the **Untitled Folder** and any other windows that are open.
- Move your mouse arrow to the in the top left corner and click once.
- Move the mouse arrow to the words **Shut Down** and click once.
- Move the mouse to **Shut Down** in the small window and click once.

All Together Now!

Glad to have everyone gathered back together. That was a huge amount to accomplish! If you are bleary-eyed, you are not alone. We covered a lot of material for your initiation, but initiated you are!

When you want to come back to the computer or tablet, you can repeat any or all of this chapter that applies to your device. Please practice the steps in this chapter for at least half an hour every day for a week. I want you to be skilled and comfortable with your mouse or touch screen and to have an understanding of your options within your device. The better your navigation skills, the better your technology experience.

Q: Why does it take my computer so long to shut down?

A: Computers can take a bit of time to start up and shut down because they need to check that everything is working properly and to put data in its proper place. If this start-up and shut-down time has lengthened dramatically, you may need to have someone do some housecleaning on your computer. (See Chapter 25.)

Q: Do I need to turn off my monitor, speakers, and/or printer when I turn off the computer?

A: You don't need to turn them off, but to leave the monitor, speakers, and printer on is an unnecessary waste of energy.

Q: I seem not to have enough space on my desk for the mouse. Do I need a bigger desk?

A: You definitely do not need a bigger desk. You need to harness your use of the mouse. Instead of sweeping all over your desk, lift the mouse up to reposition it on your desk. You'll notice that when the mouse does not make contact with the desk's surface, the arrow on the screen will stay in place.

Q: I love my laptop, but not the built-in mouse.

A: Don't despair. If you purchased a laptop computer and you continue to have trouble manipulating the built-in mouse, you have the option of purchasing an external mouse. Make sure that your new mouse is compatible with either your PC or Mac.

CHAPTER 12

GETTING TO KNOW YOU

Experimenting with what you can do with a tablet and computer

In the last chapter, you were introduced to the mouse. Congratulations on your good work! This chapter will introduce you to the Mac and PC operating systems along with Apple, Android, and Microsoft tablets, and some of the features they have to offer. For example, we'll learn about enlarging and minimizing windows and scrolling on a computer, and about the app store on a tablet.

PC users, turn to page 172. Mac users, turn to page 190. If you're the proud owner of an Android, meet me on page 164. If you purchased a Microsoft Surface, meet me on page 167 We'll start right here for those who have an Apple iPad.

Everyone will reunite on page 201 at "Job Well Done."

Welcome to the Apple iPad

In this chapter, we will experiment with adding programs, or apps, to your tablet. Feel free to move at your own pace. You can stop and start wherever and whenever you want.

The App Store

The App Store icon is on the home page screen of your iPad. If you don't see the icon, flick your finger from right to left on the screen to reveal the next page of icons. Once you've found the icon, tap on it to open it.

The App Store is where you can add more software—apps—to your tablet. When you first set up your tablet, you were probably asked to open an account with the App Store, which required you to supply your credit card information. Some apps are free and some are not. I'm super frugal and very rarely purchase an app. Whether you plan to make a purchase or not, you won't be able to download or add any apps to your tablet, even free ones, without filling in the credit card information.

If you tap on **Top Charts** at the bottom of the window, you'll be able to view apps broken into three categories: **Paid**, **Free**, and **Top Grossing**. You know which column I'm going to investigate, but feel *free* (hint, hint) to look at whatever interests you. With more than

The iPad's App Store

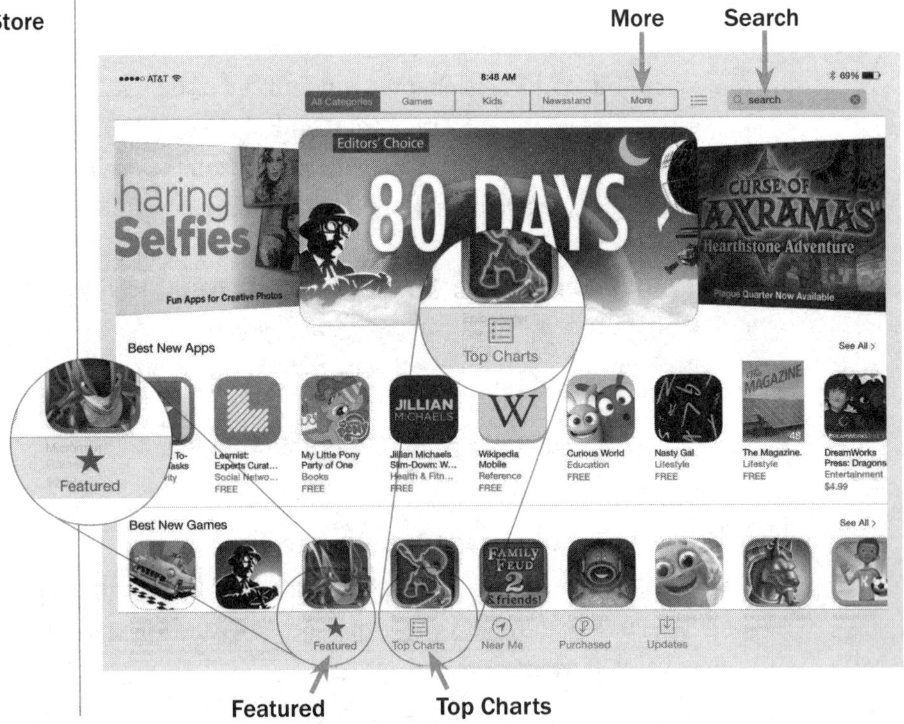

one million apps to choose from, I'm confident you'll find some that will be helpful, educational, or fun. Be sure to visit page 518 to see my list of "Over 100 Free Apps."

Top Charts

■ App Store Top Charts

Seek and Ye Shall Find

You can search for a specific app or even take a guess at what apps might be available by utilizing the Search box in the top right corner.

- Tap inside the Search box to activate it. You'll know you've done it right if a blinking line (aka the cursor) appears. That means it is ready for you to type.
- Using the keyboard that now appears on the screen, type in the name of the app that you seek. If you don't know the specific app name, make your best guess or try a keyword. Remember, if you make a typo, tap the Backspace key to delete your error.

TAP AND GO

1. Tap in Search box.
2. Type desired app name.
3. Tap Search on keyboard.

- You'll notice that as you type, suggestions will appear below the Search box in a Results list. If what you seek appears in the Results, tap on it.
- If there are no results to match your entry, tap on Search in the keyboard to view all possible apps that contain the word or words you typed.

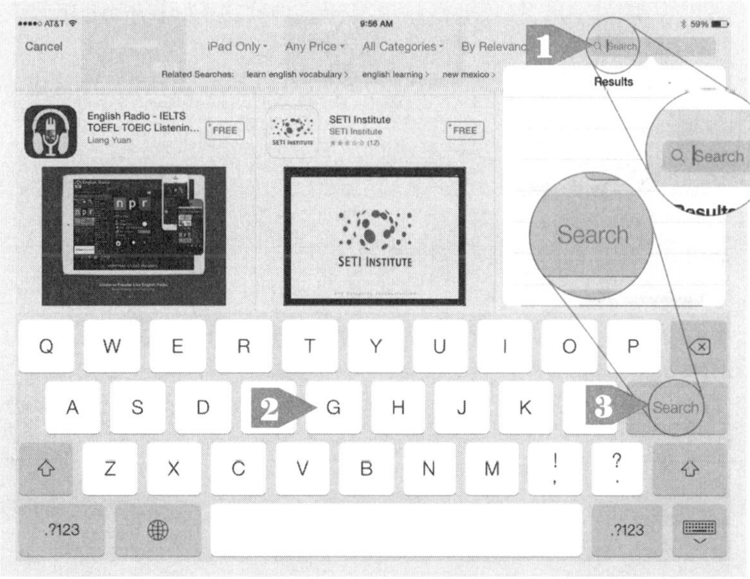

Adding an App

We're going to add one of my favorite apps to your tablet. TED (technology, entertainment, design) is a set of conferences that take place all over the world spreading inspiring stories and great ideas. Each video is only 18 minutes or less. It's a perfect nugget of time to learn something new.

Let's add the app together.

- Tap in the Search box and type "Ted talks." Tap on Ted talks, if it appears in the Results list, or tap **Search** on the keyboard.
- If you want to learn more about the app, tap on its logo or icon.
- Tap on the **Free** box in the top right of the TED conferences box to download the app to your tablet.
- Tap on **Install**.
- You will be asked to type the password that you chose when you created your account.
- A circle (■) will appear while the app is being installed. You'll know the process is complete when the word **Open** appears.
- Close out of the App Store by pressing the Home button.

Now go find the TED app on your home page or one of the other home screens and enjoy!

TAP AND GO

1. Tap in Search box and type the name of an app you're looking for.
2. Tap Search on keyboard.

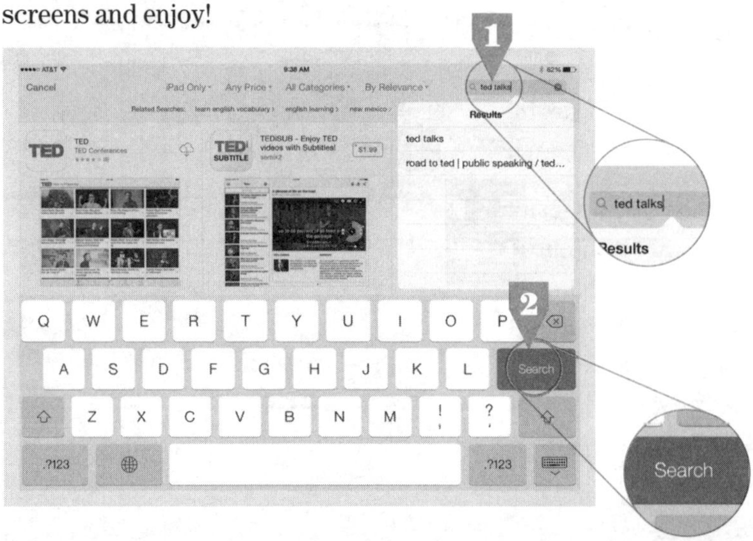

TAP AND GO

3. Tap Free.

4. Tap Install.

Well done! Let's try something else with your new toy.

Editing Text

When you've made a typo, you can delete using the Backspace key ⌫ as I mentioned above. But that is a tedious choice if the typo is deep into the text. You would have to delete and delete and delete and then retype it all. Good thing tablets have a handy editing tool.

- Tap and hold your finger on the text in question. A bubble will appear and you'll see a line (the cursor) in the text.
- Keep your finger on the screen and move across the text to the right of where you want to make your correction. Release your finger.

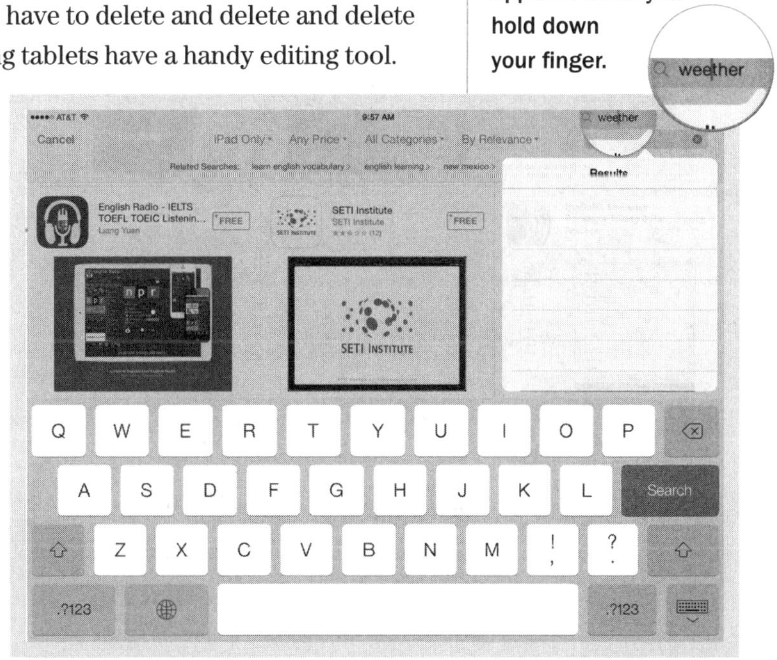

■ An editing bubble appears when you hold down your finger.

- The cursor is now in place for you to hit the Backspace key and delete.

Handy, right?

Meet me on page 201 at "Job Well Done."

Welcome to the Android

In this chapter, we will experiment with adding programs, or apps, to your tablet. Feel free to move at your own pace. You can stop and start wherever and whenever you want

The Google Play Store 

The Google Play Store icon  should appear on the Home screen of your tablet. If you don't see the icon, flick your finger from right to left on the screen to reveal the next page of icons. Once you've found the icon, tap on it to open.

The Google Play Store is where you can add more software or apps to your Android tablet. When you first set up your tablet, you were probably asked to open an account with the Play Store, which required you to supply your credit card information. Some apps are free and some are not. I'm super frugal and very rarely purchase an app. Whether you plan to make a purchase or not, you won't be able to download or add any apps to your tablet, even free ones, without filling in the credit card information.

■ The Google Play Store

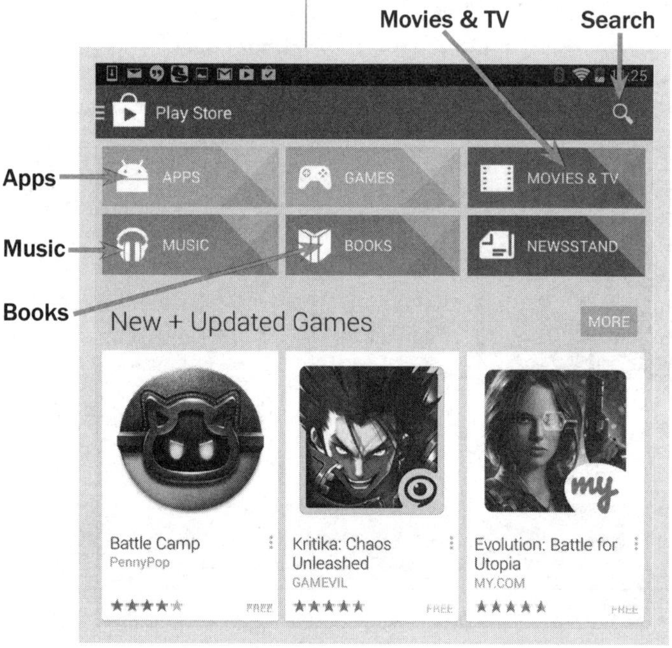

If you tap on **Apps** at the top of the window, you'll be able to view apps broken into categories: **Top**

Paid, **Top Free**, and **Top Grossing**. You know which I'm going to investigate, but feel *free* (hint, hint) to look at whatever interests you. With more than one million apps to choose from, I'm confident you'll find some that will be helpful, educational, or fun. Be sure to visit page 518 to see my list of "Over 100 Free Apps."

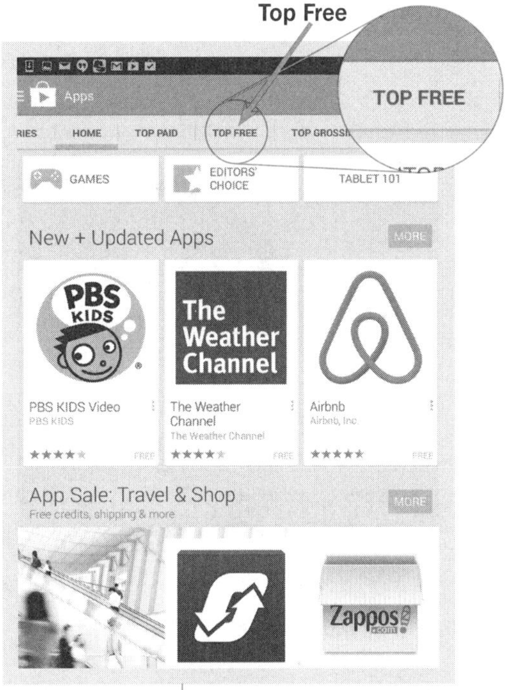

Play Store Top Apps

Seek and Ye Shall Find

You can search for a specific app or even take a guess at what apps might be available if you tap on the Search symbol on the top.

- Tap on the Search symbol at the top. You'll know you've done it right if the Search box appears with a blinking line. That means it is ready for you to type.
- Using the keyboard that now appears on the screen, type in the name of the app that you seek. If you don't know the specific app name, make your best guess or try a keyword. Remember, if you make a typo, tap the Backspace key to delete your error.
- You'll notice that as you type, suggestions will appear below the Search box in a Results list. If what you seek appears, tap on it.
- If there are no results to match your entry, tap on the Search symbol in the keyboard to view all possible apps that contain the word or words you typed.

TAP AND GO

1. Tap in Search box.
2. Type desired app.
3. Tap on Search symbol on keyboard.

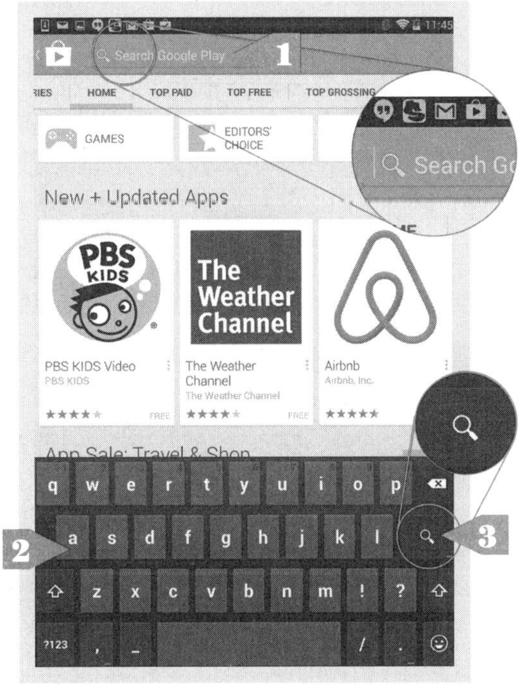

Adding an App

We're going to add one of my favorite apps to your tablet. TED (technology, entertainment, design) is a set of conferences that take place all over the world spreading inspiring stories and great ideas. Each video is only 18 minutes or less. It's a perfect nugget of time to learn something new.

Let's add the app together.

- Tap in the Search box and type "Ted talks." Tap on Ted talks, if it appears in the Results list, or tap **Search** on the keyboard.
- Tap on the **Free** box in the top right of the TED conferences box to download the app to your tablet. You can read more about the app on the page that opens to Install.
- Tap on **Install**.
- You will be asked to type the password that you chose when you created your account.
- Close out of the App Store by pressing the Home button .

TAP AND GO

1. Tap in Search box and type.
2. Tap Search on keyboard.
3. Tap Free.
4. Tap Install.

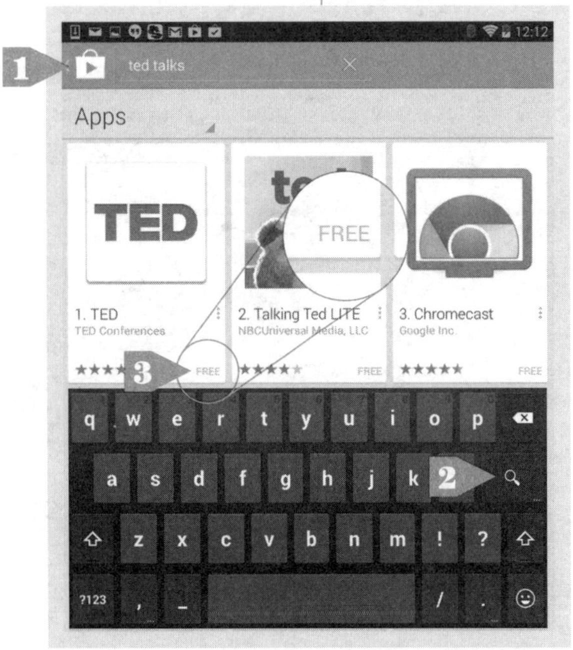

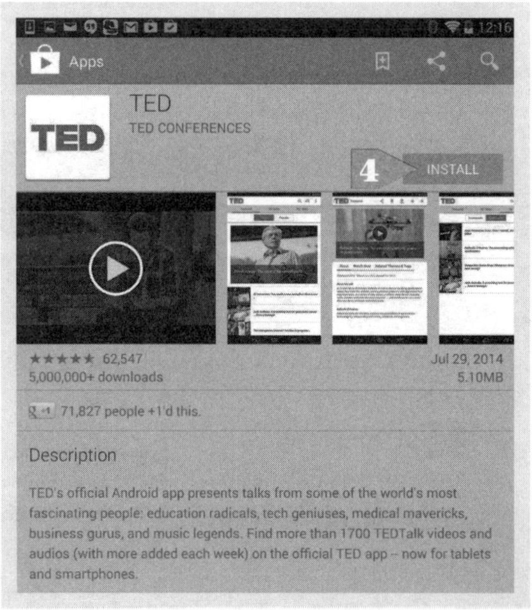

Now go find the TED app on your home page or one of the other home screens and enjoy!

Well done! Let's try something else with your new toy.

An editing pointer appears when you hold down your finger.

Editing Text

When you've made a typo, you can delete using the Backspace key, as I mentioned above. But that is a tedious choice if the typo is deep into the text. You would have to delete and delete and delete and then retype it all. Good thing tablets have a handy editing tool.

- Tap and hold your finger on the text in question. A pointer will appear and you'll see a line (the cursor) in the text.
- Tap and drag the pointer across the text to just to the right of where you want to make your correction. Release your finger.
- The cursor is now in place for you to hit the **Backspace** key and delete.

Handy, right?

Meet me on page 201 at "Job Well Done."

Welcome to the Microsoft Surface

In this chapter, we will experiment with adding programs, or apps, to your tablet. Feel free to move at your own pace. You can stop and start wherever and whenever you want.

The Microsoft App Store

The Microsoft App Store icon should appear on the Start screen of your Surface tablet. If you don't see the icon, flick your finger from right to left on the screen to reveal the next page of icons. Once you've found the icon, tap on it to open.

The Microsoft App Store

The Microsoft App Store is where you can add more software or apps to your Surface tablet. When you first set up your tablet, you were probably asked to open an account with the App Store, which required you to supply your credit card information. Some apps are free and some are not. I'm super frugal and very rarely purchase an app. Whether you plan to make a purchase or not, you won't be able to download or add any apps to your tablet, even free ones, without filling in the credit card information.

If you tap on **Top Charts** at the top of the window, you'll be able to view apps broken into categories: **Top Paid**, **Top Free**, and **Top Grossing**, to name a few. You know which I'm going to investigate, but feel *free* (hint, hint) to look at whatever interests you. With more than one million apps to choose from, I'm confident you'll find some that will be helpful, educational, or fun. Be sure to visit page 518 to see my list of "Over 100 Free Apps."

■ Microsoft App Store

Seek and Ye Shall Find

You can search for a specific app or even take a guess at what apps might be available if you tap on the Search symbol in the top right corner.

- Tap on the Search symbol . You'll know you've done it right if a blinking line appears. That means it is ready for you to type.
- Using the keyboard that now appears on the screen, type in the name of the app that you seek. If you don't know the specific app name, make your best guess or try a keyword. Remember, if you make a typo, tap the Backspace key to delete your error.
- You'll notice that as you type, suggestions will appear below the Search box in a Results list. If what you seek appears, tap on it.

TAP AND GO

1. Tap in Search box.
2. Type desired app.
3. Tap Search on keyboard.

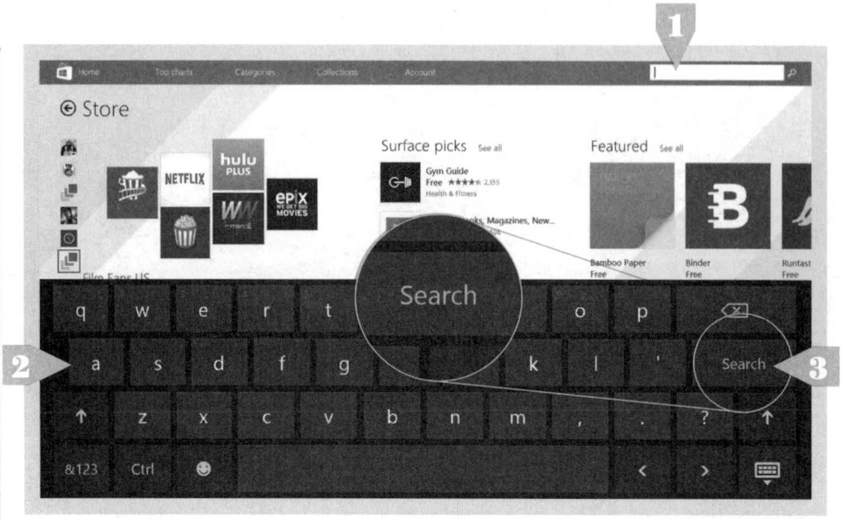

- If there are no results to match your entry, tap on Search in the keyboard to view all possible apps that contain the word or words you typed.

Adding an App

We're going to add one of my favorite apps to your tablet. TED (technology, entertainment, design) is a set of conferences that take place all over the world spreading inspiring stories and great ideas. Each video is only 18 minutes or less. It's a perfect nugget of time to learn something new.

Let's add the app together.

- Tap in the Search box and type "Ted talks." Tap on Ted talks, if it appears in the Results list, or tap **Search** on the keyboard.
- You can read more about the app on the page that opens. Tap on **Install**.
- You will be asked to type the password that you chose when you created your account.
- Close out of the App Store by pressing the Home button.

Now go find the TED App on your home page or one of the other home screens and enjoy!

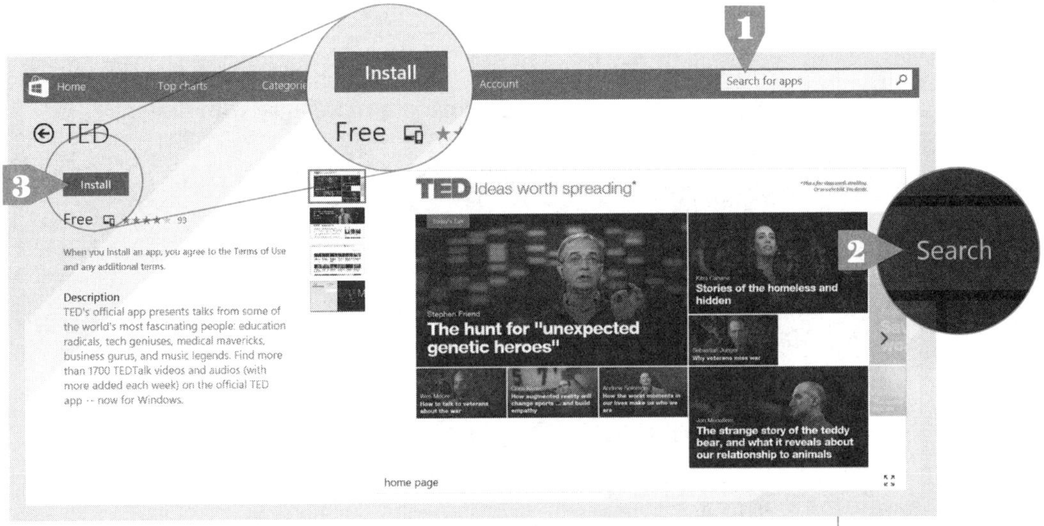

TAP AND GO

1. Tap in Search box and type.
2. Tap Search on keyboard.
3. Tap Install.

Editing Text

When you've made a typo, you can delete using the Backspace key as I mentioned above. But that is a tedious choice if the typo is deep into the text. You would have to delete and delete and delete and then retype it all. Good thing tablets have a handy editing tool.

- Tap and hold your finger on the text in question. A circle will appear and you'll see a line (the cursor) in the text.

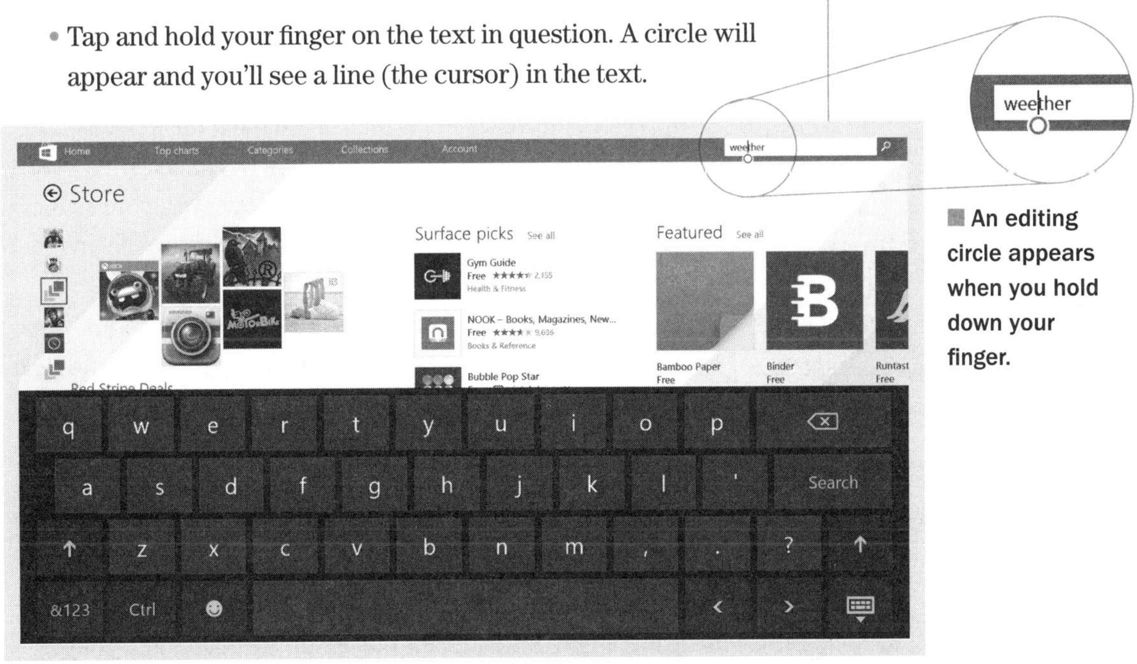

An editing circle appears when you hold down your finger.

- Tap and drag the circle across the text just to the right of where you want to make your correction. Release your finger.
- The cursor is now in place for you to hit the Backspace key and delete.

Handy, right?

Meet me on page 201 at "Job Well Done."

Welcome, PC Users

Turn on your computer. As in Chapter 11, we are experimenting with Windows 8.1, so depending on the operating system of your computer, things on your screen may vary a bit. Let's open some of the features of the computer and see specifically what they have to offer.

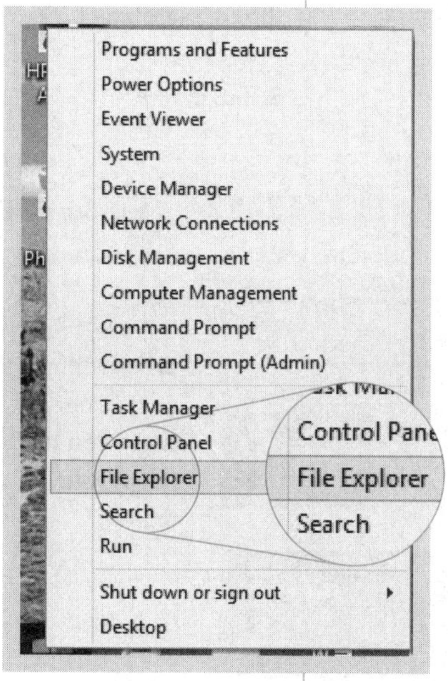

Start Menu

This PC

First move your mouse onto the Start button in the bottom left corner. Your mouse has two buttons, one on the left and one on the right. Up until now you've been using the left mouse button. Now you're going to use the right button. The right button on the mouse opens up an advanced menu allowing you to perform tasks in fewer steps—kind of like a shortcut. Try it now. With your mouse on the Start button, right-click. A menu opens up for you as seen here.

Now left-click on **File Explorer**. From this point forward, when I ask you to click the mouse, it is a left-click unless otherwise noted. The **This PC** window will open. **This PC** allows access to both the software and hardware on your computer. From here, you can get to all the information stored on your hard drive, as well as the drives that hold your CDs and DVDs.

Move your mouse onto the **Documents** folder and double-click. If the icon is highlighted in blue but the window didn't open, your

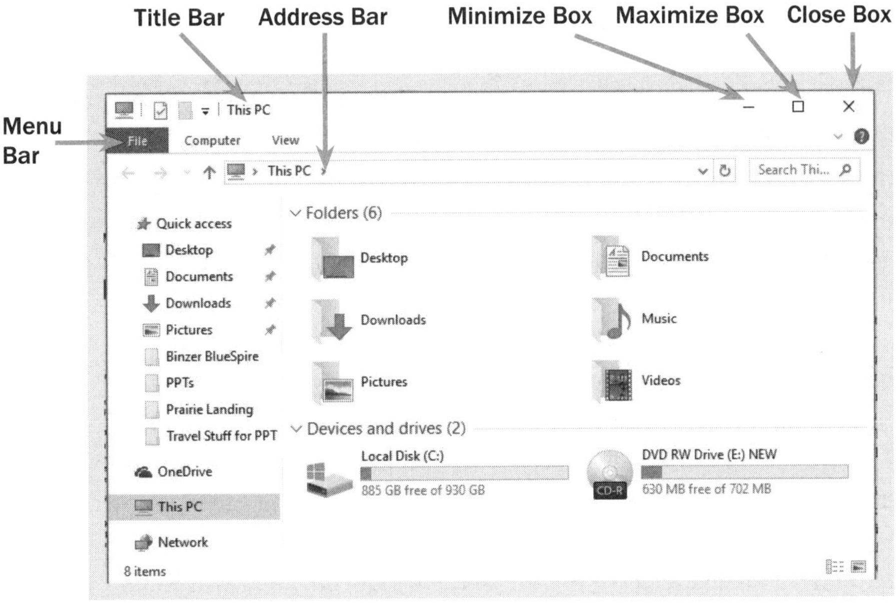

The "This PC" window. Notice that it has a Title Bar that includes Minimize, Maximize, and Close boxes. Most PC windows have these features.

double-click wasn't successful. Place the mouse arrow on the icon again and depress, release, depress, release the mouse button in rapid succession. Think knock-knock. Keep trying, and eventually you will get the timing. Click on **This PC** (a single-click) in the left sidebar to return to the **This PC** window.

As I describe each icon contained in the **This PC** window, feel free to double-click on the icon to open it and see what's inside. To get back to the **This PC** window, move the mouse onto the upper left side of the **Address Bar** and click once. If you have somehow closed the window, simply repeat the steps opening the **Start** menu with a right-click of the mouse. The **(C:)** icon allows access to anything on your computer's C: drive. Because the C: drive is the storage space for

WHEN ALL ELSE FAILS

If you absolutely cannot double-click, there is a solution. Single-click on the icon. Now that the icon is highlighted, you can depress and release the Enter key on your keyboard to open the icon.

RIGHT-CLICKS

The right button on the mouse opens an advanced menu that offers different actions depending on what you right-click on. If you accidentally hit the right side of the mouse, you can get rid of the menu that you opened by left-clicking anywhere off that menu.

everything on your computer, you can find anything you need through this icon.

Find a folder titled **Documents** above where you found the C: drive. You may also find the Documents folder in the sidebar of the **This PC** window. That folder will store whatever writing you eventually do on the computer.

Later I will explain how to view the entire contents of a window utilizing the Scroll Bar (page 179). The **DVD-RW Drive (E:)** icon allows you to hear and/or see a compact disc (CD) or digital video disc (DVD) on your computer. When a music CD is in the D: drive, this icon will offer you choices about which track you may want to listen to and the volume you prefer. We will experiment with this later in the chapter. To navigate between these windows, you can close each window when you are done and start from scratch. You may also notice an arrow in the top left of the window. That arrow, when clicked on, will also send you back to the previous window viewed.

IT'S OK NOT TO GET IT

You don't have to understand or use all of the icons offered in the Control Panel. You may only ever use one or two. The others are there for more advanced computer users or technical support to adjust things on your computer, if the need arises.

The Control Panel

Now let's visit the **Control Panel** and see what it has to offer. You can access the Control Panel two different ways. Try both. First repeat what you did to access **This PC**. Right-click on the **Start** button, then left-click on **Control Panel**. Alternatively, you can access the Charm Bar as we did in Chapter 11. Move the mouse to the bottom right corner—all the way into the corner—and five images should pop up in a sidebar on the right side of the screen: **Search**, **Share**, **Start**, **Devices**, and **Settings**. Click on **Settings**, then click on **Control Panel**. The Control Panel is where you get to customize certain aspects of your computer. I'm going to talk only about the features that you'll use most in the Control Panel window.

The **Hardware and Sound** icon allows you access to both the printer you're already using and a new printer that you might add later. This is also the place to go if you change your mind once you start printing a document and want to stop the printer (or "purge print documents," in computer-speak).

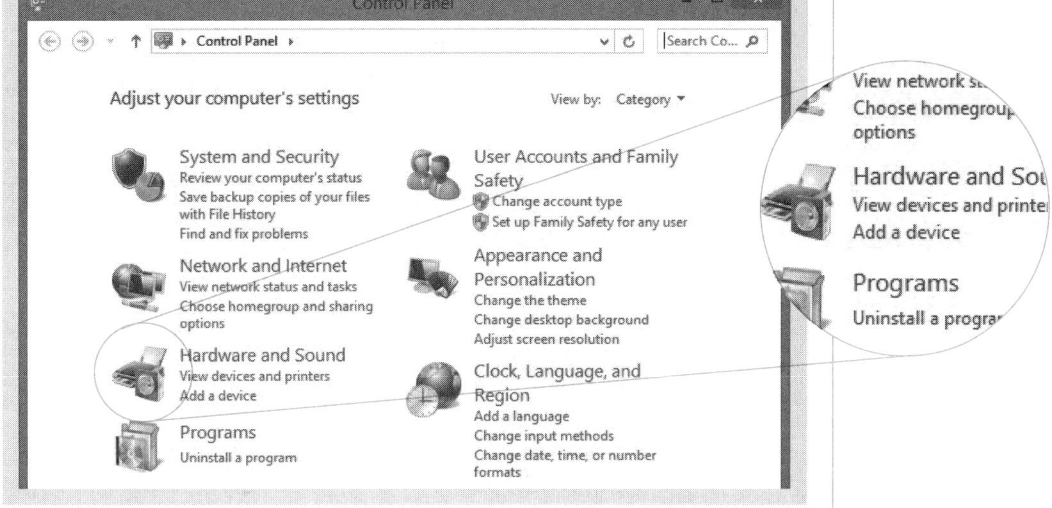

Hardware and Sound

The **Network and Internet** icon is something you will probably never use. This is where you set up your access to the Internet. If at some point you decided to reconfigure your Internet connection, you would double-click on this icon to access the area where you would make those changes.

The **Clock, Language, and Region** icon allows you to adjust the date and time. We're going to do that together in a bit, but first I want you to experiment with the parts of this window now that it is open.

What's in the Window?

You will notice that this window has the same features as the Solitaire window. It has a **Title Bar**, a **Minimize Box**, a **Maximize Box**, and a **Close Box**. What we haven't discussed yet is the Scroll Bar on the bottom and right side of the window.

If you see a Scroll Bar on the right edge or bottom of a window, it tells you that there is more in the window than you can see. (If there is no Scroll Bar on the window of your screen and there should be, don't worry. On pages 179, there are instructions on how to make a Scroll Bar appear.) You can increase the size of the window or scroll the window to see what else it contains. Students often call me in distress

You can customize certain parts of your computer using the Control Panel.

because they can't find an item that they know is supposed to be in a certain window. Usually, it is right where it should be, but they didn't see all the contents of the window. The Scroll Bar is your clue that there is more to be unveiled.

Enlarging the window. The most efficient way to see all the contents of a window is to increase its size. You can do that in a number of ways. For the sake of experimentation, try each option. Once you have seen how one choice works, follow the instructions in italics to restore the window and go on to the next option. We will experiment with scrolling after you have tried the following options.

Option 1. There is a box in the **Title Bar** that will increase the size of the window. As you may remember, it's the **Maximize Box**. Move the mouse arrow into the and click once. To restore it back to its original form, move the mouse arrow to the **Restore Box** and click once.

Option 2. Move your mouse arrow to the bottom right corner of the Control Panel window. Your arrow will become a two-ended arrow at an angle. (If the double arrow eludes you, it is because you are moving the mouse too quickly. Slow

PRACTICE MAKES PERFECT

It is a delicate business, getting the mouse arrow exactly on the edge of the window to activate the arrows that will allow you to stretch or shrink it. Move the mouse *very* slowly and you'll get the hang of it. Be patient and don't give up.

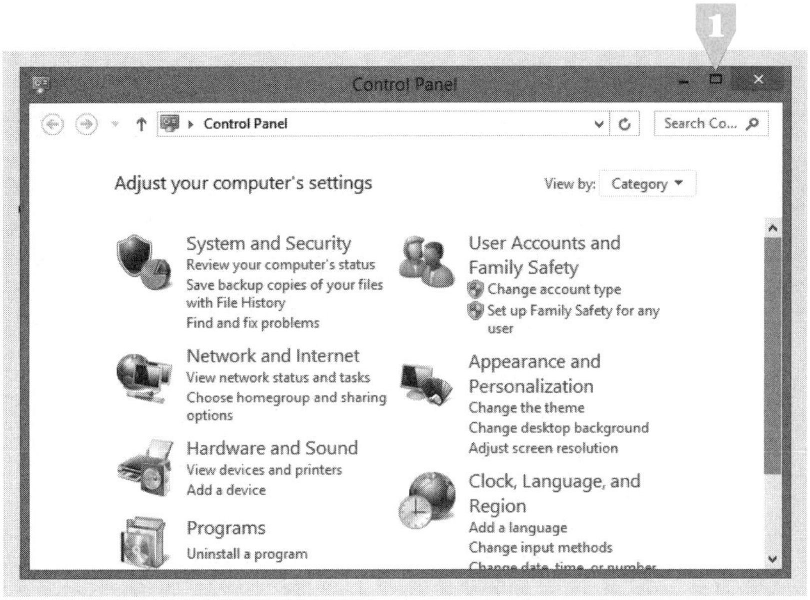

CLICK AND GO

1. Click on Maximize Box.
2. Click on Restore Box.

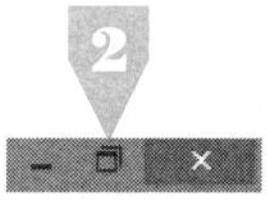

Restore Box

down.) As you did with the Solitaire cards, click and drag the arrow to the bottom right of your screen, then release the mouse button. To restore, again place the mouse arrow in the bottom right corner of the window to activate the two-ended arrow. Now click and drag the corner to the left and up until the window is the size it was when you first opened it.

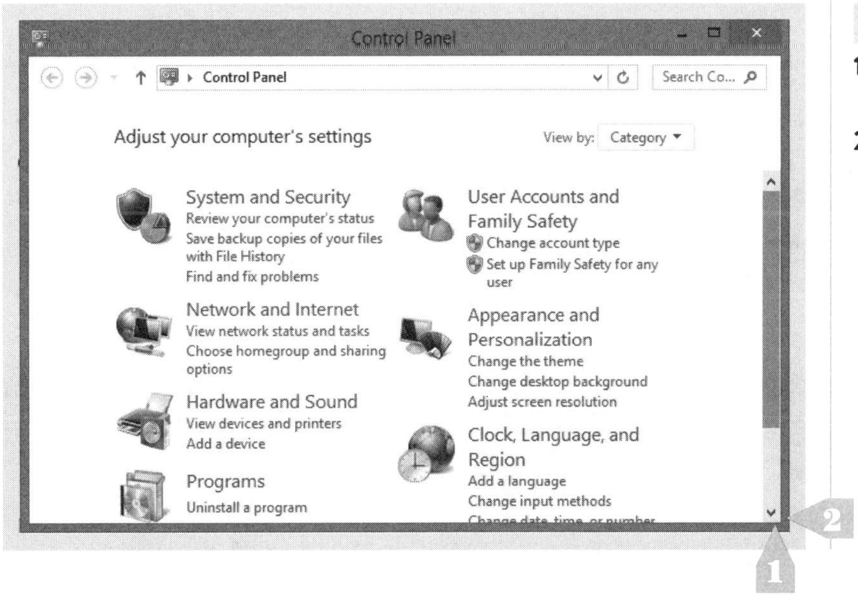

CLICK AND GO

1. Click and drag corner of window to enlarge.
2. Click and drag corner of window to restore to its previous size and shape.

CLICK AND GO

1. Increase a window's width by clicking and dragging right edge out.
2. Click and drag back to restore window to its previous size/shape.
3. Click and drag bottom edge to increase window height.
4. Click and drag back to restore window to its previous size/shape.

Option 3. Move the mouse arrow to the right side of the Control Panel window. The arrow now becomes an arrow going right and left ⟷. Click and drag the arrow to the far right edge of the screen and then release the mouse button. This increases the width of the window. (The same can be done with the left side of the window.) To increase the height, move the right-left arrow to the bottom of the window. Now the mouse arrow becomes an up-and-down arrow ↕. Click and drag the arrow to the far bottom edge of the screen and then release the mouse. (The same can be done with the top of the

CLICK AND DRAG . . . IS IT A DRAG?

Are you having some trouble with the click-and-drag maneuver? Let's review.

- Place the mouse arrow on the object you want to move and depress the mouse button.
- Keep the mouse button depressed while you drag the object (by moving the mouse) to where you desire.
- Take your finger off the mouse and the object will remain where it has been moved.

My advice is: *If you have Solitaire, keep playing.* It may seem silly (or drive you nuts), but it is the best way to master the mouse. If you haven't been faithfully doing your homework, start today!

window.) To restore, again place the mouse arrow on the right of the screen to activate the arrow going right and left. Now click and drag the edge to the left until the window is about the width it was when you first opened it. Do the same with the bottom edge of the window.

"For the longest time I couldn't use the Scroll Bar. I kept moving the mouse off the arrow or clicking too fast. Eventually, it became easier. You really can't take advantage of websites without it." —*Dan*

Scrolling Along

Sometimes there can be more icons contained in a window than you can see, no matter how large you make the window. In this case, you will have to use the Scroll Bar to see all that is available. The Scroll Bar is similar to an elevator: A button is pressed to activate it, it moves up and down, and you can get off anyplace you want.

Does your window look something like the window seen here? Make sure a Scroll Bar is on the right side of the window. If there isn't a Scroll Bar, move the mouse arrow onto the lower right corner of the window. It will now be the two-sided arrow at an angle ⤡. Click and drag the corner up and left to create a Scroll Bar on the right side and bottom of the window.

There should be a set of arrows at the top and bottom of the Scroll Bar positioned on the right edge of the window. If there is

If you see a Scroll Bar, it indicates that there's more to see in the window.

CLICK AND GO

1. Click on bottom arrow repeatedly.
2. Click on top arrow and hold mouse down until Scroll Box is at top of Scroll Bar.
3. Click and drag the Scroll Box within Scroll Bar to reveal contents of window again.

a Scroll Bar at the bottom of the window, it will also have a set of arrows positioned at the right and left. Now let's take a scroll. . . .

- Place the mouse arrow on the bottom scroll arrow on the right edge of the window and click a few times. With each click, the image on the screen moves down. Be careful that the mouse arrow stays within the box that contains the scroll arrow. If your mouse wanders, you will not be able to activate the Scroll Bar, or the window may scroll in increments larger than you desire.
- The contents within the window will move up if you place the mouse arrow on the top scroll arrow and click.
- The window will scroll left or right with the left scroll arrow and the right scroll arrow at the bottom of the window.
- If you hold down the mouse button rather than depressing and releasing it, the window will scroll very quickly. This technique is more difficult to control but faster than individual clicks.
- You can also reveal what's inside the window by placing the mouse arrow on the **Scroll Box** within the Scroll Bar and clicking and dragging the Scroll Box up or down. This is faster

PATIENCE, PLEASE

Remember that if there is a spinning circle or an hourglass, you should sit back and let the computer finish what it's doing before you use the mouse or keyboard.

than using the scroll arrows and is most convenient if you're in a very large document wanting to get from, for example, page 1 to page 40.

Scroll Bars play a big role in viewing websites on the Internet. I strongly recommend that you spend time maneuvering a Scroll Bar every time you play on the computer until you have the technique down.

Does Anybody Really Know What Time It Is?

Maximize the Control Panel window if you can't see all the icons contained in it. (Remember, you do that by clicking on ▣.) We're going to be sure that the date and time are set properly on your computer. Once set, the computer, even when it is shut off, will keep perfect time and the current date. Open the Date and Time window by clicking on the **Clock, Language, and Region** icon, then click on **Date and Time**.

At the bottom of the Date and Time window, there are three buttons: **OK**, **Cancel**, and **Apply**. These are your action choices. Sometimes a window will offer you **Help**, **Yes**, or **No** as choices. When you click on any of these buttons, you're instructing the computer to take that action. You must be **very sure** of the action you want to take—sometimes it is irreversible.

The box containing **OK** may have a slightly darker outline. In this case, the computer assumes **OK** to be the choice you'll most likely make and has preselected it for you. (You can always choose a different option—it's just trying to make life easier for you.) Be forewarned: If you depress the **Enter** key on your keyboard, whatever action the computer has preselected will be

This window allows you to set the date and time.

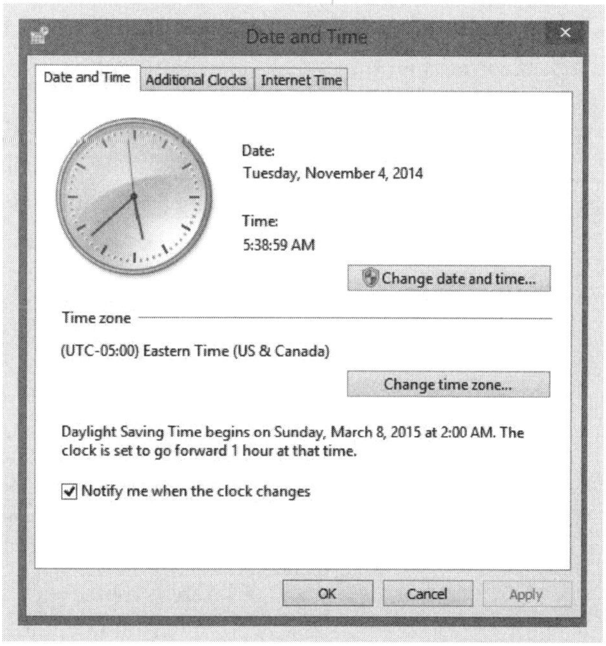

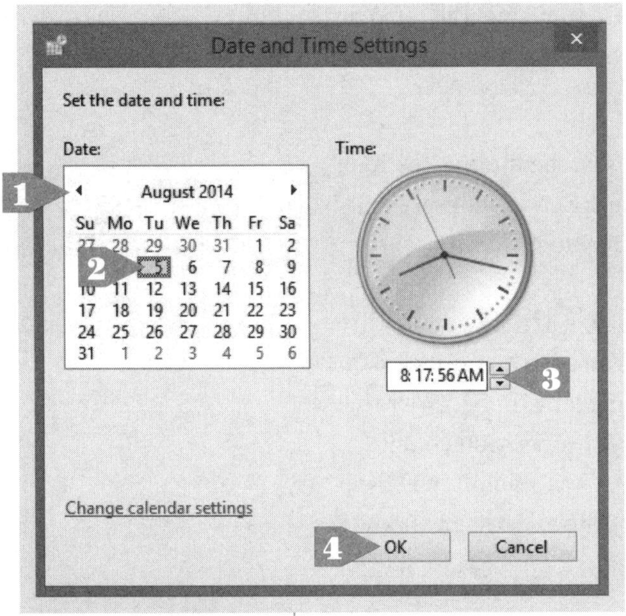

taken. *That is why it is so important not to depress the* **Enter** *key arbitrarily; you may unwittingly take an action that cannot be reversed.* (Note: It may not be **OK** that the computer preselects for you. It could be any action button that the computer deems will be your likely choice.) In the case of what we are playing with here, not to worry—nothing is irreversible.

Setting the date and time. Follow these steps to adjust the date and time on your computer.

- Click on **Change Date and Time.**
- Is the month correct? If not, click on the arrow to the right of the month until you are in the correct month.
- Is the date correct? If not, click on the correct date.
- Is the hour correct? If not, move the mouse arrow onto the hour display, then click and drag over the hour to select it. It should be highlighted in blue. You can either type the correct hour using the number keys on your keyboard or use the arrows  to the right of the time to increase or decrease the hour.
- Do the same for the minutes and seconds—highlight them and make the necessary changes.
- Once the correct hour, minute, and second are visible on the screen, click on **OK**. The window should close, accepting your changes and putting you back in the Control Panel window.
- Click once on the **Change Time Zone** button.
- There is a box with a down arrow ▼ to the right. Is the time zone that is visible your time zone? If not, click on the arrow. Find

CLICK AND GO

1. If month is not correct, click on back or forward arrow and select correct month.
2. If date should be changed, click on correct date.
3. If hour or minutes are not correct, click on each and use arrows to adjust.
4. Click OK.

your time zone (you may have to use the Scroll Bar), point to it with the mouse arrow, and click once.

- Does **Automatically adjust clock for Daylight Saving Time** have a check in the box to the left? If not, move the mouse arrow to the box and click once. Yes, like magic your computer will make the adjustment for Daylight Saving Time from now on! Adjust your screen brightness if you have difficulty seeing the map.
- At this point, click once on the word **OK**.

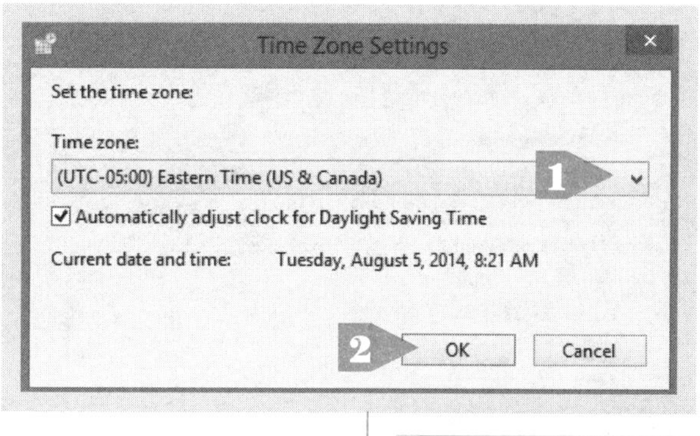

CLICK AND GO

1. Click on down scroll arrow. Click on your time zone (you may have to use the Scroll Bar).
2. Click OK.

Mouse Traps

Now we'll customize the mouse to suit you. If you prefer to have the mouse to your left, you can also reverse the functions of the mouse buttons here (see "Reversing the Buttons" on page 185). Let's adjust the double-click speed.

- Click in the **Search Control Panel** box in the upper right corner. (You may see only the word **Search**.)
- Type "mouse."
- Click **change mouse setting** in the list that appears.
- You may click on all the file tabs and read what each contains, but the one we'll focus on is **Buttons**.
- Click on the Buttons tab to adjust the double-click timing.

ATTENTION AGAIN, SOUTHPAWS

If you're a lefty, this is your chance to have the mouse cater to your needs. Some of my students who are left-handed are quite content to place the mouse to the right of their keyboard, but you can also swap it to the other side. It depends on what works better for you.

As the mouse is now configured, the left button is set up for **Click/Select** and the right button for **Context Menu/Alternate Select**. If you have an external mouse and want to position it to the left of the keyboard, these buttons are in the reverse position of how they might work best for you. See "Reversing the Buttons" on page 185.

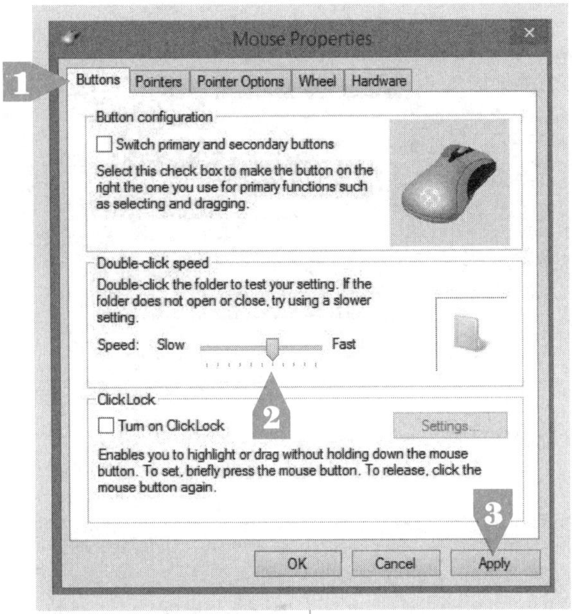

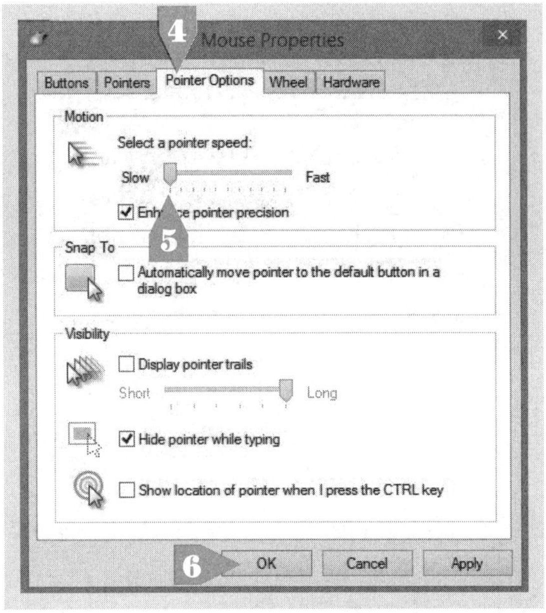

CLICK AND GO

1. Click on Buttons tab.
2. Click and drag "Double-click speed" pointer to what suits you best.
3. Click on Apply to keep changes.
4. Click on Pointer Options tab.
5. Click and drag "pointer speed" to what suits you best.
6. Click on OK to keep changes.

- Look at the pointer that indicates how slow or fast the clicking is set. If you find you need some extra time to double-click, then click and drag the pointer toward "Slow." If you naturally double-click faster than where it's set at present, click and drag the pointer toward "Fast."
- When you have found the right timing, move the mouse arrow to **Apply** and click once. (This means that your change has been accepted and the window will remain open.)
- Now let's click on the **Pointer Options** tab.
- Here we're interested in the **Motion**. There is a pointer that indicates the speed with which the mouse arrow will move across the screen (the computer may refer to the mouse arrow as a cursor here). Move the mouse arrow onto that pointer. Click and drag the pointer to the speed where you think it should be based on how quickly or slowly the mouse arrow currently moves across your screen. Mine is set on the slowest speed, which is easiest for me, but only you can judge what's best for you. You can always come back to this window and readjust it at a later date.

- Once you've selected your preferred speed, click on **OK**. Your changes will be made and the window will close.

Hanging Wallpaper

The background on your Desktop screen is also referred to as wallpaper. Your operating software comes with several different styles of wallpaper, and you can personalize your Desktop by selecting one that appeals to you.

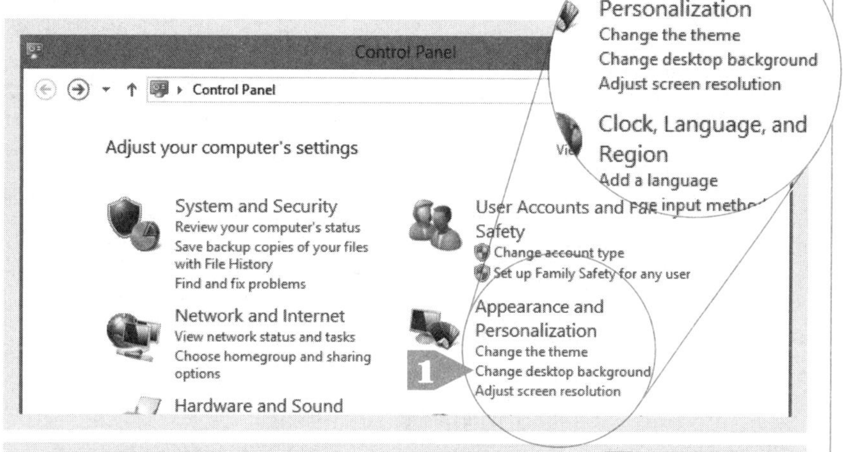

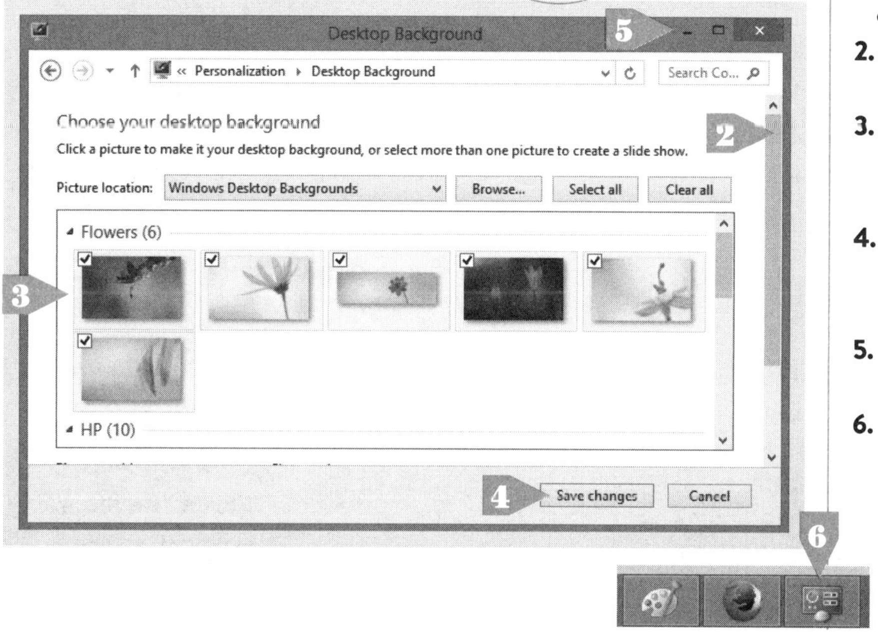

REVERSING THE BUTTONS

To reverse the functions of your mouse's two buttons:

- In the area below Button Configuration, click in the box next to **Switch primary and secondary buttons.**
- Click **Apply.**

CLICK AND GO

1. Click on Change desktop background.
2. Use Scroll Bar to reveal your choices.
3. Click on a background that appeals to you.
4. Click Save changes or OK to accept your choice.
5. Minimize window to see your handiwork.
6. Click on Control Panel icon to restore window to its previous size.

PERSONALIZE IT!
In addition to the wallpapers offered by the computer, you can create a Desktop background from photos or images that you have brought onto your computer. Chapter 19 will guide you through how to get images onto your computer.

- Click on the **Appearance and Personalization** section in your Control Panel window. (You may need to click on the left arrow at the top of the window to get back to the main Control Panel.) Here we can choose your wallpaper, change the look of the screen, and create a screen saver.
- Click on **Change desktop background**. This is where you decide the background for the Desktop screen. Click on the background choice that appeals to you. Remember to use the scroll bar to reveal all of your choices. Then at the bottom of the window, click **Save changes** or **OK**. Then minimize the **Desktop Background** window. This allows the wallpaper to be viewed at its actual size.
- The Control Panel is now minimized on the Task Bar at the bottom of the screen. Click on the icon in the Task Bar to restore it to the screen. You can now try selecting a different wallpaper. Keep repeating this process until you find the wallpaper that suits you. And remember, you can select different wallpaper whenever you please.

Choosing a Screen Saver

Now let's select a screen saver. A screen saver is an image that appears on the screen when the computer is on and has sat unused for a period of time. These steps allow you to decide what the screen saver will look like and when it will appear.

- Click on **Appearance and Personalization** to expose **Change Screen Saver** among other options.
- Click on **Change Screen Saver**.
- Under the words **Screen Saver** is a box with an arrow to the right. Click on the arrow to expose

WHAT AM I SAVING MY SCREEN FROM?
Screen savers were originally designed to protect the screen from "screen burn." Computer screens used to become damaged when the same screen image remained on the screen for too long. Improvements in the design of screens make this unlikely. Nowadays, screen savers are more for visual entertainment.

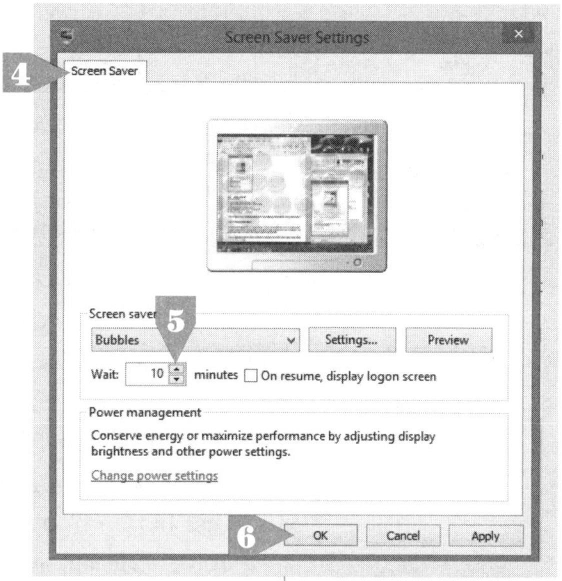

the screen saver options. You may have to use the Scroll Bar to see everything that is available. Click on the screen saver you want to see displayed and then click on **OK**.

- Click on **Settings** to see the options available to customize your choice. Some screen savers offer a choice of colors or images.
- Click on **Preview** to see your screen saver choice displayed at its actual size without having to close the window. Click the mouse button to get back to the **Screen Saver** window.
- The last decision that you need to make is how much time should elapse before the screen saver is activated. Do this by changing the number next to the word **Wait**. Click on the up and down arrows to the right of the number. Once you have decided on the length of time (I have mine set at 10 minutes), click on **OK**. Your changes have been made and the window will be closed.
- Close the **Control Panel** window. Now you're back at the Desktop screen. This might be a fine time to take a break. Just leave your computer as it is and come back when you're ready. When you return, we'll go over some more features.

CLICK AND GO

1. Click on arrow.
2. Click on your choice of screen saver.
3. Click on Preview to see screen saver in action.
4. Click anywhere to get back to settings window.
5. Adjust timing by using up and down arrows.
6. Click OK to accept your changes.

The Task Bar

The **Task Bar** is the gray or blue bar at the bottom of your screen. It offers an alternative way to access application software and other areas of the computer.

The Task Bar

The computer usually offers more than one way to skin a cat. By that, I mean that there is usually more than one way to accomplish a task or complete an action on the computer.

For instance, move the mouse arrow onto the time in the right-hand corner of the Task Bar and click the *right* mouse button. Now move the arrow to **Adjust Date/Time** and click once with the *left* mouse button. You've just opened the same **Date and Time** window that we accessed from the Control Panel. All the date and time changes that we made before can also be done by opening the window this way.

Close the **Date/Time** window. (Remember, use the **Close Box** ×.) Now with the mouse arrow on a blank spot on the desktop screen, click once with the *right* mouse button. Move the arrow to the word **Personalize** and click once with the *left* mouse button. *Ta-da!* It's the Personalize window that we used to pick your wallpaper and screen saver. Click on the **Minimize Box** -. It appears that the Personalization window has closed, but in fact it is waiting for you in the Task Bar. Click on the **Personalization** icon in the Task Bar and voilà! The window is back on the screen.

Experiment with what happens when you click the left or right mouse button on an item. You can open all the icons on the Desktop screen and see what they contain. For that matter, you can click on anything on the computer screen as long as you don't press the **Enter** key, which instructs the computer to take an action, or you don't click on an action key (**OK**, **Yes**, **Apply**). If you open a window and are concerned that you're heading into unknown territory, simply close it by using the **Close Box** ×; click on the word **Cancel**, **Finish**, or **Exit**; or click on a blank area of the screen.

Getting in the Swing

It's a lovely thing to listen to music while working (or playing) at the computer. Grab a CD that you enjoy, and let's learn how to play music.

- Open the D: drive on your computer case by pressing the button near the drive.
- Place the CD, label side up, into the CD tray and press the button again to close the tray. *You don't ever want to force the tray closed by pushing the tray in—it is a very delicate component of the computer.*
- A window will appear on the screen with options for the track you want to play and what volume you prefer. Here you will use the mouse to choose your options. For example, move the mouse onto the volume arrow. Click and drag the arrow either up or down to increase or decrease the volume.
- After you've set your preferences, click on the **Minimize Box** ▬. To maximize the window, click once on the box that contains the minimized window in the **Task Bar**.

LEARNING THE ABCS

Each computer can vary slightly. In my experience, some computers refer to the drive for the CD-ROM as the E: drive instead of the D: drive. The literature that came with your machine will clarify if your CD-ROM drive is referred to as D: or E:.

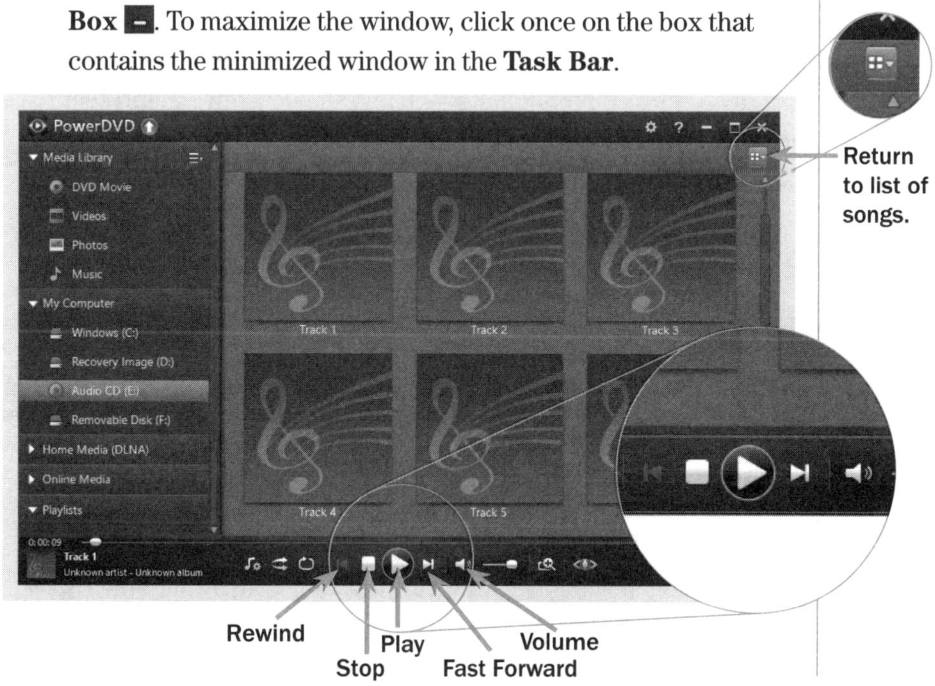

You can also access the DVD/CD drive through the Start button. Right-click on the **Start** button, left-click on **File Explorer**. Now double-click on **DVD/CD**.

There are a couple of other options for controlling the volume. If your computer came with speakers, they may have controls, or your monitor may have a volume control. Fiddle around until you find a comfortable volume. The other place where the volume can be adjusted is the speaker icon (it looks like a little horn) on the right side of the Task Bar near where the actual time is displayed. Left-click on the symbol and a box will appear where you can control the CD's volume.

When the CD has stopped (either by your choice or because it came to an end), simply press the button near or on the DVD/CD tray on your computer case to "eject" the CD. Remove the CD and press the button again to close the now-empty drive.

Meet me on page 201 at "Job Well Done."

Welcome, Mac Users

Turn on your computer. In this chapter, we will customize some features on your computer and investigate a few others. Feel free to move at your own pace. You can stop and start wherever and whenever you want.

Let's investigate what the Desktop screen has to offer. First, move the mouse arrow onto the **Finder** icon and click once.

Because the Apple mouse is quite tricky to manipulate, I have devoted a video tutorial to it on my website. To learn more about **Taming Apple's Mouse,** visit ***AskAbbyStokes.com*****.** Click on Video Tutorials at the top, then click on Video #2.

What's in the Window?

Notice that the **Finder** window has the same features as the **Untitled Folder** window you may have created back in Chapter 11. It has a **Title Bar**, a **Close Box**, a **Zoom Box**, and a **Collapse Box**. Almost every window you open will contain these elements. Remember, if you get overwhelmed and want to start from scratch, close any open windows by moving the mouse arrow into the **Close Box** and clicking once.

You can access different parts of your computer using the Finder.

The size of the window dictates how much of the information in the window you will be able to see. This is when the Scroll Bar comes in handy. The Scroll Bar allows you to move up and down (and sometimes from side to side) in a window for full viewing.

Students often call me because they can't find an item that they know is in a particular window. Usually, it is right where it should be, but they didn't see all the contents of the window. A Scroll Bar is what allows you to move up and down or across a window to reveal all its contents. We'll experiment with this shortly.

Enlarging the window. The most efficient way to see all the contents of a window is to increase its size. You can do that in two ways. Once you have seen how each choice works, follow the instructions in italics to restore the window to its original form and go to the next option. We will experiment with scrolling after you have tried the following options.

Option 1. There is a box in the Title Bar that will increase the size of the window. As you may remember, it's the **Zoom Box** ⊘. If you don't see a minus symbol in any of the three circles in the top left corner of the window, move your mouse arrow closer to the circles. Voilà! The symbols appear. Now move the mouse arrow into the **Zoom Box** ⊘ and click once. (As I said in Chapter 11, sometimes the window appears to be maximized, but it isn't actually taking up the entire screen.

PLACEMENT COUNTS

When you open an icon or folder, it's important that the arrow is placed on the icon and not on the text description or name below the icon.

CLICK AND GO

1. Click on Zoom Box once to change size of window.
2. Click on Zoom Box again to restore window to its previous size.

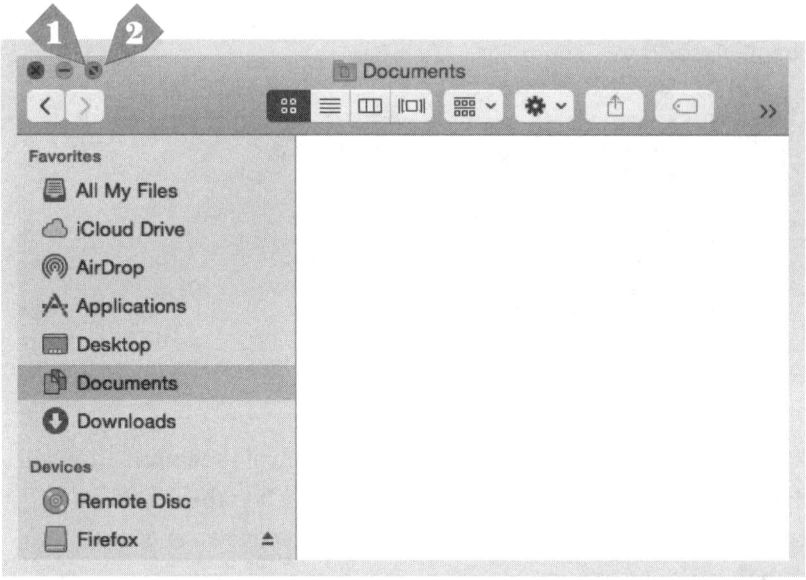

In that case, you can maximize the window as described in Option 2.) To restore, place the mouse arrow on the Zoom Box and click.

Option 2. Move the mouse arrow to any edge of the window. As you did with the Untitled Folder window, click and drag the edge to the right, so it fills the entire screen. To restore, place the mouse arrow on the edge and click and drag until the window is the size it was when you first opened it.

CLICK AND GO

1. Increase size by clicking and dragging bottom right edge out.
2. Click and drag back to restore to previous size.

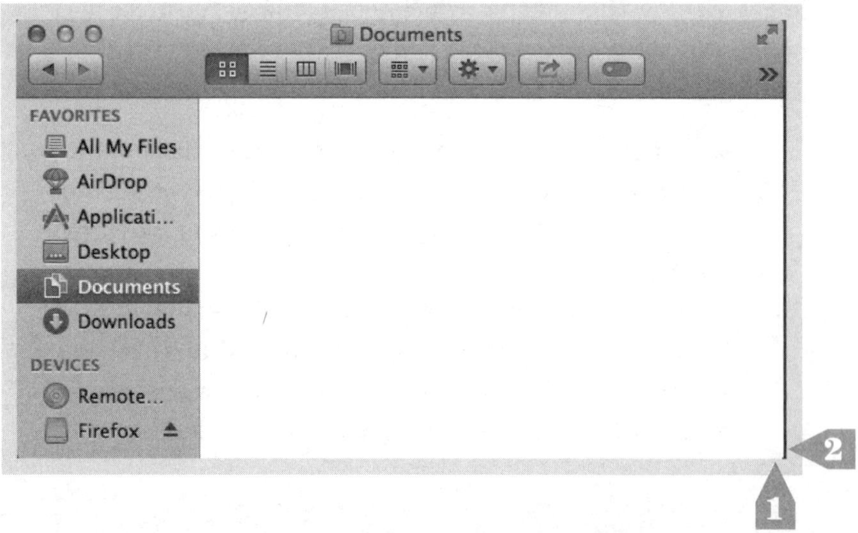

CLICK AND DRAG . . . IS IT A DRAG?

Are you having some trouble with the click-and-drag maneuver? Let's review.

- Place the mouse arrow on the object you want to move and depress the left mouse button.
- Keep the mouse button depressed while you drag the object (by moving the mouse) to where you desire.
- Take your finger off the mouse and the object will remain where it has been moved.

My advice is: *If you have Solitaire, keep playing.* It may seem silly (or drive you nuts), but it is the best way to master the mouse. If you haven't been faithfully doing your homework, start today!

Scrolling Along

Sometimes a window contains more than you can see no matter how large you make it. In this case, you will have to use the Scroll Bar to see all that is available. The Scroll Bar is similar to an elevator: It moves up and down, and you can get off anyplace you want. Click

The appearance of a Scroll Bar indicates there's more to see in the window. Mastering the Scroll Bar is critical for surfing the Internet.

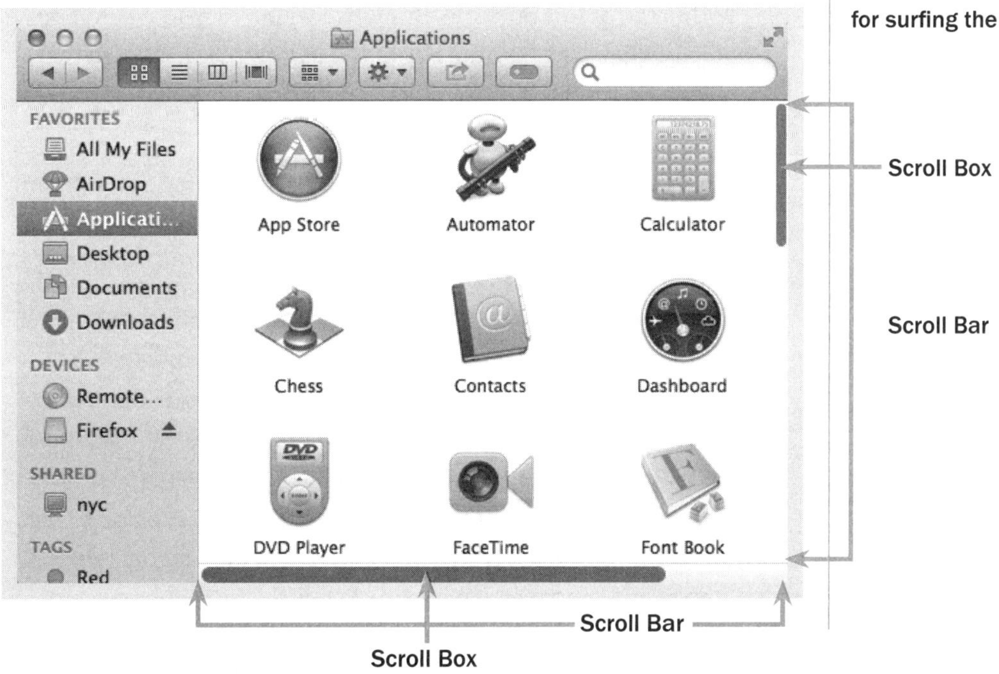

on **Applications** in the left sidebar, opening the Applications window, which will have a Scroll Bar on the right (and even maybe on the bottom). Does your window look like the window shown on the previous page? With an Apple computer, the Scroll Bar may appear only if you summon it. (Bad design, if you ask me. But no one did ask me.)

For a laptop, take two fingers and rest them on the mouse touch pad simultaneously. A Scroll Bar should become visible on the right and/or bottom sides of the window. For a desktop, move the mouse over to the right and/or bottom sides of the window and the Scroll Bar will appear.

If the Applications window opens up and is too big to reveal the Scroll Bar, click and drag the bottom right corner inward to make the window smaller. Now try it again.

Let's take a scroll.

- Once the Scroll Bar appears, you can move the mouse arrow onto the Scroll Box, the dark area within the bar that actually moves up and down. Be careful that the mouse arrow stays within the Scroll Box. If your mouse wanders, you will not be able to click and drag the Scroll Box. Now, holding down the mouse on the Scroll Box, click and drag up or down.

- The image within the window will move up if you click and drag the mouse arrow down and vice versa.

- The window will scroll left or right with the bottom Scroll Bar.

- For a laptop, you can also move what's in the window by placing two fingers on the mouse touch pad simultaneously, leaving them in contact with the pad while you press and drag them up or down. This way, you won't have to move the mouse over to the side of the window every time you want to scroll through the window. If there is more to see in the window than doing this gesture can show, you'll have to pick up the two fingers and move them higher or lower on the touch pad and repeat the dragging action. It is almost like a purposeful flicking of two fingers. This requires patience and practice.

- Close the Applications window by clicking in the **Close Box** . Scroll Bars play a big role in viewing websites on the Internet. I strongly recommend that you spend time maneuvering a Scroll Bar every time you play on the computer until you have the technique down.

MOUSECAPADES

If the mouse really has you stymied, especially if you're a PC person transitioning to an Apple, take heart. You can always purchase a standard PC mouse, plug it in, and use it on an Apple computer.

Does Anybody Really Know What Time It Is?

Move the mouse onto the in the top left corner of the screen and click once. A box with a lot of options will open. Move the mouse arrow down onto the words **System Preferences** and click once. The System Preferences window will open.

We're going to check to be sure that the date and time are set properly on your computer. Open the **Date & Time** window by single-clicking on the icon found in the System Preferences window.

Is there a check in the box to the left of **Set time and date automatically**? If so, click in the box to remove the check. At the bottom of the window are two buttons: **Revert** and **Save**. These are your action choices. Sometimes a window will offer you **Help**, **Yes**, or **No** as choices. When you click on any of these buttons, you're instructing the computer to take that action. You must be *very sure* of the action you want to take—sometimes it is irreversible.

You might notice that the **Save** button has a slightly darker outline. In this case, the computer assumes Save to be the choice you'll most likely make and has preselected it for you (you can always choose a different option—it's just trying to make life easier for you). Be

This window allows you to set the date and time.

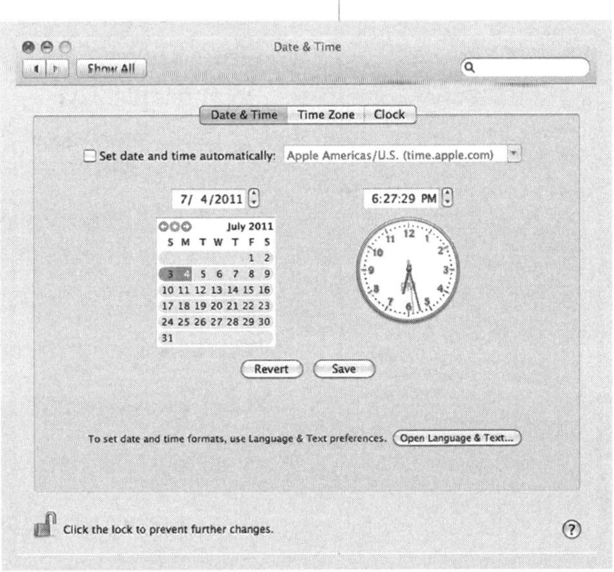

PATIENCE, PLEASE!
Remember that if there is a spinning round ball (jokingly referred to by a friend as the "spinning beach ball of death"), you should sit back and let the computer finish what it's doing before you use the mouse or keyboard.

forewarned: If you depress the **Return** key on your keyboard, whatever action the computer has preselected will be taken. *This is why it is so important not to depress the* **Return** *key arbitrarily; you may unwittingly take an action that cannot be reversed.* (Note: It may not be **Save** that the computer preselects for you. It could be any action button that the computer deems will be your likely choice.) In the case of what we are playing with here, not to worry—nothing is irreversible.

Follow the steps below to adjust the **Time Zone**:

- Click on the **Time Zone** tab.
- Click in the box beside **Set Time Zone** to remove the check.
- Click on the map in the area where you are located.
- Click on the down arrow to the right of the city listed.
- Scroll to the city nearest where you live and click once on that city's name.

Follow the steps below to adjust the **Current Date**:

- Click on the **Date & Time** tab.
- If the month is not correct, move the mouse arrow onto the arrows to the right of the month and click until the present month is displayed.
- If the date is not correct, click on the correct date.
- Is the hour correct in the **Current Time** box? If not, move the mouse onto the hour and click to select it. Hit the numbers on your keyboard to type in the correct hour or use the arrows.
- Do the same for the minutes and seconds.
- Click on **AM** or **PM** to switch between the two.
- Click on **Save** to have the clock display the current time.
- Move the arrow to **Show All** or and click to get back to the System Preferences window.

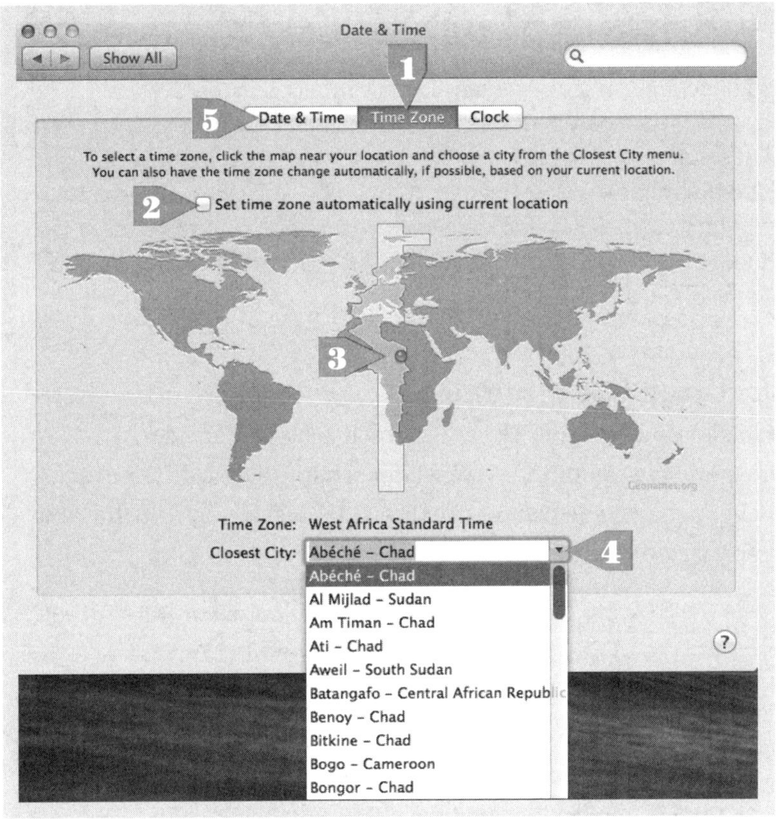

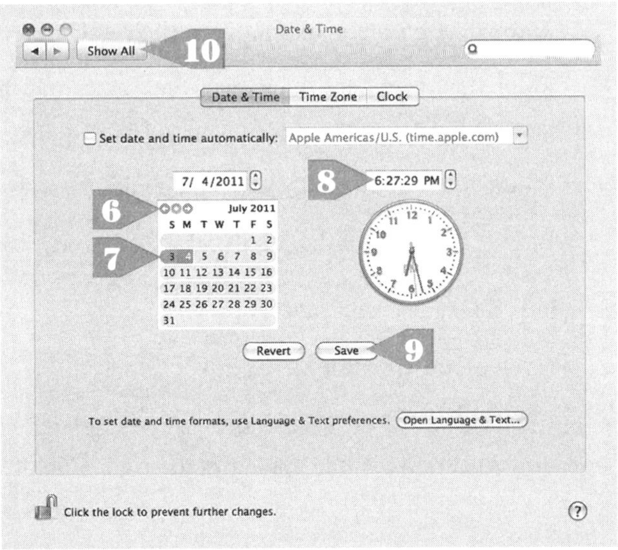

CLICK AND GO

1. Click on Time Zone tab.
2. Click in box beside Set Time Zone to remove check.
3. Click on map in the area where you are located.
4. Click on down arrow and select a city in your time zone.
5. Click Date & Time tab.
6. If month is not correct, click on arrows to choose correct month.
7. If date should be changed, click on correct date.
8. If hour or minutes are not correct, click on each and use arrows to adjust.
9. Click Save to keep your changes.
10. Click Show All or  to return to System Preferences.

EXPERIMENT

As I describe some of the many icons contained in the System Preferences window, feel free to click on each icon to open it and see what's inside. To get back to the System Preferences window, simply close the window you've opened. (Remember the Close Box ⊗?) If somehow you have closed the System Preferences window, move the mouse onto the and down to the words System Preferences and click once.

Selecting a Background

The background on your Desktop screen is also referred to as wallpaper. Your operating system comes with several different styles of wallpaper, and you can personalize your desktop by selecting one that appeals to you.

- Is the **System Preferences** window still open on your screen? If not, go to the and access the **System Preferences**, or you might have only to click on **Show All** to get there, if your **Date & Time** window is still open (start on page 195 for how to open the System Preferences). Find the **Desktop & Screen Saver** icon. Single-click on the icon to see its contents.
- You will see a menu of images to the right.
- Move the arrow into the images and press-and-drag two fingers to scroll to see what other images are available.
- When you find an image you like, click on it with the mouse.
- Bingo! There's your background.

Now, let's select a screen saver.

- Click on the **Screen Saver** tab.
- Click on any of the screen savers in the left side of the window. You will see a sample appear in the right side of the window.

- Click on the double arrows to indicate how many minutes or hours should elapse before the screen saver is activated. (Mine is set for 10 minutes.)
- Click in the to close the window and save the changes.

CLICK AND GO

1. Click on Desktop Pictures.
2. Click on wallpaper that appeals to you.
3. Click on Screen Saver.
4. Click on screen saver of your choice. Scroll down to see more choices.
5. Click double arrows to adjust when screen saver will appear.
6. Click Close Box to close window and save your changes.

WHAT AM I SAVING MY SCREEN FROM?
Screen savers were originally designed to protect the screen from "screen burn." Computer screens used to become damaged when the same screen image remained on the screen for too long. Improvements in the design of screens make this unlikely. Nowadays screen savers are more for visual entertainment.

You can open all the items in the **System Preferences** to see what they contain. For that matter, you can click on anything on the computer screen as long as you don't hit the **Return** key, which instructs the computer to take an action, or you don't click on an action key (**OK**, **Yes**, **Apply**). In fact, it is a good idea to return to the System Preferences window and make changes to the mouse and the background whenever you feel inspired. It is only through practice that you will really become comfortable with your computer. Play around here as often as you would like. If you open a window and are concerned that you're heading into unknown territory, simply close it by using the **Close Box** or clicking on the word **Cancel**, **Finish**, or **Exit**.

Getting in the Swing

It's a lovely thing to listen to music while working (or playing) at the computer. If your Mac has a D: drive, grab a CD that you enjoy, and let's learn how to play music. If you have a newer Apple computer, without a disc drive, you can purchase an external drive to listen to your CDs or watch a movie, or you can visit the iTunes Music Store to purchase music and download it directly onto your computer or device.

- Place the CD, label side up, into the CD slot and give it a gentle push. The computer will pull the CD into the slot.
- Wait a moment and an image of a CD will appear on the Desktop.
- Next, a window containing the iTunes software should open automatically.
- Click on the arrow to play the CD.
- The songs (or "tracks") on the CD are listed in the largest pane of the iTunes window. To play a specific track, move your mouse over the one you want to play and double-click it.

- There is an arrow at the top of the iTunes window that you can click and drag to increase or reduce volume. There are a couple of other options for controlling the volume. Your speakers or monitor may have a volume control. Fiddle with them to set a comfortable volume for you.
- When you want to remove the CD, close iTunes by clicking in the **Close Box**. Then simply click and drag the CD icon into the **Trash** on the Desktop, which—now that you're dragging the CD—may look like for **Eject**. If that doesn't expel the CD, you might have to depress and release the button on the top right of the keyboard.

When you insert an audio CD, a window may appear that looks something like this. It allows you to choose a CD track and adjust the volume.

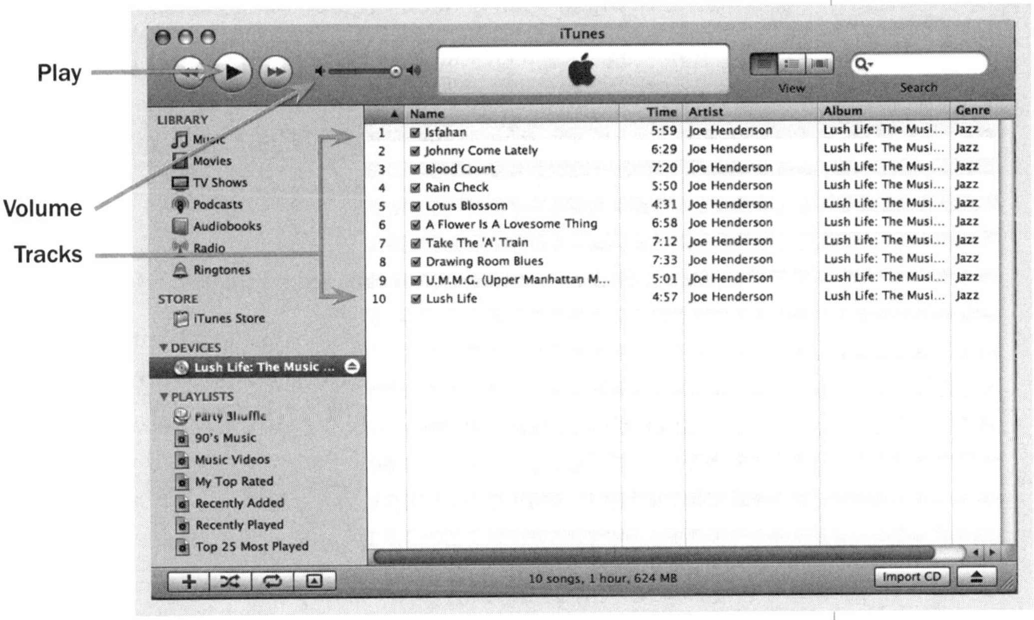

Job Well Done

If you've been using the book sequentially, at this point you should see a light at the end of the tunnel. The computer is more and more under your control. Stick with the book, and by the end you'll be in total control. Repeat any part of this chapter and the previous one until you are ready to go on the Internet. Then it's time for Chapter 13.

Q: The Task Bar at the bottom of my computer screen has moved from the bottom of the screen to the side. It works where it is now, but how did it get there and can I move it back?

A: Click-and-drag is the answer for both how it moved and for how you can move it back to its original position. Believe it or not, at some point you accidentally clicked and dragged the Task Bar (some call it a System Tray) to the side of the screen. Place your mouse anywhere on the Task Bar and click and drag it to the bottom of your screen. Release the mouse. The Task Bar should be back where you like it.

Q: Is there a way to open an icon without double-clicking?

A: Yes. If double-clicking is really a struggle for you, on a PC you can single-click on the icon and then depress and release the **Enter/ Return** key. On an Apple, you can single-click on the icon, click on **File**, and click on **Open**.

Q: Is there a way to scroll without using the mouse?

A: In addition to using the mouse to scroll, you can also move up and down a page using the arrow keys located on the bottom right of your keyboard. Sometimes it helps to click on the web page first, then use the arrow keys. But I would like you to practice with the mouse because the arrow key option does not work on all websites.

Q: What does PBKC stand for?

A: PBKC is a charming acronym to tease computer users. You ask a technician, "What's wrong with my computer?" He responds, "It's a PBKC" (pronounced *pebkack*). It stands for "problem between keyboard and chair"!

THE NEWLYWED GAME

CHAPTER 13

SPANNING THE GLOBE

"Surfing the net"—traveling around the World Wide Web

The Internet looms in front of us as the Wild West did for the early settlers. As we hear more about the Internet and its limitless possibilities, none of us wants to be left behind. It is the land of opportunity, yet it is full of unknowns and it may seem like a long, hard journey to get there. Take heart, we will access the Internet and learn about websites together, and in no time at all you'll be zipping around the Web with ease. If you are chomping at the bit to get to email, you can move on to the next chapter and come back to this one later. However, I strongly suggest that you go through this chapter first because it has information that will enhance your email experience.

A Quick Overview

As you likely know, the Internet is a huge system that connects computers all over the world. The World Wide Web is today's modernization of the old government-issue Internet, which consisted of convoluted codes on a black screen. The World Wide Web (www) was designed to make the

"I was skeptical that the Internet could follow the progress of the companies I helped develop before my retirement, as all the younger folks at the company kept saying it could. They were right. I monitor the companies' status daily and feel very much in the loop. I've never been better informed."
—Joshua

Internet accessible, with colorful graphics, sound, and a user-friendly environment.

Surfing the net (net = Internet) isn't very different from channel hopping on your television set. Sometimes something will really hold your interest; other times it's fun to change from one channel to the next; and then there are times when you can't find anything that suits your needs. The Internet, like TV, can be seductive, a great way to escape, and an opportunity to learn something new. All you need to connect to the Internet is a computer or tablet, a modem, and an Internet Service Provider (ISP).

Finding Your Internet Service Provider (ISP)

As I suggested in Chapter 8, the process of choosing an online service is another one of those cases where you might want to call in the cavalry. Ask a friend or relative for his or her advice on which company to choose and even have them come over and help you get started. Start by contacting your local phone company (Verizon, AT&T, etc.) or your cable television company (Time Warner, Comcast, etc.) to see what sort of a package they offer in combination with services they already provide you.

If you own a tablet and you want to purchase a data plan to enable you to use your tablet 24/7, whether there is a wi-fi signal available or not, you'll be choosing the carrier that can provide you with that Internet signal. Otherwise, I'm describing how you choose a provider to bring the Internet signal into your home. The wi-fi signal in your home allows you to use either a tablet or computer—both a laptop and desktop. Throughout the chapter, I'll try to let you know what information is universal to a tablet and a computer and what information is specific to either device.

I highly recommend that you choose a high-speed connection. As I mentioned earlier in Chapter 8, dial-up connections to the Internet are slow and no longer competitively priced. You can get a high-speed connection for almost the same price and zoom around the Internet with greater speed and less chance of being cut off.

Getting Connected

Depending on which Internet service provider you choose, you may have to set up the connection or they may send a technician to your home to do it for you. If you're setting it up, you will have received a box containing the modem and some cables. The modem is the device that will ultimately connect your computer to the Internet. If you're uncomfortable or timid about installing the modem or the software on your own, either call the company's 800 number and have one of their technicians on the phone while you go through the installation steps or ask a friend or family member to help you. It may even be worth it to pay someone to help you. You can often find an industrious high school or college student who would be happy to offer assistance for a lot less money than you would pay a professional computer technician. Whoever is helping you, don't let him or her leave until you've turned the computer off after installation, turned it back on, and are sure it is all working properly.

At some point during the installation, you may be asked to fill in a form on your computer screen. You'll need to provide your name, address, telephone number, and credit card information so that your online service can bill you monthly. Generally, you can move from one text box to

CUSTOMER SERVICE
As you register with your ISP, pay very careful attention: If a customer service telephone number crosses your path at any time, be sure to write it down. After you've completed the registration process, that number can be rather elusive. This may be your only opportunity to note it. Grab it while you can.

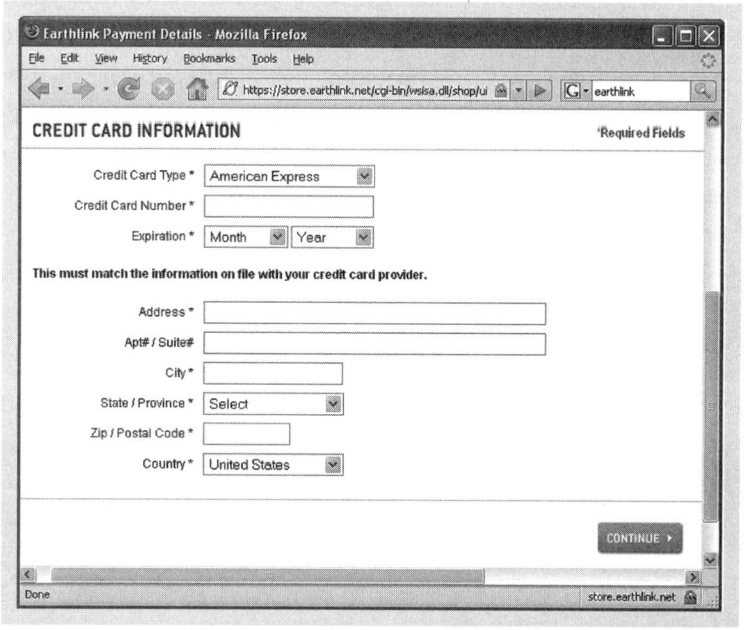

A page of the registration process for EarthLink

DON'T FORGET TO CLICK IN THE BOX!
This is a crucial thing to remember. It is the most common thing that people forget. You must click inside the text box to activate it so it will accept your typing instructions.

another by hitting the **Tab** key (located to the left of **Q** on the keyboard). If you want to access a text box out of sequence, you can move the mouse arrow anywhere inside the white part of the text box and click to activate the text box. You'll see a flashing vertical line (referred to as the cursor or blinking cursor) in the far left of the box. This indicates that you can start typing at that location. (Refer to Chapter 12 if you need a refresher on how to use the Scroll Bar.)

Wi-Fi: Whys and Why Nots

Wireless technology allows your computer to communicate with the mouse, keyboard, printer, and yes, even the Internet, all without cords and cables mucking up the room where you use the computer. A wireless setup in your home also allows you to have a network so other family members or houseguests can be online at the same time as you with no interference between the computers. And you can share a printer or scanner wirelessly.

Wireless technology isn't limited to your home. Do you remember when a hot spot was somewhere you wouldn't take a person under the age of eighteen? "Hot spots" are now also public areas where you connect your computer wirelessly to the Internet. With wi-fi technology you can bring your laptop or tablet to a coffee shop, the airport, or the mall, and, if there's a signal, you can connect to the information superhighway.

Some people would rather not see wires and cables on their desk. You can connect to your printer, mouse, and keyboard wirelessly.

It's all amazing technology and extremely convenient. The downside is that wireless connectivity increases your vulnerability to someone sneaking into your computer. When you're on a cell phone instead of a land line, your conversation is sent through the air rather than traveling through phone cables. The uncomfortable truth is that someone with the smarts and inclination can easily intercept your cell phone conversation. The same is true when you are on your computer wirelessly. The data being transmitted to and from the Internet is vulnerable to being detected and intercepted.

I don't want to take all the fun out of wi-fi, but if you choose to partake in this incredible technology, I want you to be as safe as possible.

Be sure to take standard security precautions during the setup of your wireless. Ask whoever is helping you if WPA (wi-fi protected access) and WEP (wired equivalent privacy) are activated. Both of these aid in the prevention of uninvited people piggybacking on your wireless signal or viewing any of the contents of your computer.

On the Road

Here are some measures to help you safely enjoy wi-fi when you're traveling with your laptop or tablet.

- Check that your firewall is activated (see page 266). A firewall protects you from an intruder viewing the contents of your computer. Keep in mind, however, that a firewall doesn't protect against someone seeing what you send through the Internet wirelessly.
- Delete any cookies (see pages 261–263) before you hit the road because they may contain password or credit card information that can be seen if someone gains access to your computer.
- Remove any documents from your computer that contain passwords, Social Security numbers, or credit card information. You shouldn't be traveling with that information on your computer anyway, in case it's lost or stolen.

- If you access a website requiring a login or password, be sure the website address begins with **https** instead of **http**. Think of it as **s** for security. When you see **https**, it indicates the web page is encrypted for safer transmission.
- Avoid banking online when utilizing a wireless hot spot.

I apologize if that wi-fi jargon (WPA, WEP, firewall, cookie, etc.) was a bit overwhelming. My intention is to let you know the benefits of wi-fi, along with some cautionary advice. Chapter 16 will help your computer experience be as safe as it can be. When you feel like your head is swimming in unfamiliar terms, it's time to step back and take a break.

Choosing a Username and Password

A user name is the name you use when you're on the Internet or sending email. The next chapter goes into more detail about email, but you may need to decide what your username will be now, in order to connect to the Internet. Here's an example: If I was a Verizon customer and my username was Peach, my email address would be *peach@verizon.net.*

Now that I've mentioned it, let's identify all the parts of my fictitious email address.

peach@verizon.net is the email address.

peach is the username.

@ means "at."

verizon.net is the "domain name," or mailing address.

When deciding on your username, keep in mind that people will need to know your email address so that they can send you email. It seems silly to point that out, but I've had clients pick rather embarrassing usernames and regret it when they had to tell people, "My email address is *iamanidiot@hotmail.com.*"

Be prepared not to get the username that you hoped for. With hundreds of millions of people on the Internet, it's probable that someone may already have your first choice of username. Have several options ready.

The email service will also ask for a password. A password verifies who you are each time you sign on to the service. Choose a password that comes easily to you. Please don't use the same password that you use for your bank account or ATM card.

"Case sensitivity" means that it matters whether the letters are in upper- or lowercase. At this time, most online services are *not* case sensitive when dealing with user names. But passwords are case sensitive, so be sure to type your password in the same case as you originally chose. Make sure you write down your email address and password. For safekeeping, why not stash it in your "Computer (or Tablet) Information" envelope? When writing it all down, it's a good idea to underline the capital letters so you can be sure what's upper- or lowercase when you pull out that piece of paper a year from now. What looks legible today may resemble chicken scratches down the line—so write as neatly as you can.

In Chapter 16, there's more detailed information about password security. Jump ahead to page 276 and read the "Open Sesame" section then come back here.

Once you've successfully registered, I want you to sign off and sign on from scratch. Practice, practice, practice.

KEY TO PASSWORDS

Most passwords need to be at least eight characters long. It's a good idea to make your password a combination of letters and numbers with at least one capital letter. That makes it harder to guess.

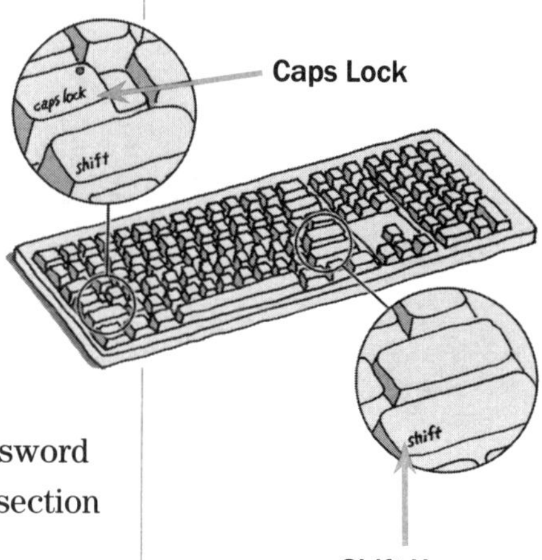

Signing Off and Signing On

Very few online services require you to sign on to access the Internet. The vast majority allow you to connect to the Internet just by double-clicking on an icon on the Desktop. Some remember your user name and password, and others ask that the information be typed in every time. If you need to type information into a text box, remember to click on the box with your mouse to activate the text box and use **Tab** to get from one text box to the next.

CLICK AND GO

1. Click in text box to activate, then type username.
2. Click in text box to activate, then type password.
3. Click Sign On or hit Enter or Return key.

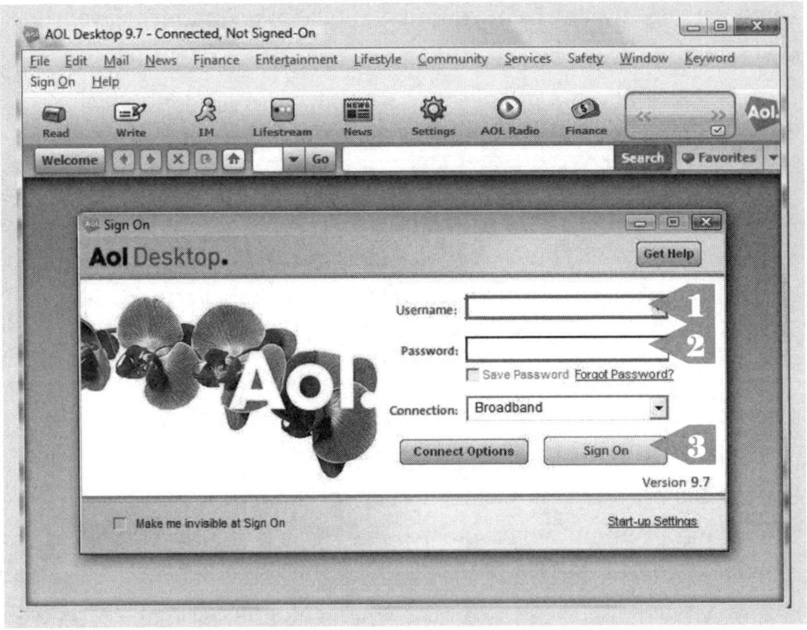

Each online service also has its own way of signing off. For some, it is simply clicking on the **Close Box**. For others, you need to maximize their box in the **Task Bar** and then click on **Disconnect**. There may be a tutorial or a tour offered that will help you discover the ins and outs of your particular service.

BROWSING WITH A BROWSER

Internet Explorer, Safari, Google Chrome, and Firefox are browsers. Browsers allow you to *browse* the Internet at no additional cost beyond what you pay to connect to the Internet. On a computer, you can choose which browser to use. Your tablet will have access to the Internet through the browser the manufacturer has chosen. (The icon could look like one of the above or something like this: .)

The Home Page

On a computer, the first page that appears when you connect to the Internet and open your browser is your home page. This is the website that the manufacturer of your computer chose to have come up first when you turn on the computer. (So, if I were a betting person, I would bet it is their website.) When you choose your ISP (Internet service provider), it may change your home page to its website.

ACTION BUTTONS

When the computer asks you questions, such as "Do you want to make Firefox your default browser?", it offers you choices of actions to take (i.e., **Yes**, **No**, **Cancel**, **OK**, **Save**). Usually, one of the action buttons is either framed in a darker box or surrounded by dots. As discussed in Chapter 12, the computer is presuming that this is the action you will take. You can take this action by either hitting the **Enter** or **Return** key or by moving the mouse arrow on the action key you want and clicking once.

Slowly move the mouse arrow around the home page. Do you notice that when it is over certain words the arrow becomes a hand? Whenever the hand appears, you are being notified that there is an item you can click on that will link you to another web page with more information on that topic. Generally, a single-click will open an item on the Internet. With a tablet, you will simply tap your finger on the different items on a website to open them. A good indication that something is "tappable" on a tablet is that it is blue and underlined.

A REAL PAGE-TURNER

Home Page = the first page of any website on the Internet. It also refers to the page that opens when you first connect to the Internet.

Web Page = any page that follows the home page of a website.

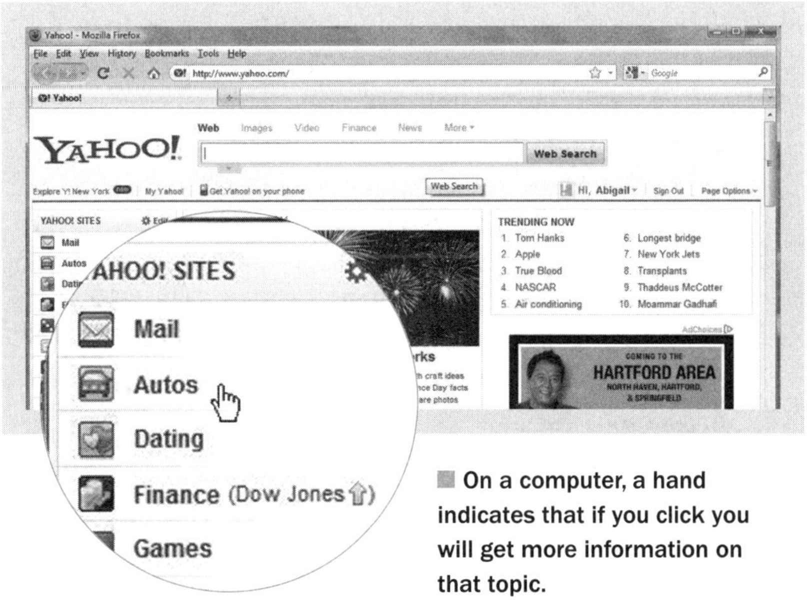

On a computer, a hand indicates that if you click you will get more information on that topic.

"One night I couldn't sign on to the Internet and none of the people I usually rely on for computer guidance were around. So I had no choice but to call for technical help. It wasn't fun and it took almost an hour. But we fixed the problem. I wouldn't ask for it to happen again, but if it does, I know I can handle it."
—*Evelyn*

Advertisements

Most online services allow advertisements to pop up. Usually, they appear when you first sign on. You do *not* want to approve any purchase by accident, but don't worry because this isn't an easy thing to do. I never even read these ads. I simply close the window or click on whatever action button indicates that I am not interested (**No**, **Exit**, **Close**, etc.). Don't click on any action button (**Yes**, **OK**, **Apply**, etc.) or hit the **Enter** or **Return** keys casually, or unexpected things may happen.

Websites and Their Addresses

Your online service connects you to the Web, and your browser (Explorer, Safari, or Firefox, to name a few) allows you to navigate it. Before we venture out to cyberspace, let's review some basic elements of all websites. A website is much like a book. It's full of information and made up of pages. The pages of a website are called web pages.

There are several different parts to a web address. Each part gives the Internet information about how to locate the website you're seeking. Don't confuse a website address with an email address. A website often starts with www. and doesn't have the @ symbol.

Here is what an email address looks like:

peach@verizon.net

Here is what the average web address looks like:

http://www.askabbystokes.com

Note: You may have noticed that in other places in the book I refer to my website as *AskAbbyStokes.com*, using some upper case letters. In fact, web addresses aren't case sensitive. I use them simply to make the name of my website clearer and easier to read and remember.

Now let's define the parts.

http:// is the hypertext transfer protocol. *AAAAaaaarrrrggghhh!* The good thing is that you don't need

MAXIMIZE
Remember to maximize your window whenever possible. It makes reading things on the Internet much easier and much more pleasant (refer to Chapter 11). You don't need to maximize on a tablet.

to know what that means. You don't even have to type it when you're inputting a web address.

www. stands for World Wide Web. Notice that there is a period after www. Many websites don't require that you type www., but I suggest that for now you do (so there is no confusion). You need to be very careful about typing the address exactly as it appears; a spelling or punctuation change can send you to a different website. It's just as if you dialed a wrong number on the phone. There will never be a space in a website address because that breaks the line of communication.

askabbystokes is the domain name, not unlike the username in your email address. If you wanted to create a website, you would start by purchasing a domain name.

.com is another part of the domain name. This extension gives you a clue to the type of website. In this case, "com" indicates that it is a commercial website. Note that it is preceded—*not* followed—by a period or "dot."

Here are the most common domain name extensions:

.com = commercial

.edu = educational

.gov = government

.org = nonprofit organization

.net = network business

So take a stab at what the website might be for 1600 Pennsylvania Avenue, Washington, D.C. You guessed it! *whitehouse.gov.*

SURFING THE NET VS. SURFING THE WEB

For practical purposes, they are one and the same (see page 9). And when you're doing either, you're on the information superhighway. (In fact, the World Wide Web is only a part of the Internet, but that is just a technicality.)

Look Out, Web, Here We Come

It's time to surf the net. At the top of the browser window, there is a long text box. It may or may not already have text in it. No matter. If you're on a computer, move the mouse arrow anywhere inside the box and click once. If you're using a tablet, tap once inside the box. (Are you beginning to see the pattern? You click with a mouse with a computer. You tap with your finger with a tablet.) If there was text in the box, it is now highlighted, probably in blue or gray. This is where you will type in a web address. Remember, you don't need to type in http://.

To access a website, you type the address in the website address box. Below are some examples of the website address boxes for Internet Explorer, Safari, and Firefox.

- Move the mouse arrow into the text box and click once. (If you are using a Mac, not a PC, you will need either to single-click on the small icon in the left of the address box or triple-click on the existing address.) When you start typing, the now-highlighted text will automatically be replaced with what you type.
- Type "cnn.com" and hit **Enter**, **Return**, or **Go**.

Before your very eyes is the home page of the website for CNN. If it hasn't appeared yet, be patient.

A website with a lot of graphics (pictures) can take some time to appear on the screen. If it's taking so long that you want to throw in the towel, click or tap on the **Stop** or **X** on the Toolbar (not to be mistaken for the Close Box in the Title Bar).

■ **Type the address in the website address box.**

Want to do something fun? Let's access my website.

- Move the mouse arrow into the text box and click once or tap with your finger.
- Type "askabbystokes.com" and hit **Enter**, **Return**, or **Go**.

Welcome to my website. Make yourself at home. Click or tap on anything that tickles your fancy. I want you to feel that my website is a safe and comfortable place for you to return to whenever you feel like it. It may be the only website that you go to for a while. That is perfectly fine. Take your time to get acquainted with this site and all it has to offer. Be sure to watch my video tutorials and don't hesitate to email me and let me know what instructions you would like to see in a video. I'm creating new videos all the time as new technologies come out. As you revisit *AskAbbyStokes.com*, you'll notice that the information is regularly updated. Websites need to be movable feasts. Why else would you go back for a second visit?

There is a list of recommended websites on page 516. Check it out and visit any of the sites that interest you. Before you know it, you'll be skillfully zooming around the Internet.

HOME PAGE

The term "home page" is used both for the first page of any website and the first page that opens for you when you connect to the Internet. Don't ask me why they didn't choose two different terms, but they didn't. I don't even know who "they" are, but sometimes I'd like to give "them" a piece of my mind!

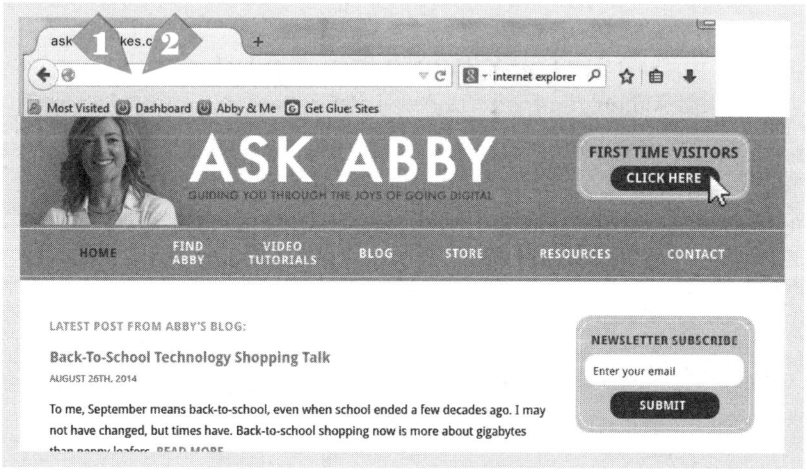

The home page of my website

CLICK AND GO

1. Click or tap inside website address box.
2. Type askabbystokes .com.
3. Hit Enter, Return, or Go.

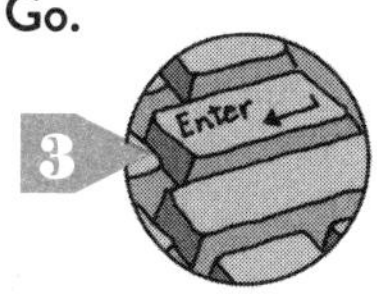

Moving Around a Website

Open up one of the websites listed on page 516. Look carefully at the website you opened. Notice that certain words may be in brighter colors or underlined. They are specifically designed that way to get your attention. Remember, when the mouse arrow becomes a hand, it indicates there is more to be found if you click on those words.

The words or images that you can click on are called links. Some links are very obvious because the text is blue and underlined. A link brings you to more information or sometimes to another website on the same topic. On my website, under **Resources** you'll find there's a page devoted to **Helpful Links** to specific categories of websites (travel, finance, etc.). When you click on one of these links, you will be taken to a different website. Those sites, in turn, may offer links to others. It just goes on and on and on. Play around with my website or others as much as you want, and then come back to the book.

Some websites have so much text it can be dizzying. Take your time. Don't feel obliged to read everything. Also don't feel obliged to stick to a website that doesn't appeal to you. That's what surfing the net is all about—riding the wave of your choice.

NAVIGATING THE NAVIGATION BAR

The Navigation Bar or Table of Contents at the top of a web page (sometimes on the side) leads you to the other pages of the website. Move your mouse over **Resources** on *AskAbbyStokes.com* and hover. You'll see a menu opens without a click of the mouse. Move onto an item in the drop-down menu and click to see that page.

Come Back Again and Again

When you read a book and you want to return to a page to continue reading, you simply stick a bookmark in that page. The same is true on the Internet. If there's a website you'll want to visit often, you can bookmark it so you won't have to type in the web address every time you want to go there. Each online service or browser has a slightly different way to bookmark a website. Usually, there is an icon in the Toolbar or in a pull-down menu. (See the opposite page for examples.)

WANDERLUST

It may be your personality to meander along without a destination. This is usually not fulfilling on the Internet. Have a website you want to visit or a topic you want to research in mind. Otherwise, you may find yourself spending a lot of time going nowhere.

When you want to open a website that you have bookmarked, you simply click on your **Favorites** or **Bookmark** icon to reveal the websites you've stored. Then click on the website you want to access, and your online service will take you directly there.

You can save website addresses for future visits. Here's a sampling of the different methods to Bookmark a website.

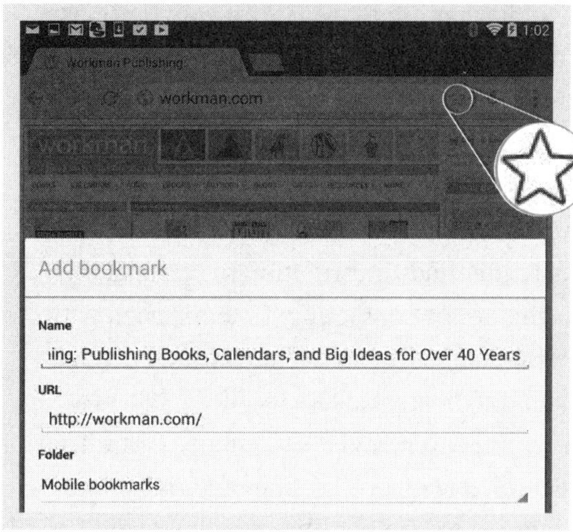

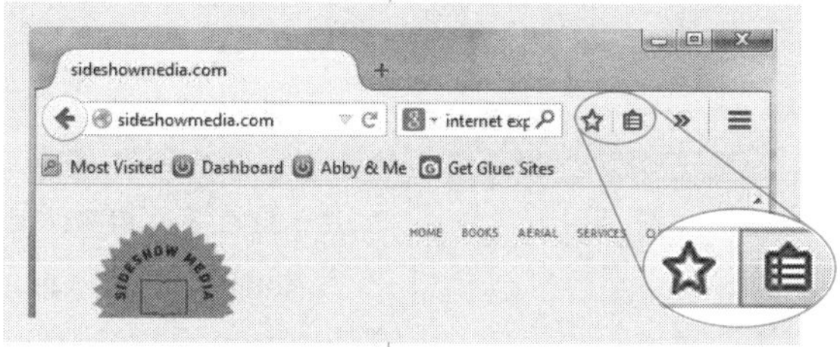

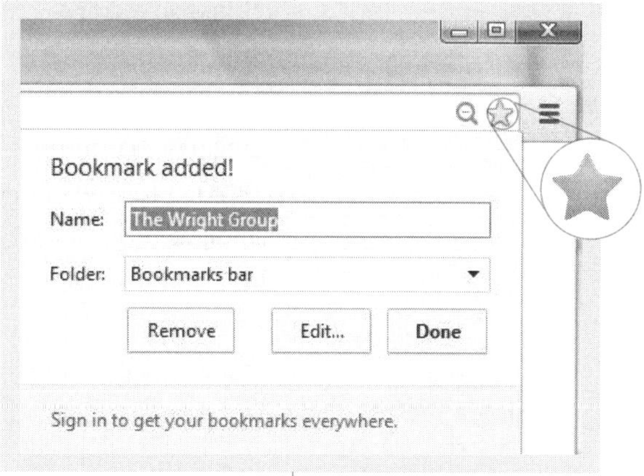

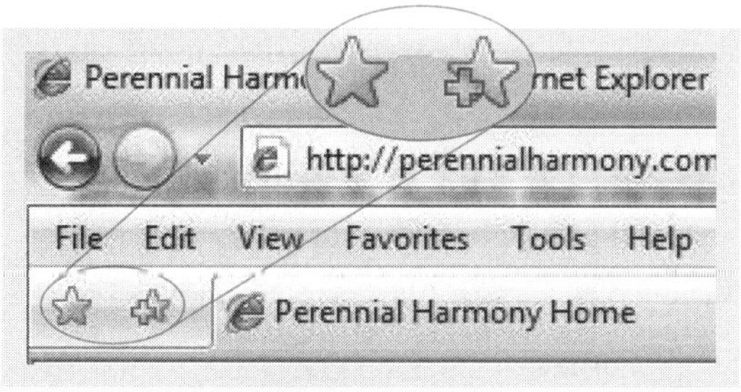

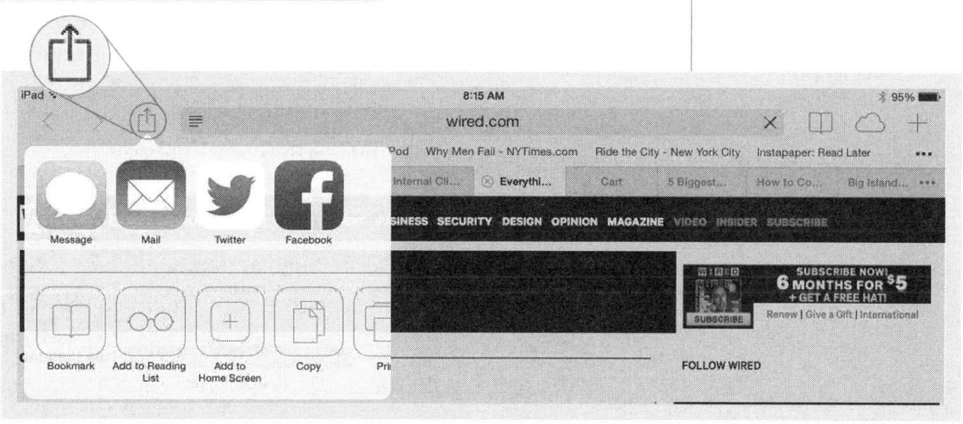

Huh? What Happened?

Strange things do happen. Sometimes after typing in a web address to access a web page, you might receive an error message. First, make sure you typed the web address correctly. If there is no mistake in the address, the error might have nothing to do with you. Perhaps the website is no longer active, or it's under construction or being updated, or the online service is experiencing difficulties. Give it another try or go somewhere else and come back and try later.

Search Engines: Seek and Ye Shall Find

A search engine is a website that finds information for you on the Internet. Think of search engines as competing libraries, each with slightly different archives and filing systems. When I found the Jack Russell terrier doormat and the theater tickets for Mom, I used a search engine. There are many search engines to choose from. Your browser probably has a search engine box on one of its Toolbars. Because each search engine has a different library, you may find different information on different search engines. See "More Than 150 Recommended Websites" on page 516 for a list of different search engines.

To learn more about **Searching Using a Tablet,** visit ***AskAbbyStokes.com*****.** Click on Video Tutorials at the top, then click on Video #3.

You can follow the same steps given below on a tablet if you're on the Internet using its browser. But Google has an app that is easier to use when searching on a tablet. Visit *AskAbbyStokes.com* to watch a video tutorial.

To see a search engine in action, we're going to visit one of my favorites—Google.

- Move the mouse arrow inside the website address box at the top of the screen and click to activate the box.
- Type in *google.com* and hit **Enter**, **Return**, or **Go**.
- When the Google home page appears, click or tap inside the search text box and type the word "recipes." Now move the mouse arrow to the words **Google Search** and click. A page will appear with the first 10 or so results of your search. Your

search word or words, in this case "recipes," appears in bold in the link (the blue title of the result), the sample contents, and the web address. The results are in a particular order, with the sites that best meet your search at the top of the list. Whichever search engine you use, these will be the basic steps.

- Remember to use the Scroll Bar to view all of the results of your search. You will notice that each search result has a title in blue that is underlined. Move the mouse onto the blue underlined title of any of the results that you want to see, and click. This will bring you to a website that pertains to your search. If it isn't what you want, use the back arrow (top left of the screen) to return to the original results of your search.

When using the Google search engine, you must click or tap in the search text box before typing in your desired search. Now type the keywords for your search and click or tap on Google Search below the text box.

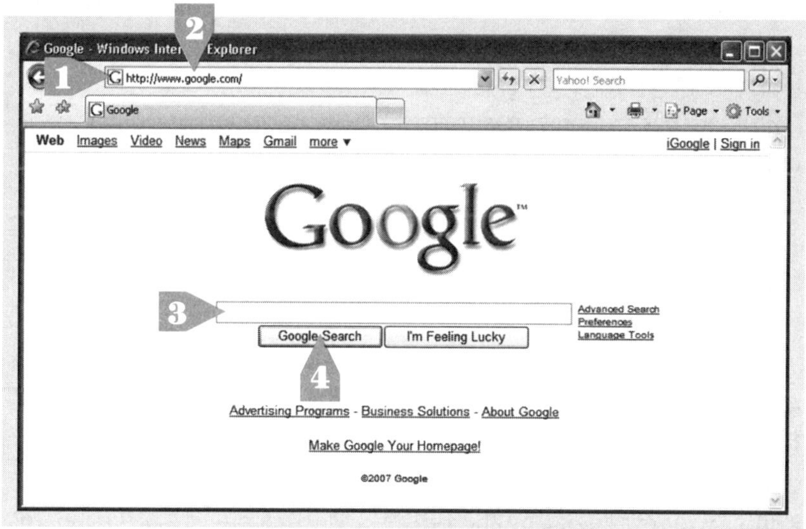

CLICK AND GO

1. Click or tap inside website address box.
2. Type google.com. Hit Enter, Return, or Go.
3. Click or tap inside text box to activate. Type "recipes."
4. Click or tap Google Search.

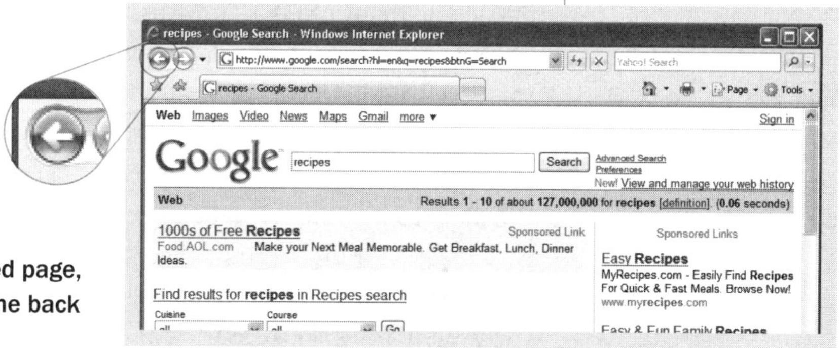

To return to a previously viewed page, click or tap on the back arrow.

TAKE THE BITE OUT OF BLUETOOTH

Bluetooth technology offers a cable-free connection among tablets, computers (desktops, laptops, and handhelds), and other peripherals (such as printers). It allows all of these devices to speak to one another without any cables connecting them, and it works with virtually every new model of cell phone.

When you type in your search, be very specific. Search engines sort the results by the percentage of how it fulfills your search, but you may still find there's a lot to weed through. Sometimes it helps to put the request in quotes. This instructs the search engine to look for websites that contain all the words in the order you typed them, not just any order. Each search engine also has categories listed on its home page. You might want to take a peek at these before you look further. We delve deeper into search engines in Chapter 22. You can either skip ahead or stick with me and we'll get there soon enough.

Print for Your Scrapbook

For those times when you want to have the information from a website to read later or perhaps to pass on to someone else, you can always use your printer to print what appears on your computer screen. To print from a tablet, your printer must be wireless with Bluetooth capability to enable them to speak to each other without being connected.

On a computer you can either click on the three stacked lines at the top right of your screen, or you may have to click on the word **File** (it depends on which browser you are using) and then move the mouse arrow down to the word **Print** and click there. When the Printer window opens, hit the **Enter** or **Return** key on the keyboard or click on **Print** or **OK**. It's as simple as that. But don't be surprised if certain parts of the screen do not print out properly. That happens on some websites and not on others.

With a tablet, tap on the icon  and then tap **Print**.

If the page didn't print at all, check that the printer is turned on and plugged into the computer. You may have to click once on the web page that you want to print. Move the mouse arrow to a blank area on the web page and click. This signals the printer that this is the page you want to print. Then go back and try to print again.

Print from the Menu Bar in Firefox.

Print from the Menu Bar in Google Chrome.

You can access the print feature in the Toolbar or the Menu Bar.

Print on an Android tablet.

TIDY PRINTING

When you want to print a web page, look around for the words *Print*, *Printable View*, or *Printer Friendly*. Not all sites have such an option, but if the one you're on does, by clicking on it you'll usually get a cleaner page—one where the advertisements aren't printed.

What Did You Do Before the Internet?

Surfing the net can get addictive. There's so much out there, and one site can lead to the next, but now and again you should sign off and do something else for a while. Seriously, a lot of time can pass while zooming around the Web. Keep track of how long you're on.

I set my kitchen timer for 40 minutes to keep myself aware of how long I have been online. Then I take a break, reset the timer, and continue my surfing. The point of the Internet is not to put you into a trance but to give you access to things you would otherwise not have available. Enjoy it, but don't let it take over your life.

Q: How do I get back to my home page?

A: There's a shortcut on your browser that allows you to return quickly to your home page without having to go to your Favorites or type in the website address. In Explorer, Safari, and Firefox, you will see an icon in the Toolbar that resembles a house. Click on the house and your home page will appear.

Q: How can I stay online to go from one site to another and not close the Internet and sign on again?

A: I see people new to the Internet do what you describe all the time. You don't close the Internet or the window you are viewing to access another website. Instead, you just click in the website address box and type the address of the new website you want to visit. Hit the **Enter/Return** key on the keyboard to open that website.

Q: Why does it take so long for the Internet to open when I double-click on Internet Explorer?

A: First, think about whether it has always taken a long time or if this is a new issue. The answer may determine the cause. Without knowing your answer I would say that if you use dial-up, connecting to the Internet can take a very long time. Alternatively, the home page you have chosen may always take a long time to open. Maybe you should change your home page. If none of that works—or if this is an issue that has come up suddenly—you might want to get someone in to look at your computer to see if it needs some fine-tuning.

Q: Where can I find information about children safely using the Internet?

A: There is a lot of very justified concern about how to keep children safe when they access the Internet. If you're going to invite your children or grandchildren to use your computer, please sit them down and explain the dangers of meeting someone over the Internet. They should never give anyone their full name, home address, or phone number. You can also call the National Center for Missing and Exploited Children (1-800-843-5678) to receive the brochure "Child Safety on the Information Highway."

HOMEWORK ASSIGNMENT

We will send email in the next chapter, so ask your family and friends for their email addresses.

CHAPTER 14

SHALL WE DANCE?

Let's send email

"Neither rain nor sleet nor gloom of night shall keep the carriers from their appointed rounds."

No matter how romantic that sounds, mail delivery via the postal service often lives up to its nickname: "snail mail." Not only does email (electronic mail) arrive anywhere in the world within the blink of an eye, but you can also send as many emails as you want, and it's included in the cost of your Internet connection. Pretty impressive.

An email you write to your daughter goes on quite a journey before it arrives on her computer screen, and yet amazingly, it all happens in seconds.

Here's how it works:

You write the email and send it to your daughter. Your email service routes the email to a central brain for the Internet. That brain reads the email address and routes it to your daughter's email service. Her email service holds it until she signs on. When your daughter signs on, any email sent to her (including yours) will arrive in her mailbox, also known as her "Inbox." She then reads the email, replies to you, and the cycle continues.

Again, recipients don't have to be home or have their computer or tablet on for you to send them email. Their email service keeps it until they sign on.

If you've chosen to skip over Chapter 13 and come straight here to send an email, be sure to go back at some point and read the previous chapter. It is full of helpful information for you to use while on the Internet.

If you didn't sign onto an email account with your Internet Service Provider, you'll want to establish an email account now. There are free web-based email services. That means you can get on any computer in the world that is connected to the Internet and access email from these sites. The three I would look into are available at *yahoo.com*, *gmail.com*, and *hotmail.com*. When you visit the website, click on the words **Sign up** and fill out the necessary form to open an email account. We discussed choosing a user name and password in the previous chapter but if it's vague to you now, revisit page 210 for tips on creating a password. I also highly recommend you jump ahead and read the "Open Sesame" section on page 276. That's where you will find more detailed information about password security.

Again, if you want someone by your side through the process, don't hesitate to ask a friend or relative to help you. You might even have a friend help you connect to the Internet on his or her device and set up an email account before you buy your computer or tablet. That way your email account is at the ready when you bring your new technology home. There is also the possibility that the salesperson will set up an email account for you at the time of purchase. This is especially true when you buy a tablet. Be sure to ask.

"Letter writing had become a lost art form. I missed it. Now with email, I am writing more and loving it!"
—*Alida*

The Email Address

Your email address is your user name (what you sign on with) plus the email service address. For example, if Judith is my username and Yahoo is the email service, my email address is *Judith@yahoo.com*.

Judith is the username.

@ means "at."

yahoo.com is the domain name or mailing address. It could have been *gmail.com*, *aol.com*, *icloud.com*, or whatever entity handles your email.

When people tell you their email address, repeat it back to them. Better yet, get them to write it down. One error in letter, number, or punctuation and your email could be sent to someone else. Be sure not to type in *Judithatyahoo.com*. "At" is represented by holding down the **Shift** key and depressing the **2** key—@ will then appear; "dot" is another way to say "period."

Time to Send a Missive

If you have a computer, you'll connect to the Internet and visit the website that hosts your email (for example: *yahoo.com*, *gmail.com*, or *hotmail.com*). Then sign into to your email account.

Sample inboxes

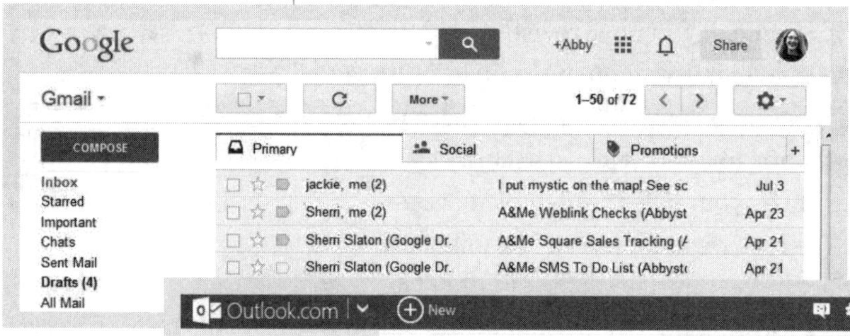

Gmail

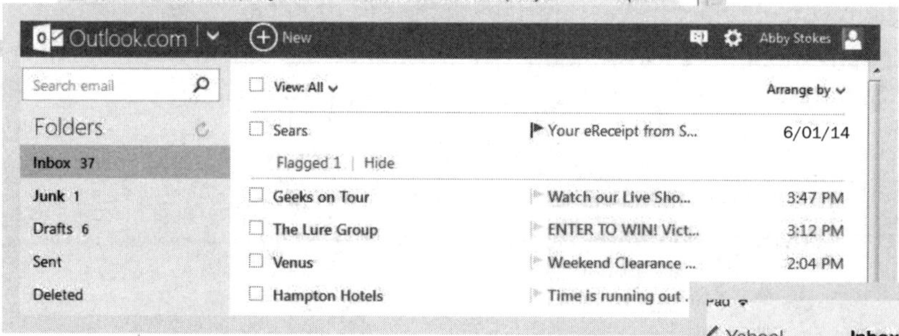

Hotmail

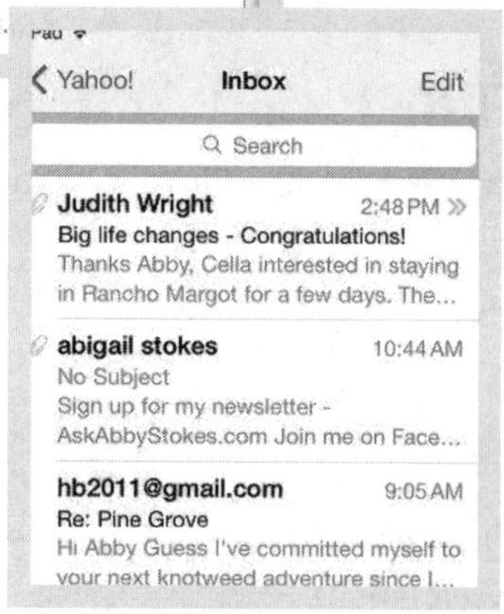

iPad

If you're using a tablet, there'll be an icon for email that you tap on to get you connected. It'll look something like one of these: .

DON'T FORGET TO CLICK OR TAP IN THE BOX!

This is crucial to remember. (But it's the most common thing that people forget.) You *must* click or tap inside the text box to activate it so it will accept your typing instructions.

When you've connected to your email provider, look around for what you click on to write an email. You should have options along the lines of **Compose**, **Create**, **New**, **Write**, or a symbol similar to this: or . Click on whichever you have. Each service is different, but they all have someplace to click to generate an email template. An email form is now on your screen, ready and waiting to be filled in. It should look something like the templates on the following page.

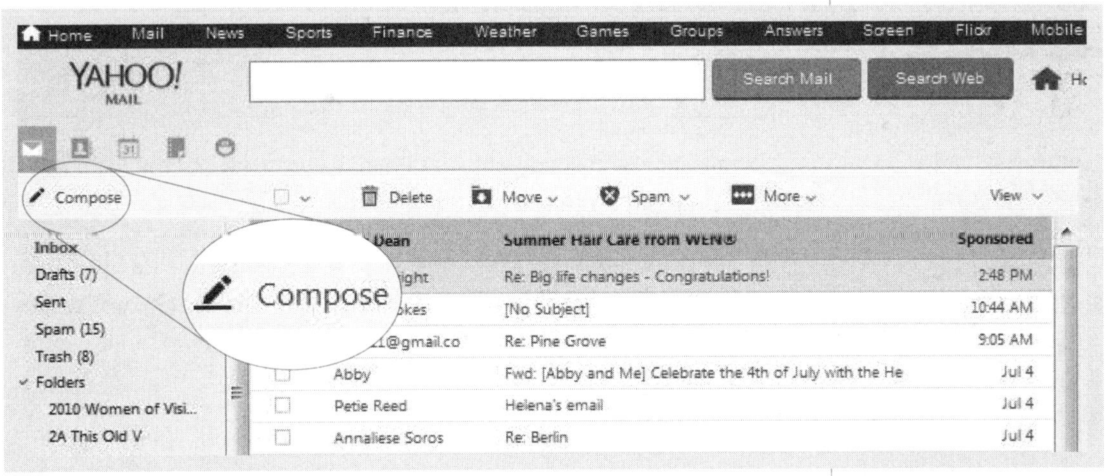

Generating an email template is different, but straightforward, for each email service.

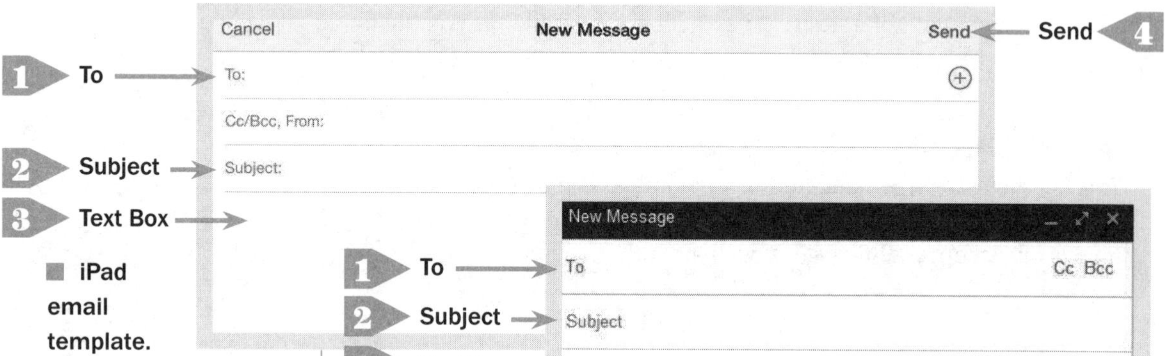

■ iPad email template.

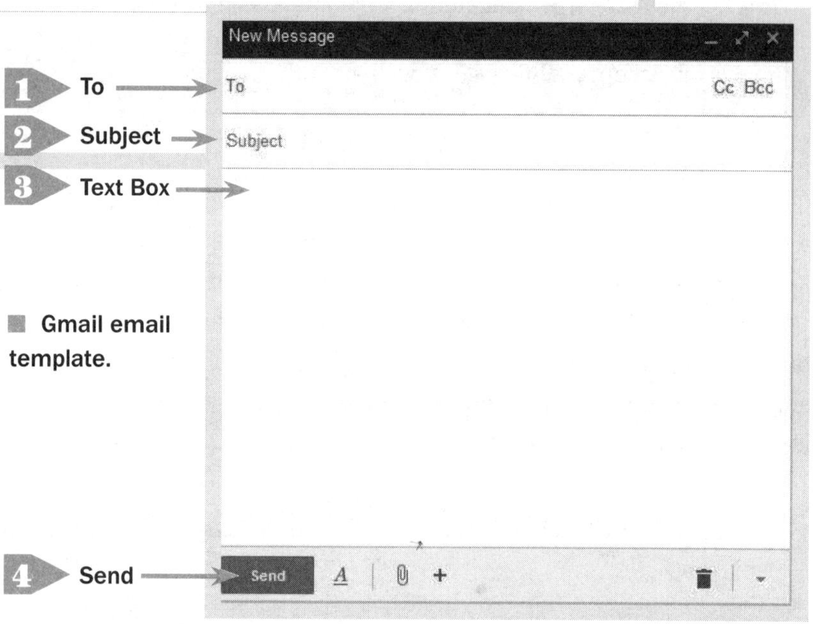

■ Gmail email template.

■ Type the recipient's email address in the **To** box and your message in the large text box below it. Click Send to send your message on its way.

CLICK AND GO

1. Click in or tap in To. Type recipient's email address.
2. Click in or tap in Subject. Type topic of your email.
3. Click in or tap in Text Box. Type your missive.
4. Click or tap on Send.

You're going to send your first email to yourself. Again, each email service is slightly different, but here are the basic steps.

- There should be a flashing vertical line (referred to as the cursor or blinking cursor) in the left corner of the **To** text box. If there isn't, move the mouse arrow into that box and click once or tap in the box.
- Type the recipient's email address in the **To** box. (In this case, because you are sending it to yourself, type in your email address.) Look at it and be sure there are no mistakes. Hit **Tab** to move the cursor to the **Subject** box or click or tap in the Subject box to activate it.
- Type something in the **Subject** box, even if it is only "Hello." Some services won't let you send an email without a subject.

The purpose of the subject box is to give the recipient a sense of the contents so they can prioritize which emails to open first.

- Now either move the mouse into the large text area and click or tap or hit **Tab** again. This is where you'll type your message.

Before we type a message, I'll explain a couple of things. One of the big differences when you're typing on a computer as opposed to on a typewriter is that you don't need to hit **Enter** or **Return** at the end of a line. The text automatically moves, or wraps around, to the next line.

You do, however, need to use the **Return** or **Enter** key to create a new paragraph or to insert a blank line between text. (The **Tab** key is still used to indent a paragraph. There may not be a **Tab** key on your tablet.)

Now we get to type a message.

- Type in whatever you would like to say. For example,

  Mirror, mirror on the wall, who is playing with the computer and having a ball?

- When you're done, move the mouse arrow onto the word **Send**, and click once or tap.

And away it goes!

Your email provider keeps a copy of your sent mail for you. If you want to see the message you sent, look for a button with the word **Sent**, probably in the left sidebar.

TO, CC, AND BCC

To is where the recipient's email address is typed.
Cc stands for carbon copy. It means that this email is also being sent to another recipient.
Bcc is a blind carbon copy. The recipients won't know that you sent the email to anyone you put in the Bcc.

OOPS—I MADE A MISTAKE

If you make a mistake, you can erase your typing (from right to left) by using the BkSp (Backspace), Delete key, or ⌫. (These can usually be found on the upper right section of your keyboard, next to the ± key.) Depress it once for each letter that you want to erase. If you hold your finger down on the key, it will continue to move and delete until you lift your finger up. You definitely have more control when you depress and release the key with each character than when you hold the key down.

You've Got Mail!

If the service is very busy, it might take a few minutes for an email to arrive, but generally it should be in your **Inbox** or mailbox almost instantaneously. There are several ways to retrieve mail, depending on which email service you use.

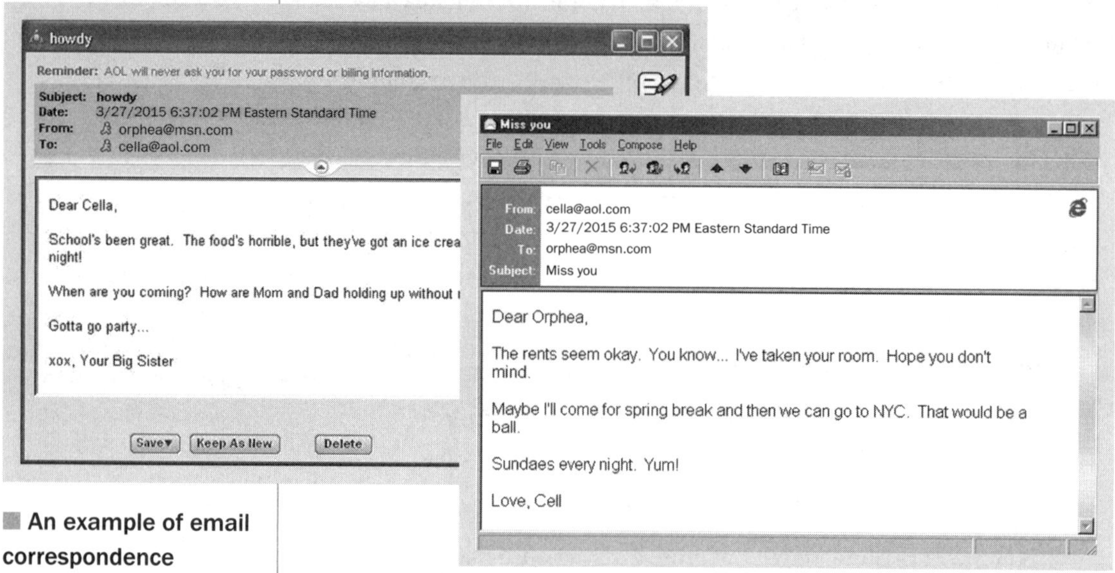

An example of email correspondence

You may have to click on either **Read Mail**, **Check Mail**, or **Mail**. Your inbox should appear on the screen. With most tablets, you tap on **Inbox**, if it doesn't automatically open to your Inbox.

Your new unread mail may be in bold to indicate that it hasn't been read. To open it with a computer, click on either the sender's name or the subject. Each email service is different. Your mouse arrow changing to a hand will help lead you to where to click. With most tablets, you simply tap anywhere on the email to open.

"I love that I can email at any time. I am often awake in the middle of the night and I would never think to call my girls at that time. When it happens now, I just sit at the computer and write them an email."
—Ed

Another Item for the Scrapbook

Let's print your new email! Is the printer plugged in and turned on? To print only the email and not all that appears on the web page, look at the top of the email for either a printer symbol or the word **More**. Some email services have made the print function rather elusive. ("Why?!" I shout.) You may also try looking for either More or, in Gmail, clicking on the down arrow to the right of the arrow pointing to the left. Mission accomplished!

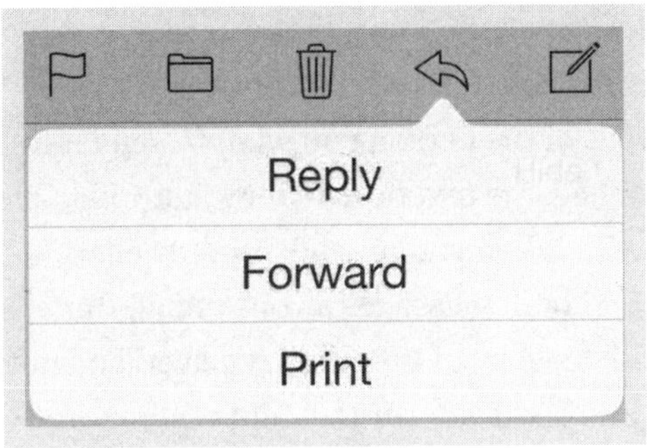

■ With an iPad, tap the **Reply** arrow to access **Print**.

Reply to Sender . . . Address Is Known

You cannot send an anonymous email. The sender's address will always appear on the email. As a matter of fact, with some services the whole routing path will appear. (That is the indecipherable code at the top or bottom of your email.)

To reply to the sender (in this case, yourself), click or tap once on **Reply** or (this will send the return email to the sender only), or **Reply All** or (this will send the return email to everyone who received the initial email, unless they were blind-copied). Each service is different, but if you take your time, you'll find the Reply button.

Look what happened when you hit the Reply button! How convenient—an email is all set up with the sender's (soon to be recipient's) email address in the **To** box. Now you can take it from here. Perhaps you want to try sending another email to yourself. Better yet, do you have someone else's email address? If you don't have anyone's email address on hand, it would be my pleasure to receive an email from you. My email address is *abby@askabbystokes.com*.

REPLY VS. REPLY ALL

If you receive a group email (i.e., you were one of multiple recipients), be aware of whether you are replying exclusively to the sender (Reply) or to everyone else who got the email along with you (Reply All). Some things are meant for only one set of eyes.

BREAK THE CHAIN
Just as there are chain letters in snail mail, there are chain emails. I hate these! My retaliation for a chain email that threatens bad luck unless it is sent to 10 other people is to return it to the sender 10 times.

Forward March

An email you receive can be passed on to others. To do this, click or tap on the button that is labeled **Forward** or look for a forward arrow →, usually at the top of the email that you received. The email you got is now ready for you to forward. Click on the **To** box and type in the email address of the person you want to send it to. You can also type a message in the large text box if you want. Click or tap on the text box and type away. When you're ready, simply click or tap on the **Send** button to send both messages as one email. But, what if you wanted to only send one part of the email received and not the entire thing? You can. You and I will go over that and other more advanced email activities in Chapter 17.

Your Little Black Book

Every email service has an address book where you can store the email addresses of people that you will correspond with frequently. As each email service is different, I can't tell you exactly where to find your address book, but I can give you some clues. Does the word **Address** or **Contacts** appear in the window? If so, click on it. If not, look for a symbol like or . You may have to bravely click on a down arrow and see what opens. When the address book appears on the screen, be extremely accurate when typing in email addresses. The last thing you want is to store a wrong address.

Click on the down arrow to access Contacts in Hotmail and Gmail.

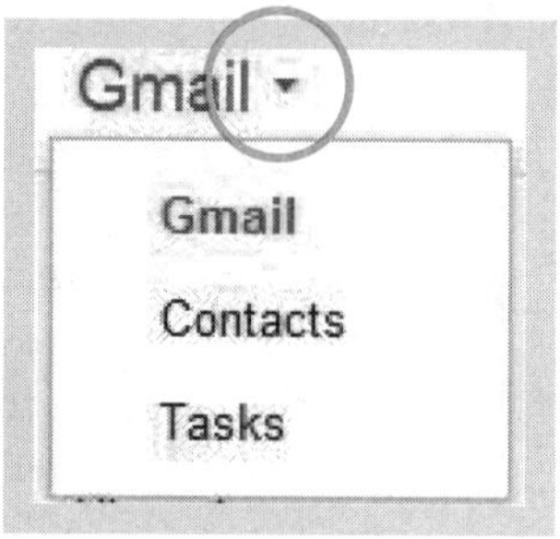

Once you've put an email address in the book, try sending an email. (You can start with mine, *abby@askabbystokes.com*, if you don't have any others.) You can either generate a new email form when you have your address book open or you can open a new email form and then access the address book from there. With most email services, you simply click or tap in the **To** box and type the first couple letters of the person's name and his or her address will appear in a list of possible addresses.

> "I love email. The only thing I don't love is getting all of those silly jokes. I wish I could ask my friends to stop, but I don't want to be rude."
> —***Virginia***

The real advantage of the address book is that you don't need to remember or keep typing email addresses. This is handy because it's easy to make a mistake in even a short email address, and just one wrong letter means your missive won't arrive.

Deleting Old Mail

Again, there are several ways to delete old mail, depending on which service you use. When email is open or even just highlighted, there might be a button with an **X** on it (not to be mistaken for the Close Box), the word **Delete**, or a trash can. Click on whatever your service offers to throw away read mail. It is wise to delete mail you don't need to keep things nice and tidy.

Of course, many people have so many emails in their Inbox that they can't find what they're looking for or forget to attend to important emails. Below are tips and tricks to help clean up your inbox by searching and deleting unwanted emails.

To delete an email without opening:

1. Click in the box to the left of the email.
2. Look at the menu above and click on **Delete**, **Spam**, **Junk,** or . (See page 256 to learn more about how to prevent Junk or Spam email from taking over your Inbox.)

Various email search boxes.

To delete multiple emails:

1. Click in the box to the left of the top email in the group.

2. Move down to the bottom of the group of emails.

3. Hold down the **Shift** key.

4. Click in the box to the left of the bottom email in the group.

5. Look at the menu above and click on **Delete**, **Spam**, **Junk**, or 🗑.

To sort and delete emails by searching:

1. Look around to find the search box for your email service. AOL's shown here. Examples of Hotmail, Yahoo, and Gmail are below.

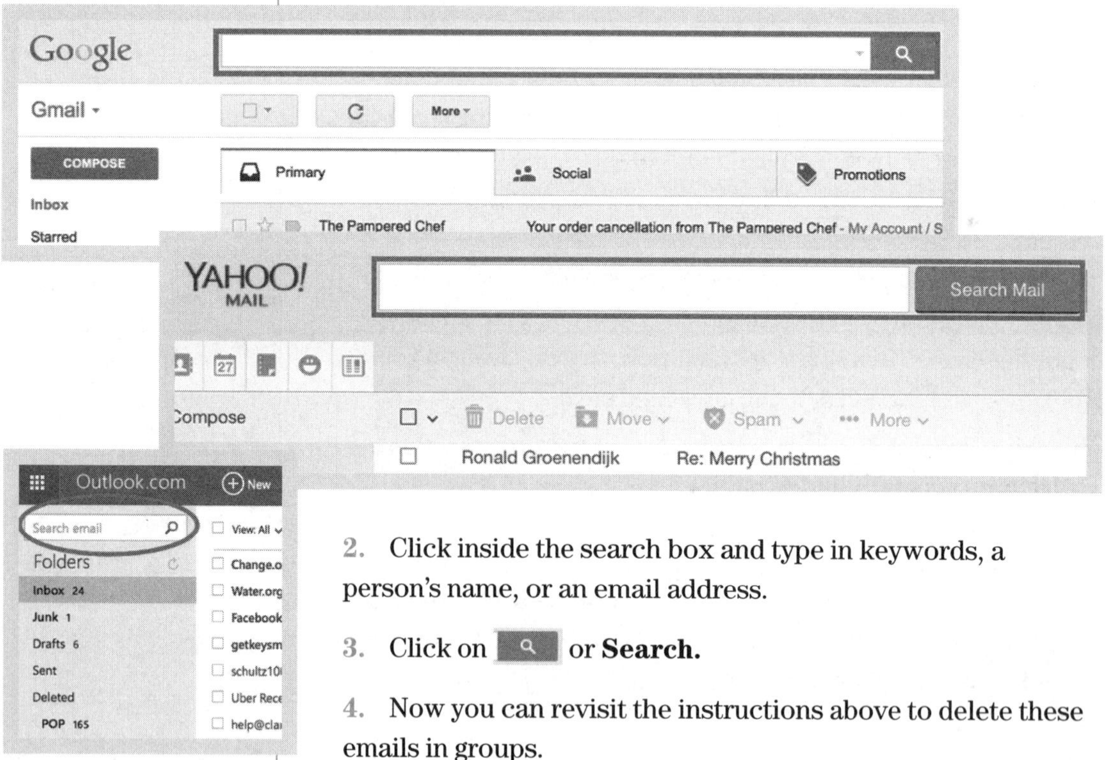

2. Click inside the search box and type in keywords, a person's name, or an email address.

3. Click on [search button] or **Search.**

4. Now you can revisit the instructions above to delete these emails in groups.

To sort and delete emails by sender, subject, or date:
Usually your Inbox is sorted by the date received, with the most recent on top. Most email services offer you the option of sorting your Inbox by Sender or Subject, as well.

Yahoo: Click on **View** (top right) then click **Sender.**
Hotmail: Click on **Arrange By** (top right) then click **From.**
AOL: Click on **Sender** or **From** on the bar at the top of the Inbox.

If you've chosen to sort your email by **Sender** or **Subject**, remember to retrace your steps to return your emails to being ordered **By Date**, with the most recent email on top.

Don't feel like you have to clean up your Inbox in one session. You can get an awful lot done by working on it for 10 minutes every day; then you won't get bored of the task and stop before you've finished the tidying.

Now, go forth and conquer!

HARNESS YOUR EMAIL
Only the emails that you still need to attend to should remain in your Inbox. All other emails should either be deleted or moved into the appropriate file folder. Take one of these four actions with each email.

1. Delete.
2. Reply and then Delete.
3. Move.
4. Leave it in the Inbox.

Email Etiquette

Email is generally more casual than letter writing, but for some, email's code of conduct is right up there with the rules of how to behave at a wedding or which fork to use at dinner. Here are some guidelines on "netiquette." Take what you want and leave the rest behind.

1. Generally, you should respond to most emails you've received, even if it's only to acknowledge that you got the message. Unless, of course, it is an unwanted solicitation—I delete these immediately.

2. Be selective about what you forward. Forwarding silly jokes you receive can be a bother for the recipient (ask if he or she wants them). Chances are, this isn't the first time these jokes have gone 'round the circuit.

3. DON'T SHOUT! When you type in all caps, it is the equivalent of shouting at someone.

4. If you send an email to multiple recipients, unless you use Bcc:, you're revealing the email addresses of all the recipients. Some people prefer to keep their email addresses under wraps. Ask before you release them into the world.

5. Be prepared to read emails without capital letters or a proper greeting and with creative grammar and punctuation. This is a very casual form of communication where you and others may take liberties with what Emily Post and your English teacher instructed.

6. Before you forward anything, try to clean it up by deleting all the gobbledygook that you may find at the beginning and end of the email. Sometimes the list of who has seen the email is longer than the message.

Again, when you join me in Chapter 17 we'll go into more detail about responsibly forwarding only a part of an email you've received.

Junk Mail

Eventually, your email address will get on someone's mailing list. Sad to say, even the Internet has junk mail. I delete junk mail right away. You can reply to the sender that you want to be taken off the mailing list, but I wouldn't hold my breath. We discuss how to manage junk mail (also called spam) in more detail in Chapter 16.

Be Adventurous

Click on and read all the different parts of your email system. You know how to get yourself out of an area that doesn't appeal to you. (Hint: Close Box!)

I have complete faith in your ability to dig deep into what your email service and the Internet have to offer you. You have all the tools at your disposal. Be brave and strike out on your own.

Q: Why do some emails get sent before I am ready?

A: Chances are you clicked on **Send** by accident. To prevent an email from being sent prematurely, don't put the recipient's address in the To: box until you've completed the email. An email can't be sent if there's no email address in the To: box.

Q: How can I correct an email address after writing a long message?

A: Nothing you draft in an email is set in stone until you click **Send**. To correct an email address, click on the existing address and make any changes you want.

Q: My emails print so small I can hardly read them.

A: Instead of finding the print function within the email, you are going up to the word File in the Menu Bar. By clicking on **Print** under **File** you are printing all that appears on the web page and not the email alone. Look for the printer and other symbols shown on pages 232–233 under "Another Item for the Scrapbook." The fact that the optimal way to print emails is not more obvious is an example of bad design. You are doing nothing wrong—it should be easier to find.

CHAPTER 15

MIND YOUR P'S & Q'S

An introduction to word processing

Many of my students, even the ones who in no way consider themselves writers, use word-processing software just about every day. Some use it for correspondence, others take notes on projects, and others use it to keep track of dinner parties, birthdays, or travel plans. Even if you don't think you need it, at some point knowing how to use a word processor will come in handy and you'll be glad you learned.

Microsoft Word dominates the word-processing software market. Introduced in the mid-1980s, it's used by most offices around the country. No other word-processing software offers as many editing features. But fear not, it's very straightforward to use. You can purchase Microsoft Word in a store, in the form of a CD, or through the Internet.

There are, however, other word-processing options available. Google Docs is free to anyone with a Gmail account (which is also free). One significant difference between Microsoft Word and Google Docs is that Google Docs is accessed through Google Drive, which is a Web-based system. Your documents don't get stored on your computer, but rather in "the cloud," which means you must be connected to the Internet to access them. (I'll talk about "the cloud" in greater detail on pages 352 and 412.) If you're interested in learning more about Google Docs and Google Drive specifically, visit *AskAbbyStokes.com*.

If you want to word-process on a tablet, Microsoft also offers Office 365, by subscription, which allows you to use Word (and other programs, such as the presentation program PowerPoint and spreadsheet program Excel) on any tablet. You could also use Pages, Apple's word-processing alternative; at this time, it is exclusively available on the iPad and other Apple products. Pages doesn't offer as many editing options as Word or Google Docs, but you may not need more than it offers. If you intend to do a lot of writing, keep in mind that the smaller screen and keyboard on a tablet aren't as comfortable to use as a larger desktop or laptop computer would be.

Most word-processing programs are modeled after Microsoft Word and use many of the same commands. In this chapter, you'll see examples of how to use some basic editing tools with Microsoft Word on a PC. You can easily apply the steps shown here to your Mac or whatever program you might be using on your computer or tablet.

There may be a trial version of word-processing software preinstalled when you buy your computer or tablet. You'll have 30 days to try it before you are required to give it up or pay for it. If you choose to buy a program at the time that you buy your device, the store may be willing to install it before you leave the premises.

"Software suites" are integrated software programs that combine word-processing, spreadsheet, database, and graphics and/or communication options. If you don't think that you will be doing a great deal more than word-processing, there's no need to spend the extra money for the suite. Stick with basic word-processing software.

Even if you're not planning on doing a lot of writing, some of the editing tips you'll learn in this chapter will come in handy when you're writing an email. So take frequent breaks, but do complete this chapter.

For the downloadable guide **Google Drive Deciphered,** visit ***AskAbbyStokes.com*.** Click on Resources at the top, then click on Helpful Guides, and lastly click on Guide #2.

Meeting Microsoft Word

Word-processing software is used to write letters, lists, memos, and whatever else a typewriter was used for in the past. We're going to open your word-processing program, create a document, and then play around with the options available to you.

After Microsoft Word has been installed on your computer, there should be an icon similar to on your Desktop. Double-click on the icon.

HOW TO I.D. OTHER WORD-PROCESSING PROGRAMS

If you've decided to go with something other than Microsoft Word, take a look at the icons shown here to identify your word-processing program.

To access Google Drive from your computer, you must sign into a Gmail account. Once signed in, look at the top right of the window and click on , then click on .

Google Drive can also be accessed on a tablet. It's preloaded on Android tablets and can be downloaded on any other tablet.

If you have an iPad or a Mac, you may want to use Pages for your tablet word-processing needs. You can find it in the App Store or on Apple's website.

In Word, you may have to click on **New** or **Blank Document**. Now we have a blank slate in front of us. Let's see what the Menu Bar and Toolbar have to offer, and then we'll work with an actual document.

USE THE TUTORIAL

A tutorial or tour may be included with your word-processing software. It will appear when you first open the software program, or you might be able to access it by clicking on the word **Help**. The tutorial can help you find your way around the program.

Slowly move the mouse arrow over the icons in the Toolbar. As the mouse rests on each icon, a small box or bubble, as it can be referred to, may appear that describes the task associated with that icon. Almost every task in the Menu Bar can also be accomplished with an icon in the Toolbar. This allows you to take an action through a text format (the Menu Bar) or through a graphic format (the Toolbar). Go with whatever suits you. I switch between the Menu and Toolbar randomly.

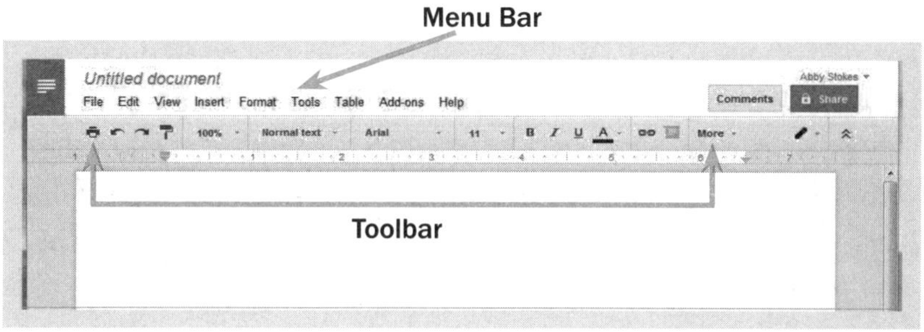

Google Doc

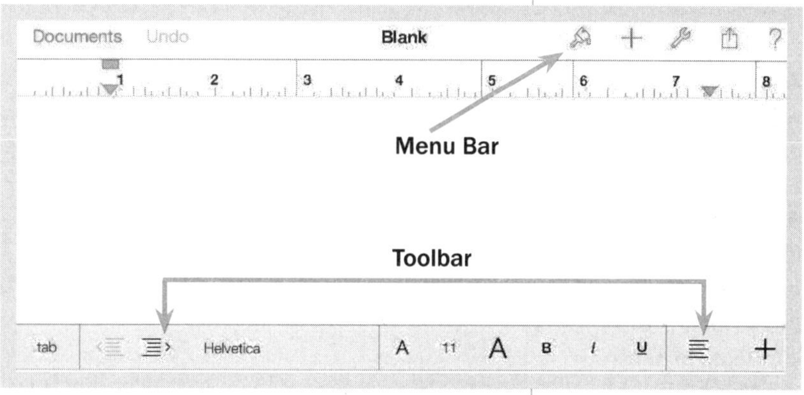

Pages

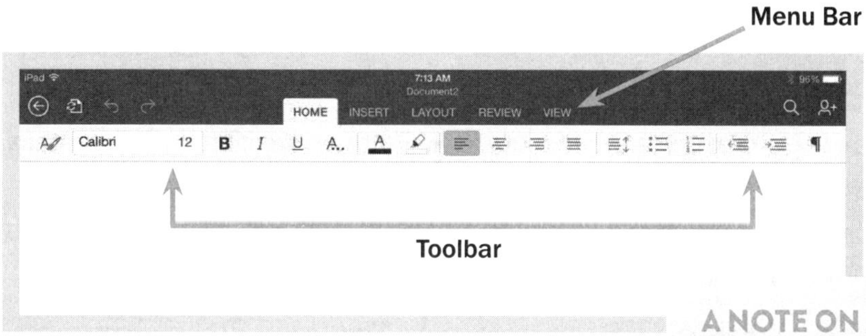

Word 365

Here are samples of different word-processing programs. All contain a Menu Bar and Toolbar. You can edit, format, and print documents with them.

What I like to do with an unfamiliar software program or app is click or tap with abandon to see what I can discover. So click or tap on each word in the Menu Bar and read the list that appears or investigate the symbols. You may not know what each of these many instructions refer to,

A NOTE ON NOTES

All computers and tablets come with pared-down word-processing software preinstalled, which may serve your needs if you're doing nothing more than simple note-taking. Notepad, WordPad, and Text Edit are perfect for a grocery list or a to-do list, but none offer enough features for you to write a letter, design an invitation, or create a travel itinerary.

but it's valuable to be familiar with what's available. When the time comes that you need one of the tasks offered in the Menu Bar, you may remember that you saw it listed when you first got to know the software. (I don't expect you to remember where you saw it, just that it exists.) If there's a feature you'd like to use later on, jot it down in case you don't remember where you originally found it.

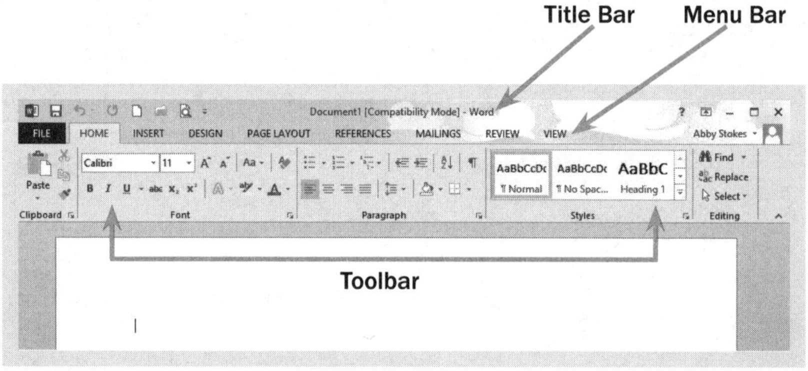

■ Microsoft Word

■ The Title Bar is where the name of your document appears. Each Menu Bar item offers you different editing functions. The icons in the Toolbar are shortcuts to items in the Menu Bar.

Nice to Meet You

Let's try creating a new document in Word on the computer. The steps here are for using Microsoft Word on a PC. If you're using a Mac, the steps will be very similar, but not exactly the same. Be flexible as you follow along.

- Move the mouse arrow onto the **New** icon, or you can move the arrow up to the word **File**, click, and move down to the word **New** or **New Blank Document** and click. A fresh, clean page will now present itself. Type the word "hi."
- The next thing we're going to do is name the document. The name of your software package appears in the Title Bar, and next to it are the words **Document 1** (or possibly **Document 2**). Keep your eye on the Title Bar. After we rename this document, the new name will appear there.

- Move the mouse arrow up to the word **File**, click, and move it down to the words **Save As**, and click. You will now get a choice of where to save the document. Click on **Computer** and, to the right of that, click on **Desktop**. A window will appear where you can rename the document. This is the moment of truth. By naming your document and giving it a home, you'll easily find it when you need it later.
- Type the word "smile," and hit either **Enter** or **Return**, or click on the **Save** button. The Title Bar has now changed to reflect the new name of the document. Nicely done.

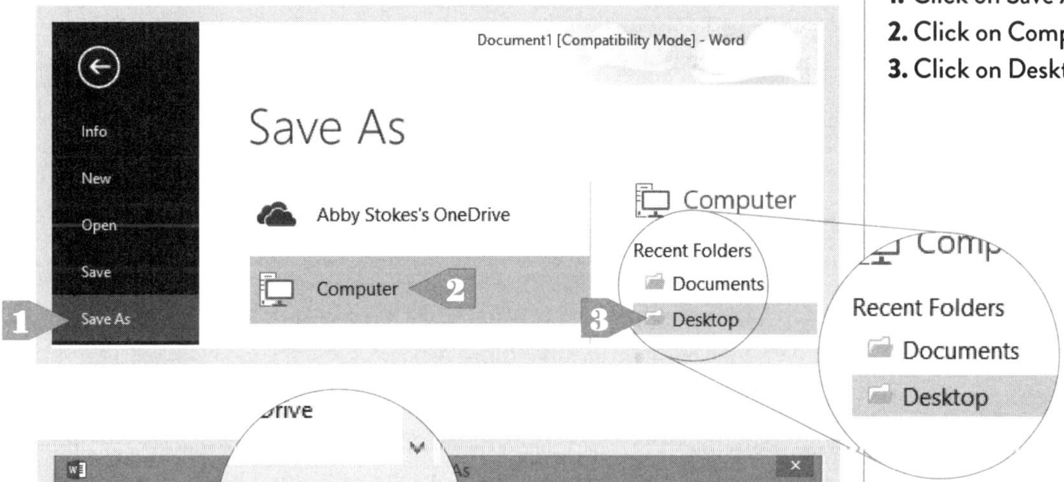

CLICK AND GO

1. Click on Save As.
2. Click on Computer.
3. Click on Desktop.

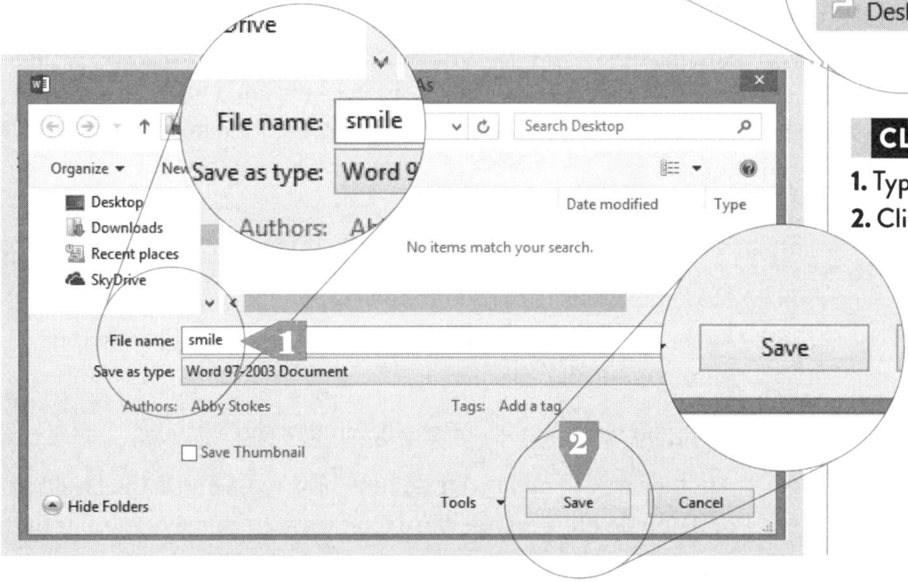

CLICK AND GO

1. Type "smile."
2. Click on Save.

OOPS—I MADE A MISTAKE

If you make a mistake, you can erase your typing (from right to left) by using the **BkSp** (Backspace) or **Delete** key. (Either can usually be found on the upper right section of your keyboard next to the ± key.) Depress it once for each letter that you want to erase. If you hold your finger down on the key, it will continue to move and delete until you lift your finger up. You definitely have more control when you depress and release the key with each character than when you hold the key down.

It's always best to name the document right at the beginning. If you get distracted or exit the program quickly and forget to name the document, you'll be stuck sifting through a bunch of Documents 1, 2, 3, and so on. It's easier to sort through documents whose names give a clue as to what they contain rather than documents with generic names.

See You Soon

I want you to now close the document that you renamed "smile." I'm having you do this so that you experience what it's like to open an existing document.

- Close the document by using the **Close Box** ☒. On some word-processing programs, there are two sets of Close Boxes. The bottom ☒ (in the Menu Bar) is for the document; the top ☒ (in the Title Bar) is for the software program itself. Or, you can move the mouse to the word **File**, click, and move down to the word **Close** and click. *Poof!* Your "smile" document is stored.

Welcome Back

To open up your "smile" document, do the following:

- Move the mouse arrow onto the **Open** icon and click. Or move the arrow to the word **File**, click, move it down to the word **Open**, and click again.
- Now you need to click on the document titled "smile."
- Another way to open your document is to find it on the Desktop and double-click on the Word icon with the name "smile." If the

ICON ALERT!
may be at the top left, instead of **File**, depending on which generation of Word is installed on your computer.

double-clicking still proves troublesome, you can single-click on "smile" and then hit the **Enter** or **Return** key or click on **Open**. Your "smile" document should appear.

Let's Get Typing

Open your "smile" document if it isn't already on the screen. You will see a flashing vertical line in the left corner of the window. This is called the **cursor**. It indicates where typing will begin.

- Please type the following:

My summer vacation

Make sure that the M is in uppercase. To do this, use the **Shift** key.

- Notice that when the mouse arrow is in the text box, it changes to an I-beam (vertical cursor— see "What It Means" on page 132) instead of the arrow; this makes it easier to position between characters. Now insert the word "hot" before the word "summer" by moving the mouse just before the "s" of "summer" and clicking once. The cursor is now before the "s" of "summer." Another way to change the location of the cursor is to use the arrow keys beside the right **Shift** key.

- Once the cursor is properly positioned, type the word "hot" and use the space bar to insert a space between the words. Did you notice that "summer" wasn't typed over but instead moved to the right to accommodate the new letters? (If this is not the case, depress and release the **Insert** key located on the top right of the keyboard.)

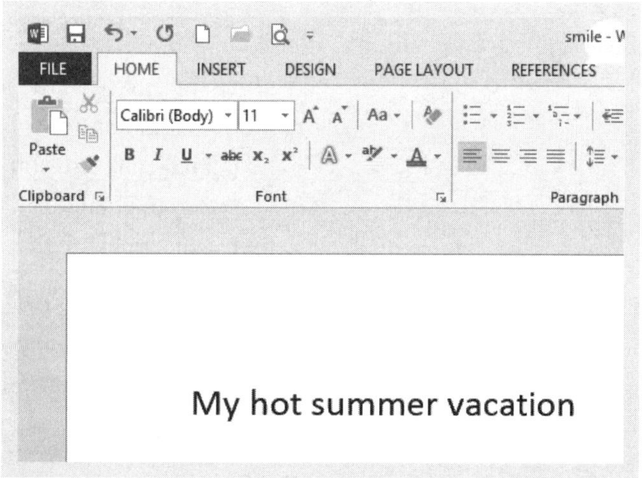

EVERYTHING IS IN CAPS. WHY?
Beware. Above the Shift key is the **Caps Lock** key. If your finger accidentally depresses **Caps Lock**, you will need to depress it again to deactivate it. For example, I HIT THE CAPS LOCK KEY AND EVERYTHING IS IN UPPERCASE. i just hit it again and everything is in lowercase.

Now your screen should read:

My hot summer vacation

Save Me!

As I mentioned earlier, it's very important that you regularly save the document you're working on. If the computer shuts off unexpectedly, the "smile" document would exist, but the new text that we just typed would be lost.

- Move the mouse arrow onto the word **File**, click, and move the arrow down to the word **Save** and click, or click on the **Save** icon in the Toolbar. It's such an important task and such an easy thing to execute.

Now we're going to move on to some editing tools. This is where the computer proves much more efficient than a typewriter. If you made a mistake with a typewriter or changed your mind about how you wanted your document to look, you would have no choice but to retype it. Not with a computer; it allows you to edit within the document before you print it out.

What if you decided that you wanted to move the first paragraph of a letter to the end of the letter? This would be accomplished by "cutting" the text from where it is and "pasting" it to a different location. Follow along and you'll see what I mean.

- Move the cursor to the left of the word "hot." Do this with the mouse (remember to click) or with the arrow keys. Before the text can be altered, you must inform the computer of what text you want to change. This is accomplished by highlighting the text. You can highlight the word "hot" several different ways.

Option 1. Click and drag the mouse arrow over the word "hot" and then release the mouse button. (This is tricky at first, but it becomes easier with practice.)

Option 2. Set the cursor at the start of the word "hot," depress the **Shift** key (on the left side of your keyboard), and hold it

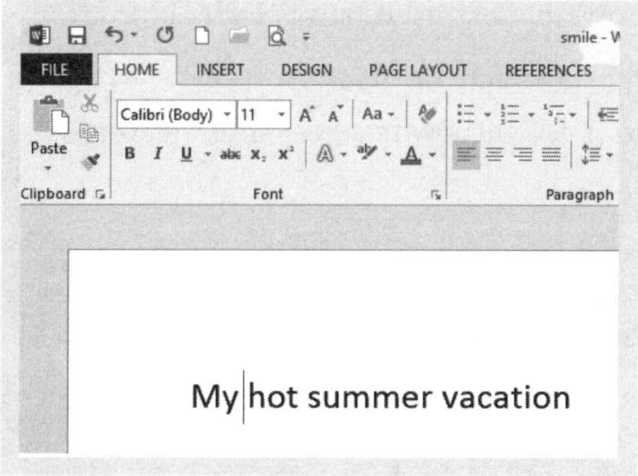

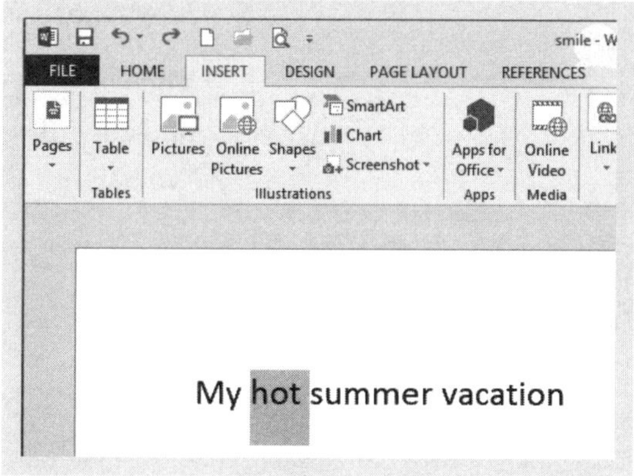

The word "hot" is now highlighted. This means the computer is waiting for your instructions for what to do with the word "hot."

down. While **Shift** is held down, use the **arrow keys** (on the right side of the keyboard) to move across the word.

Option 3. Move the mouse to the center of the word and double-click.

Using one of these methods, the word should now be highlighted. Of the three options, number 2 is the easiest to execute, but try them all and see which you prefer. You can highlight a single word, several words, or entire paragraphs and pages. Whatever you highlight will take on the changes that you instruct the computer to perform.

You Must Cut Before You Paste

Now that you have highlighted the word "hot," you are able to either cut and paste text or copy and paste text. When you cut text, the original text disappears and is held in the brain of the computer until you tell the computer where to paste it.

- Move the mouse arrow to the word **Home** or **Edit** in the Menu Bar, click, and then move it down to the scissors icon or the word **Cut**, and click. Right now the word "hot" has disappeared because the computer is storing the word until you tell it where to paste it. Now comes the paste!
- Move the cursor one space after the "n" of "vacation" by clicking the mouse after the "n" and then using the space bar.

IF YOU GOOF

If you goofed when you tried to highlight, fear not. Simply move the mouse to a blank spot in the text box and click once—that will undo any highlighting. Go back and try again.

- Move the mouse arrow to the word **Home** or **Edit** and click.
- Then move it down to the clipboard icon or the word **Paste** and click. The word "hot" will now reappear after the word "vacation."

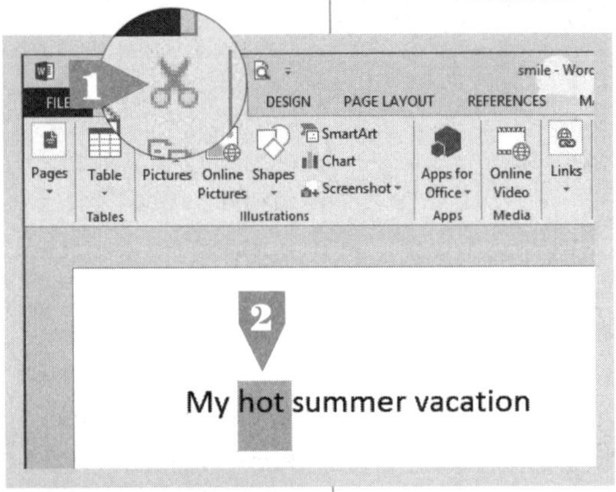

CLICK AND GO

1. Click cut.
2. The word "hot" has disappeared.

CLICK AND GO

1. Click after "n." Hit the space bar.
2. Click paste.

The word "hot" will now appear after "vacation."

Copy That

Instead of cutting text and pasting it, you might want to repeat a section of your document in another location. This is accomplished by copying and pasting the selected text.

Let's try to copy and paste.

- Go back to highlighting options 1 through 3 (pages 248–249), pick one of the techniques, and highlight the entire sentence. If you choose number 3, it takes a little practice, but it's fast; place the cursor in the middle of the sentence and click the mouse three times in rapid succession. Double-click highlights a word—triple-click highlights the whole line.

- Move the mouse arrow onto the copy icon and click, or click on **Edit** in the **Menu Bar**, and then move the arrow down to the word **Copy** and click. The sentence is still on the screen, but the computer has a copy of it stored until you tell it where you want it pasted.
- Place the cursor at the end of the sentence and click. Hit the **Enter** or **Return** key.
- Move the mouse onto the clipboard paste icon or to the word **Edit** and click.
- Then move down to the word **Paste** and click.
- Repeat the three preceding actions five times. You should have a total of seven sentences on your screen. We'll use them next to show how many ways you can change the look of your text.

In Chapter 17 on page 279, I'll show you how to copy and paste on a tablet. To learn more editing functions on a tablet, visit *AskAbbyStokes.com*.

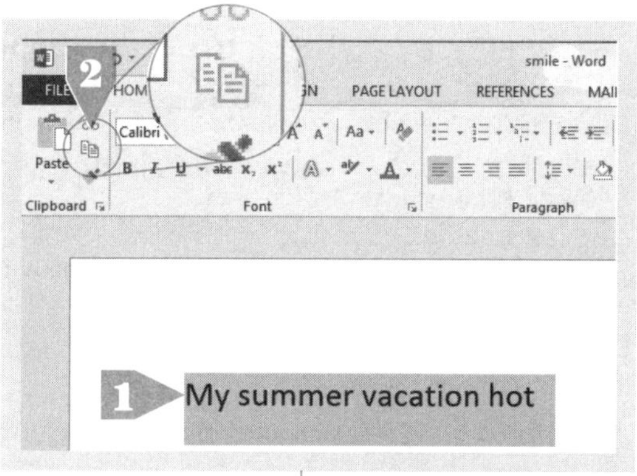

CLICK AND GO

1. Highlight entire sentence.
2. Click copy.

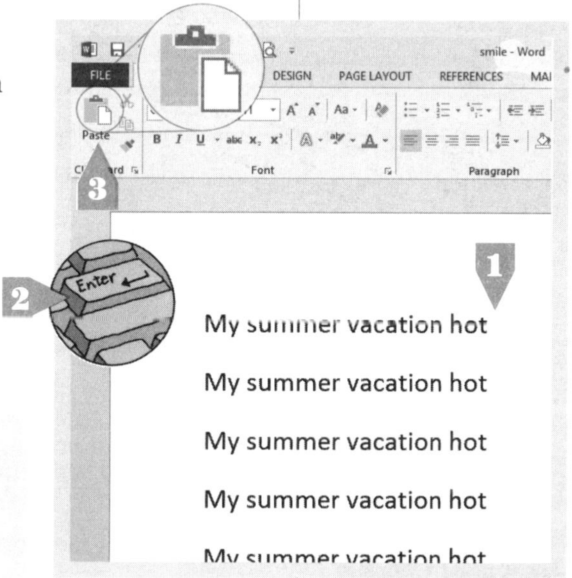

CLICK AND GO

1. Click after "hot."
2. Hit Enter or Return key.
3. Click paste. Repeat five times.

NOW SHE TELLS ME . . .

There are a few shortcuts to highlighting.

- If you click once, this is where the cursor will be positioned in the text.
- If you click twice on a word, the word will be highlighted.
- If you click three times on a word, the line or paragraph that contains the word will be highlighted.

For the downloadable guide **Word-Processing on a Tablet,** visit ***AskAbbyStokes.com***. Click on Resources at the top, then click on Helpful Guides, and lastly click on Guide #3.

Finish Your Sentence

We're going to make this into a complete sentence.

- Place the cursor just to the left of the "h" of "hot" in the first sentence, click to activate, and type the word "was." Your screen should now read:

My summer vacation was hot.

- Put a period at the end of the sentence by placing the cursor after the last word and hitting the period key. Alternatively, you could get to the end of the sentence by holding down the arrow key or the **End** key on the keyboard, and then adding the period.

Choices, Choices, Choices

There are so many different things that can be done to change the look of the text. All are done by highlighting text, which is a fundamental element in word-processing. I'll run through a series of editing choices. Try each one now. Then come back later and repeat the process until it starts to jell.

- Using whichever option you prefer (pages 248–249), highlight the word "My" in the first sentence. Move the mouse arrow up to the **Bold** icon **B** in the Toolbar and click. The word is now set in boldface: **My**.
- Highlight the word "vacation" in the same sentence, move the mouse arrow to the **Italics** icon *I* in the Toolbar, and click once. The word *vacation* is now in italics.
- Highlight the word "hot" in the same sentence, and move the mouse arrow to the **Underline** icon U in the Toolbar. The word <u>hot</u> is now underlined.

Note: You can change each word back to its original state by highlighting it and then re-clicking on the icon you used to make the change.

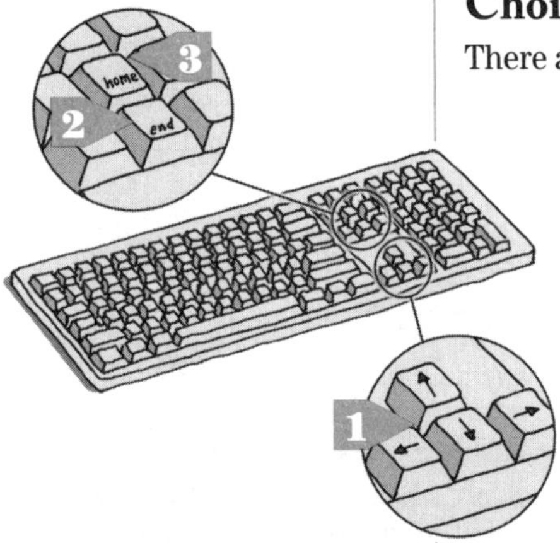

CLICK AND GO

1. Use arrow keys to move the cursor.
2. Hit End to move to the end of a line.
3. Hit Home to move to the beginning of a line.

- Using whichever method you prefer (pages 248–249), highlight the entire second sentence. Click on the **Center** icon in the Toolbar. The sentence is now in the center of the line.
- Highlight the entire third sentence. Click on the **Align Right** icon in the Toolbar. The sentence is now flush right on the page.
- Highlight the entire fourth sentence. Click on the **Align Left** icon in the Toolbar. The sentence remains flush left on the page.
- Highlight the entire fifth sentence. Click on the arrow Calibri (Body) to the right of **Font** in the Toolbar, revealing the different fonts (typefaces) (see page 254). Use the Scroll Bar to view them. Click on whichever font appeals to you.

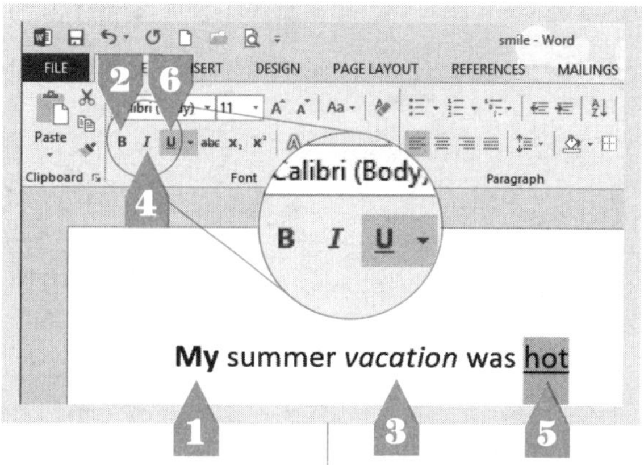

CLICK AND GO

1. Highlight "My."
2. Click on **B** for bold.
3. Highlight "vacation."
4. Click on *I* for italic.
5. Highlight "hot."
6. Click on U for underline.

The sentence could look like *My summer vacation was hot* or **My summer vacation was hot**, or countless other ways, depending on which font you choose to use.

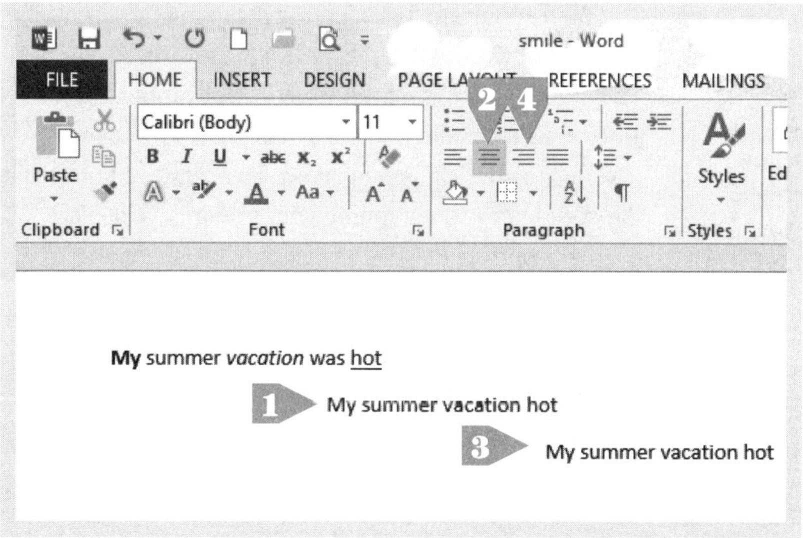

CLICK AND GO

1. Highlight second sentence.
2. Click on for Center.
3. Highlight third sentence.
4. Click on for Align Right.

Play around with your document to try out all of the many editing and formatting possibilities.

CLICK AND GO

1. Click down arrow.
2. Use Scroll Bar.
3. Click on desired font.

■ **After you highlight text, the font can also be changed by clicking on Format, then Font.**

- Highlight the entire sixth sentence. Click on the arrow ▼ to the right of the font size box in the Toolbar. Click on whichever size you want to see. This sentence could be My summer vacation was hot or My summer vacation was hot.

Play with the different styles and sizes of fonts. But if you've been at the computer for a long time, sit back, take a breath, and look around the room. When you've been focusing on the computer screen for a while, it's a good idea to give your eyes a break.

Repeat the exercises in this chapter as often as you can. It's only through repetition that you will become comfortable with your word-processing software.

Smarter Than the Average Bear

Your word-processing software is designed to make life easier. It even checks your spelling! Highlight the word "vacation" and retype it, spelling it "vaction." Note that when a word is highlighted and you start typing, the highlighted word disappears and the new word replaces it.

With some word-processing programs, a potentially misspelled word will have a red squiggly line under it. This is a heads-up that the word doesn't appear in the software's dictionary. You may also notice that some text may be underlined in green. This lets you know that the computer is questioning your grammar. Cheeky!

Let's perform a spell check on your document.

- Move the mouse arrow onto the **Spell Check** icon in the Menu Bar and click. Alternatively, you can click on the **Review** tab and then click on **Spelling & Grammar**. The spell-checker will review the document for errors. In this case, it will pick up that "vaction" is not in the dictionary and it will suggest "vacation."

HELP

If you're ever stumped about how to do something and need help, simply move the mouse arrow onto the word **Help** in the Menu Bar and click. From there you can get all kinds of information. There may also be the option of clicking on a question mark **?**, then clicking where you need help, and the screen will show some helpful hints pertaining to what you are doing.

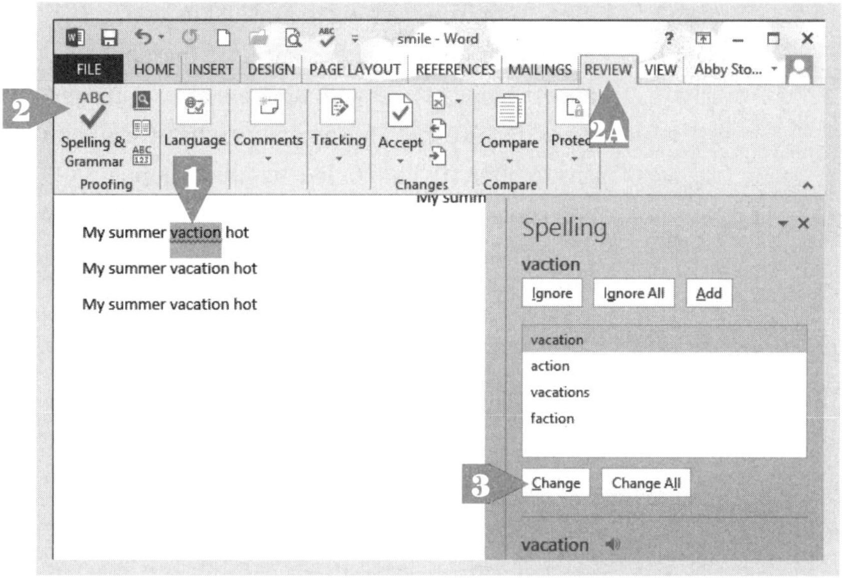

CLICK AND GO

1. Misspell "vacation" as "vaction."
2. Click on Spell Check icon.

   or

2A. Click Review, then Spelling & Grammar.

3. Click Change.

■ **Microsoft Word (and most other word-processing programs) lets you spell-check a document. Miraculous!**

- Click on the word **Change** or **Replace** in the sidebar. The computer will make the change and then either continue the spell check or let you know the spell check is complete.

The computer's dictionary may not contain a word that you have typed (such as a person's name or a technical term) and will signal that it appears to be wrong and should be corrected. However, if you know it's correct and should not be changed, you would click on **Ignore** or **Skip**.

When you're getting to know Microsoft Word, I suggest you click on each tab in the Menu Bar. Let your mouse rest on each item in the Toolbar without clicking, and a bubble will appear with a description

■ **The Menu and Toolbars of Microsoft Word 2013**

Menu Bar

Toolbar

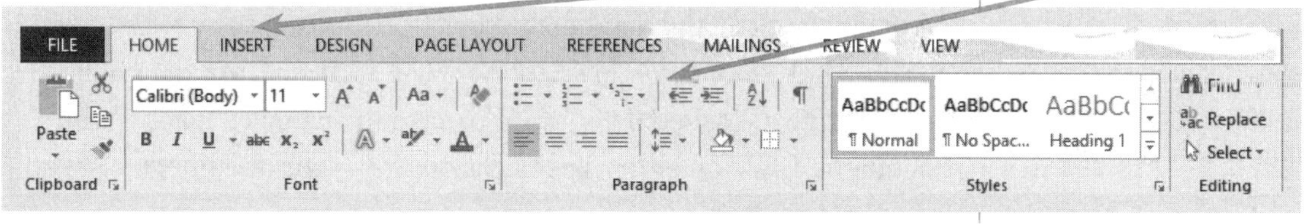

of the tool. You're going to find all kinds of goodies, such as page formatting, a thesaurus, and the ability to set up bullet points, to name just a few. Don't expect to remember what each menu has to offer. It's kind of like window-shopping—you can go back and look at what really appeals to you later.

IMPORTANT CONCEPT

You must always let the computer know where you want it to take action (accomplished by clicking on or highlighting the area), and then you must tell the computer what action to take.

A Souvenir

The last thing we'll do in this chapter is print your first document.

- Make sure your printer is on.
- Move the mouse arrow to the word **File** in the Menu Bar and click. Then move it down to the word **Print** and click. Alternatively, you can click on the Print icon, if you see it.
- There are several print options available in the Print window. You can print the current page that you're working on, all the pages of the document, or select individual or groups of pages. You can also print as many copies of the document as you want. If you want to have one copy of all the pages in your document and the Print window is open, simply hit the **Enter** or the **Return** key or click on **Print**. The **Print** icon won't offer all the choices that the **Print** window does, but it is a fast way to print the entire document.

CLICK AND GO

1. In the menu bar, click File or .
2. Click Print.
3. Click OK or Print.

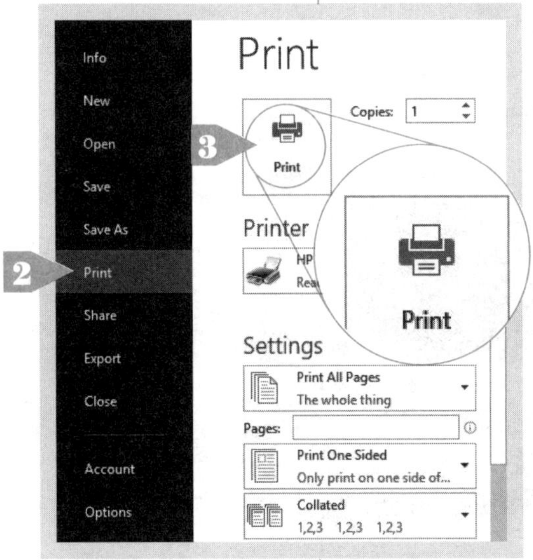

■ The Print window allows you to choose which pages to print and copies you want.

You Deserve a Break Today

It's time to close the document. Move the mouse arrow to the word **File**, click, and move down to the word **Exit** or **Quit** and click. You will now be asked if you want to save the changes made to the document. Click on either **Yes** or **Save**. Now your document is saved on your hard drive.

A CAUTIONARY TALE

Here's the scenario: You've been writing for hours, so transfixed by your own words that you neglected to click **File**, then **Save** to save your work periodically. (A bad habit you must break—it's essential to save regularly.) The phone rings—it's your neighbor, and she desperately needs you because her toe is stuck in the bathtub drain. (Strangely, this is not the first time you've received this SOS, but that's another book.)

In your haste to attend to her, you click to close the document you've toiled over. This question is posed to you: "Do you want to save the changes to . . ." What do you do? Hmmm . . . the right answer is stay calm, move your hands away from the computer, and read the question. If you want to save the changes, you click **Yes**. However, let's say that because you were in a rush to go to the aid of your neighbor, you clicked **No**. Tragically, all of the work you did since the last time you saved your changes is irretrievably lost. Gone. The fact is, it would have been better to walk away from the computer and not answer the question at all, rather than to answer it without thinking it through. The option of **Cancel** would bring you back to the document, neither saving nor losing your changes. It cancels the action of closing the document.

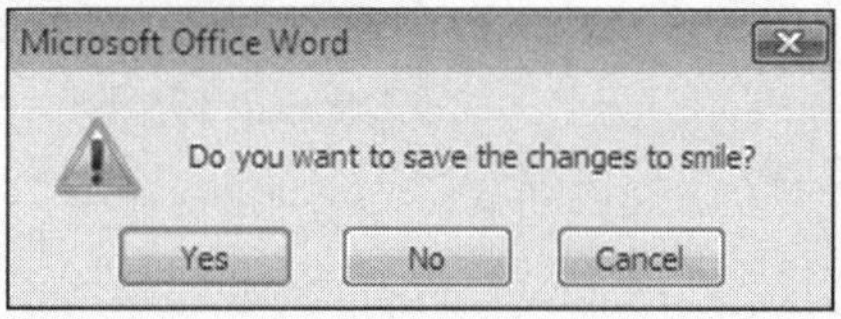

Here's the drill for the future: When the computer warns, notifies, or asks you about something and you don't know how best to respond, don't respond at all. If you're really flummoxed, leave the computer alone and call someone who might know the best action to take. If they aren't home, leave a message. Wait for them to call you back. The computer isn't going anywhere.

These are just the basic tools that your word-processing program offers. As you work more in the program, you will get better acquainted with what else it can do. If you ever get stuck, you can try to call the software manufacturer's number for technical support. If your call isn't fruitful, ask a friend or family member, or look in the local paper for computer groups or classes.

Word Processing with a Tablet

If you want to word-process on a tablet instead of a computer, Google Docs can be installed from your app store onto any tablet.

Google Docs is free, but you must have a Gmail account in order to access it. That doesn't mean that you need to change which email account you use. You'll simply have another account. (I recommend having two email accounts anyway. See page 274 for more information about the benefits of having two email addresses.)

You could also use Pages, Apple's word-processing alternative; at this time, it is exclusively available on the iPad and other Apple products. Pages doesn't offer as many editing options as Word or Google Docs, but you may not need more than it offers, and it is free. Microsoft offers Office 365, at a cost by subscription, which allows you to use Word (and other programs, such as the presentation program PowerPoint and Excel spreadsheets) on any tablet.

If you intend to do a lot of writing, keep in mind that the smaller screen and the touch screen keyboard on a tablet aren't as comfortable to use as a larger desktop or laptop computer would be. You may want to investigate an external keyboard that you can use with your tablet for easier typing.

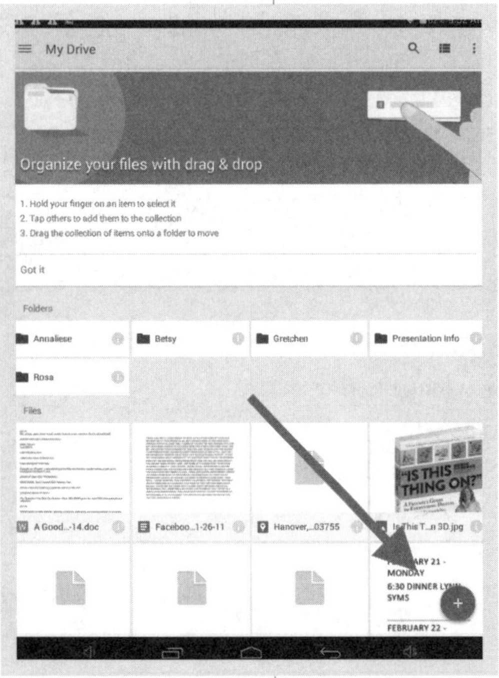

The instructions that follow are for the programs on specific tablets. If you're using either Google Docs or Pages on a different type of tablet, what you see may vary slightly, but the steps will be very similar. Let's access both programs and see what features they offer.

Introducing Google Docs on an Android

You access **Google Docs** from **Google Drive.**

To open a new document:

1. Tap on the **red plus sign** in the bottom right corner of Google Drive.

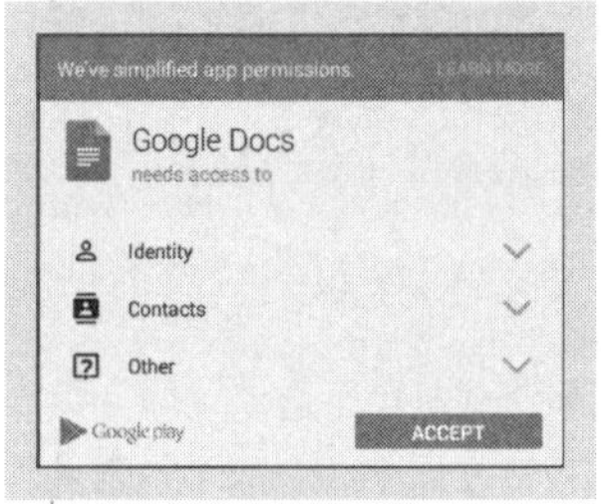

2. You may need to **Accept** whatever terms or permissions may have been updated.

3. Here are some of the editing choices offered by **Google Docs**.

 **Undo**—Deletes the last thing you typed.

 **Redo**—Repeats the last thing you typed.

 **Bold**—Makes text bold.

 **Italic**—Make the text italic.

 **Underline**—Underlines the text.

 **Format**—Opens a menu that offers you many formatting choices for the text as well as the document.

 **Insert**—Allows you to insert a table or a hyperlink.

 Three stacked dots—Brings you to more options.

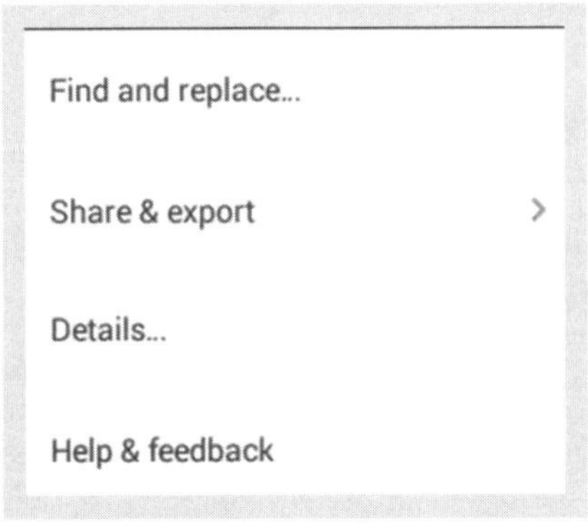

Find and replace—Lets you search for a specific word or phrase and replace it with another.

The Share & Export choices are accessed by tapping on the arrow to the right.

Share—Allows you to share this particular document with anyone of your choosing. You simply type in their email address, write a message if you want, and that person will receive an email invitation to view the document.

Send a copy—Allows you to choose the format (PDF or Word) of your document and then send it directly by email.

Save as Word—Changes the document to be a Word document instead of a Google Doc.

Print—Allows you to print the document from any nearby printer with bluetooth capability.

Make a copy—Creates a copy of the existing document.

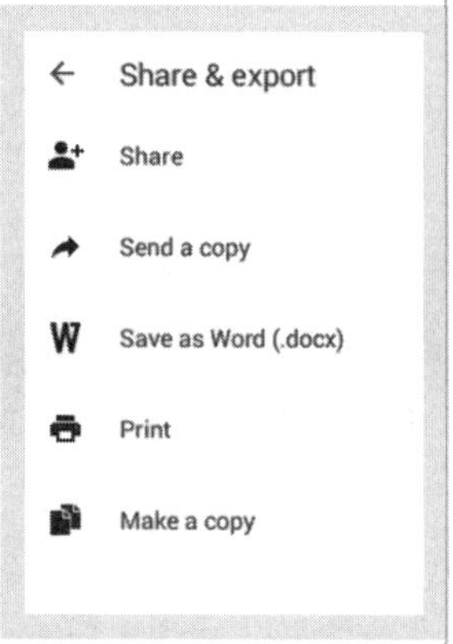

Use the arrow to the left of **Share & Export** to go back to the previous menu. You can tap anywhere on the document to get rid of the menu.

Tap on the word **Done** on the top left to save your work on the document either for good or just for the time being.

You're not finished yet. Now you must name the document. See page 414 for tips on how to best organize and name documents with Google Drive. A name should be specific enough that you don't need to open the document in order to know its contents.

To name your document:

1. Tap on the words **Untitled Document** in the top left.

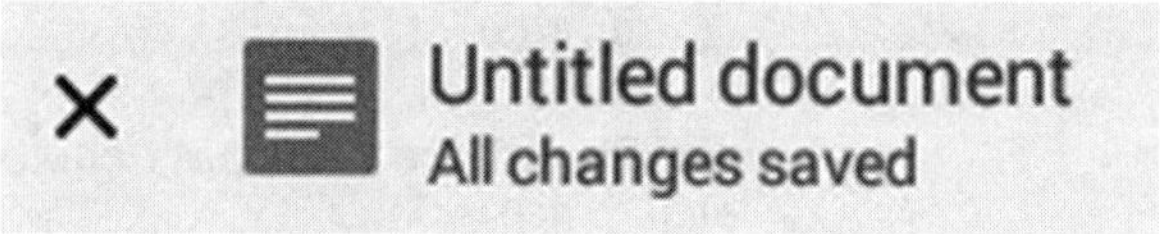

2. Type the desired name.
3. Tap **OK**.

Well done!

Introducing Pages on an iPad

Tap on the **Pages** app to open the program. 

To open a new document:

1. Tap on the **plus sign.**
2. Tap on **Blank** (unless you want to choose any of the other Templates offered).

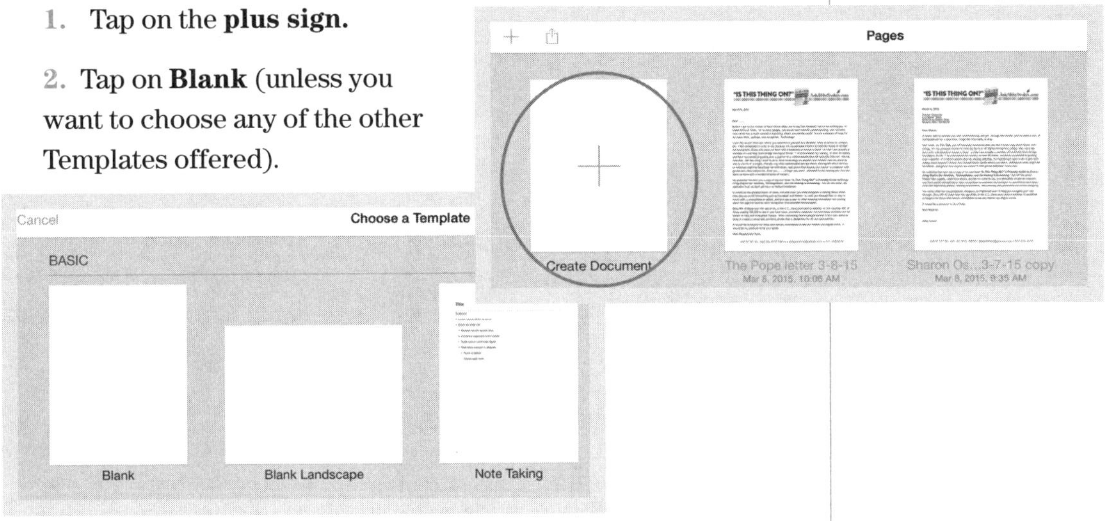

Here are some of the editing choices offered by **Pages**. These run along the bottom of the document.

Fonts—Gives you a long list of possible fonts. Be sure to scroll up and down to see all your choices.

A 11 A **Font size**—Can be changed by tapping on the larger or smaller A.

B I U Here you can change the text to **Bold**, **Italics**, or **Underline**.

≣ **Align Text**—Gives you the option of aligning left, center, or right.

\+ Here you can **Add** a **Page Break**, a **Line Break**, a **Column Break**, or a **Footnote.**

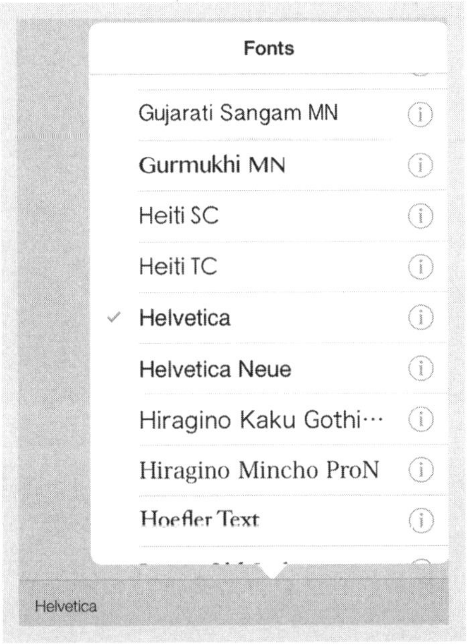

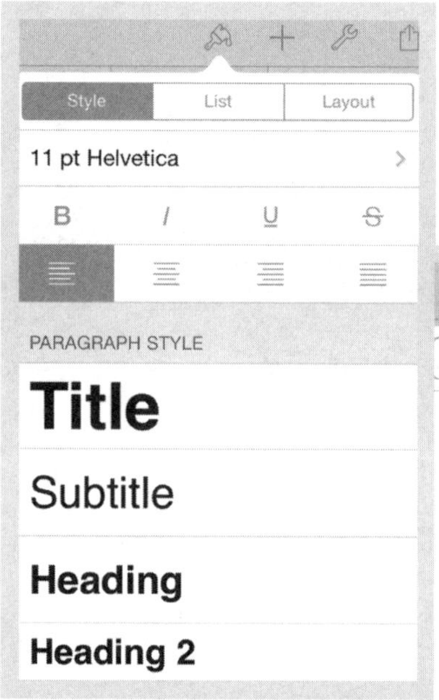

There's also a menu in the upper right corner. Here are the offerings you'll find there:

Format—Lets you format the font as well as the document layout.

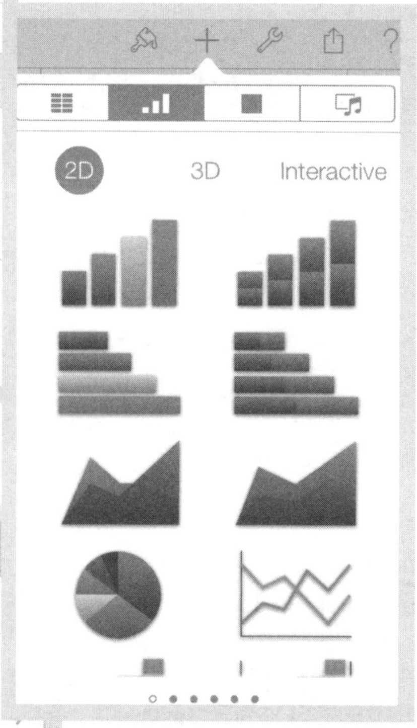

Add—If you tap on this, you can include **Tables**, **Charts**, **Text Boxes**, an **Image**, or a **Video**.

Tools—Opens a menu where you can search your document using **Find,** choose the **Document Setup**, change your **Settings**, as well as **Print** if you are within range of a Bluetooth-capable printer.

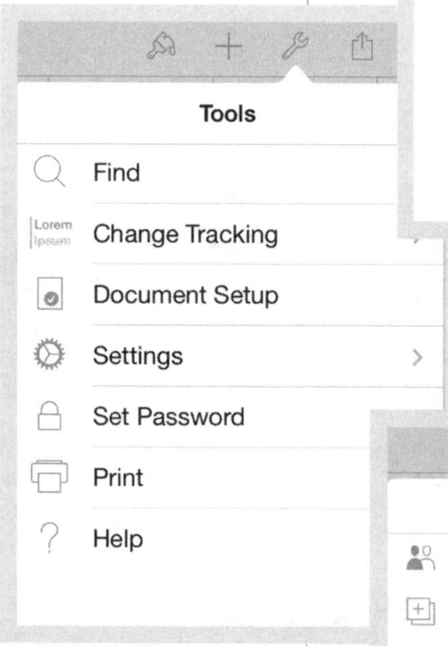

Upload—This symbol offers a menu where you can **Share** your document by either **Sharing a Link via iCloud** or **Sending a Copy**. Here you can also open the document in a different program by tapping on **Open in Another App**.

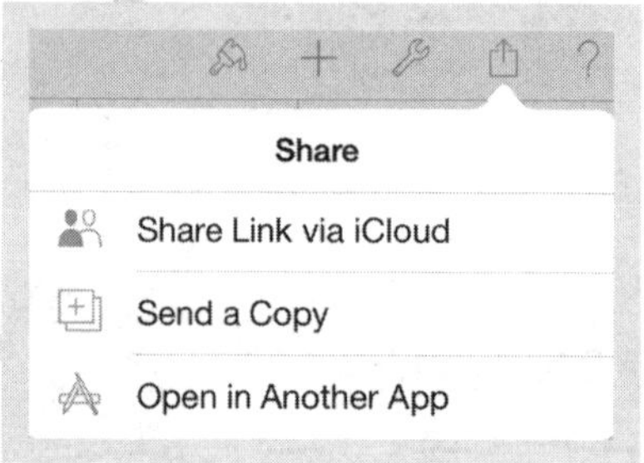

You're not finished yet. Now you must name the document. Remember that a name should be specific enough that you don't need to open the document in order to know its contents.

To name your document:

1. Tap on **Documents** in the top left.
2. Tap on the existing name of the document, which is likely to be the word **Blank**.
3. Type in the new name.
4. Tap **Done** in the top right corner.

Well done!

What Can I Say?

At this juncture in the book, I want you to take a break. It's been a pleasure joining you thus far on this exciting adventure. Try to get on the computer every day for at least half an hour to keep from getting rusty. There's also a lot of very helpful information in the back of this book. Be sure to give it the once-over so you know what resources are available. Visit my website, *AskAbbyStokes.com*, for additional guidance. If you haven't visited my website yet, please do; you can simply stop by to say Hi, watch some of the tutorial videos, or just play around to get accustomed to your computer. When you're feeling at home with your computer and are game for more, turn the page. I'll be waiting for you whenever you're ready.

Q: I tried to edit a document I wrote, but when I typed, the computer kept deleting/replacing the old text instead of just inserting the new text where I wanted to type. What is happening?

A: There is a simple fix for this very frustrating problem. Depress and release the **Insert** key on your keyboard, and all will be remedied.

Q: What is the Toolbar? I don't see one.

A: At the top of every window there is a Title Bar; below it, there is usually a Menu Bar and a Toolbar. If the Toolbar is missing, click on **View**, then click on **Toolbars**. Now click to the left of **Standard**. Repeat the same steps and click on **Formatting**. A check should appear by both.

Q: Where can I get more instruction on using Microsoft Word?

A: Unfortunately, the manufacturer does not provide a manual. You may notice the word **Help** in the Menu Bar. Help isn't always helpful, but sometimes it can be. Try it. Microsoft Word doesn't typically come with a tutorial, but if your version offers one, watch it. Lots and lots of instructional books are available for purchase, but before you buy one, sit down with it and see if it speaks your language or that of a computer geek. If you can't understand the book, it won't help you understand the computer. Another option is to contact your local library, senior or community center, or community college to see if they offer Microsoft Word classes. Also, be brave and click on the items in the Menu Bar to see how much you can understand on your own.

Q: My document keeps printing over and over again. Why and how do I stop it?

A: You control your computer and printer. The document is printing multiple times because you instructed the printer to do so. My guess is that when the printer didn't immediately spit out your document you clicked on **Print** again and, maybe, again and again. The printer is just doing what you asked it to. The simplest way to stop a print job is to turn off the printer. See page 506 in Chapter 25 for how to delete print jobs from the computer.

those skills can be used with good or bad intentions. The connotation of a hacker is usually negative and refers to someone who breaks through security codes on the computer to access otherwise protected information. Why would someone choose to hack? Some hack to gain access to a cache of credit card numbers or to gather personal data from a computer. But others hack just because they can. In the computer geek community, there is a prestige to being able to break a code. Hackers don't necessarily do any damage, but they make their mark in the hackers' hall of fame.

What can you do to protect your computer from hackers, identity theft, and other scams? Read on.

"I love the idea of having access to so many different things on the Internet. I just want to be assured that no one in turn has access to my personal information." —*Rich*

Avoid an Identity Crisis

Identity theft is not as attributable to computer use as we are led to believe. Most identity theft occurs the old-fashioned way—by sleight of hand. Your purse or wallet containing vital information about you is stolen. Your trash is rummaged through, revealing your credit card numbers and more. You give information over the phone to someone who sounds legitimate but is not. Here are ways you can protect yourself.

Guard Your Social

The key to stealing someone's identity is his or her Social Security number. You should *never* carry your Social Security number in your wallet. For some, doing so may be an old habit, but it's time to break the habit. Your full name, date of birth, and your mother's maiden name are all public record. With a little investigation, such information can be uncovered. But your Social Security number, which is often used by financial institutions as identification, is not public record. Give your Social Security number to a thief, and identity theft becomes a cakewalk. Be aware that your Social Security number appears on your Medicare card. Make a copy of your card and leave the original at home. Black out all the numbers on the copy except the last four. Bring the original Medicare card only when you visit a doctor for the first time.

Keep Copies

Make copies of the front and back of your driver's license and your credit cards. Keep the photocopies in a safe place. If your wallet is stolen, this information will facilitate the calls you should make immediately to cancel your cards. File a police report. This reinforces the validity of your claim of loss to the credit card companies. Call credit-reporting organizations to place a fraud alert on your name and Social Security number.

Here are some phone numbers to get you started:

Equifax: 800-525-6285

Experian: 888-397-3742

TransUnion: 800-680-7289

Social Security Administration (fraud line): 800-269-0271

It's also a good idea to check your credit report annually to be sure you're not carrying a bad report due to fraud or an error. Visit *annualcreditreport.com* for a free credit report.

Be Smart About What You Toss

When the time comes to throw away expired credit cards, always cut along the magnetic strip. The magnetic strip, when left intact, contains all the pertinent information for that credit card, making it way too easy for a thief to use it. Then cut up the rest of the card into small pieces and distribute them over time into different waste bins. Without sounding too paranoid, the same should be done with any correspondence revealing your credit card or Social Security numbers. Maybe this is the year to ask Santa for a paper shredder.

Mum's the Word on the Phone

What about the seemingly lovely person who calls you at home to verify information for your own protection or to enter you in a contest or to send you a promotional gift? Never, *never*, never release personal information over the phone. You have no idea who is really at the other end of the line. Have the caller give you the information to confirm, or, better yet, hang up and call the bank or wherever they claim to be calling from. That's the only way to be sure of who you are actually speaking to.

None of the scenarios just described involved a computer at all, but somehow computers receive the blame for identity theft. However, be equally cautious of dangers when surfing the net.

> **PHISHING (WEBOPEDIA DEFINITION)**
>
> **(fish´ing) (n.)** The act of sending an email falsely claiming to be an established, legitimate enterprise in an attempt to scam the user into surrendering private information that will be used for identity theft. The email directs the user to visit a website where they are asked to update personal information, such as passwords and credit card, Social Security, and bank account numbers, that the legitimate organization already has. The website, however, is bogus and set up only to steal the user's information.

Phishing Is So Very Fishy

A week doesn't go by now that I don't receive a fishy email—that is, an email that appears to be from my email service or bank and that carries an anxiety-inducing message. And at tax time, I even got an email that looked like it came from the IRS! These are all phishing scams.

A month ago I received a phone call from Switzerland. It was a student of mine. I don't want to reveal his identity, so let's call him Barnaby. Barnaby uses Yahoo as his web-based email service. He went to the expense of making an international call to me because he could no longer access his email account and suspected he knew why but wanted my advice. It all started with an email he opened that looked like it was from Yahoo, much like the one at right.

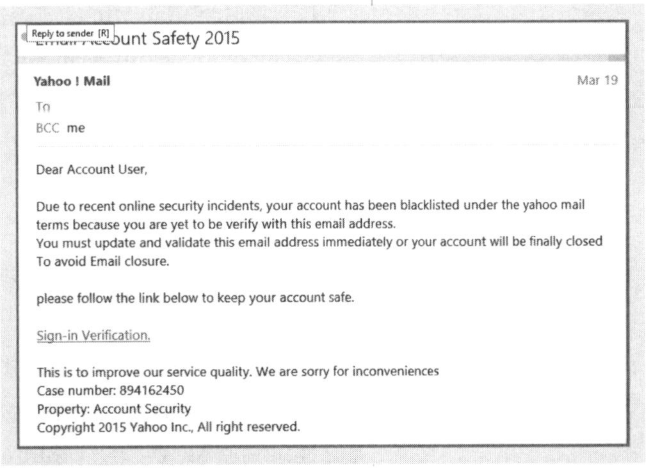

Geez. Looks serious, doesn't it? I know I don't want to be "blacklisted" and I certainly don't want my email account closed. Well, the real problem is that Yahoo did *not* send this email.

This is a "phishing" email—much like fishing, but with a "ph" not an "f." The person who sent the email at right is trolling to see if he (or she) can fool anyone into clicking on "Sign-in Verification." If you click through, the next page asks you to

MERRIAM-WEBSTER'S DEFINITION OF PHISHING

A scam by which an email user is duped into revealing personal or confidential information that the scammer can use illicitly.

type your screen name and password. Unfortunately, once you've done that, you haven't verified your email account for security, as suggested; instead you have revealed your password to the scammer.

You may not be able to tell the difference between what you might normally fill out when on a website and a phishing scam—except for one very important detail: Your email service or bank will never ask you to confirm your password in an email or through a link in an email. Let me say that again. **Your email service or bank will never ask you to confirm your password in an email or through a link in an email**. So, no matter how familiar or scary an email may look, do not **ever** confirm your password in an email or through a link in an email.

Unfortunately, Barnaby did just that. He typed in his email address and his password. The next time he went to sign into his account, he wasn't able to access his email. Within a few hours an email was sent from Barnaby's hijacked Yahoo account, written by the "phisher," to everyone in the address book. The email, appearing to come from Barnaby, stated that while traveling he had been robbed and was stranded without his wallet. It asked the recipient(s) to please send money using Western Union. Now I know you're saying, "Who would fall for that?" Truth be told, many could. And each phishing email is different—each one more compelling than the last.

Your first line of defense is to **never confirm your password in an email or through a link in an email**. (I promise I won't say it again. You get the point.) If you discover that you've unwittingly succumbed to a phishing scam, here are some resources at your disposal:

The U.S. Computer Emergency Readiness Team: *us-cert.gov/nav/report_phishing.html*

You can forward the email to The Anti-Phishing Working Group: *reportphishing@antiphishing.org*. The site is *antiphishing.org*, and the APWG is a volunteer organization devoted to helping people identify and avoid scams.

Here are some hard-to-find phone numbers. As the email services listed below are free, they have no obligation to offer tech support, but they should respond to your email account being hijacked by a phisher.

AOL: 800-827-6364	Microsoft Hotmail: 800-642-7676*
Yahoo: 800-318-0612	Google/Gmail: 650-253-0000

One last note and then we'll talk more about other ways to detect an email scam. You can imagine a phishing scammer's glee when they discover that your email password is the same as your bank PIN. Your bank password should be used exclusively for the bank and not for anything else

How to Detect an Email Scam

Once you recognize the potential for phishy people trying to lure you into responding to their emails, what else can you do? Look at it this way. Do you open the door to your home to strangers? I didn't think so. Then why would you open an email from someone you don't know? Let's learn how you can evaluate whether an email is coming from a legitimate sender *before* you open it with some examples of the type of phishy emails that are out there.

Here are two examples of emails that look legitimate but are actually phishing.

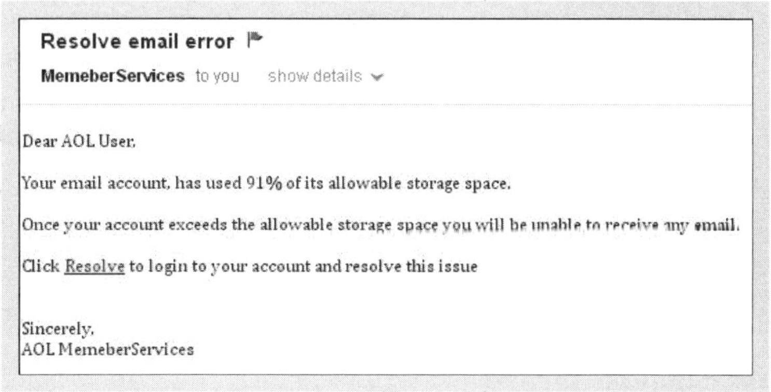

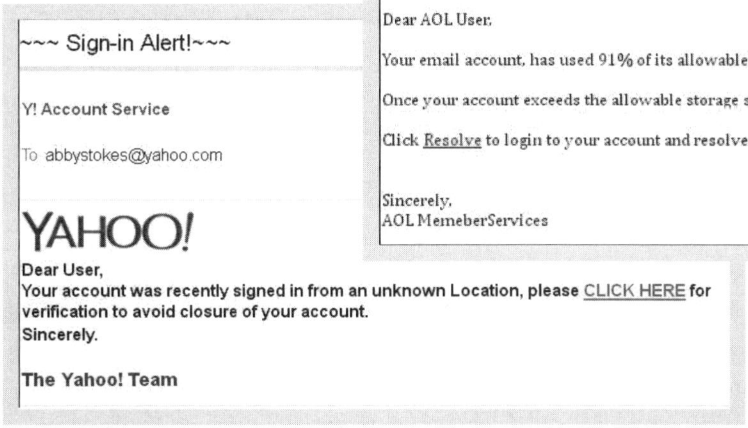

* Note: You will be directed to support.microsoft.com where you can live chat.

First of all, remember to pause before action. Do not click on any link! At least not yet. Let's take a look at the examples on the next page and check out who *really* sent the email.

You'll notice that the senders above and below look very serious—**"Sign-In Alert!," "Mail Support," "Resolve Email Error,"** etc. Let's dig just a little deeper. Move your mouse arrow over the sender's name. If the sender's email address doesn't appear, click on the name.

Well, looky looky there. Highly suspicious, right? The email addresses exposed are not those of people working in security for my email provider. I'm certainly not going to click on the link in the email sent by Uncleluckyg@aol.com, Jawsiii555@aol.com, or chrisbrown@216parasigs.org.uk, and neither should you. If you receive an email like the above and expose that it's a fraudulent sender, click on **Junk** or **Spam**, not Trash. We want to send these kinds of emails through your email server's filter so they can try to prevent further contact.

Now, when you receive an email that has a sender's name that you *do recognize* (a friend, business associate, or family member), but the email is suspicious (a vague email suggesting that you click on a link), be sure to check and see if the sender really is who you think it is. Do this by clicking on the sender's name to expose the email address.

Below is a perfect example. My name appears as the sender AND in the subject (which tips me off right away that something is fishy). Nothing in the body of the email is personal or specific to me or the recipient—it's just a ploy to get me to click.

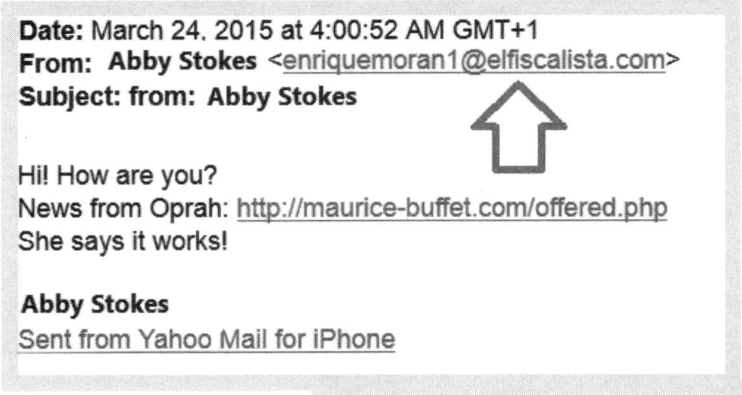

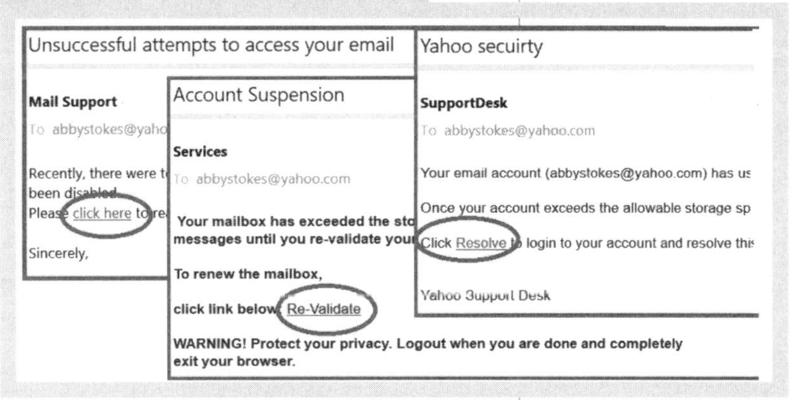

If you receive an email like the one above, **do not click on the link!** Instead, check and see who *really* sent you the email. In this case, after clicking on my name, we see that the email actually came from enriquemoran1@elfiscalista.com. Whoever that is. Again, your next move would be to click on **Junk** or **Spam**, not Trash. You won't be banishing your friend, coworker, or family member's email address to your Junk folder, but instead the rogue sender who made it look *as though* it came from someone you know. Read "Privacy Respected" on page 301 and "Break the Chain" on page 296 for steps on how to be a safer and more responsible emailer.

You may be wondering how the scammers get their grubby hands on the names that they use and abuse. It might have happened when you or someone you know didn't practice good netiquette by using the To: box instead of Bcc: when sending a mass email. Read Bcc: vs To: for Email and Tidying an Email to Be Forwarded in Chapter 14, page 226, for steps on how to be a safer and more responsible emailer.

Spam—It's No Picnic

SPAM . . . A LOT?
The debate continues about the derivation of *spam*. It could be a tribute to the Monty Python song—"Spam spam spam spam, spam spam spam spam, lovely spam, wonderful spam." Or it could be mocking the lunch meat. Spam by any other name would still be unwelcome.

Is your home mailbox flooded with mail-order catalogs? How do you think the catalog companies got hold of your mailing address? Yup. You ordered a little something from one catalog, and that catalog in turn sold your mailing address to another and another and another. Suddenly, yours is the most popular mailbox in town.

Spam is electronic junk mail and now accounts for nearly 70 percent of all email. The proliferation of spam occurs in the same way as junk snail mail. However, with email you actually have an option not offered by the U.S. Postal Service. When you create your primary email address, you can also create a second email identity to use when you shop online, join an online newsletter, or are asked for your email address by a commercial enterprise for any reason. You'll only give your primary email address to friends, family, and business associates. This will significantly decrease the spam received at your primary email address. For example:

> *janedoe@yahoo.com* = address exclusively for friends and family
>
> *janedshopping@yahoo.com* = address for shopping, newsletters, etc.

Beware that some spammers are so stealthy, spam can appear in your inbox with your email address as the sender. Not to worry. Your email address may not have been hijacked but instead "borrowed." Even so, it's a good time to change your password. We'll get to how to do that next. The spammers disguised their information targeting you specifically to entice you to open the email. Once you've opened the email and clicked through to whatever is being pitched, your email address is certain to be sold to other mailing lists. Rule of thumb: If you don't recognize the sender's email address (or if you find it suspicious) and the subject is not something very specific to you, do not open the email. Don't let your curiosity get the better of you; there is no satisfaction found in spam. Promptly trash the email.

THINK BEFORE YOU CLICK

Spammers and phishers are bad enough, but you also have to watch out for viruses. Viruses are malicious programs that can get onto your computer via downloads or opened email attachments. Don't download anything or open attachments without being 100 percent sure of the source.

Click to report spam. Your email service will be notified that you have received spam.

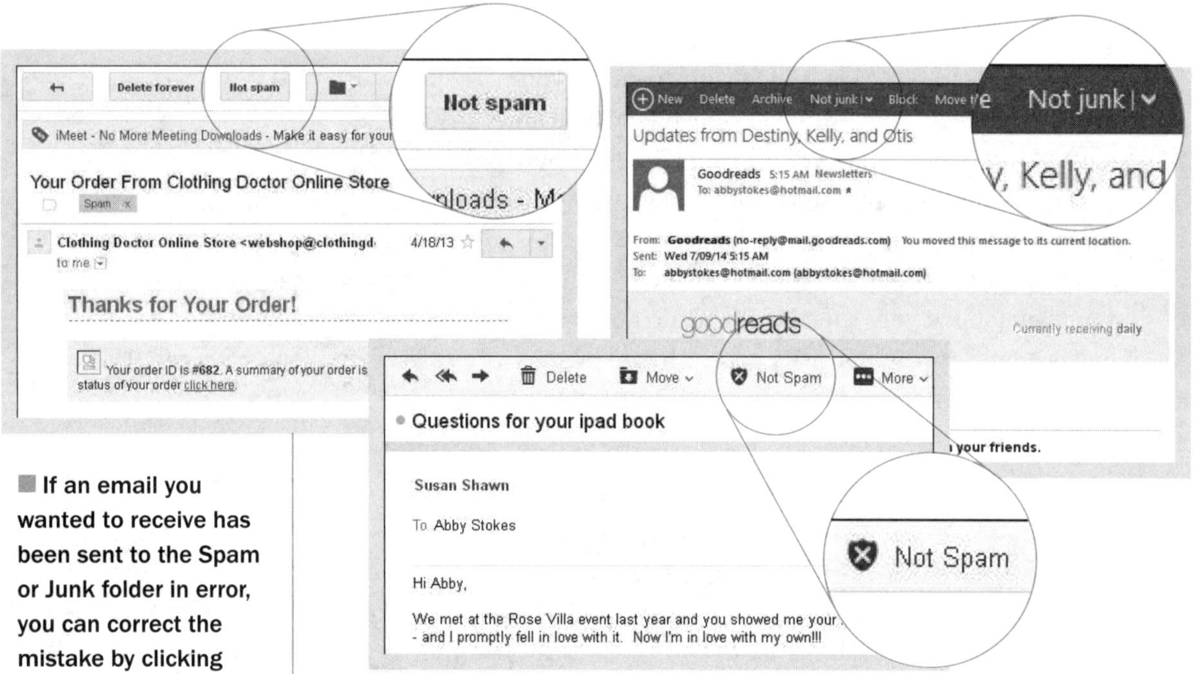

If an email you wanted to receive has been sent to the Spam or Junk folder in error, you can correct the mistake by clicking to remove the item from the Spam or Junk folder.

Most email providers now have filters to divert spam into a junk or bulk mail folder instead of your Inbox. The targeted email remains in the Junk or Spam folder for a limited time before your email company deletes it. Unfortunately, these filters cannot always identify what is junk and what is not. Junk mail may still make its way into your inbox, and sometimes an email you wanted to receive is misdirected to the junk folder. Your email service offers a method to redirect the email from the Junk folder to your Inbox. Look at the Menu bar for options like **Move**, **Not Junk Mail**, or some other option to redirect the email to the intended folder. To be sure you receive email from people you want, add their email address to your address book.

Whenever you want to take a break from all of this doom and gloom, do. Then come back so we can finish up this precautionary tale.

Glad you returned. I had faith you would.

To learn how to **Rid Yourself of Spam Emails on a Tablet,** visit ***AskAbbyStokes.com*.** Click on Video Tutorials at the top, then click on Video #5.

Open Sesame

Let's talk passwords. There are some basic dos and don'ts when choosing a password. Most passwords can be cracked in a matter of minutes. Let's see . . . your birth date or that of someone in your immediate family, a family member's name, your anniversary, some configuration of your street address. Am I getting close? Please don't make it that easy for someone who doesn't respect your privacy as much as I do.

Most important, as I mentioned on page 205, your bank or ATM PIN should not be the same as your email password. If someone were to hack the passwords of your email provider, he or she could then gain access to your bank account. Instead, have your bank PIN be an exclusive password for the bank and nothing else.

When choosing a password for your email or a website, follow these four basic guidelines.

1. Assume the password must be at least eight characters in length.

2. Use a combination of letters and numbers.

3. Because passwords are case sensitive, at least one letter should be in uppercase or capitalized to up the ante.

4. Remember to avoid public information.

The trick with any of these choices, however, is *you* need to remember your password. Write down the password before you type so there's no chance of making a mistake. No matter how speedy a typist you are, type the password one finger at a time to be sure you get it right.

My theory is you only need one *core* password to build all passwords off of so you can remember it.

The password should be memorable for you, but not easily guessed. Here are some sample passwords that, when translated, anyone can remember:

gr8Sh0eS = great shoes
Dont4g3t = don't forget
sK00bsdiK = kids books (backward)

TOO MANY PASSWORDS?

Limit yourself to three password templates: One for banking and *only* for banking, another for all email addresses, a third for every other website.

I'm not suggesting you use these sample passwords (in fact, don't), but let them inspire you. What is it that you love to do, buy, or eat? Use gr8 as a suffix to that thing. Use 4 for the word "for." Flip a 3 to replace an E. Use zero for the letter O.

When you write it down:

- Underline the capital letter (so, for example, you know it's S, not s).
- Slash zeros so you don't mistake Ø for the letter O.
- Add a hook at the top and a platform on the bottom of the number one (1) so you know it isn't the letter l.

OK, now let's harness your passwords so you don't have to remember a thousand of them.

One password for all of your email addresses. (If an email account gets compromised, you'll change them all.)

One password for banking and banking alone. (This is the only password that is a stand-alone password, to make your banking password the most secure.)

One password that can be adapted for all other websites. (A core password that will be easy for you to remember, but varied slightly for every website.)

Let's work with the password **gr8Sh0eS**. That is our core password and will be used for all email addresses. For banking, we want something relating to **gr8Sh0eS**, but not the same. How about **HighH33ls**? It meets the four rules.

Now onto the password for everything else. . . . Website addresses don't change—*facebook.com* will always be *facebook.com*, *askabbystokes.com* will always be *askabbystokes.com*, *usps.gov* will always be *usps.com*.

So let's work with that. Take your core password—**gr8Sh0eS**—choose the first two letters or the last two letters of the website you're visiting, and add them in some way to your password.

facebook.com = fgr8Sh0eSa The first letter of the site is the first letter of the password and the second letter of the site is the last letter of the password.

askabbystokes.com = egr8Sh0eSs The second-to-last letter of the site is the first letter of the password and the last letter of the site is the last letter of the password.

usps.gov = sgr8Sh0eSu The first letter of the site is the last letter of the password and the second letter of the site is the first letter of the password.

Got it? So you only have to remember the core password and whatever your "trick" is. Maybe your trick is to replace numbers for the letters. Again, write down one sample for yourself so you don't forget.

OK. Our last hurdle: How to tackle changing all your passwords?

Don't think about changing all your passwords at once. You'll never start if it seems too hard to finish. Start by changing your email and banking passwords. Then, change your passwords to any remaining websites as you naturally use them over time. Roll it out at your convenience.

Starting to get the picture?

Cover Your Tracks

This next section on history, cookies, and firewalls applies only to computers. To date, there are no settings on a tablet to manage these elements, but you might want to read about them anyway so you'll understand what people are referring to.

Like Hansel and Gretel, who left a trail of bread crumbs to follow on their way back home, your history leaves a trail for you to find a website you've visited previously; cookies leave a trail for a website to find its way back to information about your activities during previous visits to the site.

The history of the websites you've visited in the past is all well and good unless you've traveled somewhere on the Internet you'd rather not have others know about. No confessions necessary. If you don't want someone to see the websites you've visited, you can delete your history. This won't protect you if the Feds confiscate your computer and want to investigate past behavior, but it will prevent a curious spouse or grandchild from tracking your Internet activities.

To learn about **Deleting History,** visit **AskAbbyStokes.com.** Click on Video Tutorials at the top, then click on Video #6.

In a moment, I'm going to tell you how to delete cookies (as well as what cookies are). You may notice that the same window you visit to delete cookies also allows you to delete your history. Go for it! However, if you'd prefer deleting your browser history, visit *AskAbbyStokes.com*.

OK, it's cookie time! A cookie is actually a file left behind on your computer by a website that you've visited. There are advantages to a website leaving cookies behind. It allows a site to personalize your Internet experience. Here's an example: You visit Amazon (*amazon .com*) and buy an Agatha Christie murder mystery. The next time you open Amazon's website, the home page says, "Hello, (your name). We have recommendations for you" and suggests other titles you might like. It's similar to a doorman remembering your name or a salesclerk who remembers your favorite perfume. It was a cookie placed on your computer when you bought Agatha's book that provided Amazon with this information for your next visit.

Another example is if you choose to bank online, more often than not the ID the bank uses to identify you can be saved, rather than you typing your account number every time you visit the site. Your bank places a cookie on your computer so your bank ID can automatically be remembered. For security purposes, your password will be required every time you visit the site, but that is as it should be.

Cookies do not allow access to any other information on your computer besides the data the website has chosen to save. No website can view another website's cookies. A cookie is all about recognizing you and your preferences or past history with a certain website.

The only threat posed by cookies is they enable an unwelcome visitor to your computer to view information now stored on your computer by the cookies. Frankly, my shopping habits aren't anything anyone wants to know about, but your cookies may contain more significant information—possibly your credit card numbers. I choose not to allow websites to store my credit card information. If you do allow that, the information will be stored in a cookie. If you want to delete the cookies on your computer, you can do so without harm to your computer. The only downside to cleaning out your cookies is some websites that previously recognized you won't anymore. You'll just have to introduce yourself all over again. At that point, a new cookie will be placed on your computer so you'll be recognized on your next visit to that website.

When you choose to delete cookies from your computer, you could access the folder they are stored in and pick and choose what to delete, but it's difficult to always recognize what website the cookie is for and what information it contains. I prefer to delete them all and reintroduce myself to websites. (Because of the possible deletion of cookies after registration to a site, I print a document with all my registration information—website, user name or ID, and password—in case I need to refer to it later.) Let's remove the cookies accumulated on your computer.

If you use Firefox to access the Internet, follow the steps in Click and Go at right to delete cookies.

Here is how to delete cookies with Firefox.

CLICK AND GO

1. Click three stacked lines.
2. Click History.
3. Click Clear Recent History.
4. Click Details.
5. Be sure there is a check in the box beside Cookies.
6. Click Clear Now.

Firefox

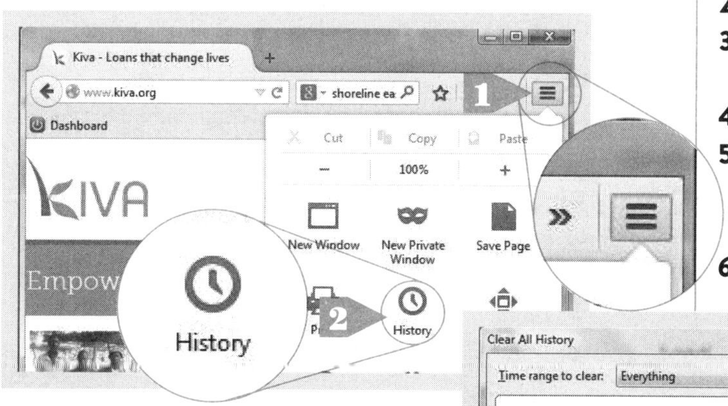

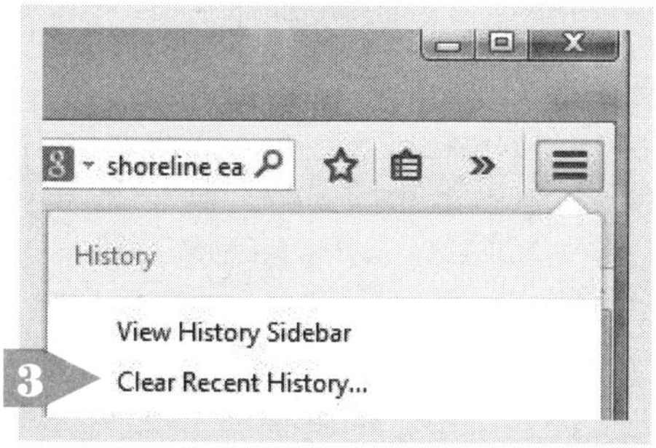

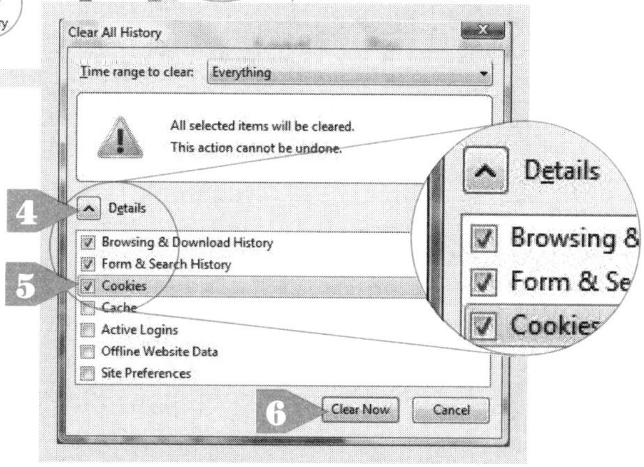

■ **Here is how to delete cookies with Internet Explorer.**

CLICK AND GO

1. Click Tools cog.
2. Click Delete Browsing History.
3. Click Delete Cookies.
4. Click Yes.

If you use Internet Explorer to access the Internet, follow the steps in Click and Go at left to delete cookies.

Internet Explorer

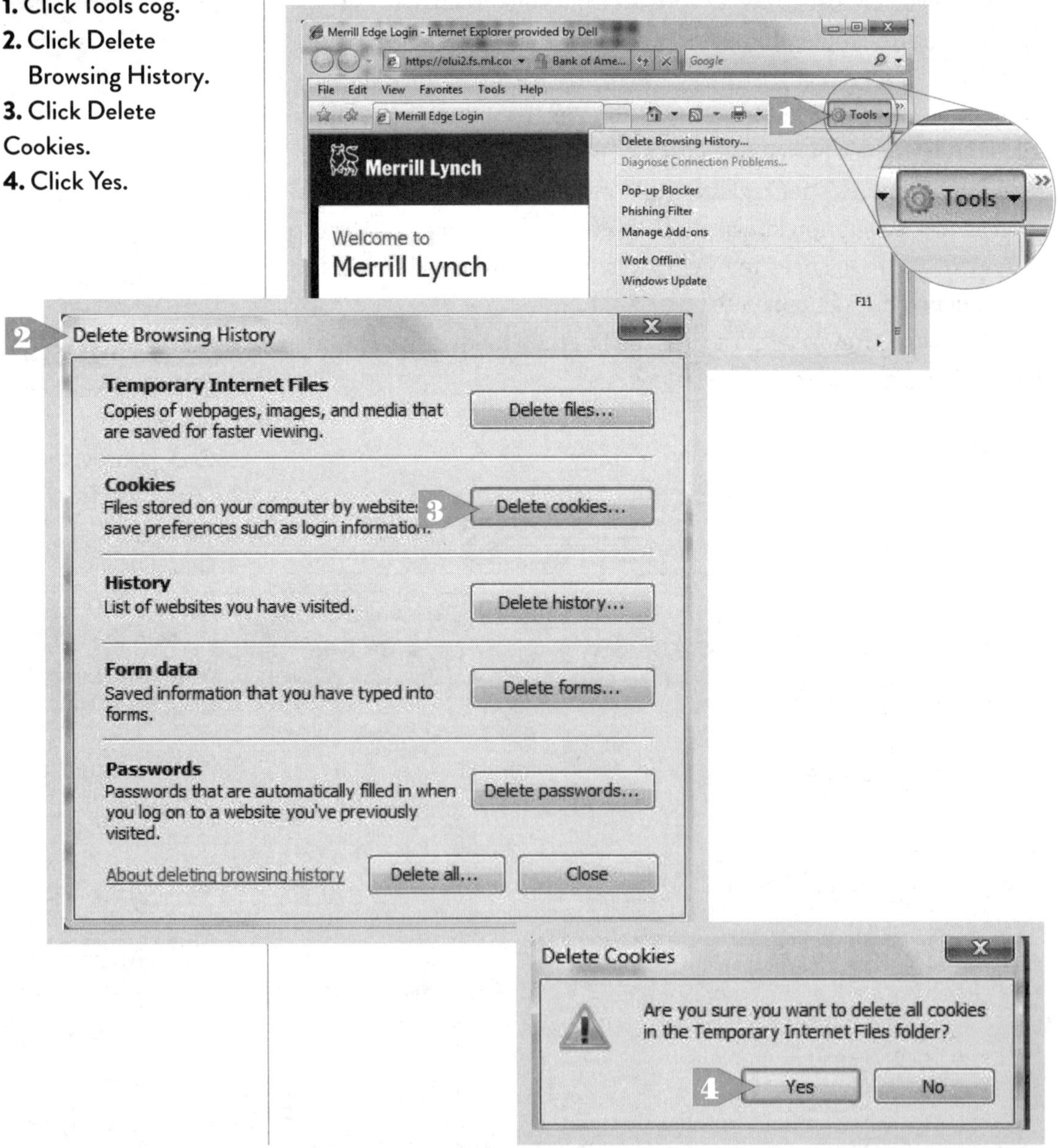

If you use Safari to access the Internet, follow the steps in Click and Go below to delete cookies.

Safari

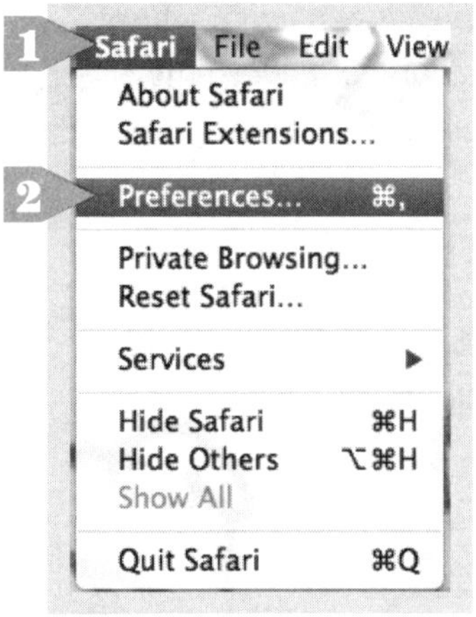

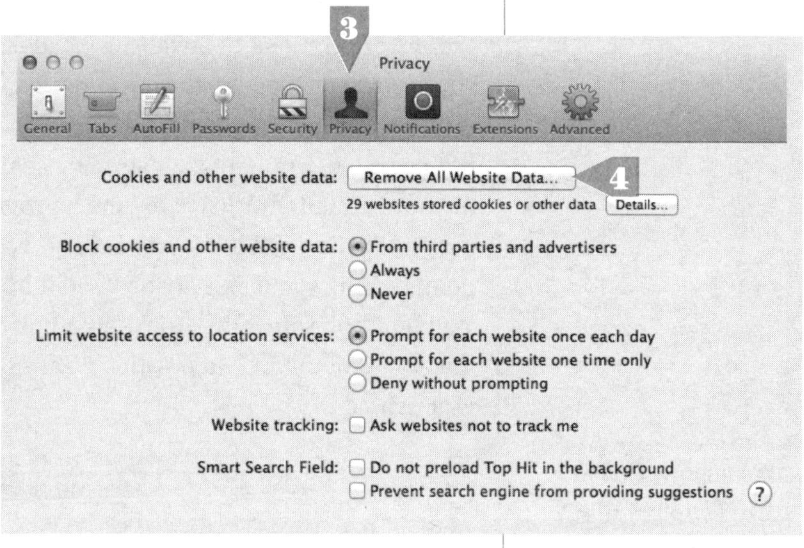

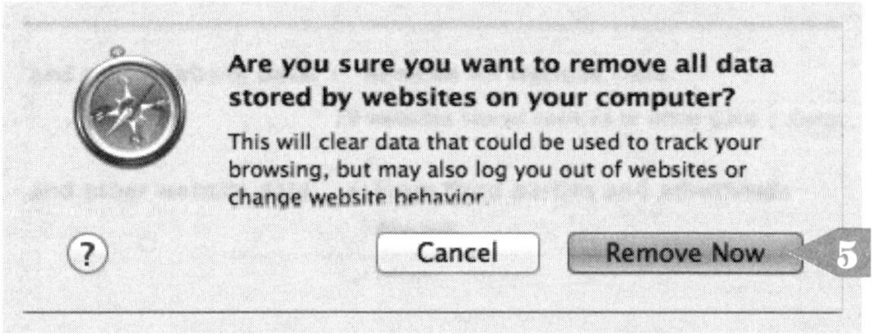

Here is how to delete cookies with Safari.

CLICK AND GO

1. Click Safari.
2. Click Preferences.
3. Click Privacy.
4. Click Remove All Website Data.
5. Click Remove Now.

While you're noodling around deleting your cookies, there may be other points of interest. Did you see a place to **Delete Files**? These refer to temporary files allowing a website previously visited to open up faster on your computer. Over time, the contents of this folder can slow down the computer. If your computer operates more slowly than it used to, access the Internet Options window and click on **Delete Files**. You may notice things run a bit faster after you've deleted those files. Other computer housecleaning tips can be found in Chapter 25, Troubleshooting.

Put Up a Firewall

Computers (not tablets) offer a firewall as a form of defense. Think of your computer's relationship to the Internet as a swinging door. It swings open when you send a request out (i.e., ask to connect to a website), and it swings open again when you receive a response to your request (i.e., you connect to the website). At both moments when the door is open, the computer is vulnerable. Uninvited guests can sneak in and view the contents of your computer or leave behind a program that may make your computer susceptible to junk mail or worse. With a firewall, these points of entry and exit are protected from intruders. (Imagine a wall built to protect fire from spreading.) Chances are very good that your computer came with a firewall preinstalled. Let's see if it is activated.

■ **Windows Security Center. Here's where you can see the status of your computer's firewall.**

To check for a firewall on your computer if you have a PC:

- Move your mouse into either the top or bottom right corner of your screen until the Settings cog appears.
- Click on **Control Panel**.
- Click on **System and Security**.
- Click on **Check firewall status**.

- If your firewall indicates that it is ON, you are protected. If it indicates that it is OFF, click on the **Windows firewall** icon . In the General options section, click the bullet next to the ON option to activate your Firewall.

To check for a firewall on your computer if you have a Mac:

- Click on in top left corner.
- Click on **System Preferences**.
- Single-click on the **Security & Privacy** icon .
- Click on the **Firewall** tab.
- Click on **Turn On Firewall** to enable your firewall. Click on **Advanced** to see more options.
- You may need to click the lock in the bottom left and type a password, if a password was created at setup.

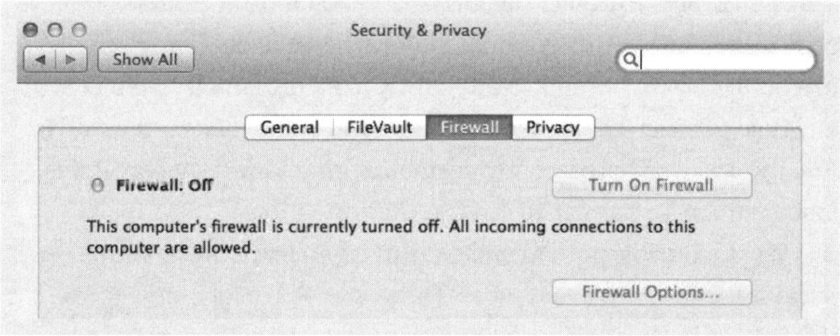

Mac Security & Privacy. Here's where you can see the status of your computer's firewall.

One thing to remember: If at a later date you decide to add software to your computer, the firewall may have to be turned off during the installation process to avoid interference.

Another preventive measure to take against hackers is to ask the provider of your high-speed connection to the Internet whether they offer any protection in the way of a router. A router is a device that also thwarts hackers by scrambling information needed to access your computer. If your ISP doesn't offer a router, you can purchase one on your own.

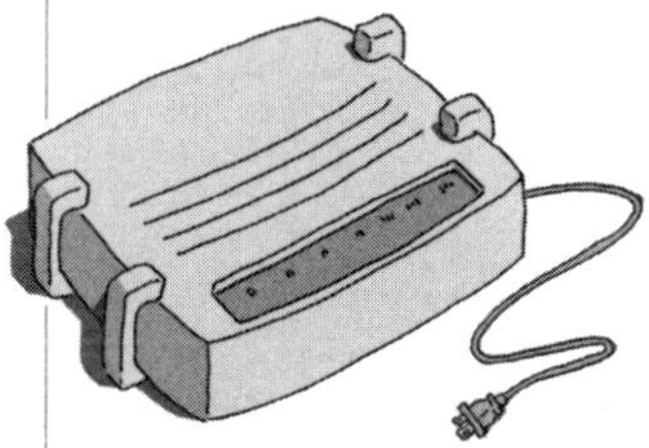

A router can protect your computer from hackers.

With these protections in place, it's unlikely that a trespasser will gain access to your computer, but it's not impossible. Therefore it is wise not to store certain information on your computer. For example, do *not* have your Social Security number, bank PIN (Personal Identification Number), or any other passwords recorded on your computer. If you can't think of any place to store your password information other than your computer, at least name the document after your first pet or your childhood hero or the person in the world you trust the most—anything other than "passwords."

Keep on Your Toes

Don't forget the old-fashioned techniques used by would-be thieves . . . their keen eyes and sticky fingers. When typing any password in a public place, try to have all of your fingers in motion over the keys to make it more difficult for someone to see what you actually type. If you have a laptop or tablet and you're in a public space, in order to protect the information on it from curious eyes, do not walk away from your computer when it is on. Frankly, when in a public place, I wouldn't walk away from my laptop or tablet at any time for fear that someone would steal it and make it their own. Finally, password-protect any portable technology. That way if it is lost or stolen no one can access your information.

What a terrible note to end on! But if you learn the potential pitfalls, it's easier to avoid them. There was also a lot of technical jargon to absorb in this chapter. Don't worry. I don't expect you to remember it all! You can always come back and review. Why not treat yourself to a few cookies (the edible kind), a cooling drink, and a break before you journey to the next chapter?

Q: Is the Internet safe?

A: Yes. It is as safe as any other place you visit in the "real" world. You just have to use the same precautions and common sense when you're visiting the Internet as you would traveling someplace you've never been before.

Q: What is spyware?

A: Spyware is software installed on your computer without your consent. Spyware can monitor your computer behavior, sending that information back to advertisers, and divert you from a desired website to another. One way to avoid spyware is not to download (or add) any programs onto your computer without being sure of the source and certain that you need the software offered. You can install anti-spyware software on your computer. This is a topic best dealt with by talking to friends or relatives in the know or a computer professional who can help install anti-spyware software and/or help remove any spyware that was found on your computer.

Q: I use a laptop computer, not a desktop. Do I need to connect wirelessly?

A: Not necessarily. You can connect to the Internet using an Ethernet cable, as you would with most desktops. (An Ethernet cable looks like a phone cable, but the cable itself is a bit fatter and the end you plug into the computer is wider.) The only advantage of a wireless connection is that you could work on your laptop anywhere in your home, free from the limitations of having to connect to the Internet with a cable.

Q: How will I know if someone has accessed my computer without my permission?

A: Unfortunately, you won't—unless they are stupid enough to change settings on your computer so it appears different to you, but that would be like leaving their glove in your home after they've broken in. You'll likely only know after they have used that information (e.g., shopped with your credit card). If you are

To learn how to **Protect Your Mobile Device with a Passcode,** visit ***AskAbbyStokes.com*.** Click on Video Tutorials at the top, then click on Video #1.

"I used to get all hung up about the names that have been given to different things on a computer, like bytes, hertz, and cookies. Now I don't give it a thought and I just have fun on my computer."
—Paul

suspicious that your computer has been hacked, call in a tech support person to check things out for you.

Q: Who do I contact if I think my computer has been broken into?

A: If you have any evidence that your credit card number(s) or your identity has been in any way jeopardized, call the police and file a report (they may want to see the computer), and also call the numbers listed on page 268 of this chapter. Bring your computer to a technical support person and have them go over the computer to see what evidence of intrusion they can find. While they have your computer, be sure to have them take the necessary steps to make it as secure as possible.

Q: I hired someone to hook up my printer. He insisted on turning off my firewall while doing the installation. Is this legit?

A: Yes. Sometimes when installing (or copying) new software onto a computer it is necessary to turn off the firewall. Just be sure to turn it back on after installation (see page 284).

Q: What can I do to let people know that the email I'm sending is from me and not someone pretending to be me?

A: The best way to thwart these email impersonators is to be specific with your subject so the recipient of your missive is assured that it is from you. The subject and the body of every email should be specific and personal. Don't send an email with the subject "hi" or "thinking of you." Instead, type "enjoyed seeing you at Yolanda's birthday" or "how's life with the new puppy?" I know that an email is from my mom because she always signs off "L, M" (Love, Mom). I always sign off "ML, P" (Much Love, Peach). It's our code, which was secret until now. Oops!

MAKE NEW FRIENDS AND KEEP THE OLD

CHAPTER 17

ADVANCED EMAIL

Let's go to the next level—web links, attachments, and more

As you've discovered by now, email is a wonderful way to stay in touch with family and friends. It's also an efficient means to communicate with co-workers and business associates. But surely it can't replace snail mail entirely. What if you apply for a job and your prospective employer wants a copy of your résumé? That would require the U.S. Postal Service, right? No, not really. What if you want your daughter to send pictures from your grandson's graduation? She'd have to mail them, right? Not anymore. Sit back and let me explain. But before we get into attachments, let's go over some other email details you should know as you become more experienced on your computer.

Email Services

Web-based email does not require software to be installed on your computer or tablet but instead allows you to access all of its features from a website. That means you don't have to use your own device to get the email. You could be on any computer anywhere in the world and access your

WHY CHOOSE WEB-BASED EMAIL?

I strongly suggest that you do not use the email provided by the company you pay to connect to the Internet. Why? If you decide to take your business elsewhere, you may hesitate because you like the email address you currently have. It's better to use a free Web-based email account so you're not beholden to your Internet service provider.

email. Many Web-based email services are free, such as Yahoo, Gmail (Google mail), and Hotmail.

As I said in Chapter 14, your computer may have come with email services already installed, such as Outlook, Entourage, or Apple Mail. Microsoft Outlook comes bundled in the Microsoft Office Suite software. Entourage is the Mac version of Microsoft's Outlook. They both offer email along with a task manager and a personal information manager that will organize your calendar, addresses, and notes, as does Apple Mail. The advantage of all these, over Web-based email accounts, is that you can access previously received or sent emails and write email without connecting to the Internet. Your newly drafted emails will be held in your computer's memory until you connect to the Internet and send them. You can access any cloud or Web-based email on your tablet.

Because free email accounts are available to you, why not have more than one email address, as mentioned in Chapter 16? Consider having a secondary email address that you use when making purchases or when being added to a newsletter or desired mailing list. This will help prevent too much junk mail from landing in your primary email account.

E-Manners

Netiquette was introduced to you back in Chapter 14, but here are some additional guidelines to keep in mind.

- **Remember that you are corresponding with a human being**. No matter how faceless and casual email may appear, abrupt and curt emails are rude. I open my emails with "hello" or "dear . . ." I close with "best," "cheers," or maybe just my initials.

- **Less is more.** Not to contradict my previous point, but convey your message in sentences rather than paragraphs. A lot of people read email at work, where time is limited, and a computer screen is no place to read a novel. If you must write a lengthy email, use paragraphs to break up the text. Avoid using indentation because the format of your email may change through transmission. Indentations can make email difficult to decipher.
- **Try to be specific in your subject line.** Unless you're writing a chatty hello, don't bother with a benign "hi" or "it's me" for a subject. Let the recipient know specifically what the email is about. This allows him or her to prioritize and identify it at a later date.
- **Watch what you say.** Email is easily forwarded, and really remarkable ones can make the rounds all the way to the news.
- **Do not lose your cool.** Serious matters of the heart or workplace warrant one-on-one interactive audio projection dialogue (in other words, speaking face-to-face). As is possible with any writing, but especially in this abbreviated form, emails can be open to misinterpretation. If you're determined to send a scathing email, send it to yourself first, and feel what it's like to receive your own harsh words.
- **Be discriminating about how and what email you pass on.** Just because you received an email doesn't mean the contents are true or worthy of being passed on to your loved ones, acquaintances, the pharmacist, your milkman, and that lady you sat next to on the bus. If you must share an email, be sure to tidy it up before you hit Send. Read "Break the Chain" on page 296 for instructions on the tidiest way to share an email.
- **Include the portion of the email you refer to.** If someone asks questions in an email, sending them the answers alone may cause confusion. Either include their entire email for reference, or include the specific text relating to your responses. You can

"It took me quite some time to get used to how casual email is. Now I appreciate the lack of formality."
—*Grant*

EMAIL IS NOT ANONYMOUS
Email can be traced to the computer where it was generated, even if you take on a false email identity.

SAY IT WITH AN EMOTICON

:-)	smile
:)	also a smile
:-D	laughing
:-}	grin
:-(	frown
:'-(	crying
;)	wink
:'-)	happy and crying
:-@	screaming
:-&	tongue-tied

To learn **How to Turn Your Emoji On,** visit ***AskAbbyStokes.com*.** Click on Video Tutorials at the top, then click on Video #7.

use copy and paste as described on pages 297–300 to bring chosen text from one email into another.

- **Reread the email address and message before you click on Send.** I've warned my students to be cautious about inputting the correct recipient for years and recently found my own face red when a slightly bawdy email I wrote accidentally made its way to an elderly student rather than the intended close friend. Oops! Check for typos and spelling errors as well. Most email services offer spell check capabilities.

How to Turn Your Emoji On

Emojis, introduced by the Japanese, are a more sophisticated version of emoticons (see box at the left for examples) used on tablets and smartphones. Instead of being made with symbols on the keyboard, emojis are tiny, simple illustrations that can help you make a point.

There are two sets of step-by-step instructions below that will help you get started using emojis in conversation. The first set is for the iPhone or iPad. The second set of instructions is for an Android device using Google's operating system.

iPhone and iPad instructions

To Activate Emojis:

1. Tap **Settings.** 
2. Tap **General.**
3. Scroll down to Keyboard, tap on **Keyboard.**
4. Tap **Keyboards** on this new page.
5. Tap on **Add New Keyboard.**
6. Scroll down to Emoji, tap on **Emoji.**

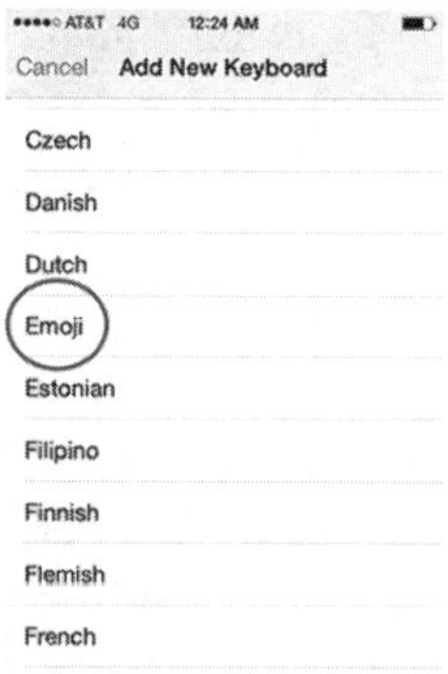

To Use Emojis:

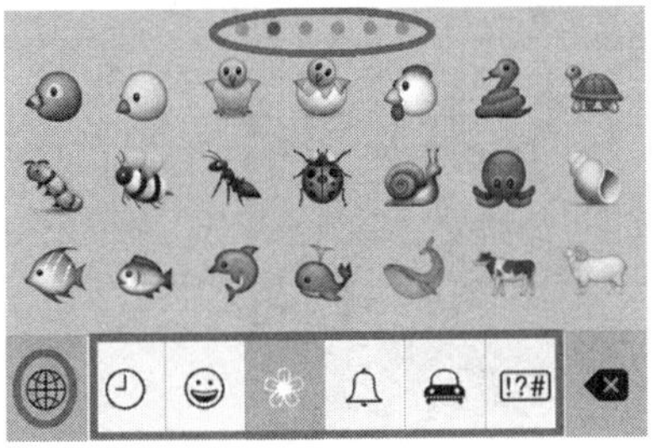

1. Tap on the **Emoji** button on the keyboard at the bottom left.

2. Flick your finger from right to left or left to right to reveal possible choices (note the small circles at the top indicate how many pages there are to view).

3. Tap on the category list at the bottom of the page to see even more (= recently used).

4. Tap on your desired emoji(s).

5. Tap to delete (if you change your mind).

6. Tap to return to the regular keyboard.

Android smartphone and tablet instructions

To Activate Emojis:

1. Tap **Settings**.

2. Tap **Language & Input**.

3. Tap on the symbol to the right of Google Keyboard.

4. Tap **Add-on Dictionaries**.

5. Tap **Emoji for English Words**.

6. Tap **Install**.

7. You may have to tap on **Refresh** in the top right corner.

To Use Emojis:

1. Tap on the Emoji button on the keyboard at the bottom right.

2. Flick your finger from right to left or left to right to reveal possible choices (note the horizontal bar that moves right and left indicating which page of emojis you are viewing).

3. Tap on the category list at the top of the windows to see even more (= recently used).

4. Tap on your desired emoji(s).

5. Tap to delete (if you change your mind).

6. Tap ABC to return to the regular keyboard.

Break the Chain

At some point, you will receive an email warning of a terribly destructive virus or relating a tragic story of a child suffering from cancer or a chain letter cautioning that if you *don't* send the email on to 10 friends, bad luck will befall you, but if you *do*, good luck or even money will come your way. It is only responsible for you to send the email on to loved ones who should be warned, may want to help, or are in need of luck or miraculous funds. Or is it?

What if the email is a hoax? Most of these types of emails are designed to see how many people can be reached. Or, even more insidious, the email addresses accumulated in the forwarded emails are culled by spammers to fill inboxes with junk mail. Before you

WARNING

If you or others you know use a work email account for personal matters, beware. (Work email can be identified by the company name as the suffix of the email address, e.g., *johndoe@westinghouse.com*.) The employer owns the email account and has a legal right to view all incoming and outgoing email. Not only can this prove embarrassing, but it also reveals, by virtue of the volume of personal email received or sent, time spent on one's private life and not work. Companies are monitoring work email accounts more and more. You should open a personal email account for yourself, if you haven't, and stop using work email for personal communications.

"I am so sick of getting emails that have obviously been forwarded several times before I was added to the heap of recipients."
—*Jimenez*

decide to pass on this type of email, check to see if it is a hoax at *snopes.com*.

If you deem the email worthy of sending on, do not click on **Forward** and possibly forward all of the past email recipients into the land of spam. Instead, copy and paste the important text into a new email. While you're at it, let's not expose each recipient to the other's email address. Use Bcc: (for guidance, see page 301) instead of using To: or Cc: when addressing the email.

The technique of copy and paste was introduced to you on page 250 in Chapter 15. If you haven't yet used copy and paste, feel free to go back and review. The techniques for copying and pasting on a computer are different from those on a tablet, so each is described in its own section below.

DO THE MATH

You send the email on to 10 people. Those 10 send it to 10 more = 100. Those 100 send it to 10 more = 1,000, and so on. By the time the email has made the rounds only six times, it will have reached 1,000,000 people!

Copy and Paste Email on a Computer

With email you've received, there's only one way to highlight the text to be copied. You must click and drag over the text. The easiest way to accomplish this is to start at the end of the text.

- Open the email that contains the text you want to copy.
- Place the mouse arrow, which probably now is the mouse I-beam, at the end of the chosen text.

CLICK AND GO

1. Highlight text.
2. Click Edit or right-click.
3. Click Copy.
4. Click Compose, Write, or New.

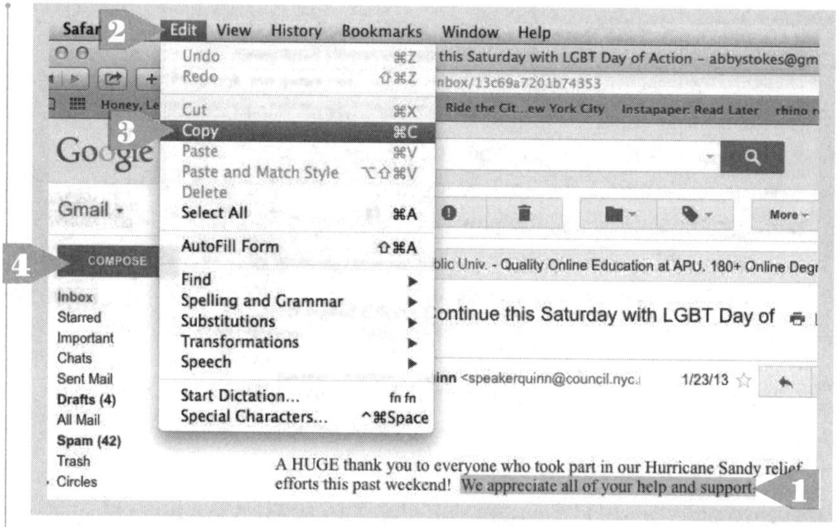

- Click and hold down the mouse while you drag across the text to the left and then straight up until you reach the start of the text. (If you're using a touch pad, this may require both hands.) This is a tricky operation and may take a few attempts before you get it right. Be patient. You will conquer it, I promise. If you don't succeed in highlighting the desired text, click the mouse anywhere in the window to eliminate the erroneous highlighting and try again at the end of the desired text.
- Once the text is highlighted, click on **Edit** in the Menu Bar or, if there is no menu bar, right-click.
- Click on **Copy**. (Most email will not allow you to cut.)
- Click on **Write**, **Compose**, or **New** to open a new email.
- Click inside the text area of the new email, where you normally type your message. A blinking line should appear.
- Click on **Edit** in the Menu Bar or, if there is no menu bar, right-click.
- Click on **Paste**.

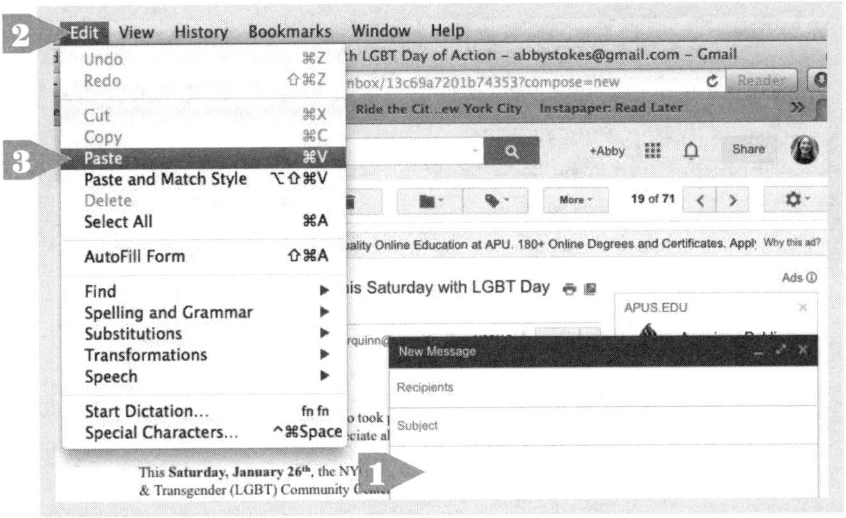

CLICK AND GO

1. Click in text area.
2. Click Edit or right-click.
3. Click Paste.

Finito! The text is now in a new email with no trace of its past journeys. Well done.

Copy and Paste Email on a Tablet

The underlying principles are the same with copying and pasting using a tablet, but highlighting is different on a touch screen. Visit *AskAbbyStokes.com* to watch a video tutorial.

- Open the email containing the text you want to copy.
- Hold your finger on a spot within the desired text. As soon as the bubble appears, release your finger.
- Highlight the desired text by keeping your finger on the screen and dragging the dot or triangle at either the beginning or end of the text. This is a tricky operation and may take a few attempts before you get it right. Be patient. You will conquer it, I promise. If you don't succeed in highlighting the desired text, tap anywhere on the screen to eliminate the erroneous highlighting and try again.
- Once the text is highlighted, tap on **Copy**.

To learn more about **How to Copy and Paste on a Tablet,** visit ***AskAbbyStokes.com*.** Click on Video Tutorials at the top, then click on Video #8.

- Tap or to open a new email.
- Put your finger inside the text area of the new email, where you normally type your message. When you release your finger, a list of options will appear.
- Click on **Paste**.

Finito! The text is now in a new email with no trace of its past journeys. Well done.

TAP AND GO

1. Activate text.
2. Highlight text.
3. Tap Copy.
4. Tap or .
5. Press and hold in text area, then release.
6. Tap Paste.

Privacy Respected

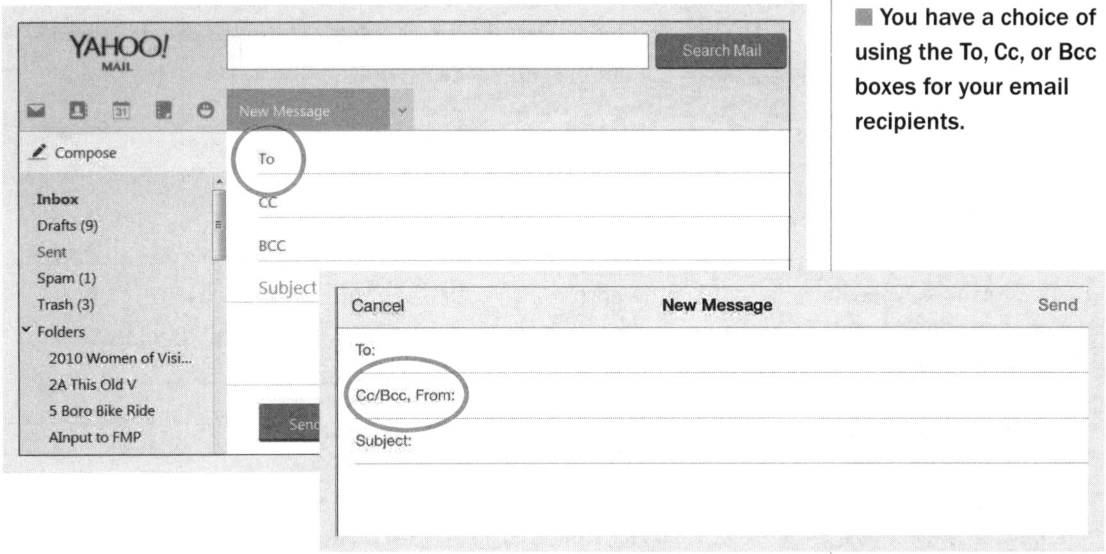

■ You have a choice of using the To, Cc, or Bcc boxes for your email recipients.

Let's send this email to a group without exposing the recipients to one another's email addresses. Each email service works slightly differently, so you may have to find where you activate Bcc instead of To when addressing an email. You might have to click on **Add Bcc** to reveal the Bcc address area. Look below or to the far right of the To box. If you select recipients from your email address book, you may choose the Bcc option at that time. Some email services require that there be at least one address in the To box. Why not type your email address in the To box and then delete the email when you receive it?

TAKE YOUR TIME

When you rent a car, the car initially appears unfamiliar and perhaps even a little intimidating. After you relax a bit, you begin to identify the location of the blinker, the emergency brake, and so on. The rental car isn't really very different from the one in the garage at home. At some point, your email service will update or redesign their website. This should not be a crippling event. Don't let it throw you off. Instead, take your time to get to know the "new look."

That's also a good way to know if the email went out, and you won't expose any of your recipients' email addresses.

Be sure to type in a subject in the Subject box so the recipients know what the email is about. Off it goes!

WHY DO WEBSITE ADDRESSES APPEAR AS GIBBERISH?

Once you have typed in a website address you may notice that with each page of the site that you look at, the address gets longer and more confusing. That's because it is actually all coding that identifies the website and the specific page you're on. You don't have to type or remember the long addresses, just the basic web address you used to access the site.

Web Links in an Email

When I'm planning a trip with my mother I'll often do online research about our destination before we depart. If I come across a website that Mom will find useful, I'll send her the website address embedded in an email. Because a website address can get very long and gibberishy, I certainly don't want to have to trust myself to retype it all. Instead I can copy and paste it into the email.

Try it yourself. Before going through the specific steps to embed the web link (copy and paste a web address into an email), open up your email account and have a blank email waiting for the link. If you're on a computer, shrink your email account by clicking on the **Minimize Box** or the **Collapse Box**. If you own a tablet, navigate from your email to your browser. With most tablets, that means returning to the Main Screen. Now open another Internet window and go to the web page that you would like to share. I'm going to send my mother the Amtrak train schedule from New York to Boston.

Embed a Link in Email on a Computer

- Highlight the web address at the top of the window by clicking once on it.
- Click on **Edit** or right-click.
- Click on **Copy**.
- Minimize the browser window and open the email window that is waiting in the Task Bar, or click on your email tab.
- Click in the message text area.

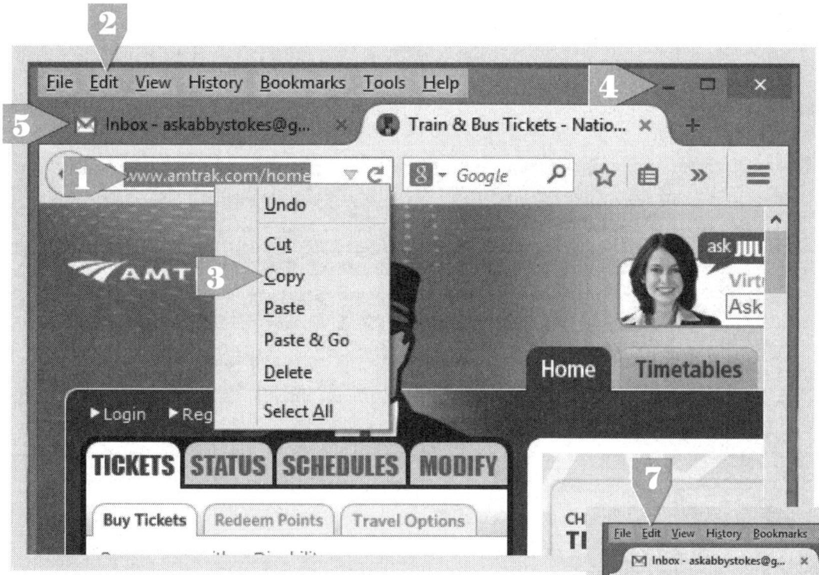

CLICK AND GO

1. Click on website address box to highlight.
2. Click Edit or right-click.
3. Click Copy.
4. Minimize window or click tab for your email.
5. Click on email window.
6. Click in text area.
7. Click on Edit or right-click.
8. Click on Paste.

- Click on **Edit** or right-click.
- Click on **Paste**.

Voilà! Now you can finish the email, type in a subject, put in the recipient's email address, and off it goes!

Embed Link in Email on a Tablet

- Highlight the web address by holding down your finger on the web address and then releasing.
- Tap on **Select All**.
- Tap on **Copy**.
- Navigate from your browser back to your email. That usually involves returning to the Main Screen.
- Hold down your finger in the message text area, and release.
- Tap on **Paste**.

TAP AND GO

1. Hold finger down in website address box to highlight, and release.
2. Tap on Select All.
3. Tap on Copy.
4. Open your email.
5. Tap on email window.
6. Hold finger down in text area and release.
7. Tap on Paste.

Voilà! Now you can finish the email, type in a subject, put in the recipient's email address, and off it goes!

When you receive an email with a link in it, you should be able to simply click on the link to go to the intended website. If for some reason the link is not active or working, you can copy and paste it into the website address box at the top of the window and then visit the suggested site. Receiving an e-vite or e-card is a common way to receive a link embedded in an email. An e-vite is an invitation via email and an e-card is a greeting card sent via email.

If the mouse arrow becomes a hand, it is an indication that the embedded web link can be accessed with a click of the mouse.

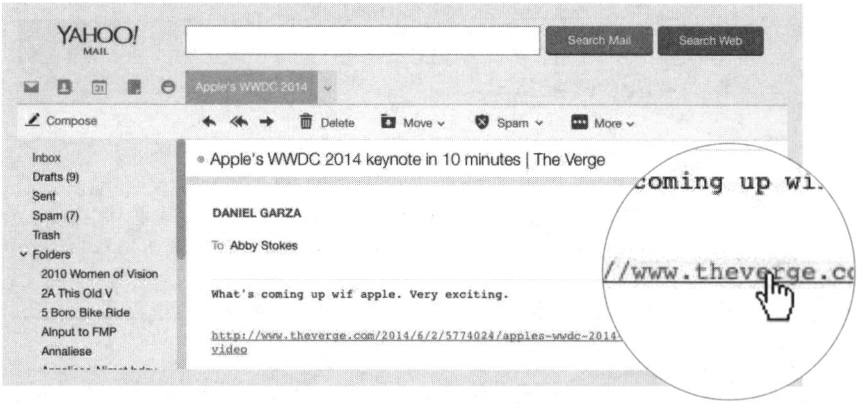

WARNING
Do not open a link in an email unless you're *absolutely* sure of the sender. Just because it appears to have been sent by a friend doesn't mean it was. Is there some content that positively identifies the sender? You, in turn, should always include a few words that assure the recipient that you, and not someone posing as you, have sent the email. If it smells fishy, it probably is.

Get Attached

An attachment is anything you send along with an email. It could be a document (a poem you wrote, driving directions, your résumé, your favorite recipe, etc.), a photograph, or even a movie or song. Let's go with the résumé scenario. In the days before computers, you'd type your résumé, then probably make photocopies of it or have a printing company produce copies for you. Next, you'd compose a cover letter either by hand or on a typewriter. Then, you would paper-clip a copy of your résumé to the cover letter. Your résumé would now be attached to the cover letter and would become an attachment.

"I was totally intimidated by attachments until I finally opened one. I felt foolish being so timid when it wasn't a big deal at all."
—Nicholas

In theory, it's no different with email. Instead of typing your résumé on a typewriter, you type it on the computer or tablet, where it's stored to print at will or, in this case, attach to an email. Next, you access your email account and compose the email that will accompany your résumé. Finally, you instruct the computer to fetch the stored résumé and attach it to the email. All you do then is click Send and off it goes! No trip to the post office, no waiting in line, and your dispatch arrives at its destination within seconds. With a tablet, the order of events is different, but the basic actions are the same. Don't worry: We'll go through the process for both step-by-step together. But before we *send* an attachment, let's discuss *receiving* one.

Receiving an Attachment

Check out the sample email shown on page 306. Your email service may look different, but all email services offer the same components. Relax, take your time, and figure out how this illustration relates to your email service.

Your email service uses a symbol to indicate that an email contains an attachment. Nearly all services use a paper clip icon, as seen here. AOL employs. Make yourself take notice of whether an email has an attachment or not.

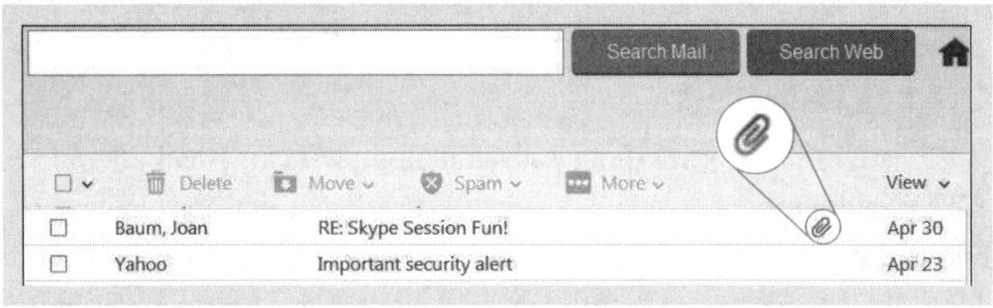

An email with an attachment in Yahoo Mail. The paper clip indicates there is an attachment.

To view an attachment, you must first open the email it was sent with. Then you open or download the attachment. Before going forward with opening the email, ask yourself, "Do I know the sender?" Email attachments are one of the ways to unleash a virus on your computer. If I receive an email with an attachment and I don't recognize the sender, I'll delete the email without opening it, to protect my computer from a possible virus. (I routinely delete unopened emails from unknown senders to lessen the spam on my computer as well.)

Here are instructions for you to follow to download an attachment. Feel free to read through them now, but don't expect the information to make sense until you're in front of the computer or tablet with an actual attachment.

- Open the email as you usually do.
- Look for attachments either at the top of the email above the main text or at the bottom of the email below the main text. If there is a paper clip and you don't see an attachment, be sure to scroll down. In all cases, when the mouse arrow is over an attachment, it appears as a hand. (Remember, the

REMAIN FLEXIBLE

If your email service appears slightly different on your screen, be flexible. All email attachments are opened with the same general steps. Take your time to check out what your email service offers. See how it works in relationship to the example here.

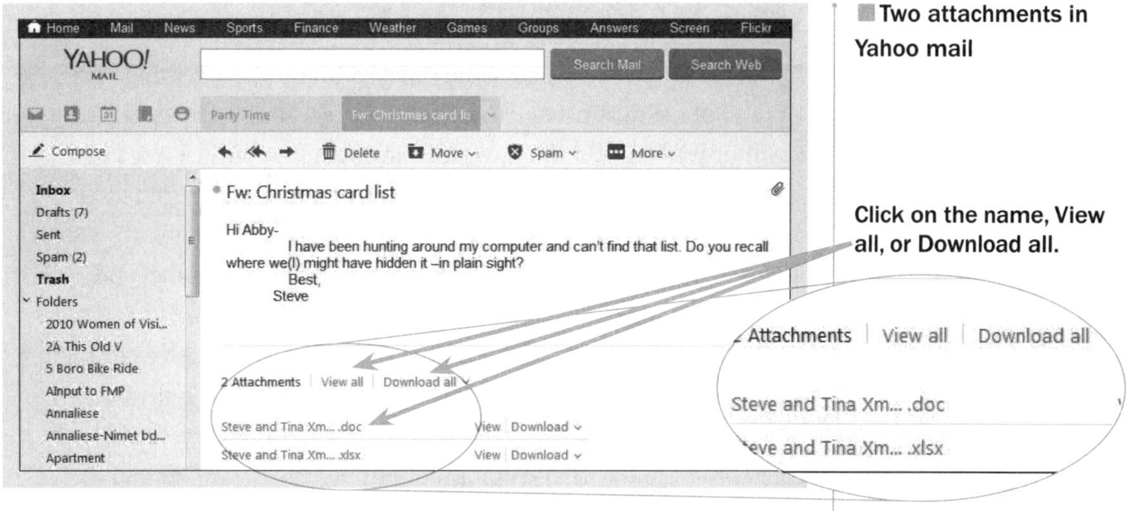

Two attachments in Yahoo mail

Click on the name, View all, or Download all.

hand is a positive indication that if you click there, something will open for you.)

- Click or tap on the attachment and you will be able to view it on your screen. If you want to move the attachment to your device (aka download it), look for the word **Download** or **Save** or one of these icons: or .
- If you're on a computer, a window may open that allows you to choose where you want to save the attachment. (This is an important step because if you don't take command of where you put the attachment, you may have trouble finding it later.) If you see the choice of **Desktop**, click on it. This instructs the computer to download the attachment to your Desktop—an easy place to find it later, but not where you'd want it to live permanently. Eventually, you'll want to organize the documents on your Desktop into a filing system. We'll get to that in Chapter 21.
- If you're using a tablet, you'll either have the option of saving the item or opening it in another program .

Notice the name of the attachment, so you can identify it later. You may also be able to change the name at this point to whatever you'll remember.

Why Won't My Download Open?

To download or upload simply means to move something from one place to another. Here's an example of downloading: The weather warms up and I download my summer clothes from the top of my closet to my dresser. An attachment gets downloaded to your computer from the email it was attached to. When you send an attachment, you upload it from your computer to an email and send it.

Sometimes, however, when people try to download an attachment, they don't succeed and they blame themselves or their computer. There are several possible reasons for this failure to download, but the most likely is that the format of the attachment isn't compatible with the computer attempting the download. This is neither the user's fault nor the computer's. Let me explain: The word "file," in computer-speak, refers to written documents, photographs, music clips, or movies. Anything that contains data is called a file (not to be confused with file folders, which contain multiple files). Every file, regardless of whether it is text or image or sound, is created using a particular software program. The same software program that was used to create the file is usually necessary at the other end to view the attachment when received. For example, if someone sends you a document written using Microsoft Word, you need Microsoft Word on your device (or a program that can read Word, like Pages) to view that document. Think of it this way: Software programs are a language. Your device needs to speak the same language as the attachment in order to read the attachment.

Hang in there while I show you the most common formats for an attachment. In Chapter 15 (on page 244) we talked about naming a document. You choose the name of a document or a photo (both known as a file) on your computer. Each file also has a suffix, or extension, that you don't choose, which identifies the format (designated software program) of that file. As an example, a Microsoft Word document ends in .docx or .doc. Remember the document we created and named "smile" in Chapter 15? In fact, "smile.docx" is its full name.

Here's a list of the most common suffixes you may encounter:

.docx or **.doc** = Microsoft Word document

.xlsx or **.xls** = Microsoft Excel spreadsheet

.pdf = Adobe Acrobat portable document file

.ppt = Microsoft Power Point Presentation

.mov = QuickTime movie

.wav = sound file

.jpg = a graphic or image

.zip = compressed data

If you receive and download an attachment and the name of the attachment ends in .docx or .doc, the Microsoft Word software program must be installed on your computer or tablet for you to be able to view and edit the attachment. A pattern will begin to emerge for you of attachment file types you can and cannot open. If you receive an email attachment but it won't open, you have the option to email the sender, let them know what attachments you have successfully opened (e.g., "I can open Word documents ending with .doc, but not .docx."), and place the burden on them to convert the attachment to a format your computer can read.

Now let's upload an attachment to an email to send. The same instructions apply whether you're sending a document or a photo. Before we can begin the process of uploading, decide what you want to attach. Do you know where it lives on your device (in Photos, Documents, etc.)? Do you know the name of it? During the upload process, you must tell the computer where to find the file to upload, so you need to know where it is and what it's called. On a computer, the process doesn't start with opening or viewing the item you want to attach. It starts with your email. A tablet is exactly the opposite—you begin the process with the item you want to attach.

Sending an Attachment from a Computer

- Open your email account and click on **Write**, **New**, **Compose**, or to generate an email. It's easy to put in the recipient's

STAY CALM
If what you see on your screen is different from what appears on these pages, stay calm. Look at your screen to see what would allow you to attach a photo, document, and so on. I bet that you can find what you need.

email address, compose the email, and forget to actually attach the file. To circumvent forgetting, we'll attach first and write later.

- Click on either the paper clip icon 📎, **Attach Files**, or **Attach**. The more comfortable you become with the computer, the more you'll be able to look around a window and instinctively find what you seek. Remember that you may need to use the Scroll Bar to reveal what you need. Take your time, remain calm, and be patient with yourself and the computer.

Click here to Attach.

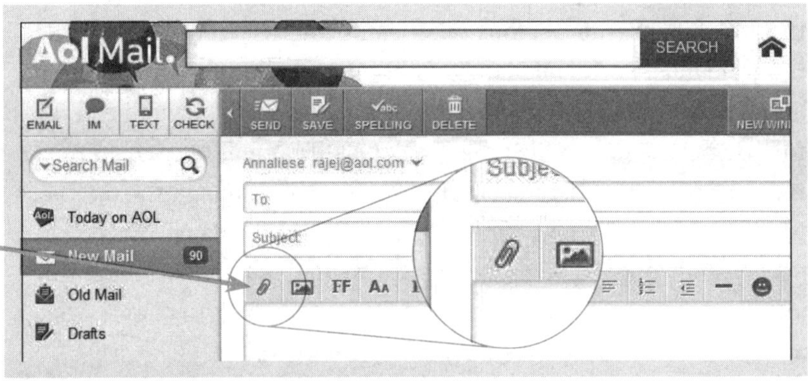

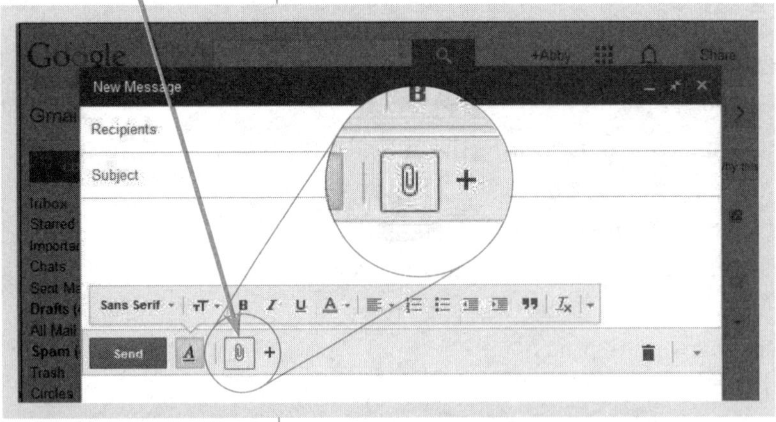

Each email service is slightly different regarding what you click on to attach a file.

- A window will appear. Once you find the item to be attached, click on the name of it, then click on **Open** or **Attach**, or you can double-click on the name.
- The attachment name will appear either near the subject area of the email or at the bottom of the email. You have attached a file to an email (you may need to scroll down to see it)! Congratulations!

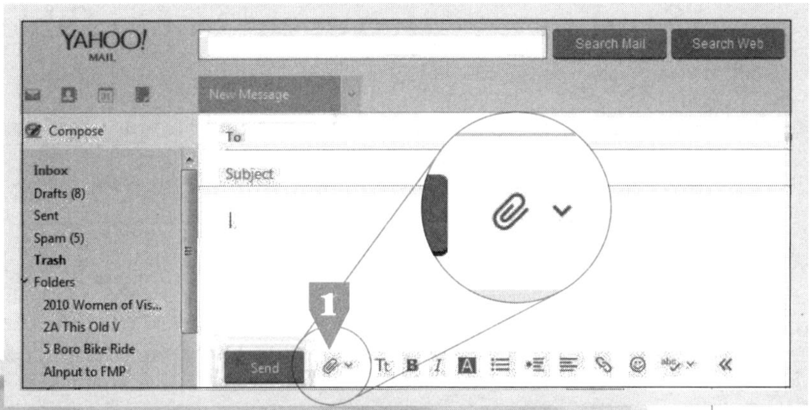

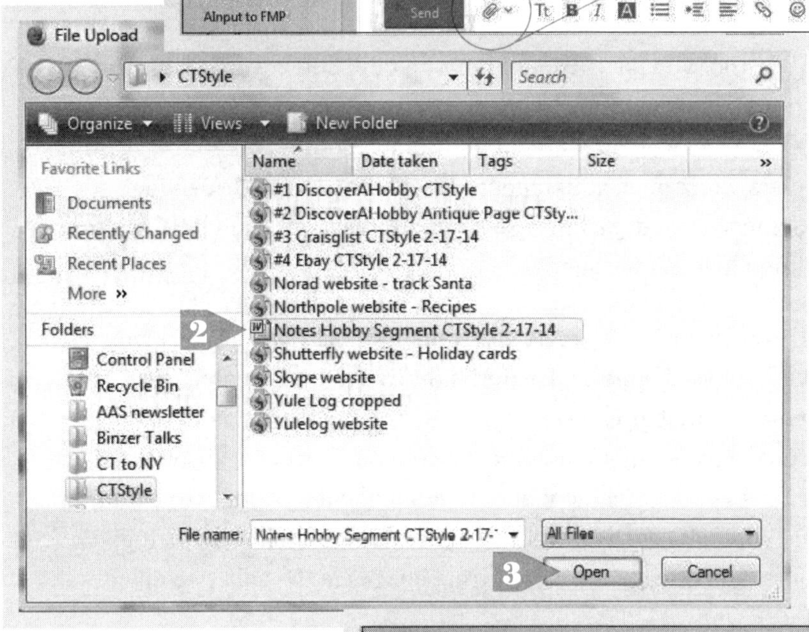

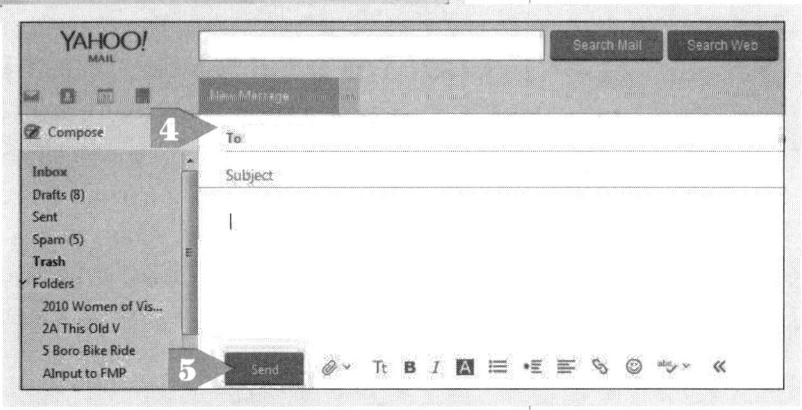

CLICK AND GO

1. Click on 📎.
2. Click on desired item to attach.
3. Click Open.
4. Fill in address, subject, and email message.
5. Click Send.

Sending an Attachment from a Tablet

- Open the photo or document you want to attach. Tap on either or . You may have the option of tapping in **Next**.
- Tap **Mail** or whichever email service you want, if you use more than one.
- The attachment will appear either near the subject area of the email at the bottom of the email. You have attached a file to an email (you may need to scroll down to see it)! Congratulations!

Whether you have a computer or a tablet, next you'll fill in the recipient's email address, subject, and your note. Be sure to mention the existence of an attachment in the subject or the message. Cautious emailers won't open attachments unless they know the sender consciously sent it, just in case it's a virus that attached itself without the knowledge of the sender.

How are you doing? Are attachments, both sent and received, making sense? I hope so. Up until now, we've been dealing with a file (document) that already exists on your computer. Hmmm . . . how do you get a document or a photo onto your computer if you don't receive it as an attachment and it's not a document you wrote and saved yourself? We'll discuss using your smartphone, tablet, digital camera, and a scanner for capturing images in the next two chapters.

Time for a Little Reflection

Wow! You've come a long way. It seems like only yesterday that you and your computer or tablet met for the first time. Now here you are uploading and downloading. Please return to this chapter as often as you need to when you've received an attachment or have a masterpiece of your own to send, and you want a little support. Don't forget to visit *AskAbbyStokes.com* for additional advice on email and attachments. It would be my pleasure to be of assistance.

Q: How do I save an email I want to keep?

A: Some email services will store your emails permanently; others may only store them for as little as a month. Be aware that the service's policy may change and you might not be notified. Some email services offer a way to set up a folder system to store emails. However, the most surefire way to know that you have a copy of an email is to print it.

Q: How do I know that the person sending an email is who they say they are?

A: You don't. It's the same as someone calling you on the phone who says they are Bill Smith when they are really John Doe. You must be cautious, as you are in any situation in life, with a stranger. Use your instincts and powers of reasoning to determine if the person you are receiving an email from is sincere or an imposter. Caution prevails! Be careful not to reveal any personal information, unless you are certain of who you are talking to and their intentions.

Q: Can I make changes to an email before I send it?

A: Yes. Until you click **Send**, you can edit your email to your heart's content. Get it just right before you decide to send it on.

Q: If I have a PC and my daughter has a Mac, can I still send her attachments?

A: Yes. It isn't the kind of computer you have that matters with attachments. What matters is if you have the necessary software on your computer for your daughter to be able to open the attachment on her computer. For example, if you send her a spreadsheet you created in Microsoft Excel, she needs Microsoft Excel or Numbers on her computer to open and view that spreadsheet.

Q: Sometimes I can't even open an email with an attachment. The computer seems to stall or says "timed out." What does that mean?

A: Your computer is having problems because either the attachment that was sent to you is very large or your Internet connection is slow. If this is chronic, it could be a sign that your computer is getting on in years. A document, no matter how large, will almost never be as cumbersome as a photograph, music file, or video sent as an attachment.

CHAPTER 18

PHONE IT IN

The scoop on cell phones and smartphones

When it comes to mobile phone technology, we've come a long way since the first cell phone was introduced in 1973, weighing in at 4.4 pounds. Imagine holding up a 5-pound bag of sugar (minus a few cups) to your ear and talking into it. As of January 2014, nearly 90 percent of people over the age of 50 in the United States use a cell phone, and almost 50 percent of the same demographic use smartphones. Those over the age of 65 account for only 20 percent, but the number of users over 65 is growing every year. In this chapter, we'll discuss both the cell phone and the smartphone.

Cell Phone vs. Smartphone

Smartphones are swanky cell phones that function not only as telephones, but also as a connection to the Internet for Web surfing and email. They also have photo, music, and GPS features. iPhones and Androids (also known as Droids) are the most common smartphones, but there are several other competitors out there. While smartphones offer many great services, almost

IS IT HANDY?
Pick up a smartphone. Put it to your ear. How does it feel to talk on it? The smartphone is a bit clunkier in the hand than a cell phone, but the large screen and keyboard may be worth it to you. As buyer, you are both judge and jury.

every cell phone has at least some of the features of a smartphone. For example, Verizon's LG enV3 is a cell phone, but it also has the capability of taking photographs, sending photos to email addresses, and exchanging information with a computer. Wouldn't you call that pretty smart?

The real difference between some "smart" cell phones and some smartphones is size—generally, a cell phone is smaller than a smartphone. Because of the size limitation, a cell phone (whether very smart or sort of smart) may offer only a phone keypad to type your text messages, etc., as opposed to a smartphone, which has a full keyboard (albeit a small one) usually on a touch screen. The screen to read your email and surf web pages is also larger on most smartphones, so your viewing experience may be more pleasant. If you're considering a smartphone, play with one in the store or ask a friend to take you for a test drive. Be sure to check if you can really read what appears on the screen.

Verizon's LG enV3 cell phone with a flip-around full keyboard

The Lowdown on Smartphones and Apps

Even if you're sure you only want a cell phone, stick with me as we talk smartphones. I don't want to change your mind, but you should know what people are talking about. A smartphone allows you to send and receive email and text messages, as well as take photos, listen to music, watch movies, and read books—and those are just the basics. Your photos or videos can be stored on the phone and shared via email. A smartphone has a calendar and an address book, and it usually comes with a bunch of other preinstalled apps (more on that in a minute). Most important, it offers access to the Internet, which means that you can visit almost any website that you can on a computer. Some websites don't read as well on a phone, but most perform pretty well in the smaller format. If you decide to buy a smartphone, be

"I could never really see the screen on my cell phone very well, but my smartphone is a huge improvement. I even text-message now."
—Irena

sure to ask if you'll be charged extra to have access to email and the Internet. I think you'll find it worth the cost, but confirm how much it will be, so there are no unpleasant surprises when the bill arrives.

You can also load apps onto your smartphone. We discussed adding apps to your tablet on page 170. Apps (or applications) are added to your smartphone from the same source—either Google Play if you have an Android phone or Apple's App Store if you have an iPhone. Some apps are free and some are not. You can get a compass, flashlight, calorie counter, movie theater finder, tide chart, international translator, flight tracker, dictionary, and games, games, games. There are more than one million apps available, and that number is growing daily. Facebook, Twitter, Skype, Instagram, and LinkedIn are all available as free apps. Ask your friends to recommend apps to add to your smartphone and be sure to check out the list of recommended apps in the back of the book (page 518).

MINI ME
Smartphones are actually a mini version of a tablet, but with cell phone capabilities. So if you're familiar with a tablet, conquering a smartphone will be a piece of cake, and vice versa.

All smartphones and most cell phones can sync information between your phone and your computer, and vice versa. ("Sync" is an abbreviation for synchronize, or to make exactly the same at the same time.) This means you can input your addresses using the standard-size keyboard on your computer and sync that information to the smartphone. If you put a date into the calendar on your phone and sync it with your computer at home, the date you booked will be on both devices. You can sync information either by linking the phone directly to the computer via a USB cable or by using wireless technology. Many mobile phones sync without your having to do a thing—they simply do it automatically. You'll want to be sure that your computer is up-to-date enough to take advantage of this feature. It would be a good idea to have the make, model, and year of your computer (as well as the version of your operating system) with you when you are shopping for your smartphone. I can't guarantee that salespeople will know your computer, but they should have some idea of which ones are compatible for syncing.

THE INTERNET IN YOUR BACK POCKET
You can buy theater tickets, watch movies, and post to Facebook from a smartphone. Many websites offer apps that mirror the content on their site, but in a format that is easy to read and manipulate on a smartphone. It's like carrying the website in your back pocket.

Buying Strategies

Buying a cell phone or smartphone can be almost as intimidating as buying a computer, but as with the computer, it is a mission you can accomplish with great success when armed with a bit of research and help from knowledgeable friends and family. Before you decide which company you want to provide your phone service (AT&T, Sprint, Verizon, or T-Mobile, to name a few), ask friends and family members to bring their cell phones to your home and see what kind of reception their phone service provider gets there. Not all cell phone companies get a good signal in all locations. They should, but they don't. Be sure before you commit to a provider that you get a strong signal so you can make and receive calls in the places most important to you.

Mobile phones come in a variety of styles and sizes. Again, test the different models your friends and family use before deciding which is best for you. Use the keypad and feel how the keys work with your fingers. Try to decide if you'll want a full keypad for texting (see page 320) or if just the numbers are enough for you. Look at the display screen and be sure you can read it clearly. Make a call and see how well you can hear. Because your own ear may block the small speaker on a cell phone, move the phone around your ear and see which position gives you maximum sound.

Ask your salesperson about the battery life of the phone. At the very least, your phone should have enough steam for three hours of talk time and nearly a week of standby time. Do a Google search on the phone brands you're considering, and read the online reviews to get an objective take on the battery life. It's a good idea to buy a spare battery, a battery booster, or a solar battery as backup when you purchase your phone. I was able to use my cell phone throughout a blackout in 2003 because I had

AT WHAT COST?
Ask at the time of purchase what your monthly "nut" will be for calling, texting, and connecting to the Internet (or whichever services you choose). If you change your mind and want to break your contract, you'll likely have to pay a penalty. Do not sign anything until you know what it will cost you.

BUYER BEWARE
Just because the sign outside the store is a familiar cell phone carrier or manufacturer doesn't mean they are an authorized dealer. Visit the website of the manufacturer or service carrier and seek out an authorized store.

a solar battery keeping it charged. My solar battery saved me again last summer when I lost power for four days during a tropical storm. As with a laptop, you should help your phone's battery last longer by letting it fully run out before recharging when you first get it. We'll cover more ways to conserve battery life on page 330.

CELL PHONE JITTERS
If all you want is a simple cell phone that's easy to use and has a large keypad, I suggest the Jitterbug cell phone. Visit *greatcall.com* to see for yourself. They also offer a specialized smartphone.

Are You a Feature Creature?

Some people want every bell and whistle available on a phone. Others just want to make a call. In either case, no one wants to pay for what they don't need or won't use, so consider the features available on a cell phone or smartphone before you decide which type is best for you. Even the most basic phone will probably have a calendar, an alarm clock, a contacts list where you store your numbers, and perhaps even voice dialing so you can speak a name into the phone rather than using the keypad.

See if you can check out the features of the phone you're considering on its manufacturer's website. You may find an online tour there that showcases all of the phone's goodies and how to operate them. Also, ask for a demonstration at the phone store before you make your purchase.

Hands-On Introduction to Cell Phones

If you've bought a smartphone, you can skip to page 323 for a hands-on smartphone introduction.

The first time I have a new cell phone in my hand, I press all of its various buttons. Is there a button that has the symbol of a reel-to-reel icon (how retro!), an envelope icon, or both icons on it? That's probably what you press to hear voice mails, or it could be for email. Maybe there's a button that says

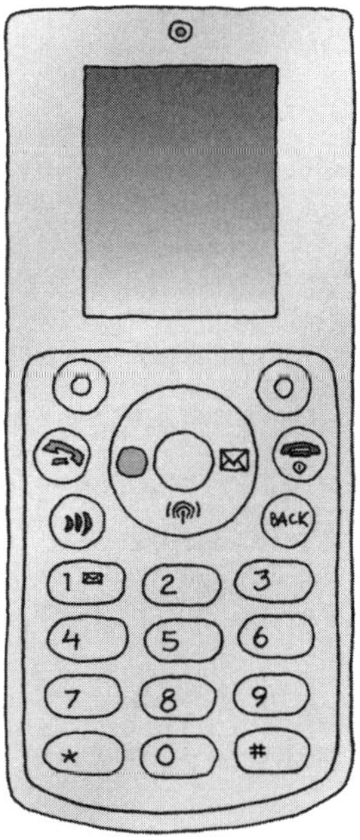

Some buttons on a cell phone are marked clearly with their function.

Voice mail or Email button

Send/Talk button

Flip phone

Candy bar phone

Slider phone with number keyboard

Slider with full keyboard

Cell phones come in a variety of styles.

Send or **Talk** (or that's green, for Go). Logic says you'll use that button to begin a call and then the **End** (or red, for Stop) button for hanging up when the call is over. I know it sounds elementary, but when you're intimidated, the obvious no longer seems obvious. So relax . . . don't think so much. Be like a kid and just play with the thing for a while. No harm, no foul.

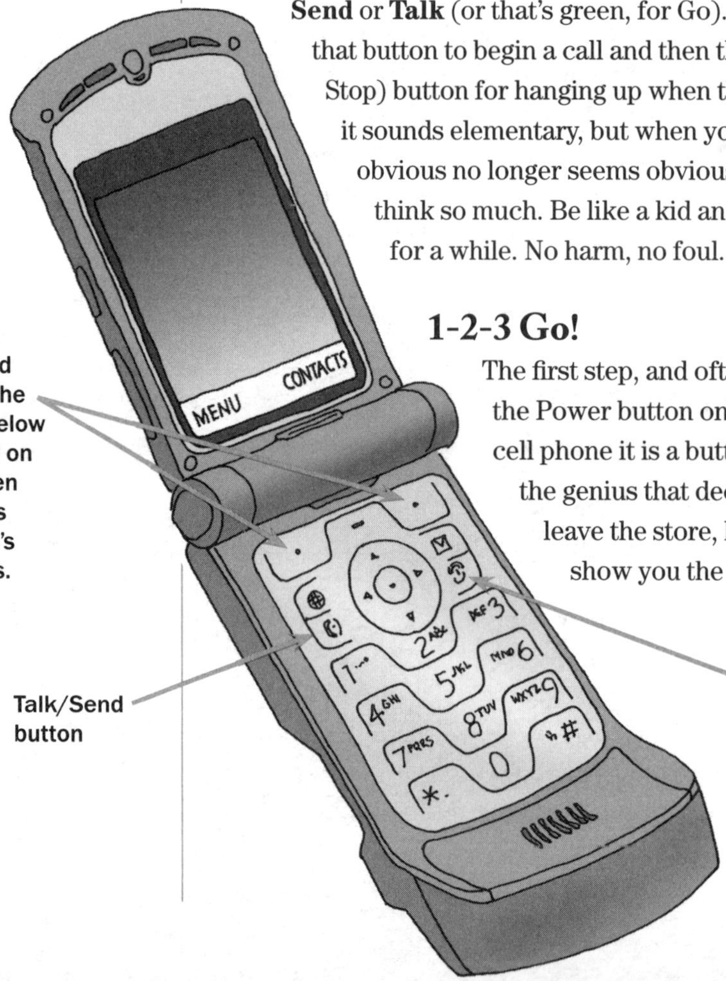

1-2-3 Go!

The first step, and often the hardest, is to find the Power button on your phone. (On my cell phone it is a button marked **End**. Who is the genius that decided that?) Before you leave the store, have the salesperson show you the on/off button, and turn the phone on and off yourself at least once. Be patient if it takes a few seconds for the phone to turn on and a few more seconds for it to turn off. The phone may chime or make some other noise to indicate that it is on, but the best way to know is to look at the screen. Eventually, the display will come to rest with an image, some text, or a bit of both on the screen.

At this stage, dial a number (your home phone number is a good one to start with) and hit **Talk** or **Send**. (Again, no two models are alike, so consult the instructions that came with your phone to find the Talk button.) Whether you need to dial a 1 and the area code first depends on where you're calling "from" and "to." Once someone in your home or your answering machine picks up, say "hi," and after you've chatted for a minute or left yourself a funny message, hang up. There is usually a button on the phone that will say **End** or that is red, or if you have a flip phone, closing it will hang it up automatically. Practice this so you know when a call has truly ended.

Now call someone you know, give that person your cell phone number, and ask him or her to call you back. (Please write down your cell number and keep it somewhere convenient. It took me months to remember mine, so I was always referring to the piece of paper in my wallet when asked. A friend taped hers to the back of her phone.) Some phone models will connect you to the caller when you open the phone cover; others require that you hit the **Send** or **Talk** button. Usually, this is a feature you can customize to your liking. Again, your instructions will tell you about your specific phone.

"I admire all that my niece can do with her smartphone, but I just want a simple phone I can use to make and receive calls. I can't see the screen well enough to read text messages anyway."

—*Emily*

Push My Buttons

When you look at the screen of your phone, you may notice that there are words at the bottom left and right of the screen. If so, below each word on the screen, there should be a button on the keypad. If you press and release this button, the phone takes the action suggested by the word. For example, say **Menu** appears on the bottom right of the screen. When you press the button below the word, a menu will open. On other phones, you'll select the feature you want on a touch screen.

Your Little Black Book

Before cell phones were around, I memorized most of my friends' phone numbers. Now, I don't even try to remember them, because they're all stored in my cell phone. All cell phones have the ability to save your recently called telephone numbers in their memories. Enter your important numbers in your phone once, and voilà, you've freed some storage space in your own memory.

KEEP YOUR NUMBERS
Many phones have a SIM (subscriber identity/information module) card that will store phone numbers. When you buy a new phone, those stored numbers can be moved from the old phone to the new one with the SIM card.

Usually, the easiest way to store a number is to dial it, but instead of hitting **Send** or **Talk**, look at the screen. Do you see the word **Menu** or **Store** there? If so, press the button below the word. Read what is offered, and press and release the key on your phone that allows you to save the number. This process may take a few steps because you'll be given the chance to type in the person's name. (Of course, or how else would you identify them in your address/phone book?)

If your phone doesn't have a full keyboard, you'll have to type the name using the keypad. You may have to hit a key multiple times to get to a given letter. To type the first letter on a button, you hit it once; to type the second, hit it twice; for the third—you guessed it, hit it three times. If you make a mistake, there's a key on your phone that allows you to backspace. It's often marked as **Back**, or it may have an arrow pointing to the left. Again, experiment. No harm done. Refer to your instruction manual. Whenever you're learning an element of the phone, repeat the steps at least three times to help cement them in your memory. It's also a good idea to take notes, so you can refer to them later. Create your own cheat sheet until the actions become second nature.

On phones without keyboards, to type the letter F, you must press and release the 3 key three times . . . once for D, twice for E, and three times for F.

In the next section, we'll discuss smartphones. Feel free to skim through the information or you can skip to "There Is No Place Like Home" on page 326, where we'll review other functions of a mobile phone that are similar on both cell phones and smartphones.

Hands-On Introduction to Smartphones

When Apple's iPhone was introduced in 2007, it was a game changer in the smartphone industry. There was nothing on the market like it. An iPhone's screen was the first to be made of glass. A glass screen offers far superior resolution to the plastic screens that were available on other smartphones, making photos and videos remarkably clear. For the first time, you could view things horizontally as well as vertically. All you had to do was turn the phone horizontally, and the screen would adjust the image automatically. And, there are no keys to speak of on the iPhone. Instead it is all operated through a touch screen that allows you to tap on the screen along with dragging your finger across the screen to activate programs or move items stored on the iPhone. Along with all of the other functions of the iPhone, it became a substitute for an iPod for listening to music. The iPhone's capacity for storing and viewing videos, movies, and songs is extraordinary.

But if you aren't interested in any of those features, the iPhone (no matter how "it" it is) may not be for you. If you don't need the cell phone feature, but everything else on an iPhone sounds appealing, you may want to look at an iPod Touch. If there isn't an Apple store near you, visit the company's website (*apple.com*) to window-shop all of their toys. If you choose to buy an Apple device, buy it either from an Apple store or from their website. It is the only way that you can ensure Apple's tech support, if you need it.

Now the Android smartphone (often shortened to Droid) is giving the iPhone a run for its money. Both function as a cell phone, camera, TV screen, connection to the Internet, music source, and whatever else you can think of in one easy-to-use, very sexy unit. Android is to smartphones what PC is to computers. There are many manufacturers (Samsung, Motorola, LG, and Sony, to name a few) supplying the hardware of the phone, but all Androids run on Google's operating system. An iPhone has both the hardware and operating system designed and manufactured by Apple.

"I thought I'd never need access to email or the Web when I was away from home, but now that I have a smartphone, I love it. It's like having a computer in your purse."
—*Carolyn*

For a brief time, Android sales surpassed iPhone sales. The biggest contributing factor to this momentary switch in status is that Android phones are usually less expensive than iPhones. The iPad remains the top seller for tablets. Only time will tell if Apple can keep the lead in the tablet market.

1-2-3 Go!

The first step, and often the hardest, is to find the Power button on your smartphone. It is usually on the top or side of the phone. Before you leave the store, have the salesperson show you the on/off button, and turn the phone on and off yourself at least once. Be patient if it takes a few seconds for the phone to turn on and a few more seconds for it to turn off. The phone may chime or make some other noise to indicate that it is on, but the best way to know is to look at the screen. Eventually, the display will come to rest with an image, some text, or a bit of both on the screen. With most touch-screen smartphones you must drag a finger across the screen to open the main display where different parts of the phone (texting, email, etc.) become accessible. Again, have the salesperson show you this and practice it a couple times to be sure you've got the idea before leaving the store.

The first time I have a new smartphone in my hand, I tap on all of the various icons on the screen and buttons on the device. Is there

All of the preloaded applications on a smartphone can be seen on the home screen.

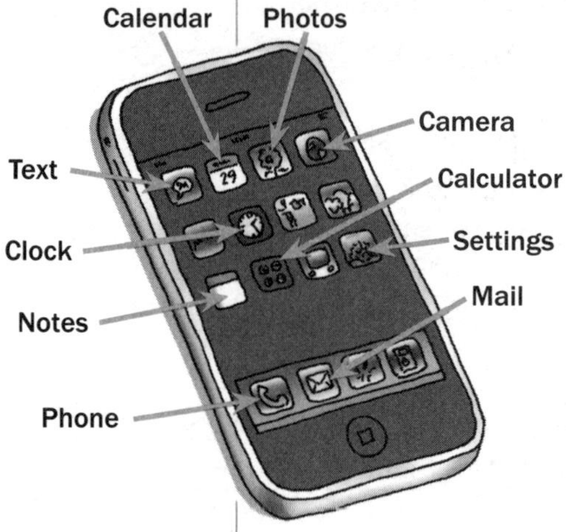

Some buttons on a smartphone are marked clearly with their function.

an icon that has the symbol of a reel-to-reel icon, an envelope icon, or both icons on it? That's probably what you tap to hear voice mails. Maybe there's a symbol of a phone's handset icon (ironically retro). Logic says you'll tap that to begin a call. I know it sounds elementary, but when you're intimidated, the obvious no longer seems obvious. So relax . . . don't think so much. Be like a kid and just play with the thing for a while. No harm, no foul.

At this stage, let's make a call (your home phone number is a good one to start with). Tap on the phone icon, type the numbers, then tap on the green call icon. (Again, no two models are alike, so consult the instructions that came with your phone, if any did.) Whether you need to dial a 1 and the area code first depends on where you're calling "from" and "to." Once someone in your home or your answering machine picks up, say "hi," and after you've chatted for a minute or left yourself a funny message, hang up. Hanging up is usually accomplished by tapping on the red **End Call** icon on the phone.

Now call someone you know, give that person your mobile phone number, and ask him or her to call you back. (It's a good idea to put yourself in your contacts so you can always find your own cell number.) When that first call comes in, take your time to read what appears on your screen. These practice calls are so important; they help you get used to the phone for when a "real" call happens. Again, your instructions will tell you about your specific phone.

Push My Buttons

If you own a tablet or have had the chance to play with one, you'll soon realize that a smartphone is simply a mini version of a tablet with calling capabilities. The screen is a collection of icons or apps (programs) for all the different tasks you can accomplish with the phone, just like a tablet. There are words below each icon or app. Take your time and read each of the apps' names. You may not know what each one means or what it can do at first, but it helps to simply have read the names to familiarize yourself with each program's existence.

Your Little Black Book

Before mobile phones were around, I memorized most of my friends' phone numbers. Now, I don't even try to remember them, because they're all stored in my phone. All smartphones have the ability to save your recently called telephone numbers, as well as street and email addresses, in their memories. Enter your important contact information in your phone once, and voilà, you've freed some storage space in your own memory.

There are several ways to store a number in the Contacts list on your phone. Here's one option for each type.

If you're using an Android, tap on the People app, then tap to add a person. Fill in the information and be sure to tap **Done** in the top left corner to complete your entry.

If you're using an iPhone, tap on the Contacts app, then tap + to add a person. Fill in the contact information and be sure to tap **Done** in the top right corner to complete your entry.

Unlike a cell phone, your smartphone will have a full keyboard so you can type a person's name like you would on a keyboard. If you make a mistake, there's a backspace key on your phone that allows you to delete. Again, experiment. No harm done. Refer to your instruction manual. Whenever you're learning an element of the phone, repeat the steps at least three times to help cement them in your memory. It's also a good idea to take notes, so you can refer to them later. Create your own cheat sheet until the actions become second nature.

DIFFERENT STYLE STYLUSES
Not every stylus works on every device. Be sure to inquire about the proper stylus for your device at the time of purchase.

You can use a stylus on the touch screen of most mobile phones.

KEEP YOUR NUMBERS
Many phones have a SIM (subscriber identity/information module) card that will store phone numbers. When you buy a new phone, those stored numbers can be moved from the old phone to the new one with the SIM card.

There Is No Place Like Home

Is there one button or key on your mobile phone that always brings you back to the main screen? You betcha. It could look like any of these: , , . Once you find that button or key, make it your friend and memorize it. If you've been fiddling with the phone and have lost your way, that is the button to bring you back home. Your other option, if you can't find your way, though it may sound extreme, is to turn off the phone and turn it back on by holding down the on/off button. But it would be better for you and the phone if you got accustomed to using the Home button. Again, ask your salesperson to point it out to you before you bring your phone home.

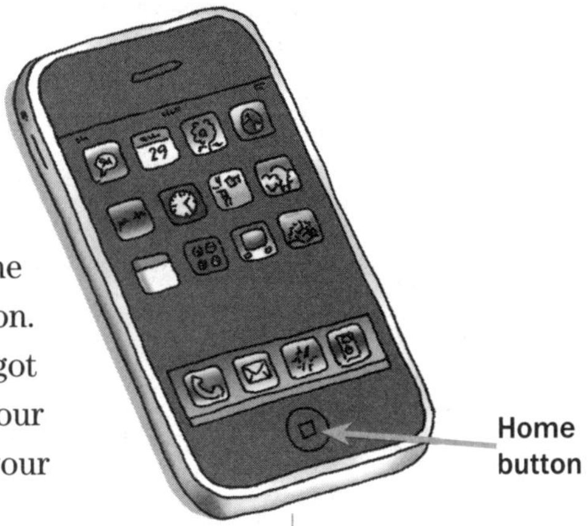

Leave Your Message After the Tone

Your mobile phone will definitely allow you to set up a voice-mail system so you can get messages from callers when you're unable to (or choose not to) answer the phone. The instruction manual will show you how to access those messages, but you can probably figure it out yourself if you fool around with the phone a bit. I cannot emphasize enough that playing with your phone makes it *yours*. This is the getting acquainted stage that comes in the beginning of any relationship. It is unnerving and exciting, and you may learn more about the phone in the first few days of introduction than in the years you spend together, so take advantage of this time of exploration and adventure!

My hunch is that there is this reel-to-reel icon , an envelope, or a combination thereof on one of the keys or the screen of your phone. Am I right? (All phones are not created equal, so the voice-mail symbol could be different.) Tap or hold down the voice-mail button, and the phone will either dial the number necessary to access your voice mail or go directly to it. Be sure to listen to all of the instructions to hear what options you have when connected to your voice mail.

This is also where you can record your outgoing message. When deciding what to say in your outgoing message, I believe honesty is the best policy. If you know that you're not likely to answer your cell phone or listen to your messages often, say so. My mother has

A variety of possible voice-mail symbols

YOUR PHONE, YOUR CHOICE

You have no obligation to use your cell phone for more than emergency calls or as a device to make calls and not receive them, but you should let your friends and relatives know, so they don't expect you to pick up.

a cell phone she keeps in her car's glove compartment only for emergencies, and I rarely answer my cell phone, unless I'm expecting a call. But many people use their cell phones all the time; nowadays some folks use their mobile phones for all their calls and don't even have a land line. To each his own.

Control Issues

Somewhere on your phone, you have access to a menu. You may be able to use a scroll bar on your phone to view all the items listed in the menu or to flip through the pages with your finger on the touch screen. In the menu, there is probably an option called **Settings**, **Tools**, **Customize**, **Options**, or **Preferences**, or you may see one of the symbols shown at left. (Whenever I see any of these words or symbols, I get curious about all that the device has to offer. And without curiosity, you'll never really take control of these gadgets, because you won't uncover the full extent of their capabilities.) This is where you get to set preferences for things like your phone's volume and ring type, whether it vibrates instead of rings when a call comes in, the number of rings before voice mail picks up, and what appears on the screen. Somewhere in the menu is probably a place where you can set an alarm clock, see other time zone times, use a calculator, and possibly even type short notes to yourself.

A variety of possible Settings or Tools symbols

Remember, we are just playing—nothing bad will happen if you change one of these settings. As a precaution, write down the original settings so you won't forget what they were. Then, if you change something and don't like it, you can change it back. This is a good rule of thumb when learning any technology. Always take notes along the way to help you remember what you did so you can either repeat it or correct it.

Phone Photography

Most mobile phones come with a built-in camera. Many also have the capability of taking short video clips. The cameras vary in quality, but overall the resolution and clarity is pretty darn impressive. It's all well and good to be able to whip out your phone and snap a photograph with it, but how the heck do you get the pictures from the phone to a computer or printer? There are a couple of options. You could email or text the photos directly from the phone. (Be sure to find out if there are additional fees if you use the email feature on your cell phone to transmit photographs to a computer. With enough add-on fees, suddenly an inexpensive phone plan isn't so inexpensive.) Some cell phones come with a USB cable that allows you to upload (or move) photos from the phone to a computer without use of the Internet. Ask about this feature at the time of purchase.

The next chapter is all about digital photography with a digital camera or a phone. So if that's an interest of yours, sit tight, because more information is coming your way.

Calendar Girls and Boys

I know that old habits die hard, but sometimes it's worth the trouble to let the old be replaced by the new. The calendar app  on your smartphone and tablet is one of these worthwhile temptations. Believe me, I'm familiar with that leather-bound thing you have—the one where you buy and insert fresh pages every year. Maybe all of your treasured addresses are in the same book. It was my bible, but I got so paranoid about losing it that I would copy pages out of it rather than take the whole thing with me on vacation.

Well, here's the thing about using technology to keep track of your events, birthdays, and doctor appointments—it won't get lost. What you input in your calendar, whether on your computer, tablet, or smartphone, gets synced across all devices almost instantaneously. So, if you lose your phone (God forbid!), you can still access the calendar from your computer. If using the app on your smartphone isn't comfortable because of the size, you can always access the calendar on your computer and do your inputting there, using that nice big keyboard.

Do what I did. Keep both the old-fashioned calendar, where you write and scratch out what's changed, and the new digital one simultaneously until you get used to the new system and trust it. For me, that took a couple of months, and then I let the old system take a permanent vacation.

A Calendar by Any Other Name Is Still a Calendar

Depending on your device and your preference, you can set up a calendar to work with Apple's iCloud, Google Calendar, or Microsoft's Outlook. Truth be told, devices are much more friendly now, so any of those choices should work on almost all devices. A good way to make the decision is to think about who is most likely to be helpful should you have questions about how to use the calendar. Ask them which calendar program they use and you use that one, too.

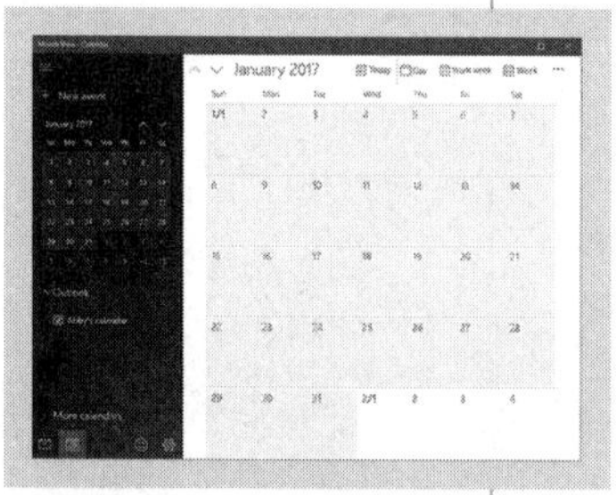

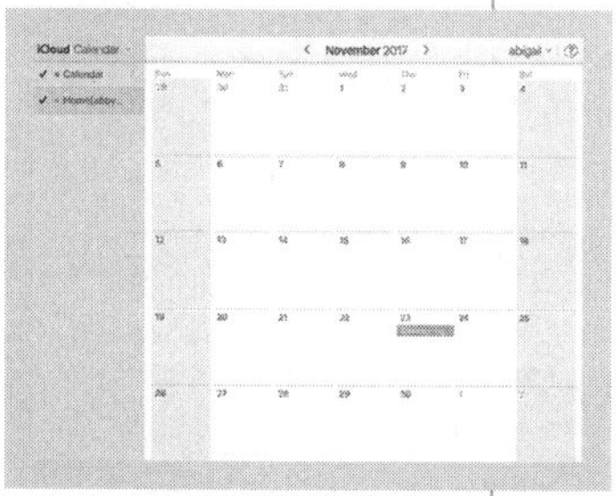

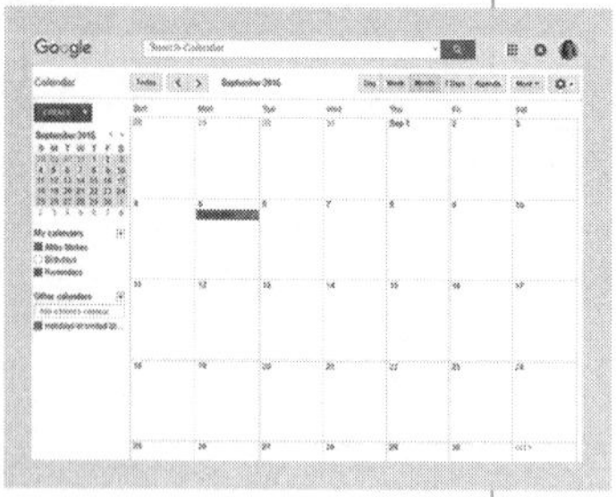

A great perk about using a calendar and having it be the same program as someone you share your life with is that you can share a calendar with them, too. Always wondering what the grandkids' schedule is? Ask to be included in the family calendar. Everything can be color-coded so you can identify which dates are your events and which are theirs.

Other Handy Calendar Features

Not only can you share calendars, but you can also send invitations from your calendar or respond to an invitation in an email. Once you RSVP via the email, the event will automatically be input into your calendar.

If the event is something that repeats, like a birthday, you can instruct the calendar to repeat it every year indefinitely. Or if it's something you'll be doing for the next 6 weeks on every Tuesday, you can customize that, as well. You can even set up alerts so you'll receive a reminder, at whatever time you desire, before the appointment.

So why not put it in your calendar that you're going to start using a digital calendar soon?

FOUR BATTERY-SAVING TIPS FOR YOUR MOBILE DEVICE

The last thing you want is for the battery on your smartphone (or tablet) to poop out when you need it most. Here are several ways you can save energy with your handheld device. There are two sets of step-by-step instructions below.

iPhone and iPad instructions

To reduce brightness:

- Tap **Settings.**
- Tap **Display & Brightness**.
- Drag circle on horizontal line to increase or decrease brightness.
- Tap the **Home** button to exit.

To turn off wi-fi:

- Tap **Settings.**
- Tap **wi-fi**.
- Tap and drag the **wi-fi** button to the right to activate.

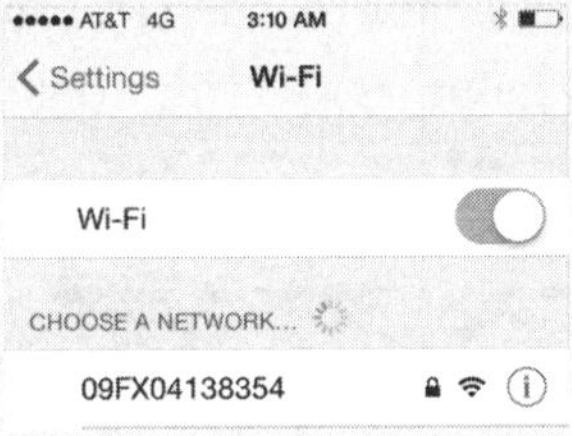

- You may need to ask for the password, if the wi-fi in the area is password protected.
- Tap the **Home** button to exit.

To turn on airplane mode:

- Tap **Settings.**
- Tap **Airplane Mode**.
- Tap and drag the **Airplane Mode** button to the right to activate.
- Tap the **Home** button to exit.

To change auto-lock setting:

- Tap **Settings.**
- Tap **General**.
- Move the screen up and tap on **Auto-Lock**.
- Choose the duration you prefer (less time gives you more battery life).
- Tap the **Home** button to exit.

Android smartphone and tablet instructions

To reduce brightness:

- Tap **Settings**.
- Tap **Display**.
- Tap **Brightness**. Brightness
- Drag circle on horizontal line to increase or decrease brightness.
- Tap the **Home** button to exit.

To turn off wi-fi:

- Tap **Settings**.
- Tap and drag the **wi-fi** button to the right to activate. Wi-Fi ON
- Tap the **Home** button to exit.

To turn on airplane mode:

- Tap on Settings.
- Tap in the box to the right of **Airplane Mode**. (You may need to tap on **More . . .** under wi-fi to find **Airplane Mode**.) Airplane mode ON
- Tap the **Home** button to exit.

To change display sleep setting:

- Tap on **Settings**.
- Tap on **Display**.
- Tap on **Sleep**.
- Choose the duration you prefer (less time gives you more battery life).
- Tap the **Home** button to exit.

AUTOTEXT OUGHT TO HELP

Some phones automatically start to suggest or guess the word you're trying to write using the keypad of the phone. This feature is called AutoTexting and can save time and keystrokes.

Texting Is Faster Than a Speeding Bullet

You may have noticed that your tech-savvy friends and relatives (especially the younger ones) opt to text rather than email. With poky old email, you compose your message, click Send, and then wait until the recipient accesses his or her email inbox and replies. There's no waiting with a text message. As fast as your fingers can tap your words and press Send, your missive appears on the recipient's cell or smartphone. Texting takes place in real time, just like actual conversations. The slowest part with texting for me is my lousy typing!

Text messages are sent to a person's cell phone number. As with email, you can send a text message to multiple people simultaneously, but be kind and make sure everyone is aware they're receiving the text as a group. Don't be surprised if a text slips through from someone you don't know. Simply ignore it like you would a wrong number.

IOW W/B (IN OTHER WORDS, WRITE BACK)

Due to the brevity of this form of communication, shortcuts are often used. Below are some abbreviations that you may want to try in addition to the emoticons found on page 294.

B4 Before

BBL Be back later

BC Because

BFN Bye for now

BTW By the way

CU See you

F2F Face-to-face

GL Good luck

GR8 Great

GTG Got to go

HAGD Have a good day

IDK I don't know

IG2R I've got to run

IMHO In my humble opinion

IRL In real life

JK Just kidding

JMO Just my opinion

L8R Later

To learn **Texting Tips,** visit ***AskAbbyStokes.com.*** Click on Video Tutorials at the top, then click on Video #10.

You may also want to revisit **How To Turn Your Emoji On,** Video #7.

Texts are quick and often abbreviated. You have an unlimited amount of space to write your text message, but a lengthy missive kind of defeats the purpose. Texting is all about fast communication. It's faster than email because you bypass the formalities of inserting a subject, email address, etc. Texting is to email what passing a note in class is to writing a letter.

A series of text messages

TAP AND GO

1. Look for blinking line.
2. Type message.
3. Tap Send.

LOL Laughing out loud

NVM Never mind

OMG Oh my God

OTL Out to lunch

NP No problem

PLS/PLZ Please

POS Parent over shoulder

PU That stinks!

ROFL Rolling on the floor laughing

RUOK Are you OK?

TSTB The sooner, the better

TTYL Talk to you later

TY Thank you

UR You're/your

WAM Wait a minute

YW You're welcome

ZZZZ Sleeping

<3 Love/heart

Try to translate this: **RUOK? WOULD <3 2 GO OTL.TSTB. IG2R. ;)**

Are you OK? I would love to go out to lunch. The sooner, the better. I've got to run. Smile and a wink.

TEXTIQUETTE

Please do not think that text messaging is less intrusive than speaking on the phone during a movie or live performance. It is still a rude distraction for those around you.

HANG UP AND DRIVE

According to one Carnegie Mellon University study, driving while using a cell phone reduces the amount of brain activity associated with driving by 37 percent. A 2011 National Highway Traffic Safety Administration study concluded that cell phones caused over 3,300 deaths and nearly 400,000 injuries that year.

Driving + Chatting/Texting on the Cell Phone = Danger Alert!

Using a cell phone while driving is a hazard, whether the phone is handheld or hands-free (using a headset rather than a handset). Cell phone use is a proven cognitive distraction to drivers. Unlike other driving distractions (e.g., conversations with passengers, radio listening, etc.), phone conversations can cause a kind of "tunnel vision" in which the driver's brain is not actually registering what her eyes are seeing. A report from Fatality Analysis Reporting System (FARS) determined that 52 percent of fatal car accidents in 2011 involved cell phone use. Simply said: Hang up and drive! If there is something so important that you must make a call or send a text, pull over and then do it. This is a personal issue for me as my sister was almost killed by a driver texting behind the wheel last year. Just don't do it.

Six Travel Tips with Smartphones

Are you planning a trip out of the country? Let's talk about precautions you should take so you don't come home to a smartphone bill that'll ruin your vacation afterglow.

1. **Call your cell phone service provider (AT&T, Verizon, Sprint, etc.)**. Before traveling overseas, talk with your cell phone service provider and ask what packages they offer for international cell phone use. I'm an AT&T customer and they have several different choices of global plans. Think about how you might want to use your phone (calling the United States, calling within the country you're visiting, texting, email, etc.) and ask how each of those is billed under your provider's international plan.

2. **Turn off data roaming.** Assuming you didn't pay for an unlimited cellular data plan, the moment you board the plane, for your international destination, go into the Settings on your smartphone and turn off Data Roaming and Cellular Data Plan. That's the best way to prevent your phone from randomly using

data to search for emails and texts throughout the day. Better that you control specifically when the cellular data is used. You can turn Cellular Data on and off as you need it so as not to exceed the plan you've chosen.

3. **Wi-fi is your new BFF.** If the hotel or home you're visiting has wi-fi, you're all set. When on wi-fi, you can check email, visit websites, send photos, text, and use the GPS feature on your phone. You want to be careful when you're outside of that wi-fi area. That's when things can get pricey. Wi-fi is a free zone where you can use almost all of the features of your phone without incurring additional charges. The one exception is voice calling. You may still be charged international fees for phone calls (in and out). You might have the option of turning on wi-fi calling, or better yet use a service like Skype.

TAKE THE BITE OUT OF BLUETOOTH

Bluetooth technology offers a cable-free connection among cell phones, computers (desktops, laptops, and handhelds), and other peripherals (such as printers and wireless earpieces). It allows all of these devices to speak to one another without any cables attaching them, and it works with virtually every new model of cell phone. But be aware that hands-free cell phone use while driving is still illegal in many states and is no less dangerous than hands-on driving and calling.

4. **Skype your phone calls.** Skype is a free website and an app that allows you to use your smartphone, tablet, or computer to call, text, or video chat internationally for free or at greatly reduced prices. (You can learn all about Skype on page 360.) When you're in a wi-fi area and communicating with another Skype user, your calls, video chats, or texts are free. Free! Using a credit card you can open a Skype account and pay a very small (and I mean *very small*) amount to call people who aren't registered with Skype. I have yet to see a phone company offer more competitive pricing than Skype for international phone calls.

5. **When in doubt, use airplane mode.** If you arrive at your destination and can't remember what your smartphone plan allows for, simply go to your Settings and turn on Airplane Mode. Airplane Mode will stop all transmission to or from the phone. So, no emails, texts, phone calls, or visiting websites. No signal = no ugly phone bills. You can still take and view photos, read your notes, or listen to any music saved on your

phone. Once you're back in the safety of a wi-fi area, you can turn off Airplane Mode and turn on wi-fi.

6. **Document with your camera.** Of course you're going to take photos of everything you love about your visit. Why not also take a photo of your passport and the back and front of your credit cards so you'll have that information on your phone at all times? I even take a photo of my rental car, when traveling, and its license plate to make it easier to identify in a parking lot full of cars.

Remember that to put away your smartphone for a day is a great vacation choice. Smell the roses, enjoy the sea breeze, or linger in a museum while your smartphone becomes your personal assistant, taking all of your messages.

Navigate Google Maps on Your Smartphone

A global-mapping app, **Google Maps** offers satellite imagery, street maps, actual traffic conditions, as well as route planning for getting from here to there by foot, car, bicycle, and public transportation. So, one way that a smartphone has improved driving safety is when it's used for navigation. Your smartphone can hang from the rearview mirror or attach to the dashboard, leaving your hands free while it guides you on your way. Much better than trying to read an unwieldy map while driving. Visit the Travel & AutoTech Store section of AskAbbyStokes.com to see suggested car-phone holders.

Google Maps vs Maps

If you have an iPhone, Google Maps may not be pre-installed. The iPhone comes pre-installed with Maps. They are very similar in purpose and use, but we'll be focusing specifically on Google Maps. Revisit Chapter 12 for a refresher on how to add an app (software application/program) to your tablet. The same instructions hold true for adding an app to your smartphone.

THREE TIPS TO PROTECT YOU AND YOUR SMARTPHONE IF IT IS LOST OR STOLEN

When a cell phone was just a cell phone, loss or theft was an inconvenience. Because a smartphone is the gateway to your emails, contact information, and much, much more, loss or theft can be a serious security breach. Here are the three steps to take to ensure protection.

- Set a **Passcode** (see page 109 for details).
- Activate **Find My Phone**.
- Set **Auto-Lock** (this will also help you save battery life).

P.S. All the same tips apply to your tablet.

Finding Your Way Around

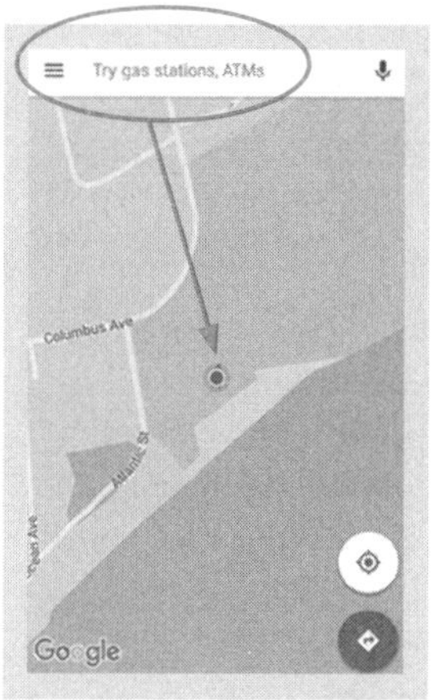

■ The blue dot shows your current location.

Before we ask Google Maps to provide directions, let's get used to some of its features. To find yourself, tap on ◎. The map will then zero in on your current location. From here you can pinch or spread the screen to zoom in or out of your location. Take a peek back at "Mastering the Touch Screen," on page 111, if you need a refresher.

The blue dot represents where you are. At the top of the screen is a text box where you type in the address of your destination. As you type, suggestions for what you seek will start to appear in a list below. If your destination appears, you can stop typing and tap on it. But be sure that it's the correct town and state—not just the street. There are a lot of 25 Main Streets out there!

Once you see your destination on the screen, tap on the blue circle in the bottom right. The next screen will allow you to choose whether you're traveling by car, public transportation, foot, or bicycle.

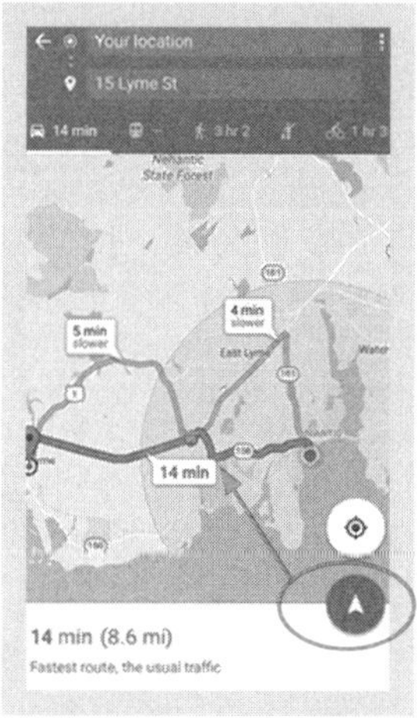

■ Choose your route, then tap the arrow to start directions.

The next screen gives you a choice of route, if there is a choice. Tap on whichever route you desire, then tap on the arrow in the blue circle at the bottom right. The screen will also show the length of the trip and the estimated time of the trip.

Once you've tapped on the arrow, you're on your way. The app will now talk you through the journey, alerting you to where and how soon your next turn will be, while the map indicates your place en route.

Any calls, texts, or emails will be held on the phone until you've arrived. So please don't be tempted to answer any overtures while you are in transit.

Phone It In or Out, but Please Don't Shout: Cell Phone Etiquette

Mobile phones can be a lifesaver or a public nuisance, depending on whether you're in control of the phone or the phone is in control of you. We've all encountered cell phone rudeness—don't be a perpetrator.

Turn off your cell phone at public performances, please.

First and foremost, keep your conversation to a dull roar. A quiet purr would be even better. Every day on the street, in the grocery store, or on a bus, many of us overhear personal conversations that we should not be privy to and, frankly, probably wish we had never heard. There are also countless cell phone users who've decided to conduct their business dealings alfresco, and we have no choice but to hear what a lousy boss they have or are. My only explanation is that Loud Larry and Shouting Shelly seem to think the cell phone is a paper cup and a string without a mechanism to project one's voice to the person on the other end. Wrong! I have tested the microphone built into my cell phone, and whispering is just as effective as shouting; no one is subjected to my conversation.

In addition, keep in mind the following cell phone civilities:

- When choosing a ringtone, remember that those around you are hearing it, too, especially if you are slow to pick up. There are only so many times we really want to hear "Macarena."
- During public performances (yes, even at the movies) turn your cell phone off—not on vibrate, so your purse seems about to take off when the phone rings, but *off*. And refrain from text messaging on your phone. We may not be able to hear your conversation, but your typing gyrations and the lit-up phone screen are a distraction nonetheless. Why did you come to the performance, anyway?
- For the sake of your dinner partner, decide you can live without the phone at the dining table. An hour or two without being disturbed by the phone should be a relief, not a punishment.

IT'S A SMALL WORLD AFTER ALL

We'll talk Skype, Facebook, Twitter, and LinkedIn in Chapter 20. You can access and enjoy all four of these forms of communication on your smartphone. Over 75 percent of Facebook users access Facebook through a mobile device. Amazing!

Q: What is Bluetooth and how do I use it with my phone?

A: Have you seen people with those *Star Trek*–like devices in their ears? Bluetooth technology allows your phone to send and receive signals between both your computer and your earpiece without wires. There is no wire going from the earpiece to the phone, but a signal is sent so the caller can use the phone through that earpiece. The wireless technology is called Bluetooth.

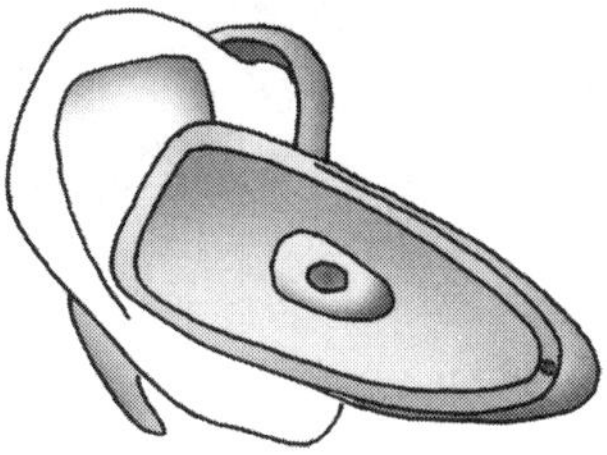

A wireless cell phone earpiece

Q: What is an SMS message?

A: SMS stands for short message service—and an SMS message is also known as a text. An SMS message can be up to 160 characters and is sent to a cell phone or computer.

CHAPTER 19

PICTURE THIS

Digital and scanned photos from A to Z

Gone are the days of Instamatic cameras, drugstore runs to drop off film and pick up photos, and costly photocopies at your local copy store. I can remember back to flashbulbs and carbon paper. Thank heavens, that is all behind us. Nowadays, modern technology offers us a digital answer to taking pictures and copying documents. A tablet, smartphone, or digital camera can capture your precious memories, and photo-editing software lets you play professional photographer. A computer and scanner bring the copy shop into the comfort of your own home.

Say "Cheese"

The popularity of digital photographs is no surprise. You don't have to buy film, you're able to view your photos instantaneously, and you can share them with friends and family without a middle man. Long before digital cameras, I stopped taking pictures entirely because my photos always looked like they were taken during an earthquake. I'd be so frustrated because I wouldn't know for a week that the pictures were lousy, and the disappointing discovery was expensive. So I threw in the photography towel. Now, however,

I'm back in the game. If you haven't played with one yet, digital cameras have a display screen, so you can view the photo seconds after you shoot it, to see if a retake is necessary. You can also take photos with your smartphone or tablet and view them immediately on the device. Amazing technology!

WHICH IS BETTER? DIGITAL CAMERA VS. SMARTPHONE

Which is the best choice for taking pictures? The answer: whichever you have with you when you want to take a photo. Smartphone and tablet cameras do a great job, but they still don't beat out the resolution or customization possible with the better lens available on a good digital camera. However, if you're not printing your photos, the difference in quality may not be a concern.

Instead of on film, digital images are stored on the memory card of the camera or the internal memory of the smartphone or tablet. You can view, edit, and delete photos on any of these devices, but that can be a drain on their battery life. A battery-saving choice would be to transfer the photos to your computer and do the edits and purge from there. When you buy a camera, it will come with software. Once the software is installed on the computer, the camera and computer communicate through a cable included with the camera that you'll plug into both pieces of equipment when you want to transfer your photos. Most smartphones and tablets sync the photos with the computer wirelessly, so none of these accessories are necessary.

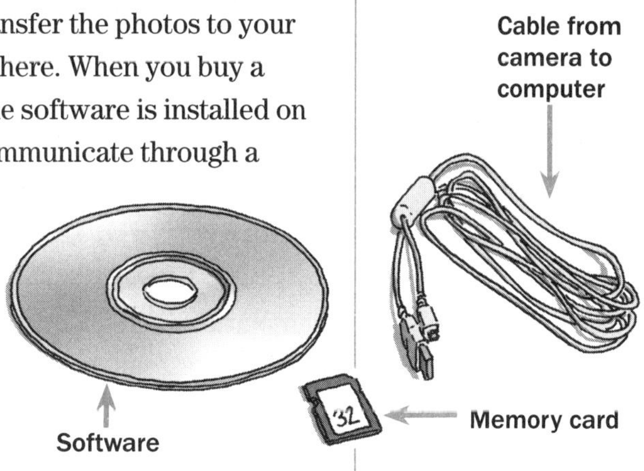

Digital Photo Basics

Digital cameras, smartphones, and tablets come in a wide spectrum of designs, styles, and prices. Consult with friends and family who are already taking digital photos, and ask what they recommend you purchase. Thankfully, all digital cameras come with simple but detailed instruction manuals that describe the device's various settings. Start snapping away as soon as you buy your device, since you can delete any bad pictures, but promise yourself that at some convenient time, you'll sit down with the camera in hand and go through the features in the instruction manual.

A SPARE PAIR
Always bring an extra set of batteries with you in your camera bag. Viewing the photos on the camera screen uses up a lot of battery power, so it's easy to wear down the batteries in a short amount of time.

IT'S A NUMBERS GAME

Do you know the size of the image you want? Are you printing it or only sending it over the Internet?

With a camera, you choose the resolution before taking the photo. Resolution refers to the number of pixels in an image. Images are commonly measured in dots per inch (dpi) instead of pixels per inch, but they are one and the same. Here's a guide for choosing the resolution measured in dpi.

- Less than 640 x 480—for Internet use only
- 1024 x 768—Internet and any size up to and including 4-inch by 6-inch prints
- 1152 x 864—Internet and any size up to and including 5-inch by 7-inch prints
- 1600 x 1200—Internet and prints as large as 8 inches by 10 inches

With a smartphone or tablet, you choose the resolution when you send the image by email or text.

Rather than numbers, you may be given the choice of small, medium, large, or actual size.

Memory Card Capacity

Your digital camera will come with a memory card, which stores the photographs taken by your camera, instead of storing the photos on film. I suggest that you purchase an additional memory card—one that offers more storage capacity than the original—so you won't worry about filling up the smaller memory card that came with your camera before you're done taking pictures of your white-water rafting trip.

A memory card

BE KIND TO YOUR MEMORY CARD

Do not remove the memory card from the camera while the camera is taking a photo or a photo is being viewed. It is best to turn off the camera first. When the camera indicates that the battery is low, believe it. Taking a picture when the battery is low can corrupt the memory card. It is always better to delete photos from your computer than from the memory card. Deleting from the memory card can cause the card to become defective.

Think about purchasing a memory card with at least 8 GB (gigabytes) of storage, but why not go for the gusto with a 32-gig card, since the price point isn't that different?

If you have a digital camera, you may want to purchase a memory card reader. It is a device that plugs into your computer by way of a USB cable. You take the memory card out of your camera and place it in the reader. Now you can transfer images from the memory card onto the computer. Transferring images from the camera to the computer directly can be a real strain on the camera's batteries.

Digital images are made up of hundreds and thousands of pixels.

Pixel This

Pixel is an abbreviation of "picture element." Digital images are made up of hundreds and thousands of small squares called pixels. Pixels establish not only the quality of the photo (more pixels equal a clearer image) but also the color and the size when viewed on a computer.

A digital camera, smartphone, or tablet with a lower megapixel count (1 million pixels) delivers images good enough for email, or to put on a website, or to look at on your computer screen, but these photos do not make good prints. Nowadays, it's unusual to find a new digital camera, smartphone, or tablet with less than 8 megapixels. The higher the number of megapixels, the higher the quality of the photo. Shop accordingly.

Snapping with a Smartphone or Tablet

Chances are very good that your smartphone or tablet will not come with specific instructions for taking photos. Let's review some of the basic photography functions on an Android and an iPhone or iPad so you can get started.

Here is the Android camera app icon  and here's the photo gallery app icon . (We'll look at Apple's on the next page.)

There are two possible symbols that will appear at the bottom of the screen when you are in the camera program. The mini camera icon indicates that, if you tap on it, you will take a photograph. That's it. One tap on the mini camera icon and you've snapped a photo that will now appear in your photo gallery. The video image icon lets you know that the device will shoot video. Tap on the video image icon to start recording. When you want to stop shooting video, tap on the box that now appears at the bottom of the screen.

To change the camera mode from photo to video or vice versa, touch and drag your finger from the left edge of the touch screen to the center. A menu appears on the left where you can tap on the camera or video icon, depending on your fancy.

There might be two camera lenses on your Android. One takes a photo in the direction that you face and another camera faces you. Tap on the three dots in the bottom right of the screen. One of the options that appears is , which redirects the camera to either focus out or right back at you.

SELFIES AREN'T SELFISH

A selfie is a self-portrait taken with a digital camera, smartphone, or tablet. It is usually taken at arm's length or with a mirror and can have more than just yourself in the photo.

Here is the Apple camera app icon and here's the photo gallery app icon on an iPhone or iPad.

Your iPhone and iPad can shoot still photos or video. To change the camera mode from photo to video or vice versa, place your finger above the word video or photo at the bottom of the screen, and touch and drag whichever format you desire into the center above the circle that appears at the bottom. The circle will be white for photo mode and red for video mode.

If you tap on the white circle icon , you will take a photograph. That's it. One tap and you've snapped a photo that will now appear in your photo gallery. Tap on the red circle to start recording video. When you want to stop shooting video, tap on the red box that now appears at the bottom of the screen.

There will be two camera lenses on your iPhone or iPad. One takes a photo in the direction that you face and another camera faces you. Tap , in the top right, to redirect the camera to either focus out or right back at you.

Plan to Scan, Stan?

You were introduced to the concept of a scanner on page 21. Now we're going to put one to use! As a refresher, a scanner works much like a copy machine. Lift the lid of the scanner, place an item on the scanner glass facedown, and the scanner makes a copy. The difference is that rather than the copy being printed, it is stored in the brain of your computer. From there, you can print the scan, email it as an attachment, or store it to refer to at a later date. The scan lives on as a file in your computer until you decide to throw it away. If you haven't already purchased a scanner, keep in mind that a flatbed scanner gives you more options because it offers the ability to make copies from a book or other bulky item, not just a single sheet of paper. I'll tell you a secret, but you have to promise not to tell my publisher. I used to tear pages out of my cookbooks to scan and send recipes as attachments (a very bad habit). Now, with a flatbed scanner, my cookbooks remain intact and I can still share recipes with friends as email attachments.

"I no longer have to gather my newspaper clippings and make trips to the library copy machine with my change in hand. Having a scanner at home has saved me so much time and money. I can also make my own copies in color!"
—*Arlene*

When you purchase a scanner or a combination scanner, printer, and copier, it usually comes with installation software. Some stand-alone scanners do not require an electrical cord—they draw power from the computer. Follow the sequence of the installation instructions included with the scanner. Don't hesitate to ask a friend to help. I believe you can install it on your own, but there's no harm in having someone by your side.

A flatbed scanner (top) allows a book to be scanned. A single-feed scanner (bottom) can scan individual pages only.

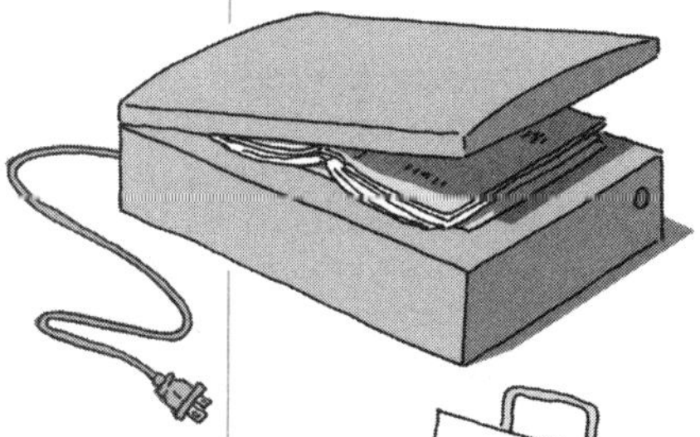

Find a photograph, document, or page from a book that you would like to scan. Place the object facedown on the scanner glass. There are usually arrows to guide the placement of an object to be scanned. Most scanners have a button that you push to initiate scanning. My experience is that if you have a choice between using the button on the scanner or initiating the scan through the software, you should go with the latter. (There's not enough room here to explain why, but trust me: The process is more intuitive and less problematic when I go through the software first.) An icon probably appeared on your Desktop screen during the installation of the software—it is the pathway to the scanner's software.

I don't know what brand or model scanner you own, so these scanning instructions will be general to all scanners. When you open your scanner software, look at what's on your computer screen and patiently try to find the equivalent of what is in the illustration of a scanner window in the steps to follow. Remember the rental car analogy? All scanners have similar components and essentially function in the same way, but your screen may look different from what you see here. Don't let that throw you for a loop. Any time you use the computer, it's important for you to be flexible and develop intuition about how you decipher what's on the screen, because there may be no consistency from one program or website to another. Adaptability and patience help you conquer something like your scanner. You're in no rush, so take your time reading everything on the screen before clicking. Take a break whenever you need one.

- Double-click on the icon for your scanner/printer. If there is no icon on the Desktop, go to your Programs/Applications and open it from there.

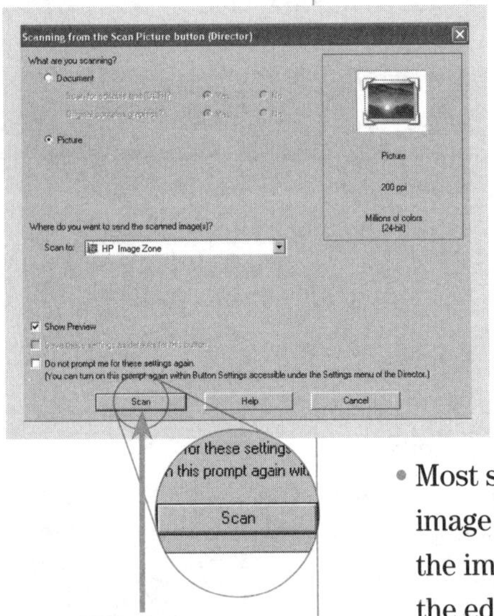

Click Scan.

- Click on **Scan**, **Scan Picture**, or **Scan Document**. If you don't see the word **Scan**, click on **File** and it should appear in the menu. If you don't see the word **Scan** anywhere, look for the word **Import**. You'll be given a chance at some point to let the scanner know whether you're scanning a picture or a document and in color or in black and white. The scanner will scan the item differently according to the nature of the item to be scanned. Text can be scanned with less definition than a photo.
- Most scanners at this point will show you a preview of the image being scanned. Often there will be a dotted line around the image. You can click and drag this dotted line to establish the edges of the item (or portion of the item) to be scanned.

You'll likely also be offered a variety of options for customizing your image (e.g., resizing, lightening/darkening).

- Be patient when scanning. The scanner may make some bumping and grinding noises while it calibrates, preparing itself to scan. Don't try to speed things up . . . wait.
- Before accepting the Preview of your image, check the resolution. Resolution is measured in dots per inch (dpi). The higher the dpi, the more detailed or clearer the image will be. However, the higher the dpi, the more space the image will take in bytes, and the larger size may make it difficult or slow to send as an attachment. Look for the word **Resolution** on the screen. If it isn't visible in the window you're viewing, click on each item in the Menu Bar to reveal where you can customize the resolution. I suggest you scan images at 100 dpi, especially if you want to email them.
- Now is the moment of truth. Click **Scan**, **Accept**, **OK**, or whatever else makes sense to continue the scanning process. Again, you'll have to wait because this step may take a minute or two.

CLICK AND GO

1. Click and drag edges to crop image.
2. Customize image.
3. Click Accept.

A preview of your scan will appear.

- If you're asked whether you have another item to scan, click **No**. (Let's not get into multiple pages on your maiden voyage.)
- Again, *wait*. At this juncture, another part of the scanning software will open, revealing your fabulous new scan, but it may take a moment to appear. Look at the Title Bar of the new window. This may give you a clue as to where to find the scan later. See if you can click somewhere on the name of this new file. (It is probably scan.jpg or scan1.jpg.) Click on the name and see if you can change it to whatever would make sense to you. This is important so you can identify your scan later.

Congratulations! You created a scan of a photo or document. While you're viewing the scanner's software, click on every item listed in the Menu Bar. Read the drop-down menus for each item. Even if you don't understand most of what you see, some of it will look familiar to you (Print, Save As, etc.). A little investigation goes a long way in becoming familiar and comfortable with your computer and its programs.

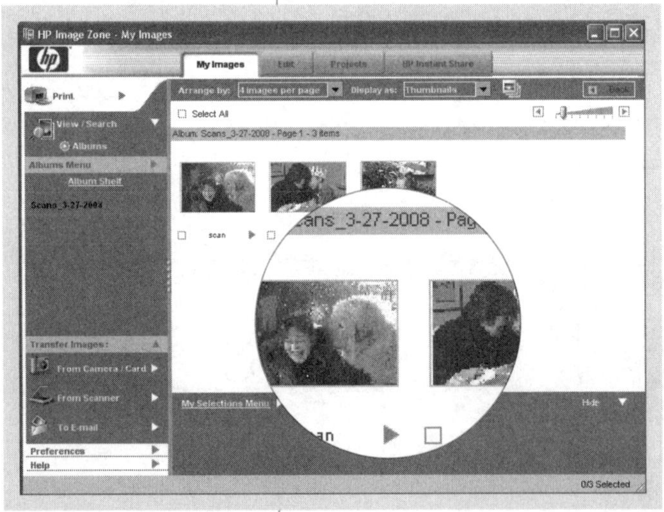

A few examples of completed scans

If your first attempt didn't work properly, don't be hard on yourself (or your friend, the computer). You are learning. It is inevitable that things won't always go your way along this journey of discovery. Don't be discouraged. Try again. Write down the steps you take so you can follow them or amend them as necessary. A week or longer may pass before you have the need to scan again. It's always helpful to have clear notes at the ready to assist you next time, in case you forget the sequence of steps that worked.

Send and Receive Photos and Scans

Once you have an image living on your computer—whether it came there by way of a cable from your digital camera, smartphone, or tablet, from a scan you made, or because someone emailed it to you—I suggest you give it a name that you'll recognize down the line. Why? Imagine how many photographs you'll accumulate over the time you have your computer. Now imagine if all of them had different numbers as their names. How on earth would you be able to quickly find that adorable photograph of Samantha with birthday cake all over her face?

"A few years ago I couldn't imagine ever needing a scanner, but I was given one as a gift and I use it all the time." —*Lillian*

In Chapter 21 we're going to create folder systems for what you have stored on your computer. That way you can organize your photos and documents to access them readily, but for now let's rename an image on your computer. We're also going to discuss storing on the cloud (i.e., the Internet). (For more about "the cloud," sit tight. You'll learn more in Chapter 21.)

When you receive photographs as attachments from someone, the name of each image is often a random number designated by their camera. You can rectify the situation after the image has been downloaded to your computer. (If you skipped Chapter 17, go back and read it to find out how to download attachments.) The numerical designation also happens with photos taken on a smartphone or tablet.

The easiest way to rename an image is to move your mouse onto the icon for the image. Click once to highlight the icon, wait a second or two, and then click once directly on the name of the image. Now all the text below the image should be highlighted. Whatever you type will replace the current name. Once you've typed the new name, depress and release the **Enter** or **Return** key on the keyboard. May I suggest that you include in the name the subject of the image and the date (at least the year) and perhaps something about where it was taken or what they are doing? The ideal name tells you all you need to know about the photo without having to open it to see what it is.

WHAT'S IN A NAME?

As you've learned on page 308, every file on your computer has a suffix or extension that identifies the type of item it is or the software it needs in order to be read. Most images end with either .jpg, .bmp, .gif, or .tif.

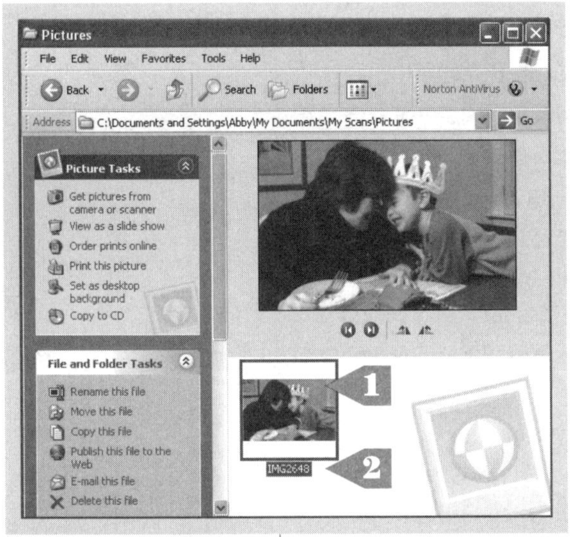

Now that you've renamed your photos, feel free to send them to friends or family as email attachments following the steps in Chapter 17. Whoever you send them to will appreciate that you have given the images names rather than sent them on with the random numbers the camera gave each image.

Save Me!

Let's talk about some safety measures for your treasured memories. After you transfer your photos from the camera to the computer, you'll want to empty the memory card so there's plenty of room for you to snap away. The camera's instruction manual will walk you through those simple steps. You may or may not want to delete the photos off of your smartphone or tablet. Some people like to continue to view them (and show them off) from their device as long as they have enough memory. Either way, now the photos you took live on your computer. Right? What happens if your computer is stolen or breaks down? The photos of the family reunion you documented could be lost forever. It is crucial to back up your photographs (and all your important files) regularly.

We haven't really discussed backing up the computer before. You should back up your computer at regular intervals, depending on how

CLICK AND GO

1. Click on image.
2. Wait a second and click on name. Type new name to replace highlighted text.
3. Hit the Enter or Return key on keyboard.

NOW CUSTOMIZE YOUR DESKTOP

In Chapter 12, we set the Background or Wallpaper on the Desktop of your computer. Now that you have photographs on your computer, smartphone, or tablet, those photos can be chosen as the background on your Desktop. Return to Chapter 12 to refresh your memory of how to customize your Desktop. But this time, instead of selecting from the images offered, click on **Browse** or **Choose** to find a photo from your collection.

you use it. If you only use your computer for email and to surf the Internet, there's really not much to back up. If you have web-based email, your email service keeps your emails on their computers. (That's why you can access your email from any computer, not just yours at home.) However, if you use your computer to write documents, create spreadsheets, and store photographs and/or music, you'll want to save that information onto a backup periodically, in case something happens to your computer.

DEAR SOUTHPAW
If you reversed the features of the mouse, as described on page 185, reverse the instructions here.

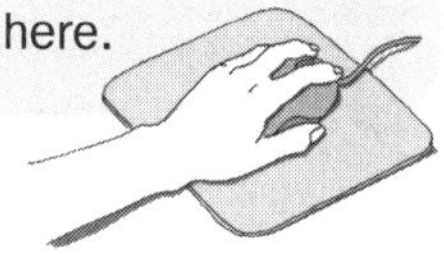

Backing Up onto a CD or DVD

If your desktop or laptop has an internal media drive, a writable CD or DVD is a great way to back up a whole lot of information. A couple of different methods are available to copy data from your computer onto a CD or DVD. Here's one method.

If you have a PC:

- Open the CD or DVD drawer. Be gentle, as it is a fragile piece of equipment, and yet be firm enough, if you have a laptop, that the CD or DVD snaps into place. Close the drawer.
- A window may automatically open. Close the window by clicking on the **Close Box** ☒ in the top right corner.
- Make sure any documents or photos you want to back up are closed. You can't back up something if it's open.
- Move your mouse onto the icon of the folder or file you want to back up.
- Remember from Chapter 12 that your mouse has two buttons, one on the left and one on the right. Up until now you've mostly been using the left mouse button (see "Dear Southpaw," above). Now you're going to use the right button. The right button on the mouse opens up an advanced menu, allowing you to perform tasks in fewer steps—kind of like a shortcut. Try it now: Right-click on the item to back up.

PC USERS—TRY TO RIGHT-CLICK
You right-click the mouse to get the advanced menu. Once the advanced menu is available, you left-click from that point forward.

CLICK AND GO

1. Right-click on folder icon.
2. Left-click on Send To.
3. Left-click on CD or DVD Drive.

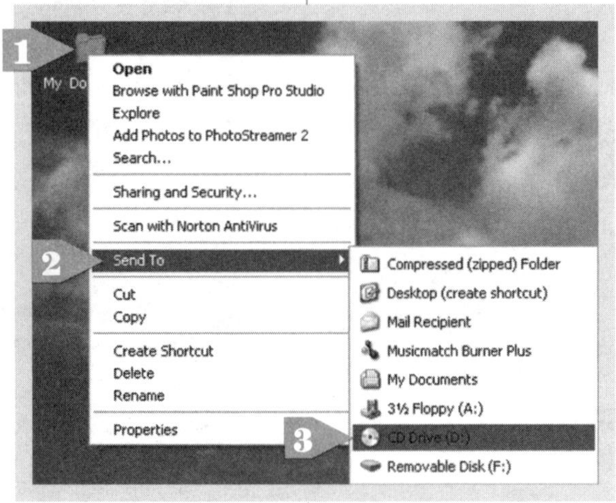

- A menu opens. Move your mouse onto **Send To** and left-click.
- Another menu has opened to the side. Move your mouse into that menu and left-click on the **CD Drive**. (It may read **DVD/CD-RW Drive**.) Give the computer a minute to copy.
- To remove the CD or DVD, open the drawer.

If you have a Mac:

- Push the CD or DVD into the slot. The computer will grab the CD or DVD from you. An icon for the CD or DVD will appear on the Desktop.
- Click and drag the folder or file you want to back up onto the CD or DVD icon. Release the mouse.
- Give the computer a minute to copy.
- To remove the CD or DVD, click and drag it to the Trash.

That's all it takes to copy something from your computer onto a CD or DVD! At some point, you'll back up your entire system, but for now we'll stick with this simple method to back up desired files such as the first draft of your memoir or those adorable photos of Fido.

Backing Up onto the Cloud

I live in New York City, where apartments are small and many people have more stuff than they can fit in their tiny spaces. One option available is to rent space at a mini-storage facility. Those extra boxes of books, your golf clubs, and Aunt Millie's china are kept safe and sound under someone else's roof. That's similar to what the cloud is . . . an option for storing your documents or photos on someone else's computer rather than taking up space on yours. Essentially, you open an account (some are free, some are not) with a website where you can upload, or move, your photos and documents to be stored.

I'm telling you about this *after* describing how to copy your photos onto a CD or DVD because there is no guarantee that whatever website you choose (*dropbox.com* or a specific photo site such as *shutterfly.com*) will not have some catastrophic failure and lose your stuff, the same way the mini-storage facility could have a tragic fire. Both the cloud and mini-storage take every precaution, but stuff happens.

If your photos really matter to you, why not safeguard them with every method possible? Back them up onto CDs or DVDs—clearly marked and tucked somewhere in your home—*and* upload your photos to the cloud, where you can access them from any computer with an Internet connection. Better safe than sorry, right?

"I didn't even know I wanted to take photographs, but when I was given a digital camera for my sixtieth birthday from my grandkids, a whole new world opened up for me. I'm now the official family photographer."

—Oliver

Backing Up onto an External Hard Drive

Another option is an external hard drive, which is a small storage device that you plug into your computer. In much the same way that photos can be moved onto a CD or DVD or into the cloud, you transfer and store photos onto an external hard drive for safekeeping. An external hard drive does not require electricity and once the photos are transferred onto it, you can unplug it from the computer and stash it away until you want to add more photos to it or look at the ones you have stored on it. An external hard drive holds many more photos than a CD or DVD. The advantage to an external hard drive over the Cloud is that you have full control over it.

Enhance My Experience

You may get so into digital photography that to take a picture, print it, and send it on as an attachment may not be enough for you. You may decide you want to enhance or manipulate your photographs. What inspired me to buy my first scanner was a friend's impending nuptials. With the scanner, I was able to scan existing childhood photographs of the soon-to-be bride and groom onto my computer. Once the images were on my computer, I copied the bride (sitting Indian style at about age 5) from her photo and pasted her on to the handlebars of the groom's picture (riding a bike also at about age 5). It was so much fun!

The scanner transferred the images onto my computer like a camera transfers images onto a computer. It was photo-editing software—not the scanner—that enabled the copying and pasting of the images. If you're interested in altering the images you've brought onto your computer, ask friends and relatives who do the same what software they recommend. Some well-known programs are iPhoto (for the Mac), Adobe Photoshop, Corel PaintShop, and Serif PhotoPlus. You can edit directly on your smartphone and tablet.

You'll be able to draw that mustache you miss so much back onto Uncle Charlie's face and erase the unfortunate one on Aunt Charlene. The sky is the limit with what you can do with photo editing. If you're really gung ho about it, you may want to track down an adult education program in your area to jump-start your photo-editing abilities.

An image can be altered once it is on the computer.

Enhance Your Photos

There are several very good software programs that you can purchase to help you edit your photographs. But that's not necessary for most people who just want to crop or tweak their photos in a fairly straightforward way. If you have an Apple computer, the program that is preinstalled on your computer is **Preview**. If you have a computer running Microsoft Windows, the program is **Paint**. Let's first look at Apple's Preview.

Apple's Preview 

To crop:

1. Move the mouse above and to the left of the area that you would like to crop.
2. Click and drag across the area until desired area is contained in that box.
3. Release the mouse.
4. Click **Tools**.
5. Click **Crop**.

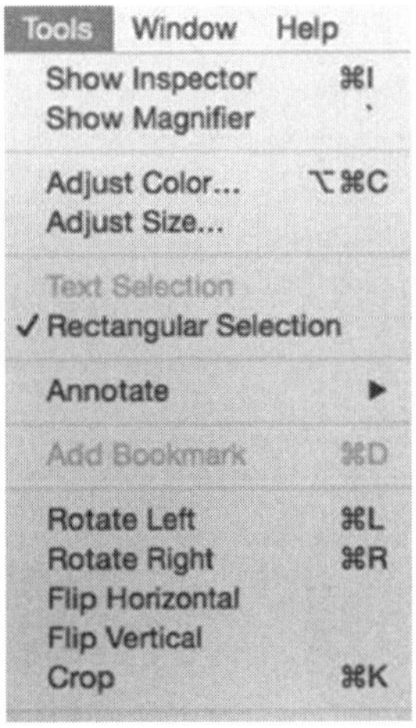

Well done!

When you click on **Tools** in the Menu Bar, you can also choose to **Adjust Color** and **Adjust Size** of the image, as well as **Rotate Left** or **Right** and even **Flip Horizontal** or **Vertical**. The best way to get familiar with these editing tools is to open a photo and simply play with it. Try everything out. Get a feel for what tools you might like to use and take notes so you don't forget what you liked. (So copy and print/scan and print this and write on the backside.)

For those of you with a computer running Microsoft Windows, let's look at Paint.

Microsoft's Paint 

To crop:

1. Move the mouse above and to the left of the area that you would like to crop.
2. Click and drag across the area until desired area is contained in that box.
3. Release the mouse.
4. Click **Crop.** 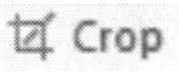

Well done!

The Microsoft **Paint Ribbon** offers you the tools to **Resize** and **Rotate** your image. The best way to get familiar with these editing tools is to open a photo and simply play with it. Try everything out. Get a feel for what tools you might like to use and take notes so you don't forget what you liked. (You can print this and write on the backside.)

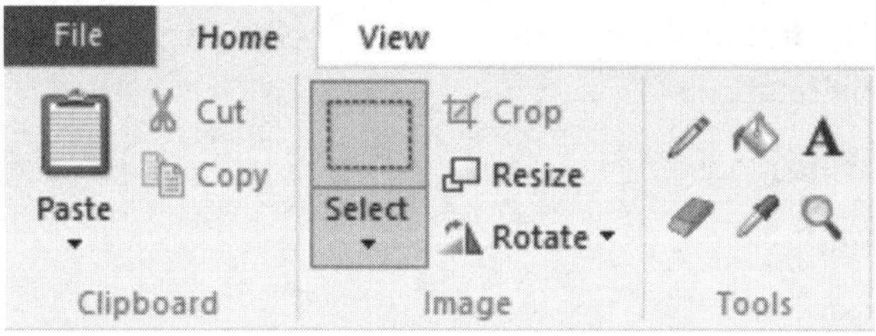

A Disappearing Act

Do you remember the original fax paper? It was shiny and thin. What a shock to discover faxes disappeared off the paper before our very eyes a few years after their composition. No one can be sure about the flaws or longevity of new technology. I say this as a warning about printing photo images at home. It's very satisfying to take a picture of a memorable event, race home, attach the camera to the computer, transfer the image onto the computer, and print the photo (or to send it directly from your smartphone or tablet to your printer). Seconds later, the image is printed on photo paper with your home printer. It really is incredible. But what do we know about how long that image will last on that paper? Ten years? Twenty years? It may be more, but maybe not. I tell my students if it's a really important photo, bring the backup CD or photos on a flash drive to a professional photo shop and have them process a set of pictures as they would from a set of negatives. I could be wrong. Your printed image could last until the next ice age, but why take a chance?

There's another way you can save your images. Some websites offer to store and process your photos if you upload them onto their website. Again, be sure to choose

PHOTO-FRIENDLY WEBSITES

Here are four websites worthy of a visit. You can store, order, and share photos at:

flickr.com
photos.google.com
shutterfly.com
photobucket.com

BACK ME UP!

Use the same steps described here to back up the masterpieces you've written when word processing (discussed in Chapter 15). You don't want to lose your writing any more than you want to lose your photographs. By the way, just to add a new bit of computer jargon to your vocabulary, what you just did was back up data, copy data, or "burn" data to a CD or DVD. That's all burning means—to copy onto another format, in this case onto a CD or DVD. Once a CD or DVD is burned or information is backed up on it, the CD or DVD should be labeled. An indelible marker like a Sharpie is the best writing tool to mark a CD or DVD because most regular markers and pens smudge, and pencil isn't dark enough. Always date a CD or DVD, including the year, and be specific about what it contains. You might not look at the CD or DVD for a very long time, and you'll want to be able to identify the contents without having to put it into the computer. Store the CD or DVD in a safe place. If it holds vital financial information, you may want to store it in a home safe or a safe-deposit box.

a reputable company. It would be tragic if the company went out of business with all your pictures stored on their computer.

Q: If I delete all the photos on my camera, is there any way to get them back?

A: Unfortunately not. If you haven't transferred them to your computer and you delete them from the camera, they are gone.

Q: Will my camera lose the photographs I've taken if the batteries run out?

A: No. The photographs are stored on the memory card inside the device. It holds the photographs regardless of the battery power. However, low batteries can affect the memory card's ability to do its job, so change the batteries as soon as you see that they are running low. Using rechargeable batteries is both environmentally and economically smart.

Q: What is the difference between a scanned image and a photo?

A: Well, they are both images in the mind of the computer. The only difference is how they got onto the computer. One is a photograph taken by a camera. The other is a photo taken by a scanner.

Q: What about backing up onto a flash drive?

A: A flash drive (also known as a thumb drive or USB drive) isn't a good choice for backing up. Its small size makes it easy to misplace and hard to label clearly. But it's a great choice for moving documents or photos from one computer to another or even to or from a tablet that has a USB port. All you do is insert the flash drive into the USB port on your computer or tablet. If you have a PC, a window will open on your screen. If you have an Apple, an icon will appear on your screen. Double-click on the icon to open it. Now, simply click and drag whatever document, folder, or photo you want to move into the window of the drive. Close the window. With an Apple, click and drag the icon into the trash, then unplug the drive. With a PC, in the bottom right corner of your screen there's a symbol resembling a USB plug . Click the symbol, then click on **Eject USB Drive**. Now you can safely unplug the flash drive.

USB flash drive

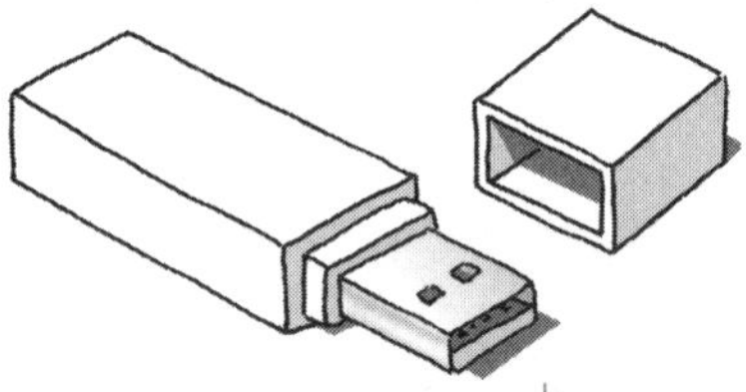

CHAPTER 20

JOIN THE CONVERSATION

Skype, Facebook, Twitter, blogs, online dating, and more

From online dating to video chatting to photo sharing with friends, computers, tablets, and smartphones offer lots of different ways to meet people, communicate, and express yourself. No more waiting for the postman: Now you've got email, and if email doesn't reach enough people, you can tweet your message. Do you feel like visiting with someone who's far away? Use Skype to video chat—it's the next best thing to being there. Want to share your views? Tell the world via social networking or on your own blog. And there's no need to wait for Cupid's arrow to find you: Start dating online. But before you jump into these ever-evolving means of communication and connection, let's understand how each works.

Say It Face-to-Face with a Webcam

A webcam, as we discussed in Chapter 2, is a camera capable of shooting video that can be viewed on the Internet in real time using a computer, tablet, or smartphone. It's a great tool for communicating with family and friends who are far away, because you can see them face-to-face while you speak. I have a friend here in the States whose dad lives in Ireland. She and her children take turns at their computer in San Francisco while Granddad is at his computer in Belfast, and they hear and see and interact with one another by using a webcam and a program called Skype (more on that in a minute).

Most computers come with a webcam built directly into the monitor. If your computer didn't come with a webcam, you can purchase one and connect it to your computer. You'll plug it in using the attached cable and follow the simple instructions for installing it (or get a friend to help). Most people place their webcams near or on the monitor because that's where they face when they're at the computer. Some webcams have sound capabilities. If your webcam doesn't, you'll need to plug a microphone and speakers into your computer in order to be heard and to hear others. Almost all tablets and smartphones have a built-in webcam.

Here's a web address where you can see Times Square 24/7 captured by webcams set up in the area: *earthcam.com/usa/newyork/timessquare*. If you're not interested in Times Square, *earthcam.com* has cameras all over the world. Or for animal lovers, here's a webcam where you can see a live African wildlife safari, 24/7: *africam.com*. These are one-way operations. You can see what's happening in Times Square or Tunisia in real time on these websites whether you have a webcam or not. Some people set up webcams in their homes and keep tabs on things remotely with their smartphone or tablet.

What's the Hype with Skype?

Skype is a program that allows voice and video calls over the Internet, along with instant messaging (which is a lot like texting via Skype) and video conferencing. Contact between Skype users online is free (at least at the time of my typing this), while contact between a Skype user and a landline or cell phone can be made for a fee using a debit-based account system.

I recently traveled to Germany and used Skype to contact my sister in Connecticut during my trip. We both sat in front of our computers (she with a microphone, speakers, and webcam plugged in; me with all those features built into my laptop) and chatted for 45 minutes absolutely free through Skype and our high-speed Internet connections. When my 8-year-old nephew joined my sister, I picked up my laptop and walked around my hotel room to show him the view of the Opera House from my window in Berlin, and he was able to show me his Halloween costume. At that time, my mother had not yet joined Skype, so when I wanted to call her landline, I purchased credit through Skype. The 30-minute international call to Mom cost me only a couple of dollars—much less than using my cell phone overseas.

"Skype has changed everything for me. I love video calling! Now I understand why everyone thinks the computer is a miracle."
—*Nimet*

Skype isn't the only service that allows you to connect via video online. There are several others—Apple offers FaceTime, for instance. I've used *oovoo.com* for webinars where I present a topic to several computer clubs at once when I can't physically visit any of the locations. The groups connect their computers to a projector, so the entire audience can see me, and I sit in my living room with my webcam. Up to six different locations can connect through the website to see and hear one another in real time. It truly is a miracle of modern technology!

Get Skype Started

To join Skype, visit *skype.com*. As when you registered with your web based email, you'll provide Skype with some contact information, plus whatever profile information (personal details, such as date of birth, hometown, etc.) you would like to share. This is an opportunity for you to use your secondary email address (the email address you opened for shopping and newsletters), as suggested on page 274. If a password is required, the same rules we discussed earlier apply (see page 276). Do not use the same password you use for any financial transactions. At this time, the Skype password needs to be at least six characters—better to use eight (longer is harder to crack)—and a combination of letters and numbers. To really scramble things, since passwords are case sensitive, add a couple capital letters here and there.

ASTERISK = MANDATORY

When you see an asterisk (*) on an online form, it is an indication that you *must* fill in that information. If you don't see an asterisk, the information may be optional.

Skype's sign-in window

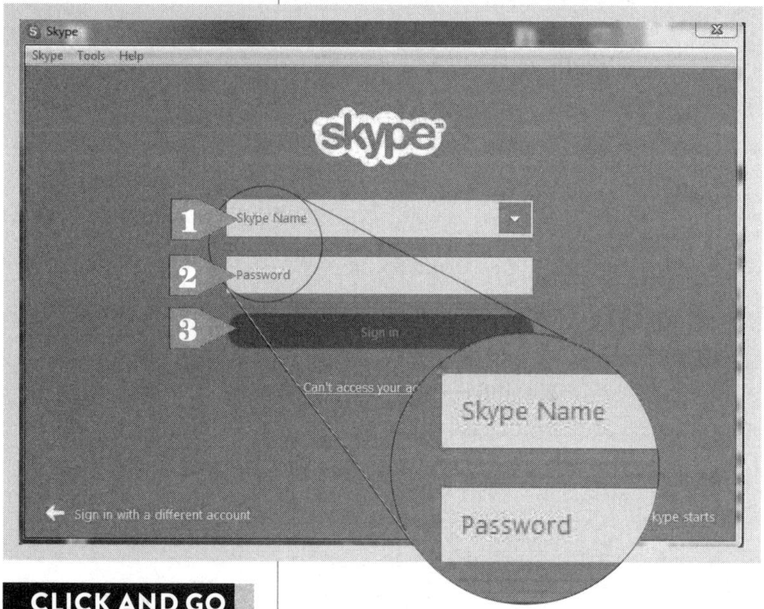

You will also need to choose a Skype Name. Review the guidelines on page 210 about choosing your email username.

After you've created an account with Skype, you'll have to download the program from the website to your computer or add the app to your tablet (see page 170) or smartphone (see page 316).

Once Skype is downloaded, you should receive a confirmation email from Skype at the email address that you listed with them. As soon as these steps are complete, you can open the program and sign in. Skype functions pretty much the same whether you're on a computer, a tablet, or a smartphone. Just be sure to hold the handheld device steady so you don't cause motion sickness for the person who is watching on the other end!

Take a tour of Skype's many features.

CLICK AND GO

1. Click in Skype Name text box. Type your Skype name.
2. Click in Password box. Type your password.
3. Click on Sign in.

Skype's website offers lots of guidance to help you set up your account and get familiar with how the program works. Click on Explore to learn about each of the features offered.

TIME CHANGES ALL THINGS

Websites and software programs are updated on a regular basis. Be prepared for what you see in this book not to match exactly what you see on your computer. The basic elements, however, will be the same.

I Accept Your Invitation

Skype status options

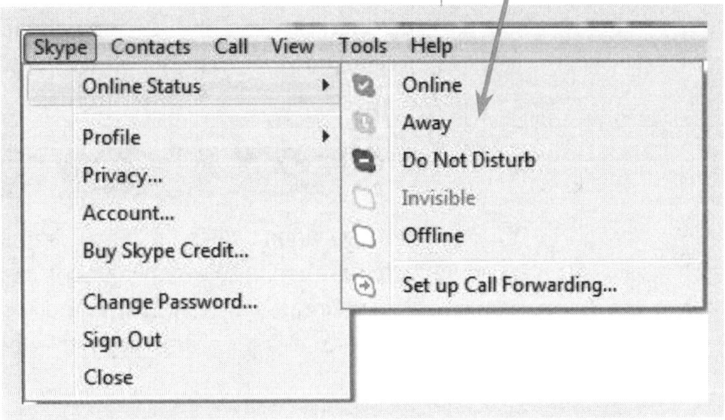

Ask anyone you know who is already a "Skyper" to invite you to join his or her contact list. (When you are new to Skype, it's easier for you to accept an invitation than to send one.) When you next sign into Skype, you'll have the opportunity to accept the invitations, at which point your friends' names, will be automatically added to your Contacts/Address Book on Skype.

Status Symbol

When you sign into the program, your Skype contacts can see that you're available. If you don't want to be seen as available, you can change your status. You have the option of **Online**, **Away**, **Do Not Disturb**, **Invisible**, or **Offline**.

Changing your status on Skype can be done one of two ways. Your first option is to:

- Click on the **Status Symbol** beside your name.
- Click on the desired status.

Your second option is to:

- Click on **Skype**.
- Click on **Online Status**.
- Click on the desired status.

Skype allows you to video call or voice call. You can also instant message.

Once you're up and running, Skype offers three choices for communication. Double-click on the person you want to communicate with in your Contacts, then you can **Video Call** or **Call** by clicking on the appropriate button, or start typing an Instant Message at the bottom of the window. Try each option at least once so you get the lay of the land.

You're going to love being able to contact friends and family through Skype. But all good calls must come to an end. When it's time to say good-bye, simply click on the red hang-up icon to end the call.

LOOK AT THE BIRDIE

When video calling on Skype or using a webcam in general, the temptation is to watch your computer screen. If your camera is on top of your monitor, this means the person watching you will see only your eyelids. When talking, eyes up—look directly into the webcam.

Social Networking

I refer to social networking as the "green beans of the Internet." You know when you hand a kid a plate of food they gobble up the hamburger. They'll devour the mashed potatoes. But they won't touch their green beans.

"Do you not like green beans?"

They decidedly shake their head.

"Have you ever tasted green beans?"

They shrug and shake their head again.

A lot of you may have very strong opinions about social networking without actually having tried it. Hang in there with me.

I'm not here to convince you to use Facebook or Twitter. I simply want to walk you through the pros and cons and then you can try it if you think it's right for you.

Recently, a friend decided to host a dinner party. A matchmaker at heart, she hoped to help people make new friends, and she had some potential couples in mind. She also thought some of her guests might benefit from knowing one another professionally. Her idea was to get together a handful of smart, creative, hardworking people, most of whom didn't know one another, and see if any love, friendship, or business connections could be made. By the end of the night, phone numbers and email addresses were exchanged many times over.

I know you think I've diverted from the topic, but I haven't. What happened that night was good old-fashioned socializing. Certain websites are designed after the same idea—they're referred to as social networks. Social networking has many purposes—create a discussion around a topic, share news and ideas, find a like-minded soul, discover a long-lost classmate, build your business, make a love connection . . . and the list goes on. Facebook, Twitter, and LinkedIn are three popular social networking websites, each with its own design and slightly different purpose.

A POST, OR TO POST A MESSAGE
When you publish your words online in a forum, newsgroup, or message board, you are posting a message, and the text is referred to as a *post*.

Social networking can't duplicate the benefits of connecting in person, but it does have its place. If you have a product or company to promote, social networking is a wonderful tool. If you have old friends whom you would like to find, or if there are folks you'd like to keep in better touch with, social networking may prove to be the fastest and cheapest way to do so. If you have ideas that you would like to share with more people than can fit around your dining room table, social networking allows you to reach a lot of people all at once—hundreds, thousands, maybe even millions. Using social networking to hard-sell your wares or force your views on others is frowned upon, as is ranting and raving on a particular topic.

As with any interactions online, where you can't be certain of the identity or intentions of the person you are interacting with, avoid revealing too much personal information, including your home

"I pooh-poohed Facebook when I heard everyone talking about it. I must confess, now that I'm using it, I am hooked. It's so much more interesting and useful than I expected." —*Meredith*

address or phone number. You also don't want to somehow let slip your birthday (including the year), where you were born, or your mother's maiden name. Those pieces of information can be used to confirm your identity with credit card companies and banks. Keep those tidbits to yourself for your own safety. *Never* share your Social Security number online. And keep in mind the fact that your conversation is being read by many.

OMG! I Have 500 Friends on Facebook

What is this Facebook thing everyone is talking about? Facebook is going to require a bit of explanation, so get comfortable. As I've said, online social networking isn't that different from socializing in our three-dimensional world. You discuss what you've been up to, exchange ideas, share family photos or articles that have caught your interest, whatever comes to mind, but it all happens online while visiting a website, rather than over afternoon tea in your living room. Facebook (*facebook.com*) is the most popular social networking website in the world. As I type this, there are over 1.3 billion Facebook users and counting. 1.3 billion! OMG! (If you don't remember what OMG means, see page 333). That is more than four times the population of the United States. Facebook's site is translated into over 70 languages, and 75 percent of its users live outside of the United States. It is a global phenomenon.

You're going to discover that with Facebook, much as with the rest of technology, familiar words are used in unfamiliar ways. The word "friend" in this case doesn't necessarily mean someone you like, see on a regular basis, or even know. For some on Facebook, a friend could even be someone you have never met or had any previous contact with at all. Facebook friends are people you have invited or who have invited you to view what you or they share on Facebook. I know this may seem strange, but some people like to share, whether it's with people they know intimately or anyone who will listen. Hang in there with this concept—it'll make more sense as you get to know the website better.

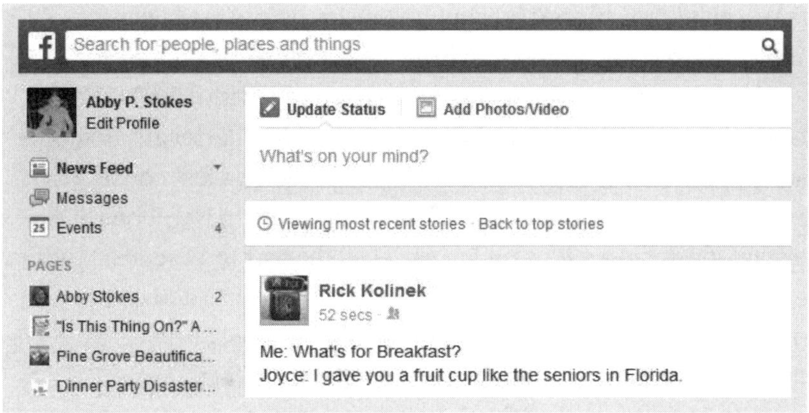

Sample Facebook page

What people share on Facebook runs the gamut from innovative ideas to great life philosophies to fun self-expression to promotion of their endeavors to tiresome overexposure to moment-to-moment thought processes. People share photos of themselves and photos they like, as well as links to articles and videos they find interesting. Accordingly, you may discover that what is posted is truly worthwhile, or you may perceive it as a huge waste of time. For me, it's a mix of the two.

Imagine, if you will, walking around town holding a bulletin board in front of you. Every time you want to share an idea, a website you like, or a photo, you thumbtack it on your bulletin board for everyone to see. On Facebook, everyone's personal page has a wall where they can share whatever comes to mind for all to enjoy or ignore as they see fit. You can see what your friends post on their walls on your News Feed (more on that in a minute).

A wonderful feature of Facebook is the ability to search for and find people. I organized my 30th high school reunion on Facebook, a great tool for that purpose. I was able to search for and find more than half of my graduating class on the site. I created a special page called LOLHS Class of 1980 Reunion, where everyone could get in on the act and give feedback on where and when the reunion should take place. By the time the reunion happened, many of us had already caught up on who had kids, what careers or marriages had come and gone, and even who had gained a little extra weight. Something about getting that preliminary information out of the way before the big event allowed everyone to relax and have a great time.

Many people use Facebook to share photos with friends and family who are spread out all over the world. It's like magic: Someone snaps a photo of Aunt Ruthie dancing with her long-lost cousin at a family reunion and moves (or uploads) the photo to Facebook. Those distant loved ones who couldn't travel all the way to Wisconsin for the event see the photo online, and if they want, they can add comments or click **Like** to give the photo a thumbs-up. Soon it all starts to feel as though everyone is in the same room at the same time.

You can also use Facebook to join groups to share information on a particular interest, hobby, or topic. I have a Facebook page with helpful and up-to-the-minute information about technology and other fun stuff: *facebook.com/AskAbbyStokes*. I would love for you to join me there, and then I can answer any questions you might ask. I suspect your relationship with Facebook, if you choose to join it, will evolve as you become familiar with all it has to offer.

Facebook's sign-up form

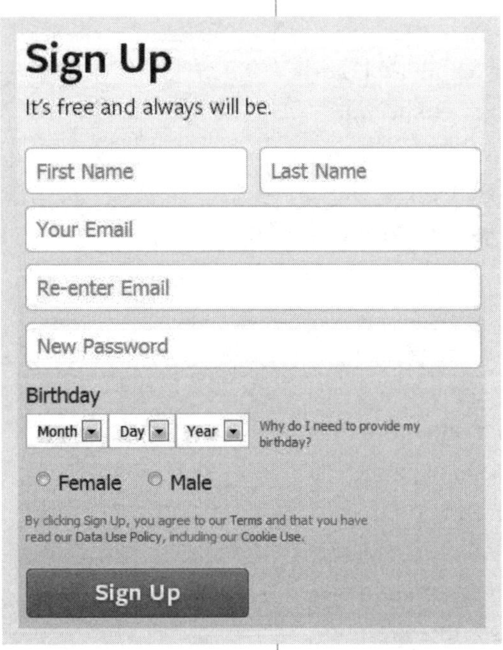

How Facebook Works

Facebook is free for the cruising . . . I mean, using. You will need, however, to register with *facebook.com*, by filling out a form (see example at left). I suggest, if you can, that you register with Facebook on a computer, then add the app to your tablet or smartphone. Forms like these are more difficult in the smaller format. But, if you have no choice, this is a great time to use a stylus to be more precise with your navigation.

All the same rules apply as discussed on page 276 about choice of email address, password, and divulging private information. Unlike message boards, Facebook frowns upon false identities. The whole principle behind the site is to present yourself, with your real name and any truthful information that you want to share with others.

After you've registered, you're given the opportunity to create a **Profile**. You decide how much information you want to reveal about yourself: birth date (with or without year), hometown, school history, photographs, phone number, interests, etc. You may share as much or as little as you want. I err on the side of caution and don't reveal my phone number or address. (However, if someone is determined to find that information about me, it isn't hard, as it's all publicly available.)

Here are the steps to follow to fill in your Facebook profile.

- Click in each text area and type whatever information you would like to share.
- If a down arrow is available, click on the arrow to see what options are offered.
- Click on the desired item in the drop list.
- When you're happy with what you have typed in, click on **Save Changes**.
- When you're all finished, click **Done Editing**.

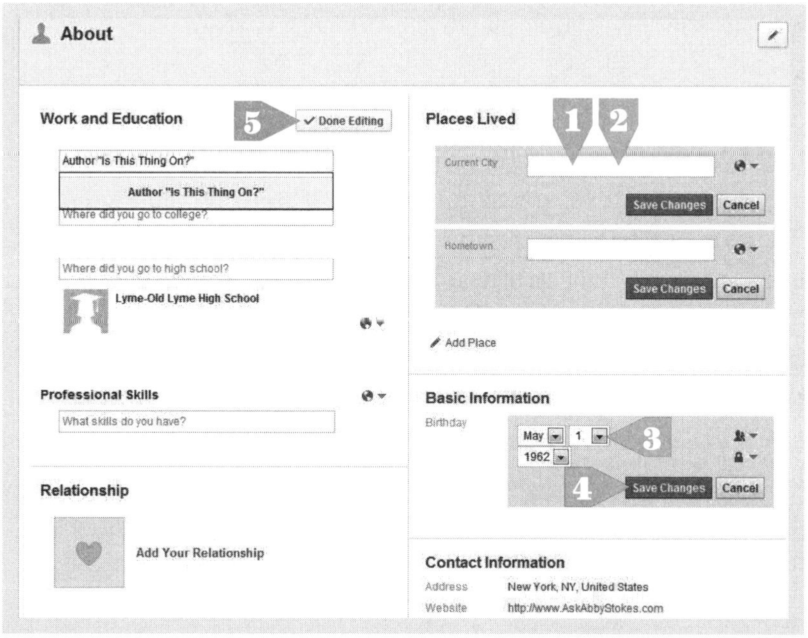

CLICK AND GO

1. Click in text areas.
2. Type information you want to share.
3. Click down arrows to choose month, day, and year.
4. Click Save Changes.
5. Click Done Editing.

PRIVACY RULE OF THUMB
Share on a website only what you are comfortable sharing with the whole world.

Facebook offers settings that allow you to customize your account. You can decide what notifications you would like to receive, who can post to your wall, and what email address people can use to contact you. For example: You may want to receive an email if someone invites you to be a friend on Facebook or sends you a private message, but you may not want to receive an email when someone posts something on your wall. I prefer not to clutter my email with notifications from Facebook, so I find out what people are posting or what invitations I received only when I visit the site.

To get to your **Notification Settings**, follow these steps:

- Click on the **Down Arrow** in the top right.
- Click on **Settings** in the menu.
- Click on **Notifications** on the left.
- Click on **Edit** to the right of each notification topic.

Your decisions are not written in stone—you can revisit your Settings and Notifications at any time to make changes.

TMI = Too Much Information

Let's take a break from setting up Facebook to discuss the very important issues of sharing information and protecting your privacy. I've sat in on daylong workshops detailing how to tweak Facebook in such a way as to be as private as possible. I've read a multitude of magazine and newspaper articles listing countless tips on how to prevent overexposure while enjoying online social networking.

My one rule of privacy for *all* online social networking, not just Facebook, is The Front-Door Test: *Do not put anything on a website that you would not feel comfortable having taped to the outside of your front door.* Simple. Easy to remember. No confusing instructions.

If you're OK with telling anyone and everyone who passes by your front door that you'll be on vacation for two weeks, put it on

Facebook. If the details of your recent breakup are acceptable on your front door for all to see, add them to your Facebook page. If you have no hesitation venting about your boss on your front door for whomever might stroll by, then by all means share it on Facebook. Are you beginning to get the idea?

The safest thing you can do is to assume that there is *no privacy* when you post *anything* to *any* website. You may want to share with only your friends on Facebook or your followers on Twitter, but what's to stop any of them from printing your confidences and sharing them with a total stranger, or with your ex, your boss, or your local cat burglar? When you share online, you are potentially sharing with the entire world. Does what you want to say or show pass The Front-Door Test?

By the way, no one is obliged to join Facebook, regardless of how much press it gets or how many other people enjoy it. If you have any hesitation about using the site, follow your gut. However, if the feeling in your gut is simply butterflies because you're nervous you won't be able to figure out Facebook, you are underestimating yourself and me!

Set Your Settings

Let's learn how to customize your privacy and account settings on Facebook. As with many websites and software programs, you'll find you can customize different elements by clicking on the down arrow to the far right at the top of the window. A drop menu will appear; click on **Settings**.

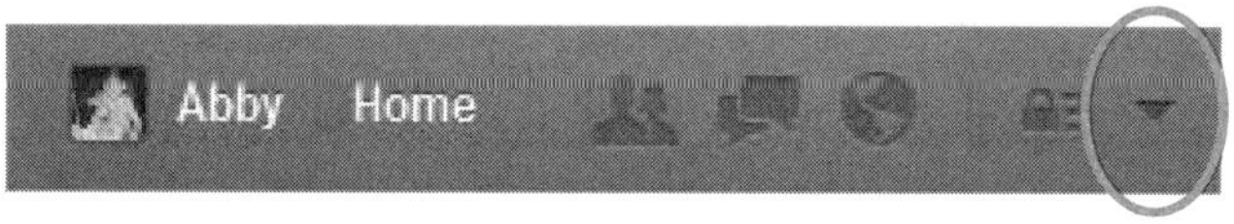

The down arrow will lead you to where you can customize Facebook features.

The safest thing to do when experimenting with settings (anywhere, not just on Facebook) is to write down the current settings *before* you change them. That way, if you decide you don't like the changes you've made, you can revert to the previous settings. Take a peek at the Facebook **Privacy Settings and Tools** on the next page, so you know what's there.

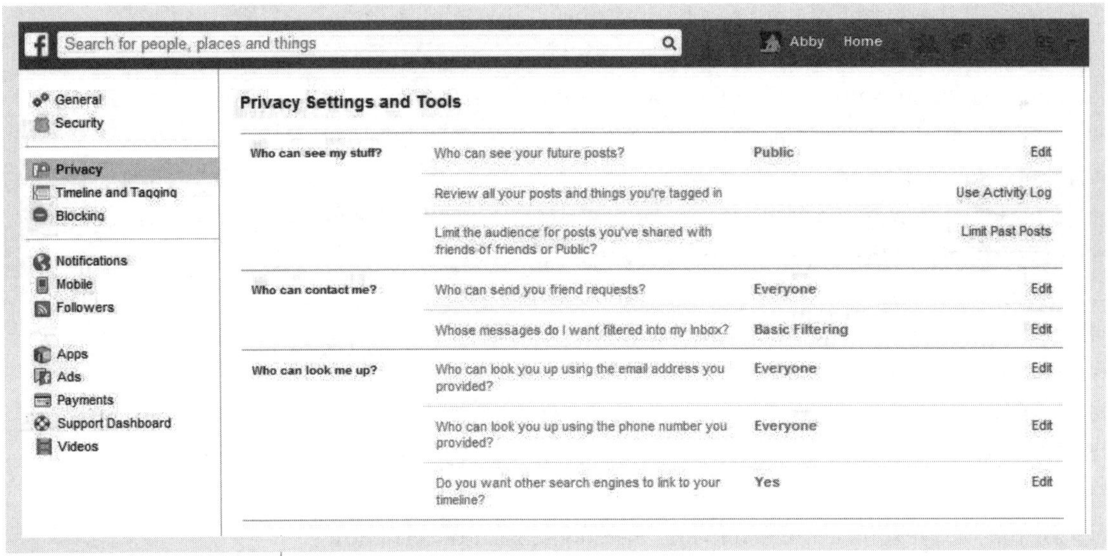

Take a tour of your Facebook Privacy Settings and Tools.

Complete Your Profile

There's one more task to be completed before you're ready to search for friends on Facebook.

A **Profile Picture** is standard fare on Facebook. From a practical aspect, because there are many people who share the same name, a photo can reveal whether you've found the Bob Smith, Juan Alvarez, or Mary McGillicuddy you're looking for. Is there a good photo of you stored on your computer? If not, you can turn back to the previous chapter and review digital photography, or you can have someone email you a photo of yourself and then download it (see page 349). If your computer has a webcam, you can take a photo right now. As you can see on the left, my

CLICK AND GO

Option 1. Click on Choose from Photos to find a photo already stored on your computer.
Option 2. Click on Take Photo to snap a photo with your webcam.

photo isn't current, but my smile remains identifiable. Some people use photos of their pets or views from their porches as their profile pictures. Like your notification settings, you can change your profile picture at any time.

Networking, Here We Come

Once you're happy with your profile, it's time to start networking. To become someone's Facebook friend, an invitation must be sent and accepted. There is no obligation to say yes to someone whose interests you don't share or with whom you don't want to share information. You can search for someone on Facebook by typing in their name, email address, workplace, or school in the search box at the top of the page then clicking on the magnifying glass to the far right. Once you find the person you're looking for, click on **Add Friend** to send them an invitation to share with you on Facebook. I've reconnected with old friends on Facebook whom I may never see face-to-face again, but it's fun to catch up on what's been happening in their lives and see pictures of their families, vacations, artwork, etc. You may want to use Facebook exclusively for your family to view photos and stay in touch. If that's the case, you'll decline any invitations to become friends with people who aren't in your family. You can always send a message explaining your choice to whoever has made overtures. It's all up to you.

Let's meet some of the features of Facebook. Feel free to click on any of these elements—it's the best way to get the lay of the land.

Edit My Profile—Click here to make changes or additions to your profile.

Events—Here is where you can see upcoming birthdays and other events and where you can create an event invitation of your own, if you want to invite all or some of your Facebook friends to something.

Friends—If you click on your name at the top, you can then click on Friends to see all of your Facebook friends and edit them as you see fit. (That means to add or delete friends. It sounds decidedly unfriendly, but that's how it works.)

Home—Returns you to the News Feed page.

Like—As with "friend," the word "like" has a Facebook-specific meaning. If you click on Like under someone's posting of a photo, a link, or something they've written, you're letting them know you give it a thumbs-up or you agree. You can also Like a group or fan page (devoted to a celebrity, TV show, author, etc.) so that those posts will appear in your News Feed.

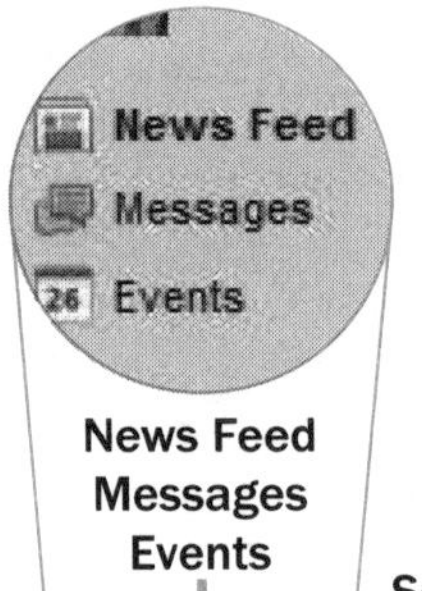

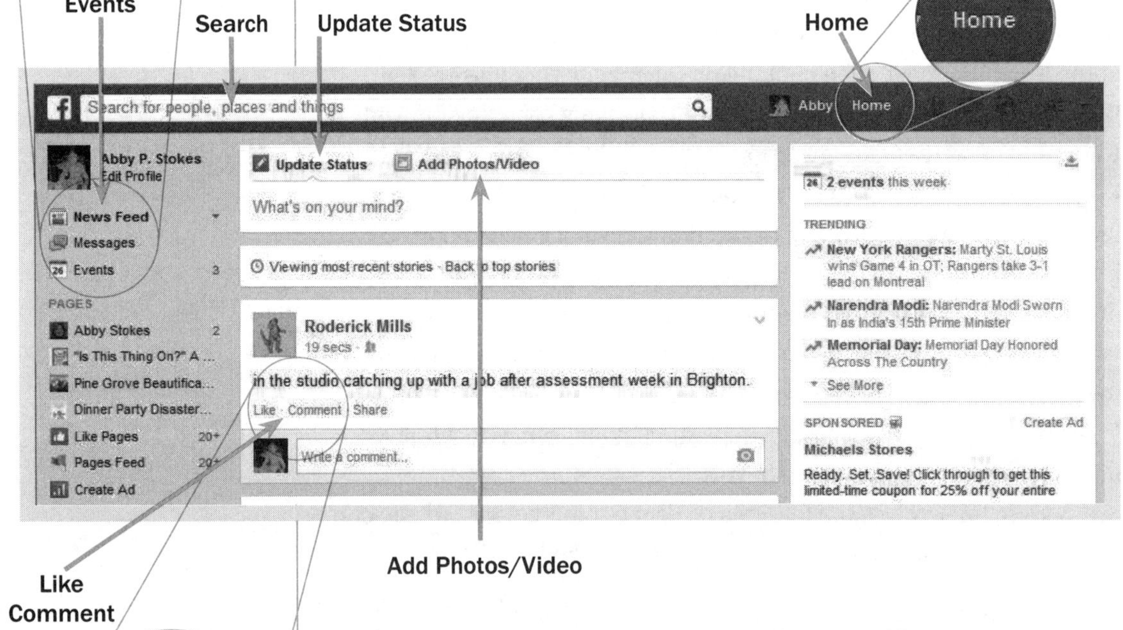

Messages—This is an internal email service. Messages are seen only by the sender and the recipient(s).

Most Recent Stories—Sorts all your friends' posts in chronological order with the most recent on top. You can also access Recent Stories by clicking on the down arrow beside News Feed.

News Feed—Considered the home page of Facebook, this is where you'll see all of your friends' and your own status updates, along with birthdays, invitations, and other announcements.

Search—Click in the text box and then type in an individual's name, a business's name, or a keyword, and search to see what you can find on Facebook.

Top Stories—Sorts posts based on an algorithm for what posts are getting the most views and comments.

Update Status/What's on Your Mind—Type in whatever you want to share with your friends. You can also add a photo, a link to a webpage, a video, or a question. These updates will appear on your wall and in your friends' News Feeds.

Your Name—Brings you to your wall, where only things you have posted or posts directed specifically to you appear.

News Feed vs Your Page

Many of my students are confused about the difference between the **News Feed** on Facebook and the page that shows only what they've posted. If you click on **Home**, at the top right, what appears in the center of the page is the News Feed. This is where you see all of the posts from your friends and any organizations that you follow. There will also be some advertisements now and again.

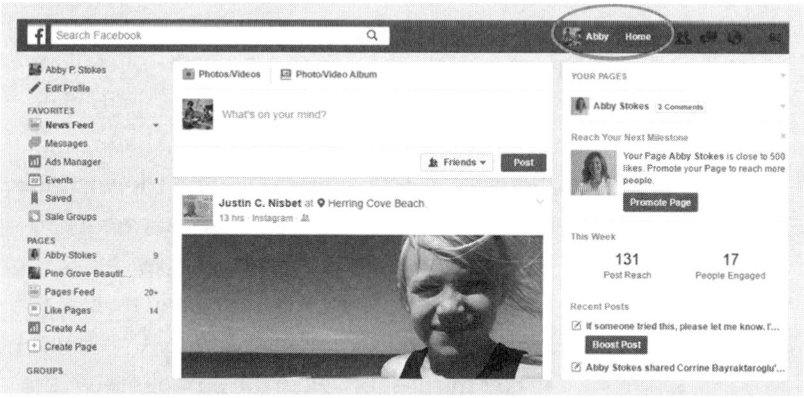

If you click on your name in the top right (to the left of **Home**), the center of the page will change. You'll see the most recent item you shared on top. Everything else you've shared will be below that, sorted chronologically from newest to oldest. This is your page on Facebook and shows only what you have contributed. To revert back to the News Feed, where you'll see what other people have posted, click **Home** in the top right.

You have a choice on the News Feed of whether the order of what's shown is chronological or what's trending—that is, being viewed by the most people. Look in the left sidebar. There's a small, grey arrow to the right of News Feed. Click on that arrow and a menu will drop down offering you **Top Stories** or **Most Recent.** Click on whichever you fancy—you can always change your mind.

Not What You Bargained For

Socializing online is not so different than socializing in our three-dimensional world. Sometimes you sit next to a great conversationalist and sometimes you'd do almost anything to get away from the person talking your ear off. The good news is there is a feature with Facebook where you can hide all of the posts from people you no longer want to hear from or you can unfriend them entirely. (They will not receive any notification that you have unfriended them.)

Next time a post pops up from the person who can't stop talking about their cat's morning somersaults, move your mouse up to their name, then across to the right. You may not have noticed before but there is a very faint arrow pointing down. Click on that arrow. A menu drops down where you can click on **Hide Post** or **Unfollow**.

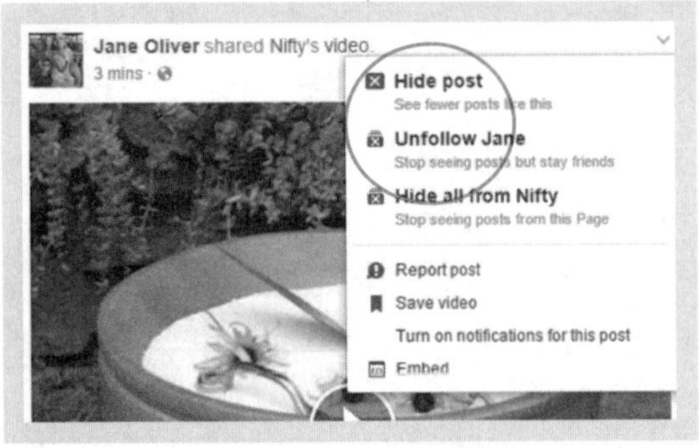

What if you post something and realize, after the fact, that you have a typo, so you want to edit the post or delete the post entirely? The same tool is available…that discreet down arrow to the right of your name. Click on it and

a menu opens with several different options for what you can do to your post, including **Delete**. You must keep in mind, however, that you can't erase what someone has read from their memory. So always ask yourself if your post passes the Front Door Test (page 370) before you pull the trigger and share it.

Facebook Scams

The last thing I want to do is alarm anyone or put you off using Facebook, but I do want to arm you with an understanding that some people use Facebook and other social networking websites to take advantage of people. The most important thing to do is listen to that voice in your head that says, "This doesn't seem right." Often when people hear that voice, they ignore it, sure that somehow whatever they see on their screen is OK, deferring to their intimidation with technology over their own instincts. I say, "Always go with your instincts!" If something seems hinky, it usually is. Don't click on what you don't understand or sounds too good to be true.

A common Facebook scam is to impersonate someone who already has a profile on Facebook. Often money is the big motivator. Once the imposter has lured in your existing friends, they plead a sob story and try to extort money. But some of these imposters do it just because they can. So, besides the creep factor, it is inconvenient, but often harmless. Nonetheless, you want to be on the lookout.

If you receive a friend request from someone you're already friends with on Facebook, that is the tip-off. Do *not* accept the second request. Instead, by private email, phone, or text, let your friend know about the fake request. Then they or you should notify Facebook. This is a common enough occurrence that Facebook has it in the Q&A and Help sections. Here's Facebook's response to:

How do I report a fake account that's pretending to be me?
Impostor accounts aren't allowed on Facebook. If someone created an account pretending to be you:

1. Go to the impostor profile. If you can't find it, try searching for the name used on the profile or asking your friends if they can send you a link to it.
2. Click on the cover photo and select **Report**.
3. Follow the on-screen instructions.

Facebook will act promptly (it's in their best interest) and the fake profile might disappear before you have a chance to ask, "What kind of creeps are out there, anyway?"

Don't be lured in by ads that tout some insider way to see who is viewing your profile on Facebook or invite you to view some ghastly, morbid photos or offer the possibility of big prize money. Scam, scam, scam. Be selective about what you click on and you'll be fine. There's so much to enjoy about Facebook. Don't let these bad apples spoil the benefits.

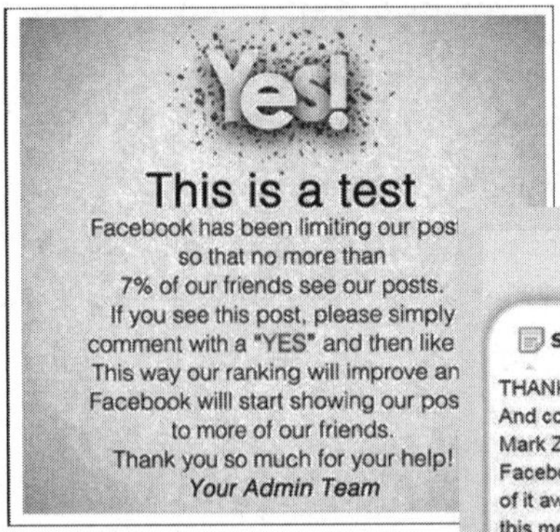

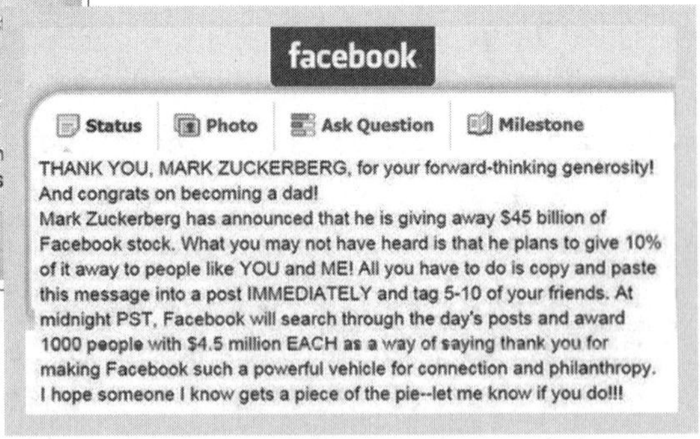

If you're interested, now's the time for you to actually get on Facebook, if you haven't already. Facebook is much easier to understand in practice than in theory. If you'd like to friend me on Facebook, my username is *AskAbbyStokes*. When you send me a friend request, include a message letting me know you've read this book. In that case, we've been through so much together already, I consider us friends.

Come on back to this page when you have the time and energy, and I'll introduce you to Twitter next.

Let's Talk Twitter

Merriam-Webster (*merriam-webster.com*, the company's website, is a great resource) defines the noun "twitter" as:

1. a trembling agitation
2. a small tremulous intermittent sound (as of birds)
3. a. a light chattering; b. a light silly laugh

A sample of some tweets on Twitter

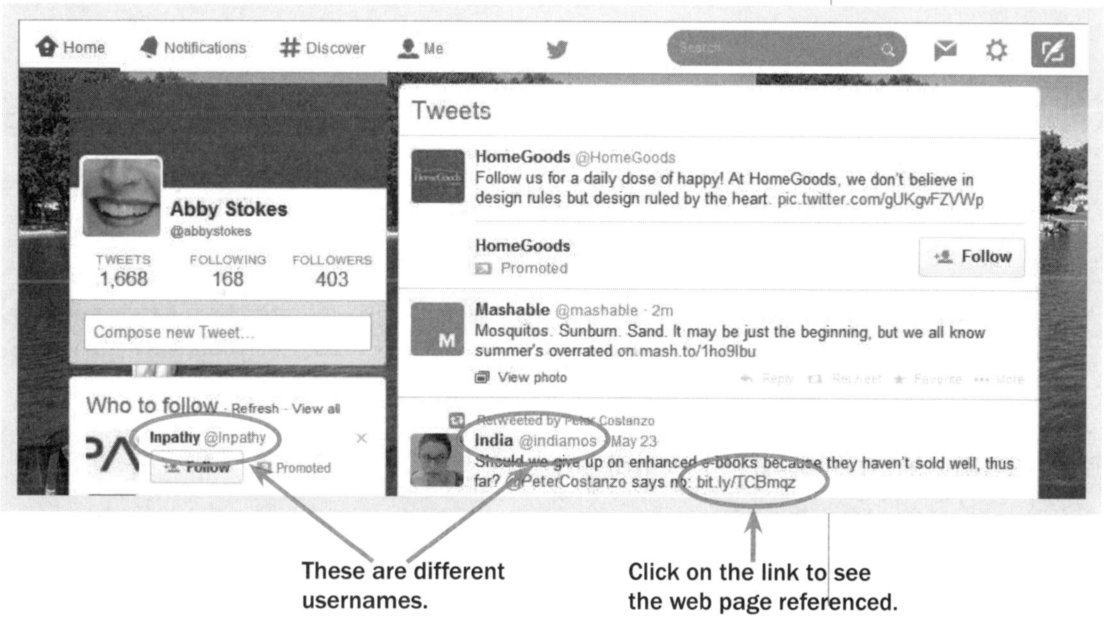

"Tweeting sounded so silly, but now that I've joined Twitter, I learn something new every day."
—***Murphy***

As an example, Merriam-Webster gives, "Our grandmother gets all in a twitter if she doesn't get her weekly phone call right on time." In my opinion, Merriam-Webster should update the example to: "Our grandmother gets all in a twitter trying to figure out Twitter."

The creators of Twitter describe their site as a social networking and microblogging service that allows you to answer the question, "What are you doing?" by sending short text messages called "tweets" to your friends, or "followers." In actuality, people send out tweets on far more than just what they're doing. Tweets are the entries that you type on Twitter (*twitter.com*) to share with others. Each entry is limited to no more than 140 characters, not including the username and the colon that appears before every tweet. Twitter is designed so tweets are quick, like cell phone texts.

You can invite people to view your tweets (people who choose to receive your tweets are known as your "followers"), and you can decide whose tweets you want to read (or "follow"). Twitter is a constantly evolving stream of information similar to the News Feed on Facebook. I follow a wide variety of folks—a few friends and family, but mostly news (CNN, NPR, etc.), several bookstores, other authors, and some really helpful computer geeks. Some people like to follow celebrities or their favorite writers. There's everything under the sun on Twitter for you to search out and discover. I'll help you get to know Twitter, and then you can decide what's right for you.

Here's where you compose a tweet.

Take a look at the Twitter page at left.

To tweet, click in the box with **What's happening?** and type your missive. You don't need to worry about counting characters. The number **140** decreases as you type, to reflect how many characters are still available. Once you're ready to share your thoughts, simply click **Tweet** at the bottom right of your post.

Many tweets include a link to a website. (To review links, refer to page 302.) The use of links explains how the limit of 140 characters doesn't really limit how much information can be included in a tweet. If you click on the suggested link, a website with more information on the subject will open.

One of the biggest differences between Facebook and Twitter is that on Twitter you may choose to follow someone who does not follow you, and vice versa. On Facebook, which is more reciprocal, only mutual friends see one another's posts, unless you join a group or a fan page. For me, Twitter is more for information, news gathering, or pure entertainment and less for personal sharing than Facebook.

Setting Up Twitter

The steps you take to set up Twitter are much like those you take for Facebook. You'll register with the site, choosing a username and password and giving an email address. All the same rules apply that did with Facebook and Skype. Again, this is slightly easier on a computer than on a tablet or smartphone, simply because of the size. Here is another opportunity for you to use your secondary email address (the email address you opened for shopping and newsletters). Do not use the same password you use for any financial transactions. As with Skype and Facebook, your Twitter password needs to be at least six characters and a combination of letters and numbers.

You'll notice that the two options below **Choose Your Username**, in the sign-up window, already have checks in the boxes. If you do not want those options, click in the boxes to remove the checks.

Unlike the world of Facebook, anonymity is not frowned upon on Twitter. I'm not suggesting that you lie about yourself, but Twitter is an environment where one tends to share less personal information than on Facebook. I choose to use my real name on all social networking sites because I want people, whether they've read this book or want some technology advice, to easily find me. You may want to stay in the shadows a bit more—or not.

Twitter Lingo

Let me introduce you to some lingo specific to Twitter.

@—The **@** sign is used to call out usernames in tweets, like this: "Hello @abbystokes." When a username is preceded by the @ sign, you can click on the name and visit the person's Twitter profile.

FF—The character sequence #FF stands for Follow Friday. Twitter users often suggest whom others should follow on Fridays by tweeting with the hashtag #FF. Consider it very flattering if someone suggests you for #FF. (See below for an explanation of "hashtag.")

Follow—When you "follow" someone on Twitter, you've chosen to see his tweets or updates on your Twitter page.

Follower—A "follower" is someone on Twitter who has chosen to add you to the list of people whose tweets she sees on her Twitter page.

Hashtag—The hashtag symbol (#) is used directly before relevant keywords in a tweet to help categorize tweets so they show up more easily in a Twitter Search. If #kiwis appeared in a tweet and you clicked on #kiwis, you would be brought to every recent tweet that contained #kiwis to see what people are saying about kiwis.

Mention—When you refer to another tweeter with the @ sign, it is referred to as a mention. Example: "Attended a great lecture at @nypl. @jamieoliver was so interesting."

Message (aka **Direct Message** or **DM)**—A message is a tweet that is private, between only the sender and recipient.

Retweet (noun)—A tweet by another tweeter, reposted by someone else.

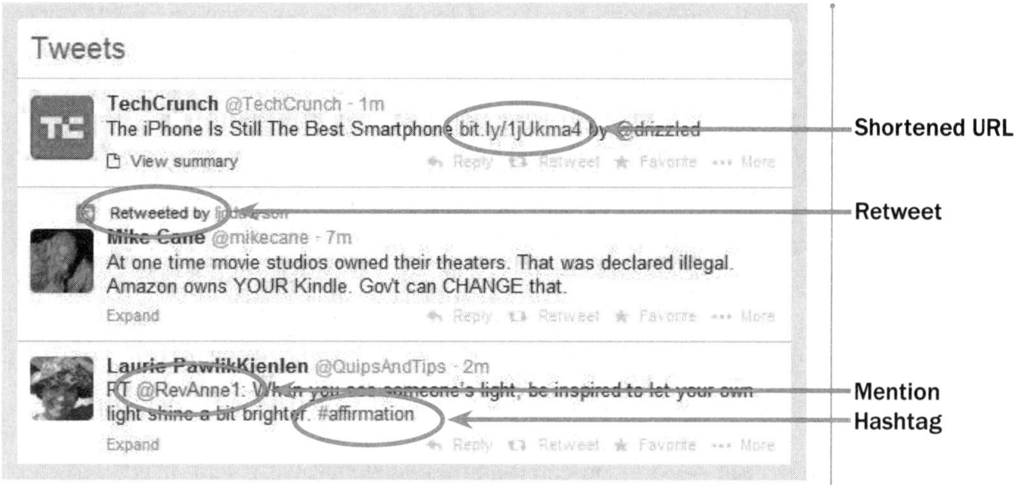

Retweet (verb)—To retweet; retweeting; retweeted. (Say that five times fast!) When you retweet, you are forwarding another tweet to all of your followers.

RT—Abbreviated version of "retweet."

Trending Topic—A subject algorithmically determined to be one of the most popular on Twitter at the moment. When a certain awards show or a big game is being played on TV, you'll see hashtags like #oscars or #worldseries trending.

Unfollow—To stop following someone on Twitter. His tweets will then no longer show up on your page.

URL—A uniform resource locator (URL) is a web address that points to a specific page on a website. (I normally avoid techspeak, but I had to introduce URL in order for you to grasp a URL shortener, below, which is a really important tool for Twitter. My apologies.)

URL Shortener—Because some website addresses can be long (and Twitter limits us to 140 characters), a URL shortener is used to convert or truncate long URLs into shorter ones. The link *http://www.nytimes.com/2011/09/07/dining/grilled-london-broil-try-it*

"I still don't understand all the Twitter jargon, but I really enjoy reading my favorite journalists' tweets."
—Irwin

-spicy-and-smoky.html?_r=1&hpw is 120 characters in length, but it can be reduced to *http://tinyurl.com/3qgmg4s*, a mere 26 characters. *Tinyurl.com* and *bitly.com* are two common sites where you can shorten a web page address, but there are others.

I don't expect you to understand everything listed above without a visit to Twitter to see it all in action. Just have this list handy when you go to the site.

Here's a breakdown of some of the elements on Twitter's website. Be adventurous and click on anything your heart desires—it's the best way to learn what the site has to offer.

—Here you can read messages that were sent directly to you or write a message privately to someone on Twitter.

Compose new Tweet—This is where you type your tweet of no more than 140 characters.

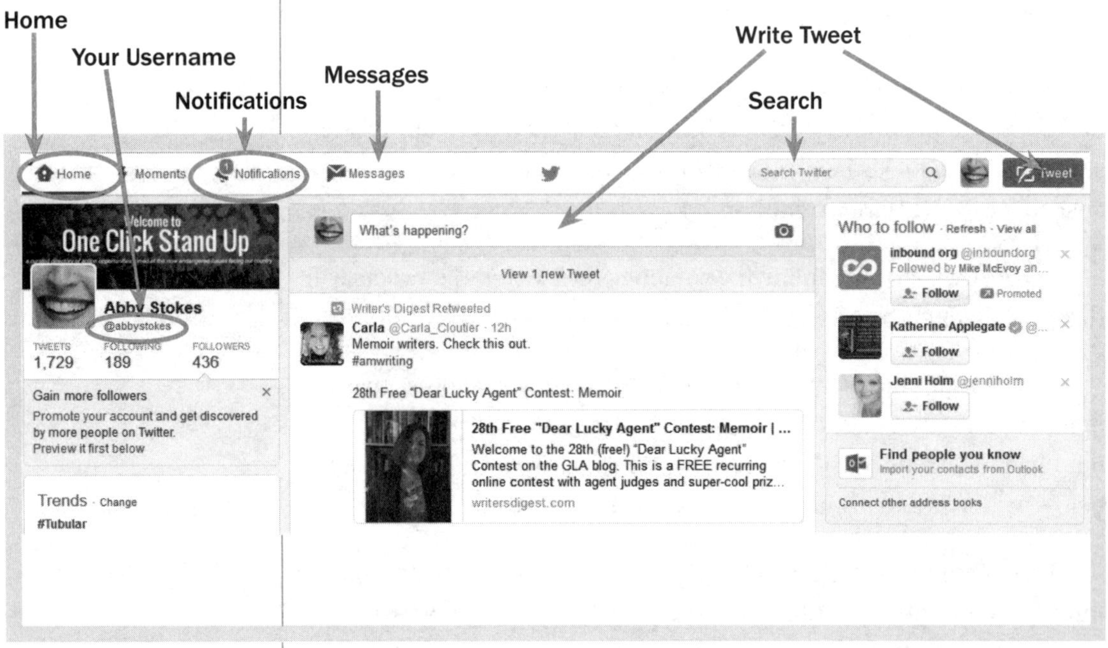

Home—This will take you back to the home page on Twitter.

Me—Brings you to your page of tweets, followers, and whom you're following.

Notifications—If someone has mentioned you in a tweet or retweeted you, it will appear here.

Search—Click here and type in keywords for what or whom you would like to find.

Who to follow—Twitter suggests people you might want to follow based on your activity on the site.

Your Username—Here you can access your account settings and sign out of Twitter. (Signing out is especially important if you're using a shared or public computer to visit your Twitter account.)

Enough already! If you choose to join Twitter, it's time for you to get your feet wet. As you experiment and have questions, you can always tweet me at *twitter.com/AskAbbyStokes*.

Come back when you're done playing with Twitter, and we'll talk a little bit more about social networking, blogging, and online dating.

Aren't There Better Things to Do with My Time?

Absolutely! As my mother would say, "Go outside! It's a beautiful day. There's no reason for you to be in the house." One of the complaints about Facebook and Twitter is that they can consume an enormous amount of time. Remember, you're the one who controls

BECAUSE IT IS WORTH REPEATING

Do not put anything on any social networking site that you would not feel comfortable having taped to the outside of your front door.

how much time you spend on your computer and on any given website. I check out Twitter and Facebook at the beginning and the end of my day—sometimes more often, if I have free time. But I'm the one who decides how much time to spend. If you aren't the best at time management, limit your visits to Facebook to as long as it takes you to drink a cup of coffee, or set a kitchen timer for 15 minutes. After it rings, go do something not computer related. You can always come back for another 15-minute visit when your time allows.

Get Connected with LinkedIn

Of all the social networking sites, LinkedIn (*linkedin.com*) may be the most practical. As the site says, it's "The world's largest professional network: 300 million strong." LinkedIn is not as social as Facebook or as information-based as Twitter. It is really a site for professionals to meet, greet, and see how they can help one another out. If you're looking to change jobs, hire someone, or even just stay abreast of what's going on in your field, joining LinkedIn would be a very good idea. It would be an oversight for anyone seeking employment to not join LinkedIn.

LinkedIn's Setup

Getting started with LinkedIn is almost exactly the same as setting up Twitter and Facebook. You'll register with the site by providing your email address and choosing a password. All the same rules apply. In this case, however, you may choose to use your work email instead of your personal or secondary email address. Do not choose the same password you use for any financial transactions. Choose a password that's at least six characters (eight is better) and a combination of letters and numbers.

RECORD YOUR PASSWORD
Please write down your selected password *before* you even type it to be sure you have the *exact* password you want. Be precise about what letters are uppercase and lowercase.

The most significant difference between LinkedIn and the other social networking sites will be what you choose to share in your profile. Because of the professional nature of LinkedIn, people tend to share their employment history, education, and whatever other affiliations and associations they have. You can provide quite a lot of detail (although not an unlimited amount) about yourself and your areas of expertise and experience.

Instead of Facebook **friends** or Twitter **followers**, LinkedIn is made up of **connections**. The features offered on LinkedIn's website reflect the more professional focus of the site.

—You can receive or send private messages on LinkedIn. Invitations to become connected are also received and responded to here.

Home—Brings you back to your main page on LinkedIn, which summarizes your connections' recent updates.

Here's a sample LinkedIn profile. (Full disclosure: That's my sister.)

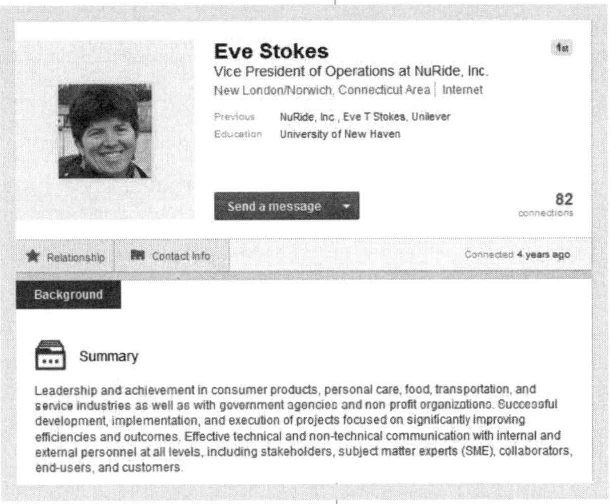

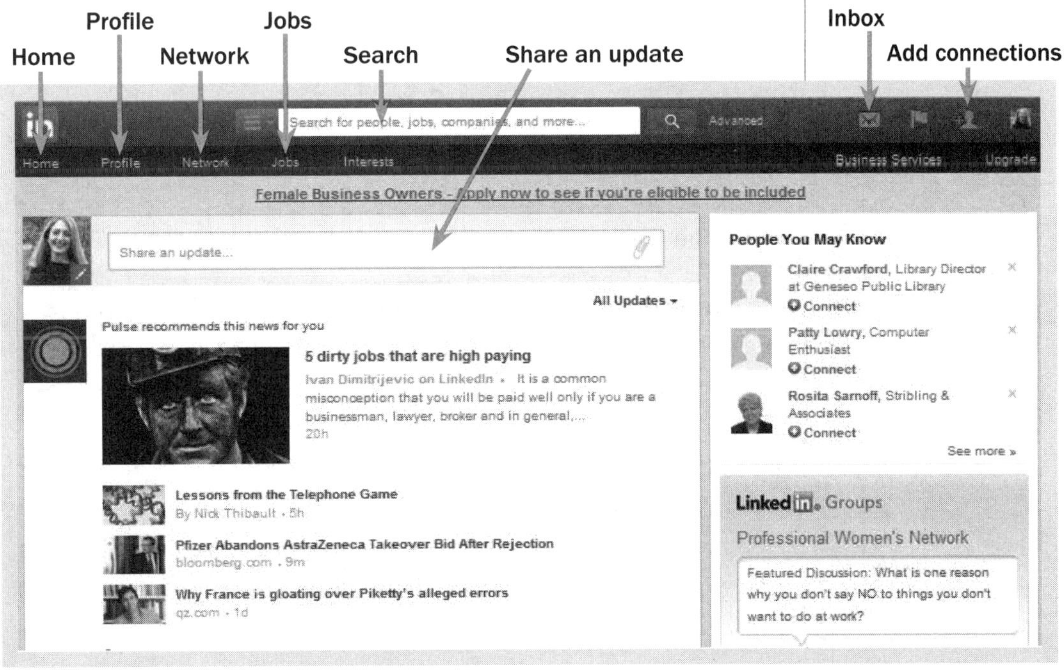

"I didn't really pay attention to LinkedIn after I opened my account. But about a year later, when it came to hiring a new employee, it was the perfect resource."
—*Kimberley*

Interests—Here you can find groups or companies that might be of interest to you.

Jobs—Where you would go to post or find available jobs.

Network—Here you view your existing connections and add more.

Profile—Click here to view and edit your profile. You can also make and request recommendations from here.

Search—Notice the down arrow next to People. You search, using keywords or names, under any of the categories listed.

Share an update—Here's where you share your thoughts or activities, as you would on Facebook or Twitter.

Another way to think of LinkedIn is as an electronic résumé. Because of this, accuracy and honesty are of the utmost importance. Exaggerating may get you in the door, but lying will get you the boot and may damage your professional reputation.

What Else Is Out There?

I've described the three most popular social networking websites, but there are many more that you might want to investigate. Let's talk about a few of them.

Google+ works in much the same way as Facebook, but you organize who you share with into Circles distinguished by your common interests. For example, you can organize your colleagues and other work connections into one circle, family members into another, etc. Google+ in no way competes with the billions of people on Facebook, but there are over 540 million Google+ users, which is nothing to sneeze at. If you are social networking for your business, you would be remiss to overlook Google+.

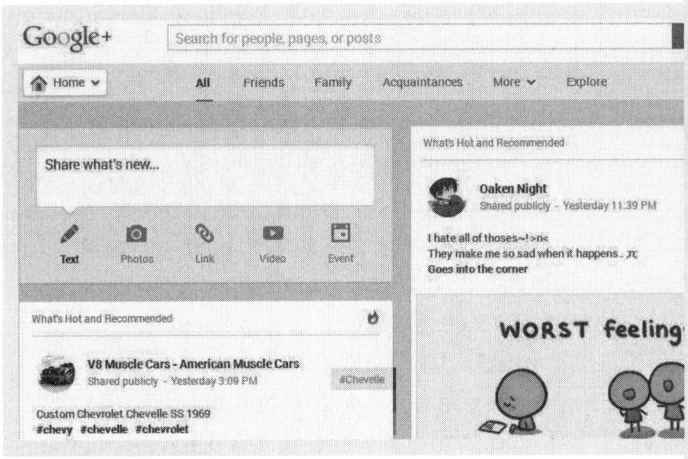

■ Google+ website

■ Instagram App

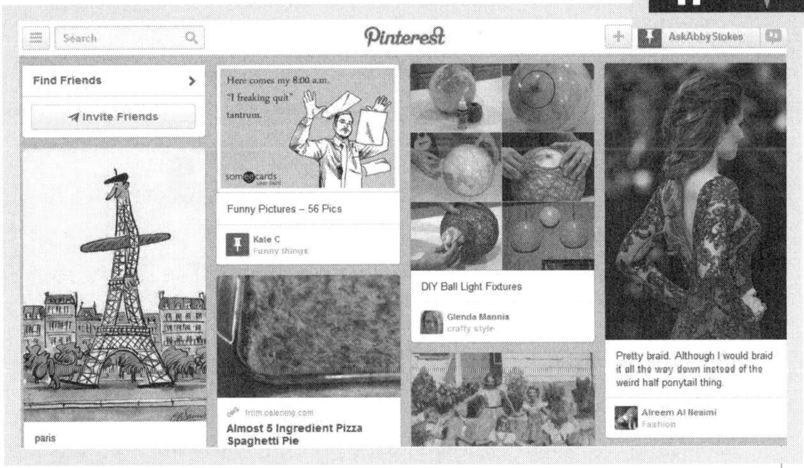

■ Pinterest website

Pinterest is primarily a visual site, using images rather than words to share ideas. Remember how I compared Facebook to a bulletin board? Pinterest is even more like one. You can "pin" pictures that interest or appeal to you onto your board and view others' boards. Your board can be practical or just for fun. Say you need new light fixtures for your kitchen—you can search the Web for images of lights that appeal to you and pin any that pique your interest to your board. At the end, you can assess what you've pinned and make a purchase. Or you can simply pin images that you love and create your own inspiration board.

To learn **How to Use Instagram** visit ***AskAbbyStokes.com***. Click on Video Tutorials at the top, then click on Video #12.

Instagram is another largely visual site where people share photographs and videos. Instagram offers all kinds of fun digital filters to easily enhance photos. You can change your photos to black-and-white or tint them in various ways. Because Instagram is all about images usually taken with a smartphone, you use the app on a smartphone or tablet—rather than a computer—to visit or share on Instagram. There is an area, below the photos shared, where you can let someone know what you think of the photo they shared. (Remember what your mother told you: "If you don't have something nice to say, don't say anything at all.")

We'll talk about **YouTube**, the video-sharing website, a bit later (see page 475). The list of social networking sites goes on and on—and some brilliant computer geek is probably thinking up some new format as I'm typing this!

The process of setting up an account at all of these sites is very similar to how you set up Facebook, Twitter, and LinkedIn. And the privacy concerns are the same—just remember The Front-Door Test!

Lift the Fog About Blogs

Blogging is another way to communicate and express yourself online. Originally known as a web log, a blog may read like a professional article written for a newspaper or magazine or like a personal journal entry that someone might once have kept under lock and key. Someone who writes a blog is called a blogger. A blogger can post his or her thoughts, observations, and opinions for millions of readers, if the blog is popular, or for a few, if it isn't. Blogs are usually updated daily, every few days, or weekly, and the majority offer readers an opportunity to post a reply. Often there is no editor, publisher, or filter for the information. So while freedom of speech prevails, the quality of writing and subject matter can vary widely.

For instance, most of the numerous blogs that appear on the Huffington Post website, which has over 43 million visitors a month, are written by professional bloggers and take on the tone of an article or op-ed piece. The Huffington Post editors approve each blog before it appears on the site. But anyone who wants to can set up a website and blog there. One blog I visit regularly is maintained by a very dear friend who battled breast cancer for the second time. She created her blog so we could be kept up to date on her health without her fielding phone calls all day. Now that she's cancer-free, she still maintains the blog, sharing what else is happening in her life. I love to read her updates. The movie *Julie & Julia*, starring Meryl Streep, was based on a blog that was adapted into a book before becoming a film. Most blogs, even those written by professional writers, are not going to get made into books or movies, but blogging is a great way for writers to get their words out there to be read.

"Blogs have opened up my entire world. I can't get around on my own, so reading blogs makes me feel like I'm in on a conversation even though we are miles apart."
—*Claire*

Most blogs are conversational in tone and may contain videos, photographs, or other graphics, and links to other websites. Some may have more photos and videos than text. A blog may be used to promote a project, share experiences, voice opinions, or chronicle a journey. The possibilities are endless. To date, there are more than 250 million blogs on the Internet. (OMG!)

YOU ARE CORDIALLY INVITED

Visit *AskAbbyStokes.com* and click on Blog at the top of the page. I await your feedback!

To get an initial sense of what a blog is, check out my blog at *AskAbbyStokes.com/blog*. After you've gotten the feel of my blog, visit *google.com* and type in a topic of interest to you and take a tour of the scores of blogs listed. Or give any of these a try:

- *getrichslowly.org/blog*
- *huffingtonpost.com*
- *janefonda.com*
- *mashable.com*
- *smittenkitchen.com*

Here are some samples.

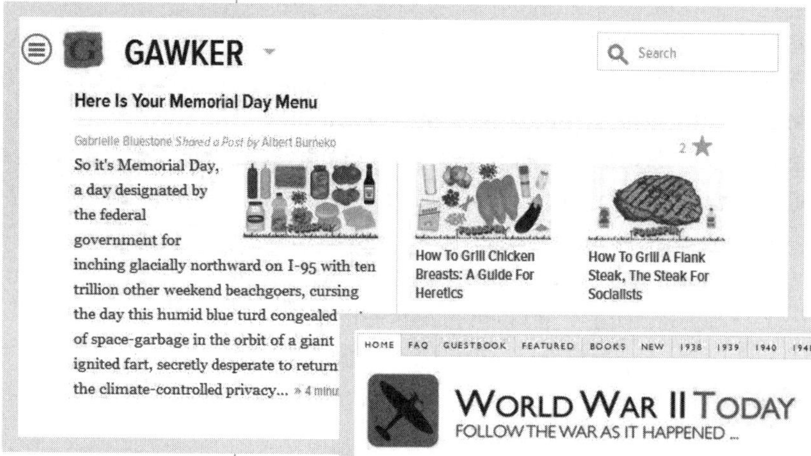

■ Gawker focuses on celebrity and media news.

■ World War II Today's tagline is "follow the war as it happened."

■ The actress Felicity Huffman is behind What the Flicka.

If you're considering creating a blog of your own, there are plenty of websites that will provide you with a free platform (i.e., a place to house it). To start, take a look at these three free blog sites:

- *blogger.com*
- *weebly.com*
- *wordpress.com*

Each of these will walk you through creating your own blog step-by-step. Alternatively, visit *google.com*, search for "free blog," and see what you find. Or when you visit a blog you like, see if it shows who powers or hosts it.

If you start a blog and few Internet travelers visit at the outset, remember that Rome wasn't built in a day. It takes time for people to become aware of a blog and for you to establish an audience. Send a link to your blog, via email, to all your friends, and post the link on your Facebook and Twitter pages. Comment on other blogs to introduce yourself, and invite people to visit your blog. Remember, it is socializing, so you have to reach out to people and engage them.

Again, be very careful not to send private information into cyberspace. The unfortunate reality is that scammers, hackers, or worse may be lurking to take advantage of your forthright exposure of who you are. Never give information on your blog revealing your home address or phone number. Also, avoid hanging other people's dirty laundry out on your blog. You may be willing to tell all, but are your friends and family?

Intergenerational Ideas to Bridge the Digital Divide

As you grow more comfortable using the Internet, you may find it becomes a very useful tool for helping to stay in touch with younger family members (those born with a keyboard and mouse in hand). From documenting memories to scheduling quality time, the Internet offers an endless array of options to help you build a richer connection with loved ones. I like to refer to this section as my "Grandparent Cheat Sheet," but the reality is, these suggestions will work for anyone, regardless of age. Here are some ideas to get you started.

Make a Date

- Schedule a regular date to connect in real time online, whether it is through a Skype video call or instant messaging (see page 359 for more instructions).

- Be prepared with open-ended questions that promote conversation, such as: "Why is she your favorite teacher?"; "If there is something you could change about yesterday, what would it be?"; or "What is a perfect day for you?"

Create a Ritual

- Touch base with computer questions on Tech Tuesday.

- Website Wednesday is when you email the link of a website that you enjoy and think others would like, too (see page 291 for more instructions). And for suggestions to get you started, there are more than 150 websites listed on page 516.

- Schedule time to play a game online on Fun Fridays, alternating who chooses the game. Don't forget to play the old favorites—checkers, hangman, chess, and Go Fish. Play the same games, but use the actual 3-dimensional board games when you get together face-to-face.

Chronicle Family History

- The Internet is a great tool for swapping memories and sharing family history between generations. Digital Natives can share a recent photo online—either as an email attachment or on Facebook. Digital Immigrants, in turn, can share an old photo taken well before the birth date of the younger partner (see page 309 for instructions on sending photos). You should each write a few sentences describing the photo. It can be a great conversation starter for your next Skype session.

- Work together to design a family website for everyone to share photos and blog postings. Include a family calendar with birthdays, recitals, school vacations, and more.

- Collaborate to create a questionnaire for each family member to answer and share. Include questions such as, "What's your favorite food?"; "What were you doing the day I was born?"; and "Did you have a pet when you were little?"

Send a Surprise

- Just for fun, shop online and send all the supplies necessary for a party (hats, balloons, etc.) even when there is no event on the calendar. (See page 441 for instructions on shopping safely.)
- Video-record yourself reading their favorite story.
- Send an e-card for no occasion at all.

Go Retro

Some traditions are irreplaceable! Send a postcard or a box of homemade cookies via snail mail.

Affairs of the Heart

You can use the Internet to keep up to date with people you already know, but it's also great for meeting new people. Some of the people you encounter online you may never want to meet face-to-face, but others may become great friends, or more. Wedding bells and engagement rings aren't out of the question: One-third of married couples in the United States met online. I know a lovely older couple who met online and married a couple of years later. Even if you're not in the market to get hitched, a dinner companion or an online flirtation might be just what the doctor ordered.

You decide what type of person's profile you want to see.

Online dating uses the same technology as the original computerized dating services in the 1960s. You answer a series of questions to create a profile. Most of the online dating sites then compare the qualities you describe in yourself and those you desire in another with the rest of the profiles on the site and, presto, matches are made. If you would rather not have a machine make your match for you, you can take your time to find and view profiles that you feel

> "When I first started online dating I thought I wanted to get married again. Now I'm having so much fun dating, I don't want to limit myself to one person."
> —*Shelly*

fit your criteria without anyone's guidance. You can search the profiles listed based on your own criteria, such as age, physical attributes, location, education, likes, dislikes, etc.

A few of the leading online dating sites are:

- *chemistry.com*
- *eharmony.com*
- *match.com*
- *okcupid.com*

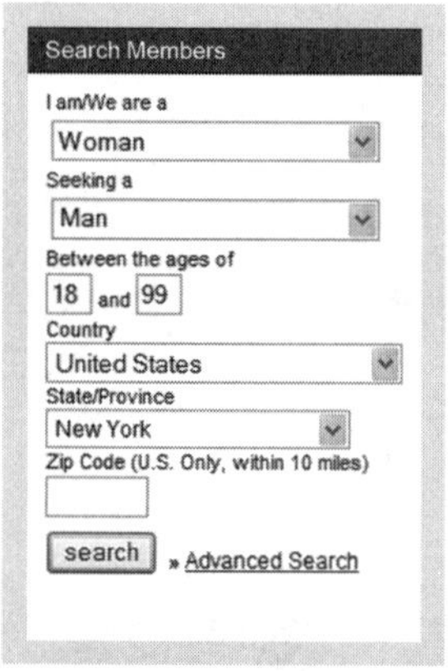

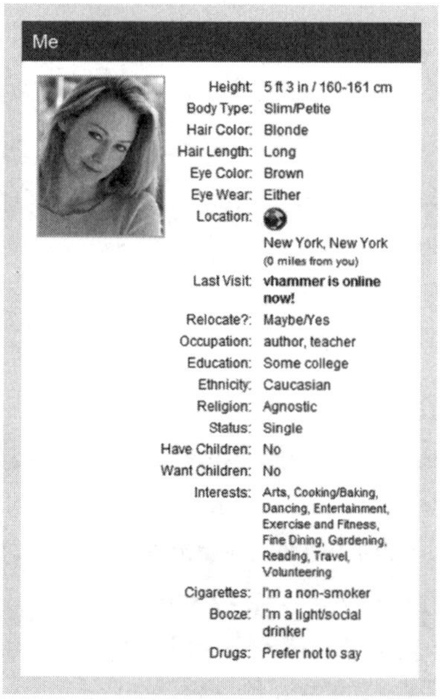

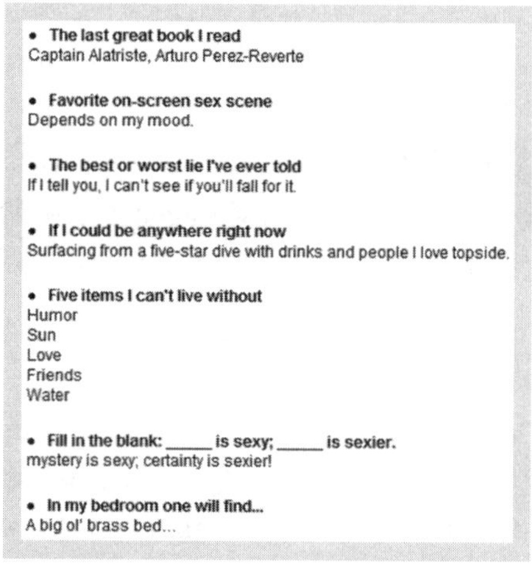

A sample online dating profile

As you can see in the example above, there is usually a photo of the prospective match. (I never bother to read a profile if the person isn't willing to include a photo. It makes me wonder what he or she is hiding and why.) Most dating websites have their members answer standard questions about height, weight, body type, smoking and drinking habits, education, location, and so on. Then you have the option to list things like recently read books, favorite musicians or songs, what five things you can't live without, what kind of person you're looking for, and what you have to offer. The specific questions asked may vary from site to site, but each dating site tries to gather as much information as possible to paint a detailed picture of who you are and whom you're hoping to meet.

> **PLAY = HANKY-PANKY**
>
> You might be asked what you are "looking for": Friendship, Dating, Marriage, or Play. Don't make the same mistake I did. Choosing "Play" means an interest in fooling around and not much else. I chose it once on a dating site and proceeded to receive graphic photos from the men who were interested! Silly me; I thought "Play" meant "have fun," not "have sex."

Some online dating services like *okcupid.com* or *plentyoffish.com* are free, but the majority charge a fee. Fees vary and usually cover a period of time or the number of contacts made. Most sites allow a free trial or limited use before you need to give credit card information. I highly recommend that you take advantage of a sneak peek before you commit yourself financially to a site. Just as individuals have personalities, so do dating websites. Some are based on age, religion, race, or sexual preference—*jdate.com*, *gay.com*, and *seniorfriendfinder.com* are some examples of dating websites that cater to specific groups. Specifically, *jdate.com* is the leading Jewish singles networking site; *gay.com* is a dating site for gays and lesbians; and *seniorfriendfinder.com* is a site where older adults can create new relationships. Some sites are racier than others. Here in Manhattan, *match.com* is considered a bit tamer than *ashleymadison.com*. Ask around to see if you know anyone who has taken the plunge to look for companionship or more on the Internet. If you find someone, ask about his or her experiences.

Here are some simple guidelines to online dating.

- Never divulge your last name or home address before meeting face-to-face.
- If you choose to chat by phone, give a cell phone number so your home address cannot be traced.
- When arranging a meeting, agree to make it brief (a cup of coffee or a cocktail), in a public place, and make sure a friend knows what you're doing, when, and where.

WHILE AWAY

Don't limit yourself to meeting people only in your hometown. The website you've listed your profile on may have members from all over the country (maybe even the world). So if you're traveling, check out the profiles of people near your destination. It might be nice to arrange a meeting for coffee or a drink when you arrive, to kick off your time away.

- Under no circumstances should you get into a car with this person or meet in an isolated place.
- Listen to your gut and your head. Your heart doesn't have eyes and ears.

Statistically, profiles with a photograph are viewed more often than those without a photo. In the previous chapter, we talked about how to get photographs onto the computer. Once your picture is on your computer, you can copy (or upload) it to a website. Please use a photograph that's flattering but that honestly represents what you look like *now*. You'll do yourself a disservice if you post a 20-year-younger or 20-pound-lighter photo. If someone shows interest and you would like to meet, imagine his or her disappointment at realizing you've posted a misleading photo. Your suitor will feel lied to, and justifiably so. You would feel the same way if the person you met didn't look like the person you'd taken a shine to in the photos. Have more faith in yourself than that. Put the true you online for potential matches to see.

If you find a profile of interest, there are usually two routes you can take to make contact. You can send an email through an anonymous email account that is set up through the dating website. The person won't know your real name, and you won't know hers or his, until you both decide to reveal them.

Some sites let you send a person a "wink" or a "like." This is an unwritten message to notify the other party of your interest. Based on your profile, he or she can then decide to make contact or not.

You have no obligation to respond to everyone who contacts you, and vice versa. Try not to be hurt if you don't hear back from someone. You may not be her type, or he may have already found someone and forgotten to take his profile off the website. If you'd rather be the date shopper and not have your profile window-shopped by others, you can also make your profile private. Then if, and only if, you find someone of interest you can allow him or her to see your profile.

Caution should prevail, however, when you venture into online dating. A broken heart heals, but a fraud that results in your retirement savings being swindled out from under you by a cunning Romeo or Juliet requires a much longer recovery. Have fun. Date and be merry. But think long and hard about what you really know about your new friend before you make any legal arrangements or lend money. Tragic stories of people marrying before actually meeting sound improbable, but it happens. Bask in the attention, but let your head and not your heart guide your decisions.

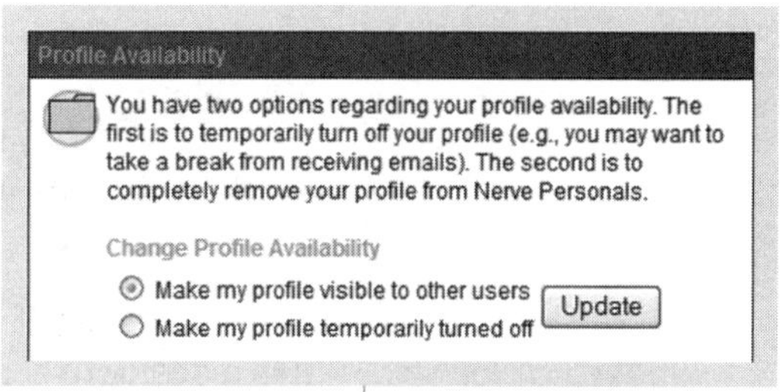

You can decide to reveal or hide your profile from others.

I've taken all the romance out of it, haven't I? Not at all! Online dating is a wonderful way to make friends, develop relationships, and possibly find love. I want you to have a good, even great, experience. However, as is true with any affair of the heart, you shouldn't be reckless. The cyber world of the Internet has just as many Gallants as it does Goofuses. Take advantage of the varied ways in which the computer and the Internet can connect you to a world few of us could imagine even 20 years ago. Just exercise a bit of caution until you're more familiar with the ways of this new world.

What Will the Future Bring?

My crystal ball is a bit foggy about what might happen in the future. Five years ago, I could not have imagined all the new ways we now share online, but not to worry—the instructions you followed in this chapter can be used to guide you through the features of new sites and help you customize them to meet your specific needs. I have faith that you can go with the flow as new ideas and ways to communicate come down the pipeline. And, hey, keep in touch!

TOO MANY TO NAME

There are many social networking sites not mentioned in this chapter. For a comprehensive list of sites, visit *wikipedia.com* and type "list of social networking websites" in the search box.

Q: Why would someone participate in a blog under a false identity?

A: Some people who write a blog want to remain anonymous for the sake of privacy, but their input is valid and well intended. Others contribute false information to a blog for no other reason than a desire to screw around with people. Remember that kid from grammar school who put the frog down your shirt? Some people never change. So be discriminating when you read something on the Internet. Not everything you read is true.

Q: Is there any recourse when people misrepresent themselves on a dating website?

A: Every online dating site offers a way to contact the people who administer the site and let them know if someone's behavior warrants preventing him or her from being listed on the site. However, a little fibbing about height, weight, finances, and so on probably will not get someone banished from the site.

Q: If I remove a photo of me from Facebook, can it be found elsewhere?

A: The uncomfortable fact is that once a photo or text is posted on Facebook, it is out there. When you delete a photo from your album, someone else may have already printed it or captured the image from Facebook. You should know that Facebook owns anything posted on the site. So even if others can no longer see the photo in your album, it remains in Facebook's archives.

Q: Can I control who can read my tweets on Twitter?

A: Yes! After you have signed into your account, click on the icon in the top right corner that looks like a cog ⚙. Next click on **Settings** in the menu that pops up in the left sidebar, and then **Security and**

Privacy. Click inside the box to the right of Tweet Privacy. A check should appear in the box. Last, click on **Save Changes** at the bottom of the page. Keep in mind that someone you allow to read your tweets can copy or print your tweet and pass it on. So you still want to be discreet and thoughtful about what you tweet.

LET'S REVIEW

blog
a website where contributors share ideas and opinions

Facebook
a social networking website where you and your "friends" can view whatever ideas, photos, or links to websites you all choose to share

Google+
a social networking service owned by Google that allows you to organize people into groups called "circles"

Instagram
an online photo-sharing, video-sharing, and social network that enables its users to take pictures and videos and share them on a variety of platforms, including Facebook and Twitter

LinkedIn
a social networking site for professionals to make connections and list or find jobs

Pinterest
a virtual bulletin board where you can "pin" images that appeal to you

post
to submit text that appears on a blog, message board, or social networking website

profile
a web page on a social networking site where you list your interests, hometown, and whatever other details you choose to share with anyone who has access to your information on the site

Skype
a program that allows you to call, IM, or video call other users at no cost over the Internet

social networking
connecting with friends and family, meeting new people, and sharing ideas, photos, etc., on the Internet

Twitter
a social website where you "follow" whoever's thoughts (140 characters or less) are of interest to you and where others may in turn follow you

CHAPTER 21

PUT IT ALL IN ORDER

Use your computer and the cloud to create a filing system to keep everything backed up and organized

You don't need to be a neatnik for the sake of your buddy, the computer. It couldn't care less whether you can find the documents you "penned." Nor does it have any investment in whether your photographs are organized in a folder on the Desktop or if they live higgledy-piggledy all over your machine. Your computer will not lose sleep over whether you've copied your photos and documents onto CDs for safekeeping or not. *You* are the sole beneficiary of an organized computer. Knowing where things are stored makes your computing experience manageable and more pleasant. Don't you deserve that? As for the computer, what matters is that you do some regular housekeeping to help it function at its best. First, let's take care of *your* needs. Unless the computer is misbehaving, it can wait. (For housekeeping and troubleshooting advice, visit Chapter 25.)

I don't mean to ignore those of you with tablets. When, later on in this chapter, we discuss "the cloud" for storage, that's when you tablet folks are going to want to perk up your ears—but take in the conversation about creating a filing system even if you don't have a computer.

File vs. Folder

Files and folders have been referred to several times in this book. Let's get to the nitty-gritty of exactly what the difference is between the two and how you can make use of both.

A file can be a word-processing document, a digital or scanned photograph, a video clip, an audio or music recording, a PowerPoint slide show, or a movie. It could be a multipage document containing text, graphics, and photos. In every case, a file must have a name. Ideally, that name clearly describes the contents of the file, thereby eliminating the need to open the file to reveal the gist of its contents. It's a good idea to include who, what, and when in the filename (e.g., Betty Xmas 2014). A file name can contain spaces and may be uppercase and lowercase, but punctuation can sometimes be tricky. You can't use slashes or question marks. If you must have a means to divide text, use the hyphen key (e.g., accountant final letter 4-14-2015).

PUNCTUATION IS NOT WELCOME

For simplicity's sake, avoid punctuation when you name a file or folder. Slashes (/) are a coding used by the computer to designate the location of an item on the computer, and for some reason the computer won't accept question marks, either. It's easiest to steer clear of punctuation when you name a file (aka document, photo, etc.) or folder. Period!

One folder containing three files

FILE NAME EXTENSIONS

.docx or .doc = Microsoft Word document

.xlsx or .xls = Microsoft Excel spreadsheet

.pdf = Adobe Acrobat portable document file

.ppt = Microsoft PowerPoint Presentation

.cwk = AppleWorks document

.mov = QuickTime movie

.wav = sound file

.jpg = a graphic or image

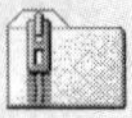
.zip = compressed data

"My actual desk is a mess, yet somehow I'm able to keep my computer quite organized. Who knows why I can do it with the computer and nowhere else, but it definitely eliminates computer confusion for me."
—***Daniel***

FILE OR FOLDER
Drop the phrase "file folder" from your lexicon, and it will be easier to understand dealing with a file *or* a folder.

In Chapter 15, I described how to use **File** and **Save As** to name a Microsoft Word (MS Word) document. Using **File** and **Save As** as file-naming devices is not exclusive to MS Word. Both options appear in many different software programs. Feel free to click on **File** in any program when curiosity calls to see if **Save As** appears in the drop-down menu. At the end of a file name is a suffix or extension that identifies the software program used to create the file. Above is the same list from our discussion on attachments in Chapter 17.

Notice there is an icon beside the suffixes listed in the above box. The icon represents each software program. Becoming familiar with these different icons can help you identify the types of files on your computer. There are many more extensions than those shown here. The ones listed are ones you'll see most often.

A folder is *not* a file. I know it's confusing, but to the computer, a file is a file and a folder is a folder. There is no such thing as a "file folder" on the computer. A folder is a means to store and organize one or more files. (For example, you might have a folder called "travel" and in it a document titled "packing list" and another called "Italy itinerary." Those two items are files contained in the folder "travel.") To assist in the identification of the contents, you will assign the folder a name. Again, specificity counts. The icon for a folder  helps clarify things because it looks like a manila folder and it functions like one.

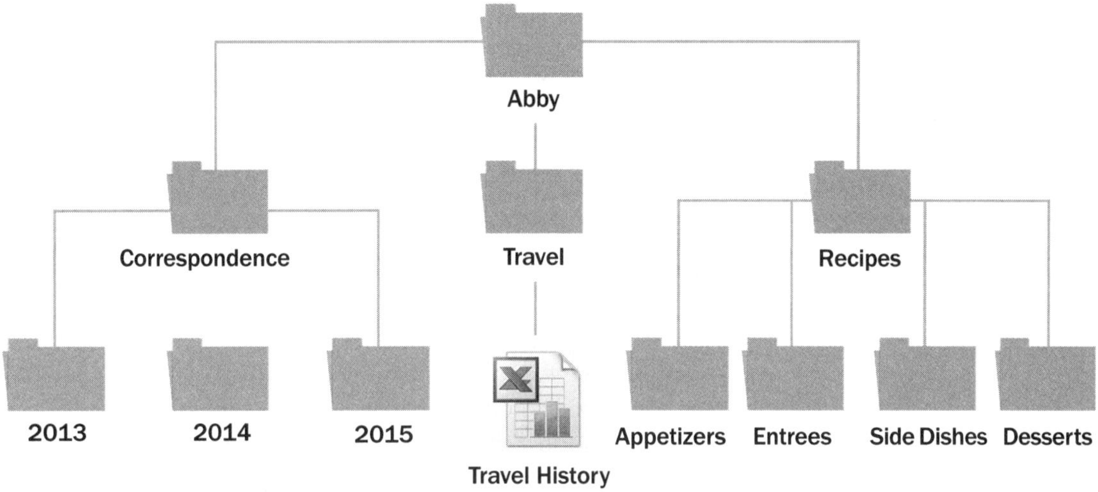

The Abby folder branches out into subfolders that contain folders and documents.

You can even have a folder system within a folder, similar to a family tree, as in the illustration here. On my computer, the main folder is named "Abby." Within that folder are folders titled "Correspondence," "Travel," and "Recipes," to name a few. Inside the correspondence folder are folders designated by year that store the correspondence of each year. Within the Travel folder are various itineraries and conversion charts. The Recipes folder contains separate folders for appetizers, main courses, side dishes, and desserts—each folder with recipes in it. Starting to get the picture?

Essentially, there is no limit to the number of files or folders a single folder can store, as long as your computer has enough memory. Here's the rule of thumb to keep things organized: If you have three or more files that can be grouped, make a folder to store them.

Create a Folder

Let's create a folder on the Desktop, so you can see what this business is all about.

If you have a PC:

- Move your mouse to a blank spot on the Desktop.

- Click with the *right* button of the mouse.
- Left-click on **New** (all other clicks will be with the *left* button after this point).
- Move the mouse into the menu that opened next to **New**.
- Click on **Folder** at the top of the list. A folder will now appear on the Desktop.
- Do *not* click the mouse at this stage. Instead type the desired name of the folder. For this exercise, simply type your first name. (If you did click the mouse, even though I told you not to, your folder is now officially named New Folder. Don't worry. We will learn how to rename a folder next. Sit tight.)
- Hit the **Enter** key to save the new name.
- Double-click on the folder to open it.

■ Creating a New Folder on a PC

CLICK AND GO

1. Right-click on any blank space on Desktop.
2. Left-click on New.
3. Left-click on Folder.
4. Do not click mouse; type desired folder name.
5. Hit Enter key.

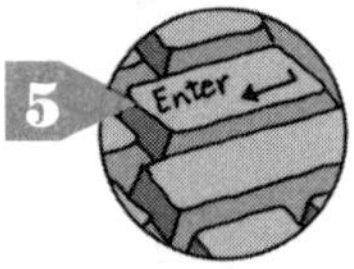

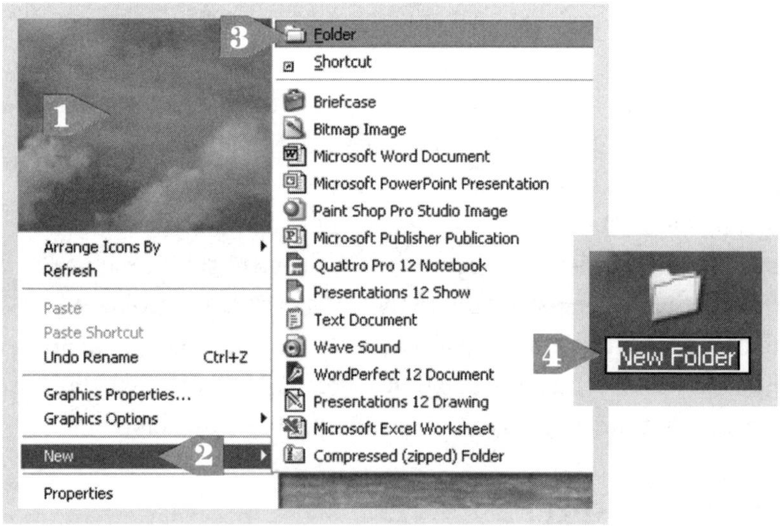

If you have a Mac:

- Click on the Desktop.
- Click on **File** at the top of the window.

- Click on **New Folder**.
- Do *not* click the mouse at this stage. Instead type the desired name of the folder. For this exercise, simply type your first name. (If you did click the mouse, even though I told you not to, your folder is now officially named New Folder. Don't worry. We will learn how to rename a folder next. Sit tight.)
- Hit the **Return** or **Enter** key to save the new name.
- Double-click on your folder to open it.

Well done! Repeat these steps anytime you want a new folder to appear on your Desktop. These are the same steps you would follow to create a folder within a folder anywhere on your computer. Open the existing folder where you would like a new one to appear. If you have a PC, right-click inside the folder where you want the new folder to appear and then follow the preceding steps. With the Mac, open the existing folder and then click on **File**.

BE FLEXIBLE
Remember, the steps I go over might be slightly different on your computer, but the underlying principles are the same. Do your best to apply the instructions here to what appears on your screen.

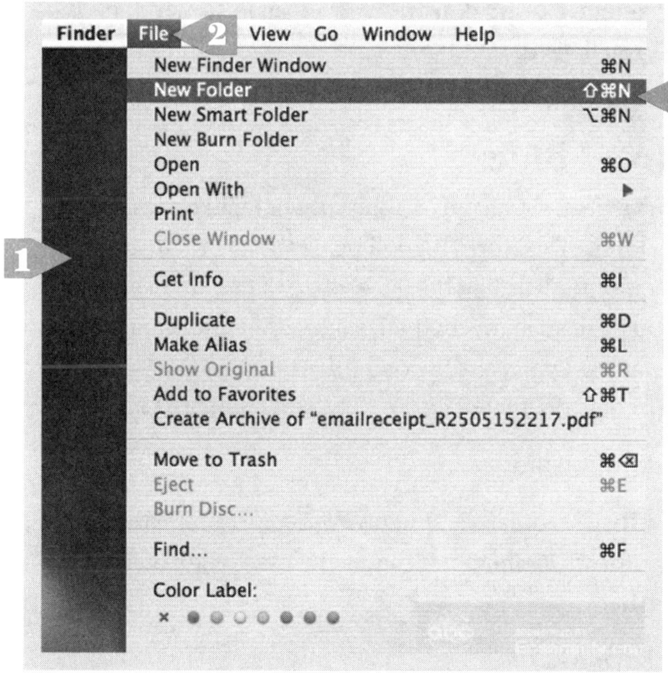

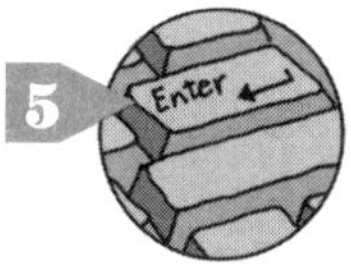

Creating a New Folder on a Mac

CLICK AND GO

1. Click on any blank space on Desktop.
2. Click File.
3. Click New Folder.
4. Do not click mouse; type desired folder name.
5. Hit Return or Enter key.

A PHOTO BY ANY OTHER NAME
As mentioned in Chapter 19, if you give a photograph a specific name that indicates the subject, location, and date, you won't play a guessing game as to what the image is or have to open it over and over again to find out. This is also true for any file or folder.

Rename a Folder or File

You can change the name of an existing folder or file (aka document, photograph, etc.) at any time. The same steps apply to both a file and a folder. Folders and files must be closed while changing their names.

- Place your mouse on the text below the icon of the file or folder to be renamed.
- Click once on the file or folder name. The computer now knows what item you want to modify.
- Click once, again, on the file or folder name. Only the name is now highlighted. You can either click within the name, if you want to modify only part of the name, or start typing to replace the entire name. For this exercise, replace your first name with your last name.
- Hit the **Enter** or **Return** key to save the change. Pretty good, huh? If that didn't work, don't fret. Try it again slowly and carefully. You'll get it.

Move into a Folder

Let's say you've been saving all of your attachments or new documents on the Desktop. (A good place to save them at the onset of your computer learning because you can find them easily.)

But now you have so many on the Desktop that you want to tidy things up. You can easily move a file or a folder into an existing folder. First, let's open a new document so we have something to play with.

- Open Microsoft Word.
- Click on **File**. (An older version of Word may require that you open a New Document. If that is the case, click on **New Document**.)
- Click on **Save As**.

- Choose the **Desktop** as your destination.
- Name the document "Move Me."
- Click **Save**.
- Close Microsoft Word.

Great! Now we have a document on the Desktop titled "Move Me" and a folder with your name.

- Move your mouse onto the "Move Me" document (aka file).
- Depress the mouse and keep it depressed (poor sad mouse) while you drag the "Move Me" file on top of the folder with your name.
- When "Move Me" is smack on top of the folder, highlighting both of the icons and text, release the mouse.
- Double-click on the folder with your last name. *Shazam!*

There is your "move me" document (aka file) inside the folder. Close the folder.

Repeat the steps in "Create a Folder" on page 405. Name the new folder "Bertha." Then keep reading.

Let's move the Bertha folder into the folder with your last name. It's as easy as click, drag, and drop. (You can sneak a peek at the previous instructions, if you want. They are there to help you.)

The Bertha folder should no longer exist on the Desktop. Now you can open the folder with your name.

Bertha and "Move Me" should be inside. Click and drag "move me" into "Bertha." Get it now? I thought so.

Because you can also use this method of moving items for moving files into a folder, it makes tidying up the Desktop very easy. When you're not sure where to save a photo, document, or folder, why not save it to the Desktop? You now know you can move it from there into an already existing folder or one you create.

Moving a file into a folder

CLICK AND GO

1. Move mouse onto "Move Me."
2. Click and drag onto folder.
3. Release mouse.

CLICK AND DRAG
If you need a refresher on click-and-drag, return to page 151 and play a hand or two of Solitaire.

Delete a Folder

Nice work so far! Now close whatever folders you have open on the Desktop.

I apologize for what you're about to do, but I'd like you to practice deleting a folder. Don't feel that all of your hard work has gone for naught because we're about to throw it away.

You can repeat the preceding steps to create as many folders as you like. But what if one of your folders and its contents become obsolete? You want to be able to clean up your Desktop or any other area of your computer, don't you?

First, find your target for where to put unwanted files and folders. On a PC, it is the **Recycle Bin** . On a Mac, it is the **Trash** . Let's get rid of the Bertha folder. Make sure it's closed. Click, drag, and drop the folder onto the Recycle Bin or Trash. Simple as that. Gone!

Be aware that there is more than one method available to create, rename, move, and delete a file or folder. As is true with so many actions on the computer, there are several ways to accomplish each of these tasks. The more you experiment with your computer, the more easily you can decide which method you prefer. You may choose to mix and match, as I do. You can also choose to store things anywhere on the computer that you desire. A folder called Documents already exists on your computer. You may want to store documents you've written there instead of creating a new folder with your name. How you decide to organize is your choice. I just strongly suggest that you *do* organize as you begin your journey rather than having to do a massive cleanup further down the line.

Two things to keep in mind:

- If you delete a folder, you will also be deleting *all* the files and folders within that folder.
- If you move a folder, you will also be moving *all* the files and folders within that folder.

Trash Picking 101

What happens to the file and folders you've thrown away? They remain stored in the trash or recycle bin until you or the computer, if scheduled to do so automatically, empties it. If you have a Mac, and you want to empty the Trash, click **Finder**, then click **Empty Trash**. If you have a PC, right-click on the **Recycle Bin**, then left-click on **Empty Recycle Bin**.

If you feel remorse about something you threw away, you can roll up your sleeves and retrieve it from the trash, unless it has been emptied. Double-click on the **Recycle Bin** or the **Trash** to open it. Click and drag the desired item out of the folder, back onto the Desktop. (You may want to wash your hands afterward!)

What do you do when the message below appears on your screen?

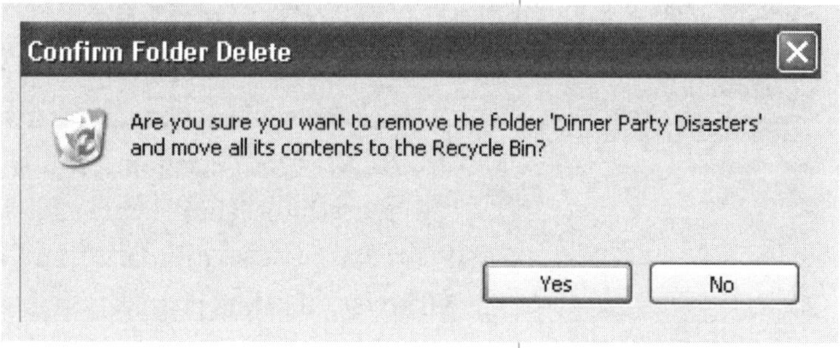

The computer may ask you to confirm that you want to throw something away.

The safest thing to do is to move your hands away from the keyboard and mouse. A hand hovering over the mouse, with its owner in an agitated state, can lead to an accidental click. The result of that click may be irreversible. In the case of this example, if you chose **Yes** and later realized your error, the item in question could be retrieved from the trash, but in other situations you might not be so lucky.

Don't Throw Out the Baby with the Bathwater!

More than one student has come to my class with the same sad story. Their computer seemed to be running slower than usual. So, they decided to delete items they didn't think were necessary in the hope that it would make the computer run more smoothly. Much to their disappointment, the computer stopped working entirely. What they did was delete items they didn't *think* they used on their computer. The number of files and/or folders on your computer doesn't make a big difference in the operation of the machine, unless you have an older computer with little memory. Unwittingly, a program that works in the background of the computer can get tossed in the purging process. By deleting this necessary but unfamiliar element, you risk negatively impacting how the computer functions. Files ending in .exe, .config, .sys, .bak, and .dll should *never* be altered, modified, renamed, copied, moved, or deleted. I don't expect anyone to commit that list to memory. So, instead, here is the policy I suggest: If you didn't create it or receive it as an attachment, don't delete it. When in doubt, don't throw it out!

A SAVING PLAN
Go back to Chapter 19 (page 350) to review backing up. Consider purchasing an external hard drive, which can store much more than CDs or DVDs can.

The Cloud Really Does Have a Silver Lining

So, everything is named and organized on your computer. It feels great, doesn't it? Just when you get nice and comfy—*BAM!*—your computer is lost or stolen or a rogue virus deletes everything. That is why a backup of your data is so important. I didn't mean to be so dramatic, but I did want to get your attention.

The cloud offers an additional way to back up your material, but it is much more than that. As I described in Chapter 19, the cloud is to your computer what mini-storage is to your home—an off-site location that does its best to protect your belongings. Is it foolproof? No. Could everything you've stored on the cloud be lost? Yes. That's why we keep the really important data (family reunion photos, contracts, love letters) in multiple formats. Back up what's crucial onto a CD or DVD or external hard drive, print it, *and* store it on the cloud. Surely all three methods can't fail you—at least not all at the same time.

Backing up is not the only function of the cloud. It also allows you access to your materials from any Internet-connected device at any time, anywhere in the world. If you want to share files with someone else, but not email the files, you can do that with the cloud, too, by giving them access to the "place" they're stored.

There are many file-hosting services available. We'll zero in on Dropbox and Google Drive, as both are free and among the most popular, but don't hesitate to ask friends and family for recommendations of which storage and sharing websites they trust and prefer.

How to Begin with Google Drive

To access Google Drive from your computer, you must sign into a Gmail account, which is free. If you need help choosing a safe but memorable password, review the instructions on page 210.

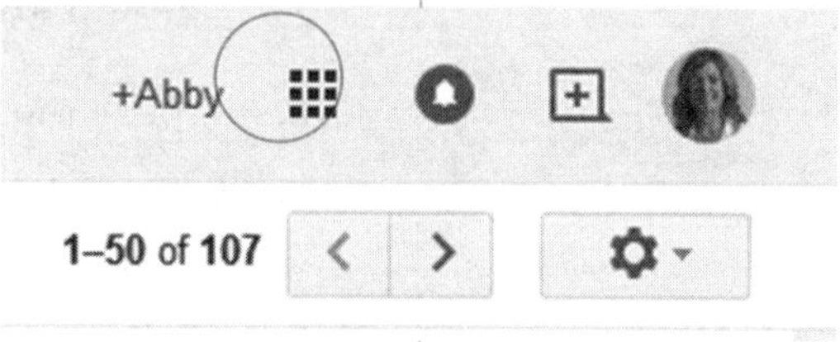

Once signed into Gmail, look at the top right of the window and click on , then click on . You are now in Google Drive.

How Does Google Drive Work?

Once you're into your Google Drive account, you can upload (or move) documents, folders, or photographs from your computer to Google Drive.

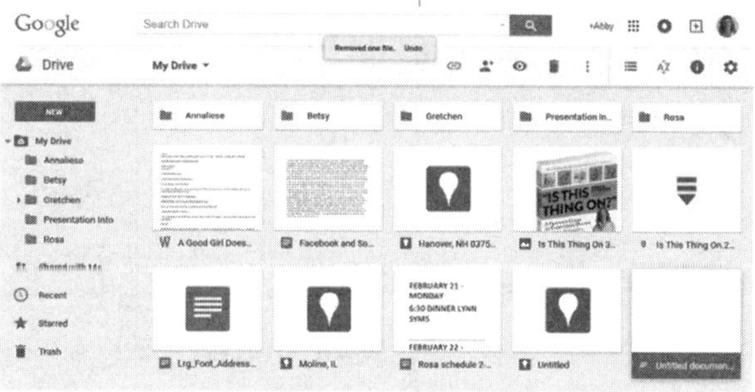

To upload to Google Drive:

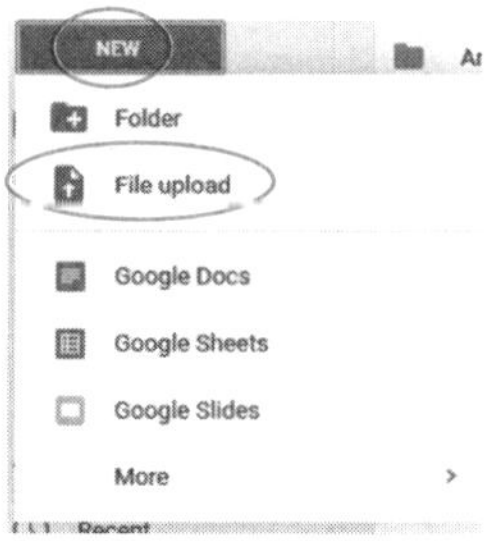

1. Click on **New** (in red in the upper left corner).
2. Click on **File Upload**.
3. Find the item you want to move. Click on the item, then click on **Open** in the bottom right.
4. Give Google Drive some time to complete the task. The larger the item, the longer it will take to upload.

You should now see the item on the Google Drive page. Well done!

Keep Everything Organized

Depending on how many items you choose to bring onto Google Drive, you may want to create a folder system. If you don't give an item a solid name and a logical place on your computer, it is so much harder to find later on. The ideal name tells you enough about the item that you don't need to open it to identify what it is.

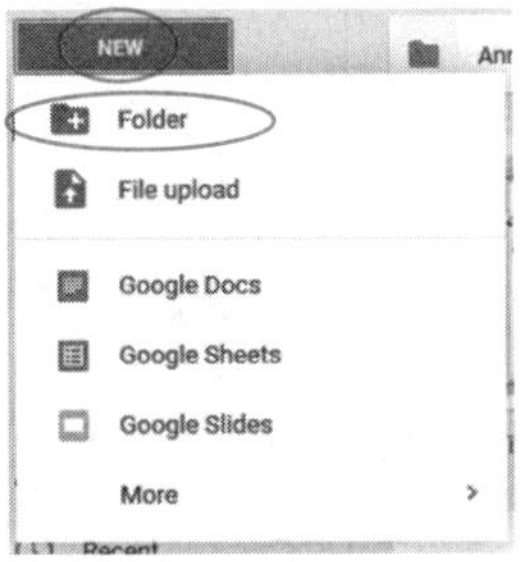

To create a folder:

1. You can create a folder by clicking on **New** again.
2. Click on **Folder**.
3. Type in the name you want to give the folder and click **Create**.

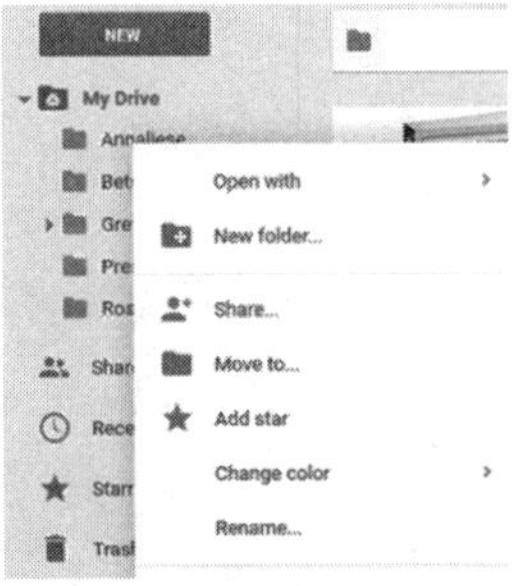

Who, What, and When

The ideal name for a document or photo tells you whom it is of or to, what the content is about, and when it was taken or written. For example: *Mom Xmas pajamas 2015* or *Dr. Farley test results 5-12-13.*

Once you've created a folder, it will appear in the sidebar along the left. If you don't see a list of folders, click on the arrow to the left of **My Drive**. That menu also allows you to zero in on what items have been **Shared** with you and the most **Recent** items.

As is often true with websites and the computer, there is more than one way to accomplish a task. You can also **Upload Files** and create a **New Folder** if you open the **My Drive** menu by clicking on the down arrow to the right of **My Drive**.

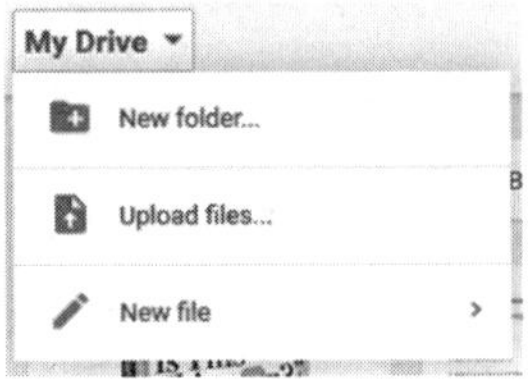

What Are Your Options?

Once you have a document, photo, or folder on Google Drive, there are several actions you can take.

If you *single click* on a document or photo, a new set of actions will appear in the top right corner:

Get Link—gives you a link to the document or photo that you can send to whomever you want to share the item with.

Share—is another way of sharing the document or photo, but in this case you would type the recipient's email address and the item would be sent directly from Google Docs.

Preview—lets you see the item without actually opening it.

Trash—is just what it sounds like—where things you have deleted go.

View—gives you a choice about how you would like to view your documents and photos.

Sort—lets you choose what order you would like the items to appear in.

This set of stacked dots opens up the **More Menu** where you can **Move** items, **Rename** them, and **Download** (or move) them onto the computer that you're visiting Google Drive on.

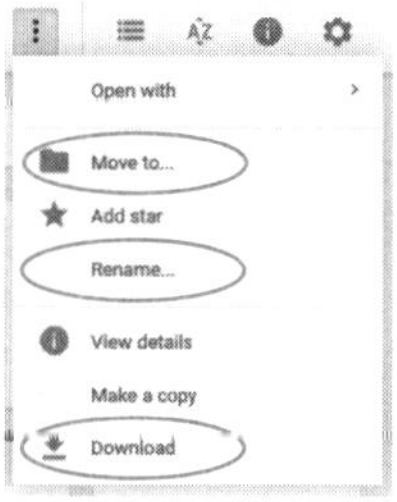

If you *double-click* on a document or photo, it will open and a new set of actions will appear across the top.

Let's review each of these features.

Print—directs the Google Drive to print the document or photo.

Share—is yet another option for sharing the item.

Download—lets you move the item onto the computer that you're currently using.

Zoom—is where you click to make the image larger on the screen.

Pop Out—opens a new tab for what you're viewing.

This set of stacked circles brings you to another **More Menu** where you can **Rename** the item among other things.

That should be enough to get you started with Google Drive.

P.S. Google Drive can also be accessed on a tablet. It's preloaded on Android tablets and can be downloaded on any other tablet.

Dropping In on Dropbox

As I mentioned, Dropbox is a file-hosting service, which means you can store your files there and access them from any device connected to the Internet. You can also use Dropbox to share them with others.

To create an account with Dropbox, visit *dropbox.com*. As when you registered on Skype or Facebook, Dropbox requires an email address and you must choose a password. This is an opportunity for you to use your secondary email address (the email address you opened for shopping and newsletters). Follow my previous guidelines for creating a password, and most importantly, do not use the same password you use for any financial transactions.

Once your account is set up you can add it to your mobile devices. Yup—file-sharing services like Dropbox are cloud-based storage systems accessible from any device with Internet access.

Dropbox's Create an Account page

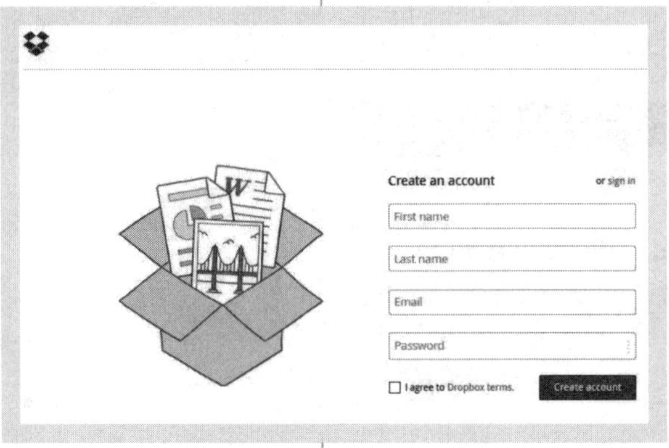

There is an app for Dropbox available for your tablet or smartphone. (Revisit page 170 for the steps to add an app to your tablet. The same instructions hold true for smartphones.)

Let's Take a Look Under the Hood

You can move (upload) documents, photos, and other files onto Dropbox. And of course, what goes up, must come down—you can also download files from Dropbox onto your computer. This is particularly useful when someone shares a file with you via Dropbox. Say your nephew took a lot of photos at a family reunion. He could upload them to Dropbox and share them with you, who could then download them to your device.

The most important symbols to get under your belt are:

= upload. It is what you click on when you want to bring something from your computer onto Dropbox.

= new folder. You can put folders within folders. Click on this symbol to create a new folder.

= share link. When you click this symbol you will be prompted to input the email addresses of those you would like to share your file with. You can share as many of your files as you like. There is also a space for you to write a note to your recipient.

The home page of Dropbox

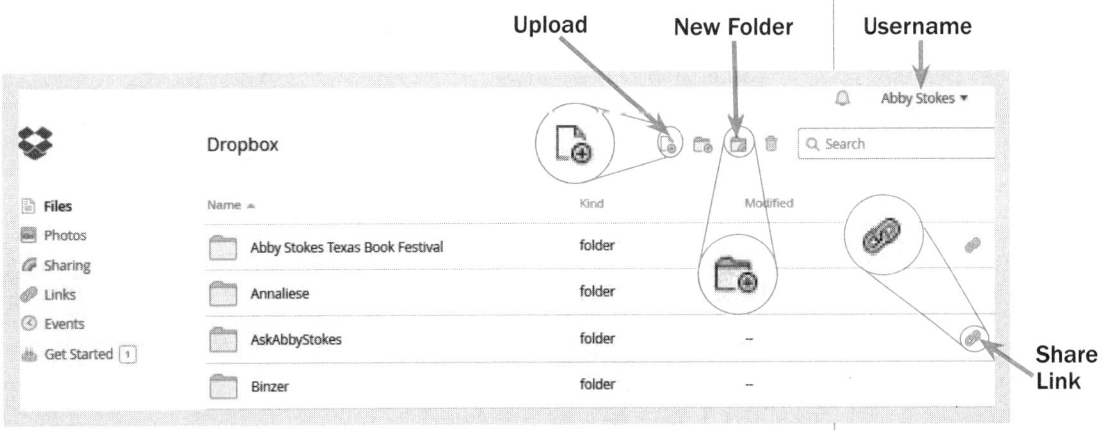

Download **Download**—allows you to move something from Dropbox onto your computer or device.

Move... **Move**—Once you've created a folder system, you can **Move** items into or out of a folder.

Rename **Rename**—Over time, you may want to **Rename** an item or folder.

Share **Share**—When you click the **Share** symbol, you'll be prompted to input the email addresses of those you would like to share with. There is also a space for you to write a message. Alternatively, you can copy and paste the share link into an email (see pages 250 and 297 for step-by-step instructions to copy and paste).

It's a good idea to review what you've stored on Dropbox periodically and delete what is out-of-date or no longer needed.

This allows you to move documents, photos, videos, and folders from your computer into your Dropbox account.

To upload to Dropbox:

1. Click on **Upload**.
2. Click **Choose Files**.
3. Find the item (document, photo, or video) that you want. Click on it.
4. Click on **Open**.
5. Click on **Done**.

To share from Dropbox:

1. Click on the item you want to share in Dropbox.
2. Click on **Share** to the right of the item.

3. You can either fill in the form that opens with the email address of your recipient, type a message, and click on **Send**, *or* copy and paste the link into an email (see pages 250 and 297).

Clear Skies

I hope that helps you understand what the cloud is and how you might benefit by using it to back up or share your files. The harnessing and organizing of your documents and photos can't come too soon. It's like dirty laundry—the pile just keeps getting higher and higher. Tackle a few folders a day and before you know it you'll make Melvil Dewey proud. (Melvil is the creator of the Dewey decimal system.)

Q: I can't seem to locate documents that I've written. How can I find them?

A: If you have a PC, you can right-click on the **Start** button and then left-click on **Search**. A sidebar will open on the right side of your screen. Type all or part of the name of what you're looking for. A list of items containing the keywords you typed will appear below. If you click on the Search icon, you'll see results for those keywords beyond what is stored on your computer. If you have a Mac, click on the **Desktop**, then click **File**, and finally click **Find**, or click on the Search icon in the upper right corner and type in what you're looking for. The window that opens will indicate the location of the file at the bottom of the window. To prevent losing a document or file, always make a conscious decision about where it should live during the **File**, **Save As** stage.

Q: I've decided I don't want a folder to be inside another folder. How do I get the one folder onto the Desktop?

A: It's as easy as clicking and dragging. Just click and drag the desired folder out of its present home and onto the Desktop, and release the mouse. Once the folder is on the Desktop, you can leave it there or click and drag it into another folder.

Q: Somehow when I click and drag, the document never goes inside the folder. What am I doing wrong?

A: It's all about the aim. Use a steady hand and don't release the mouse until the target (the folder) is highlighted. Then, without moving the mouse, release your finger. You can also open the target folder and drag the document into the folder rather than onto the icon. Be sure the document itself is not open when you try to move it.

Q: I've tried a few times to rename a document, but the computer keeps refusing the name.

A: Be sure there's no punctuation in the name. Instead of punctuation, use spaces to divide up characters in a file or folder name.

Q: If I buy a new computer, how do I get all my files from one to the other?

A: If your new computer has a CD/DVD drive, you back up all your documents, photos, and files onto a CD or a DVD, and then take that CD or DVD and copy all the information from the old computer into the new one. As discussed on page 358, another device that is perfect for moving information from one computer to another is a USB flash drive (aka a thumb drive or a memory stick).

USB flash drive

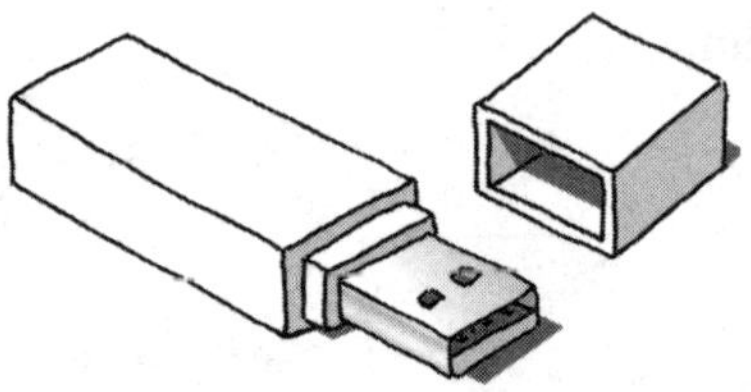

EXPLORATION AND DISCOVERY

CHAPTER 22

DETECTIVE WORK WITH YOUR TECHNOLOGY

Get the most out of your searches

A milestone was reached in October 2006. That month marked the existence of 100 million websites on the Internet. By the end of 2014, there were over *1 billion* websites. I think this thing called the Internet is catching on!

There's no denying the wealth of information on the net to be researched and enjoyed. The conundrum is how to navigate, sift, and discern what is available in relationship to what you want to find. You'll find this is a process of trial and error that will improve with practice. Searching the Internet requires a sense of adventure, curiosity, and a positive attitude. Say to yourself, "I think I can. I think I can." And you know what? You can!

Search and Recover

On page 220, I introduced the concept of search engines, but let's refresh. Not so long ago, if you walked into the hallowed halls of your local library in search of information on heart disease, you would have headed

GIVE IT YOUR BEST SHOT

Search engines aren't the only way to find a website. Word of mouth, advertising, and sometimes guessing may get you to a website that meets your needs. For example, you love to shop at Brooks Brothers. Hmmm . . . what could their Web address be? You got it: *brooksbrothers.com.*

straight for the "card catalog," which is now found on a computer, or to the informative person behind the desk. You would use these resources to locate books and periodicals relating to heart disease. Search engines on the Internet work basically the same way. You access a search engine and type keywords pertaining to your query, and the search engine finds websites that contain those keywords. Instead of a few books on the subject, you'll likely have hundreds, if not thousands, of websites with all their information at your fingertips in your own home.

■ **Do not confuse the text area of a search engine with the website address box.**

If you haven't taken a glance at the recommended websites on page 516, do so when you have a chance. Among the various

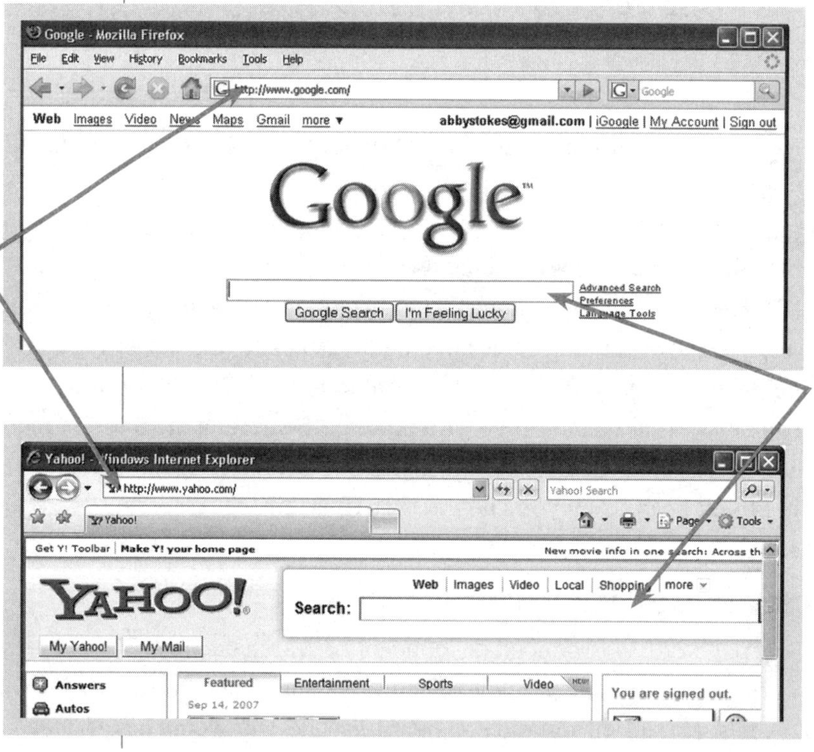

Website address box, where you click and type a website address

Text area where you type in keywords for your search

categories are eight search engines for you to try. Of course, new ones can pop up at any time, and if they're really good, you'll hear about them. Even before you picked up this book, I bet you'd heard of Google. You may not have known what it was, but the buzz had probably gotten to you.

We'll use *google.com*, *bing.com*, and *yahoo.com* for our searching adventures. You can see from the windows below that although each search engine performs the same basic task, they are designed differently. Yahoo! offers many additional resources above and beyond searching on its home page. At the time of this writing, Bing and Google's home pages look very lean and at first glance appear only to offer searches. But, in fact, both offer much more than just search results. Besides searching, you can find maps, blogs, news, and more if you click on the items above where you type in your search.

SHORTCUT

Can I let you in on a secret? You don't usually need to type "www." before website addresses—most websites open without the w's. But, if you have trouble opening a site, type the address again with "www." at the beginning.

Choose Your Words Carefully

On all three sites, the procedure is to click your mouse inside the long text box to activate it. You'll know the site is ready for you to type when the blinking line (the cursor) appears. Simply type the keywords that succinctly describe what you're looking for, and

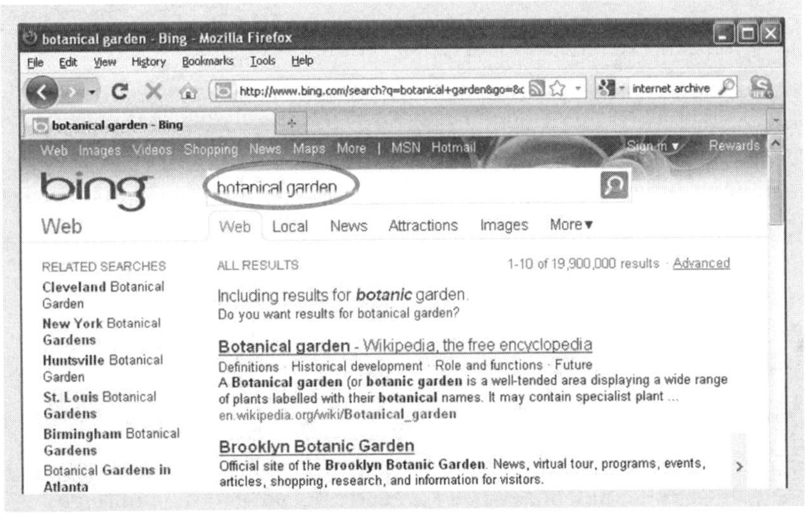

Search results for "botanical garden"

EXCLUDE IT!
If there is a word you want eliminated from your search, add that word to the end of your search preceded immediately by the – (minus) symbol. For example, you want to find a website with information on hurricanes excluding information about hurricanes on the island of Bermuda. Type "hurricane –Bermuda." This search will render all websites that contain the word "hurricane," excluding those containing Bermuda.

then click on **Search**. Before you type your first search, let's discuss the keywords to best find what you seek. Let's say you love visiting botanical gardens. You're thinking of organizing a vacation around the locations of botanical gardens. You might begin your search with the keywords "botanical garden."

Here are the numbers of websites I found searching for "botanical garden":

Yahoo! = 20,700,000

Bing = 19,300,000

Google = 21,200,000

Why would one search engine's results vary in number so dramatically from anothers? Relatively speaking, a difference of 100,000 isn't so great when you take into account that there are 1 billion websites out there. The seeming discrepancy is because each search engine has its own system and resources for performing a search. That is precisely why you may want to try more than one search engine to cover your bases when seeking information. Choose specific words to best describe what you seek.

For example:

- Type "Italian renaissance art" instead of "antique paintings."
- Try "top 10 laptops" instead of "computers."

To search for an exact phrase, insert quotation marks (single and double both work) to frame two or more words. You can have a combination of phrases and individual words. For example, free "New York City" "ice skating rink."

Are You on the Internet?

Out of curiosity you might check and see if there's information about yourself on the Internet. No matter how certain you may be that a search for you will come up dry, you might be in for a surprise. You could appear on a website because of the political contribution made during the last presidential race or the random interview with the *San Francisco Chronicle* about busing. Try a search with your name and see what you can find. While you're at it, click on the word **Images** at the top of the window. If you or someone else with your name has any photos on the Internet, you can see them! Remember to click on **Web** to get you back to your text results.

Here's something to take into consideration when formulating your search. My full name is Abigail Pemberton Stokes. (Please don't make fun of my middle name. Thank you!) I wouldn't search for my formal name because no one ever refers to me by that name, so it's unlikely I would be found by that name online. Even being addressed as Abigail is a rarity for me, unless my mother's mad at me. You may want to try a couple of different versions of your name and nickname and see what you discover.

"When I first found myself on the Internet I didn't like it at all. It felt like an invasion of privacy. However, now I realize that the Internet offers information that is already public."

—*Ronald*

Every Letter Counts

Every letter you choose matters. Try a search for "hanger" in the singular. Now try a search for "hangers" with an s. The difference in the number of results is significant as a result of one little letter. Interesting, right?

Instead of keywords, you can also type your search in sentence form. Experiment with both. Type "what is an eclipse." No need for a question mark, and you can play around with whether the quotes help or hurt your results. Now try only "eclipse."

If you don't find what you're looking for, try another search engine and/or using different keywords or phrases. With practice, you'll improve at zeroing in on your searches.

SEPARATE YOUR WORDS

Search engines are not case sensitive. You do not need to use capital letters. But unlike a website, you do need to separate each word with a space.

Consult Your Results

OK. Let's try a search together. Using either Google, Yahoo!, or Bing, type the words "free rice."

You'll see different results with each search engine, but in all cases the results will be displayed in the same way. In

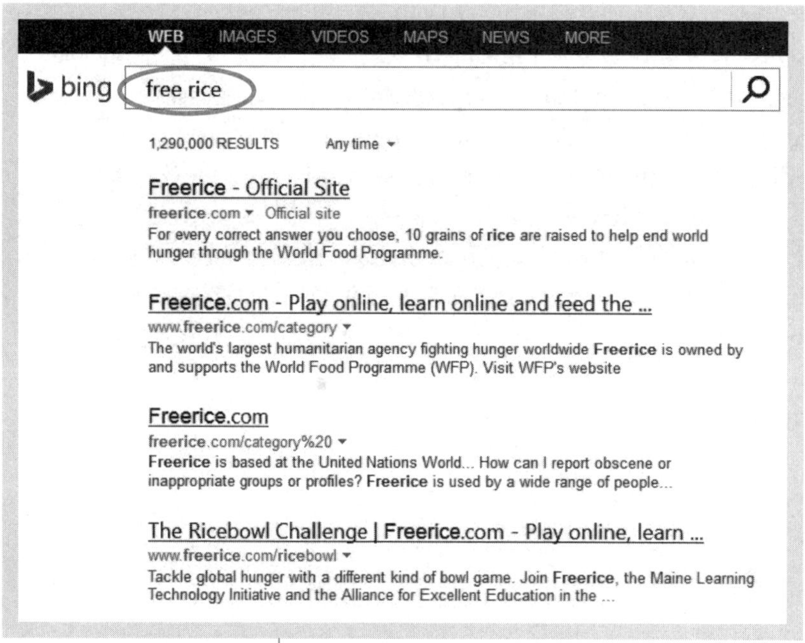

Bing search results for "free rice"

most search engines, the top line of each search result is usually blue and underlined. Remember, websites are usually designed so that the links, where you click, stand out from other text. Links are often featured in blue and underlined, but not always. Each website is at liberty to make a link noticeable in any way they choose.

Move your mouse over the top line, and you'll notice the mouse arrow has changed to a hand—positive confirmation that if you click there, you'll be taken to more information on the subject. This is the link to the search result.

Below the link, in black text, is a short summary of the contents of the site pertaining to the keywords in your search.

The bottom line in green is the actual website address. It's important to look at that address because it may be a deciding factor for which link you choose to check out. If one result has a recognizable website (e.g., *foodnetwork.com*) versus an unknown entity, I'll go with the familiar website.

Our search for "free rice" has brought us literally millions of websites (look at the results number at the top left of the page). Each search engine shows us those results 10 to a page. Generally, the order of search engine results is based on a set of rules and an algorithm that takes into consideration the number of terms matched and their relevancy. At the bottom of each page, you can click **Next** or the following page number to see the next set of results. Of the websites that fit your criteria,

KEEP AN OPEN MIND

If any of these screen images look different from what's on your computer, don't fret. Websites are updated and redesigned regularly. Look carefully at your computer screen and you'll soon find the same elements referred to here. Remember to scroll!

generally most will appear early in the list. I rarely view more than the first three or four pages of results before I restructure my search or have found what I need.

Once you've found a website you want to view, click on the blue underlined link. Scroll down the pages of your results and read the web addresses until you find *freerice.com*. Click on the link for that site. Voilà!

This is a wonderful site where, for each answer you get right, the website's sponsors donate 10 grains of rice through the World Food Programme to help end hunger. You can click on **Subjects** at the top of the page to choose which subject you would like to answer questions about. The better you do, the more rice is donated to the World Food Programme. Truly amazing, isn't it?

My mother and I visit this website daily and answer questions until we've hit 1,000 grains of rice.

Don't forget to bookmark a website you may want to visit again. (See page 218.)

SPONSORED LINKS

Sponsored Links, Sponsored Results, or Ads are websites that paid the search engine to appear on the site. I click on them only when I've exhausted all the other likely possibilities because the websites that open from a sponsored link often have nothing to do with the search made. They want to lure you to their site in hopes that, once you're there, you'll decide to buy what they're selling, regardless of whether it was what you were looking for.

The back arrow takes you to the previous page.

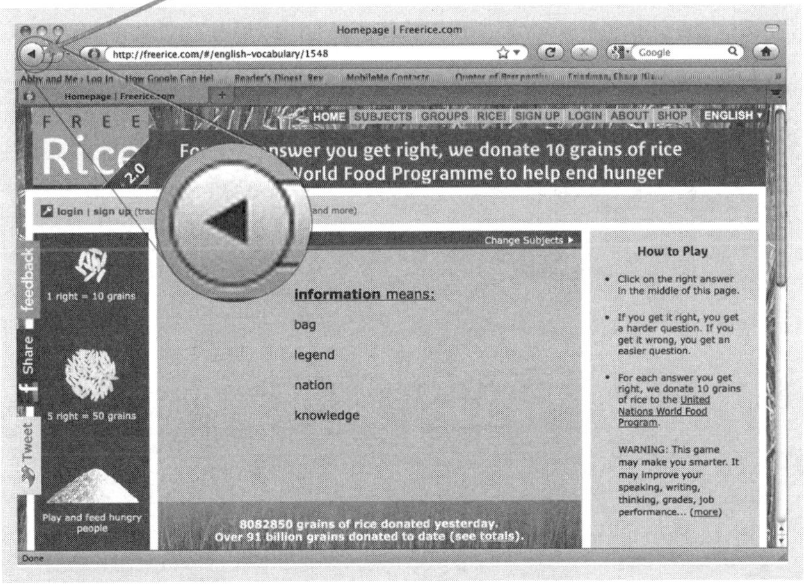

Click to choose an answer to donate free rice. Visit *freerice.com* every day to make a donation of food and more without ever opening your wallet.

You've Got My Number

What if you find a piece of paper in your wallet with a phone number you've scribbled down, but no name? Visit *reversephonedirectory.com* and be sure to use hyphens when you type in the number. If the site offers you the name associated with the number for a fee, use the back arrow to return to *reversephonedirectory.com* and scroll down until you reveal the form for "white pages." Click in that text box to activate it, type the phone number, and click **Lookup**. Now, you see the information and no one is asking for money. Remember, unless a website is selling something, most make their money from advertisers. Some of these advertisers deliberately make their ads look like they're part of the website. If you find yourself being solicited for money, close the website or use the back arrow. Start your journey again and look at the entire page (don't forget to scroll!) before you click on anything.

In Google, you can also type in a telephone number to find a person. Try it with your home phone number. Use the dashes between each set of numbers—it improves the search. Click **Google Search**. Did your name and address come up? If your number is unlisted, you'll come up dry, but for those of us that are listed in the telephone book, our names, phone numbers, and addresses are public information. Try the same search in Yahoo! and Bing.

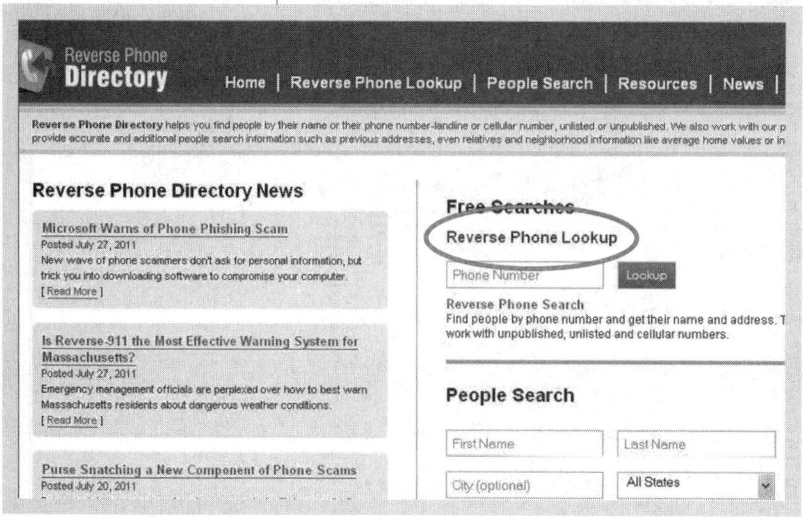

■ Reverse Phone Directory website

If this revelation upsets you, keep in mind that you didn't uncover anything private. A phone book would have revealed the same information (albeit by searching by name, not phone number), but I understand how it can put you off to feel so exposed. Public information is just that. The Internet makes public information more easily accessible, but it doesn't reveal anything that isn't already available.

MISSING PERSONS
If you're trying to track down that long-lost someone, start your search with these websites: *switchboard.com*, *whitepages.com*, *peoplefinders.com*, and of course there's also *facebook.com*.

Detective Work Continues . . .

Search engines aren't the only way to find people, places, or things on the Internet. There are websites designed to offer specific information depending on what you seek. What if you have someone's mailing address but not the zip code? Visit *usps.com*. Click on the down arrow of Quick Tools, then click **Look Up a ZIP Code**. Fill out the form with the information you do have and click **Submit**. Handy, isn't it?

Next challenge. You have the street address of your destination, but you want to see where it is on a map. Visit *mapquest.com*. Click on **Find Places,** then type the address in the search box. Move your mouse onto **Find Places** and click, or hit the Return button. Amazing! MapQuest also offers driving directions, which include length of trip, estimated travel time, and turn-by-turn instructions, along with a map for cars, public transportation, and bicycles. Play with this site to see all it has to offer. It's one of my favorite websites. (Accordingly, I put it into my Favorites! See page 218.) Come back to the book when you're ready for more.

Click on **Look Up a ZIP Code.**

The U.S. Postal Service's website, where you can search for a zip code and buy stamps

■ MapQuest provides driving directions as well as maps.

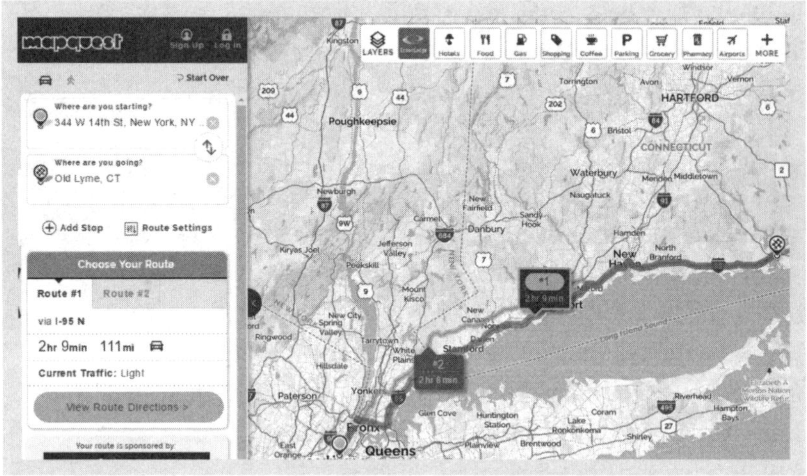

Elementary, My Dear Watson

Let's go to *barnesandnoble.com* now. Look across the top of Barnes and Noble's home page to see if there's a table of contents, in the form of a list of topics or shopping areas, to guide you where to go. The table of contents can also appear as a sidebar on the left or right of a window. If you click on an item to see where it leads you, remember to use the back arrow (at the top of the window) to return to the previous web pages.

Some websites offer a text box built into the site where you can type keywords to search for information on that particular website.

■ The table of contents gives you choices of where to visit on a website. The internal search engine allows you to search for keywords within the website, not the entire Internet.

Internal search engine

Table of contents

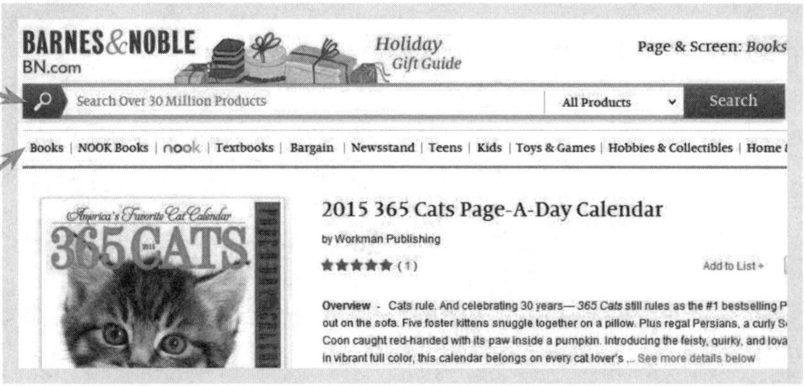

These are internal search engines. An internal search engine points you to where you want to go on that site (as opposed to the entire World Wide Web). Some of the same rules apply: Type keywords for your search. The text box is not case sensitive, so caps don't matter. Type quotes on either side of your keywords to narrow your search results.

Less talk and more search . . .

HOME SWEET HOME
To return to the first page of a website, click on the word **Home** or **Main.** Either word could appear at the top or bottom of the page.

The Doctor Is In

One of my favorite websites for medical information is *mayoclinic.org*. My confidence in the site is based on the extraordinary reputation of the wonderful Mayo Health Clinics located in Scottsdale, AZ, Jacksonville, FL, and Rochester, MN. Their website is one of the best-designed for finding information about ailments, symptoms, treatments, medications, and more. Join me at *mayoclinic.org* to practice some searching techniques.

Click on **Patient Care & Health Info** at the top of the page. The search box is to the left, and an alphabetical search is in the center. I prefer the alphabetic search method because it doesn't require that I spell the ailment—instead I need only know the first letter. Let's look up De Quervain's tenosynovitis. (See my point about spelling?)

- Click on D in the alphabet.
- Scroll down the page to De Quervain's tenosynovitis.
- Move your mouse onto De Quervain's tenosynovitis and click. (Did you notice your old friend, the hand, indicating the cursor was on a link?)

Look at the wealth of information available on this condition! They've broken down the information into manageable chunks. You can click on the section that interests you or read each small article and click at the bottom of the page to continue. Notice that at the top of the page it lets you print either just this section or all sections, and it offers you the opportunity to view the site in larger type. Very thoughtful and

■ **The Mayo Clinic's website offers information on medical conditions, treatments, and much more.**

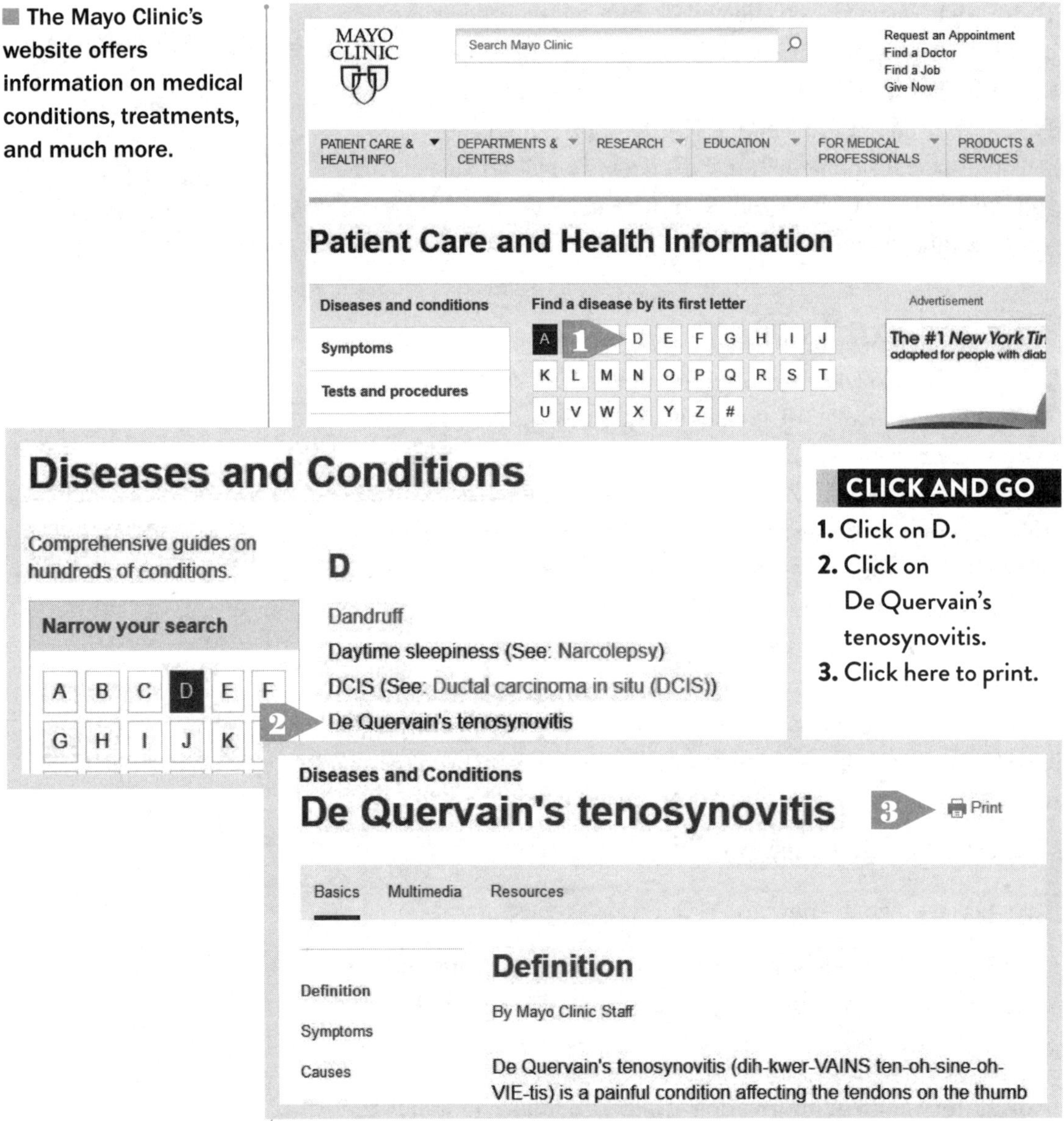

CLICK AND GO

1. Click on D.
2. Click on De Quervain's tenosynovitis.
3. Click here to print.

practical of the website designers. If you click on **Print**, the page is modified to have only the text of the article and none of the additional information on the page, simplifying the reading and saving you ink.

Linger on this site as long as you want. When you're ready, we'll sleuth out some more information from the Internet.

Encyclopedia Brown

Have you ever wished you had an encyclopedia at your fingertips to support your version of the facts? Just the other night at dinner, my sister and I could not agree about when the first crossing of the English Channel happened by air (1909 by French aviator Louis Blériot). You don't have to always search around the Internet for what you seek. You can go directly to a known source of information, as you would if you were in a library. Feel free to access the many encyclopedias offered on the Internet.

Here are a couple to start:

- *britannica.com*
- *wikipedia.org*

I've always considered the text in an encyclopedia to be unquestionable and almost sacrosanct. Wikipedia, which launched in January 2001, is an exception to that rule. It is self-described as "the

SEARCHING WITH A TABLET

You have a browser on your tablet, but you might want to search your App Store for other good research apps, such as Google, Wikipedia, and Merriam-Webster.

Encyclopaedia Britannica's home page

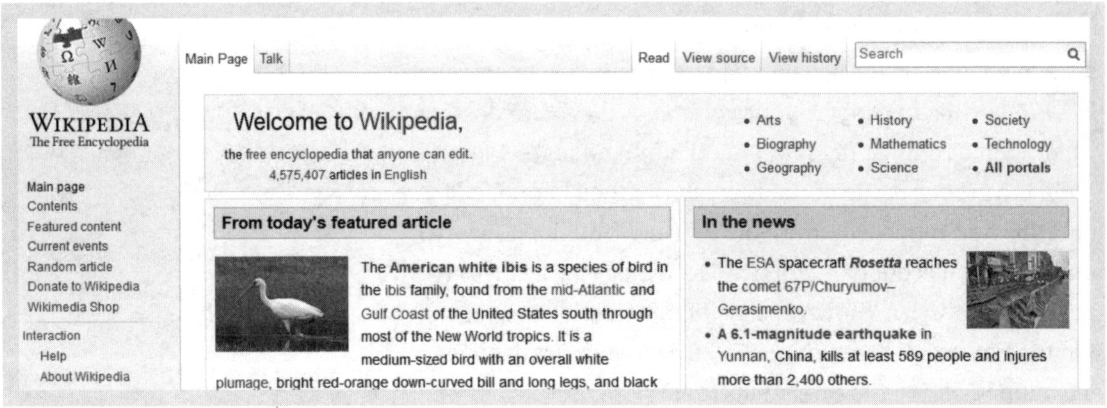

Wikipedia's main page

free encyclopedia that anyone can edit." Interesting notion, but it does make me a bit leery about what is fact and what is opinion, or even a prank. That said, I haven't heard much about people abusing the power given to them to edit the facts, and in my experience, Wikipedia has proven a great resource every time I've visited. Still, proceed with open eyes.

Variety Pack

Whatever your interest, there's a website chock full of information for you. Start to notice and make note of interesting website addresses that cross your path. Web addresses are often referred to in newspapers, magazines, and on TV. If there's the slightest chance the site mentioned is of interest to you, jot down the address. Computer magazines, as I said earlier in the book, can be overwhelming. However, if you see a magazine cover with "100 Best Websites" or some other in-depth review of the Internet, it may be worth picking up. Because the Internet is constantly evolving, there is no single directory listing all websites. If you're considering buying a book with a directory to websites on the Internet, be sure to check out the copyright date and buy the most recent book published.

Here's just a sampling of what's out there for you to enjoy. When you're ready for more surfing, take a look at the more than 150 websites listed (by category) on page 516 or visit my website, *AskAbbyStokes.com*, for other recommended sites.

- For movie buffs, one of the best sites is *imdb.com* (Internet Movie Database). Here you can look up a movie using the names of the people involved both in front of and behind the camera, the movie title, the plot, and so on. I've found the most consistent results come from searching for an actor, director, or character name. This website has settled many a movie trivia debate!

- If words are what you seek, there are a multitude of resources. Here are a few:
  - *merriam-webster.com* (Merriam-Webster's site)
  - *rhymezone.com* (rhyming dictionary)
  - *oxforddictionaries.com* (Oxford dictionaries)

- The sports-minded can look up scores, view schedules of competitions, and get the inside scoop on *espn.com*. From the editors of *Golf* magazine, there's *golf.com*. The complete TV listing of ice skating events is available on *usfigureskating.org*.

- Foodies, make sure you spend some time at *foodnetwork.com* and *epicurious.com*. They are both excellent sites for finding recipes, cooking instruction videos, and party ideas.

- There are websites for every hobby and interest: For toy soldier collectors, there's *toysoldiersgallery.com*. Siberian husky owners will want to check out the Siberian Husky Club of America's site, *shca.org*. There's even a site devoted to a man getting slapped by an eel (*eelslap.com*). I kid you not.

- The jackpot of all research websites is *refdesk.com*. If there was only one website on the Internet to lead you to all other sites, this would be it. The amount of information it contains is extraordinary, but a bit overwhelming when you pay your first visit. Take your time and enjoy it in small bites. Anything in blue may be clicked on to lead you to more information on the subject. The home page is very long—be sure to utilize the Scroll Bar to its fullest. During my first visits to this site (found

"As a retired librarian, I had no idea of the impact of search engines and other research tools on the Internet. It's extraordinary."
—Rhonda

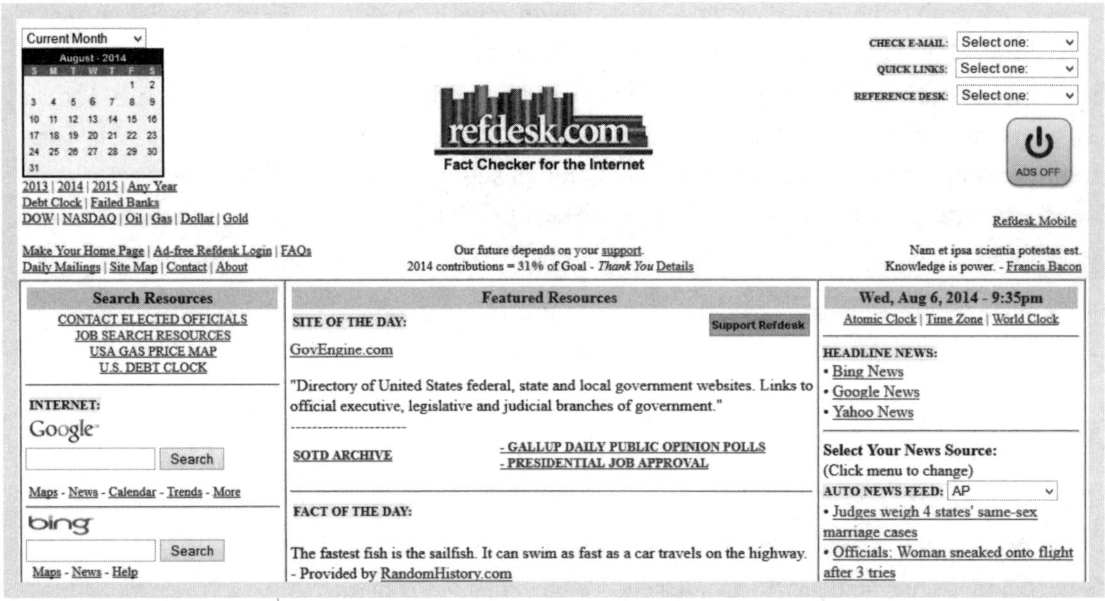

***Refdesk.com*'s home page**

by my mother, by the way), I would alternate starting at the top of the page and then the bottom to be sure to take advantage of all it offers.

Are you beginning to get the picture? You name it and you'll find it on the Internet. Each of the sites I mentioned offers a way to navigate and search the site. The more you travel the Internet, the more adept you'll become at finding what you need.

The Guessing Game

Never underestimate your own powers of logic. Let's say there's an organization you'd like to find on the Web. Feel free to take a stab at its web address. Type *(yourguesshere).com*. If your guess doesn't work, try typing *www.* before your guess, in case it's necessary for the website to open. Keep in mind that there are no spaces in a website address. Revisit page 214 for web address basics. If you're wrong, either a website you're not interested in will open or you'll get an error message because no website exists under that address. (Is it possible that you could be led to a fraudulent website that registered a similar name hoping to snag viewers who made typographical errors? Yup. And beware: These websites are often pornographic.) If you really get muddled up, close everything until you're back at your Desktop, and make a fresh start. Losing your way, bungling a website address, and ending up someplace completely unexpected is part of the learning process. Every time you turn on the computer, have a research challenge at the ready so you can hone your skills. Do I have to repeat myself? OK, I will. It is only with practice that you will tame the computer beast. Practice, practice, practice!

HOMEWORK ASSIGNMENT

I'm sending you on an Internet Treasure Hunt. See if you can find the answers to the quests below (FYI: The answers are at the end, but don't peek):

1. Do a good deed—help save the rain forest. (How many square feet did you save today?)

2. Read a headline—find out what's going on in the world.

3. Check the weather for tomorrow—here or somewhere else.

4. Find yourself—remember to use the exact listing from the phone book. Are you correctly listed in the Web directory?

5. Find yourself by using only your phone number.

6. Figure out if you are notable enough to be listed on a search engine.

7. Get directions—how do I get to Carnegie Hall (57th Street and 7th Avenue) in New York City from Faneuil Hall (75 State Street) in Boston?

8. Go shopping—look for this book.

9. Find out how batteries work or why biting aluminum foil is painful.

Possible answers (remember, there's usually more than one route to the information you want):
1. *therainforestsite.org*; 2. *cnn.com* or *nytimes.com*; 3. *weather.com*; 4. *switchboard.com*;
5. *reversephonedirectory.com*; 6. *google.com*; 7. *mapquest.com*; 8. *bn.com*; 9. *howstuffworks.com*

Q: Is there a website where I can find someone's cell phone number or email address?

A: At the moment the answer is no. Tracking email addresses is particularly difficult because people register new addresses every day, and they do not always use their real names to do so. I'm not sure why there isn't a registry of all cell phones, but there isn't.

Q: Is there a definitive website to visit for research?

A: Of all the search engines we've discussed in the chapter, my favorite research site is *refdesk.com*. My mother found the site when I was working on this book. The site is so jam-packed with information that you have to take it in small bites or you can get overwhelmed. This is the one site to visit if you need to find a doctor by area of expertise, to contact your congressional representative, to convert a cooking measurement, to read a Tel Aviv newspaper, to see the time in Hong Kong, to do today's crossword puzzle, to translate a German word, to get stock quotes . . . Are you starting to get the picture? Visit the site and don't forget to use the Scroll Bar to reveal all it has to offer.

Q: Can someone trace what I've researched online?

A: The websites that you've visited shouldn't be tracing your steps, but your computer keeps a history of what websites you've visited. So, if someone has access to your machine, they can see where you've been. Fortunately, it's easy to clear your history at any time and set your browser's Preferences to automatically do it for you.

CHAPTER 23

SHOP TILL YOU DROP

Shopping, auctions, airline reservations, prescriptions, and online banking

Shopping online may be one of the greatest assets the Internet has to offer. No lines to stand in, no one trying to hard-sell you, and no need to leave your home. I have a student who likes to get out of the house to grocery shop, but she has trouble managing all the bulk items, like paper towels and cleaning products. She buys those items online, along with heavy canned and bottled goods, but goes to the store for fresh produce, milk, and meats. (She could buy those things online as well, but she chooses not to.)

However, if you're not comfortable shopping online for any reason, don't do it. There is no rule that mandates you must shop online merely because online shopping exists. Most of us don't climb a mountain just because it's there.

Having said that, let's investigate what's available and how to shop efficiently and safely on the Internet, if you choose to do so. Shopping online isn't limited to clothes and housewares. Anything you can imagine is available online. My most obscure purchase was a set of shower curtains. Doesn't sound obscure, right? Well, I needed nine shower curtains in very specific colors. No,

"I don't want to sound like a Scrooge, but over the years I'd started to dread Christmas shopping. Now it's a breeze. I sit at my computer for an hour or two and in one evening purchases are made. I even opt for the gift wrapping and ship directly to my kids!"
—*Vernon*

I don't have nine showers—I wanted shower curtains for my screened porch because they are waterproof, and I thought they would make practical curtains. I searched dozens and dozens of websites and viewed hundreds of shower curtains before I finally found the perfect ones.

Unfortunately, the online store that sold them only had three in stock and they weren't able to order more. From their website, I copied the exact name of the shower curtain and product number and pasted it into Google where, with a little hunting, I found the name of the manufacturer . . . in China! The end of the story is, after the loveliest email correspondence with a woman named Rain (and an invitation to visit her in China!), the shower curtains were shipped to my home directly from China. I certainly would not have been able to accomplish that task without the Internet. By the way, they look adorable.

Why Shop Online?

You can't see or touch the merchandise, so what makes online shopping so appealing? Well, the following three aspects for starters:

- **Comforts of home:** You don't need to leave your home (or office) to shop. Therefore, no parking hassles, no waiting in long lines, and no fighting for the last iPhone on the shelf.
- **Global access:** Stores all over the world are at your fingertips. A student of mine wanted an out-of-print CD that a jazz-musician friend of hers had recorded nearly 40 years ago in Denmark. She was able to track down the recording studio's website and place an order for the CD online. Even the musician himself didn't know his original recordings were still available for purchase.
- **Savings:** Online retailers save on personnel and other overhead costs. They often pass the savings on to you. This is especially true with travel arrangements. Shopping online should save you money—you're doing most of the administrative work!

Start with the Familiar

Get your feet wet with a visit to the website of a "brick-and mortar" store you frequent in your area. If you shop at Home Depot, visit their website: *homedepot.com*. Is Macy's one of your shopping spots? Visit *macys.com*. Or you could pop into the website of a catalog that you patronize. Perhaps you are a Crate & Barrel (*crateandbarrel.com*) fan or a Harriet Carter (*harrietcarter.com*) loyalist.

Right now, you and I, together, are going to visit L.L.Bean (*llbean.com*) to simulate the purchase of a canvas tote. Connect to the Internet and access *llbean.com*. Let's see what their website has to offer.

A POLICY ON POLICIES
It's a good idea to click on and read the website's policies. You'll find out what the procedure is if you need to return an item, along with any guarantee information.

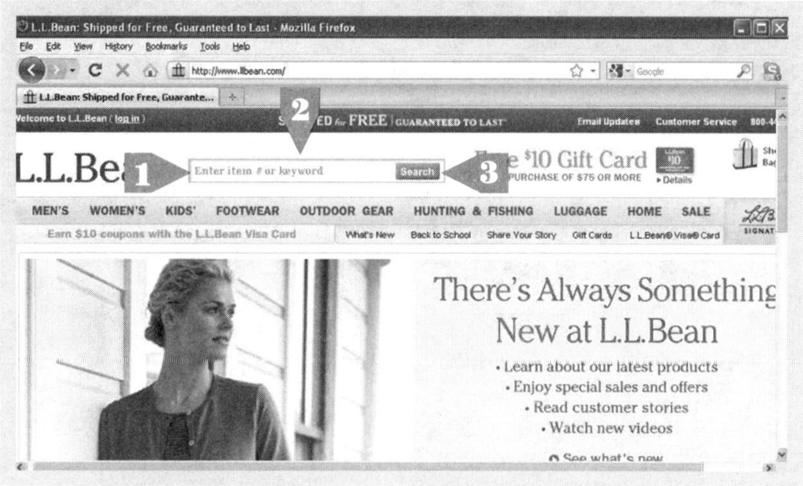

■ L.L.Bean's website

CLICK AND GO
1. Click in Search box.
2. Type "canvas tote."
3. Click Search.

Wow . . . there's a ton of information on their home page. It's almost too much to take in, but there is strength in numbers and together we can navigate these new waters. I spy an internal search engine. Do you? Perfect. Click inside the text box to activate and type "canvas tote." Click on **Search**.

The new page reveals a selection of canvas totes. Click on **Boat and Tote Bag**, **Open Top**. Be sure to scroll all the way to the bottom of the following page so you don't miss anything. When you

FLEXIBILITY PREVAILS
It may be that L.L.Bean redesigned their site after this image was captured for the book. If that's the case, take your time to look around the page and find the same elements seen here.

have viewed the entire page, scroll back up and join me at the top of the page. You get to choose your tote's size, color, and handle length. You can even have the bag monogrammed! Let's say you want two medium-size totes with dark green handles in the regular length.

CLICK AND GO

1. Click Medium.
2. Click on Regular or Long handles.
3. Click on desired color.
4. Click Quantity box, hit Backspace to erase 1, type 2.
5. Click Add to Bag.

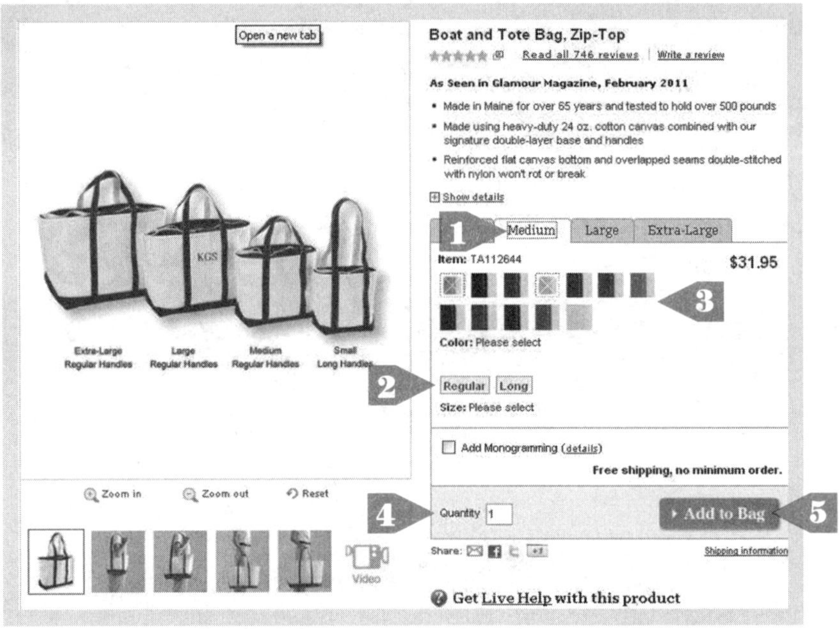

- Click on the **Medium** tab. Give the window a chance to update your order.
- Click on either **Regular** or **Long** for handle length.
- Click on your desired color.
- Click after the number 1 in Quantity. Depress and release the **Backspace** or **Delete** key on your keyboard to eliminate the "1." Type the number "2."
- Click on **Add to Bag**.
- Most websites, as this one does, give you the option to **Continue Shopping** or to **Check Out**. Click on **Check Out**.

The website will offer to ship the bag to someone other than you. Click on the arrow to the right of **Ship All Items to: Me** then click on **Add New Recipient**. A box will appear where you type a nickname for the recipient of this item. Now, we're not really buying the tote; we're only practicing. Choose whomever you want to "pretend" to send a tote to. I will choose my sixth-grade teacher, Mrs. Ballek. She always carried home our quizzes in a canvas tote to grade. (I can remember that but not the movie I saw last night?!)

You can now view the contents of your shopping cart and make any changes necessary regarding quantity.

Did you happen to notice the shipping costs? It isn't common, but some online retailers really gouge you on their shipping fees. Before you complete your purchase, decide if the shipping costs listed are reasonable. This is especially true when shopping for airfares. The lowest airfare may end up being equal to or even exceeding its competitors' fares when the taxes and fees are tallied.

THE BEST OF BOTH SHOPPING WORLDS

Many stores offer an app to download (or add) to your tablet or smartphone. (See page 160 for a refresher on using the App Store.) On the smaller handheld devices, the store's app is often easier to navigate than the website. You be the judge.

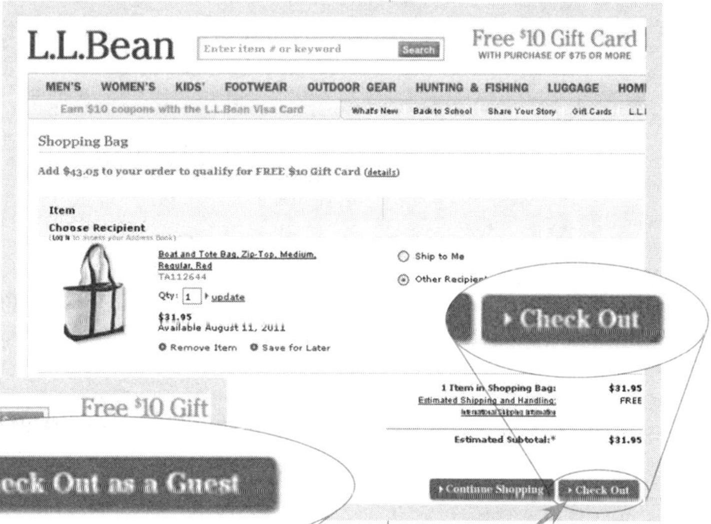

Click on Check Out.

Click on Check Out as a Guest.

REMINDER
Use the Scroll Bar to view all the page has to offer.

- Next, click on **Check Out**. (You may have to scroll down to find it.)
- The page that opens next is an interesting one. You're offered the chance to **Log In** or **Check Out as a Guest**. If this is a website you'll shop at frequently, you might consider registering with the site. This involves an online form you complete with your name, mailing address, telephone number (possibly home and cell phone), billing address, and email address. The convenience of registering is that your information is kept on file and you don't need to type it every time you come back to make a purchase. Let's not register with the website this time around. (Some websites require you to register to make a single purchase. It's a bit irritating, but you may not have a choice.)
- Next click on **Check Out as a Guest**.

You will need to type your billing information. Notice that any text box with a red asterisk is a required field (you must fill it in). Those areas without an asterisk are sometimes optional.

The credit card company uses the billing address to confirm that the credit card is in the hands of the authorized cardholder. Be sure you type your correct billing address—for some people, that is different from the mailing address. You will be asked for the shipping address later.

Fill in the form. These forms are not case sensitive so you don't need to capitalize, unless you have a burning desire to use the Shift key. Enter the address as you would on a mailing envelope and don't use nonstandard abbreviations. When you arrive at **State**, click on the down arrow and use the Scroll Bar to find your state. Click on your state. (It could be that the city and state fill in automatically when you enter your zip code.)

A SHORTCUT
Use the Tab to key move the cursor from text box to text box, instead of clicking in each box to activate before you type.

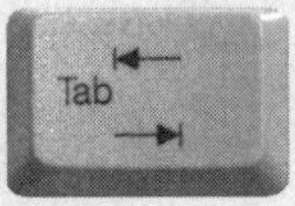

Certain websites require you to type your email address in twice to be sure there are no typos (typographical errors). Your email address is used to send a confirmation of your purchase and to update you on the shipping status. Because this may lead to future solicitations, I use my second email address—the one I created for any correspondence other than with friends, family, and business contacts. You may want to do the same.

Notice on some sites there is a choice about whether you receive email updates, along with an offer to store your information for future purchases. If you see a check in the box, it indicates that you accept their offer. If there is a check in the box and you don't want to accept the offer, click on the check to make it vanish. *Poof!* It's gone.

- Now, click on **Continue**.
- For the sake of practice, fill in the shipping form. You can input a fictitious address because we have no intention of completing this order.
- Next, click on **Continue**.

CHOOSE YOUR STATE
Instead of scrolling from Alabama to Wyoming, click in the box and type the first letter of your state. Scroll to your state and click. Less scrolling makes for fewer mouse mishaps.

You can see your entire order for review before you type your credit card information. Remove your hands from the keyboard, lest you accidentally order an unwanted tote bag! Notice where your credit card information would be typed, but remember we're not actually shopping. In the future, when you input your credit card number, ignore the spaces or dashes—type it as one long number—and examine what you typed to be sure there are no errors.

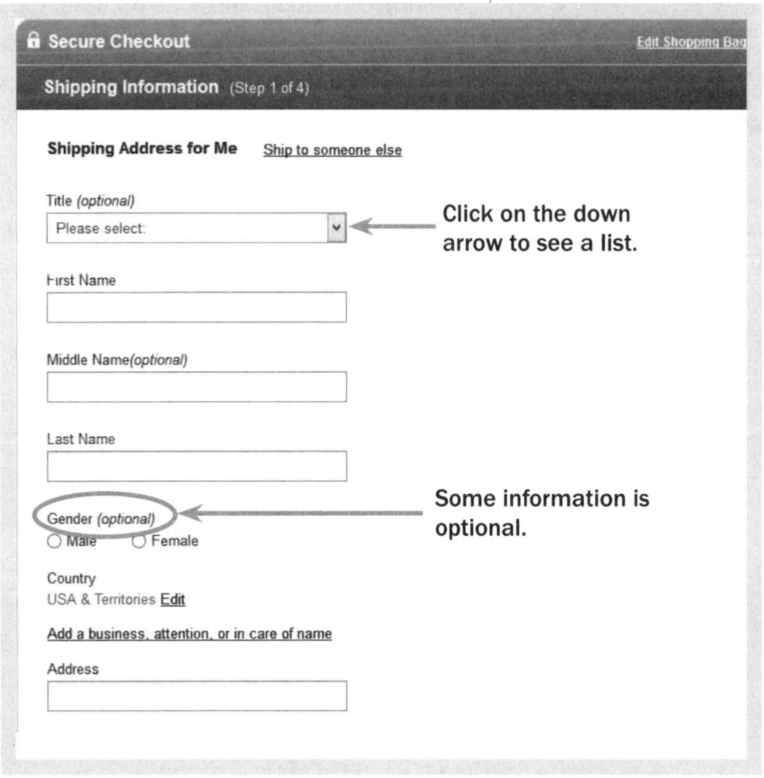

You may be asked for the code on your credit card. If you use American Express it will be the four numbers above and to the right of your credit card number. If you use MasterCard or Visa it is the three numbers to the right on the back of your card. The last step after entering all the credit card information would be to click **Continue**. The website then sends an email confirmation of your order, which you should promptly print and keep for your records until delivery occurs.

Be on the Lookout

If, at any time, you see a customer service number, jot it down. Websites are notorious for concealing their contact numbers. For reasons of cost, most sites prefer all correspondence be by email. I may be old-fashioned, but when I have a complaint or question, I'd like the option to speak to a human being. If you return to the website seeking out their telephone number, look for **Contact Us**, **Customer Service**, or **About Us**. Scroll to the bottom of the page. Sometimes, what you seek (and they hide) is in very small letters at the end of the web page.

■ Here is where you would give your credit card information.

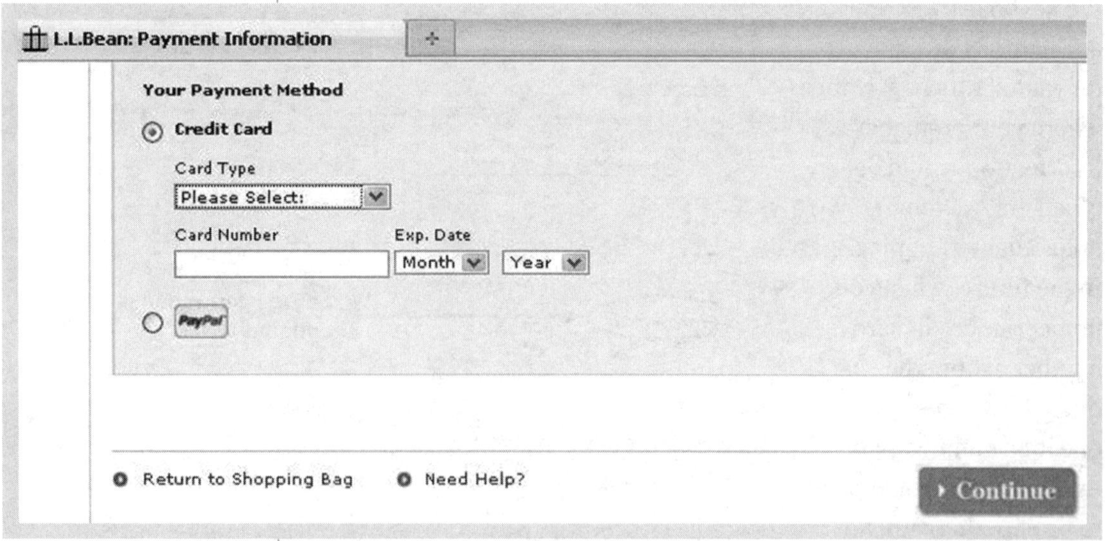

Satisfaction Guaranteed

To ensure that your credit card information is safe, websites employ SSL (Secure Sockets Layer), which encrypts data, making it safer for transmission. You'll know the page is protected by SSL when the **http** in the web address has an added "s" (**https**) for security. A closed padlock might appear at the bottom of the browser window. An open padlock or a broken key at the bottom of the window indicates you are not on an encrypted page.

CONSUMER REPORTS
Visit *consumerreports.org* for unbiased ratings and reviews of a huge array of products. A subscription to the site or magazine will give more in-depth information.

If the unfortunate happens and someone has abused your credit card (and, remember, the Internet may not have even played a role in the event), under federal law your liability is limited to $50. If a breach of security on the part of the website revealed your credit card information, the website should pay this amount for you. The American Bar Association has created an informative website, *safeshopping.org*, for information about online shopping. (Note: It is .org, not .com.) Visit their site for more information before you start shopping on the Internet.

If something happens that warrants you bringing in the big guns, contact the Better Business Bureau at *bbbonline.org* (or call your local Better Business Bureau). You could also fill out a complaint form with the Federal Trade Commission at *ftc.gov*. Type "complaint" in the internal search engine. Another option is to contact your state attorney general. Contact information can be found at the website of the National Association of Attorneys General, *naag.org*. (Notice their website acronym almost reads like "nag"!) If your complaint crosses international lines, head to *econsumer.gov* and click on English.

A closed padlock indicates you are on a secure website.

Registration Considerations

When you register on a website you are required to establish an identity (ID) with the website. Some websites will use your email address for your ID; others may allow an ID of your choosing. You will also be asked for a password. Do I have to tell you *not* to use your bank password? Good. You've been paying attention! A+!

"I couldn't believe it when I found the American Heritage plate of my mother's that I had broken years ago. You should have seen the look on her face when I gave it to her. I love shopping on the Internet."
—Georgia

If at any time during the ordering process you are uncomfortable or confused, most shopping sites allow you to complete the order over the phone. Don't be hard on yourself. If the site is difficult to navigate, it is poorly designed. You are not the ninny, the website designer is.

Relax while I relate a funny, and possibly helpful, story about a student of mine. Gloria, with great trepidation, ventured onto a website to purchase a gift for her nephew. In the course of filling in the registration form, the site asked her to type her email address. She dutifully did so in the appropriate text box. Next, she was asked to type a password.

She did. The next step read "Confirm your password" with a text box beside those words. (As you may have noticed by now, when you type a password you can't see what you type. That's for your own protection, so no one can peek over your shoulder and read your password.) Gloria responded to the request for her to confirm her password. The website rejected her. She tried, and tried, and tried again. She finally gave up in frustration. In our next class together, she shared her saga. I asked, "What did you type in the box that asked for you to confirm your password?" She answered logically, "I confirm." A completely understandable mistake—the website, of course, wanted her to "retype" her password as confirmation, but the language the website designer chose made that less than perfectly clear. Shame on the designer, not on Gloria!

The burden, unfortunately, falls on you to interpret the text of a website or software program. If at first you don't succeed, try a different interpretation, then try, try again.

Same Moves, Different Dance Partner

The steps we took with L.L.Bean are essentially the same as what you'll do with any shopping website you visit, whether ordering tulip bulbs, vitamins, or a bicycle built for two. Be sure to notice if the website offers, at the top or the side of the window, different categories of what they sell. Nose around the site until you find something of interest, and then click on the item for more

Click in either place to see more items offered from Zappos.

Table of Contents with Categories

Sidebar of Categories

information. Next, instruct the site to place the item in your shopping cart, bag, or basket. When you're done shopping, fill in the necessary shipping and billing information. When you're certain you want to complete the purchase, fill in your credit card information. Soon after, you'll receive an email confirmation to be printed and kept until your doorbell rings when the package arrives. The convenience is fantastic, and you can't deny the efficiency of the process.

Let's Make a Deal

Before you pay top dollar for an item, perhaps you should shop around for the best deal. The same item is often sold on several different websites. Could it be that there is competition on the Internet? You bet your bottom dollar! Competition breeds competitive pricing, and that's good news for all of us. Comfort and/or loyalty may lead you to shop at a tried-and-true website. There is nothing wrong

NO PURCHASE REQUIRED

If a website is really confusing or poorly designed, feel free to abandon the mission at any time. In most cases, you can find the same item being sold on several different websites.

YOUR PRESCRIPTION IS READY

It is now possible for you to purchase prescription medication online. The most common reasons why people choose to buy prescription medications with a click of their mouse rather than a trip to the pharmacist are convenience and privacy. However, it may also appeal to you because you're able to compare prices and access more written material about the drug in question.

The steps to checking out are a little more involved than the steps to purchasing a tote bag, but not by much. You will at some point be asked about allergies to medications to be sure that you can take the medication prescribed. There will also be a point where you decide how the website will verify your prescription. You can mail in your prescription, have your doctor call or fax the website, have the website walk you through the steps to transfer the prescription from your present pharmacy, or ask the site to contact your doctor directly to confirm the prescription.

Ask your doctor what pharmacy site he or she recommends. Be cautious about buying prescription medication from a foreign country's website because the drug may not be exactly the same as it is in the United States. The Food and Drug Administration (FDA) regulates the quality of drugs made in the United States but not elsewhere. If you have more questions, visit the FDA's website at *www.fda.gov* and use the site's internal search engine to look up "buying prescription medicine online."

You decide how the website will deliver your prescription.

with that. But, if you want to buy a particular item and you have no website allegiances, why not find the best deal? There are search engines to hunt the World Wide Web in its entirety (e.g., *google.com*, *yahoo.com*, *bing.com*) and there are search engines that specialize exclusively in shopping:

- *mysimon.com*
- *pricegrabber.com*
- *shopping.com*
- *shopzilla.com*

Try any of these on for size. Each site allows you to type in the item you seek by name, product number, or description. The site will look up the item. If it finds it, it will let you know the different websites you can purchase from and let you see an estimate of the price.

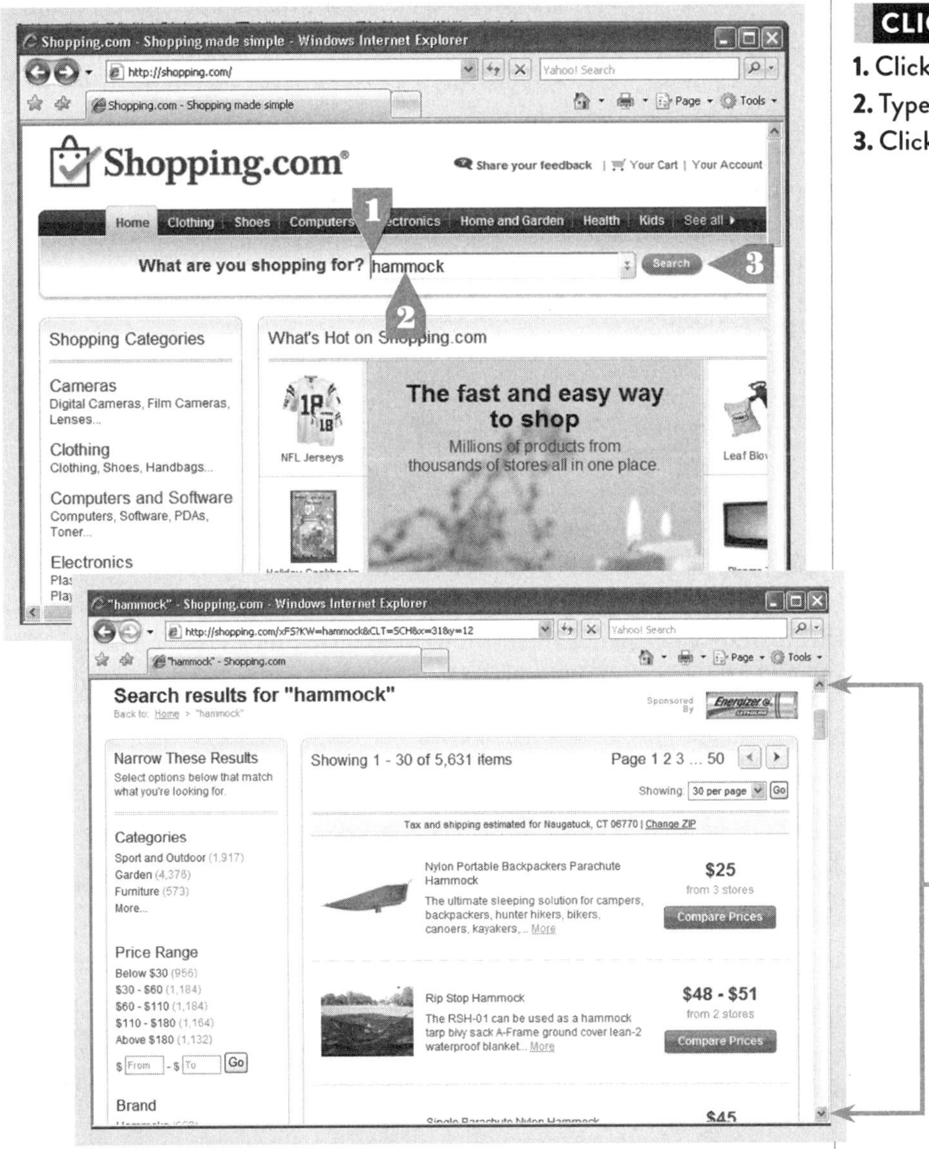

CLICK AND GO

1. Click in box.
2. Type "hammock."
3. Click Search.

■ Use the Scroll Bar or the up and down keys to see the results of your search for a hammock.

Scroll Bar

COUPONS

There are many websites with coupons for the printing. Here are a few to try:

- *couponcabin.com*
- *coupons.com*
- *thecouponclippers.com*

Do *not* pay for coupons. That is not a coupon. That is a rip-off. If registration is required, give your secondary email address. Registering will likely result in you being added to an emailing list, which may lead to you receiving advertising and spam. Not to worry, as long as it doesn't clog up your personal email account. Groupon put a whole new twist on the "coupon" world. For more information, see page 470.

Feel free to also experiment with Google, Yahoo!, Bing, or any other search engine. The results, however, from a general search engine may be less specific than a search engine designed specifically for shopping. Shopping search engines usually hit on the type of product you seek (e.g., microwave) and list the various models, with a link to direct you to the websites selling those products. Remember to take shipping costs into consideration before you decide where to make your purchase.

Going Once, Going Twice, Sold!

There is an alternative to paying a set price asked for an item. You can decide to do your shopping on an auction website such as eBay. These sites operate very much as a live auction does. If there is an object you are interested in purchasing, you place a bid on the item. You watch the bidding to see if someone bids higher and then you can decide if you want to go higher, and so on. This goes on until the deadline for the bidding is reached. The highest bidder then pays for the item and it is shipped to them.

Many people buy and sell on auction sites with happy results all around, but you must have your guard up. It is extremely important that you click on and read the **Terms of Use**, **Rules**, or **Policies**. The rules of the auction site must be perfectly clear to you before you become involved in buying or selling.

Although you view an auction item on a given auction website, who is responsible if the item doesn't arrive, is broken, or is not what it appeared to be? Often that responsibility is with the seller, not the auction site. How comfortable are you with that situation? Who is this seller anyway?

These issues illustrate why it is so important to familiarize yourself with an auction site's policies and stick with reputable websites. Although eBay may be one of the best-known auction websites, it isn't the only good one.

Here are some other auction sites to visit.

- *biddingforgood.com* (a portion of the proceeds goes to charity)
- *skyauction.com* (specializes in travel auctions)
- *ubid.com* (a general auction site)

WHAT'S IN A NAME?

Why "eBay"? Rumor has it the founder of the site, Pierre Omidyar, wanted to name it *echobay.com* after his company, Echo Bay Technology Group. Someone had already registered that domain name, so he settled for eBay and the rest is history.

For now, let's use eBay as our gold standard. Visit *ebay.com* (no need to type the b in caps). Scroll to the bottom of the page and click on **Policies**. Take the time to read everything this page presents. The policies for whatever site you use to buy or sell should be as clear and specific as eBay's.

eBay policy page

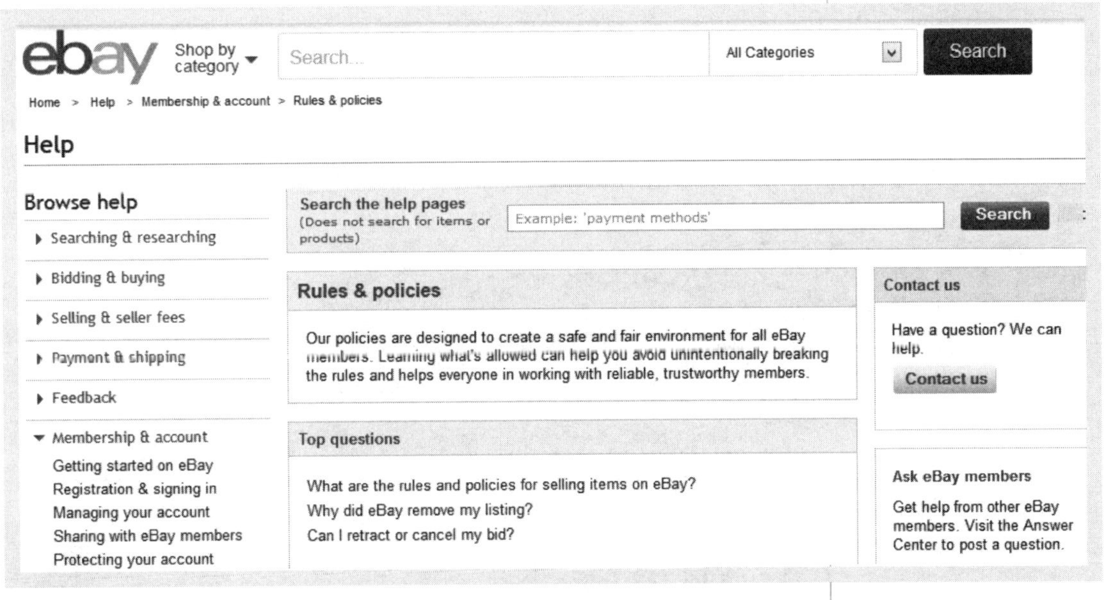

Standard Procedures

Auction sites usually charge a fee to the seller. The fee may apply whether your item sells or not, or the fee may only apply if the item sells. There is a time limit for how long an item is at auction. If you really want the item, get your final bid in just before the bidding closes. My heart is racing just writing about it! The reserve price, which is typically unknown to the bidders, is the lowest price the seller will accept. Some sellers also list a "buy-it-now" price, eliminating the hassle and nerve-racking auction process. Frankly, I would rather buy the item outright than play the auction game. The suspense is too much for me.

Both sellers and buyers are required to register with the auction website. (Use the same registration and password guidelines that I have suggested throughout the book.) As a matter of fact, you will be using a lot of the same skills discussed previously to get the most out of your auction experience. For example, use the internal search engine of an auction site to compare prices on what you want to sell

You can either browse a site's categories or use the internal search engine to find what you want.

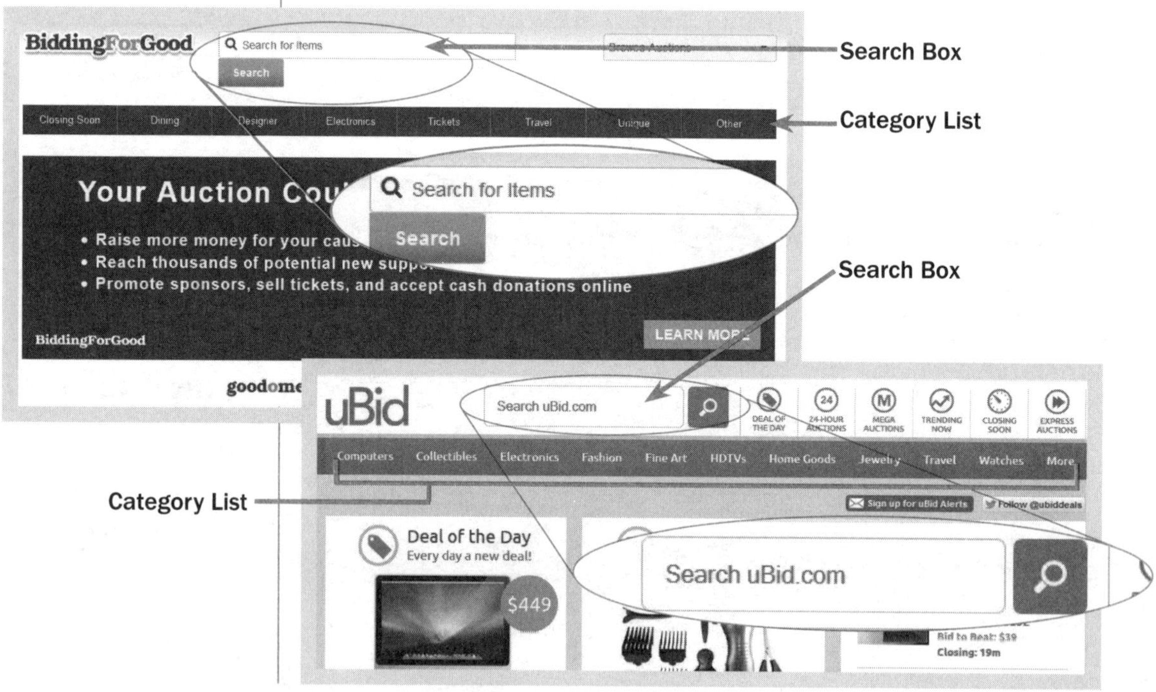

or buy. Also, be on the lookout for a list of categories at the top or sides of the window to narrow your search.

Armed with the preceding information, find and buy the vintage Louis Vuitton handbag your mother gave away before you were old enough to appreciate it. Sell the awful lamp your sister-in-law gave you, because there is someone out there who will think it's beautiful. Bid on the missing Hummel to complete your collection. Good luck!

You name a collectible and you can find it on the Internet.

Advice for the Buyer

Before you decide to participate in an auction, watch a few auctions online from start to finish. Get the lay of the land. Here are some more helpful tips for buyers.

- Do not be lured away from the auction site you know and trust by the promise of that same item at a lower price by a private seller. That is called "bid siphoning." Once you leave the auction site, you leave the protection it guarantees.
- Stick with the top price you set for yourself. Sellers may have "shills" who drive up prices with no intention of buying. (Shills are a violation of most auction policies.) They rely on buyers to get caught up in the moment and overbid.
- Always check the shipping cost for an item. Sometimes sellers create the illusion of a bargain by lowering the price but hiking up the shipping expense to more than is necessary.
- Take heed of other people's experiences. Usually a website offers a place where people can review their experiences with a particular seller. The rating scale (another term for review) should be near the ID or email address of the seller.
- Do not assume the rules are the same from one auction site to another. Some websites offer a tour of how the site works or a tutorial on how to use the site. If there is a bidding tutorial offered, take advantage of it.
- Investigate shipping costs, warranties, and return policies.

Advice for the Seller

Before you list your baseball card collection on an auction website, get familiar with how these websites work. There are as many shifty buyers as there are sellers. You need to have your head about you as a seller. Here are helpful tips for sellers.

- Be as specific as possible about the condition of the item. You don't want to give the buyer the opportunity to return something using the excuse that the description was inaccurate.
- A good photo will save you a thousand words about the object.
- Be clear about who incurs the shipping expense. If you're selling a large or heavy object, you may not want to be the one to pay to ship it cross-country.
- Decide on and post a clear return policy. The more transparent your policies, the less wiggle room for the buyer.
- If the buyer suggests an online payment service that you've never heard of, check it out with a phone call or a visit to the website before you agree. Don't accept a payment arrangement that makes you uncomfortable. The standard website to facilitate payments is PayPal.
- Be on the lookout for fraudulent checks or money orders.

If there is any question about a check's authenticity, bring it to your bank and ask a bank officer to have a look before you ship to the buyer. Most sellers stipulate a seven-day waiting period to make sure the check clears before shipping an item.

Born Free

The Internet is sort of a mixed bag when it comes to what is free and what appears to be free and ends up not free at all. Here's a good example: You want to design an invitation for Bastille Day. You search on a search engine (i.e., Google, Yahoo!, etc.), as described in the previous chapter, hoping to find free clip art that relates to Bastille

Day. Holy smokes! More than 39 million websites come up on Bing. I don't want to disappoint you, but most of the clip art sites in your results aren't free at all. Sure, you can use some of the (how shall I say this and remain polite?) "less attractive" clip art, but the good stuff? That you'll have to pay for. It's a sneaky technique. Based on principle, I don't buy from a website that touts "free" and then doesn't live up to it. I find it underhanded and disingenuous.

Freecycle.org**'s description on their home page**

Here's the good news: There are websites that offer free advice, free information, and, yes, free stuff for free. One of my all-time favorite websites is *freecycle.org*. At *freecycle.org*, you'll find all kinds of things that people want to dispose of and are willing to give away rather than sell. The whole spirit of the website appeals to me. (Although there is no law governing the use of .org, it is intended to be used only with nonprofit sites. If you type "freecycle.com," you will arrive somewhere else entirely.)

Even though the site is full of free stuff, become acquainted with their site procedures by clicking **About Us** or **FAQ** (frequently asked questions).

THE CLASSIFIEDS

Just as your local paper lists classified ads, the Internet offers the same convenient way to advertise to sell or buy a used car, rent your apartment, or find a masseur. All of the same precautions we've discussed previously should be taken here. If the website or transaction seems fishy, walk away. If it all seems right, go for it! Some better-known classified websites for you to visit:

- *classifiedads.com*
- *craigslist.com*
- *oodle.com*

Up, Up, and Away

The Internet offers you not only the opportunity to research where you might want to go on vacation, but also the best way to get there, where you should stay, and how you should get around while you're there. What more can you ask?

There are several really good travel websites that you might recognize because the same companies that supply travel books host them:

- *fodors.com*
- *frommers.com*
- *lonelyplanet.com*

I'm also a big fan of *tripadvisor.com* for firsthand traveler feedback. Most hotels have their own websites with a photo gallery, the location of the hotel on a map, and the capability of making reservations online.

One of the more intimidating transactions to complete online is the reservation and purchase of airline tickets. Almost all airlines have a Web storefront where you can purchase airline tickets directly from the carrier. There are also websites that compare airline, hotel, and rental car prices for you. You can make your reservations through these websites and be offered some great discounts. However, be aware that you may be subject to the website's policies and not the airline, hotel, or rental car company's policies.

Being able to track down the flight that best meets your travel needs is miraculous. (You could stop the process there and call the airline or your travel agent with the flight information to finalize the purchase. I did that for years before I decided to take the plunge and actually purchase the airline tickets online. But now that most travel agents charge a fee to issue tickets, I almost always buy online.)

Once you've purchased your ticket, the common practice is to email you an e-ticket (electronic ticket), which you print and bring to the airport in lieu of having the airline mail you a ticket. You don't have to print out your e-ticket—you can pick it up at the airport—

but I get nervous without some acknowledgment I can carry in my hand to the check-in desk. There are electronic kiosks in most airports where you can use your credit card to get your boarding pass, or if you have proper identification, the representative at the ticket desk will print your boarding pass for you. And nowadays, many airlines have apps that enable you to get your boarding pass on your smartphone or tablet.

A PENNY SAVED . . .
Airline carriers have taken to charging a fee for tickets purchased over the phone, so if you buy your ticket online rather than over the phone, it's almost as if it's discounted.

There are many travel sites out there, and new ones sprout up all the time. Here are some of the better-known discount airline websites:

- *expedia.com*
- *kayak.com*
- *orbitz.com*
- *priceline.com*
- *travelocity.com*

When I shop for airfares, I experiment with several sites to compare prices and flight times. Once I decide on the flight, I usually visit the airline carrier's website to check if they can match the lowest price. Be sure to add up any fees and taxes before you decide which is the better deal.

Take your time filling in the search form. Specify options like one-way, round-trip, or multiple cities, and look for **Expand Search Options**, **Advanced**, or **More Search Options** to set a preference for specific departure times, airlines, whether you want to go nonstop or are willing to change planes, and so on. When you type your destination, avoid abbreviations unless you know the airport code; otherwise, type the full name of the city, state, and country. The more specific your departure and arrival dates and times, the leaner your results.

The list of available flights can be sorted by price, departure time, and/or length of flight. Pay attention to whether there are stopovers. How long is the stopover? Too tight for the connecting flight or so long that you lose a day of your vacation?

In the event that you need to cancel or change your reservation, the change fees with discount tickets can run over $100. If there is an opportunity to buy travel insurance at the time of purchase, you may want to consider it. Investigate travel insurance when making hotel and car rental reservations as well.

Happy trails!

Some travel websites

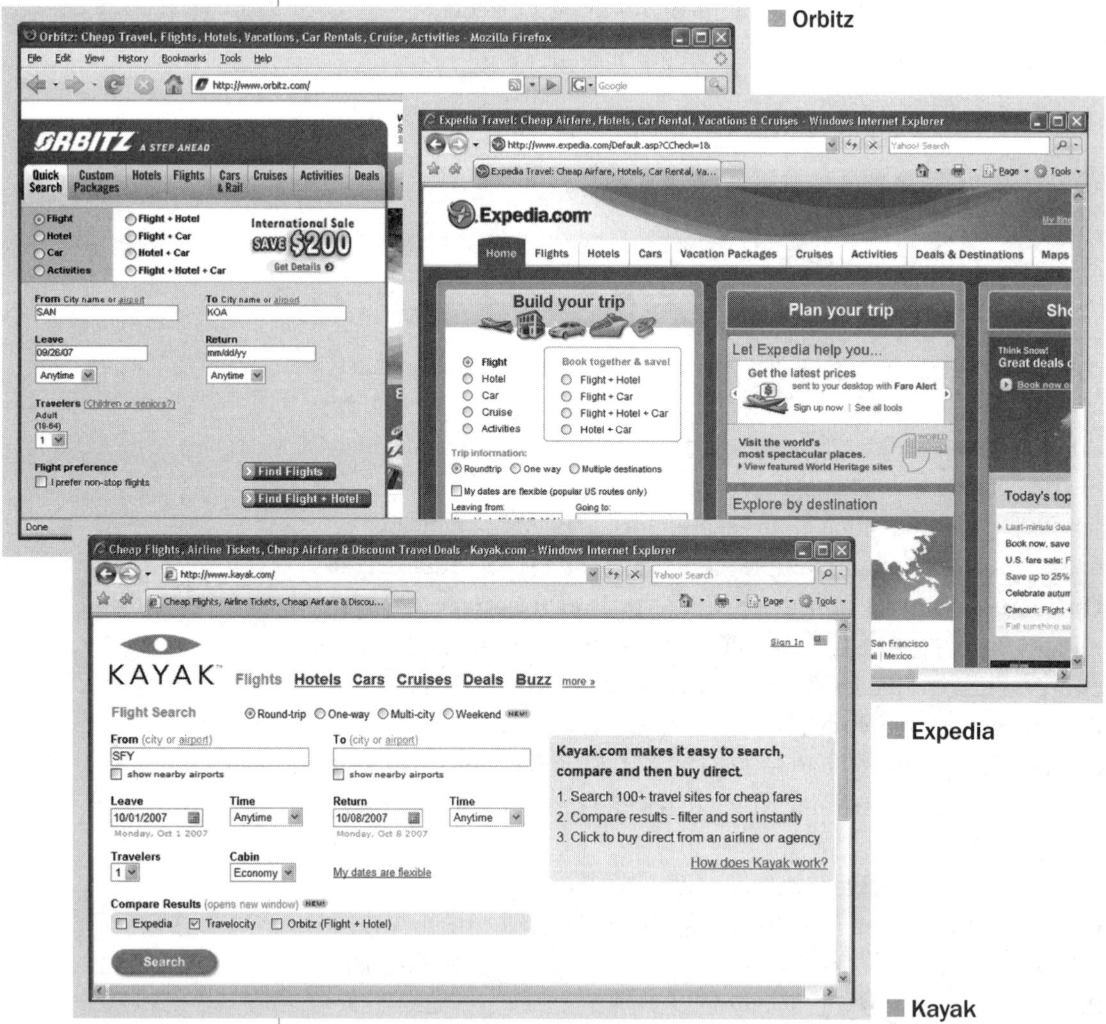

Orbitz

Expedia

Kayak

The Buck Stops Here

At some point, the day of reckoning arrives and you have to pay for your purchases. That's where online banking comes in handy. No more writing checks, licking the yucky envelope, or paying postage. In one fell swoop, you can pay all of your bills online in a few minutes. Contact your bank and find out if they offer online banking. You may be pleasantly surprised to learn that because online banking saves the bank money, many banks share the savings by not charging a fee to pay bills online. Ask if that's true at your bank.

If your bank does offer online banking, you will be able to go to their website to view your account balance, see any recent transactions, look up past transactions, order checks, transfer from one account to another, and pay both monthly bills and onetime bills. Other than actually getting hard cash in your hands or making deposits to the bank, there isn't much that can't be done with online banking.

"I no longer have to spend hours balancing my checkbook at the end of the month. I view my balance online every day and always know the status of my account."
—*Marlena*

Do I Need the Payee's Account Number?

Whether it is your telephone company or your local florist, the bank can make a payment from your checking account to the payee online. All you need to give to the bank is the mailing address of the payee along with any account number you may have with them. You do not need any bank account information from the person or company that you want to pay online.

The bill payment window of Bank of America's website

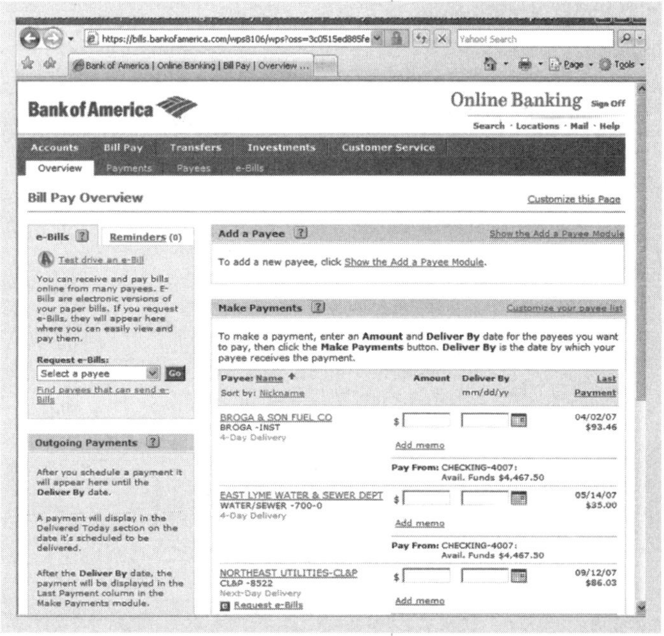

Register with Your Bank

Access your bank's website to register to view your account and pay bills, among other things. Some banks issue an ID and password. Others let you choose it yourself. (I will resist the urge to remind you *again* about password protocol.) This is one of the rare times that you may be asked to type your Social Security number. The bank uses that number to confirm your identity. Once you have gotten past that stage, you should never be asked for your Social Security number online again. If you are, call the bank directly to be sure it is a legitimate request.

After registration, you will log on to your account with your ID and password.

Follow your bank's instructions about how to input each payee for bill paying. Double-check everything you type (account name, account number, mailing address, and telephone number) to be sure it is correct. A typo can cause a payment to go astray. Eventually, the problem would be corrected, but extra care during account setup will prevent possible difficulties.

I know for some of you there is too much uncertainty with banking online. Will my payments really go through? How can I be sure? What if I make a mistake with a transaction? Do I get a receipt?

■ The registration page of HSBC's website

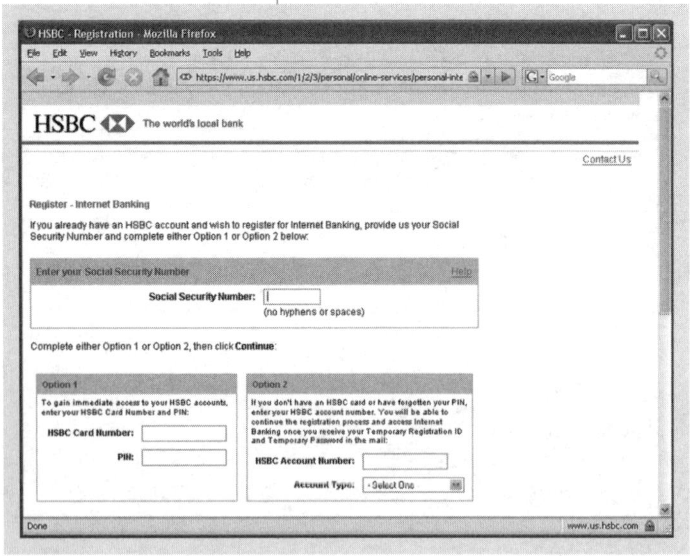

Start small. If you want to experiment with banking online, start with a utility bill or two until you get the hang of it. Once you've honed your online banking skills, add your credit cards, then your mortgage payment, and before you know it, you won't be able to remember the last time you wrote a check! Continue to note transactions in your check register, however, to keep on top of your bank balance. When you make an online payment, you may be given a transaction number. Note that number in your check register or on the paid

The Sign-On window of Citibank's website

bill. It will be your reference number with the bank if something goes wrong with the transaction.

Let me fess up: I still walk into the bank and wait in line for the teller to process my deposits. I can't explain why I don't use the ATM machine to make my deposits, but it's somehow comforting to me to hand my money to a live person. So I completely understand if online banking does not appeal to you. Conduct your bank transactions in whatever manner is comfortable for you.

CLICK AND GO

1. Click in box. Type your User ID.
2. Click in box. Type Password.
3. Click on Sign On.

Credit Cards Online

Consider accessing your credit card statements online. The process to sign on to your credit card accounts online is very similar to that of online banking. You can also pay the credit card company directly, if you don't mind giving them your checking account number. (I personally prefer doing all my payments from my bank site and not directly on my credit card company's site because I'm afraid I'll forget to note the payment in my check register.) You can monitor your credit card spending daily, rather than nearly passing out when the monthly statement arrives. You'll also have ample time to make up some really good excuses for your overspending before your spouse sees the statement!

The Gift of Online Giving

While shopping online can be very rewarding and handling your bills online is certainly convenient, there's another aspect to online transactions you may want to consider: Nonprofit organizations have made it very easy to make donations online. But how do you know that your gift is going to the right place? Here are five ways you might consider using the Internet to make an impact on the causes you care about.

1. Visit *Give.org* and review their Charity Reports to be sure your donation is going where you would like it to go. Ideally *at least* 65% of your donation should go to the programs and not administration.

2. **Small Token** is the first mobile app designed to let you use your smartphone or tablet to make a contribution to a nonprofit as a gift to someone important to you. Small Token is committed to passing on 100% of the proceeds. Visit the App Store on your device to download. It's free!

3. There's nothing more fulfilling than donating your time as an individual or as a family. Visit *VolunteerMatch.org* to find a worthy project. You can specify interests, skills, and preferred distance from home.

4. Increase your donation by asking if your employer offers a matching gift program to stretch your dollar.

5. If you donate online, be sure to print the receipt and hang on to it for your records.

I've also compiled a list of websites you might like to visit.

Kiva *(Kiva.org)*—This site provides a great opportunity to teach children and grandchildren about both investing and making a difference. "Kiva is a nonprofit organization with a mission to connect people through lending to alleviate poverty. Leveraging the Internet

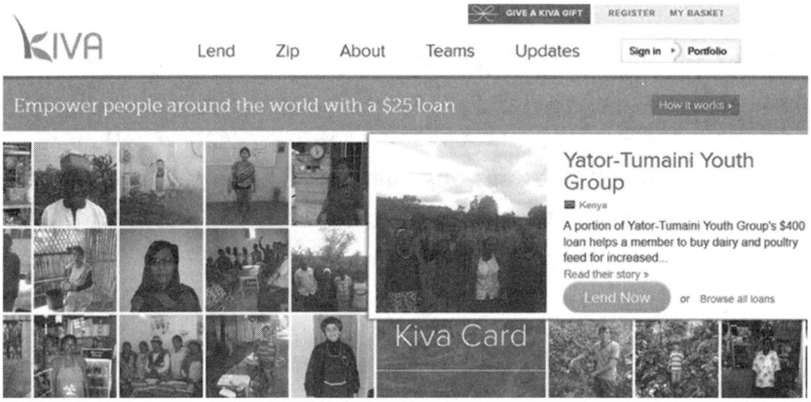

and a worldwide network of microfinance institutions, Kiva lets individuals lend as little as $25 to help create opportunity around the world." (They have a 98.45% repayment rate!)

Senior Planet Exploration Center and *SeniorPlanet.org*—is one of the groundbreaking flagship programs of the Older Adults Technology Services (OATS). "OATS harnesses the power of technology to change the way we age. Since 2004, they've innovated one of the nation's most powerful models to shape the future of aging. The OATS approach begins with a strong commitment to creative and responsive program design. We develop programs that engage seniors as change agents—in the classroom, in the community, and at home." (They donate 80% to programs.)

Rhino Rescue Project *(rhinorescueproject.org)*—I found out about this when I had the good fortune of enjoying an African safari. "Rhino Rescue Project's mission is to offer a sustainable, cost-effective defensive strategy to protect rhinos in South Africa and elsewhere from poaching. Their all-inclusive, holistic protection program is focused largely on the devaluation of rhino horns as commodities by infusing them with an animal-friendly toxin and indelible dye as well as adding security measures like microchips, tracking technology, and DNA sampling and storage."

National Alliance to End Homelessness *(endhomelessness .org)*—This is a leading voice working to prevent homelessness in the United States. "The Alliance analyzes policy and develops pragmatic, cost-effective policy solutions. The Alliance works collaboratively with the public, private, and nonprofit sectors to build state and local capacity, leading to stronger programs and policies that help communities achieve their goal of ending homelessness. They provide data and research to policymakers and elected officials in order to inform policy debates and educate the public and opinion leaders nationwide." (They give 94% to programs.)

Human Rights Watch *(hrw.org)*—"Established in 1978, [Human Rights Watch] is known for its accurate fact-finding, impartial reporting, effective use of media, and targeted advocacy, often in partnership with local human rights groups. Each year, Human Rights Watch publishes more than 100 reports and briefings on human rights conditions in some 90 countries, generating extensive coverage in local and international media. With the leverage this brings, Human Rights Watch meets

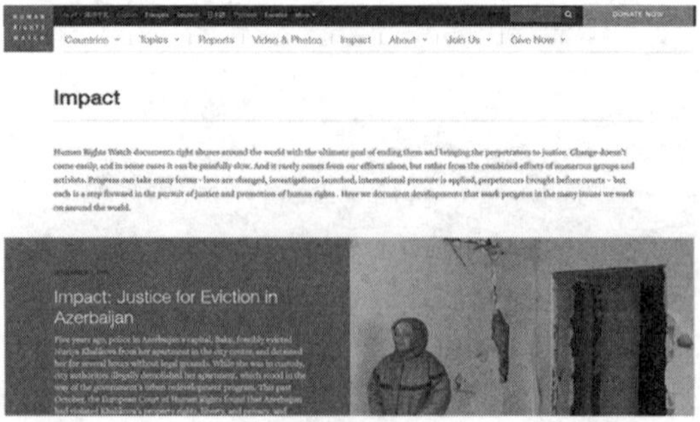

with governments, the United Nations, regional groups like the African Union and the European Union, financial institutions, and corporations to press for changes in policy and practice that promote human rights and justice around the world." (They give 78% to programs.)

A Final Word on Shopping

Your online shopping experience will probably start out slowly, with small purchases. That is as it should be. Take it at whatever pace works best for you. I hope that I've given you some tips on how to make your online shopping less confusing and safer. However, no one can save you from your own bad shopping habits.

Step away from the mouse when considering the 1980s sweater that glows under black lights. It wasn't a good idea back then, and it certainly isn't a good idea now. Do you really need *another* circular saw? Aren't two enough? Yes, I know it was a great deal, but stand firm. The convenience of the Internet can definitely feed the impulse shopper in all of us. Practice restraint and enjoy your purchases.

Q: What if I buy something online and it arrives broken or I don't like it?

A: Before you make your purchase, check the website's return policy. Usually you can return the item in the box it came in for replacement or refund within a certain number of days.

Q: Is it safe to bank online?

A: Banks have done everything they can to ensure that their websites are safe and secure. If they didn't trust the safety of their site, they wouldn't have you bank online at all. Obviously, if there is a breach of security that is due to the site not being designed securely enough, the results of that would be the bank's responsibility. However, if you have any hesitation about banking online, don't do it.

Q: If I start paying my bills online can I still write checks?

A: Yes. There are still certain bills (like my rent) that I prefer to write a check for. You have no obligation to pay any bills online, even if you access your account online. It is your decision if you only want to view your account online, rather than actually "use it."

Q: What is Groupon?

A: Groupon (derived from "group coupon") offers daily discounted gift certificates on their website. If enough people sign up for any of the "deals of the day," they become available to everyone who signed up. If too few people sign up, no one gets the discount. Usually, the deals involve paying a fee for a more valuable discount from a specific retailer. For example, you might pay $25 for $50 worth of clothing at Nordstrom.

Q: What is an e-ticket?

A: E-ticket means "electronic ticket." Rather than have an actual ticket in your hand, a record of your ticket is in the computer system of the company you bought the ticket from. E-tickets are used for airline reservations, theater, and other entertainment venues. It is smart to print the record of your e-ticket purchase as proof of your transaction.

CHAPTER 24

EXTRA! EXTRA! READ ALL ABOUT IT!

The wide, wide world of entertainment, fun on the Web, and what's new

After all of the research, downloads, and shopping you've done online with your computer or tablet, it's time for you to use technology for fun, fun, and *more* fun! We're going to visit entertainment websites in this chapter. We're also going to venture into the somewhat murky waters of other modern technological innovations and devices. You may never choose to connect your TV to the Internet, track your exercise with a wristband that talks to your computer, or use an e-reader, but it can't hurt to at least understand what these things are and how they might enhance your life.

For those of you who do decide to forge ahead: Before we discuss each offering, relax and take a deep breath. Much of conquering these little beasts comes down to relaxing and using your instincts rather than trying to memorize each step necessary to accomplish the task at hand. This chapter is a tasting menu and you can decide what you want to consume.

SENIOR AND JUNIOR SAVINGS
Be sure to specify if you're purchasing tickets for a child, adult, or senior. The prices vary just as they do at the cinema box office.

Did you know you could tune in to full episodes of major network TV shows online, rent movies directly onto your computer or tablet, and buy movie tickets online? The Internet, along with everything else it offers, is your gateway to many forms of entertainment.

Let's Go to the Movies

It's Friday afternoon. How about if you hop on the Internet and see what's playing at your local cinema tonight? You may want to find out what movies have been recently released; you may know what movie you want to see, but not the show times; or you may want to purchase tickets in advance for a show that may sell out. Both *fandango.com* and *moviefone.com* meet most of your movie needs.

When the list of movies appears on the screen, click on the name of a film for a description, or click on the movie time you desire to begin the purchase process. Next, you'll be asked how many tickets you want to buy, your email address, and, eventually, your credit card information. Take note that there is a surcharge for purchasing tickets online. (This always bugs me, as you've done all the work to purchase the tickets. Why should you pay extra? Oh well, *que sera, sera.*) Follow all the online buying procedures and precautions noted in Chapter 23 and you shouldn't run into any unexpected surprises.

CLICK AND GO

Option 1.
Click on down arrow to select movie from list.

Option 2.
Click here to type movie title, actor's name, or your zip code. Click GO.

Go to Fandango's website to get movie information, purchase tickets, and locate theaters.

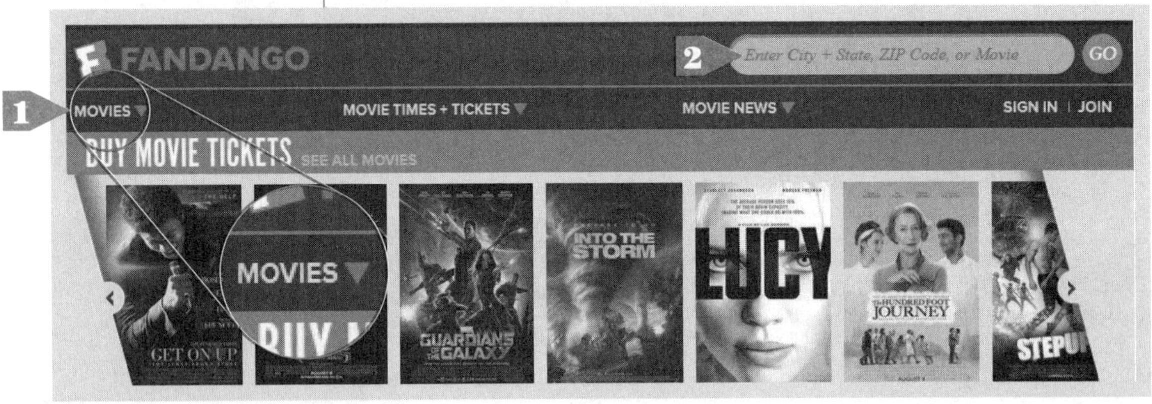

Home Theater

If you bought a computer with a built-in DVD drive, you have the capability to watch movies on your computer as well as on the DVD player you may have attached to your television set. Depending on the size of your monitor, you might even be able to transform your computer into a mini home movie theater. The sound from your computer can be hooked up to your home stereo system for surround sound. (Visit *pricegrabber.com* to order a hot-air popcorn popper and you've got it made!)

You can borrow DVDs from your local public library or rent them at a Redbox in the supermarket, but the Internet offers you the ability to rent DVDs without leaving the comfort of your home. *DVD.netflix.com* is the leading online video rental site—it will mail you the movies that you select among the more than 90,000 movies it offers. Rental plans are as low as $7.99 per month.

Visit *netflix.com* to view the many movies offered. Even if you don't use them as your DVD rental company, their list of movies may inspire your next movie night.

"When I used to visit the video store I'd rack my brain for what movie to rent. My memory just isn't that good anymore. Now, with a movie list online, I don't feel as much pressure and I can change it at any time."
—*Jules*

Search box where you can type keywords

You can rent DVDs online using *DVD.netflix.com.*

Live Streaming

Netflix.com and other websites like it are not limited to using snail mail to send and receive movies. Now, with high-speed Internet connections, you can **live stream** movies and TV episodes on your computer, tablet, or even your smartphone. Live streaming requires the power of a high-speed Internet connection. The magic of live streaming is that there's no waiting for a movie or TV series to arrive in the mail or leaving your cozy home to make your choice at the local video store. Instant gratification is just a keyboard and mouse click away.

CRITIC'S CHOICE
Visit *metacritic.com* for reviews of movies, DVDs, books, and more.

DON'T FORGET THE VOLUME
Your computer may have come with speakers. If the sound quality isn't good enough for movie watching, you can buy very good quality speakers to attach to your computer. Just be sure to tell the salesperson of your intentions so they can help you find the right ones.

No TV, No Worries

I gave away my television set way back in 2001 and I haven't missed it since. Between watching DVDs on my computer and catching complete episodes of television online using my tablet, I don't feel at all out of the loop. Yes, I said "watching television online." ABC, CBS, and NBC, along with HBO, Showtime, and most other cable stations and satellite TV providers, offer select episodes free online. Visit each of the network's websites (you know how to search for them on Google, if you can't guess their web address) to see what they offer online. If you are already paying for a cable or satellite service on your TV, you can access all of their programming on your computer or tablet by creating an online account. The steps are similar to those for Facebook or Dropbox (see pages 368 and 416). You'll give them an email address and create a password. All the same rules that we discussed in Chapter 16 apply. *Hulu.com* is another website where you can access television shows for free—as long as you don't mind viewing them a day or more after they've aired.

You can also buy episodes of television shows from iTunes (see page 200 for more on iTunes) and download episodes onto your computer or tablet. (Remember, downloading is just moving or copying from one place to another. In this case, you are downloading from the iTunes website to your device.) As of this writing, a TV episode usually sells for $1.99. Once you download it to your iTunes library, it is yours to watch over and over again.

If I want to catch up-to-the-minute news, I visit *cnn.com* and watch their online videos of

■ Hulu's home page

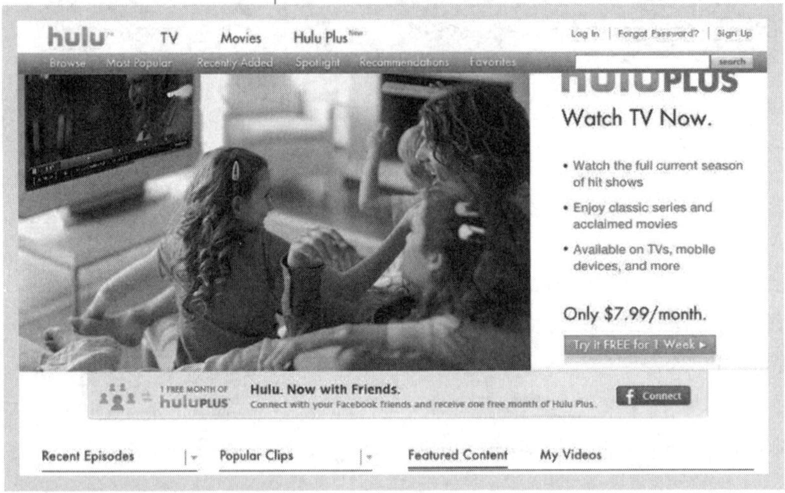

breaking news. All major news organizations—the *New York Times*, the *Wall Street Journal*, the BBC, and many more—have websites that they update frequently. Check out your local network's website to see what they have to offer. The real advantage of watching online versus on TV is that usually there are fewer commercials interrupting the show when you watch online.

■ *Cnn.com* offers online videos of breaking news.

Do You YouTube?

Speaking of watching video online . . . *youtube.com* allows *anyone* to upload favorite video clips onto the website to be shared with the world at large. (Upload is just like download—to move or copy files from one place to another—but in this case it's *from* your computer *to* the Web, not the other way around.) These clips aren't usually more than a few minutes long.

Be warned: YouTube runs the gamut from nostalgic clips of past television shows, to Maria Callas singing at the Met, to newsworthy current events, to practical how-to videos, to juvenile, armpit-fart pranks and worse. You select video clips to view based on your interests, segments most recently added to

YOURS TRULY

Search for me on YouTube and you'll discover video clips of my classes, lectures, and TV interviews (clue: *youtube.com/user/AskAbbyStokes*)! My YouTube clips can also be accessed by visiting *AskAbbyStokes.com* and clicking on Video Tutorials at the top of the page.

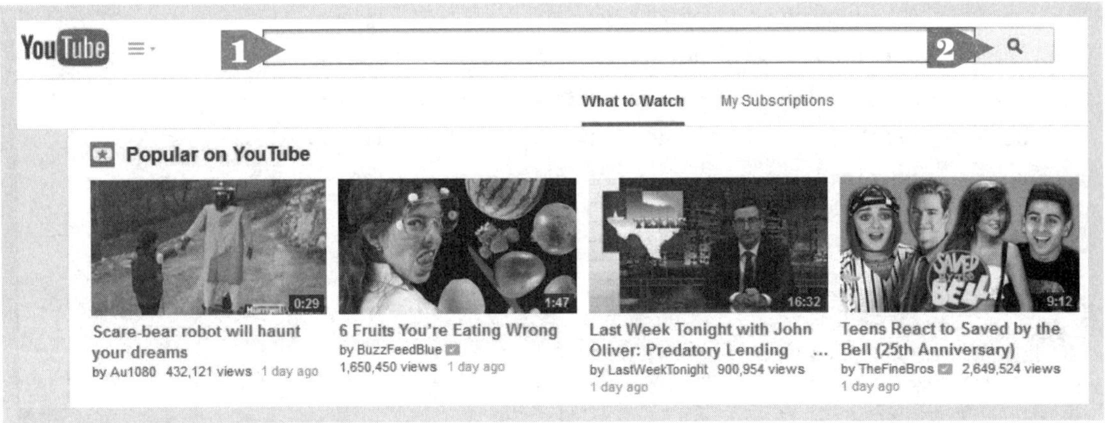

YouTube's home page

CLICK AND GO

1. Click and type keywords in Search box.
2. Click on Search.

the site, most viewed, top rated, and so on. Click on the **Video** tab at the top of the home page to see your choices.

If you want to upload a digital video file onto YouTube, it's free. Just be careful about what you choose to share. You don't want to post anything that gives away too much personal information about you or anything that might jeopardize your job, relationship, or, in the case of younger folks, chances of getting into the college of their choice. Anyone can visit YouTube, so your submission is there for all to see. Remember, Uncle Bert may not appreciate that impersonation of him being seen worldwide.

THERE'S AN APP FOR THAT

If you want to watch cable or satellite channels on your tablet or smartphone, visit the App Store on your device. You'll find HBO GO, WatchESPN, and many more listed. If you already pay for the service on your TV, you won't have to pay extra to watch it online through your computer, tablet, or smartphone.

The Best of Both Worlds—TV *and* the Internet

What if you could have it all—the luxury of your big, beautiful television and access to everything the Internet has to offer? It is yours for the taking with the latest digital entertainment network devices. (That was a mouthful.) Simply plug a small box into the back of your TV. It connects to your Internet signal and pulls movies, TV, games, and radio off the Internet and into your home. The two devices leading the market are Roku and Apple TV. You can pay as little as $50 and up to $100 for the device, but there is no recurring monthly fee. The only extra cost is if the channel you are accessing requires a monthly

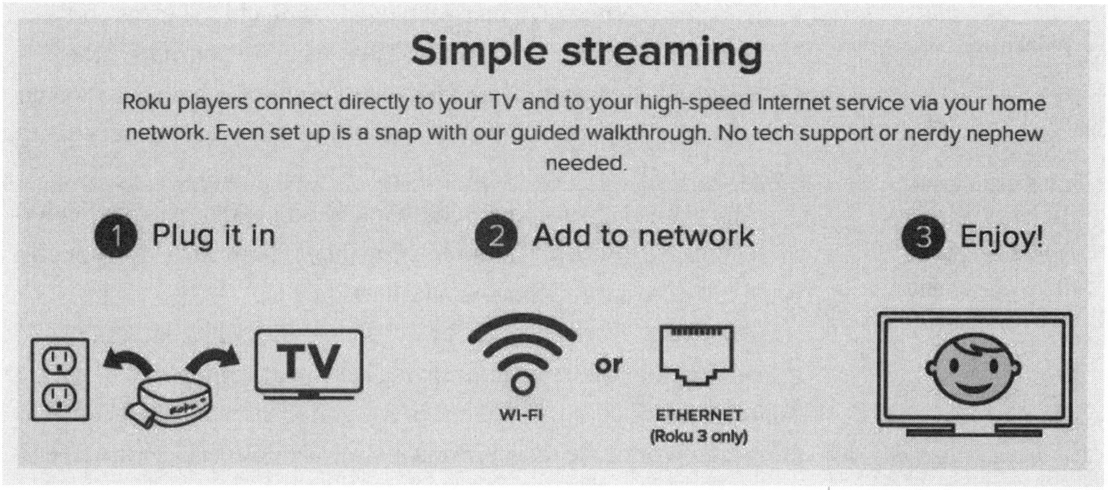

Roku's simple installation instructions

subscription. And with over 1,000 channels to choose from, there are plenty that are free.

The concept might seem complex, but the steps for setup are really simple.

- Plug the device into the back of your TV. (Both Roku and Apple TV have very clear instructions and access to tech support if you need help.)
- Connect the box to your Internet signal either wirelessly or with an Ethernet cord. If you are connecting through a wi-fi connection, you'll need to know the password to gain access.
- Once it is up and running, you can start to enjoy the same channels you view on your TV and the Internet. You'll have to use a sign-in ID and password to access the services you already pay for, such as HBO and Showtime.

Music to Your Ears

A smartphone or tablet allows you to listen to music anytime, anywhere, and if you plug into a speaker or use a wireless Bluetooth speaker, it's an instant party! There are several different methods for storing and accessing music on a smartphone, tablet, or computer.

MINI ME
Smartphones are actually a mini version of a tablet, but with cell phone capabilities. So, if you're familiar with a tablet, conquering a smartphone will be a piece of cake, and vice versa.

"Aw shucks. Can't I store more than 100,000 songs?" If you listened to 5 hours of music every day, it would take 4 years to listen to all 100,000 songs.

The first method is to take all those CDs on your shelves and convert them to a digital collection by copying (or "burning") the CDs into a music library stored on your computer, which can then be shared with your smartphone or tablet. That way you can carry every song from your CD collection with you wherever you go.

Alternatively, you can purchase music online that you download (move) directly onto your devices. You *own* that music even though you don't have a three-dimensional version.

Or, you can *borrow* music by live-streaming it. Live streaming means sending music, without saving it, to your computer, smartphone, or tablet. You listen to songs instantaneously while they *stream* onto the device. Some live-streaming services are free (I love free!), but you may have to endure advertisements. Some live-streaming services are available at a nominal subscription fee.

Let's walk though how each of these options work.

Listening Through the Ages

We evolved from listening to music on LPs to CDs, with 8-track and cassette tapes tossed in between, and now we can carry our entire music collection in our pocket. One of the most popular methods for transferring CDs to a computer is the software program **iTunes** . iTunes is an Apple product, which means it comes pre-installed on Apple computers, iPhones, and iPads, but iTunes is available for non-Apple devices as well. With iTunes you create a music library that stores up to 100,000 of your favorite songs.

Copying Your CDs into iTunes

You might not have **iTunes** pre-installed if you don't have an Apple computer. Visit *itunes.com* and click on **Download** to add the program to your computer. Along the way you'll need to agree to their **Terms & Conditions**. If you're not comfortable downloading the program to your computer, this is a good time to offer to make dinner for your more tech-savvy friends or family members and have one of them do it for you.

Once iTunes is installed, look through your CD collection and choose your favorite CD. (For a refresher on how to play a CD on your computer, revisit page 189, for a PC, or page 200, if you have a Mac.)

If you have a PC:

- Open the CD/DVD drawer. Place the CD, label side up, into the drawer. If you have a laptop, the CD snaps into place. Close the drawer.
- If iTunes doesn't open up automatically, double-click on the iTunes icon  on your desktop.

If you have a Mac:

- Push the CD into the CD/DVD slot. The computer will grab the CD from you.
- iTunes will open automatically.

Import CD

Okay. Now we're all together. iTunes has opened and you see a list of tracks. This is the list of songs on your CD. Each song has a check in the box to the left. If you want to copy all of the songs into iTunes, click on **Import CD**. If there's a song you don't want copied, click on the check to remove it.

An **Import Settings** window may open; simply click **OK**. The title bar of the window now reads **Importing "Track 01"** and will continue with the number of each track. Notice that once a track has been added, a green check appears to the left.

A green check indicates that a track has been copied.

If the correct name of the song wasn't added during the import, you can change the name. Single click on **Track 01** (or whatever number you want). The entire line will be highlighted in blue. Click again on the name and now only the name will be in blue. You can go directly to the keyboard and type in the song name. Now hit the **Enter** or **Return** key on the keyboard. Well done!

The Down Low on Downloading Music

You can purchase music from iTunes in the same way you purchase movies or TV episodes. When music is purchased online, you download (move) that music onto your computer, smartphone, or tablet. All the music is organized in a music library and can be sorted by song or album title, composer, or artist. If you've copied your CDs onto your device, the downloaded songs can be integrated into the same music library as your CDs. Your first steps will be to create an account with iTunes. They require an email address (perfect time to use your secondary email address), a password, and your credit card information.

SOMETHING FOR EVERYONE

Don't think that just because the technology is new that the songs are, too. iTunes has a catalog of 30,000,000 songs. I'm guessing you'll find that little ditty you're looking for.

To purchase music from iTunes:

Once you have an account with iTunes, you can start buying individual songs or entire albums.

- Open iTunes.
- Click on **iTunes Store**.
- Type either the artist, composer, song title, or album name in the Search box or toodle around, using the scroll bar, to see what iTunes is recommending.
- Click on the price associated with the song or album you desire.
- If you haven't signed into your iTunes account, they'll ask you now to type your Apple ID and Password.

- Click **Buy** and the credit card you listed with Apple will be charged and the song or album will be copied into the **My Music** area of iTunes along with your other music.

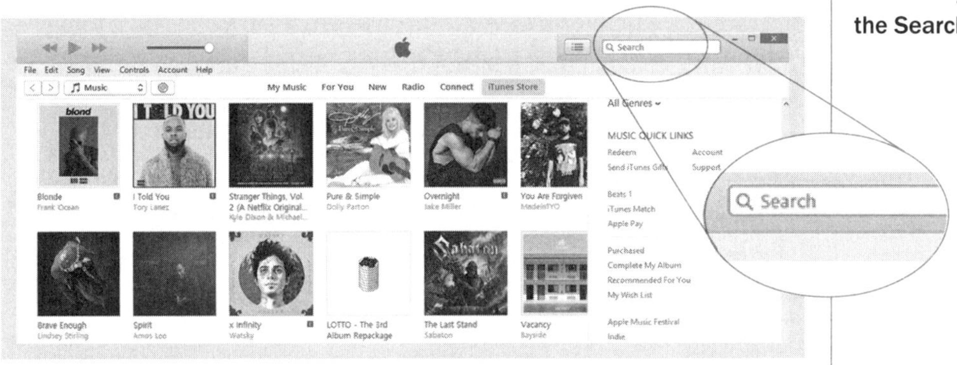

Type the song, artist, or album you seek in the Search box.

For those of you with an Android smartphone or tablet, **Google Play** offers you the ability to purchase and download music just like iTunes, if you'd prefer to purchase from Google rather than from iTunes.

Ride the Wave of Live Streaming

Below are some of my favorite music apps for live streaming. You might want to consider adding some, or all, to your smartphone or tablet. Revisit Chapter 12 for a refresher on how to add an app (software application/program) to your tablet. The same instructions hold true for adding an app to your smartphone.

Apple Music—Apple's next step up from iTunes. For a fee (at present, $14.99 a month) you can live-stream anything your heart desires from Apple's 30,000,000 song library. Apple Music has the added bonus of a radio station—**Beats 1**—if you like the nostalgia of listening to a proper radio station.

Spotify—A great *free* option to live-stream single tracks or entire albums. For a monthly subscription fee ($9.99) you can download songs for offline listening.

APP = APPLICATION

The term *application software* is often shortened to *software* when referring to programs added to a computer. The nickname *app* (short for *application*) is most commonly used when referring to software added to a tablet.

Pandora—Provides personalized online radio. You start listening to music and indicate what you like and what you don't and Pandora will start to filter songs accordingly. It creates the equivalent of a radio station based on your favorite artists. If you decide to pay ($54.89 per year or $4.99 per month), you'll enjoy music ad-free.

TuneIn Radio—Gives you access to more than 100,000 live radio stations from all over the world. There's music, talk radio, sports, news radio, and podcasts. Chances are very good that you'll have access to your local radio stations, which you could then stream directly onto your smartphone or tablet.

Shazam—One of my all-time favorite music apps. Imagine this: You hear a song playing and, for the life of you, you can't remember the title or who recorded it. Hold up your phone, open the Shazam app, and it will detect the song in a matter of seconds, giving you the title and lyrics, along with purchasing or streaming options.

Speaking of Speakers

At the start of this section I mentioned listening to music with speakers. You can plug computer speakers into the headset jack on your smartphone or tablet and fill whatever room you're in with sound. But wireless—or Bluetooth—speakers are really the cat's pajamas. Using Bluetooth technology you can place the speaker wherever it suits you and control what music plays and at what volume from your computer, smartphone, or tablet.

Your entire home can be rigged with a wireless speaker system that allows you to control what rooms play what, when, and how loud. Sonos is one of the top manufacturers of in-home wireless speaker systems.

Maybe it's time to take a break and put on your dancing shoes. I'll meet you right back here when you're done cutting a rug!

TAKE THE BITE OUT OF BLUETOOTH

Bluetooth technology offers a cable-free connection among tablets, computers (desktops, laptops, and handhelds), and other peripherals (such as speakers). It allows all of these devices to speak to one another without any cables attaching them, and it works with virtually every smartphone or tablet.

More Listening Pleasure

While we're talking about listening, let's discuss **Podcasts**. A podcast is an audio (sometimes video) file that can be downloaded (copied) from the Internet to your computer, smartphone, or tablet. There are a couple of things that set podcasts apart from the live-streaming radio referred to in the previous pages. Podcasts are typically available as a series, with new installments being received by subscribers automatically. I'll get into how that happens in a minute.

Most podcasts are free of charge to listeners and are usually in a talk-radio format instead of all music. This is primarily because of copyright law. If you broadcast music that you don't have the rights to, you're breaking the law. But many podcasts are *about* music, like the example we'll look at after I explain about this automatic component.

What Is RSS?

RSS originally stood for *Rich Site Summary*, but now stands for *Really Simple Syndication* and that is exactly what it is. Instead of returning over and over to a favorite website to see what new content has been added, you can have an RSS feed to that blog, podcast, or newsletter and the content will automatically come to you. The whole point of syndication is to make it easier and more efficient for you to consume your favorite content. Having said that, you can listen to podcasts without using RSS. Take a look at the list of RSS Readers on page 518.

Standard RSS icon.

Where Can You Find Podcasts?

Your smartphone and tablet already have an app to tap on for you to search for, subscribe to, and listen to podcasts.

Keep your eyes peeled when you're visiting a website. You might see the RSS icon or the word **Subscribe**.

Android's GooglePlay Podcast app

Apple's My Podcast app

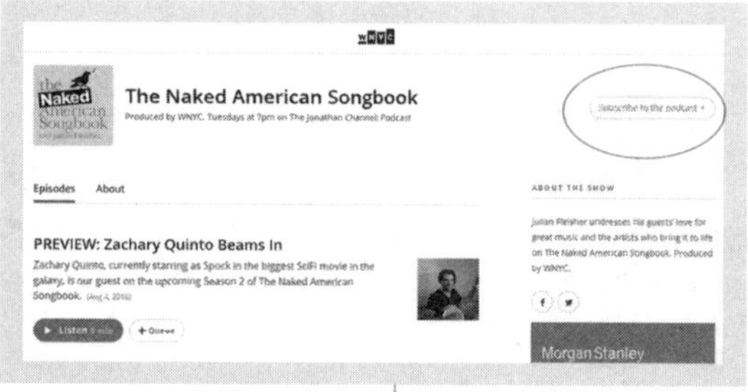

■ Click or tap on **Subscribe**.

Let's visit a website with one of my favorite podcasts. Search for *Naked American Songbook* or type *wnyc.org/shows/americansongbook* in the website address box. You can see at left where to click in the upper right corner on **Subscribe to the podcast** once the webpage is open.

From there you can choose to use iTunes or an RSS feed. Next time you have your smartphone or tablet in hand, trying searching for the *Naked American Songbook* through the podcast app.

I'm a big National Public Radio (NPR) fan, and they have many great podcasts to choose from. Visit *npr.org/podcasts* to see what they have to offer. I suggest starting with *Serial*, *Radio Lab*, or *This American Life* to get your feet wet. Otherwise you can simply Google a topic of your choosing and add the word "podcast" at the end. You'll have plenty of podcast choices to keep you busy.

It's only by playing around that you'll get familiar and comfortable with this or any other technology. You won't hurt anything. I promise. Happy listening!

Book It, Danno

Not all entertainment needs to move or make noise. An e-reader may be just the ticket for you. The major players in the field of e-readers are Amazon's Kindle and Barnes & Noble's Nook, but there are many other worthy brands to consider. E-readers range in price from $99 to almost $500 and can weigh anywhere from 6 ounces to a pound. An e-reader is definitely one of those devices that you should try on for size before you commit to a purchase. Only you can tell whether the e-reader is too heavy, the screen is too small, or the feeling is just right. Some questions to ponder: Which style of turning pages appeals to you? Does the keyboard suit your fingers? What else do you want to read on the device besides books? How heavy is too heavy? Where will you be reading? Some devices are better in sunlight than others.

But I'm getting ahead of myself. The first question to be answered is, "What is an e-reader, really?" Essentially, it is a portable device that enables you to read digital versions of books and periodicals. You can download books, newspapers, and magazines onto the device using a wi-fi connection or a 4G or 5G connection. To clarify, a wi-fi connection is an Internet connection dependent upon being within range of a wi-fi signal. Both 4G or 5G are cellular network signals, as you use with your cell phone. They offer service in more areas than wi-fi, but usually at an additional cost.

The same technology that allows you to send an email attachment enables you to download a digital book. It flies through the air with the greatest of ease. For many people, an e-reader will never replace the pleasure of reading a physical book. Similarly, electric light will never completely replace candlelight, but that's no reason not to turn on the lights. I use an e-reader for travel. The benefits are twofold—I keep the weight of my suitcase to a minimum, and every morning the *New York Times* arrives on my reader, regardless of where I am on the globe. The Kindle is capable of storing up to 3,500 books. Astonishing when you think about it!

When comparing e-readers, you really want to get your hands on each to see what suits you best. The features and screen quality are improving every day, so what your neighbor had last year may be very different from what is being sold this year. You don't need to buy books to read on an e-reader. You may also download them from your local library's website. Go in and ask for a demonstration. Or start

"I love that as my eyes get tired from reading I can increase the size of the text on my e-reader, then decrease it later. You can't do that with a book!"
—*Felix*

by going to the websites listed below to get a better sense of which e-reader might be best for you.

- *amazon.com/kindle*
- *barnesandnoble.com/nook*

How Do E-Readers Work?

I'm using the Kindle Fire as my example here because it currently leads the market in sales—I have no allegiance to any brand of e-reader. If you choose to purchase a different e-reader, the general function will be similar to what I'm explaining here.

At the time of purchase or after receiving the Kindle as a gift (lucky you!), you'll be required to register it at *amazon.com/kindle.* Doing so establishes a relationship with Amazon so you can purchase and download books to the Kindle. (You must purchase books for your Kindle exclusively from Amazon.) Amazon will store your credit card information for your convenience. As is true with just about all of the large online shopping sites, Amazon takes precautions to protect your credit card information, but if you are squeamish about having your credit card information stored, you may want to consider a different e-reader.

You can choose from among nearly a million books to download to your Kindle.

Once you've registered with Amazon, visit the **Kindle Store**. Over one million books are available for the Kindle—including this one! You'll find that not only can you buy books, but certain magazines and newspapers are available as well. The miraculous part is that less than a minute after you buy the book or periodical of your choice, it wirelessly arrives on the Kindle. *Poof!* If you download the Kindle app to your computer or smartphone, you can also access your library there. Pretty incredible, isn't it?

Life's a Game

As I mentioned earlier in the book, you can play mah-jongg, cribbage, and almost any other game you can imagine on your computer. You either buy softwarc that allows you to play against the computer (unless your computer came preinstalled with the game

SOME ENTERTAINING WEBSITES TO GET YOU STARTED

espn.com
Get the latest sports scores and news.

nytimes.com
Read the *New York Times* online.

people.com
Find entertainment news and human interest stories.

secondlife.com
Explore a 3-D virtual game-world created by users.

theonion.com
Enjoy a satirical look at the news.

usatoday.com
Read *USA Today* online.

wired.com
Keep up with technology news.

you want to play) or visit websites where you'll actually play against other people sitting at their computers somewhere in the world. Again, Google may be your best resource to search for the game you want to play. Or look at the list of websites in the back of this book for guidance. The more specific you are with your search on Google, the more specific the suggested websites. If you type in "games" in Google, the results will show millions of websites. Good heavens, that's way too many choices. Better to type in "scrabble," "bridge," or "chess." Remember, specificity counts.

Some gaming sites require a membership fee, but most don't. Most will, however, ask you to register with the site. This is when you'll decide on the name you want to be called when you're on the site. Again, be wise about how much you tell about yourself. That lovely elderly woman you've been playing bridge with could be the big bad wolf in disguise, waiting to blow your financial house down.

There's No End to the Fun

The resources for entertainment on the Internet are as endless as your imagination is boundless. Whatever hobby, activity, or distraction you seek, it can be found with some detective work on the World Wide Web.

Do you have it in you to learn about more gadgets? Take a break and come back for the grand finale.

What the Future Will Bring

A friend of mine has a pacemaker in his chest that he tests remotely, using a device similar to the one you use to turn on your TV (but with fewer buttons). I've been consulted to review the design of in-home health devices that monitor your vital signs, medication dosages, and fitness activity and send the information directly to your physician. People wear glasses or a watch that records their every movement, and based on that data, anticipate their next steps and can share their whereabouts with others. Now there's no need to carry your wallet—you can simply hold up your smartphone and your credit card gets charged. I kid you not. Many of the innovations are straight out of *The Jetsons* or some sci-fi thrillers.

Let's take a look at a few of the latest technologies and gadgets.

Voice Recognition

Voice or speech recognition software has been in development for a long time. I know several authors who dictate their books, rather than type them, using *Dragon NaturallySpeaking* software. The development was slow because it took time to create software that could detect and transcribe so many different accents and cadences. Every year the software improves in its accuracy. Dragon also has an app for your smartphone or tablet. Some other leaders with dictation apps are *Dictadroid* and *Speech to Text.*

But the really amazing new feature on your smartphone is a "voice assistant." Siri is the iPhone's assistant, Google Now is for Androids, and Cortana is the assistant on a Windows phone. You can ask your assistant to dial a phone number for you, send a text, find the nearest gas station, or play a song. Short of fetching you a cup of steaming coffee or peeling you a grape, you can ask the personal assistant in your hand to help with a lot of small tasks.

Speaking with Siri: If you want to try speaking with *Siri*, here are two sets of step-by-step instructions to get you started. The first set is for the iPhone or iPad. The second set of instructions is for an Android device using Google's operating system. Be patient when

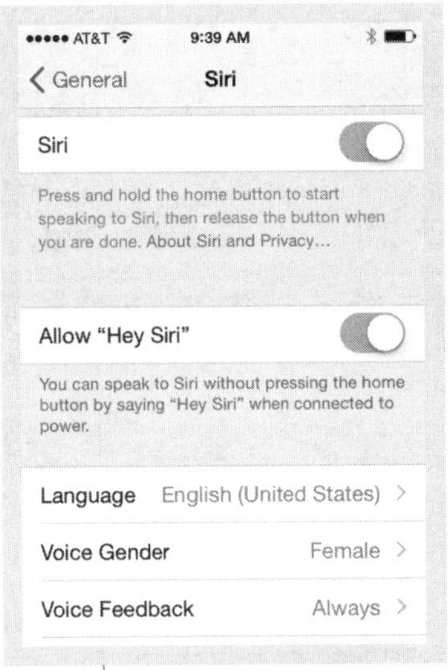

using any voice recognition services. The technology is still a work in progress and is definitely imperfect.

To turn on Siri:

1. Tap **Settings**.
2. Tap **General**.
3. Tap **Siri**.
4. Turn on Siri by tapping on the circle to the right.

To use Siri:

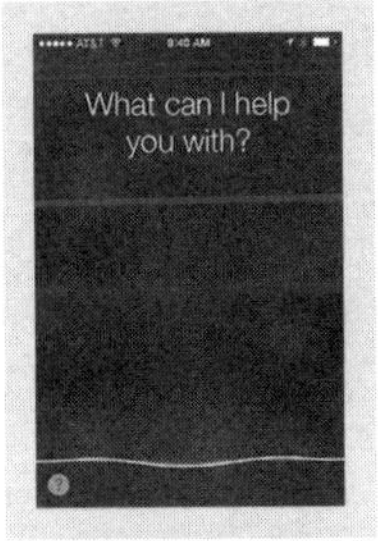

1. If the microphone is already there, tap on it. If not, hold your finger down on the **Home** button at the bottom of the iPhone.
2. Wait for the microphone and the words "What can I help you with?" to appear.
3. Slowly and clearly speak your question or command.
4. Be sure to give a quiet pause before you say anything not intended for Siri, so it will stop recording.
5. When you hear two beeps. you know that the recording of your question or command is complete.

Try these commands and questions to get started:

- Write a text.
- What's the weather where I am? Or, is it going to be cold today?
- Where's the nearest movie theater?
- When is Easter this year?

Google Now Search is the voice-activated feature on Androids running Google's operating system. If *Google Now* is not pre-installed on your device, go to the **Google Playstore** and install the launcher.

To use Google Now Search:

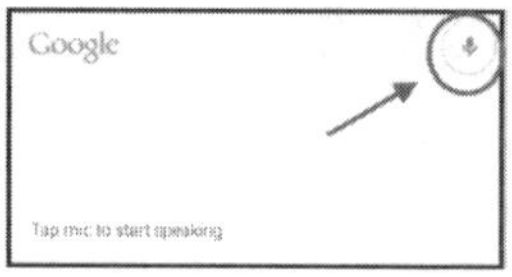

1. Tap on the mic in the top right.

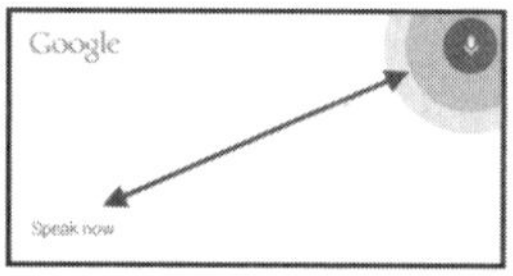

2. Start speaking when the mic turns red.
3. Be sure to give a quiet pause before you say anything that does not relate to your question, so it will stop recording.

Don't be discouraged if you see an error message like this one. Just give it another go and chances are it will work the second (or third) time around.

Try these commands and questions to get started:

- How many calories in a slice of pizza?
- How late is the nearest drugstore open?
- What is gluten?
- Show me the steps for the fox-trot.

Wearables

Yes, you can now wear your technology. There are watches, eyeglasses, and even rings that transmit information over the Internet and back to your computer or tablet.

Apple recently introduced the **Apple Watch**, which literally brings the world to your wrist and you to the world. You can text, email, and call from the watch. But that's not all . . . it also checks your heart rate, tells you if you're on schedule, and lets you send a gentle

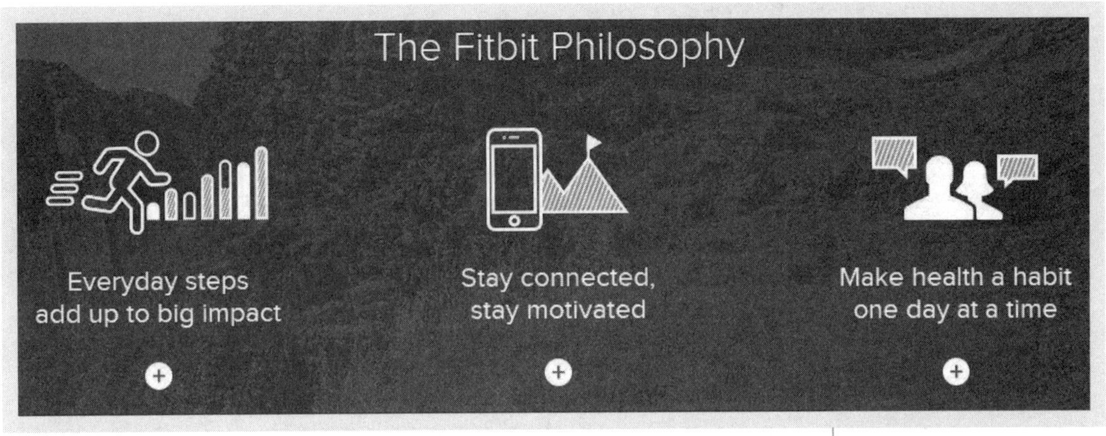

vibration to someone else wearing an Apple Watch so they know you're thinking of them, or sketch a heart to zap to your honey. Your credit card information is stored on the watch so you can use it to pay at stores or restaurants and, I almost forgot, it also tells time!

Fitbit and **Sony's Smartband** are wristbands that monitor your physical activity, food intake, and sleep. They then share that information with your tablet, smartphone, or computer, and suggest how you can improve your health based on the data collected.

Moving from your wrist to your head, meet OHMD (optical head-mounted display). **Google Glass** is the most well-known device of this kind at the moment, but there are several others in design that you wear just as you would a pair of eyeglasses. Utilizing voice recognition software, you speak your commands or questions—driving directions, movie start times, how much to tip a barber—and the device will either display or say the answer. There's a built-in webcam so what you see can be instantaneously shared online with one person or with millions. For obvious reasons, this is controversial. Only time will tell how many people adopt these wearable and all-seeing technologies.

Fitbit Band

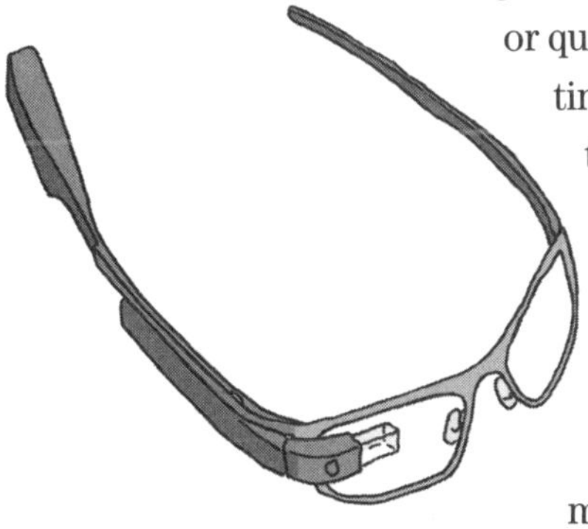

Google Glass

Until We Meet Again

Before we move on to the troubleshooting chapter, I just want to let you know what a pleasure it's been to go on this journey of discovery with you. If you can believe it, there was a time when you didn't know what a computer or tablet could do, let alone the basics of texting or what the heck Twitter is! You've come a long way, baby! But remember, you have no obligation to try or adopt anything you don't want to, especially if it isn't ultimately helpful to you.

Please do take the time to visit and revisit me at my website, *AskAbbyStokes.com*. Join my newsletter, and I'll keep you up to date while you keep in touch. Bon voyage!

Q: Are there websites for those of us who would like to learn how to play bridge or other games like it?

A: Most interactive gaming websites have different skill levels, including beginner, intermediate, and advanced. The great thing about using the interactive sites, as opposed to buying software, is that you can ask questions on the website and get expert guidance from other players. If you do opt to buy software instead, it will probably either come with a manual or have a tutorial built into the software that you can watch on your computer. You can also find sites that will help teach you the strategies of certain games.

Q: My grandchildren love their Xbox, PlayStation, Wii, and Nintendo 3DS. What are these things?

A: None of these game systems run on your home computer, but they all utilize computer technology to function. The Xbox, Sony PlayStation, and Wii are independent consoles that connect to your television and are played using a controller to guide your movements (games include car racing, combating villains, etc.). A Vita is a handheld PlayStation device on which you can play a variety of games, not unlike the Nintendo 3DS. Just as with a computer, game time should be limited, with regular breaks in between sessions. To get a better sense of each device, visit their websites to see demonstrations.

A few game systems

"I now play chess with opponents all over the world. Online chess has changed my life."
—*Vittoria*

Q: Is there any downside to playing games on the Internet?

A: It's hard to say. For some people, playing computer games increases their contact with the outside world because they can make friends living in places they may never get a chance to visit; for others, it diminishes it. Only you can judge whether the games you play online add to the quality of your life or not. The computer and what it has to offer should never replace face-to-face interaction with live human beings. Nothing beats quality time spent with friends and family.

CHAPTER 25

TROUBLESHOOTING

"I think it has a fever"—what to do if something doesn't seem right

Error messages that appear on a computer or tablet screen can cause the bravest souls to quake in their boots. These messages are generally as harmless as a spooky movie, but they can be just as frightening.

It's a good idea to keep a diary of any problems you have with your computer. Make a note of the date, time, and what happened. If an error message shows up, write it down exactly as it appears. In the unlikely case that you bought a lemon, it will also be helpful information when you return the computer.

This chapter will go over some of the problems that you *might* come across with your device. I want you to be aware of them and to show you that they can be solved. Be assured that most of these problems *will not* happen. There is even the possibility that none of them will ever happen (although the chances of that are about the same as you winning the Publishers Clearing House sweepstakes).

I don't expect you to understand the logic behind the solutions; just read along to get a feel for how to troubleshoot problems. Consider this chapter your first-aid kit for your computer experience.

TAKE ADVANTAGE OF TECHNICAL SUPPORT SERVICES!

Technical support is yours for the taking, based on your warranty agreement. There is no question too big or too small to be asked. Read through the scenarios in this chapter, but know that you can always call for technical assistance instead of trying to troubleshoot on your own. You paid for the service—take advantage of it!

A Little TLC Goes a Long Way

Keep your device free of dust and animal hair, and far away from liquids. I mentioned this back in Chapter 5, but it warrants repeating.

Better Safe Than Sorry

As I mentioned in Chapter 5, technology has several enemies.

- Magnets can damage the screen and other components. My advice: Keep your magnets on the fridge and nowhere near your technology.
- Liquids should be kept far away. As you may recall, just a few drops of milk from my cereal spoon caused a huge amount of damage to my computer. Don't take that chance. Instead, take regular breaks from your device and enjoy your refreshing drink in another room—or at least a few feet away. Any excuse to break from technology helps prevent bleary eyes and fatigue anyway.
- Little kids are the *wunderkinder* of technology. However, they may not be gentle with your touch screen, keyboard, or mouse. Never let young children use your device unsupervised.

- Static electricity is another villain. I recently read an article that a woman's computer at work conked out every day at 4:45 p.m. Several technicians tried to find the problem, but to no avail. Finally, a technician decided to observe her at that hour. What he discovered was that as her workday came to a close she would get more and more anxious about finishing her work on time. She would cross and recross her legs, conducting static electricity from the thick carpet below her desk, which in turn fouled up her computer. For this reason, it isn't wise to have the computer in a room with a heavy pile carpet.
- Be sure to protect your CDs and DVDs from any extremes. They don't respond well to direct sunlight or heat (neither does your computer or tablet). The safest thing to do is to store CDs or DVDs in a box or on a bookshelf. I used to keep mine on a shady windowsill until a friend accidentally sent them on a four-story kamikaze drop. *Splat.* Now I have them safely stored under my desk. You can purchase shelves, boxes, or albums designed to store and organize CDs and DVDs.

Your computer will also benefit from some routine maintenance. Tablets don't offer the maintenance tools below. Meet me on page 507 and we'll discuss tablet-specific issues and solutions.

PCs and Apple computers differ in what regular maintenance you should provide. If you have a PC, read on. If you have an Apple, you can skip the disk cleanup and defrag section—Macs do this automatically—and meet up on page 499 at "Mac and PC Updates."

PC Maintenance

Disk Cleanup

Disk Cleanup is a tool built into the computer to help the computer remain as lean and smooth-running as possible. When activated, Disk Cleanup sweeps your computer to find unnecessary files it can safely delete to free up space on your hard drive. Rest assured the Disk Cleanup would not suggest deleting any files you added to the computer. Primarily, it finds temporary Internet files and the like. The frequency with which one should perform a cleanup is directly related to the amount of computer use, not the calendar.

However, because that's hard to judge, you could perform a disk cleanup once every one to three months. (I'll bet you a new ream of paper that some people you ask *may* do it once a year, but most have *never* done it at all!)

Here are the steps to clean up your PC computer:

- Close all programs that are open.
- Right-click on the **Start** button.
- Left-click on **Control Panel**.
- Double-click on **Disk Cleanup**.
- Click **OK**. Wait while it evaluates your computer.
- A window opens, with check marks indicating what files the computer proposes to delete. If there are any files you do *not* wanted deleted, click in the box with the check to remove the check.
- Click on **OK**.
- Click **Delete Files**.

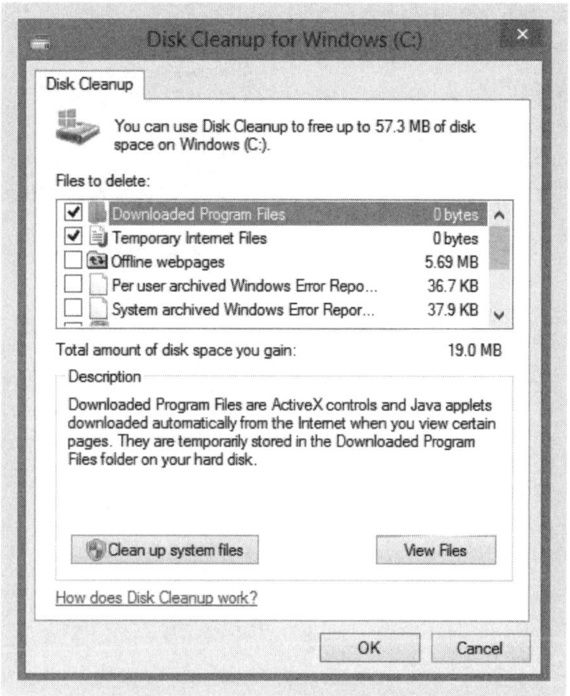

The Disk Cleanup window on your PC computer

Defrag

Every time you open or close a program, bits of the data used in the program move from their place of origin to another location in the computer. This is called *fragmenting*. When fragmenting occurs, it slows down the computer because now it has to search

■ The Optimize window to defrag your PC

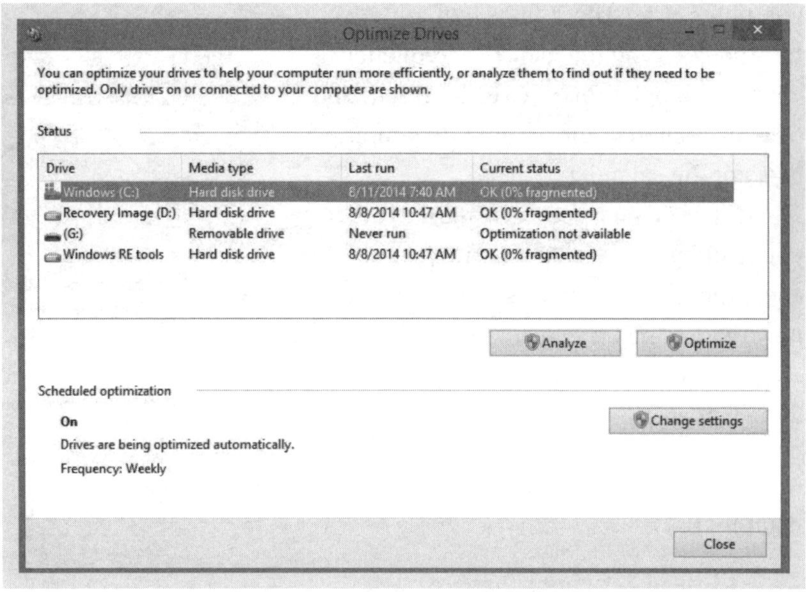

for all the fragments scattered hither and yon on the computer. To return these bits of data to where they belong, the computer must be defragmented. Why not defrag your computer every time you perform a disk cleanup? Choose your computer housecleaning day to be something you can remember . . . perhaps the first of the month or when you pay your quarterly taxes.

Here are the steps to defrag your PC computer.

- Close all programs that are open.
- Right-click on the **Start** button ⊞.
- Left-click on **Control Panel**.
- Double-click **Defragment and Optimize Drives**.
- Click on **Analyze**. If the analysis says you don't need to defrag, close both windows. Otherwise, click **Optimize** and *wait*. This could take minutes or hours.
- Eventually, it will notify you that the defragging is complete and you can close all windows.

Mac and PC Updates

If you have a PC, the Microsoft operating system regularly offers updates. These updates are fixes or patches from Microsoft to make your computer run more smoothly. It's a good idea to allow these updates to occur.

To instruct the computer to do just that, follow these steps:

- Right-click on the **Start** button.
- Left-click on **Control Panel**.
- Click on **System and Security**.
- Click on **System**.
- Click on **Windows Update** (bottom left).
- Click on **Check for updates**.
- From here you can check for updates and schedule when the updates will be downloaded and installed.

Windows Update window on a PC

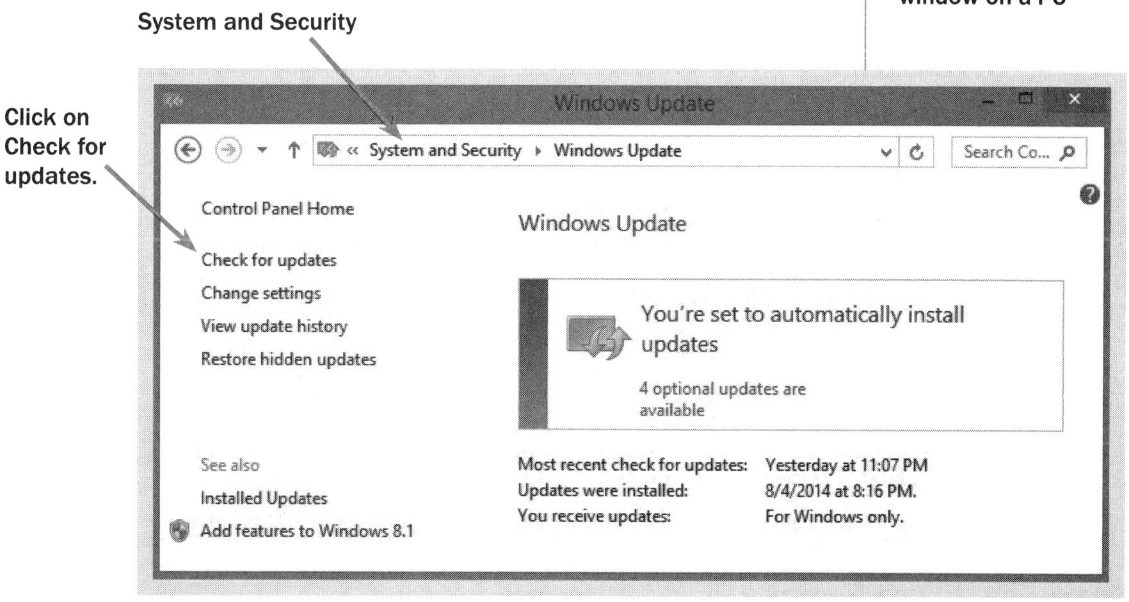

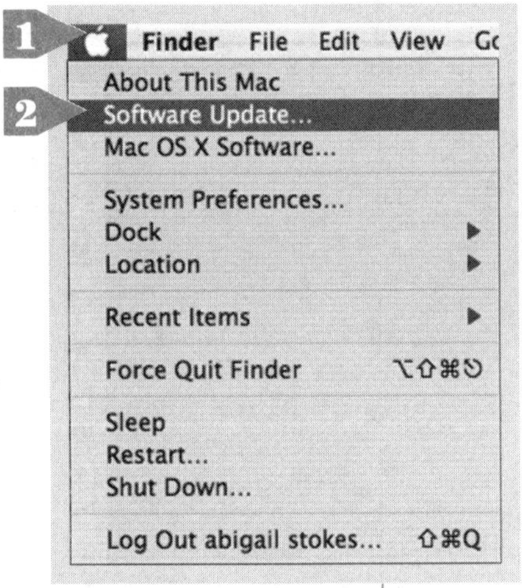

CLICK AND GO

1. Click .
2. Click Software Update.
3. Click Install.

Apple also offers regular updates, but you access them differently.

- Click on the **Apple** in the top left of the screen.
- Click on **Software Update**.
- The Software Update program will evaluate what is on your computer. If it determines that there are updates available, click **Update All** to download and install what is suggested for your computer. This may require that you sign into your iTunes or iCloud account.

Remember, if you take care of your computer, it will take care of you. With both PCs and Apples, be cautious if, when on the Internet, you are offered to update software on your computer. How does the website know what's on your computer or what you need? Resist the temptation to download anything unless you know what it is and that you want it.

NO NEED TO RUSH

When an error message appears on your screen and does something you don't understand, there's usually no need to rush to fix it. Write down the error message, if one has appeared, then just leave the computer on (error message and all) until you get help. You won't do it any harm.

Computer Troubles

When I turned on the computer, the screen remained black.

Most monitors have a small light that indicates if the monitor is on. If this light is not lit, it means the monitor is not getting electricity.

- Is the monitor turned on?
- Is the computer plugged in?

- Is the monitor plugged into the computer?
- Is the computer plugged into a working outlet?
- If it's plugged into a surge protector, is the surge protector plugged in and turned on?
- There may be a dial or button to increase or decrease the brightness of the screen somewhere on the monitor. Perhaps that is turned to the darkest choice.

These solutions may seem too obvious to solve the problem, but that is often the case with computers. Because computers seem so complex, the simple solutions are sometimes overlooked. If only I had a dollar for every time a client called in distress and the culprit was a part of the computer that had been unplugged by accident.

My keyboard or mouse doesn't work.

Again, chances are something isn't plugged in correctly. Trace the path of each cord. Unplug the cord from its port and then replug it into the port. Sometimes even I find myself wondering why a document won't print, and then I remember I unplugged the printer the last time I took my laptop on the road. Oops.

If it's still not working, try restarting your computer.

My mouse, keyboard, or screen is frozen.

This remains one of the great mysteries of the computer. Sometimes it just freezes up on you. It's a bit like when a part of my brain can't come up with the name of a person I've known for years.

Something stops working momentarily. The computer might fix itself in a few minutes, but if it doesn't, you can bring it back to life.

Option 1. Rather than continue to click the mouse or hit the **Enter** key (on a PC) or the **Return** key (on a Mac), just get up from your desk and walk away. Some people

CHECK YOUR BATTERY

If your wireless keyboard or mouse stops working, the solution could be as simple as replacing the battery.

BOOTSTRAPS

Are you familiar with the saying "pull yourself up by your bootstraps"? That's what inspired the term "to boot" the computer. When you "boot" the computer, you're either straightening out a problem, restarting the computer, or shutting it down. **Soft Boot** – to restart the computer without turning the power off. **Hard Boot** = to shut down the computer by either turning it off or cutting off the electrical supply. **Boot up** = to turn on the computer.

get very frustrated when the computer freezes up. Be warned—computers cannot withstand the Samsonite stress test. Do not pound on your keyboard or your mouse. It will only make matters worse. If you need to take five, do so. By the time you come back to the computer, it may have adjusted itself.

Option 2. You can try gently depressing the **Esc** (Escape) key a couple of times (the Esc key is usually at the top left of the keyboard). The Esc key is used to get out of a program or to stop an action before it is completed.

SERGEANT, GIVE ME 60

Count to 60 after you've turned off the computer and before you turn it back on because that gives the computer a chance to catch its breath. When a computer shuts down, it needs to file what was open on the screen. Giving the computer a little rest time ensures that it has caught its breath and is ready to get back to work. A 60 count also gives you a chance to drop any feelings of frustration over what has gone awry with the computer. In other words, those 60 seconds may prevent you from throwing the machine down a flight of stairs! Now, you wouldn't want to do that, would you?

Option 3. If the Esc key doesn't help, you will need to "soft boot" (or "force quit," in Mac speak) the computer. To soft boot means to close a program that isn't responding or, if that doesn't work, to force the computer to restart or shut down without pulling the plug. To "hard boot" the computer is a last resort and involves cutting off the electricity (by shutting off the computer or unplugging it) rather than following the proper shutdown process. My interpretation is that you're giving the computer a swift kick with a soft boot as opposed to a hard boot. We won't hard boot the computer unless absolutely necessary. Of course, you should never really kick the computer, with or without footwear!

To soft boot a PC:

- Find the **Ctrl** (Control), **Alt** (Alternate), and **Del** (Delete) keys on your keyboard.
- Hold down all three simultaneously, and then release.
- A window opens; click on **Task Manager**.
- A Windows Task Manager window will appear. It will list all the programs that are open or running.
- Click (select) the program you want to close down. Hit the **Enter** key on your keyboard. That instructs the computer to **End Task**. That means the computer will close the program

that is highlighted in blue. (This program may have the words "not responding" next to it.) You'll then be asked to confirm this choice. Hit the **Enter** key again to confirm.

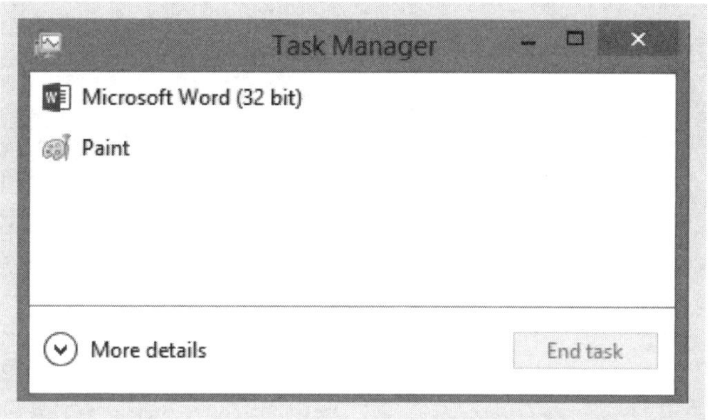

- If that doesn't work, hold down the **Ctrl**, **Alt**, and **Del** keys again and release.
- Click on the Power symbol .
- Click **Restart**. This will instruct the computer to turn off and turn on again. It's a more gentle solution than hard booting the computer, which involves turning the computer off by cutting off the electrical current.

When a PC freezes, first try the Windows Task Manager window to close a program that is not responding.

To soft boot a Mac:

- Find the **Command ⌘**, **Option Alt**, and **Esc** keys on your keyboard.
- Hold all three down simultaneously, and then release.
- A **Force Quit Applications** window will appear. It will list all the programs that are open or running.
- Hit the **Return** key on your keyboard. That instructs the computer to **Force Quit**. That means the computer will close the program that is probably causing the problem.
- If that doesn't work, hold down the **Control** key and the Power button.
- Then you can instruct the computer to Shut Down or Restart. It's a more gentle solution than hard booting the computer,

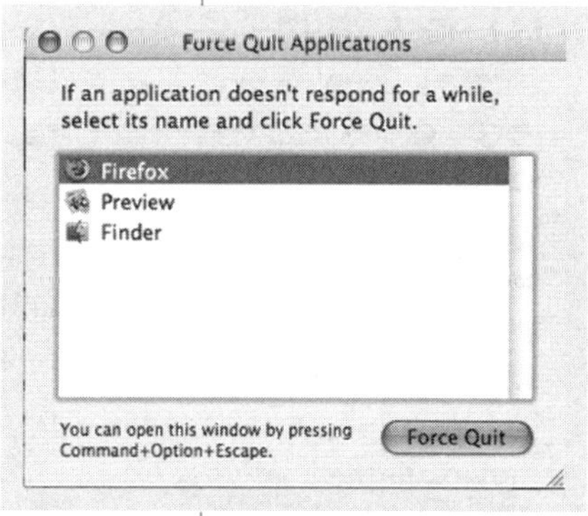

When a Mac freezes, the Force Quit Applications window will help you to soft boot the machine.

which involves cutting the electrical current by turning the computer off.

The computer may have frozen because the program you were in had a hiccup of sorts, not because the computer has any real problems. That's why we first look at the programs that are open and see if closing one of them will unfreeze the computer.

Option 4. If a soft boot fails, you have no choice but to hard boot (shut down) the computer. You do this by turning the power switch off on the computer. If that doesn't work, you'll have to unplug the computer or turn off the surge protector. Count to 60 and then turn the computer back on. Everything should be fine now.

Note: When you close a program through a soft or hard boot, you can't save any of the changes that you've made. For example, say you are writing a letter to your son and the computer freezes. You soft or hard boot the computer to unfreeze it. The parts of the letter that you had not saved probably won't be there when you retrieve it. Yet another reason to save often.

MY COMPUTER IS POSSESSED!

I had a student unplug her computer as a last resort and it *still* wouldn't turn off. She called me completely spooked that the computer was still on even after she had unplugged it. It turned out the computer was a laptop. When she unplugged it, the computer remained on because it was running on the battery!

My PC screen has a strange disk error message.

Don't worry! This window will only appear if your computer has a floppy disk drive (which new ones will not). If you have a floppy disk drive and you see this message, you simply forgot to take your floppy disk out of the A: drive. Remove the disk and press any key (whatever key that your little heart desires) on the keyboard. Your computer should continue the start-up process without a glitch.

A "Startup Settings Menu" appeared on my PC screen.

This window will appear on a PC if something went wrong during the start-up process. For right now, we don't care what went wrong. We just want to get the computer back on track.

In this case, the first thing to do is to hard boot (turn off) the computer, count to 60, and turn it back on.

- If the box appears again, choose Option 4, **Safe Mode**, by typing the number 4 and hitting the **Enter** key.
- Now let's shut down the computer by right-clicking on the **Start** button.
- Left-click on **Shut Down** or **Sign Out**.
- Click on **Shut Down**.

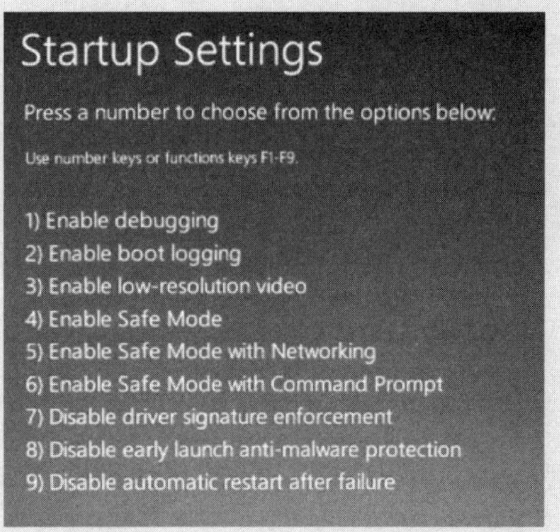

I'm sure all of this sounds a bit unappealing, but it really isn't that bad when you're doing it. Trust me.

My computer won't let me delete a file or document.

Chances are the document or folder you want to delete is still open. Make sure that you've closed the document or folder and quit the program that it lives in.

Achoo! Is It a Cold or a Virus?

A computer can get a virus (a program or piece of code that is loaded onto your computer without your knowledge), and that virus can reproduce itself inside the computer or move from one computer to another via an email attachment or a CD.

The nasty truth about viruses is that they are created by humans. They are the result of some computer geek wanting to see how insidious his or her virus can become. Viruses can be debilitating, but they can also be detected and destroyed with virus software. Your computer probably came with virus detection software. If not, ask your salesperson about it.

You are the first line of defense against a virus. The most likely way to infect your computer with a virus is by opening

UP WITH UPDATES

Your computer may notify you that there are updates available. As I mentioned earlier in the book, these updates are corrections, adjustments, and improvements to the operating system of other programs you run on your computer. Accept the updates and your computer may run more smoothly.

UPDATING YOUR VIRUS DETECTION SOFTWARE
Because new viruses are being created every day, you will need to update your computer to protect it from the newest incarnations. The virus software that you buy will offer this feature. Be sure to take advantage of it by either sending in your registration card or accessing their website.

an email attachment that is carrying a virus. Be sure your email service offers virus scanning for attachments. If you receive an email with an attachment and you don't recognize the sender, immediately throw the email away.

A virus can manifest itself in a variety of ways. You may notice that your computer functions more slowly than usual or that certain tasks aren't being carried out properly. Unfortunately, a virus can also destroy information stored on your computer. If your computer begins to misbehave (i.e., it suddenly turns off repeatedly, programs shut down without your instruction, it moves at a snail's pace when it used to be a jackrabbit, etc.), get thee to a technician and have them run diagnostics to see if it has been infected.

My printer won't stop printing.

Your printer hasn't gone mad. The most likely explanation is that you actually asked it to print and print and print, by repeatedly clicking on the Printer icon. The printer now has several print jobs in its queue and wants to print them all.

If you have a PC, follow these steps to stop the print jobs:

- Right-click on the **Start** button in the bottom left corner of your screen.
- Left-click on **Control Panel**.
- Click on **Hardware and Sound**.
- Click on **Devices and Printers**.
- Right-click on your printer's icon.
- Left-click on **See What's Printing**.
- Click on **Print** in the menu bar (top left).
- Click on **Cancel All Documents**.

If you have a Mac, follow these steps to stop the print jobs:

- Click on the **Printer** icon in the Dock.
- Click the **Pause** icon .
- Click on the name of the item printing.
- Click on the Delete icon  to the far right of the name to end printing. (This icon is not to be confused with the Close button at the top left of the window.)

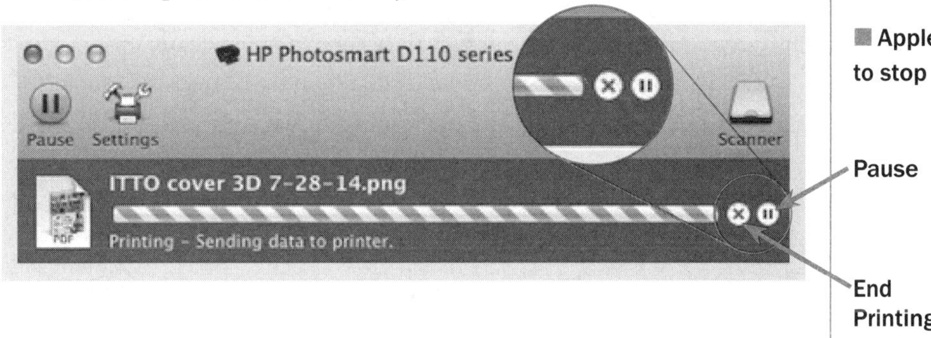

Apple Printer window to stop printing

It may take some time for the printer to obey your commands and stop printing. Be patient. If you've followed the steps above and it still won't stop printing, turn everything off, unplug the printer from the computer, and count to 60. Then plug everything back in and turn everything on again. Everything should be back to normal now.

Computer users, let's all meet up again on page 509 at "My computer/tablet can't open a website."

Tablet Troubles

When I tried to turn on the tablet, the screen remained black.

The most likely issue is that the battery has run down so low that the device cannot turn on. Plug in the electrical cord and try again. That may seem too obvious to solve the problem, but the simple solutions are sometimes overlooked. If only I had a dollar for every time a client called in distress and the culprit was a dead battery or something not being plugged in.

My tablet has frozen and won't shut down.

This remains one of the great mysteries of the technology. Sometimes it just freezes up on you. It's a bit like when a part of my brain can't come up with the name of a person I've known for years. Something stops working momentarily. The tablet might fix itself in a few minutes, but if it doesn't, try the steps below.

First try to hold down the Power button for 20 to 30 seconds. That may just do the trick.

If you have an iPad and it is still frozen, hold down the Power button and the Home button until the device shuts down.

If you have an Android tablet, hold down the Power button and the volume buttons until the device shuts down.

Give the tablet a solid minute before you turn it back on.

An app is misbehaving and buggy.

There's really no telling why an app or program on your tablet may misbehave or start acting buggy. The first thing to try is to stop and shut down the app.

If you have an iPad, follow the steps below to **close an app**:

- Double-tap the Home button. Any open apps are now seen on the screen.
- Flick your finger from the right to the left to reveal the app you would like to close.
- Place your finger on the image of the app screen above the icon for the app. Keep your finger down and swoop the app up. The app will now be closed and no longer on the screen.
- Tap the Home button. Try to reopen the app and see if it behaves better.

If you have an Android, follow the steps below to **close an app**:

- Tap on the Settings icon.
- Tap **Apps** or **Applications**.

- Tap on the desired app.
- Tap on **Force Stop**.
- Tap on **OK**.

If that doesn't help, try shutting down the app with the steps above and then also turn off and restart the tablet. If the app is still a problem, you may want to delete it from your tablet and upload it again from your App Store. You should not be charged a second time, if it is an app that you've already purchased.

My battery life seems short.

There are a couple of easy things you can do to increase battery life.

Lower the brightness on your screen with an iPad:

- Tap on the **Settings** icon .
- Tap on **Wallpapers & Brightness**.
- Tap and drag the circle to make the screen a bit darker.

Lower the brightness on your screen with an Android:

- Tap on the **Home** button .
- Tap on the **Brightness** icon to change the brightness.

Try this and see if things improve. If you're in a pinch to keep what little battery you have left, don't turn off the tablet. Turning it back on may use up what little battery you have. Instead, put the device into Airplane Mode. Airplane Mode stops the device from receiving or transmitting a signal. You can find it under Settings.

My computer/tablet can't open a website (aka "server not responding").

The first thing to do is try to visit another website. That determines if the original website you were trying to access is acting up or there's a different problem. I usually try *cnn.com* as my test site, because it's lush, and if it opens up, that means that you, your technology, and your Internet connection have no problems, but the website you were trying to visit was having a hiccup. Give the site some time to get its act together and try again later.

If you're using a computer and you have no success opening *cnn.com*, close the window and try connecting to the Internet with a different browser on your computer. If you have a PC, you will have **Internet Explorer** (the blue E) already on your desktop. If you have a Mac, you'll have **Safari** (the compass). They are both browsers, allowing you to "browse" the Internet. If you haven't already, download **Mozilla Firefox** (*firefox.com*) or **Google Chrome** (*google.com/chrome*). They are browsers that work well on both Macs and PCs. If Internet Explorer or Safari won't open, try to open Firefox. If Firefox opens, try to access the desired website. If you succeed, the problem was with your other browser.

With a tablet, try opening a different app that requires the Internet for use (like Skype, Google Maps, Pandora, etc.) and see if you can connect that way.

If you're still not able to connect, the problem could be your modem. The best thing to do at this stage is to turn off the device. Turn off your modem, and unplug all of the plugs in the back of the modem. (Take note of where each one is plugged in before removing it. If you haven't already, you can mark each cord by labeling it with masking tape to ensure there will be no mistaking what it plugs into.) Let it all sit for a full minute, then plug the cords in again and turn the modem on. Wait another full minute for the modem to reset itself. Now turn on your computer and try to connect to the Internet again.

It's a good idea to make a note of the lights on the modem when it is working well. That way, if you can't connect to the Internet, you may be able to identify the problem quickly with just a glance at the lights. ("Eureka! What should be green is yellow or not lit at all.") If restarting the modem doesn't work, call the company that provides your Internet service, and see if they can troubleshoot things from their end.

My connection to the Internet is sooo sloooow.

It could be that there's something slowing down your device from within, but before digging too deep, test whether the signal coming from your Internet service provider is up to snuff. Visit *speedtest.net* and click on **Begin Test**. Note the download and upload speed results. Call the company you use to connect to the Internet, share the results, and see if that's the best they can do for you. Recently, I changed Internet service providers because my previous service just couldn't deliver.

My printer says my ink cartridge is empty.

Even if your printer is telling you that your ink cartridge needs changing, wait until you notice the ink is light on your printouts before replacing it. Printers tend to notify you that new ink is needed when there's still a bit of life left in the existing cartridges, and printer ink is expensive. But when your cartridge really is running out, follow these steps.

- Be sure the printer is on.
- To remove the ink cartridge you'll either lift the lid off your printer or pull down the front panel (each printer model is different).
- Push down on the old cartridge with your thumb (be firm). Once the cartridge has disengaged, pull it forward and remove it from the printer.
- Take the new cartridge out of the wrapper and remove the little piece of plastic that covers where the ink comes out. Be careful not to touch that part of the cartridge. (The oils from your fingers can clog it.)
- Place the new ink cartridge into the slot from which you removed the old one. It'll most likely start with the back tipped slightly up or down, and you'll have to push on the front. It can feel like it takes a bit of force.

- If your printer is a scanner/copier as well, when you close the lid or front panel, your printer is probably going to ask you to print out an alignment page or something similar to that.
- Follow the directions on the page printed to align the cartridge.

If this all seems like too much, call in the cavalry. But, have your knight in shining armor show you how to change the cartridge so you can do it yourself next time.

If you must call tech support . . .

Have all pertinent information about your device at the ready when calling tech support. You may need to provide the tech person with the specs on your system. It's a good idea to have written down the make and model of your computer and the operating system.

If you took advantage of the Test-Drive Form on page 60, all the information you need is already written on that. Handy, isn't it?

Ask if the tech support person is familiar with your system. I'm all for learning on the job, but not when it comes to tech support. With so many different computer systems being used and a lot of compatibility problems, it is essential that you start your search for answers with someone who knows your device well. If the technician is not familiar with your technology, please feel empowered to ask for someone who is. Without hesitation, I will request a *tier-two technician*—tech talk for someone more knowledgeable or a supervisor.

Doom and Gloom

I just threw a lot of "ifs" and bad scenarios at you. Rather than make you anxious, this is all meant to empower you, knowing that you have the resources available should something go wrong with your computer.

I would love to tell you that your computer will never have a problem, but I would be lying to you. Computers and tablets were made by humans and they have flaws. I hope that, between this book, my website, and the instructional book that (maybe) came with your machine, a solution is never too far away.

RESOURCE LIST

Here are phone numbers you may find useful, whether or not your computer is acting up.

Unfortunately, these numbers are subject to change, but not to worry—if you can't find the customer service number you seek, visit: *customerservicenumbers.com* or *gethuman.com*.

Computer Manufacturers and Technical Support

Acer 800-816-2237

Apple 800-692-7753 (customer service)

Apple 800-275-2273 (AppleCare tech support)

Dell 800-624-9897 (customer care)

Dell 800-999-3355 (technical support)

Hewlett Packard (HP) 800-474-6836

IBM 800-426-7378

Keytronics 800-262-6006 (ergonomic keyboards)

Toshiba 800-457-7777

Printer Manufacturers and Technical Support

Brother International 800-276-7746

Canon 800-828-4040

Epson 800-533-3731

Hewlett Packard (HP) 800-474-6836

Online Services

America Online (AOL) 800-827-6364

AT&T 800-288-2747

EarthLink 800-395-8425

Hotmail 800-672-4551

Microsoft Network 800-936-5700

Software Manufacturers and Technical Support

Word-processing Suites

Microsoft 800-642-7676

Financial Management Software

Microsoft Money 800-642-7676

Quicken—Intuit 800-446-8848

Virus Protection Software

McAfee 866-622-3911

Symantec—Norton Anti-Virus 800-441-7234

Mail-Order Houses

Dell 800-624-9897

PC Connection 800-800-0014

Mac Connection 800-986-4420

APPENDICES

More Than 150 Recommended Websites

Antiques
goantiques.com
icollector.com

Auction
biddingforgood.com
ebay.com
ubid.com

Blogs
blogger.com (must log into Google)
boingboing.net
huffingtonpost.com
livejournal.com

Cars
autobytel.com
cars.com
kbb.com
nada.com
nhtsa.gov

Community
facebook.com
linkedin.com
twitter.com

Dating
eharmony.com
gay.com
jdate.com
match.com
seniorfriendfinder.com

Email (free)
google.com
hotmail.com
yahoo.com

Entertainment
fandango.com
imdb.com
metacritic.com
netflix.com
playbill.com

Family
ancestry.com
brainpop.com
family.disney.com
fastweb.com
grandparents.com
parenting.ivillage.com
discoverykids.com

Finance
tdameritrade.com
bankrate.com
bloomberg.com
irs.gov
morningstar.com
worldbank.org

Find Someone
pipl.com
reversephonedirectory.com
switchboard.com
whitepages.com

Food
americastestkitchen.com
cooking.com
epicurious.com
foodnetwork.com
menupages.com
stilltasty.com
topsecretrecipes.com
whfoods.com
yelp.com

Fun(ny)
howstuffworks.com
pogo.com
secondlife.com
stumbleupon.com
theonion.com
youtube.com

Good Deeds
globalvolunteers.org
heifer.org
hungersite.org
kiva.org
makeitrightnola.org
mowaa.org
unitedplanet.org

Greeting Cards (free)
123greetings.com
evite.com

Grocery Shopping
netgrocer.com
peapod.com
shaws.com
stewleonards.com

Health
clinicaltrials.gov
healthfinder.gov
mayoclinic.org
medscape.com
nlm.nih.gov
quackwatch.com

realage.com
webmd.com

History
ellisisland.org
fold3.com
historynet.com

Magazines
acttwomagazine.com
bhg.com
life.com
newyorker.com
people.com
tvguide.com
wired.com

News
bbc.co.uk
cnn.com
msnbc.com
npr.org
nytimes.com
thepaperboy.com
usatoday.com
weather.com

Photos
flickr.com
instagram.com
shutterfly.com
snapfish.com
touchnote.com

Research
annualcreditreport.com
britannica.com
legaldocs.com
merriam-webster.com
oxforddictionaries.com
refdesk.com
rhymezone.com
snopes.com
usps.com
webopedia.com
wikipedia.org

Search Engines
ask.com
bing.com
dogpile.com
duckduckgo.com
google.com
webcrawler.com
yahoo.com
yandex.com

Seniors
aarp.org
agefriendlycollege.org
grandmabetty.com
nsclc.org
roadscholar.org
seniorplanet.org
ssa.gov
thirdage.com

Shopping
bbbonline.org
consumerreports.org
couponcabin.com
freecycle.org
groupon.com
mysimon.com
pricegrabber.com
safeshopping.org
shopzilla.com
thecouponclippers.com
ftc.gov

Sports
espn.com
golf.com
si.com
sportingnews.com
usfigureskating.org
takemefishing.com

Travel
expedia.com
flightarrivals.com
fodors.com
frommers.com
hotels.com
kayak.com
lonelyplanet.com
mapquest.com
priceline.com
roadfood.com
rvtravel.com
skyauction.com
travelocity.com
tripadvisor.com
tripspot.com
vrbo.com

Weather
nhc.noaa.gov (National Hurricane Center)
radar.weather.gov
weather.com
wunderground.com

More Than 100 Free Apps

Books
Audible
iBooks
Kindle
Nook
OverDrive

Communication
Google Voice
Skype
Snapchat
WeChat
WhatsApp

Education
Duolingo
History Here
Lumosity
Memrise

Entertainment
Flipboard
Movies by Flixster
HBO Go
Netflix
SHO Anytime
StumbleUpon
TED
Vine

Finance
Apple Pay
Mint
Spending Tracker
PayPal

Fitness and Health
GAIN fitness
iFirstAid
Lose It!
MyFitnessPal
Runkeeper
Touchfit: GSP
WebMD

Food
CheckPlease
Dirty Dozen
Foodgawker
MenuPages
Seafood Watch
Urbanspoon

Fun and Games
2048
CheckWord
Comics
Draw Something
TapWord
Temple Run

Kids
My Talking Mom
Peppa Pig: Paintbox

Music
Pandora
Shazam
SoundCloud
TuneIn Radio

News
BBC News
CNN
HuffPost

Photo
Adobe Photoshop Express
Instagram
Pic Stitch
Touchnote

Productivity
Any.Do
Dragon Diction
Dropbox
EasilyDo
Evernote
Google
Google Drive

Radio
GuguRadio
iHeartRadio
Podcasts

Research
Google Search
Mention
Wikipedia
Yelp

RSS Readers
CommaFeed
Digg
Feedly
Inoreader
The Old Reader
Reedah
Reeder 3 (for Mac)

Shopping
Quick Scan
RetailMeNot
Slickdeals
Soap

Social Networking
Facebook
Hangouts
Instagram
LinkedIn
Pinterest
Twitter

Sports
ESPN Score Center
Team Stream
theScore
Ubersense (video analysis and coaching)
Yahoo Sports

Travel and Navigation
Flights
GateGuru
Google Maps
iTranslate
Navfree
TripAdvisor
TripIt
Uber

Utilities
Free WiFi Connect
myLite
USPS Mobile
Speedtest
Units

Weather
MyRadar
WeatherBug
Yahoo Weather

Glossary

4G or **5G** cellular network signals that allow data to be sent to smartphones, e-readers, tablets, and other devices

Android an operating system for smartphones and tablets that are not Apple or Microsoft products

antivirus program software that helps detect and destroy viruses

app software program for tablets and smartphones

Apple company that makes Mac, or Macintosh computers, which run on a different operating system than PCs. They also produce the iPhone, iPad, and iPod.

application (application software) computer software designed to help the user to perform specific tasks

arrow keys keys on the keyboard that allow you to move the cursor around the screen

attachment file sent along with an email

bits per second (bps) measurement of a modem's data-transmission speed

blog (web log) regularly updated website where an author and/or contributors share ideas and opinions

Bluetooth short-range radio technology between communication devices

bookmark website address saved to be revisited (also referred to as "favorite")

boot up to turn on the computer

broadband high-speed communication network that allows for multiple transmissions simultaneously

browser software program (such as Google Chrome, Mozilla Firefox, Safari, or Internet Explorer) that allows your computer to communicate with the World Wide Web

bug error or defect in software or hardware that usually results in the computer not working properly

byte measurement of space. A byte equals a single alphabetic or numeric character.

caps lock key key on the keyboard that allows you to type in uppercase without holding down the shift key. It is deactivated by depressing and releasing the key again.

CD-R functions like a CD-ROM, but you can also copy information from your computer onto it

CD-ROM (compact disc, read-only memory) type of disk that holds files or software that can be transferred onto your computer

CD-RW (compact disc re-writable) blank CD that is used to copy information to/from your computer

central processing unit (CPU) computer part that serves as the pathway for all information

click depressing and releasing the mouse button to initiate an action onscreen

click and drag action taken with the mouse to move items on the screen, such as a file or an icon

close box box in your title bar where you click to close a window

cloud cloud computing refers to programs and services offered over the Internet, including online storage and backup services

collapse box box in a title bar where you click to shrink a window

computer case computer part that houses the CPU, hard drive, RAM, modem, and disk drives

copy editing tool that allows you to duplicate text and place it elsewhere in a document

crashing when an error occurs and an application or the whole computer unintentionally shuts down

cut editing tool that allows you to remove text from a document

cyberspace figurative reference to the intangible world of the Internet, such as the World Wide Web and email

D: drive or **E: drive** computer part where you insert a CD or DVD to read, listen to, view, or install its contents (*see* disk drive)

desktop (1) non-laptop computer; (2) name for the main screen display on the computer (whether it is a laptop or a desktop)

digital certificate attachment to an electronic message used for security purposes

disk drive computer part that reads information or software from a disk

domain name person's or organization's chosen website name, including the suffix that identifies the type of website (for example: *whitehouse.gov*)

double-click quickly depressing and releasing the mouse button twice on an icon or text to take an action, such as to open a document or a software program

download transfer data or files from one location to another (for example, from a website to your computer)

dpi (dots per inch) refers to the resolution of an image. The more dpi, the more detailed the image.

drag *see* click and drag

Droid smartphone that uses the Android operating system

DVD (digital versatile disc) disk that holds 26 times the data of a CD; most commonly used to view movies

email (electronic mail) to send or receive typed messages via the Internet

email address person's or organization's address used to receive email (for example, *abby@AskAbbyStokes.com*)

emoticon playful use of keyboard characters and symbols to represent emotional responses (also referred to as smileys), usually used in email or text messages (for example, >: -(means angry)

encryption secret code added to data for data security

Enter or **Return key** keyboard feature that performs actions; also can be used like a return key on a typewriter when typing a document or an email

e-reader device used for reading electronic books

error message message from the software indicating that an error has occurred. Sometimes a code or number is given in the message so a technician can identify the problem.

Ethernet port used to connect a computer to a DSL or cable modem as well as another computer or a local area network

external hard drive a storage device that plugs into your computer to transfer and store documents, photos, or music to save space or for safekeeping

external modem modem that is housed separately from the computer case and is connected by a cable

Facebook social networking website where you and your "friends" can view whatever ideas, photos, or links to websites you each choose to share

Facetime Apple program that allows you to call, IM, or video call other users over the Internet at no cost

favorite *see* bookmark

file collection of information stored in one named grouping. There are many different kinds of files (for example, data files, text files, and image files).

firewall security measure that can be turned on to protect a computer from unauthorized users

Fitbit mobile wrist device that records and wirelessly transmits physical activity

font style of type

forum online discussion site where people can read posts from others—often concerning a particular topic—and respond with their own posts

freezing when the mouse and keyboard become temporarily inoperative

function keys set of keys on the keyboard, rarely used nowadays, that carry out special commands

gigabyte (GB) measurement of computer hard-drive space; roughly 1,000 megabytes

Google+ social networking website that utilizes circles to organize people by groups where they share ideas, photos, or links to websites

hacker highly skilled computer user who gains access to information on computers not intended for them by "cracking" the programming codes

hard boot to shut down the computer when it is frozen, either by switching it off or by cutting off the electrical supply

hard drive (C: drive) place in the computer where information is permanently stored

hardware physical pieces of a computer (i.e., monitor, mouse, keyboard, computer case)

hashtag (#) symbol that is used directly before relevant keywords in a tweet. Hashtags help categorize tweets so they show up more easily in Twitter searches.

hertz measurement of computer processor speed

home page first page of any website on the Internet

hotspot location providing public wireless connection to the Internet

http (hypertext transfer protocol) prefix to a website address (which no longer needs to be typed in) that helps direct your browser software to the website

I-beam one of the many faces of the mouse; cursor that fits between the characters of text to allow you to make changes

icon small picture or image seen on the screen that represents a software program, a document, or a command

information superhighway nickname for the World Wide Web, referencing its seemingly limitless information

Instagram social networking website where users can edit and share photos

installing process where the computer reads and stores software onto the hard drive

instant messaging (IM) real-time communication with an individual on the Internet that allows faster transmission than an email and is often briefer in content

internal modem modem that is housed inside the computer case

Internet huge, worldwide, ever-growing system of computers linked by telecommunications networks that share data

ISP (Internet service provider) company that provides access to the Internet

keyboard used to type information into the computer

Kindle portable e-reader designed and sold by *amazon.com* that allows you to download and read digital books, newspapers, magazines, and other electronic publications

laptop portable non-desktop computer that combines the drives, keyboard, mouse, and monitor into one much smaller unit

link website feature that allows you to click on text and be transferred to another page with information on the subject indicated

LinkedIn social networking site used by professionals to network and list or find jobs.

live streaming sending music or videos to your device to be listened to or watched in real time, but not saved to the device

login name unique name chosen by a user to identify him- or herself while on the Internet

login password private set of letters or numbers used to confirm the identity of the computer user

log off disconnecting from the Internet (also referred to as signing off)

log on connecting to the Internet (also referred to as signing on)

Mac or Macintosh *see* Apple

maximize box box on a PC title bar that allows you to increase the size of a window

megabyte (MB) measurement of computer space

megahertz (MHz) measurement of computer processor speed

menu bar bar that appears below the title bar in a window and offers menus of different commands

message board *see* forum

minimize box box on a PC title bar that allows you to shrink a window

modem computer part that allows you to connect to the Internet through a phone or cable line

monitor computer part that houses the screen; measured diagonally from top corner to opposite bottom corner

mouse handheld device used to move the pointer on the screen

mouse buttons controls on the top of the mouse that you click to carry out a command (*see* click)

mouse pad pad that sits underneath the mouse and helps you to control its movement

netbook small portable computer designed primarily for wireless Internet access and with most but not all the features of a larger computer; contains no media drive

netiquette network etiquette; guidelines for how to communicate your ideas or feelings via email or chat rooms (for example, USING CAPS INDICATES THAT YOU ARE SHOUTING)

newbie person who is new to using the Internet or a particular program or website

Nook portable e-reader designed and sold by Barnes & Noble that allows you to download and read digital books, newspapers, magazines, and other electronic publications

notebook computer smaller version of a laptop

online service provider *see* ISP (Internet service provider)

operating software system (such as Windows 10 or Mac Yosemite) that organizes and manages your computer

paste editing tool that allows you to place text that you have cut or copied

patch computer code created to correct a problem (i.e., bug) within an existing program

PC compatible software or hardware that works with a PC (versus a Mac)

peripherals additional pieces of hardware, such as a printer or scanner, attached to the computer

personal computer any computer intended to be used by an individual (rather than, say, a large business)—includes PCs and Macs

phishing scam email sent to elicit private information from the recipient to be used for identity theft

Pinterest social networking website where users post (or pin) images of ideas, collections, and projects to share

pirated software software that has been illegally copied

pixel (abbreviated from "picture element") tiny dots that together make up images on computer screens and digital photos

podcast audio (and sometimes video) file that can be downloaded from the Internet onto a computer, smartphone, or tablet

pointer arrow that appears on the screen and moves according to the manipulation of the mouse; also referred to as the arrow, mouse arrow, or cursor

port place on the computer where the cable from a different computer part is plugged in

post to submit text (often in the form of a comment or update) to a blog, message board, forum, or social networking website

ppi (pixels per inch) relates to the resolution of an item as seen on the computer screen

printer allows you to print text and images from the computer

profile web page on a social networking site where you list your interests, hometown, and whatever other details you choose to share with your "friends," "connections," or "followers"—anyone who has access to your information on the site

QR code ("Quick Response code") type of matrix barcode that consists of black modules arranged in a square pattern on a white background and that, with a QR scanner or smartphone, can be used to access encoded information or serve as a link to a website

RAM (random access memory) temporary memory used when the computer is on

resolution describes the sharpness and clarity of an image

right-click function offered on the PC mouse that allows for more advanced tasks

router device used to route information to or from the computer and to connect networks. It also provides a firewall.

RSS (really simple syndication) feed automatically populates a blog, podcast, or newsletter, making it easier and more efficient to consume your favorite content

scanner device that copies images and text and converts them into a digital image that can be stored on a computer or emailed

scroll bar feature that allows you to move a page up and down in order to view all its contents

scroll box part of the scroll bar that allows you to control the movement of the page

search engine website where you can search the rest of the Web for information on a given topic

shift key key on the keyboard that performs several functions, including typing in uppercase and highlighting text

Siri "voice assistant" utilizing voice recognition software to perform hands-free tasks on Apple mobile devices

Skype program that allows you to call, IM, or video call other users over the Internet at no cost

smartphone mobile phone that, in addition to making calls and texting, allows users to surf the Internet, access email, download apps, take pictures, and more

SMS (short message service) *see* text

snail mail nickname for mail delivered by the postal service that negatively refers to the time it takes to be delivered in contrast to the speed with which an email is sent

social networking connecting with friends and family, meeting new people, and sharing ideas, photos, etc., on the Internet

soft boot to close a program or restart the computer without completely shutting it down

spam unsolicited commercial/junk email

spyware software that covertly gathers user information when connected to the Internet without the user's knowledge

SSDs (solid state drives) nonmechanical storage device that is more reliable and smaller, uses less power, makes no noise, and lasts much longer on a single battery charge than computers that use hard drives

SSL (secure sockets layer) format for transmitting private documents over the Internet. It uses a cryptographic system that involves two keys.

streaming allows you to play audio or video without it being completely downloaded first

surfing the net traveling the Internet from site to site

surge protector device that protects the computer from irregular electrical currents

sync abbreviation for "synchronize." In the context of smartphones and computers, it means to transfer information to and from the devices so they have identical copies.

tablet small, lightweight portable computer contained entirely in a flat screen that has many, but not all, of the features of a full-size personal computer and is often equipped with a rotatable touch screen instead of a keyboard or mouse

tap depressing and releasing you finger to initiate an action on a touch screen

task bar bar that appears at the bottom of a PC screen that contains the start button as well as access to other programs and features

text to send a short text message on your cell phone

title bar bar that appears at the top of a window and indicates the name of the software program and the document; also contains the close box

touch point type of mouse used on a laptop that uses a small rubber button for control (*see* mouse)

touch screen computer monitor or device screen that can be operated by finger touch

trackball type of mouse that uses a ball for control (*see* mouse)

tweet post written on Twitter that contains 140 characters or less

Twitter social networking website where users post messages of limited length and "follow" whoever's thoughts are of interest to them

URL (uniform resource locator) technical term for a website address

upgrading hardware increasing the memory capacity or functionality of the computer

upgrading software installing a new and improved version of a software program already installed on the computer

upload to transfer data or files from a computer to a network (for example, to transfer photos from your computer to a website)

USB (universal serial bus) most common type of port on a computer; used to plug in a printer, scanner, etc.

username *see* login name

user password *see* login password

virus computer problem created by malcontented computer geeks. Viruses are meant to damage computers and are spread by opening email attachments or links or using someone else's disks.

virus protection software *see* antivirus program

voice recognition software software that responds to voice commands to take an action and transcribes dictated text to a written format (emails, text, documents)

wearables devices worn on the body that connect to the Internet (examples: Apple Watch, Fitbit)

webcam video camera that feeds its images in real time to a computer where they can be viewed online

web page any page that follows the home page of a website

welcome page *see* home page

WEP (wired equivalent privacy) data encryption that utilizes a password to protect wireless communication

wi-fi (wireless fidelity) enables a computer, e-reader, or smartphone, among other devices, to connect to the Internet without being tethered to a modem

window visual frame that appears on your computer screen to contain an application

Windows 8.1 operating system used on older PCs

Windows 10 operating system used on more recent PCs

World Wide Web (www) cyberspace library of information organized by website

worm program, not unlike a virus, that replicates itself over a computer network and usually performs malicious actions

WPA (wi-fi protected access) *see* WEP

wrist pad pad placed in front of a keyboard or mouse pad that helps position your hands in a way that prevents wrist strain

zoom box box on a Mac title bar where you click to increase the size of a window

Keyboard Shortcuts

Mac

Command and + (zoom in to enlarge)

Command and A (select all)

Command and B (bold)

Command and C (copy)

Command and down arrow (bottom)

Command and F (find)

Command and F3 (show Desktop)

Command and G (find next)

Command and I (italic font)

Command and M (minimize)

Command and N (new document or window)

Command and O (open file)

Command and P (print)

Command and Q (quit)

Command and S (save)

Command and Shift + 3 (capture the screen)

Command and U (underline)

Command and up arrow (top)

Command and V (paste)

Command and X (cut)

Command and Z (undo)

Option and F1 (open display options)

Option and F10 (open sound options)

PC

ALT and F4 (close the active item, or quit the active program)

ALT and Tab (switch between open items)

CTRL and A (select all)

CTRL and C (copy)

CTRL and Down Arrow (move the insertion point to the beginning of the next paragraph)

CTRL and ESC (display the Start menu)

CTRL and Left Arrow (move the insertion point to the beginning of the previous word)

CTRL and Right Arrow (move the insertion point to the beginning of the next word)

CTRL and Up Arrow (move the insertion point to the beginning of the previous paragraph)

CTRL and V (paste)

CTRL and X (cut)

CTRL and Z (undo)

F2 key (rename the selected item)

F3 key (search for a file or a folder)

F10 key (activate the Menu Bar in the active program)

Windows Logo (display or hide the Start menu)

Windows Logo and D (display the Desktop)

Windows Logo and F (search for a file or a folder)

Index

<u>Underscored</u> page references indicate boxed text. **Boldface** references indicate illustrations.

F

G

K

L

M

N

R

S

T